The Book of
the Thousand Nights
and One Night

The Book of
the Thousand Nights
and One Night

RENDERED INTO ENGLISH FROM
THE LITERAL AND COMPLETE
FRENCH TRANSLATION OF
DR J. C. MARDRUS
BY POWYS MATHERS

Volume II

LONDON AND NEW YORK

Reprinted ten times
Second edition 1964
Reprinted 1972
First published as a paperback in 1986
by Routledge & Kegan Paul plc

Reprinted 1989, 1993, 1994, 1995 by
Routledge
11 New Fetter Lane, London EC4P 4EE
29 West 35th Street, New York, NY 10001

Printed in Great Britain by
The Guernsey Press Co. Ltd,
Guernsey, Channel Islands

ISBN 0-415-04540-1 (vol. II)
ISBN 0-415-04543-6 (set)

Contents of Volume II

CONTENTS OF VOLUME II

The Tale of Kamar al-Zamān and the Princess Budūr, Moon of Moons

But when the hundred-and-seventieth night had come

LITTLE DUNYAZĀD, who could not contain her impatience, rose from her carpet and said to Shahrazād:

'Sister, I pray you hasten to tell us the tale which you have promised; for its title alone has filled my heart with joy.'

Shahrazād smiled at her sister, saying: 'I wait the good pleasure of the King.'

King Shahryār, who that night had hurried over his usual embrace because of his anxiety to hear the story, said: 'O Shahrazād, you may begin the fairy tale which you have so agreeably announced.'

So Shahrazād told the following tale:

It is related, O auspicious King, that there was once, in the antiquity of time, a sultān called Shahrimān, master of armies and great wealth, who ruled over the land of Khālidān. Although he was in all other things happy, and possessed seventy concubines and four wives, he suffered the grief of being childless; for he had already reached a great age, and the marrow had begun to dry within him without Allāh having granted him an heir to the throne.

One day he confided his secret sorrow to his grand-wazīr, saying: 'I can find no reason for this torturing sterility.' The wazīr reflected for an hour before raising his head and answering: 'The problem is a delicate one, soluble by none save Allāh. I can only think of one remedy. Before you enter the women's quarter to-night, fulfil the duties of faith with unusual care, make your ablutions fervently, and pray to Allāh with a submissive heart, so that your union may become fertile through His blessing.'

'Master of wise words,' cried Shahrimān, 'your remedy is an excellent one.' He gave the wazīr a robe of honour; and that evening chose the youngest of his women, a virgin with remarkable hips, and lay with her after having meticulously performed his rites before the Creator. Thus it was that the woman conceived and bore a man-child in nine months to a day, amid the rejoicings of the people and the sound of fife, clarinet and cymbal.

The child was so beautiful that his father marvelled and called his name Kamar al-Zamān, moon of the time.

As a child he was the most beautiful of created things; as a youth it was easy to be seen that beauty had scattered all the flowers of the garden upon his fifteen years; as he grew older his perfection increased in degree, remaining the same in kind, so that his eyes had all the magic of the eyes of the angels Hārūt and Mārūt and the seduction of the eyes of Tāghūt; and his cheeks were more pleasant to the regard than Spring anemones. His waist was more pliant than a bamboo, finer than a silken thread; but you would have taken his croup for a mountain of moving sand; nightingales sang when they beheld it.

You must not be astonished, then, that his waist sometimes complained of the weight which went below it, and made mouths in its weariness at his behind.

Nevertheless his cheeks remained as fresh as the corol of roses, as pleasant as the evening breeze; so that all the poets of the time tried to paint his beauty. Here is one out of a thousand of the songs they sang:

> Across his cheek with trailing flowers
> The rose has written: 'He is ours.'
> And the people cry: 'Ah, ah!'

> Crisped on his forehead nobly pale,
> In each black tress the scorpion's tail
> Has written: 'If my venom fail . . .'
> And the people cry: 'Ah, ah!'

> God wrote a new moon in the sky,
> His silver nail paring; but I
> (Who wait the full moon anxiously)
> And the people cry: 'Ah, ah!'

King Shahrimān loved his son and could not bear to be separated from him. Fearing that he might dissipate his strength and beauty in excess, he wished to marry him during his lifetime and to rejoice in his posterity. One day, when this idea weighed on his mind, he opened his heart to his grand-wazīr, who replied: 'Marriage reduces the humours of the body, and therefore your idea is excellent.' The King sent for his son, who came and, after wishing his father peace with all respect, stood silently before him with lowered eyes, as a submissive son should always do.

At this point Shahrazād saw the approach of morning and discreetly fell silent.

But when the hundred-and-seventy-first night had come

SHE SAID:

Shahrimān said to him: 'My son, I wish to see you married during my lifetime, that I may rejoice in you and gladden my heart in your wedding.' Kamar al-Zamān changed colour and answered: 'My father, I have no inclination towards marriage and my heart feels no delight in women. Apart from the distaste I have for them, I have read so much in the books of the wise concerning the wickedness and perfidy of that sex that I would rather die than allow a woman to approach me. Our best poets have said on the subject:

> She has overthrown
> A thousand forts of steel and stone
> Calling 'My own!'
>
> Her eyes are black decoys,
> Her hairs are hunting-nets for boys;
> But she names them joys.

And again:

> You ask me about women, I reply:
> 'Look at this wagging lip, this sunken eye,
> The early white upon this scanty hair,
> The rot of this strong body which was I.'

And again:

> Woman: that is to say
> A body which the birds of prey
> Disdain to take away.
>
> Woman: the word implies
> A thing which lies
> With you at night, about you at sunrise.

Therefore, dear father, even at the risk of grieving you, I would not hesitate to kill myself if you wished to force me into marriage.'

Though King Shahrimān grieved at this answer and the light changed to darkness before his face, he so loved his son that he answered: 'I do not wish to force you, Kamar al-Zamān, if the project is disagreeable to you. You are still young, and will have time to reflect and to consider how happy I would be to see you married and the father of children.'

For a whole year he spoke no more of marriage to Kamar al-Zamān; but loved him as before and coaxed him with presents.

At the end of the year he called his son to him, and said: 'Have you reflected on the recommendation which I made to you and the joy which your marriage would give me?' Kamar al-Zamān bowed before his father, saying: 'How could I have forgotten your words or have entertained the least thought of disobedience, seeing that Allāh Himself commands my respect and submission in all that concerns my father? I have thought upon marriage for a whole year; and my reflections, fortified by the books of both ages which I have read, have convinced me that women are immoral, foolish and disgusting, and that death were better than to have anything to do with them.'

King Shahrimān understood that it would be harmful to constrain the obedience of his dear son; so he sorrowfully called his grand-wazīr and said to him: 'What fools fathers are when they desire children, for a son is a deception and a grief incarnate. Kamar al-Zamān is more set than ever against marriage; what must I do now?'

The wazīr reflected a long time before answering: 'O King of the age, have patience for another year and then, instead of talking to your son in secret, assemble all your amīrs and wazīrs, your nobles and the officers of your palace, and in their full assembly declare your intention of marrying Kamar al-Zamān without delay. I warrant that in front of so many honourable people he will prove himself obedient enough.'

At this point Shahrazād saw the approach of morning and discreetly fell silent.

But when the hundred-and-seventy-second night had come

SHE SAID:

The King witnessed his joy at this suggestion by giving his wazīr a fair robe of honour. He waited for another year and then called his son before an assembly of all the chief people of the kingdom. The boy came in; was not the hall lighted? What beauty-spot upon his chin! What perfume, yā Allāh, as he passed among the people! He kissed the earth three times between his father's hands and stood attentive. 'My child,' said the King, 'I have brought you hither into the presence of all these honourable gentlemen to tell you that I am about to marry you to some princess worthy of your blood, and to rejoice in your posterity before I die.'

Kamar al-Zamān was stricken with a sort of lunacy which made him give so disrespectful an answer to his father that all who were present lowered their eyes in shame; and the King himself, not being able to pass over so public an insolence, cried in a terrible voice: 'You shall see what happens to impudent and disobedient sons!' He ordered his guards to bind the boy's arms behind him and to shut him in an old ruined tower which was near the palace. This was done, and one of the guards stayed at the door of the prison to watch over the prince and attend to him if he needed anything.

Kamar al-Zamān said sadly to himself: 'Perhaps it would have been better to obey my father and consent to this marriage. At least I should have escaped being shut up in an old tower. It only proves that women are the cause of all misfortunes.'

King Shahrimān retired to his own apartments, mourning for the imprisonment of his dear son; he wept because he had already forgotten the boy's insolence and his heart was filled with fury against the wazīr who had suggested the idea of the assembly. He sent for him and said: 'You are to blame! If it had not been for you I should never have been betrayed into a position where I had to be harsh to my son. Speak now, if you have any excuse or suggestion to make; because I cannot bear that my son, my heart's desire, should undergo such punishment.' 'My King,' answered the wazīr, 'leave the boy shut up for fifteen days, and I guarantee that he will come out a most obedient son.' 'Are you sure?' asked the King, and the wazīr answered: 'I am sure.' Shahrimān sighed and lay down on his bed, where he passed a sleepless night, for you must know that his only son was the greatest joy in his life; he was accustomed to sleep with the lad at his side, making a pillow for him with his arm and watching over his slumbers. Therefore that night he turned from side to side without closing his eyes.

An excellent bed had been spread for the prince in the place of his confinement; when night fell, the slave at the door entered with a lighted torch, which he placed at the foot of the couch and retired. Then Kamar al-Zamān made his ablutions, recited certain chapters of the Koran, and undressed himself till he was clothed in nothing but a light shirt. He passed a piece of blue silk round his brow and thus became as beautiful as the moon upon her fourteenth night. He lay down upon the bed and, although he was sorrowful at having displeased his father, soon fell into a sound sleep.

He did not know (how could he even have dreamed?) what was going to happen to him that night in an old tower haunted by Jinn of the earth and air.

At this point Shahrazād saw the approach of morning and discreetly fell silent.

But when the hundred-and-seventy-sixth night had come

SHE SAID:

The tower in which Kamar al-Zamān was shut dated back to the time of the ancient Romans and had been abandoned for a great many years. At the back of it was a well in which lived a young Ifritah of the seed of Iblīs, whose name was Maimunah. She was the daughter of Dimiryāt, King of the subterranean Jinn; a Believer, famed throughout all the unknown spaces for her power and her virtue.

Towards midnight Maimunah left the well to take the air as was her custom, and flew up towards the higher levels of the sky that she might the more easily start thence for whatsoever place she desired to visit. As she went by the top of the tower, she was astonished to see a light in a place which had been so long neglected. She said to herself: 'There must be some reason for this light; I will go and see.' Swerving in her flight, she entered the tower and passed over the sleeping body of the guard into Kamar al-Zamān's chamber. Words cannot describe her joyful surprise on seeing the youth stretched out half-naked upon the couch. She paused on tip-toe, lowered her wings which were inconvenient in so narrow a space, and gently approached the bed. She lifted the covering from the boy's face and was thunderstruck at his excess of beauty. For a full hour she held her breath, lest she should wake him before she had had time to learn his perfections by heart. In all her ages of existence she had never seen cheeks so delicately touched with red, eyelids with such long cool shadows, or such assembly of lights as there was upon

As the three Nights before this occupied only a few lines in the Arabic text, Mardrus suppressed them in order that the narrative should not be unnecessarily interrupted. Such omissions in future will not be noted.—P.M.

that perfumed body. She might have made use of the words of
the poet:

> Dark grow the eyes of folly in my head,
> The white flowers in my garden turn to red;
> I cry to the respectable and wise:
> 'Then try to find some rapture in its stead.'

Maimunah's eyes filled with tears; she praised Allāh, crying:
'Blessed be the Creator of such perfection!' Then she thought to
herself: 'How can the mother and father of this boy bear to be
separated from him, or be so cruel as to shut him in this tower?
Do they not know the wicked practices of the ruin-haunting Jinn?
As Allāh lives, if they have no concern for their child, I will take
him under my protection and guard him from any Jinnī who would
abuse his loveliness.' After this oath, she bent over Kamar al-Zamān
and kissed him very gently on the lips, the eyelids, and the cheeks;
then covered him again without waking him, and flew through the
highest window.

She reached the middle region of the air and was refreshing herself
with calm flight as she thought of the sleeping youth, when she
heard a furious beating of wings. Turning towards the sound, she
recognised the Ifrīt Dahnash, a lewd Jinnī who did not believe in the
supremacy of Sulaimān ibn Dāūd. He was the son of Shamhūrīsh,
swiftest flier of the Jinn.

Maimunah was afraid this base Dahnash might see the light in
the tower and perpetrate some nameless thing, so she swooped
down upon him like a sparrow-hawk and was about to dash him to
the ground, when he made a sign of surrender, crying: 'O Maimunah, O daughter of the King, I conjure you, by the name of the
Sacred Seal of Sulaimān, not to harm me. I promise on my part that
I will do nothing shocking.' 'Be it so,' answered Maimunah, 'I will
spare you, if you tell me whence you come so late and what you are
thinking of doing. Only speak the truth, O Dahnash, or I will tear
out your wing feathers, scorch your skin, and break your bones. A
lie will not help you, Dahnash.' Then said the Ifrīt: 'O mistress, you
have met me at the right moment for hearing something very
strange. But first promise me that I may go in peace after I have
satisfied your curiosity, and that you will give me a safe-conduct
serviceable against my foes of earth, air, and sea, O powerful
daughter of Dimiryāt.'

Maimunah made answer: 'I promise upon the engraven stone in the ring of Sulaimān ibn Dāūd (prayer and peace be upon both of them!). Now speak!'

The Ifrīt Dahnash slackened his speed and ranged himself alongside Maimunah. Then he told her this adventure:

'Glorious Maimunah, I have just come from the last back of the furthest beyond, a land behind the confines of China, where rules Ghayyūr the Great. He has below his powers many remarkable towers, from each of which lowers a company of soldiers each greater than an army of ours; his women are fairer than flowers after showers; and even my flight, which devours a thousand leagues in as many hours, has never before beheld anything to be compared with his only daughter, the lady Budūr.

'My tongue would become furry before it could paint you the whole beauty of this princess; if you will listen, I will try to give you the pale shadow of the truth of certain details.

'I will tell you of her hair, of her cheeks, of her mouth, of her breasts, of her belly, of her croup, of her middle, of her thighs, and of her feet.

'In the name of Allāh!

'Her hair is dark as the separation of friends; she let it fall in three rivers to her feet, and I thought I looked upon three nights at the same time.

'Her face is as white as the day when lost friends meet again. The moon shone on it; or, maybe, it shone upon the moon.

'Her cheeks are an anemone, parted into two petals; her nose is a sword; there is purple wine running cool below the crystal of her skin.

'Her lips are coloured agate, eloquent with a water which cures all thirst.

'Blessed be Allāh who made her breasts twin fruit of ivory, each fitted for the grasp of a lover's hand.

'Her belly has dimples of shadow, as cunningly placed as are the Arabic characters in the life work of a Coptic scribe.

'Her croup; oh, oh, I shiver and I recollect. It is so heavy that it makes her sit down when she would rise, and rise when she would lie down. A poet has said:

> Her sumptuous bottom calls for a less frail
> Waist than is common,
> Whereas her waist is frailer:

> Therefore when she would rise and take regale
>   Among her women
>   Her slim white ankles fail her . . .
> There is a thing I cannot keep in gaol,
>   Being but human,
>   Of which my drawers are gaoler.

'Such is her croup; her thighs are two branches of marble marrying in the air. I wonder that her feet, though beautiful, can bear such beauty.

'As for the middle and fundament: tongue can but say that one is All, and the other Absolute; gesture is dumb before them.

'Such is the lady Budūr, daughter of Ghayyūr, O my princess.'

At this point Shahrazād saw the approach of morning and discreetly fell silent.

But when the hundred-and-seventy-ninth night had come

SHE SAID:

'I must tell you that King Ghayyūr so loves his daughter that his only pleasure in life is to find some new amusement for her. Recently, when he had exhausted other kinds of joys, he had a series of seven miraculous palaces built for her, each of a different material. The first is entirely of crystal, the second of diaphanous alabaster, the third of porcelain, the fourth of stone mosaic, the fifth of silver, the sixth of gold, and the seventh of diamonds. Each is wonderfully furnished according to the style of its building, so that a day therein may be a dream; and is completed with gardens and waterfalls.

'In order to please his daughter, the King caused her to live but a single year in each palace, that she should never grow tired and that pleasure should succeed to pleasure.

'I saw the child among the beauty of her palaces: do you wonder that I have lost my head?

'All the kings about have sought this magnificently-behinded maiden in marriage; but, when her father has told her of these proposals, she has answered: "I am queen and mistress of myself. How shall my body, which can hardly bear the touch of silks, tolerate the rough approaches of a man?" So the King, who would rather die than discontent his daughter, has been obliged to send her suitors away. Once, when a young king, more powerful and handsome than the rest, sent gifts and proposed for the hand of Budūr, she broke out in reproaches against her father, crying: "I see but one way to rid myself of these continuous tortures: to take this sword and plunge it in my body, that it comes out at my back." She even set about committing this violence upon herself, so that the King rolled the whites of his eyes in fear and confided his child to the keeping of ten wise old women, including her own nurse: and since then one at least of them has never left her, even sleeping at the door of her chamber.

'That is the state of affairs at present, Mistress Maimunah. I go every night to open my heart with the contemplation of her beauties, nor is temptation lacking to mount her and rejoice in her un-paralleled behind; but I refrain, thinking shame to attempt such loveliness. I content myself most discreetly while she sleeps; I kiss her between the eyes very gently, though I am burning to press my lips strongly upon her. I do not do so, because I distrust myself; I would rather abstain altogether than find that I had harmed her.

'Come with me, Maimunah, and see this paragon; I warrant that her perfections will amaze you!'

Thus spoke the Ifrīt Dahnash, son of swift Shamhūrīsh.

At this point Shahrazād saw the approach of morning and discreetly fell silent.

But when the hundred-and-eightieth night had come

SHE SAID:

Young Maimunah heard his words without replying; when he had finished, she burst into a mocking laugh, dug him in the belly with her wing, and spat in his face, saying: 'Your remarks about this young pisser are all very disgusting. I ask myself how you dare to speak of her in the same breath as the handsome youth I love.' Wiping his face, the Ifrīt answered: 'Dear mistress, I was absolutely ignorant of the existence of your young friend; and, although I ask your pardon, I will have to see him with my own eyes before I can believe that he rivals the beauty of my princess.' 'Will you be quiet, evil one?' cried Maimunah. 'My friend is so handsome that, if you saw him even in one of your dreams, you would fall into an epilepsy and bubble like a camel.' 'But who and where is he?' asked Dahnash, and the Ifrītah answered: 'O beast, he is in the same trouble as your princess, and is shut in the old tower behind which I live; but, if you think you are going to see him without me, disabuse yourself, because I know how wicked you are and would not even trust you to stand guard over the bottom of a holy man. I will show him to you myself, as I want your opinion; but I warn you that if you dare to lie and defy the truth of your own vision, I will tear out your eyes and make you the most miserable of Afārīt. At the same time, I shall expect you to pay a large forfeit if my friend is fairer than your princess, and shall be prepared to do the same myself if the positions are reversed.' 'I accept!' cried Dahnash. 'Come with me to see the lady Budūr.' 'But,' Maimunah objected, 'it will be quicker to go to the tower which is just below our feet, and afterwards we can compare.' So the two dropped down until they came to the top of the tower, and then entered the chamber of Kamar al-Zamān by the window.

'Do not move, and above all behave yourself,' said Maimunah to Dahnash, as she went up to the sleeping boy and removed his covering. Then she turned her head and continued: 'Look, O evil one, and be careful not to fall on the floor in your emotion.' Dahnash turned his head and then jerked it away in stupefaction; he looked a second time long and long. 'Mistress Maimunah,' he said at last, shaking his head, 'I find that it was excusable in you to think your friend incomparable, for I have never seen so many perfections in a boy, and I think I may claim to know something about them; and yet I tell you this, the mould which made him was not broken until it had cast a female copy also, Princess Budūr, daughter of Ghayyūr.'

Hearing these words, Maimunah threw herself upon Dahnash and gave him so violent a blow with her wing about the head that one of his horns was broken. 'Vilest of Afārīt,' she cried, 'I command you to go at once to the palace of this Budūr and bring her back with you; I will not put myself out for the silly little thing. When you return, we can compare the two; go quickly or I will cut your flesh into strips and throw them to the hyenas and the crows.' Dahnash picked up his horn and made off, grumbling and scratching his bottom. He plunged through the air like a javelin and returned in an hour with his burden.

The sleeping princess lay upon the shoulders of Dahnash, clothed solely in her chemise; and her body glimmered whitely beneath it. Worked in gold thread and many coloured silks on the wide sleeves of this chemise, were to be read these verses in interlacing character:

> Three things alone
> Prevent her black eyes saying yes:
> Fear of the unknown and horror of the known
> And her own loveliness.

'I think that you have been amusing yourself with this young girl by the way,' said Maimunah to Dahnash, 'it should not take an hour for a good Ifrīt to go and come between Khālidān and China. But be that as it may, hasten to place the little one by the side of my friend that we may make our examination.' So Dahnash, with infinite precaution, laid the princess on the bed and took off her chemise.

The child was as beautiful as Dahnash had painted her, and Maimunah was forced to admit that the two upon the couch might be twins, save in the matter of their middle parts. Each had the same moonlit face, the same slim waist, and the same rich round croup; if the girl lacked the youth's central ornament, she made up for it with marvellous paps which confessed her sex.

Maimunah said to Dahnash: 'I admit that it was possible to hesitate between the two, but you must be a fool or blind not to know that, if there is equality between a male and a female, the male bears off the prize.' But Dahnash answered: 'I know what I know, and I see what I see; nor will time make me deny the witness of my senses. Nevertheless I am ready to tell a lie if that would please you.'

Maimunah broke out into angry laughter and, recognising that she and the foolish Dahnash would never agree through a simple examination, she said: 'Let us decide which of us is right by putting the matter to the arbitrament of our inspiration. Let each of us prove our contention by saying beautiful verses in praise of our favourites. Do you consent, or are you incapable of a subtlety which is usually only found among refined people?' 'I was about to propose the same thing myself,' replied Dahnash. 'My father, Shamhūrīsh, taught me the rules of poetic construction and the art of rhythmical verses. You begin, charming Maimunah.'

The Ifrītah bent over the lips of Kamar al-Zamān and kissed them lightly; then, with her hand among his hair, she said:

> This body is born of branches
> And the scent of jasmine:
> No woman was made so.

Night threw a handful of stars
Into black tarns:
No woman was made so.

To drink the aromatic honey of his mouth,
To feed my flesh on his, to feel his hair . . .
No woman was made so.

Dahnash ecstatically applauded these lines, convulsing himself
with emotion at their beauty; then he approached Budūr and,
inspiring himself by kissing her breasts, sang:

The myrtles of Damascus smile and shine
And lift my heart like wine,
But you . . .

The roses of Baghdād are fed on dew
And moonlight. Oh, but you,
If you were mine . . .

At this point Shahrazād saw the approach of morning and
discreetly fell silent.

But when the hundred-and-eighty-second night had come

SHE SAID:

When Maimunah heard this delicious little poem, she was surprised that so much talent could be concealed by so much ugliness;
and, as she had a certain amount of judgment, although she was a
woman, complimented Dahnash, who swelled with delight. Then
she said: 'Although you have a delicate soul under your strange
exterior, you must not think that you excel in verse or that Budūr
excels in beauty.' 'Is that so!' cried Dahnash. 'Yes, it is,' she
answered. 'I do not believe you,' he replied, and she said: 'Take
that!' and poked him in the eye with her wing. 'That is not proof!'
he howled. 'Look at my arse!' she screamed. 'It is little enough,' he
retorted.

Maimunah wished to throw herself upon Dahnash and do him
some real injury, but in the twinkling of an eye he changed himself
into a flea and hid below the two forms on the bed. The Ifrītah was
therefore obliged to swear a truce and Dahnash warily returned to
his own form. 'Listen, good Dahnash,' said Maimunah, 'there is only
one way to end our dispute, and that is to refer it to a third party.'

Dahnash was willing; so Maimunah stamped upon the flooring, which opened and emitted an Ifrīt of woeful ugliness. On his head were six horns, each four thousand four hundred and eighty cubits in length, and he had three forked tails which were not an inch shorter; he was hump-backed and lame, and his eyes were where his nose should have been; one of his arms was five thousand five hundred and fifty-five cubits long, and the other only half a cubit; his hands were greater than cauldrons, with claws like a lion's; he had hoofs which made him limp; and his zabb, which was forty times larger than that of an elephant, ran between his legs and rose triumphantly behind him. His name was Kashkash ibn Fakrash ibn Atrash, of the line of Abū Hanfash.

When the floor closed, Kashkash kissed the earth between Maimunah's hands and, standing humbly before her with crossed arms, said: 'Mistress Maimunah, daughter of our King, your slave awaits your bidding.' 'I wish you, good Kashkash,' she said, 'to judge between myself and the wicked Dahnash. The matter is such and such. Cast an impartial eye upon this bed and say whether the youth or the maiden is more beautiful.'

Kashkash regarded the two young people sleeping, calm and naked, on the bed; and was seized with such an emotion that he grasped his thing above his head with his left hand and, holding his triple tail with his right, danced about the chamber. At last he said to the other two: 'As Allāh lives, they are equal in beauty and their difference is one of sex alone. I know only one way of settling your dispute.' 'What is that?' cried they; but he replied: 'First let me sing something in honour of this most disturbing girl.' 'There is not time,' said Maimunah, 'except perhaps for some song about the youth.' 'That would be a little irregular,' objected Kashkash. 'Sing what you like then,' retorted Maimunah, 'as long as the lines are short and well-balanced.' Thereupon Kashkash sang this obscure and complicated song:

> The prudent lover slips,
>   Dear lad, from out that kind
>   Of love which asks for constancy.
>   Behave like me:
> Drink sugar as it drips,
>   But keep in mind
> That salt were sweeter on less easy lips.

'I cannot be bothered to understand you,' said Maimunah, 'hasten to tell us how we may know the truth.' 'It is quite simple,' answered Kashkash, 'wake one after the other, while we three remain invisible, and the one who shows greater love and hotter passion for the other will prove himself or herself vanquished in the test, by confessing that the charms of the other are more powerful.'

At this point Shahrazād saw the approach of morning and discreetly fell silent.

But when the hundred-and-eighty-third night had come

SHE SAID:

Maimunah cried: 'O excellent idea!' and Dahnash, exclaiming: 'The idea is excellent!', changed himself again into a flea, and bit the handsome Kamar al-Zamān in the neck. The youth woke with a start and carried his hand to the place; but he found nothing, for Dahnash, after having avenged the affronts of Maimunah on the youth's white skin, had returned to his own invisible form.

What happened after this was certainly remarkable.

Kamar al-Zamān, who was still half asleep, dropped his hand from his neck and it came to rest on Budūr's naked thigh. The boy opened his eyes and then shut them again, for they were dazzled. He felt against him a body more tender than butter, and breathed another's breath sweeter than musk. In pleased surprise he raised his head and looked long at the unknown sleeper by his side.

Leaning on his elbow, all unmindful of his hatred, he detailed with charmed eyes the girl's perfections. First he compared her to a fair citadel topped by a dome, then to a pearl, then to a rose; he could not at first make a true comparison, as he was ignorant of the forms and graces of women; but soon he realised that his last analogy was the truest, his second the pleasantest, and his first ridiculous.

He leaned over the rose, inhaling the perfume of its delicious flesh, passing his nose over the whole of its surface. This he found so pleasant that he ventured his fingers over all the contours of the pearl and found that this touch set his body on fire, causing movement and beatings in various parts of his person. He felt a violent need to give rein to his nature; therefore, crying: 'Be it as Allāh wills!', he made ready to couple with Budūr.

Thinking it very astonishing that the girl should have on no chemise, he took her and felt her and turned her in every way. 'Yā Allāh, Yā Allāh, what a rare behind!' he exclaimed, and then, as he caressed her belly, 'It is a marvel of tenderness!' Her breasts tempted him, and he filled his hands with them, crying: 'As Allāh lives I must wake her up; it is strange that she is not awake already.'

Now it was Dahnash who had plunged the girl into a deep slumber, in order that Kamar al-Zamān might go to work the more easily.

The boy set his lips to the lips of the princess and took a long kiss; but still she did not wake. He took a second and a third without result, and at last spoke to her, saying: 'Rise up, my heart, my eye! Awake, O liver of me, for I am Kamar al-Zamān.' But the young girl did not move. So the prince stretched himself upon her, saying: 'As Allāh lives, I cannot wait; I must penetrate her while she is asleep.'

Maimunah, Dahnash and Kashkash were watching all this while; and the first was getting ready to say, in case the boy achieved his deed, that it did not count.

At this point Shahrazād saw the approach of morning and discreetly fell silent.

But when the hundred-and-eighty-fourth night had come

SHE SAID:

The girl was sleeping on her back, dressed only in her dishevelled hair; the prince clasped his arms about her, and would have been at it, when suddenly he shivered and disengaged himself, saying: 'Surely my father has placed this girl in my bed and now watches through some hole in the wall. To-morrow he will say: "Kamar al-Zamān, you pretend to abominate women; what then did you do to that girl last night? You delight to couple in secret; but refuse marriage in order to thwart me of my joy in your posterity." And I shall be considered a liar and trickster. Therefore to-night I will refrain, although I do not wish to; and to-morrow I shall ask my father to give me this fairest of all girls in marriage. He will be happy, and I shall be able to use this alluring form without repenting of it.'

With that, to Maimunah's great delight and to the powerful disappointment of Dahnash, who was already dancing for joy, Kamar al-Zamān kissed Budūr upon the lips, slipped a costly diamond ring from one of his fingers on to one of hers, to show that he considered her his wife already, and then regretfully turned his back and went to sleep.

After this Maimunah changed herself into a flea, jumped on to Budūr's thigh, reached her navel, and then, going back four inches on her track, paused at the little hill which overlooks the valley of roses. Concentrating her jealousy and revenge in a single bite, she caused the young girl to spring up wide awake, carrying both her hands to the seat of her pain. The princess gave a cry of terror and astonishment when she saw a young man lying beside her, but her first glance changed into a second of admiration, her second into a third of joy, her third into a fourth of delirium.

In her first fright she thought: 'You are compromised for ever, for there is a young stranger in your bed. For this audacity, the eunuchs shall cast him from the window into the river! . . . and yet, perhaps this is some youth which my father has chosen for me: let me look at him before I have recourse to violence.' Thus it was that she took her second glance and was overcome by his beauty. 'O my heart, how pretty he is!' she whispered. Bending over his lips which smiled with sleep, she kissed him, saying to herself: 'As Allāh lives I wish him for my husband. Why has my father delayed so long in giving him to me?' She took one of his hands within her own, and said quietly: 'Wake, wake, delightful friend; arise, sun of my soul; come kiss me, my dear; come kiss me, my life; awake, awake!'

But Kamar al-Zamān was kept in a deep sleep by Maimunah, and therefore did not move; so the beautiful princess thought that the fault lay with her, and that she had not put enough warmth into her appeal. Without caring whether any watched or no, she opened the silk chemise with which she had covered herself on waking and slipped herself all along the young man, clasping him in her arms, pressing her thighs to his, and whispering in his ear: 'Take me, take me; I will be sweet and obedient. See, here is the narcissus of my breasts, the garden of my belly is very tender. Lo, here is my navel, ready for the refinement of love. The first fruits of me are yours; the night shall not be long enough. We shall still be sweetly happy in the morning.'

At this point Shahrazād saw the approach of morning and discreetly fell silent.

But when the hundred-and-eighty-fifth night had come

SHE SAID:

Then, as Kamar al-Zamān still slept, the princess thought that it was a trick of his; half laughing, she said: 'Come, come, dear friend, do not play with me like this. Is it so that my father has taught you to punish my pride? But now it is enough, because your beauty, O fawn, has turned me into a faithful slave of love.'

The prince still remained motionless, and the lady Budūr, more and more in love, exclaimed: 'Open your eyes, O master of beauty. I also am considered beautiful; all life about me lives in an admiration of my cold, serene perfection. You alone have lighted a fire within me; why will you not wake, adorable boy, why will you not wake? I feel that I am dying.'

With that she thrust her head beneath his arm and amorously nibbled his ear and in his neck; then she passed her hand between his legs and found his thighs so full that her fingers might not pass along their surface. By chance she met so new a thing while she was doing this, that she looked at it with wide eyes and perceived that it changed form every moment beneath the examination of her hand. At first she was frightened, but very soon she understood the use of the thing; for, even as desire is greater in women, so is their intelligence quicker to seize the correspondence between certain charming organs. She lay along him, taking it in her hands, and, while her lips sucked his, that happened which happened.

Afterwards, the lady Budūr covered her sleeping lover with kisses until not a part of him was ignorant of her lips. Being calmer, she kissed the palms of his hands and, nursing him upon her breast so that their breaths mingled, fell into a smiling sleep.

The three Afārīt had lost not a single gesture of all this; and Maimunah was delighted to have proved to Dahnash that he had lost his wager. Nevertheless she was magnanimous, saying: 'I let you off your debt, O evil one. Also I grant you the safe conduct which you require about the airy ways. Do not abuse it, and try always to behave well.'

Then, turning towards Kashkash, she said sweetly: 'I thank you for your advice, and name you chief of my messengers. My father, Dimiryāt, shall confirm my choice. . . . Now both of you take this girl back to the palace of her father; for her development has been so swift before my eyes that I make her my friend and prophesy fair things for her in the future.'

At this point Shahrazād saw the approach of morning and discreetly fell silent.

But when the hundred-and-eighty-sixth night had come

SHE SAID:

The two Afārīt approached the bed and, taking the girl upon their shoulders, flew with her to the palace of King Ghayyūr and deposited her gently on her couch. Then they went off in different directions.

Maimunah, after kissing her young friend on the eyes, returned to her well.

In the morning Kamar al-Zamān awoke with his mind filled by the adventure of the night. He turned to right and left, seeking his bride, and, when he did not find her, said to himself: 'This is some trick of my father's to prove me, and hurry me on to marriage. Therefore I did well to wait for his consent like a good son, before accomplishing my desires.' He called to the slave at the door: 'Rouse up, you rascal!' and the fellow staggered in, half asleep, carrying the ewer and the basin for his master. The prince took them and went to the privy, where he did what he needed, and then performed careful ablution. Returning to his room, he prayed and ate a morsel, before sitting down to read a chapter of the Koran. When he had finished, he said to the slave in an indifferent voice: 'Whither have you taken the young girl, O Sawwāb?' 'What young girl, my master?' asked the astonished slave, and Kamar al-Zamān raised his voice, crying: 'Give me a straight answer, you scamp! Where is the young girl who passed the night upon my bed?' 'As Allāh lives I have seen no young girl,' exclaimed the slave. 'No one could have entered, for I was sleeping across the door.' 'Eunuch of misfortune,' cried the prince, 'do you also thwart me and heat the humours of my blood? I see that they have instructed you to lie; but I command you to speak the truth.' The slave lifted his arms to heaven, crying: 'Allāh alone is great! I do not understand anything of what you are saying, my master.'

'Come here, you wretch!' shouted Kamar al-Zamān; and, when the eunuch approached, he threw him to the floor and heaped blows upon him till he broke wind. When the blackamore was half dead and answered the prince's questions with inarticulate cries, the latter fetched the stout hempen rope which was used for the well and, passing it under the slave's arms, let him down into the water.

It was winter, the water was unpleasant and the air cold; so the eunuch began to sneeze violently, howling for pardon. But the prince dipped him up and down several times, crying: 'You shall not come out until you tell me the truth.' 'Surely he will do what he says,' thought the eunuch, and called aloud: 'Pull me up, and I will tell you the truth, O Prince.' Kamar al-Zamān hoisted him to the surface, and he stood there shivering like a reed in the wind, with chattering teeth and bleeding nose. Feeling himself for the moment out of danger, he obtained leave of his persecutor to change his clothes and stanch the blood; but, instead of doing so, he ran to the palace and found the King.

At this moment Shahrimān was saying to his wazīr: 'I have passed a bad night, for my heart was heavy lest so tender a youth as my son might have come to harm in the old tower.' The wazīr answered: 'I assure you that no harm has come to him; he is better where he is, if you have any wish to tame his pride.'

Even as the wazīr spoke, the eunuch fell at the King's feet, crying: 'O our master the Sultān, misfortune has come into your house! My young lord woke this morning in a state of madness. As a proof, he said such and such and did to me such and such. Now I swear by Allāh that I never saw any young girl.'

When he heard this, King Shahrimān supposed that his fears were realised and cried to his wazīr: 'A curse be upon you, O wazīr of dogs! It was you who suggested I should shut up my son, the light of my heart! Rise up now, see what has happened, and immediately bring me word.'

The wazīr made all haste to the tower, asking questions of the eunuch by the way. His replies were so disquieting that the old man entered the room with boundless precaution; first his head, and then his body, bit by bit. You may picture his surprise when he saw Kamar al-Zamān sitting calmly on his bed and reading the Koran with reverent attention.

At this point Shahrazād saw the approach of morning and discreetly fell silent.

But when the hundred-and-eighty-seventh night had come

SHE SAID:

The wazīr went up to the bed and sat down on the floor beside it, saying: 'This pitch-dark eunuch has put us all in a great fright. Would you believe that he ran to us like some scabby dog and frightened us all with news so indecent that I would not repeat it before you. I am still all of a tremble through his false reports.' 'Indeed,' replied Kamar al-Zamān, 'he cannot have been more of a nuisance to you than he was to me. I should be interested to hear what he said.' 'Allāh preserve your youth!' the wazīr answered. 'Allāh strengthen your understanding! Allāh preserve you from heedless acts and from words which have no salt to them! This son of a bugger said that you had suddenly gone mad, that you spoke of a girl who had lain by you all the night, that you had beaten him and thrown him into the well. Oh, what insolence from a putrescent black man!'

Kamar al-Zamān smiled knowingly and answered: 'Have you not had enough of this joke, you dirty old man, or do you want to visit my new hammām at the bottom of the well? I warn you that, if you do not tell me at once where my father has hidden my divine, my rose-cheeked, my black-eyed mistress, I will treat you worse than I treated the eunuch.'

The wazīr recoiled in fear, saying: 'May the name of Allāh be upon you and about you! Why do you speak in this way, O Kamar al-Zamān? If it is some dream that you have had through indigestion, clear your mind of it, I pray; for these are not the remarks of a sane person.'

'Sinister old man,' cried the prince, 'I did not see her with my ears, but with these two eyes; I did not touch or smell the roses of her body with my eyes, but with these fingers and this nose. So take that!' He butted the wazīr in the belly with his head, so that the old man fell over; then, getting a good grip on his long white beard, he beat him until his own strength failed.

The unhappy wazīr, feeling his beard giving way hair by hair and his soul slipping away from him bit by bit, thought to himself: 'Now I had better lie myself out of the hands of this young maniac.' Aloud he said: 'Master, I beg your pardon for having deceived you; only your father forbade me, on pain of being hanged instantly, to reveal the place where he has concealed the girl. If you will let me go

I will run to him and beg him to release you from this place and marry you to the child: surely he will rejoice in doing so!'

Kamar al-Zamān let go, saying: 'Run now, and return immediately with my father's answer.' The wazīr incontinently leapt from the room, double-locking the door behind him, and hurried, clothed as he was in indignation and torn garments, to the throne-room of the King.

Shahrimān looked at him and said: 'I see you ill-treated and without your turban. Some terrible thing must have happened to you.'

'A more terrible thing has happened to your son,' answered the wazīr, 'for he has gone quite mad, past peradventure.'

The King saw the light change to darkness before his eyes and said: 'Allāh help me! In what way is my child mad?' The wazīr told him, and the King at once flamed out into a great anger, crying: 'O pestilence among wazīrs, this news shall cost you your head! If my son be as you say, I shall crucify you on the highest minaret in the city, to teach you what advice it is meet to give and what to leave ungiven.' With that he ran to the tower and entered the chamber of Kamar al-Zamān with the wazīr at his heels.

The young prince rose in honour of his father and stood before him with folded arms, after having kissed his hands as a good son should. The King, delighted to see him so calm, threw an arm about his neck and kissed him between the eyes with tears of joy. Then he made the youth sit beside him on the bed and, turning with wrath to the wazīr, exclaimed: 'Now you can see for yourself that you are the last of the very last of wazīrs. How dared you tell me that my son was such and such, making my heart afraid and crushing my liver to fragments? Now you shall hear with your own ears the most sane replies of my dear son.' He looked at Kamar al-Zamān paternally and asked:

'My child, what day of the week is to-day?' 'It is Saturday,' answered the other. 'You hear that?' cried the King, with a terrible glance of triumph at the wazīr; then he continued:

'And what day will to-morrow be; can you tell me that, O Kamar al-Zamān?' 'Indeed, I can,' replied the prince, 'to-morrow will be Sunday; the next day Monday, the next Tuesday, the next Wednesday, the next Thursday, and the next Friday which is a holy day.'

At this point Shahrazād saw the approach of morning and discreetly fell silent.

But when the hundred-and-eighty-eighth night had come

SHE SAID:

The delighted King cried: 'Heaven defend you from all evil, my son! Now tell me, in good Arabic, in what month we are?' The young man answered: 'This is Dhul-Kadah. It will be followed by Dhul-Hijjah, that by Muharram, that by Safar, that by Rabīa the First, that by Rabīa the Second, then come the two Jumādas, and afterwards Rajab, Shaabān, Ramadān and Shawwāl.'

The King in his relief and joy spat at the wazīr's face, saying: 'You are the only madman here, detestable old man.' The wazīr shook his head and answered nothing, considering that this was not the end.

Then said the King to his son: 'My child, if you will believe it, this wazīr and this pitch-black eunuch came and reported such and such of you, and that you had said a girl had been with you in the night. Tell them to their faces that they lie!'

'Father,' said Kamar al-Zamān with a bitter smile, 'I cannot enjoy this joke any more. I pray you spare me any further humiliation, for I feel the humours of my body changed with what you have already made me endure. I have determined to obey you, and I willingly consent to marry the lovely woman whom you sent to my bed last night. My blood boils with her still; I find her admirable.'

At these words of his son the King cried: 'May the name of Allāh be upon you and about you, my child! May he preserve you from the evil of madness! What nightmare is this? Did you eat so heavily yesterday that the consequent dreams have played havoc with your wits? Return to your right senses, my son; I shall never go against your wishes again. Accursed alike be marriage and the hour of marriage, and any who dare in the future to talk of marriage!'

Kamar al-Zamān answered: 'Your words are before my eyes, O father. But first swear to me, I pray you, that you know nothing of the adventure of this night; for I can prove to you that it has left traces.' 'I swear by the truth of the sacred name of Allāh, God of Moses and Abraham, who sent Muhammad among His creatures to be a promise to them of Peace! Amen!' cried the King, and Kamar al-Zamān repeated: 'Amen!' Then he said to his father:

'If someone came to you, saying: "Last night I woke and saw before me a form in act to wrestle with me till the blood came and, although I did not wish to fight with this figure, an unconscious

23

movement of my sword took it in the middle of its naked belly, so that this morning my blade was still foaming and bloody," and proved his statement by showing you the bloodstained sword, what would you say, my father?' 'I would say,' answered the King, 'that the sword without the body of the victim was but half a proof.'

Then said Kamar al-Zamān: 'My father, when I woke this morning I found the lower part of my belly covered with blood. The basin is still in the privy which will prove this to you; and, as further witness, here is the girl's ring which I found upon my finger. My own has disappeared.'

At this point Shahrazād saw the approach of morning and discreetly fell silent.

But when the hundred-and-ninety-first night had come

SHE SAID:

The King hurried to the privy and, seeing that the basin of his son's ablution held a great quantity of blood, said to himself: 'I think that the victim of that duel must have been very healthy; it is a royal wound. I see the hand of my wazīr in this.' He returned to his son and, taking the ring from him, turned it over and over for a long time, before he returned it to him and said: 'This is a proof which troubles me.' He remained silent for a whole hour, before he cried to the wazīr: 'Old bawd, you have arranged this mystification!' But the wazīr fell at his feet, swearing by the Holy Book and by the Faith that he knew nothing of the business; and the eunuch swore to his ignorance with the same oaths.

'Allāh alone can solve this mystery,' cried the perplexed King to his son; but the other answered in a trembling voice: 'I beg you to hunt out this girl, for my soul cannot forget her. Have compassion upon me and find her, or I shall die.' The King wept and answered: 'O Kamar al-Zamān, only Allāh is great, only He can know that which is not known. There is nothing left for us but to mourn together; you for a hopeless love, and I because I am powerless to cure your pain.'

The King led his son out of the tower by the hand and returned with him to the palace, where he refused to pay attention to the affairs of the kingdom. Instead he mourned by the bed on which Kamar al-Zamān lay despairing for his lost and unknown mistress.

In order that he might remove himself further from the people

and concerns of the court, and might occupy himself with nothing
but the care of his dear son, he had a palace built in the midst of the
sea, joined only to the mainland by a pier twenty cubits wide. There
they lived together alone, far from all noise, dreaming of their misfortune. Kamar al-Zamān found no consolation save in reading
romances about love and reciting the verses of inspired poets. This
was one out of a thousand:

> Brave child, who wins
> Each skirmish in the battle of the roses,
>   Your loot lies purple on your brow;
> And one supposes
>   The captives of the garden now,
>   The vanquished each and all,
>   Lean down to kiss your feet, as small
> And sweet as sins.

> O princess maid,
> The winds of evening get their sweet
> By kissing your two feet.
>   We have lost many a summer breeze
>   Which ventured underneath your light chemise
> And stayed.

> O not large queen,
> The necklace of your naked throat has felt
> Wantonly jealous of your belt;
>   The golden bracelets of your either wrist
>   Are envious of your anklets, which have kissed
> And seen what they have seen.

The night was already far spent when the two Afārīt placed the
lady Budūr on her bed, so that in three hours morning came, and she
woke. She smiled and stretched herself in that delicious waking by a
lover's side. While her eyes were still shut, she put forth her arms
to him, and clasped the empty air. Then she became wide awake on
the instant, and her heart and mind were so troubled by the disappearance of the youth that she uttered a great cry, which brought
her nurse and the nine other old women running to her side. 'What
is it, my mistress?' called the frightened nurse.

At this point Shahrazād saw the approach of morning and
discreetly fell silent.

But when the hundred-and-ninety-third night had come

SHE SAID:

Budūr cried out: 'You ask me as if you did not know, O cunning one! Tell me at once what has become of the sweet young man who lay in my arms all night; for I love him passionately.' The scandalised old woman thrust out her neck to hear better, and said: 'Allāh preserve you from all improper matters, O princess! This is not your usual kind of conversation; if it be a joke, please tell me.' Budūr half rose on her bed and answered in a threatening voice: 'Nurse of misfortune, I order you: tell me what has become of that youth to whom last night I gave my body, my heart, and my virginity.'

The nurse saw the world diminishing before her eyes; she beat her face and fell with the other nine old women to the ground. While these called out: 'O black morning! O prodigy! O loss! O tar!' the nurse said through her tears: 'In Allāh's name, dear lady Budūr, collect your wits, for such conversation is unworthy of you.' 'Will you be quiet, wicked old woman!' cried the princess. 'Tell me what you have done with my black-eyed lover. His brows were arched and turned up at the corners, he lay with me until the morning, and he had something below his navel which I have not.'

The nine old women raised their hands to heaven, crying: 'O confusion! Allāh preserve our mistress from madness, from snares, and from the evil-eye! Her joke goes a little too far this morning!' And the nurse, beating her breast, said to the princess: 'If these naughty words came to the ears of the King, he would kill us all; we would never be able to escape his wrath.' 'I ask you for the last time,' answered Budūr, with trembling lips, 'to tell me what you have done with the boy whose traces I still bear upon my body.'

The old woman shrieked: 'That one so young should have gone mad,' and the princess was so angry at these words that she unhooked a sword from the wall and threw herself upon the collection of dames. These at once fled from the apartment, jostling each other and bellowing, until they came into the presence of the King. The nurse, with tears in her eyes, told the monarch what had happened to Budūr, and added: 'She would have killed us all if we had not fled.' 'This is a terrible thing!' cried Ghayyūr. 'But are you really sure that she has lost what she says she has lost?' The nurse hid her face between her fingers, and said: 'I saw for myself. There was a great deal of blood.' 'It is extraordinary,' said the King and, dressed as he was, with naked feet and his night-turban upon his head, ran to his daughter's apartment.

The King looked sternly at Budūr, saying: 'Is it true, as these old fools say, that you lay with someone last night, and still bear traces of his passage? That you have lost what you have lost?' 'Indeed it is true, my father, and I am sure that it was your doing. You chose the young man well. He is so beautiful that I burn to know why he has been taken away from me. See, here is the ring which he gave me when he took mine.'

Then the King, who, as you will remember, already thought that his daughter was half mad, said to himself: 'Never was such complete lunacy!' and added: 'My child, I wish you to explain the reason for your undignified conduct.' At that Budūr tore her chemise from top to toe and beat her cheeks amid a storm of sobs; therefore the King ordered the old women and the eunuchs to hold her hands, in case she should do herself an injury, and even, if she became worse, to chain her with an iron collar to the window.

Then, in his despair, Ghayyūr returned to his own palace, cudgelling his brains to think of some cure for the daughter whom he loved with his whole heart, and whom he could not believe to be irremediably deranged.

He called together all the learned men of his kingdom, the doctors, astrologers, chemists, and those versed in the books of old, and said to them: 'My daughter, the lady Budūr, is in such and such a state. Who cures her shall have her to wife, and inherit my throne after my death; but who goes to her and does not make her well, shall have his head cut off.'

These promises were proclaimed throughout the city and neighbouring states, so that many doctors, learned men, physicians, and chemists, came to the test; and very soon forty heads were arranged in a fair pattern along the front of the palace. 'This is not a good sign,' said the others, 'we consider the disease incurable.' Not another of them dared risk his head: surely that is an excellent way to treat doctors.

Now the Princess Budūr had a foster brother, the son of her nurse, whose name was Marzawān. Although he was a good Believer, he had studied magic and sorcery, Hindu and Egyptian books, talismanic characters, and the art of stars; then, when he had no more to learn, he had travelled through far countries and conferred with the masters of secret sciences. At this point in the tale he had just returned to his own country.

The first thing he saw on entering the city were the forty heads fastened to the gate of the palace; and, when he asked what these might mean, the passers-by told him of the notable ignorance of the doctors, which had so justly been punished.

At this point Shahrazād saw the approach of morning and discreetly fell silent.

But when the hundred-and-ninety-fourth night had come

SHE SAID:

When Marzawān had kissed his mother the nurse, he asked for news of Budūr, and was confirmed in what he had heard. Therefore he became sorrowful, for he loved the princess with a love which is unusual between brothers and sisters. After reflecting for an hour, he asked his mother if it were possible for her to introduce him into the presence of the princess, that he might see if her illness were curable. 'It is difficult, my son,' answered the old woman, 'but, since you wish it, hasten to dress yourself as a woman and follow me.' Without delay Marzawān disguised himself and followed his mother.

The eunuch on guard wished to prevent them entering Budūr's apartment, but the old woman slipped a substantial present into his hand, saying: 'O chief of the palace, our dear princess, who is so sick, told me that she wished to see my daughter who was brought up with her. Therefore let us pass, O father of politeness.' So the eunuch, doubly gratified, told them not to stay too long, and they entered.

As soon as he saw the princess, Marzawān lifted the veil which covered his face and brought from under his garments an astrolabe, some magic books, and a candle. He was about to cast Budūr's horoscope before questioning her, when she threw her arms about his neck, saying: 'Do you also think I am mad, my brother? If so, you are mistaken. Reflect on these words of the poet:

> They said: 'She is mad.'
> I answered: 'Would that I had
> Followed the madman's rule
> Of looking on life from another angle
> To find it beautiful.'

When he heard these lines, Marzawān understood that Budūr was in love and nothing more. 'A wise man only needs a sign,' he said. 'Tell me your story, and, if Allāh wills, I may bring you health and consolation.' Budūr told him all the details of her love, adding tearfully: 'Such is my sad lot; I weep by night and day; my burning heart is hardly refreshed by love songs.'

Marzawān lowered his head and stayed for an hour in deep thought, before he said: 'As Allāh lives, your tale is clear enough, though it is not easy to understand. I think that I can satisfy your desires, but you must be patient until you see me again. I swear that, when you look upon me next, I will be leading your lover by the hand.' With that he retired precipitately and, on the same day, left the city of King Ghayyūr.

For a whole month Marzawān journeyed from city to city and from island to island, hearing nothing talked of but the strange tale of the lady Budūr's indisposition. At last, however, he came to a great city by the sea, the name of which was Tarab, and there the people were not talking of Budūr, but of the surprising illness of a prince called Kamar al-Zamān, who was the son of the King of those countries. Marzawān found the details of this story so like those which he knew concerning Budūr, that he at once asked where the prince might be found. Being told that he could make Khālidān in six months by land and in one month by water, he chose the sea way and embarked on a boat which was just setting sail for the islands of King Shahrīmān.

A favourable breeze followed the boat until the last day of her voyage, when she was actually in sight of Khālidan; then a terrible storm smote the sea and, lifting the ship in air, broke her to pieces on a pointed rock. Marzawān was an expert swimmer, so that he alone was able to save himself by clinging to a mast which was left floating on the sea. The waves bore him to a tongue of land on which was built the mourning palace of Kamar al-Zamān and his father.

Fate willed that the wazīr, who had just been reporting on the state of the kingdom to Shahrīmān, should be looking out of the seaward window. He saw the young man come to shore, and ordered his slaves to go to his assistance. These soon brought Marzawān to the wazīr, who gave him a change of garments and made him drink a glass of sherbert to calm his spirits.

The wazīr was delighted with the appearance of this handsome stranger; he questioned him and greatly approved of the wise answers he received. 'Surely,' he said to himself, 'this young man must know something of medicine.'

At this point Shahrazād saw the approach of morning and discreetly fell silent.

But when the hundred-and-ninety-sixth night had come

SHE SAID:

The wazīr said to Marzawān: 'Allāh has led you here that you may cure a sick man, whose distemper greatly grieves his loving father and all of us. I refer to Prince Kamar al-Zamān, son of King Shahrimān.'

'Destiny is on my side,' said Marzawān to himself, and added aloud: 'From what illness does the King's son suffer?' 'For my own part,' answered the wazīr, 'I am persuaded that it is madness pure and simple; but his father believes rather in the evil-eye, and seems almost to give credit to the strange story which his son told him.'

Marzawān rejoiced as the wazīr told him the tale of Kamar al-Zamān; for he was persuaded that the prince was none other than the young man who had left so sweet a memory within the bed of princess Budūr. He was careful, however, to say nothing of this to the wazīr; but contented himself with remarking: 'If I saw the young man, I could tell better what remedy should be applied to him. Under Allāh's grace, I might even be able to cure him myself.'

Without a moment's delay the wazīr introduced Marzawān into the presence of the prince, and the first thing which struck him was the extraordinary resemblance between Kamar al-Zamān and Budūr. He could not prevent himself from exclaiming: 'Blessed be Allāh Who has created two beauties so alike, giving them the same kind and the same perfection!'

Kamar al-Zamān, who was lying weakly upon his bed with half-shut eyes, started when he heard these words, and listened attentively while Marzawān improvised these verses, which should explain his coming to the young man, while leaving King Shahrimān and the wazīr in ignorance:

> Because I wish to remember
> I will sing a certain song.
> They told me that I was wounded,
> But that the cup waited,
> And the lute waited for me.

Why should the blue chemise
Which has done nothing
Lie so close,
Or the insensate cup
Be so long against those lips?

Do not be angry with me:
Joseph broke fewer hearts,
David was less melodious before Saul,
Mary the mother of Christ
Had not her tenderness.

Cures,
Do not talk to me of cures!

When Kamar al-Zamān heard these verses, a soothing freshness descended upon his heart, and he signed to his father to seat the young man by his side and leave him alone with him. Delighted to see his son interested in something at last, Shahrimān seated Marzawān by the bedside and left the chamber, winking to his wazīr to follow him.

Marzawān whispered in the prince's ear:

'Allāh has led me hither that I may serve as a link between you and the woman you love. Here is the proof of what I say.' He gave such details of the night which the two young people had passed together that there could be no room for doubt in the prince's mind. 'The girl's name is Budūr,' he added. 'She is the daughter of King Ghayyūr, and my own foster-sister.'

Kamar al-Zamān felt his strength come back to him; he rose from the bed and took Marzawān by the arm, saying: 'I will set out with you at once for the land of King Ghayyūr.' 'It is rather far,' answered the young man. 'First get completely well, and then we will set out together, for you alone can cure the princess.'

At this point Shahrazād saw the approach of morning and discreetly fell silent.

But when the hundred-and-ninety-ninth night had come

SHE SAID:

Led by curiosity, King Shahrimān re-entered the hall at this moment, and the breath halted in his throat for joy when he saw the shining face of his son and heard him say: 'I wish to dress and go to the hammām.'

The King threw himself upon Marzawān's neck and kissed him, without thinking to ask how he had wrought this cure. He showered him with gifts and honours; he illuminated the whole city and distributed a prodigious quantity of robes of honour to his nobles; he opened all the prisons and let the captives free, so that the kingdom was filled with joy.

When Marzawān judged that the prince was strong enough, he took him aside, saying: 'The moment has come for departure; therefore make your preparations.' 'But,' answered the other, 'my father will never let me go, for he loves me too much. Yā Allāh, what a misfortune! Surely I shall become ill again.' Marzawān consoled him, saying: 'I had foreseen that difficulty, and have invented a benevolent lie which will favour our escape. You must tell the King that you wish to hunt with me for a few days and breathe the good air into a breast too long narrowed by the sick-room. Surely he will not refuse.' Kamar al-Zamān went delightedly and asked permission from the King, who did not dare to refuse him, but stipulated that he should lie away from home only for one night. 'I would die of grief if you were absent any longer,' he said, and prepared two magnificent horses, with six relays, for his son and Marzawān. Also he loaded a dromedary with hunting gear and a camel with food and water-bags.

The King embraced the two young men with tears in his eyes, and saw them leave the city with their company. Once outside the walls, the youths pretended all day to be in search of game, in order to delude their grooms and huntsmen. That night they had the tents pitched and, after eating and drinking, fell into a sound sleep. At midnight Marzawān gently woke his friend, saying: 'Let us be gone while our people are asleep.' Each mounted one of the relay horses and left the encampment without having been noticed.

They proceeded at a good pace till dawn, and then Marzawān halted and begged the prince to dismount. Kamar al-Zāman did so and, when Marzawān asked him to take off his shirt and drawers, obeyed without question. 'Give them to me, and wait here a little,' said the young man, as he tucked the garments under his arm and set off towards a place where the road branched into four. He had brought an extra horse with him from the camp; when he reached the cross-roads, he led it a little way into the forest and cut its throat.

Then, staining the shirt and drawers with the animal's blood, he threw them into the dust of the road and rejoined the prince. When Kamar al-Zamān questioned him as to his plan, he answered: 'First let us break our fast.' They ate and drank, and then Marzawān explained: 'When two days pass without our returning and our huntsmen report that we left them in the middle of the night, the King will send men to seek us. These will find your clothing at the cross-roads, covered with blood and containing a little horse-flesh and two broken bones which I had the forethought to place within them. They will think that you have been devoured by some savage beast and that I have fled. I know that this supposition will be a terrible blow to your father; but think of his later joy when he hears that you are alive and married to the Princess Budūr!' 'O Marzawān,' exclaimed the prince, 'it is an excellent plan, but how shall we pay the expenses of our journey?' 'Do not trouble yourself for that,' returned the other, 'for I have brought my most beautiful jewels with me, and the least of them is worth two hundred thousand dīnārs.'

They journeyed for many days and came at last to the city of King Ghayyūr, which they entered at full gallop by the great gate of the caravans.

Kamar al-Zamān wished to go at once to the palace, but his companion bade him be patient and led him to a khān which was much used by rich strangers. They rested there for three days from the fatigues of their journey, and during that time Marzawān had a complete astrological outfit in gold and precious metals made for the prince. On the fourth day he conducted him to the hammām and, after they had both bathed, dressed him in the garments of an astrologer. Only then, and after giving him minute instructions, did he lead him to the palace and leave him at the door, in order to go himself to his mother, that she might advise the princess of his return.

At this point Shahrazād saw the approach of morning and discreetly fell silent.

But when the two-hundredth night had come

SHE SAID:

Kamar al-Zamān came up to the door of the palace and proclaimed in a loud voice to the crowd in the square and to the sentinels and door-keepers:

Remember me:
I am the master of astrology,
The chief of wizardry,
The cord of blackest curtainry,
The supreme key
Of every treasury,
The pen by whose calligraphy
Black book and amulet come to be,
The hand which subtilely
Spreads out the sands of prophecy
And draws electuary
From written charactry;
Being talismanic energy
My word is victory.
I make the malady
Turn aside and flee
To the emunctory;
I scorn contemptuously
In my great artistry
Either inflammatory,
Or any vomitory,
Or sternutatory,
Prayers jaculatory,
Or words of suppliancy,
Or modes propitiatory;
Thus I can guarantee
With certainty
Immediate remedy.
I am the chief of wizardry;
Come speedily,
I take not currency
Nor any other fee,
But work entirely
For notoriety:
Remember me!

The people, the guards, and the door-keepers were stupefied by such eloquence; especially as they thought that the race of doctors and magicians had ceased to be. They surrounded the young astrologer and, seeing the perfection of his beauty, were charmed and

grieved at the same time; for they feared that he would suffer the
same fate as those who had gone before him. They who were
nearest to the velvet-covered car on which he stood, begged him
to be gone, saying: 'By Allāh, lord magician, do you not know the
fate which awaits you here? The King is certain to command you to
try your science on his daughter, and then your head will go to join
those others.'

Kamar al-Zamān only answered by crying:

> Remember me,
> I am the chief of wizardry;
> I scorn contemptuously
> In my great artistry
> Or tube injectory
> Or bag suspensory
> Or burning pungency.
> Therefore come speedily!

And those who were round became convinced of his knowledge and
yet feared to see him fail before an incurable disease. They beat their
hands together, crying: 'Woe for his youth!'

The King heard the tumult outside his window and, seeing a
crowd surrounding an astrologer, sent his wazīr to fetch the man
into his presence. As soon Kamar al-Zamān stood before the
throne, he kissed the earth between the King's hands, and made him
this compliment:

> There are eight things
> Which make the wise
> Bow before kings:
> Knowledge and strength and power,
> To give at the apt hour,
> Good luck and victories,
> A bird's voice on bird's wings,
> A taste for subtleties.

King Ghayyūr looked attentively at the astrologer, and shut his
eyes for a moment at so much beauty. Then he commanded the
youth to sit by his side and said to him: 'My child, you would look
better without these medicinal garments. I would be very happy to
give you my daughter to wife if you cured her; but I doubt if you
will succeed, and do not wish to have to do with you that which

I have sworn to each who should look upon her face and fail to make her well. Therefore tell me if you consent to the conditions.'

'O auspicious King,' answered Kamar al-Zamān, 'I have come from far away to prosper by my art and not to hide it in silence. I know what I risk, but I will not draw back.' Then said the King to his chief eunuch: 'Take him to the prisoner, since he insists.'

As the two went towards Budūr's apartment, the eunuch, seeing his companion hurry, said to him: 'Unhappy boy, do you really think that you will become the son-in-law of the King?' 'I hope so, indeed,' answered the prince. 'I am certain that I can cure the princess, without even seeing her, and spread the fame of my art abroad among all this people.'

'If you can do that,' answered the astonished eunuch, 'you will deserve everything which can be given to you.' Then said Kamar al-Zamān: 'As I am anxious to see the princess who shall be my wife, let me go in quickly; I will cure her from behind a curtain in her room.'

The eunuch did as he was requested, and the prince, sitting on the floor behind the curtain, took paper and writing materials from his belt and wrote the following letter:

At this point Shahrazād saw the approach of morning and discreetly fell silent.

But when the two-hundred-and-fourth night had come

SHE SAID:

'*These lines are from the hand of Kamar al-Zamān, son of the Sultān Shahrimān, King in the lands of Mussulmān over the Isles of Khālidān.*

'*To Princess Budūr, daughter of King Ghayyūr, master of al-Buhūr and of al-Kusūr, showing his love for her.*

'If I would tell you of all the fire in my heart, there is no reed in the world hard enough for the expression. Yet if the ink failed, my blood would not fail; and it is the colour of flame, a fire which has burnt me ever since that magic night when you appeared to me in sleep.

'Under this cover is your ring. I send it as certain proof that this letter comes from that young man, whose heart your glances burnt as fire burns bran, who is as yellow as saffron because he cannot yet reach you for the whirlwind's ban. He cries to you *Aman* and signs himself as

Kamar al-Zamān.

'I lodge at the Great Khān.'

The prince folded this letter and, slipping the ring inside it, sealed it and handed it to the eunuch. The slave gave it at once to his mistress, saying: 'Madam, there is behind your curtain a certain young astrologer, so audacious that he pretends to be able to cure folk without seeing them. He has sent this paper to you.'

No sooner had the princess opened the paper than she recognised her ring and cried aloud; pushing aside the eunuch, she ran through the curtain and knew her lover. Then it might have been thought that she was really mad; she threw herself upon his neck, and they kissed like two doves which had been long away from each other.

The eunuch ran to tell the King what was happening, and said: 'That young astrologer is more learned than any of them; he has cured your daughter without even seeing her.' 'Is that true?' cried the King, and the slave answered: 'My lord, I have seen it with my own eyes.'

Ghayyūr ran to his daughter's room and, seeing that she was indeed cured, kissed her between the eyes because he loved her; then he embraced Kamar al-Zamān, asking whence he came. 'I come from the Isles of Khālidān,' replied the prince. 'I am the son of King Shahrimān.' And straightway he told the whole story to the King.

'By Allāh,' exclaimed Ghayyūr, 'this tale is so marvellous that if it were written with a needle in the corner of an eye, yet would it teach prudence to the circumspect.' Straightway he ordered the cleverest scribes of the palace to write the story in the annals, that it might be handed down for future generations from century to century.

He called the kādī and his witnesses to write out the marriage contract of the lady Budūr with Kamar al-Zamān. The city was decorated and illuminated for seven days and seven nights; the people ate, drank, and rejoiced; and the two lovers loved each other at ease in the midst of festivities, thanking Him who had created them for one another.

One night, after a feast at which all the chiefs of the Inner and Outer Isles had been present, Kamar al-Zamān made use, even more marvellously than was his wont, of the sumptuous perfections of his wife, and fell into a deep sleep. His father, King Shahrimān, appeared in his dreams, saying: 'Is it thus that you abandon me, O Kamar al-Zamān? See, I am dying of grief.' The prince wakened with a start and, rousing his wife, fell into a storm of sighs. 'What is the matter, O eye of me?' asked Budūr anxiously. 'If you have a belly-ache, I will make you a decoction of aniseed and fennel; if you have a headache, I will put a vinegar compress on your forehead; if you have eaten too much this evening, I will put a hot loaf wrapped in linen upon your stomach and give you a mixture of rose-water with water of flowers.'

At this point Shahrazād saw the approach of morning and discreetly fell silent.

But when the two-hundred-and-sixth night had come

SHE SAID:

Kamar al-Zamān answered: 'To-morrow we must set out for my own country, where the King, my father, lies sick. He has appeared to me in a dream, and waits me weeping.' 'I hear and I obey!' answered Budūr, and, although it was still full night, rose up to seek the King, who was in his harīm.

At her order the eunuch at the door went in, and the King, on seeing him, cried: 'Surely you come to announce some disaster, pitch-face?' 'The princess wishes to speak to you,' replied the eunuch, and Ghayyūr answered: 'Wait till I put on my turban.' When he had done so, he went out and said to his daughter: 'My child, what kind of pepper have you been eating that you should be about at this time of night?' 'Father,' answered the princess, 'I wish permission to start at dawn for the land of Khālidān, which is the kingdom of my husband's father.' 'I have no objection to make,' said Ghayyūr, 'provided that you return at the end of a year.' The princess kissed her father's hands by way of thanks and called Kamar al-Zamān, who thanked him also.

By dawn the horses were harnessed, the dromedaries and camels loaded, and every other preparation made. The King recommended his daughter to her husband in his farewell and, giving them numerous gifts in gold and diamonds, saw them a little upon their way. When the sun was well up, he made his last recommendation with tears in his eyes, and returned towards the city, while the young people continued their journey.

The tears of Kamar al-Zamān and Budūr were soon dried by joyful expectation of seeing King Shahrimān. They went forward for thirty days, and at last reached a pleasant meadow which tempted them to pitch their camp and rest for a few days. When her tent had been made ready in the shadow of a palm tree, the lady Budūr, who was weary, ate a light repast and went to sleep.

When Kamar al-Zamān had given orders that the other tents should be pitched far off, so that he and his wife might benefit by the isolation, he also entered the tent and saw Budūr lying in calm slumber. This sight recalled the first wonderful night which they had had together in the tower, for the young girl lay upon the carpets, with her head resting on a pillow of scarlet. She was dressed only in a chemise of apricot gauze and ample drawers of Mosul silk. From time to time the breeze lifted the filmy chemise to her navel, showing her belly, which was as white as snow, with dimples in delicate places, each large enough to hold an ounce of powdered nutmeg.

Kamar al-Zamān recalled these delicious lines of a certain poet:

> Sleeper, the palm trees drink the breathless noon,
> A golden bee sucks at a fainting rose,
> Your lips smile in their sleep. Oh, do not move.

> Sleeper, oh, do not move the gilded gauze
> Which lies about your gold, or you will scare
> The sun's gold fire which leaps within your crystal.

> Sleeper, oh, do not move; your breasts in sleep,
> Allāh, they dip and fall like waves at sea;
> Your breasts are snow, I breathe them like sea foam,
> I taste them like white salt. They dip and fall.

> Sleeper, they dip and fall. The smiling stream
> Stifles its laugh, the gold bee on the leaf
> Dies of much love and rosy drunkenness,
> My eyes burn the red grapes upon your breast.

> Sleeper, oh, let them burn, let my heart's flower.
> Fed on the rose and santal of your flesh,
> Burst like a poppy in this solitude,
> In this cool silence.

Kamar al-Zamān burnt with a desire for his wife which might not be slaked by all the cold water-springs of the world. He leaned over her and, undoing the silk cord of her drawers, stretched his hand towards the warm shadow of her thighs, where it encountered a small hard object. This he drew towards him and found to be a carnelian, held by a silken cord just above the valley of roses. In his astonishment he thought to himself: 'If this stone had not extraordinary virtue and were not very dear to Budūr, she would not keep it so carefully in the most precious part of her body. Surely it must be some talisman given her by her brother, Marzawān, to ward off the evil-eye and all miscarriage.'

Before going further with his caresses, he untied the silk cord and took the stone outside the tent to examine it. Just as he had discovered that the carnelian had four faces, engraved with talismanic characters and unknown symbols, a great bird swooped down from the sky and, more quickly than lightning, snatched it from his hand.

At this point Shahrazād saw the approach of morning and discreetly fell silent.

But when the two-hundred-and-seventh night had come

SHE SAID:
Then the bird perched out of reach on the branch of a great tree and regarded the prince with silent mockery, holding the talisman in its beak.

At this disastrous accident, Kamar al-Zamān's mouth fell open, and he stood still for some moments without being able to move; for he thought of the grief which Budūr would feel when she heard of the loss of so dear a treasure. When he was a little recovered from his consternation, he picked up a pebble and ran towards the tree on which the bird had perched; but, as soon as he came near enough to throw, the bird flew to a further tree; and then, as the prince still pursued, to a still further one. 'He must see the stone,' thought Kamar al-Zamān, 'I will throw it away to show that I wish him no hurt.' And he suited the action to the thought.

The bird, seeing the prince throw away the stone, hopped to the ground; but, when Kamar al-Zamān put forth his hand, it fluttered out of reach. The prince jumped forward and the bird jumped away; the bird jumped away and the prince jumped forward; and this went on for hours and hours, from valley to valley and from hill to hill, until nightfall. 'There is no help save in Allāh!' cried the prince, as he halted out of breath and saw the bird halt also, just out of reach on the top of a little mound.

Kamar al-Zamān sweated more from despair than from fatigue, and was in half a mind to return to the tents; but he said to himself: 'My dear Budūr might die of grief if I announced to her the loss of this talisman, whose powers, though unknown to me, may seem very precious to her. Also, if I return now that darkness has set in, I may lose my way or be attacked by savage beasts.' Not knowing what to decide, he stretched himself wearily on the ground. As he lay he watched the bird, whose eyes shone strangely in the night; each time he moved or tried to crawl nearer, it beat its wings and cried out to signify that it was also watching. At length, worn out with fatigue and emotion, the prince slept.

As soon as he woke he decided to catch the bird at all costs; and the pursuit of the day before began again with no greater success. On the second evening Kamar al-Zamān beat his breast, crying: 'I will follow as long as there is a breath in my body!' and, having eaten certain plants and herbs, he slept again with his face turned towards the bird, who watched him with luminous eyes throughout the night.

For ten days the pursuit continued and, on the morning of the eleventh, the bird led the prince to the gates of a city built by the sea. Here it paused and, laying down the carnelian, uttered three cries which sounded like 'Kamar al-Zamān.' Then it took up the talisman again in its beak and, rising in the air, flew out to sea. For some hours the prince lay raging upon the ground, broken by sobs; then he washed his face and hands in a stream, and lastly walked towards the city, thinking of Budūr's grief and all the dark forebodings which she would entertain at the disappearance of himself and the carnelian. As he went, he murmured poems of separation and the pains of love, of which this was one out of a thousand:

> Not to hear the fools who said:
>   'Ah, you loved too fair a being,'
> Not to see the shaking head
>   Wag: 'She trusted to her seeing,'
> I stopped my ears with the enchanted song:
>   'Though death come after . . .'
> And hid my eyes with the verse: 'Life is long
>   And made for laughter.'

Kamar al-Zamān entered through the gates of the city and walked about the streets, without receiving from a single one of the many inhabitants a kindly glance such as Mussulmāns bestow on strangers. He walked straight ahead, and passed through the opposite gate which led to the suburban gardens.

Finding the gate open in a garden larger than the rest, he went in and was greeted by the gardener in Mussulmān fashion. Kamar al-Zamān wished him peace and greedily drank in the Arabic which was addressed to him; after they had bowed to each other, the prince asked the gardener why all the people of the city looked so coldly and fiercely upon a stranger. The good old man replied:

'Glory be to Allāh, my child, that you have come safely out of their hands. The people who live now in the city are invaders from the black lands of the West; they came up suddenly out of the sea one day and massacred all the Faithful. They worship strange and incomprehensible things, and speak an obscure and barbarous language; they eat evil-smelling, putrescent things, such as rotten cheese and game which they hang up; they never wash, for, at their birth, ugly men in black garments pour water on their heads, and this ablution, accompanied by strange gestures, frees them from all obligation of washing for the rest of their lives. That they might not be tempted by water, they at once destroyed the hammāms and public fountains, building in their place shops where harlots sell a yellow liquid with foam on top, which they call drink, but which is either fermented urine or something worse. And their women, my son, are the abominations of calamity. Like the men they do not wash; but they whiten their faces with slaked lime and powdered egg-shells. They do not wear linen or drawers to protect them from the dust of the road, so that their presence is pestilential and the fire of hell will never clean them. Such are the people among whom I, the last Mussulmān here left alive, must pass what rests to me of earthly existence. Yet I praise the Highest who allowed me to be born in a Faith as pure as the sky from which it comes.'

When he had made an end of these words, the gardener saw, by his listener's face, that the young man was tired and hungry; so he led him to his modest house at the bottom of the garden, and gave him food and drink. After his guest had eaten, he discreetly questioned him concerning his reason for coming to that place.

At this point Shahrazād saw the approach of morning and discreetly fell silent.

But when the two-hundred-and-eighth night had come

SHE SAID:

Kamar al-Zamān was moved by the generosity of the gardener to such an extent that he told him the whole story of his adventures, and ended by bursting into tears.

The old man did his best to console him, saying: 'My child, the Princess Budūr is certain to make her way to Khālidān, your father's kingdom. Here in my house you will find affection, protection and rest, until Allāh send you a boat to take you to the neighbouring Isle of Ebony. There you will find many ships plying to Khālidān. I myself will go every day to the harbour, until I find some merchant who will consent to journey with you to the Isle of Ebony; you might wait for many years before finding one whose destination was Khālidān.'

The gardener kept his word; but first days and then months passed without his finding any vessel bound for the Isle of Ebony.

I hasten to return to the lady Budūr, because her adventures were more than marvellous. When she woke, she opened her arms to clasp Kamar al-Zamān; great was her surprise at not finding him and greater when she saw that her drawers were undone and that the talisman had disappeared. For the time being she only thought that her husband had taken the carnelian outside to examine it, and therefore she waited patiently.

When hours passed and the prince did not return, she became very anxious; and when night fell, she said to herself: 'Yā Allāh, some strange thing is keeping Kamar al-Zamān away from me. But why has the talisman gone also? O evil stone! O wicked brother, to give me as a present the cause of all my grief!'

After two days of waiting, Budūr, instead of collapsing as any other woman would have done under the circumstances, found an unusual strength. She said nothing of her husband's disappearance, for fear that she might be betrayed or badly served by her slaves; and she forbade her maid to say anything of it either. Knowing how perfectly she resembled Kamar al-Zamān, she put aside her woman's garments and dressed herself in a fair striped robe of his, which fitted exactly and left the neck at liberty. In a belt of carved gold she placed a dagger having a jade hilt encrusted with rubies; she covered her head with a rainbow-coloured silk turban, fastened about the brow with a triple cord of young camel's hair. Making her slave dress in the garments which she had discarded, she took a whip in her hand and left the tent. The other walked behind her, so that all thought that she herself was the lady Budūr and that it was Kamar al-Zamān who gave the order for departure.

The princess, in the likeness of her husband, voyaged for many days until she came to a city by the sea. She had her tent pitched near the gate and asked what the name of the city might be. When she was told that it was the capital of the Isle of Ebony, she asked what king ruled over it. 'Our King's name is Armānūs, and he has one daughter of surpassing loveliness, whose name is the lady Hayyāt al-Nufūs,' answered the stranger whom she had questioned.

At this point Shahrazād saw the approach of morning and discreetly fell silent.

But when the two-hundred-and-ninth night had come

SHE SAID:

She sent a letter to King Armānūs, in which she announced herself as Prince Kamar al-Zamān, son of Shahrimān, lord of Khālidān. As King Armānūs was on the best of terms with Shahrimān, he was pleased to do the honours of the city for his son. Therefore he went out to the tents, followed by the principal people of his court, and welcomed the princess with every honour. He even persuaded her, in spite of her hesitation, to accept a lodging in his own palace, and made her entry the cause for three days' sumptuous festivity throughout the whole court.

On the fourth day Armānūs spoke to Budūr of her journey and asked her intention in making it. That day also the princess went to the palace hammām, without calling for the services of a rubber, and came from it so shining and beautiful that people stopped to catch their breath and thank her Creator as she passed by.

King Armānūs sat by her side and, as he spoke with her, her perfection and eloquence so wrought on him that he said: 'My son, it is Allāh Who has sent you to my kingdom that you may be the consolation of my declining years and act towards me as a son and heir. Will you do so, my son? Will you marry my daughter Hayyāt al-Nufūs? No one in the world is so worthy as you of her fortune and her beauty. She is just marriageable, having crossed the threshold of her fifteenth year; an exquisite flower which I would delight to see you breathing. If you accept, I will abdicate my throne in your favour at once, because my great age is wearied by the burden of kingship.'

Princess Budūr was naturally embarrassed by this generous offer and, to prevent her perturbation being seen, cast down her eyes as if reflecting, while a cold sweat like ice stood out upon her brow. 'If I tell him that I, Kamar al-Zamān, am already married to the lady Budūr, he will answer that the Book allows me four wives,' she said to herself. 'If I tell him the truth, he may force me into marriage with himself, and the story is bound to be noised abroad to my ever-lasting shame. If I simply refuse his paternal offer, his love will turn to great hatred and, when I leave his palace, he will set snares to destroy me. Therefore I must accept, and let Destiny work itself out in its own way; for who knows what the gulf of the future may hide? At least, by becoming King, I will have acquired a fair land for Kamar al-Zamān when he returns. As for the consummation of my marriage with the child, I shall have to think out a way.'

She raised her head, with a fine colour which the King attributed to modesty, saying: 'I am the submissive son of the King. I answer that to hear is to obey.' King Armānūs rejoiced exceedingly at this reply and insisted on the marriage taking place at once; before all his wazīrs, amīrs, and chamberlains, he abdicated in favour of Kamar al-Zamān, and announced the change of dynasty in the city and the provinces by means of heralds. In less time than it takes to tell, festivities were organised on a scale which had never been seen before, and, amid cries of joy, to the sound of fifes and cymbals, the marriage contract was written for the new King and Hayyāt al-Nufūs.

That evening the old queen, surrounded by her maidens who cried 'Lū-lū-lū!' for joy, brought the young bride to Budūr's room, and the pretended husband took her gently and, for the first time, raised the veil from her face. Those who were by grew pale with desire and emotion when they saw this wonderful couple; they discreetly retired after a thousand compliments and good wishes, leaving the bridal pair alone in the torchlight of their chamber.

At this point Shahrazād saw the approach of morning and discreetly fell silent.

But when the two-hundred-and-tenth night had come

SHE SAID:

After a rapid inspection, Budūr was delighted with the girlish charms of Hayyāt al-Nufūs; she saw great black frightened eyes, a colouring as pure as water, and little breasts childishly lifting the light gauze which covered them. The young bride smiled timidly with lowered eyes when she knew that she had pleased her husband; though she hardly dared to move, she had herself taken stock of the virgin cheeks of her companion, and found them more beautiful than any which she had yet seen in the palace. She was stirred to the depths of her being when she saw her husband approach and sit down beside her on the carpet-covered mattress.

Budūr took the girl's little hands in her own and gave her a kiss upon the mouth which was so delicious that Hayyāt did not dare to return it, but shut her eyes and sighed for happiness. Taking the small head in the curve of her arm and leaning it against her breast, Budūr softly sang lullabies to the child until she went to sleep with a happy smile upon her lips. Then she freed the slender body from its veils and jewelry and, lying down beside it, slept till morning.

The lady Budūr, who had kept on most of her own clothes and even her turban, hastened to make her necessary ablutions as soon as it was light and, putting on the insignia of royalty, went to her throne-room to receive the homage of the court, to do the business of the state, to put down abuses, to give office and to take it away. Deeming these reforms urgent, she abolished tolls, customs, and prisons; therefore her new subjects loved her and prayed for her prosperity and long life.

In the meanwhile King Armānūs and his wife hastened to ask their daughter news of her bridal. They questioned her as to whether her husband had been gentle; they asked her if she was too tired, for they did not wish to come to the important point at once. 'My husband was delightful,' answered Hayyāt. 'He kissed me on the mouth and I went to sleep on his breast to the rhythm of his lullabies. How tender and gentle he is!' 'Is that all that passed?' asked Armānūs, and she answered: 'That was all.' 'Were you not even undressed?' stammered the queen. 'No, I was not,' replied the little princess. Then her father and mother looked at each other without saying a word, and left the apartment.

When the royal business was over, Budūr returned to the

marriage chamber and asked her bride what the King and Queen had said to her. 'They asked me whether I was undressed,' answered Hayyāt. 'As to that, let me help you,' said Budūr and, undressing the little girl garment by garment, lay down with her naked on the mattress.

Very gently she kissed her between the eyes, asking: 'My lamb, do you love men very much?' 'I have never seen any except the eunuchs of the palace,' answered the other, 'but it appeared to me that they were half men. What is it that they lack?' 'Just what you lack yourself, sweet eyes,' said Budūr, and the child said: 'What is that?' 'A finger!' laughed the false bridegroom.

Little Hayyāt al-Nufūs uttered a stifled cry of terror and, taking her hands from under the coverlet, spread out the ten fingers before her frightened eyes; but Budūr pulled her close and said, kissing her hair: 'As Allāh lives, I was only jesting!' She covered her with kisses until she was quite reassured, and then said: 'Kiss me, gentle one.' Their lips met and stayed. Thus they slept till morning.

At this point Shahrazād saw the approach of morning and discreetly fell silent.

But when the two-hundred-and-eleventh night had come

SHE SAID:

When Budūr went forth to look after the affairs of the nation, the King and Queen came to their daughter, and Armānūs said: 'The blessing of Allāh be upon you, my child. I see that you are still in bed. Did he wound you too much?' 'Not at all,' answered Hayyāt. 'I slept wonderfully well in his beautiful arms; this time he undressed me and covered all my body with delicate little kisses. Yā Allāh, I still feel all tingling and shivery. It is true that he frightened me once by saying that I lacked a finger, but that was only a joke. His kisses were so pleasant, his fingers so sweet upon my naked flesh, his lips so warm, that I thought myself in Paradise.' 'But where are the napkins? Did you lose much blood, my dear?' asked the Queen. 'I did not lose any!' replied the astonished child. At this her father and mother beat their faces, crying: 'Oh the shame, the unhappiness! Why does your husband so despise us?' Little by little, the King entered into a violent passion of anger and, as he withdrew, he cried so loud to his wife that Hayyāt al-Nufūs heard: 'If he does not do his duty to-night and take our daughter's virginity, thus saving our honour, I will find a way to chastise him. I will take away the throne which I have given him, I will drive him from the palace; let him beware lest I do something worse.'

When night came, Budūr found the bride sobbing with her head among the cushions of the bed; when she kissed her brow and wiped away her tears, asking the reason for her despondency, Hayyāt al-Nufūs answered in a dolorous voice: 'Dear my lord, my father wishes to take away the throne which he gave you, and even hinted at worse things, because you do not take my virginity and save the honour of his name. He says that the thing must be done to-night. I only tell you this, sweet master, as a warning, and to persuade you to the act which he requires. All day I have been weeping at your danger. I pray you hasten to take my maidenhead and make the napkins red to delight my mother's eyes. I trust to you entirely and place my body and myself between your hands.'

'Now is the time,' thought Budūr to herself, 'there is nothing else to be done; I put my faith in Allāh.' Then to the young girl she said: 'Sweet eye, do you love me very much?' 'As I would love Paradise,' answered the other. Budūr kissed her on the mouth, asking: 'How much more?' And the little one replied under the kiss: 'I do not know; but very much.' 'Since you love me so,' said Budūr, 'would you be happy if, instead of being your husband, I were only your brother?' 'I would die of happiness,' cried the little one, clapping her hands. 'And supposing, my gentle one,' went on the princess, 'instead of being your brother, I were your sister, would you love me as much?' 'More, more!' exclaimed Hayyāt, 'for then I could be always with you, always play with you, always sleep with you, and never be separated.' Budūr drew the girl to her and covered her eyes with kisses, saying: 'O Hayyāt, can you keep a secret to prove your love for me?' 'Since I love you, everything is easy,' cried Hayyāt al-Nufūs.

After a final kiss which robbed them both of breath, Budūr stood up and, crying: 'Look at me, child, and be my sister!' opened her robe from neck to waist and pulled out two shining white breasts crowned with roses. 'See, I am a woman like yourself, my dear,' she said. 'I am disguised as a man, because of a most strange adventure, which I shall recount to you at once.'

Sitting down again and taking the bride on her knee, she told her the whole story from beginning to end. But nothing would be gained by repeating it here.

Little Hayyāt al-Nufūs marvelled at this tale and, as she lay in the breast of Budūr, took the other's chin in her small hand, saying: 'Dear sister, what a delightful life we are going to live together while waiting for your Kamar al-Zamān. Allāh hasten his coming that our joy may be complete!' 'May He indeed hear your petition, dear,' said Budūr. 'I shall give you to him as a second wife, and the felicity of all three of us will be perfect.' The girls embraced each other and played a thousand games together, so that Hayyāt was astonished at the many beauties which she found in her friend. Taking hold of Budūr's breasts, she said: 'How beautiful they are, dear sister. Look, they are much bigger than mine. Mine are quite tiny; do you think they will ever grow?' After that she examined Budūr everywhere, questioning her about the discoveries which she made; and the elder girl, amid a hundred kisses, clearly exposed to her the use of many things. 'Yā Allāh,' exclaimed Hayyāt, 'now I understand perfectly. When I used to ask the slaves: "What is this for?" and "What is that for?" they were accustomed to wink for sole answer. Sometimes even they would click their tongues, which drove me into a great rage; I used to scratch my cheeks and cry louder and louder: "Tell me what that is for?" Once, hearing my shout, my mother ran in and the slaves said to her: "She is yelling because she wants us to tell her what that is for." Although I promised repentance, the Queen was very angry and, baring my little bottom, gave me a furious slapping, and said: "That is what that is for!" So I ended by believing that its only use was for slapping.'

The pair said and practised a thousand follies, so that by morning Hayyāt al-Nufūs had nothing to learn of the charming uses which her most delicate organs were destined to fulfil.

At this point Shahrazād saw the approach of morning and discreetly fell silent.

But when the two-hundred-and-twelfth night had come

SHE SAID:

When the hour approached for a visit from the King and Queen, Hayyāt al-Nufūs said to Budūr: 'My sister, what shall I say to my mother when she wishes to see the blood of my virginity?' 'That is easy,' smiled Budūr and, going out secretly, she returned with a fowl. She cut its throat and bathed the girl's thighs and dipped the napkins in the blood, saying: 'You need only show her these; for happily custom does not allow any further examination.' 'But why will you not take it yourself, with one of your fingers?' asked Hayyāt. 'Because, my sweet,' replied Budūr, 'I am keeping it for Kamar al-Zamān.'

As soon as the supposed King had departed to his hall of justice, the King and Queen entered to their daughter, ready to give rein to violent anger if the marriage had not been consummated. But, when they saw the blood and reddened thighs, their happiness knew no bounds and they ran to set open all the doors of the apartment. The women of the palace trooped in with cries of joy and triumph, and the proud Queen placed the ensanguined napkins on a velvet cushion, and bore them in procession round all the women's quarter. The King, for his part, gave a great feast and slaughtered countless sheep and young camels for the poor. The Queen and the female guests returned to the young bride and, kissing her with many tears, stayed with her till the evening, when they led her to the hammām, closely covered against the cold.

The lady Budūr sat every day upon the throne of the Isle of Ebony, reigning so justly that all her subjects loved her; but in the evening she joyfully returned to her young friend and, taking her in her arms, lay with her upon the mattress. Clasped together as if they were really husband and wife, they consoled each other with every kind of attempt and pretty game, still waiting for the time when Kamar al-Zamān should come to them.

All this while the prince lived in the house of the Mussulmān gardener, outside the city of the unclean and inhospitable western invaders. At the same time his father Shahrimān, in the islands of Khālidān, being bitterly convinced of his death, made all his kingdom assume mourning and built a funeral monument, in which he shut himself to grieve silently for his child.

In spite of the companionship of the old gardener, who did his best to distract him and to make him believe in the arrival of a boat that should carry him to the Isle of Ebony, Kamar al-Zamān became progressively sadder as he recalled his happy past.

One day, while the gardener was away at the harbour as usual, Kamar al-Zamān sat sadly in the garden and said over verses to himself, as he watched the birds fighting. Suddenly his attention was attracted by the harsh cries of two great birds; he lifted his eyes and beheld them battling in the branches of a tree, with cruel strokes of beak and claw and wing. Very soon one of them fell lifeless at his feet, while the victor flew far away in the sky. Immediately two other birds, which were larger still, flew out of a neighbouring tree and alighted by the side of the dead. One of them stood at his feet, one at his head, and both wept loudly with bowed beaks. Seeing this, Kamar al-Zamān also wept out of sympathy; then, after a few minutes, he saw the two birds dig a grave with their claws and beaks and bury the dead. This done, they flew away and returned carrying between them the murderer, who struggled violently to escape and uttered piercing cries. They held him down over the grave and, ripping up his belly with a few rapid strokes of their beaks, pulled forth his entrails and flew away, leaving him struggling in agony upon the grave.

At this point Shahrazād saw the approach of morning and discreetly fell silent.

But when the two-hundred-and-sixteenth night had come

SHE SAID:

Kamar al-Zamān stayed motionless with surprise at such an extraordinary sight; but, when the birds had flown away, he curiously approached the place where the dead criminal was lying and, while looking at the corpse, saw in the middle of the split belly some red and sparkling thing. He picked it out, and fell in a faint upon the grass; for he had recovered his wife's carnelian talisman.

When he came to himself, he hugged the precious relic to his breast, crying: 'Allāh grant that this be a good omen and that I will find my love again!' He kissed the stone and carried it to his forehead; then he wrapped it carefully in a piece of linen and fastened it safely round his arm, jumping for joy the while.

When he became calmer, he remembered that the good gardener had requested him to cut the roots of an old locust-tree, which bore neither leaves nor fruit. He girt himself with a hempen belt and, taking an axe and basket, set to work with hearty strokes on the roots of the old tree. Suddenly he felt the iron of his tool strike against a metallic object, which gave out a low grumbling sound beneath the earth. Shovelling aside the mould and stones, he found a large plate of bronze, which he hastened to lift. The hollow thus exposed showed him a stair of ten steps, hewn in the living rock; he quickly climbed down and discovered a large square cave, dating from the time of Aad and Thamūd. In this cave were ranged twenty gigantic vases; lifting the cover of the first, he found it filled with ingots of red gold; a second was heaped to the brim with gold dust; and the remaining eighteen held gold in one of these two forms.

As soon as he had recovered from his surprise, he left the cave and, replacing the bronze plate, went on with his work of watering the trees in the garden, until his old friend returned at night fall. The gardener's first words were filled with good news. 'My child,' he said, 'it delights me to tell you that you will soon return to the land of the Mussulmāns. I have found a vessel, freighted by rich merchants, which will set sail in three days and bear you to the Isle of Ebony.' Kamar al-Zamān cried aloud for joy and kissed the old man's hands, saying: 'Father, I also have good news which will rejoice your heart, although I know that you are removed from the greed of this century and that your soul is set above ambition. Come with me to the garden and I will show you the fortune which a compassionate providence has prepared for you.'

At this point Shahrazād saw the approach of morning and discreetly fell silent.

But when the two-hundred-and-nineteenth night had come

SHE SAID:

He conducted the gardener to the locust-tree and, lifting the bronze plate, led him, in spite of his astonished fears, down into the cave. When the gardener saw the twenty jars of gold, he lifted his arms and opened his eyes, crying: 'Yā Allāh!' in front of each vessel. 'Thus is your hospitality rewarded by the Great Giver,' said Kamar al-Zamān. 'That same hand which a stranger held out to you that you might lift him from his adversity, has caused a river of gold to flow into your dwelling. This is the work of Destiny, which loves actions coloured by the beauty of kindness.'

Tears flowed from the old man's eyes and ran down into his beard, before he could say: 'My child, what should an old man like myself do with all this treasure? It is true that I am poor, but my happiness is great enough; it will be complete if you give me a dirham or two with which to buy a winding-sheet. I can lay it by my side when I come to die alone, and the first charitable stranger may dress me in it for the Judgment Day.'

This time it was Kamar al-Zamān who wept. At last he said to the gardener: 'Father of wisdom, old man with perfumed hands, the holy solitude in which your quiet days have passed has made you forget those laws of Destiny which bind the cattle of Adam's seed, both the just and the unjust. But I am myself returning shortly to the company of greedy mortals, and I must not forget the rules which govern them or I shall be devoured. This gold belongs to you in the sight of God; but, if you wish, we will share it. Only if you will not take half, I will touch none of it.'

'My son,' replied the gardener, 'ninety years ago my mother bore me in this place; she died, and my father died also. The benevolent glance of Allāh followed my footsteps as I grew up in the shade of this garden, to the murmur of this native stream. I love the stream and the garden; I love the sighing of the leaves and the sunshine and the grass on which my shadow moves at liberty, and the moon which shines above these trees and smiles upon me until the morning. All these things speak to me in voices which I understand better than the voice of man. You know that I cannot voyage with you to the country of the Mussulmāns, because I am myself the last Mussulmān in a land where many lived of old. I pray to Allāh that my bones may whiten here, and that the last Believer may die with his face turned towards that sun which shines upon an evil world, soiled by the barbarity of the West.'

The old man's hands trembled as he continued:

'As for those precious jars which you admire, since you desire it I will leave ten of them in the cave as a recompense for the stranger who wraps me in my shroud and buries me. The difficulty is not in this; it lies in shipping your jars without exciting the black hearts of this city. Now the olive trees in my garden are heavy with their fruit, but olives are rare and much sought after in the Isle of Ebony. I will buy you twenty large jars, which we will half fill with gold and then complete with olives. Thus we can safely have your treasure carried to the ship.'

Kamar al-Zamān took his friend's advice and spent the day in preparing the new jars. While he was working on the last one, he thought to himself: 'This talisman is not safe upon my arm; it might be stolen during my sleep or lost in some other way. It will be better to place it at the bottom of this jar, and cover it first with gold and then with olives.' This he did, and stoppered the last jar with its cover of white wood. Then, so that he might remember which one it was, he first made a notch in the leather near the bottom of it and then, being started, cut the whole of his name in fair interlacing characters.

When all was finished, he sent his old friend to advise the sailors to come for the jars in the morning. The gardener did as he was asked, and then returned to the house in a state of some fatigue. He lay down shivering, with a light fever upon him.

In the morning the old man, who had never been ill in his life before, felt that his fever had increased; but he said nothing, as he did not wish to sadden Kamar al-Zamān's departure. He lay upon his mattress, growing weaker every hour, and understood that his last moments were not far off.

During the day the sailors came to the garden and asked Kamar al-Zamān to show them what they had to take. He pointed out the twenty jars ranged by the hedge, saying: 'They are filled with olives of the finest quality. I beg that you do not knock them about too much.' Then the captain, who was with his men, said: 'Above all, my lord, do not be late, for to-morrow morning's wind will blow from off shore and we shall be obliged to set sail.' After this the men departed with the jars.

At this point Shahrazād saw the approach of morning and discreetly fell silent.

But when the two-hundred-and-twenty-second night had come

SHE SAID:

Kamar al-Zamān went back to the gardener and found that his face was very pale, though marked with a great serenity. In answer to his enquiries, he learnt of his friend's illness and was much disturbed by it, in spite of the reassurances of the invalid himself. He prepared various decoctions of green herbs, which did little good, and watched over him that day and all through the night, seeing the fever increase every hour. In the morning the good gardener called to him and took his hand, saying: 'Kamar al-Zamān, my son, listen! There is no God but Allāh! And Muhammad is His Prophet!' Then he fell back dead.

Kamar al-Zamān burst into tears and stayed some time weeping by the old man's side; then he shut the eyes of the dead, performed the last rites, made him a white shroud, dug a grave, and buried the last son of the Faith in that idolatrous land. Not till then did he think of going to join his ship.

He collected provision for the journey, locked the gate of the garden, and ran in haste to the harbour; the sun was already high and he saw the ship that should have carried him making, with all sails set before a favourable wind, for the open sea.

His grief and despair were boundless, but he hid them so that the low fellows about the shipping should not laugh at him. He went back to the garden which was now his and, lying down on his bed, wept bitterly for himself and for Budūr and for the talisman which he had just lost for a second time.

In his grief at knowing that he was doomed to stay in that inhospitable country for an unknown length of years, he said to himself: 'My misfortunes began with the loss of the talisman, luck came back to me when I recovered it; and, now that it is gone once more, who can tell what calamity hangs above my head? Yet there is no help save in Allāh!' With that he rose and bought twenty new jars, as he did not wish to risk the loss of the rest of his treasure. He filled the jars with gold covered by olives, saying to himself: 'They will be ready for the day on which Allāh sends me a ship.' After this he took up the old life again, and spent his days in watering the garden and declaiming sad verses about his love for Budūr.

The ship met favourable winds and made a good passage to the Isle of Ebony; it dropped anchor alongside a jetty, overlooked by the palace where Princess Budūr lived in her character of Kamar al-Zamān. Seeing the vessel arriving under a spread of sail and windy flags, Budūr was seized with a desire to visit it, especially as she was always hoping that one of the ships which came to her over the sea would bring her husband back to her. Therefore she ordered some of the chamberlains to accompany her, and went down to the ship.

When she was alongside, she called the captain and went aboard; all too soon she learnt that Kamar al-Zamān was not among the passengers. Through idle curiosity, she said to the master: 'What cargo have you got?' The captain answered:

'My master, beyond our lading of merchants, we have in the hold: beautiful fabrics and silk from all countries, brocades and embroidered velvets, painted cloths in the old style and the new, which make an excellent show; Chinese and Indian drugs, medicines in leaf and powder, salves, pomades, collyriums, unguents, and precious balms; diamonds, pearls, coral, and yellow amber; choice spices and every kind of aromatic thing, musk, amber, incense, transparent tears of mastic; unrefined benzoin, and essences of every flower, camphor, coriander, cardamoms, cloves, cinnamon from Sarandīb, Indian tamarind and ginger; and, at our last port, we took on a quantity of bird-olives, those with the thin skins and sweet flesh, filled with juice and coloured like blond oil.'

At this point Shahrazād saw the approach of morning and discreetly fell silent.

But when the two-hundred-and-twenty-fifth night had come

SHE SAID:

Now Princess Budūr had a passion for olives; so, when she heard the word, she stopped the captain in the middle of his list and asked him, with bright desirous eyes: 'How many of these bird-olives have you?' 'Twenty large jars,' he answered. Then she said: 'Tell me, are they very large? Have they stuffed olives among them? You know the kind; they are stoned and filled with tart capers; my soul prefers them to the ones with stones.' 'I expect there are some of that kind among the rest,' answered the astonished captain.

Budūr felt her palate filled with the water of unsatisfied desire and told the captain that she wished to buy one of the jars. 'As the owner missed the boat,' he answered, 'I cannot sell them; therefore our lord the King has the right to take what he wills.' Then, turning to the crew, he cried: 'Hi, there! Bring one of the twenty olive pots out of the hold.'

This was done on the instant and, when one of the covers had been knocked off, the princess, seduced by the appearance of the fruit, cried: 'I will buy the whole twenty! How much would they fetch in the open market?' 'Olives are much sought after in your kingdom, my lord,' answered the captain. 'I should say that they would fetch a hundred dirhams the jar.' Then said Budūr to her chamberlains: 'Pay the captain a thousand dirhams for each jar!' She departed, followed by porters carrying the jars, and saying over her shoulder to the captain: 'When you return to the owner's country, you will hand over the price to him.'

Budūr ran to tell her friend Hayyāt al-Nufūs of the arrival of the olives; when they were carried into the harīm, the two women had the largest conserve plate brought to them and ordered the slaves to separate on its surface the olives from the first jar, so that they might distinguish between the natural and the stuffed. Great was their astonishment when they saw the olives mingled with gold dust and ingots. Also they were a little disappointed, as they feared that the fruit might have been harmed by this mixture. Budūr commanded other plates to be brought, and had all the jars emptied. While the slaves were dealing with the twentieth, the princess saw, first the name of Kamar al-Zamān carved upon it, and then the talisman, shining red among the yellow olives. She uttered a great cry and fell fainting into the arms of Hayyāt al-Nufūs; for she had recognised the carnelian which had stayed so long fastened to the silk knot of her drawers.

When she came to herself through the ministrations of her friend, she carried the stone to her lips with sighs of contentment and then, dismissing her slaves, said to Hayyāt: 'Dear sweetheart, this is the talisman which separated me from my husband; now that I have found it again, I feel in my heart that he will return to me and fill the souls of both of us with happiness.'

She sent for the captain of the ship and, when he appeared before her, asked him what the owner of the olives did in his own country. 'He is an assistant gardener,' answered the other, 'he should have come with us to sell them in your kingdom, but missed the boat.' Then said Budūr: 'The best of the olives were stuffed. As I tasted them, I recognised that they could only have been prepared by my old cook, for he alone of all men could make a stuffing of capers which at once raises the appetite with its sharpness and soothes the palate with complete softness. This wicked cook of mine fled one day, for fear that I should punish him for having split a kitchen boy while trying hard and disproportionate embraces upon his form. You must set sail at once and bring him back to me, and I will pay you well if you are diligent in the search. If you are not, you shall never land in my kingdom again; or, if you do land, you shall be put to death with all your crew.'

At this point Shahrazād saw the approach of morning and discreetly fell silent.

But when the two-hundred-and-twenty-eighth night had come

SHE SAID:

The captain was constrained to undertake this mission and, although he knew his departure would prejudice his sales, he comforted himself with hopes of the King's liberality. Allāh permitted his ship to make a swift voyage to the unbelieving city, and, a few nights later, he disembarked with the strongest of his crew.

He hastened to the garden where Kamar al-Zamān was living and knocked at the door. The prince was sitting sadly, after his day's work, reciting verses on the subject of separation; when he heard the knocking on the door, he rose and cried: 'Who is there?' The captain answered in a feigned and sorrowful voice: 'One of Allāh's poor!' The prince felt his heart beat compassionately when he heard one asking for help in his native tongue; therefore he opened the door and immediately fell into the hands of the sailors, who pinioned him. Seeing twenty olive pots ranged by the hedge as before, they took them up and bore them to the ship, which immediately set sail.

The captain came up to Kamar al-Zamān, followed by some of his crew, and said: 'So you are the lover of boys, who split the child in the King's kitchen? As soon as we get in, you will find an impaling post ready to return the compliment, unless you would rather be broached in the meanwhile by these jolly fellows, who are filled with abstinence.' As he said this, he pointed to the sailors, who winked at the young man and considered him an excellent windfall.

Although his bonds had been unfastened as soon as the vessel sailed, Kamar al-Zamān had so far said no word; but now, being unable to remain silent under such an accusation, he cried: 'I take refuge in Allāh! Are you not ashamed to speak in this way? Pray for the Prophet!' 'I do pray for Him,' answered the captain, 'I pray that the blessing of Allāh be upon Him and upon His people. Yet it was certainly you who outraged the boy.'

Kamar al-Zamān cried out afresh: 'I take refuge in Allāh!' and the captain said: 'May Allāh be merciful to us all!' Then exclaimed the prince: 'I swear before you all, on the life of the Prophet (upon whom be prayer and peace!), that I understand nothing of what you say, and that I have never set foot in the island to which you are taking me. Pray for the Prophet, good people!' Then all replied according to custom: 'May the blessing of Allāh fall upon Him!'

'Am I to understand, then,' continued the captain, 'that you have never been a cook and never split a child in your life?' Kamar al-Zamān spat indignantly on the deck, saying: 'I take refuge in Allāh! I shall answer no more.' 'That is as you like,' said the captain, 'my business will be done when I hand you over to the King. If you are innocent, you must get out of your scrape in the best way you can.'

Soon the ship came to the Isle of Ebony, and the captain at once led Kamar al-Zamān to the palace, where he was immediately conducted into the presence.

Now Princess Budūr had hit upon a plan, which was really a very clever one for a woman, to safeguard the interest of both of them. As soon as she saw the captain's prisoner, she recognised her beloved and became as yellow as saffron. Her courtiers put down this change of colour to anger; while the prince, in his old gardener's robe, trembled before the monarch who looked at him so closely. He was far from guessing that he was in the presence of her for whom he had shed so many tears.

At last Budūr gained control of herself and said to the captain: 'You may keep the price which I paid for the olives as a reward for your faithful service.' 'And what shall be done with the other twenty pots which I have in my hold?' asked the delighted sailor, as he kissed the earth before the throne. 'Send them to me and you shall receive a thousand dīnārs of gold,' said the supposed King, as she dismissed the captain.

At this point Shahrazād saw the approach of morning and discreetly fell silent.

But when the two-hundred-and-thirtieth night had come

SHE SAID:

Turning towards Kamar al-Zamān, who stood before her with lowered eyes, Budūr said to the chamberlains: 'Take this young man to the hammām and then habit him sumptuously; bring him before me to-morrow at the first hour of the dīwān.'

The princess hastened to her friend Hayyāt al-Nufūs and said to her: 'My lamb, our well-beloved has returned. As Allāh lives, I have thought of a plan which will prevent his recognition of me. I do not wish him to betray us in the sight of any who see one day's gardener made King upon the next. My scheme is such that were it written with needles on the inside corner of an eye, yet would it serve as a lesson for the circumspect.' Hayyāt threw herself joyously into Budūr's arms, and that night the two girls behaved moderately, so that they might later receive their lover in all freshness.

Next morning, as Kamar al-Zamān stood in his rich robes before the throne, his face shining from his bath, his slight waist and mountainous croup shown off by the well-fitting tissues, the amīrs and chamberlains were not surprised to hear the King say to his grand wazīr: 'Give this young man a hundred slaves to serve him, with allowances from the treasury worthy of the rank to which I

raise him from this moment.' Then Budūr named her husband a
wazīr among the wazīrs, and gave him a complement of horses,
mules and camels, of well-filled cupboards and chests.

After this she withdrew. But next morning, still in her character
of King, she called Kamar al-Zamān before her and, taking away his
appointment from the old grand wazīr, invested it upon the prince;
so that he sat in council straightway and began the direction of
affairs of state.

When the dīwān rose, Kamar al-Zamān went aside and reflected
deeply, saying to himself: 'The honour and friendship with which
this young King has loaded me in the presence of all his people
must certainly have some cause. But what is it? The sailors who
brought me here said that I was accused of having harmed a boy;
and the King, instead of punishing me, sends me to the hammām
and richly rewards me. What can lie behind so strange a happening?
. . . As Allāh lives, I have found the reason, and it is a wicked one!
The King, who is young and handsome, must think that I am a lover
of boys and has treated me thus splendidly on that account. But I
swear that I will never undertake such duties. I will discover his
plan and, if he wishes either himself or myself to suffer the shameful
thing, I will return all his gifts and go back to my garden.'

Kamar al-Zamān went to Budūr and said: 'O auspicious King,
you have loaded your slave with honours and positions which are
usually only accorded to the white hairs of wisdom, while I am still
a young boy. If there be not some unknown reason behind all this,
then the thing passes my understanding.'

Budūr smiled and looked at Kamar al-Zamān with languorous
eyes, saying: 'O handsome wazīr, there is, as you say, a reason
behind all this; it is the sudden fire which your beauty has lighted in
my heart. The colouring of your cheeks is both calm and delicate;
I am quite in love with the colouring of your cheeks.' 'Allāh lengthen
the days of Your Majesty,' said Kamar al-Zamān, 'but your slave
has a wife whom he loves with his whole heart, weeping for her
throughout every night since Fate has parted them. Your slave
requests permission to journey on across the sea, after having
given back those delightful things with which you wish to honour
him.'

Budūr took the young man's hand, saying: 'Be seated, O fairest of
wazīrs. Do not speak of departure; rather stay here with one who
burns for the beauty of your eyes and who is very ready, if you

return his passion, to seat you on the throne beside himself. I, even I, only became King because of the love which the old King bore me and the complacence with which I answered it. Gentle youth, you must learn something of the customs of our country; for it is one in which beauty is the sole title to eminence . . .'

At this point Shahrazād saw the approach of morning and discreetly fell silent.

But when the two-hundred-and-thirty-second night had come

SHE SAID:

'Do not forget this truth of one of our greatest poets:

> Our time recalls the age of Lot,
> The Friend of Allāh, who had got
>> A beard
> On cheeks like roses bending to the waters;
> When angels came to visit him
> He kept the lovely cherubim,
>> Nor feared
> To throw the naughty populace his daughters.
>
> God recompensed his charming fault,
> By turning his good wife to salt,
>> A dame
> With shrewish tongue and feminine opinions.
> Our age like his, as I repeat,
> Has learnt to cultivate one sweet
>> Clear flame
> For little boys and paint-and-perfume minions.'

When Kamar al-Zamān heard these verses and recognised their trend, he blushed like a coal under the bellows, and said: 'O King, your slave must confess that he has no taste or aptitude for such things; he is too slight to bear weights and measures which would break the back of an old porter.'

The lady Budūr laughed heartily at this, and continued: 'I do not understand your backwardness, delicious lad. Listen and I will tell you about the thing. Either you are a major or a minor: if you are a minor, you have no responsibilities and cannot be blamed for anything you do; if you are a major (and, to hear you discourse so well,

I imagine you to be so), why do you hold back, for you are master of your own body and may do with it what you will? Nothing happens which was not written; and I myself might more reasonably be backward, seeing that I am smaller than you are. But, on the contrary, I apply these charming verses to myself:

> As the boy looked at it, my thing
>   Moved and he whispered: 'It is splendid!
> Do let me try its love-making.'
>   I answered: 'Such an act is reprehended;
>
> In fact, a lot of people call it awful.'
>   He said: 'Oh, they—oh, they!
> With me all things are lawful.'
>   And I was too polite to disobey.

Kamar al-Zamān saw the light change to darkness before him as he heard these lines; he lowered his eyes, saying: 'O glorious King, you have many young women and beautiful virgins in your palace; no other monarch has ever possessed the like. Why then would you neglect all these for me? Do you not know that it is lawful to use women in any way which desire, curiosity or experiment may suggest to you?'

Budūr smiled, looking sideways at the prince through half-shut eyes. 'Nothing could be more true, O wise and handsome wazīr,' she retorted, 'but when taste changes desire, when our senses become refined and our humours alter their direction, what is to be done? Yet let us leave a discussion which is certain to come to nothing, and listen together to the verses which our chief poets have made upon this subject. One of them has said:

> Come with me to the fruit-seller's green shade:
> Here on cool palm-leaves you may see displayed
>   Ripe figs with their emotional brown bums;
> And in the place of honour you may find
> The small and rosy sycamore's behind,
>   Yea, fruit of sycamore for each who comes.

A second has said:

> Ask the girl whose breasts grow big,
> While consciousness invades her fig,
> Why she prefers the taste of lemons
> To pomegranates and water-melons!

Another has said:

> Though my full and present joys
> Are concerned with tender boys,
> Taste for women never ends
> And my less observant friends
> When they see me go without
> Think I have become devout.

Another has said:

> Brown-breasted Zainab, Hind whose hair is dyed
>   With youthful art, both say that I neglect them
> By finding roses in my friend's backside
>   Fairer than any rose which ever decked them;
> Hind cannot tempt my senses to abide,
>   And Zainab's razored slice cannot affect them;
> Even their bottoms now entice in vain
> One who has learnt of muscles and a mane.

Another has said:

> Who says this fawn of boyish grace
>   Is lovely as a girl,
>   Commits a blasphemy:
>   There is a difference.
> You take a girl at face to face,
>   But the fawn has to curl
>   Round and stoop pleasantly:
>   There is a difference.

Another has said:

> I freed you, child, because your flanks
> Cannot conceive an answer to my wooing;
> Oh, I abominate those tunnelled fats
> Which at the first excitement of my pranks,
> Even before I know what I am doing,
> Hurry indecently to birth
> And fill the suffering earth
> With ranks and ranks and ranks and ranks
> Of useless brats.

Another has said:

> A wife is that unpleasant thing which gets you
> To lie with her and, when no child is born,
> Ignores your deathly lassitude and frets you
> By saying in a voice of peevish scorn:
> 'If being hard for women so upsets you,
> I promise you another kind of horn.'

Another has said:

> A man lifts up his arms to God
> Asking that bliss
> Be his;
> A woman lifts her legs in air
> With the same prayer.
> Is it not odd?

And yet another has said:

> Some women think, because they have
> Bottoms like men, that they can save
> Their faces by analogy.
> I showed one child her fallacy
> The other day, or rather night;
> She showed a grotto sweet and tight,
> And when I said: 'That's out of fashion,'
> Instead of flying in a passion
> She turned quite round and smiled. 'I know
> That modern men do not do so;
> See, I am up-to-date,' she said.
> 'Although you turn your maidenhead,
> I am unworthy,' answered I,
> 'Of such great hospitality.'

Hearing all these poems, Kamar al-Zamān thought that there could be no doubt as to the intentions of the King, and decided that it would be useless to resist any further. Also he was a little tempted to experience for himself this new fashion of which the poets spoke.

At this point Shahrazād saw the approach of morning and discreetly fell silent.

But when the two-hundred-and-thirty-fourth night had come

SHE SAID:

So he answered: 'King of time, I ask you to promise me that we shall do the thing together once and once only. If I consent, it is that I may show you how much better it would be to return to the old fashion. I beg you to give me a formal undertaking that you will not ask me to commit a second time an act for which I ask Allāh's pardon in advance.' 'I give you my formal promise,' cried Budūr, 'and I also pray to the Merciful One that He may lead us from the darkness of error into the light of true wisdom. Nevertheless it is absolutely necessary that we try the thing once, for the reason which the poet gives:

> The good, the friends of Allāh, countless times
> Accuse us of unknown and nameless crimes.
> God says false accusation is a sin,
> Come let us save them from it, dear. Begin!

With that she rose and dragged the prince towards the great mattress, as he tried to defend himself a little and shook his head, sighing: 'There is no refuge save in Allāh! This would not happen if He did not mean it to.' Hurried by the impatient princess, he took off his baggy trousers and linen drawers, and found himself, in the twinkling of an eye, up-ended by the King upon the mattress. The supposed Sultān clasped him, saying: 'You are about to know a night such as the angels could not give you. Oh, close your legs . . . Give me your hand, put it between my thighs to waken the sleeping child!' 'I do not dare!' said Kamar al-Zamān, and the King answered: 'I will help you.'

When Kamar al-Zamān felt his hand touching the King's thighs, he realised that he had found something very delicious, softer than butter and sweeter than silk; so he explored high and low on his own account and found a dome, which seemed both animated and delightful. But, though he let his fingers wander everywhere, he could not find a minaret. He said to himself: 'The works of God are hidden; how can there be a dome without a minaret? I think this charming King is neither man nor woman, but a white eunuch. That is much less interesting.' He presently said aloud: 'O King, I do not know how it is, but I cannot find the child!'

At this point Shahrazād saw the approach of morning and discreetly fell silent.

But when the two-hundred-and-thirty-fifth night had come

SHE SAID:

Budūr burst into such a peal of laughter that she almost fainted. Then she became serious and, resuming her sweet and woman's voice, said: 'O my dear husband, have you so quickly forgotten those fair nights of ours?' She rose and, throwing aside her masculine garments, appeared naked with her heavy hair falling down her back.

Kamar al-Zamān recognised his wife Budūr, daughter of King Ghayyūr, master of al-Buhūr and al-Kusūr; they embraced, they clasped each other, they wept for joy, they confused each other with kisses on the mattress. The princess said many verses, and this was one of them:

> My beloved dances,
> Setting one foot before the other.
>
> This is my beloved,
> The flowers are a carpet for his dancing.
>
> The dust of his dancing
> Is a balm upon my tired eyes.
>
> I have seen the dawn dancing
> Upon the face of my beloved:
> O daughters of Arabia,
> How could I be unmindful of him?

When Budūr had told all her story to Kamar al-Zamān and he had answered with his own adventures, he began to blame her, saying: 'That which you did to-night was most extraordinary.' 'As Allāh lives, it was only a joke,' she replied; and they continued between each other's arms and thighs until the morning.

With the coming of dawn, Budūr went to King Armānūs, father of Hayyāt al-Nufūs, and told him the truth about herself, adding that his daughter was still a virgin. Armānūs marvelled to the limit of marvel and ordered the whole prodigious story to be inscribed in golden letters upon parchment of exceeding whiteness. Then he turned to Kamar al-Zamān, saying: 'O son of Shahrimān, will you become one of my family and take my maiden daughter, Hayyāt al-Nufūs, as your second wife?' 'I must first consult the lady Budūr,' answered Kamar al-Zamān, 'for I owe all my respect and love to her.' Turning to the princess, he said: 'Have I your consent to marry the child?' 'Indeed you have,' answered Budūr, 'I myself have kept her for you, that she might gladden your return. I am so grateful to her for all her kindness that I will willingly take the second place.'

Then Kamar al-Zamān turned to King Armānūs, saying: 'My wife willingly consents, saying that she would be happy to be your daughter's slave.'

The old King rejoiced with a greater joy than he had known in all his life, and went to sit once more upon his throne, that he might tell the whole story of Kamar al-Zamān and Budūr to the wazīrs, amīrs, chamberlains, and notable persons of his kingdom. He informed them of his intentions with regard to Hayyāt al-Nufūs, and solemnly proclaimed Kamar al-Zamān King of the Isle of Ebony in the place of Budūr. All who heard him kissed the earth between his hands and answered: 'Since Prince Kamar al-Zamān is the husband of our dear King, we accept him joyfully and will be his faithful slaves.'

King Armānūs moved all his limbs with joy and, sending for the kādīs and their witnesses, had a contract of marriage written upon the instant for Kamar al-Zamān and Hayyāt al-Nufūs. He ordered general rejoicing and held marvellous feasts, killing thousands upon thousands of animals to feed the poor and sorrowful, and presenting gifts of money to the army and the people. There was not one soul in all the land who did not pray for the long life and happiness of Kamar al-Zamān and his two Queens.

Kamar al-Zamān governed his kingdom as perfectly as he contented his two wives, with whom he passed alternate evenings. Budūr and Hayyāt lived together in harmony, allowing the nights to their husband, but reserving the days for each other. Kamar al-Zamān sent messengers to his father, King Shahrimān, to tell him of his happiness, and to promise that he would visit him as soon as he had put to death all the western invaders in that city by the sea which had once been inhabited by Mussulmāns.

In the course of time Queen Budūr and Queen Hayyāt al-Nufūs, who had been wonderfully impregnated by their King, each gave birth to a man-child as excellent as the full moon. All lived together in complete happiness until the end of their days. Such is the marvellous tale of Kamar al-Zamān and Princess Budūr, Moon of Moons.

At this point Shahrazād smiled and fell silent.

Little Dunyazād, whose cheeks were usually so white, had grown very red at the last part of this tale; her eyes were round with pleasure, curiosity and confusion; so that at last she covered her face with her two hands, but looked through the fingers.

While Shahrazād was refreshing her tired voice with an iced cup of raisin juice, Dunyazād clapped her hands, crying: 'O my sister, what a shame that this delightful tale should be so soon finished! This is the first of its kind that I have heard you tell and . . . I do not know why I am blushing like this.'

Shahrazād, after swallowing a draught, looked at her sister out of the corners of her eyes, saying:

'What will you think when I have told you the Tale of Alā al-Dīn Abū Shāmāt? . . . Only first I mean to tell you the tender Tale of Happy-Handsome and Happy-Fair.'

Dunyazād jumped for joy, crying: 'O sister, please tell me about Alā al-Dīn Abū Shāmāt before you recount the tale of those people with delightful names, Happy-Handsome and Happy-Fair.'

'But Alā al-Dīn Abū Shāmāt was a boy, my dear,' answered Shahrazād.

Then King Shahryār, whose sadness had quite disappeared at the opening sentences of the tale of Budūr and who had heard it through with the greatest attention, said: 'O Shahrazād, I must confess that the tale which you have just told pleased me, even rejoiced me, even incited me to find out more about that new fashion which Budūr described in prose and verse. If the stories which you promise us contain explanatory details of this unknown pastime, you may begin at once.'

But at this point Shahrazād saw the approach of morning and discreetly fell silent.

King Shahryār said to himself: 'As Allāh lives, I will not kill her until I have heard many more details of the new fashion, for at present it seems to me both obscure and complicated.'

But when the two-hundred-and-thirty-seventh night had come

DUNYAZĀD CRIED: 'O Shahrazād, dear sister, please begin!'

Shahrazād smiled at her sister and then, turning towards King Shahryār, said:

The Tale of Happy-Handsome and Happy-Fair

I T is related—but Allāh is all-wise and all-knowing—that there was once a rich and respected merchant in the city of Kūfah, whose name was Spring. A year after his marriage the blessing of the Highest descended upon his house, for a handsome son was born to him. As the child came into the world smiling, his father called him Happy-Handsome.

Seven days after the birth of his son, the merchant Spring went down to the slave market to buy a handmaiden for his wife and, looking over the women and boys exposed for sale, saw a pleasant-faced slave, who carried her little daughter fastened on her back by a broad belt. Saying to himself: 'Allāh is generous,' he approached the broker and asked how much the two would cost him. 'Fifty dīnārs, neither more nor less,' said the broker, and at once the merchant answered: 'I will take them. Write out the contract and receive the money.' When these formalities had been gone through, the merchant said kindly to the young woman: 'Follow me, my child,' and led her to his house.

As soon as his wife saw the slave, she exclaimed: 'O husband, why have you gone to this useless expense? For, although I have just risen from childbed, I can still manage the affairs of the house as I did before.' 'Dear wife,' answered the merchant, 'I bought this slave because of her little daughter, whom I intend to bring up with our own Happy-Handsome. I prophesy that, when she has grown up, she will not have her equal for beauty in all the lands of Irāk, Persia and Arabia.'

The merchant's wife asked the slave her name, and the other answered that she was called Prosperity. 'As Allāh lives, it suits you!' cried the delighted wife. 'And what is your daughter's name?' 'Fortune,' answered the slave. Pleased by this omen, the mistress exclaimed: 'May it be so! I pray that Allāh will continue prosperity and fortune upon those who have bought you, O white auspicious face!'

Then, turning to her husband, she said: 'As it is the custom for folk to give a new name to the slave they buy, what will you call the little girl?' 'It is for you to choose the name,' answered Spring. 'Then let us call her Happy-Fair,' exclaimed his wife. 'An excellent name!' said the merchant.

Happy-Fair was brought up with Happy-Handsome, on exactly the same footing. The two grew every day in beauty and called each other brother and sister.

When Happy-Handsome was five years old, it was time to celebrate his circumcision, but the merchant waited for the birthday of the Prophet (upon whom be prayer and peace!), so that all possible beauty might attend the precious rite. With due solemnity the child was circumcised and, instead of crying, found the operation pleasant and smiled sweetly. An imposing procession was formed of relations, friends and acquaintances, which walked through all the streets of Kūfah with flags and clarinets at its head. Happy-Handsome was perched on a red palanquin borne by a mule with brocaded trappings, and little Happy-Fair sat by his side, fanning him with a silk handkerchief. Amid the joyful 'Lū-lū-lū!' of his friends, the merchant Spring walked proudly, leading the docile and important mule.

As soon as the procession returned to the house, the guests came one after the other to take leave of the merchant and congratulate him, saying: 'Blessing and honour be upon you! May every joy that your soul desires continue with you throughout a long life!'

At this point Shahrazād saw the approach of morning and discreetly fell silent.

But when the two-hundred-and-thirty-eighth night had come

SHE SAID:

When the children were twelve years old, the merchant Spring found Happy-Handsome in act to play the husband with little Happy-Fair. Therefore he took him aside, saying: 'Thanks to the blessing of Allāh, my child, you have now reached the age of twelve. Henceforth you must not call Happy-Fair your sister, for I must tell you that she is the daughter of our slave, Prosperity, although she was brought up in the same cradle with you. Your mother tells me that the child last week reached her marriageable epoch. Now she must veil her face until a husband be found for her who shall add to the number of our faithful slaves.'

'As Happy-Fair is no longer my sister,' said Happy-Handsome to his father, 'I would like to have her for my own wife.' 'We must ask your mother's permission,' answered the merchant.

Happy-Handsome ran to his mother and kissed her hand, saying: 'I wish to have Happy-Fair as my secret wife.' 'She belongs to you, my dear,' answered his mother, 'your father bought her for you.'

Delighted to have gained his point, the boy hurried to his one-time sister and took her by the hand; that night they slept together as happy married folk.

For five blissful years they lived together, and in the whole city of Kūfah there was not to be found a girl more beautiful, more sub-missive, or more learned than the daughter-in-law of the merchant Spring. Happy-Fair had used her leisure to learn the Koran, various sciences, Kūfic and ordinary character, literature and poetry, and the practice of stringed instruments. She had studied singing to such purpose that she was perfect in fifteen ways and, if she were given a single word of the first stanza, could, from her own invention, pro-long a song for several hours or even all night, with infinite varia-tions and ravishing rhythms.

Happy-Handsome and Happy-Fair spent the warm hours of each day sitting in their garden, on the naked marble of the fish-pond, refreshed by the cool water and the cool stone. There they ate the light melting flesh of water-melons, almonds and nuts, roast and salted corn; there they would pause in their nibbling to smell the roses and jasmine, or to recite exquisite verses. Sometimes, for instance, Happy-Handsome would beg the girl to play a prelude on her double-stringed guitar, and the two would sing alternate stanzas such as these:

> Girl,
> It is raining flowers
> And small coloured birds,
> Let us wander with the wind
> To warm Baghdād,
> To the rose domes.

> Not so, lord;
> Let us stay in the garden

Under the gold palms
And dream.

Girl,
Diamonds fall on the blue leaves,
The curves of the branches are beautiful
'Against the sky.
Rise,
Shake the drops from your hair.

Not so, lord:
Lay your head upon my knees,
Taste the flowers of my breast
Among my garments,
And listen to the light wind.

Or they would sing verses such as these:

I am happy and light
Like a light dancer.

Breathe no more,
O lips red upon flutes;
Be still,
Fingers on silver strings;
That we may hear the palms.
The palms are girls
Standing under the night
And whispering to each other,
Their green hair dances
To the flute-playing of the west wind.

I am happy and light
Like a light dancer.

Perfumed delight,
The singing of your voice
Builds up a palace of living marble
For Him who bade love be beautiful,
Perfumed delight.

You who are darkness about my eyes,
I will paint the lids of them azure
With a stick of crystal,

And in a bright paste of henna
Stain my fingers,
My hands shall be date-coloured
For your pleasure,
I shall burn a delicate incense
Below my breasts for
You who are darkness about my eyes.

Thus Happy-Handsome and Happy-Fair passed their mornings and evenings in the calm and sheltered life of a garden.

At this point Shahrazād saw the approach of morning and discreetly fell silent.

But when the two-hundred-and-thirty-ninth night had come

SHE SAID:

Alas, alas! That which the finger of Allāh has written upon the brow of man, the hand of man can in no wise efface; though he had wings, no creature could escape his Destiny. The buffets of Fate were made ready for Happy-Handsome and Happy-Fair, but the benediction of their birth was such that they would escape final and incurable misfortune.

The Khalīfah's governor in Kūfah, hearing of the beauty of Happy-Fair, said to himself: 'I must find some way to abduct this paragon, this charming musician; for she will make a splendid present to give to the Commander of the Faithful, Abd al-Malik ibn Marwān!'

When the day came on which the governor finally determined to put his plan into execution, he sent for a very cunning old woman, whose usual business was the recruiting and special instruction of young slaves, and said to her: 'I wish you to go to the house of the merchant Spring and get to know a slave belonging to his son, a girl called Happy-Fair, who is said to be both musical and beautiful. By hook or by crook you must bring her here to me, for I wish to send her as a present to the Kahlīfah.' 'I hear and I obey!' answered the old woman and at once went out to make her preparations.

Early next morning she dressed herself in drugget, hung round her neck a prodigious chaplet of thousands of beads, fastened a gourd to her belt, took a crutch in her hands and made her way with dragging steps towards the house of the merchant Spring. At

every few paces she would stop with a loud and holy sigh: 'Praise
be to Allāh! There is no other God but Allāh! There is no help save
in Allāh! Allāh is the Highest!' Thus were all the people upon the
road she took edified in the extreme. She came at last to the house
and knocked at the door, saying: 'Allāh is generous, O Benefactor,
O Giver!'

A respectable old man, who had been for a long time in the
service of Spring, came to the door and, inspecting the devout caller,
determined that her face did not bear the imprint of piety. For her
part, the old woman took an instinctive dislike to the door-keeper
and gave him a sidelong glance. To protect himself from the evil-
eye, he said beneath his breath: 'My left five fingers in your right
eye, the five others in your left!' and then aloud: 'What do you wish,
old aunt?' 'I am a poor old woman whose sole concern is prayer,'
she answered, 'and now that the time of prayer is at hand I wish to
enter this house and make my devotions.' The good door-keeper
objected, saying harshly: 'Walk on now! This is not a mosque or an
oratory but the house of the merchant Spring.' 'I know that well,'
answered the old woman, 'but is any mosque or oratory more
worthy of prayer than the blessed house of Spring and his son
Happy-Handsome? Also, I would have you know, O dry-faced
door-keeper, that I am a woman well thought of in the palace of the
Commander of the Faithful at Damascus. I only journeyed thence
to visit the sacred places and to pray upon all those spots which are
worthy of veneration.' But the door-keeper answered: 'I can see
that you are a holy woman but that is no reason why you should
come in here. Walk on now!' The old woman insisted loud and
long until the noise reached the ears of Happy-Handsome, who came
out and heard the old woman saying: 'How can you prevent a
woman of my quality entering the house of Happy-Handsome,
when the most closely guarded doors of the great are ever open
to me?'

Happy-Handsome smiled as was his wont and, begging the old
woman to follow him, brought her in and led her to the apartment
of Happy-Fair. The old dame looked at the girl while she wished her
peace, and was stupefied by her beauty.

Happy-Fair, seeing the saintly old woman come in to her, rose in
her honour and returned her bow respectfully, saying: 'May your
coming be a good augury, O excellent mother! Be so obliging as to
rest yourself.' 'The hour of prayer is at hand, my daughter. Let me

pray!' answered the old woman, as she turned in the direction of
Mecca and threw herself into the attitude of prayer. She stayed so
without moving until the evening, and none dared interrupt so holy
an occupation; during that time she took no notice of what was
going on round her, because of the depth of her ecstasy.

At last Happy-Fair plucked up courage to approach the saint,
saying sweetly: 'My mother, rest now, if it be only for an hour.'
'My child,' answered the old woman, 'those who do not fatigue their
bodies in this world may not hope to taste that rest which is laid up
for the chosen pure in Paradise.' Happy-Fair was much edified, and
said: 'We beg you to honour our table with your presence and to
share bread and salt with us.' 'I have made a vow of fasting, my
daughter,' replied the other. 'Think no more of me but rejoin your
husband; when one is young and beautiful it is right to eat and drink
and care for happiness.'

At this point Shahrazād saw the approach of morning and
discreetly fell silent.

But when the two-hundred-and-fortieth night had come

SHE SAID:

Happy-Fair went to her husband and said to him: 'Master, let us
beg this saint to make her home with us, for the piety of her face
will light up all our house.' 'Take no thought for that,' answered
Happy-Handsome, 'I have already set aside a room for her and
furnished it with a new mat and a mattress, with a basin and an ewer.
No one will disturb her there.'

The old woman passed the night in praying and reading the
Koran at the top of her voice; at dawn she washed and went to her
hosts, saying: 'I have come to say farewell. May Allāh guard you!'
'But, mother,' said Happy-Fair, 'how can you leave us thus easily
when we are so delighted with the thought of having our house
made permanently sacred by your presence, and have already set
aside our best room for your quiet prayers?' 'The blessing and the
grace of Allāh be upon you, my children!' said the dame. 'Now that
the virtue of Mussulmān charity holds the chief place in your hearts,
I desire to be sheltered by your hospitality. Only I would beg you
to command your dry-faced and unobliging door-keeper not to
oppose my entrance at the hour when I can return. I go now to visit
the sacred places of Kūfah, where I will pray to Allāh that He may

reward you according to your deserts; after that I shall return to sweeten myself with your charity.' The two young people kissed her hands and carried them to their brows; and she departed.

Alas, poor Happy-Fair! Had you but known the reason of this foul old woman's coming, the black plans which she nourished against your peace! But who may divine what is hidden, or unveil the future?

The beldame went straight to the governor's palace and into his presence. 'O unweaver of spiders' webs, O subtle and sublime practitioner of evil, what have you accomplished?' asked the governor. 'Such as I am, O master,' answered the old woman, 'I am but your pupil ... I have seen the girl Happy-Fair; the womb of fecundity has never before brought forth such beauty.' 'Yā Allāh!' cried the governor, and the old woman continued: 'She is steeped in delights, she is a running river of sweetness and unconscious charm.' 'O beating of my heart!' exclaimed the governor, and the old woman answered: 'What then would you say if you heard the ring of her voice, which is more refreshing than the sound of water under an echoing arch? What would you do if you saw her antelope eyes, which are modestly cast down?' 'I am afraid that I could not do more than admire,' said the governor, 'for, as I have told you, I intend her as a present to the Khalīfah. Make haste with your plots, I beg you.' 'I must ask a whole month for them,' she said. 'Take the month, but mind that you succeed,' he replied. 'Here to begin with are a thousand dīnārs, as earnest of my generosity.'

The old woman fastened the money within her belt and began a daily series of visits to the house of Happy-Handsome and Happy-Fair, who, as time went on, showed her more and more respect and consideration.

When she had become, as it were, perpetual adviser to the household, she said to Happy-Fair: 'My daughter, conception has never visited your young thighs. Would you like to come with me to ask the blessing of holy ascetics, old men loved by Allāh, saints and walīs who are in communication with the Highest? These walīs are known to me and I have experienced their great power to do miracles and accomplish prodigious matters in the name of Allāh. They cure the blind and infirm, they raise the dead, they swim through the air, they walk on the water. As for the fecundation of women, that is one of the least privileges which God has given them. It suffices to touch the skirt of their robe or to kiss their beads, and the thing is done.'

Happy-Fair felt her spirit tremble with a desire for child-bearing as she answered: 'I must get leave from my master to go with you, therefore let us wait till he comes back.' 'Tell your mother-in-law, that will be enough,' said the old woman. The young wife ran to Happy-Handsome's mother, saying: 'In Allāh's name give me leave to go forth with this holy saint to visit the walīs, the friends of Allāh, and ask for a blessing from them in their pure abode. I promise to return before Happy-Handsome.' 'My daughter,' answered the older woman, 'think of your husband's grief if he returned and did not find you. He would blame me for having given you permission.'

Here the old woman interrupted, saying: 'I promise that we will make a quick round of the sacred places, without stopping to sit down, and that I will bring her back in no time at all.' So Happy-Handsome's mother gave her consent with a sigh.

The old woman led forth Happy-Fair and conducted her to a lonely pavilion in the palace garden. There she left her alone and went to inform the governor of what she had done. He hurried to the building and halted, thunderstruck upon the threshold by the beauty of his captive.

At this point Shahrazād saw the approach of morning and discreetly fell silent.

But when the two-hundred-and-forty-first night had come

SHE SAID:

Happy-Fair, seeing a strange man enter the place, veiled her face and burst into sobs, as she looked round in vain for a way of escape. As the old woman did not come back, she suddenly realised her perfidy and called to mind certain words of the good door-keeper concerning the guileful eyes of the pretended saint.

As soon as the governor had satisfied himself that it was really Happy-Fair, he shut the door upon her and gave rapid orders. He wrote a letter to the Khalīfah Abd al-Malik ibn Marwān and intrusted the letter and the girl to the commander of his guards, bidding him set out immediately for Damascus. The soldier forcibly placed Happy-Fair in front of him on a fast dromedary and rode off, followed by a few slaves. Throughout all the journey Happy-Fair hid her face in her veil and sobbed silently, paying no attention to the pace, to halts or departures, and replying with neither word nor sign to her conductor. As soon as they reached Damascus, the latter left the slave and the letter with the chief chamberlain of the palace, took a receipt, and returned to Kūfah.

Next morning the Khalīfah entered the harīm and told his wife and sister of the arrival of the new slave, saying: 'The governor of Kūfah has sent her as a present; he informs me that he bought her from certain merchants and that she is a king's daughter whom they abducted in some far country.' 'Allāh increase your joy!' answered his wife. 'What is her name? Is she brown or white?' asked his sister. 'I have not yet seen her,' said the Khalīfah.

The King's sister, whose name was Dahīa, hastened to the apartment where the girl had been lodged, and found her bent in an attitude of dejection, her face burnt by the sun and glistening with tears. Being of a tender heart, she leaned over the child, saying: 'Why do you weep, my sister? Do you not know that you will be safe here and that life will be easy for you? What better fate could you have hoped for than that which brought you to the Commander of the Faithful?' Happy-Fair raised her eyes, saying: 'My mistress, since this is the palace of the Commander of the Faithful, in what city am I?' 'In Damascus. Did you not know that?' answered Dahīa. 'Did not the merchant tell you that he had sold you to be a gift to the Khalīfah Abd al-Malik ibn Marwān? You are now the property of my brother the King; therefore dry your eyes and tell me your name.' 'O my mistress, in my own country I am called Happy-Fair,' answered the young woman through her sobs.

Just as she was speaking, the Khalīfah entered and, coming towards her with a kind smile, sat down by her side, saying: 'Lift your veil, young girl.' But instead of doing so, Happy-Fair drew her robe round her with a trembling hand. The King did not wish to take offence at so strange an action, so he said to his sister: 'I leave this child in your charge and hope that in a few days you will have made her accustomed to you and persuaded her to be less timid.' He threw a glance at Happy-Fair and could see nothing of her save the joints of her tender wrists; yet he loved her hotly, for wrists so beautiful had need belong to an exquisite body. But though he was inflamed with passion, he departed.

Dahīa led Happy-Fair to the palace hammām and, after she had bathed, dressed her in delightful robes, and sprinkled pearls and diamonds among her hair. All that day she kept company with her, but the girl, being confused by her attentions, continued to weep and would not tell her the cause of her weeping. The poor captive imagined that nothing she could say would change her destiny, and therefore consumed her own grief day and night, until she fell seriously ill and the best medical science of Damascus despaired of her life.

Happy-Handsome, the son of Spring, returned on that first evening to his house and threw himself on the couch, calling: 'O Happy-Fair!' As no one answered, he sprang to his feet and called a second time: 'O Happy-Fair!' No one dared enter to him, for all the slaves had hidden. Therefore he hurried to his mother and, finding her thoughtful and dejected with her chin in her hand, asked anxiously: 'Where is Happy-Fair?'

His mother burst into tears, stammering: 'Allāh protect us, my child! Happy-Fair asked my permission to go out with the old lady to visit some sacred walī who performs miracles; she has not yet returned. O my son, my heart has never been at ease since that hag came into our house. Our door-keeper, the good old man who brought us all up, never could regard her without suspicion; and I myself have always had a presentiment that she would bring misfortune upon us with her over-long prayers and sidelong glances.' Happy-Handsome interrupted his mother, saying: 'When exactly did she go out?' 'Early this morning, soon after you left for the market,' she answered, and the youth cried: 'You see what comes of changing our habits and giving liberty to women when they do not know how to use it! Oh, why did you let her go out? Who knows, she may have lost herself, or fallen into the water, or stood under some minaret while it was falling. I shall go to the governor and make him undertake an immediate search.'

Beside himself with grief, Happy-Handsome ran to the palace and was received without delay, because of the respect in which his father was held by the governor. Neglecting all formal greeting, he cried: 'My slave disappeared from my house this morning, in company of an old woman to whom we had given lodging. I pray you to help me find her.' The governor adopted a tone of the greatest interest, and answered: 'Certainly, certainly, my dear boy; there is nothing that I would not do for the son of so worthy a father. Go to my chief of police and tell him your trouble; he is a clever and experienced man; he is certain to be able to find your slave in a few days.'

Happy-Handsome hastened into the presence of the chief of

police, and said: 'The governor sent me to you, that you may find a slave who has disappeared from my house.' The chief of police, who was sitting upon his carpet with his left leg crossed over his right, blew through his mouth two or three times, and then asked: 'With whom did she go away?' 'With an old woman whose distinguishing marks are such and such,' answered Happy-Handsome. 'She is dressed in drugget and has a large chaplet of many beads about her neck.' Then said the chief of police: 'As Allāh lives, tell me where the old woman is and I will find your slave for you.' 'But how do I know where the old woman is?' cried the distracted youth. 'Would I come here if I knew?' The chief of police changed the position of his legs, crossing the right over the left, and said: 'My son, only Allāh can search out the invisible!' 'By the Prophet!' cried Happy-Handsome angrily, 'I shall hold you responsible. If necessary I shall tell the governor, even the Khalīfah of the attitude which you adopt.' 'You can do what seems good to you,' answered the other. 'I never learned sorcery, therefore I cannot find out hidden things.'

The unhappy son of Spring returned to the governor, saying: 'I went to the chief of police and such and such happened.' 'Impossible!' exclaimed the official. 'You there, my guards! Bring that son of a dog to me at once!' When the chief of police appeared before him, he said: 'I order you to make the very closest search for the slave of this young man, who is the son of the merchant Spring. Send horsemen in all directions, set off yourself and look everywhere; you must find her at any cost.' At the same time he gave the man a wink which signified: 'Do not stir in this matter.' Then he turned to Happy-Handsome, saying: 'My son, I trust that it will be through me alone that you get back your slave. If by any extraordinary chance she be not found, I myself will give you ten virgins exactly as old as the hūrīs, with firm breasts and buttocks like stone cubes. Also I shall make this chief of police give you ten of his slaves as virgin as my eye. Calm yourself now, and remember that Destiny will ever render to you what is intended for you and, on the other hand, that you will never receive anything which was not destined for you.'

At this point Shahrazād saw the approach of morning and discreetly fell silent.

But when the two-hundred-and-forty-second night had come

SHE SAID:

Happy-Handsome took leave of the governor and returned in despair to his house, after wandering about the city all night in search of Happy-Fair. In the morning he had to take to his bed with a weakness and fever, which increased day after day in measure as his faith in the researches decreed by the governor lessened. The doctors who were consulted decided that there was no cure for him except the return of his wife.

About this time there arrived in the city of Kūfah a Persian, who was a past master in the art of medicine, chemistry, the science of the stars, and sand divination. Called by the merchant Spring to the bedside of his son with many honourable promises and compliments, this learned man felt the boy's pulse, looked in his face, and then turned with a smile to the merchant Spring, saying: 'The illness lies in his heart.' 'As Allāh lives, you speak truly!' cried the merchant, and the sage continued: 'And it is caused by the disappearance of some loved one. I will soon tell you, by the aid of my mysterious powers, the place in which this person is to be found.'

With that the Persian squatted on the floor and sprinkled a packet of sand in front of him; in the middle of the sand he placed five white pebbles and three black pebbles, two sticks and a tiger's claw; these he arranged on one plane, on two planes, then on three planes; and, after murmuring some words in the Persian tongue, said: 'All you who hear me, know that the person is to be found at Basrah . . . No, no, these three rivers mislead me; she is to be found at Damascus, in the King's palace, and she is in the same state of debility as this young man.'

'What must we do, O venerable doctor?' cried the merchant. 'Help us in this, and you will have no cause to complain that avarice abides here. As Allāh lives, I will give you enough money to live opulently for three lives.' 'Calm your spirits,' answered the Persian, 'let quiet eyelids cover quiet eyes. I undertake to bring these two young people together; the matter is much easier than you suppose. Give me four thousand dīnārs.' The merchant undid his belt and handed five thousand to the Persian, who said: 'Now that I have enough for all expenses, I will set out immediately for Damascus and take your son with me. If Allāh wills, we shall return with the one he loves.' Then he turned to the boy on the bed, saying: 'O honourable son of the merchant Spring, what is your name?' 'Happy-Handsome,' replied the other, and the sage continued: 'Well then, Happy-Handsome, rise up and let your soul be at peace; you may look upon your slave as already returned to you.' The humours of the youth were stirred by the good influence of the doctor, so that he sat up, while the other said: 'Be of good cheer; eat, drink, and sleep. In a week, when your strength has returned, I will come back for you and carry you with me.' With that he took leave of father and son, and went away to make preparations for the journey.

The merchant gave his son five thousand dīnārs, bought him camels which he charged with rich merchandise and pleasantly coloured Kūfah silks, and provided him with horses. At the end of a week the boy had become well enough to travel; he said farewell to his father and mother, to Prosperity and the old door-keeper, and set out with the Persian sage, followed by the prayers of the whole household.

You must know that by this time Happy-Handsome had reached the perfection of adolescence; seventeen years had left their light touches on the carnation of his cheeks in a powder of down; all who beheld him stopped suddenly short with a feeling of ecstasy. It was not long before the Persian doctor came under the boy's delicious spell and loved him with all his heart; therefore he deprived himself of any luxury upon the journey which might add to his companion's comfort, and took great pleasure when the lad was pleased.

At this point Shahrazād saw the approach of morning and discreetly fell silent.

But when the two-hundred-and-forty-third night had come

SHE SAID:

Under these conditions the journey passed pleasantly, and the two travellers arrived in health and safety at Damascus. At once the Persian sage went with Happy-Handsome to the principal market and hired a large shop, which he caused to be redecorated and fitted with velvet-covered shelves. On these he arranged with careful art his precious flasks, his salves, his balms, his powders, his syrups held in crystal, his fine theriacs contained in pure gold, his pots of Persian porcelain which shone with a glaze of silver and held to ripen old pomades made up of the sap of three hundred rare kinds of herb. Among the greater jars, retorts and alembics, he gave a place of honour to his golden astrolabe.

He dressed himself in the full robes of his profession and bound his head with a turban of seven folds. Then he clothed Happy-Handsome in a blue silk shirt with a cashmere jacket, and fastened about his wrist a rose silk apron worked with threads of gold, that he might stand by his side as an assistant, fill prescriptions, pound drugs in the mortar, make little bags of scent, and write magic cures to his dictation. When all was ready, he said to the youth: 'From this moment you must call me father and I will call you son, as we do not wish the inhabitants of Damascus to think we practise you know what.' As soon as the shop was open, the people crowded to it, some with diseases, some to see for themselves the beauty of the assistant; and all were stricken with a happy surprise to hear the boy converse with the sage in the Persian tongue, which seemed to them beautiful enough on such lips. But the thing which caused the greatest amazement throughout the city was the way in which the wise man could diagnose diseases.

He would look at the whites of the patient's eyes for a few moments and then hold out a great crystal bowl towards him, saying: 'Piss!' The sick man would piss in the bowl, and the Persian, lifting it to the height of his eyes, would say, after a moment's examination: 'You have such and such disease.' The patient never failed to cry: 'As Allāh lives that is so!' and then all who were by would lift their arms, crying: 'Yā Allāh, what a prodigy of learning! We have never heard tell of the like! We cannot see diseases in our piss.'

With such a beginning it is hardly to be wondered that the fame of the Persian came in a few days to the ears of the Khalīfah and his sister Dahīa. One day, as the sage was sitting in his shop dictating a prescription to Happy-Handsome, who stood pen in hand by his side, a noble-looking old woman, mounted upon an ass whose saddle was of red brocade starred with diamonds, stopped at the door, knotted the bridle of her mount to the copper ring on the pommel, and signed to the physician to help her dismount. He rose quickly and, taking her hand, helped her from the ass and led her into the shop, where he begged her be seated, while Happy-Handsome brought forward a cushion with one of his discreetest smiles.

The old woman took a flask filled with urine from the folds of her robe and handed it to the doctor, saying: 'Is it not you, venerable old man, who have come from Irāk to perform wonderful cures in our city of Damascus?' 'Your slave is even such as you describe,' answered the sage, and the old woman continued: 'None is a slave save of Allāh! Sublime master of the sciences, this flask contains you know what; it was made by the virgin favourite of our lord, the Commander of the Faithful. Our own doctors could not determine the illness which has kept her to her bed since the first day of her arrival at the palace; therefore lady Dahīa, sister of the King, has sent you this that you may discover the disease.' 'Mistress,' answered the old man, 'I must know the name of this patient, otherwise I cannot calculate an auspicious hour for her to drink my cures.' 'Her name is Happy-Fair,' answered the royal messenger.

The sage began to trace row after row of figures upon a piece of paper which he held on his hand, some in red ink, others in green ink; then he added up the red figures and the green figures and did something with the totals, saying: 'Mistress, I have discovered the disease. It goes by the name of Trembling of the Fans of the Heart.' 'As Allāh lives, that is so!' cried the woman, 'for we can hear the fans trembling in her heart.' 'Before I can prescribe for her,' continued the physician, 'I must know the land from which she comes. That is very important, for I must needs determine the lightness or heaviness of the air in its influence upon the fans. Also that I may ascertain the state of preservation of those delicate organs, I must know how long she has been in Damascus and her exact age.' 'It appears that she was brought up in Kūfah, a city of Irāk,' replied the woman. 'She is sixteen years of age, I know, for she told me that she was born in the year of the fire of Kūfah market. She has only been a few weeks in Damascus.'

At this point Shahrazād saw the approach of morning and discreetly fell silent.

But when the two-hundred-and-forty-fourth night had come

SHE SAID:

The Persian doctor turned to Happy-Handsome, whose heart was beating like a mill, and said: 'Prepare such and such remedies, good fellow, after article seven of the formula of ibn Sīnā.'

The woman looked at the boy who was thus addressed, saying: 'As Allāh lives, my child, she who is ill is very like you; her face is beautiful and agreeable in the same way as yours . . . Tell me, noble

Persian, is this your son or your slave?' 'My son and your slave,' answered the sage, and the old woman, charmed with this flattery, continued: 'In truth, I do not know which to admire more, your science or your son.' She went on conversing with the physician while Happy-Handsome put up the cures in small packets and arranged these in a box, into which he also slipped a note telling Happy-Fair of his arrival in Damascus. He sealed the box and wrote his name and address on the cover in Kūfic character, which the people of Damascus could not read and his dear slave could. The old woman took the box, placed ten dīnārs of gold upon the doctor's desk and, bidding farewell to this obliging couple, hurried to the palace.

Finding the eyes of the sick girl half-shut and moistened at the corners with tears, she went up to her, saying: 'Dear child, may these cures do you as much good as he who prepared them gave me pleasure! He is a youth as fair as an angel and the shop is a place of delights. Here is the box.' Happy-Fair, not wishing to offend the old woman, stretched out her hand for the box and threw a careless glance upon the cover; suddenly all the colour of her cheeks changed, for she saw these words traced in Kūfic character: 'I am Happy-Handsome, son of the merchant Spring of Kūfah.' Calling together all her strength so as not to faint or betray herself, she asked smiling: 'What like was this fair youth of yours?' 'He is such a mingling of all delights,' said the other, 'that I could not possibly describe him. He has eyes! He has eyebrows! Yā Allāh! But the very soul melts at a beauty-spot on the left corner of his mouth, and a dimple which appears on his right cheek when he smiles.'

At this description Happy-Fair recognised her dear lover beyond any doubt. 'Since that is so, may his face be a good augury for my cure,' she said. She took the contents of the packets and swallowed them immediately; as she did so, she saw the note, opened it and read it. Straightway she jumped to the bottom of her bed, crying: 'Good mother, I feel that I am cured! These drugs are miraculous! O happy day!' 'As Allāh lives, this comes by His blessing,' exclaimed the old woman, and Happy-Fair continued: 'I pray you to bring me something to eat and drink, for I am dying of hunger after my thirty days' fast.'

The old woman served Happy-Fair with trays of roast meats, fruits, and drinks, and then hurried to the Khalīfah to tell him that his young slave had been cured by the unheard-of learning of the

Persian sage. 'Carry him at once these thousand dīnārs,' said the Khalīfah, and the old woman hastened to do as she was told. First she returned to Happy-Fair, who gave her a present for the doctor in a sealed box, and then ran to the shop, where she gave the thousand dīnārs to the sage and the box to Happy-Handsome. The youth opened his present and saw within it a letter which described the abduction of his beloved by order of the governor of Kūfah and her transmission to the Khalīfah. He burst out sobbing and fell into a swoon.

'Why does your son weep and faint?' asked the old woman, and the Persian replied: 'How could it be otherwise, when the slave I have cured belongs to this boy whom you deem my son, but who is no other than the son of the illustrious merchant Spring of Kūfah. We came to Damascus for the sole purpose of looking for the young girl, who was raped from her home one day by a wicked old woman with treacherous eyes. Now, dear mother, we place our dearest hopes in your benevolence and beg that you will help us to recover this most precious of possessions. As an earnest of our thanks, here are the thousand dīnārs which the Khalīfah sent to me. You can count on further gratitude in the future.'

At this point Shahrazād saw the approach of morning and discreetly fell silent.

But when the two-hundred-and-forty-fifth night had come

SHE SAID:

The good old woman helped the sage to recover Happy-Handsome, saying: 'You may count on my good-will and devotion.' Without further delay she left the shop and returned to Happy-Fair, whom she found brilliant with joy and health. 'My daughter,' she said smiling, 'why did you not trust your mother from the beginning? I would never have blamed you for shedding so many tears at being separated from that delightful Happy-Handsome.' Seeing the girl's surprise, she hastened to add: 'My child, you can rely absolutely on my discretion and maternal good-will towards you. I swear to return you to your lover, even if I risk my life in doing so. Put aside all anxiety and let the old woman act according to her cunning.'

She left Happy-Fair, who had kissed her hands and wetted them with tears of joy, and, after making up a packet of female garments, jewelry and articles of toilet, went out again to the sage's shop and signed to Happy-Handsome to go apart with her. The youth led her behind a curtain at the back of the shop, and heartily approved the plan which she unfolded to him.

She helped him to dress as a woman, lengthening his eyes with kohl and increasing the mole on his cheek with a black pigment; then she put bracelets upon his wrists and jewels among his hair beneath its Mosul veil. She cast a last glance upon her handiwork and found the boy more ravishing than all the women of the palace put together. 'Blessed be Allāh in His works!' she said. 'Now you must walk as a young virgin walks, with little steps, bringing the right hip forward and the left hip back, and making small learned wriggles with your bottom. Practise awhile before we go forth.'

Happy-Handsome practised these things in the shop and acquitted himself so well that the old woman cried: 'As Allāh lives, women need not be so proud in future; the bottom moves marvellously and the hips superbly! Now, that nothing shall be lacking, you must give your face a more languorous expression, thrusting your neck a little forward and looking out of the corners of your eyes. There, that is perfect; you can follow me.'

When they got to the door of the harīm, the chief eunuch stepped forward, saying: 'No stranger may enter without a special order from the Commander of the Faithful. Either retire with this girl or go in without her.' 'What has become of your wisdom, O crown of eunuchs?' cried the old woman. 'You, who were ever urbanity itself, now adopt a tone which ill matches with your delightful face. O nobly-mannered man, this slave is the property of the Lady Dahīa, sister of our Khalīfah, and if she hears of your lack of courtesy towards her favourite I am afraid she will have you decapitated, or at least thrown from office. I regret to have to confess that it will be your own fault.' Then, turning to Happy-Handsome, she said: 'Come, good slave, forget the rudeness of our worthy master, and above all say nothing about it to your mistress. Come!' She took him by the hand and led him through the door, while he thrust his head forward from left to right in an enticing manner, and threw an eye-smile to the chief eunuch, who shook his head and let them pass.

As soon as they were in the court of the harīm, the old woman said to Happy-Handsome: 'My son, we have reserved a room for you in the harīm itself, and from this point you must go to it alone. The way is quite simple; go through that door, take the gallery in front of you, turn to the left, then to the right, then again to the right, count five doors and open the sixth. That will be your room, and I will send Happy-Fair to join you there. After the two of you have met, I will myself help you to leave the palace without being noticed by the guards or eunuchs.'

Happy-Handsome entered the gallery and, in his exaltation, forgot which hand was which; he first turned to the right, then to the left into a parallel corridor, and entered the door of the sixth chamber which he found there.

At this point Shahrazād saw the approach of morning and discreetly fell silent.

But when the two-hundred-and-forty-sixth night had come

SHE SAID:

He found himself in a lofty hall, topped by a narrow dome whose interior was ornamented by verses written out in gold with a thousand interlacing lines. The walls were covered with rose silk, the windows curtained with gauze, and the floor spread with immense carpets of Hind. Cups of fruit were set on stools, and on the carpets themselves were ranged platters covered with silk but teeming with suggestion, both in form and odour, that here were famous pastries meet for the tenderest throats, such as only the art of Damascus can confect with entire sympathy.

Now Happy-Handsome was far from suspecting that this hall held unknown powers for him.

The only visible furnishing was a velvet-covered throne, so the youth, who did not dare to retreat in case he should be found wandering about the corridors, seated himself on this throne and waited his Destiny.

He had not been there long before a noise of silks reached his ears, and he saw a young woman with a royal look enter by one of the side doors. She was dressed only in house garments, so that her face and hair might be seen; and was followed by a delicious little slave with naked feet, who was crowned with flowers and carried a lute of sycamore-wood in her hand. This woman was none other than the lady Dahīa, own sister to the Commander of the Faithful.

When she saw a veiled woman sitting upon the throne, she went towards her softly, saying: 'Who are you, stranger? And why do you sit thus veiled in the harīm where no unlawful eye may see you?' Happy-Handsome rose precipitately to his feet and, as he dared not speak, pretended to be dumb. 'Why do you not answer, girl with beautiful eyes?' asked Dahīa. 'If you are by any chance some slave sent back from the palace by my brother, tell me so and I will intercede for you. He refuses me nothing.' Happy-Handsome remained silent; so Dahīa, thinking that the unknown would not speak in the presence of the little slave, who was regarding the pair of them with round eyes, said to the child: 'Go behind the door, my pretty one, and do not let any enter.' When the little girl had left them, she went closer to Happy-Handsome, who was trying to wrap himself more and more in his large veil, saying: 'Tell me who you are, dear girl, and why you came to this hall which is reserved for myself and my brother. You may speak freely, for I find you charming. Your eyes are delightful. I think you are perfectly beautiful, little one.' With that Dahīa, who was partial to white delicate virgins, drew the veiled figure towards her by the waist and, raising one hand to caress the breasts, undid the robe with the other. You can picture her stupefaction when she found the breast of the young girl as flat as a boy's. First she recoiled and then, returning, wished to lift up the robe altogether and to look more closely into the matter.

Seeing this movement, Happy-Handsome judged it more prudent to speak; so he carried Dahīa's hand to his lips, saying: 'Mistress, I throw myself upon your kindness and beg for your protection.' 'I grant it already; speak on,' said Dahīa, and the youth continued: 'Dear mistress, I am not a girl; I am Happy-Handsome, son of the merchant Spring of Kūfah. I came here at the risk of my life to see my wife again, Happy-Fair, a slave stolen by the governor of Kūfah and sent as a present to the Commander of the Faithful. I conjure you by the life of the Prophet, compassionate lady, to pity your two slaves.' With that he burst into tears.

Dahīa straightway called the little slave, saying: 'Run as fast as you can, pretty one, to Happy-Fair's apartment and tell her that I wish her to come to me.'

At this point Shahrazād saw the approach of morning and discreetly fell silent.

But when the two-hundred-and-forty-seventh night had come

SHE SAID:

Then she turned to Happy-Handsome, saying: 'Be of good cheer, O youth, I have in store for you nothing but happiness.'

Now, while all this had been happening, the good old woman had gone to Happy-Fair, saying: 'Follow me quickly, my child, for your beloved is in the room which I reserved for him.' She led her, pale with emotion, to the place where she supposed Happy-Handsome to be, and the two were terrified not to find him. 'He must be wandering about the corridors,' said the old woman. 'Return, my child, to your own apartment, while I go to look for him.'

Just as Happy-Fair had regained her room in a state of great anxiety, the little slave came in, saying that Princess Dahïa wished to speak to her. Poor Happy-Fair thought that she was indeed lost and her husband with her, and was hardly able to follow the delightful little girl with naked feet.

As soon as she came into the hall, the King's sister ran to her smiling and led her by the hand to Happy-Handsome, saying to both of them: 'Here is happiness!' The two young people recognised each other and fell fainting into the arms which each stretched out.

Dahïa, with the little girl's help, sprinkled rose-water on their faces and, when they came to themselves, left them alone together. She returned in an hour and found them sitting side by side in each other's arms, their happy cheeks moistened by tears of joy and gratitude. 'Now we must drink together,' she said, 'to celebrate your reunion, and that your happiness may last for ever.' The laughing little one filled cups with rare wine and, as they drank, Dahïa said: 'How you love each other, my children! Surely you must know admirable songs of love and lovers. Take this lute and sing me something, I beg. Let me hear the soul of its melodious wood!' Happy-Handsome and Happy-Fair kissed the princess's hand and sang these wonderful alternate stanzas:

> I bring light flowers
> Under my veil of Küfah silk
> And fruits still powdered with their gold.

> All the gold of Südän shines upon you,
> O well-belov'd,
> Because the sun has not ceased to kiss you.

The velvet of Damascus
Is woven from your past glances.

I come to you in the cool of the evening,
The light air
Stirs the blue veil of the night;
There is a murmur of leaves and waters.

You are here,
Gazelle of nights;
My spirit dips toward your eyes
As a white bird to the sea.

Come near and take these roses;
I slip like a flower
From the bud of my green silks.
I am naked for you.

Beloved!

I am here,
A young moon stealing to you through the trees,
A summer sea
Flown over by quick rejoicing birds.

Hardly had the last notes of this song died away upon the lips
of Happy-Fair, when the curtains parted and the Khalīfah himself
stepped into the hall. All three sprang to their feet and kissed the
earth between his hands. He smiled at them and sat down among
them, calling to the little slave to bring wine. 'We must drink
together,' said he, 'to celebrate the recovery of Happy-Fair.' Then,
lifting his cup with a 'For love of your eyes, my dear!' he drank
slowly. As he put down his cup he noticed the veiled slave, and
turned to his sister, saying: 'Who is this girl whose light veil promises so much beauty?' 'She is a friend who cannot bear to be
separated from Happy-Fair,' answered Dahīa. 'They can neither eat
nor drink unless they are together.'

The Khalīfah parted the youth's veil, starting back before the
beauty of him; for Happy-Handsome had no hair upon his cheeks,
but there was a very light down upon them which gave an adorable
texture to their whiteness: also you must not forget the beauty-spot
which smiled upon his chin.

'As Allāh lives, my sister,' cried the delighted Sultān, 'henceforth

I take this new slave as a concubine and reserve for her, as for Happy-Fair, an apartment worthy of her beauty and a following equal to that of a lawful wife.' 'Indeed, my brother,' answered Dahīa, 'she is a morsel worthy of you . . . It just occurs to me that I would like to tell you a tale which I read in a book written by one of our wise men.' 'What tale is that?' asked the Khalīfah, and the lady Dahīa said . . .

At this point Shahrazād saw the approach of morning and discreetly fell silent.

But when the two-hundred-and-forty-eighth night had come

SHE SAID:

'O Commander of the Faithful, there was once in the city of Kūfah a youth named Happy-Handsome, son of Spring, who had a slave to wife. They loved each other, for they had been brought up together from the same cradle and had possessed each other at the moment of puberty. For years they were happy together, until an evil day came to separate them. A wicked old woman, acting as the hot hand of Destiny, stole the slave and delivered her to the governor of the city, who sent her as a present to the King of that time.

'The son of Spring took no rest after she had gone, until he had followed her up and found her in the very harīm of the King's palace. Just as the two were congratulating each other and shedding tears of joy, the King surprised them together and, without waiting to discover the full meaning of what he saw, furiously cut off both their heads.

'The sage who wrote this tale gives no judgment upon its ending; therefore I beg you to tell me your opinion of the act of this King, and whether you would have done the same in his place.'

The Sultān Abd al-Malik ibn Marwān answered without a moment's hesitation: 'The King should not have acted so precipitately; he should have pardoned the two young people for three reasons: first, because they had long and truly loved each other; second, because they were his guests at that time; and third, because a king should always act prudently and circumspectly. I conclude, therefore, that the action of that King was unworthy of his rank.'

The lady Dahīa threw herself before her brother's knees, crying: 'O Prince of Believers, without knowing it, you have already prejudged yourself. I conjure you, by the sacred memory of our noble ancestors and our august father, to abide by that judgment in the case which I put before you.' 'Rise, my sister; you may speak without fear,' answered the surprised Khalīfah. Dahīa rose and, making the two young people stand up also, said to her brother: 'My lord, this beautiful and charming girl is, beneath her veil, none other than that young man Happy-Handsome, the son of Spring. Happy-Fair was brought up with him and became his wife; her ravisher was even Yūsuf al-Thafakī, governor of Kūfah. He lied when he said in his letter that he had bought her for ten thousand dīnārs. I demand his punishment and the pardon of these most excusable children. Be good to them, remembering that they are your guests, sheltered by your sacred shadow.'

'It is not my custom to go back on the spoken word,' said the Khalīfah. 'Tell me, Happy-Fair, is this in truth your master, Happy-Handsome?' 'Even as my Lord says,' she answered, and the Khalīfah cried: 'I give you back to one another.'

Then he looked at Happy-Handsome, saying: 'I should be interested to learn how you succeeded in reaching this place, and how you knew that your wife was in my palace.' 'Commander of the Faithful,' replied Happy-Handsome, 'listen but for a few minutes, and I will tell you all the tale.' With that he related the whole adventure to the Khalīfah, without omitting a single detail.

The King was astonished and, sending for the Persian sage, named him his own physician and loaded him with honours. He kept Happy-Handsome and Happy-Fair for seven days and seven nights of festivity and rejoicing in the palace, and then sent them back to Kūfah with many presents. He debased the governor of that city and named in his stead the merchant Spring, father of Happy-Handsome. All concerned in this tale lived at the height of happiness throughout long and fortunate lives.

When Shahrazād fell silent, King Shahryār exclaimed: 'O Shahrazād, the tale has pleased me and the verses in it have inspired me. But I was a little surprised not to find any details of that other way of love.'

Shahrazād smiled lightly, saying: 'O auspicious King, you will find those details in the Tale of Alā al-Dīn Abū Shāmāt, which I will tell you if you still continue to be troubled by your insomnia.' 'What is that you say, O Shahrazād?' cried King Shahryār. 'As Allāh lives, I would rather die of insomnia than not hear the Tale of Alā al-Dīn Abū Shāmāt. Begin at once.'

But at that moment Shahrazād saw the approach of morning and postponed her tale.

So when the two-hundred-and-fiftieth night had come

SHE SAID:

The Tale of Alā al-Dīn Abū Shāmāt

I T is related, O auspicious King, that there was once in Cairo a venerable old man, who held the office of syndic among the merchants of the city. All the market respected him for his honesty, his grave politeness, his thoughtful language, his wealth and the number of his slaves. His name was Shams al-Dīn.

One Friday, before the prayer, he went first to the hammām and then to a barber's shop. At the latter place he had his moustaches cut to the border of the upper lip and his head carefully shaved. He took the mirror which the barber offered him and, after having recited the act of Faith against pride, looked within it. Sadly he considered the white hairs of his beard, which were now more numerous than the black, and noticed that at length the black were indeed hard to find. 'A white beard is a sign of age,' he thought to himself, 'and age is an advertisement of death. Poor Shams al-Dīn! You are at the door of the tomb and have no children. You will be snuffed out like a candle and no more seen.' Filled with these desolate thoughts, he made his prayer at the mosque and then returned to his house. His wife, who knew his usual hour of return and had prepared herself to receive him with bath and perfume and careful depilation, ran to meet him with a smile, saying: 'A happy evening attend you!'

Instead of returning his wife's wish, the syndic said sharply: 'What talk is this of happy evenings? Is there any happiness left for me?' 'The name of Allāh be upon you and about you!' cried his astonished wife. 'Why this gloom? What happiness do you lack? What is the cause of your sadness?' 'You are,' he answered. 'Listen, woman, and try to imagine my bitter pain when I go to the market every day and see the merchants sitting with two, three, or four little children by them, bright promises growing up in the sight of happy paternal eyes. They are proud of their issue, and I alone have not that consolation. Often I wish for death rather than such a life as this, and pray to Allāh, Who has called my fathers to His rest, to put a term to my suffering.'

'Do not think of such distressing things,' answered his wife. 'Come and do honour to the cloth which is spread for you.' But the merchant cried: 'As Allāh lives, I will neither eat nor drink and especially I will accept nothing at your hands. You are the sole cause of our sterility. Forty fruitless years have passed since our marriage, and you have always forbidden me to take other wives; you even profited on the night of our wedding by the weakness of my flesh to make me swear never to know another woman. Also, worse and worse, you kept me to my oath, which, when you saw your barrenness, you should at once have forgiven. I swear by Allāh that I would rather cut off my zabb than ever give it to you or even kiss you. I see that it is lost labour to work with you; I would as likely get children by thrusting my concern into a hole in a rock as into a dry field like yours. Yes, it is all wasted seed that I have generously dropped within your bottomless pit.'

His wife saw the light change to shadows before her eyes and cried, with the bitterest voice that anger could give her: 'Scent your mouth before you speak, old cold one! Allāh preserve me from all ugliness and false imputation! If you think that I am the backward one, undeceive yourself, old uncle. If you want to complain, complain of yourself and your cold eggs; for, as Allāh lives, they are as ice, secreting a liquor all too clear and absolutely worthless. Buy something to heat them and thicken their sap, and you will see whether my fruit has excellent seed or not.'

These words somewhat shook the syndic in his conviction and, in a hesitating voice, he said: 'Admitting that my eggs are cold and transparent, and that their sap is cold and worthless, can you by any chance tell me where to buy a drug to thicken the stuff?' 'At the first druggist you come to,' answered his wife, 'you will find a mixture to thicken the eggs and make men apt to get children upon their wives.'

At this point Shahrazād saw the approach of morning and discreetly fell silent.

But when the two-hundred-and-fifty-first night had come

SHE SAID:

'As Allāh lives,' said the syndic, 'to-morrow morning I shall go to a druggist and buy a little of this mixture.'

As soon as the market was open next morning, the old man took a porcelain bowl and brought it to a druggist, saying: 'Peace be with you!' 'The morning is blessed which brings you for my first customer. What may I have the pleasure of selling you?' answered the man, and the syndic held out his bowl, saying: 'I want an ounce of that mixture which thickens a man's eggs.'

Not knowing what to think, the druggist said to himself: 'Our syndic is very solemn as a rule, but I think that he wishes to jest this morning, so I will answer him in his own vein.' So aloud he said: 'As Allāh lives, I had plenty of it yesterday, but it is so popular that to-day my provision has run out. You had better go to my neighbour.'

The syndic went to a second druggist, then to a third, and finally to all in the market. Each one gave him the same answer, laughing behind his hand the while.

Disappointed in his search, the old man returned to his shop and sat down to dream disgustedly upon life. As he sat in his black humour, there alighted before his door the sheikh of the brokers, whose name was Samsam. He was a phenomenal hashīsh eater, a drunkard, a user of opium, a model of debauchery for all the lowest in the market; but he respected Shams al-Dīn and never passed his shop without bowing to the ground with polished words of compliment. This morning he saw that the syndic answered all his salutations with bad grace, so he said: 'What disaster has so troubled your spirit, O venerable syndic?' 'Come, good Samsam,' answered the other, 'sit down by my side and listen to me; you will see if I have good cause to be afflicted or no. I have been married for forty years and have not had so much as a sniff of a child. Now they tell me that I am the cause of this lack, because my eggs are transparent and their sap too clear and worthless. I have been to every druggist in the market for a mixture to thicken these things, but not one of them has it. I am very unhappy, because I cannot find anything to give a proper density to this most important humour of my body.'

Instead of being astonished at what the syndic said or laughing at him, the broker Samsam stretched out his hand, palm upwards, saying: 'Give me a dīnār and your bowl, and I will do the business myself.' 'By Allāh, is that possible?' answered the syndic. 'I swear by the life of the Prophet that your fortune is made if you succeed. Here, to begin with, are two dīnārs instead of one.' And he handed two gold pieces and the bowl to Samsam.

On this occasion that creature of fabulous debauch showed himself more learned in medicine than all the druggists of the market. He bought what he needed and set himself to prepare the following mixture:

He took two ounces of Chinese cubebs, one ounce of fat extract of Ionian hemp, one ounce of fresh cloves, one ounce of red cinnamon from Sarandīb, ten drachms of white Malabar cardamoms, five of Indian ginger, five of white pepper, five of pimento from the isles, one ounce of the berries of Indian star-anise, and half an ounce of mountain thyme. These he mixed cunningly, after having pounded and sieved them; he added pure honey until the whole became a thick paste; then he mingled five grains of musk and an ounce of pounded fish roe with the rest. Finally he added a little concentrated rose-water and put all in the bowl.

After this work was completed, he carried the bowl to Shams al-Dīn, saying: 'Here is a sovereign mixture which will harden the eggs and thicken the sap when it has become too thin.'

At this point Shahrazād saw the approach of morning and discreetly fell silent.

But when the two-hundred-and-fifty-second night had come

SHE SAID:

Samsam continued: 'You must eat this paste two hours before the sexual approach; but, for three days before that, you must eat nothing save roast pigeons excessively seasoned with spice, male fish with their cream complete, and lightly fried rams' eggs. If, after all that, you do not pierce the very walls of the room and get the foundations of the house with child, you can cut off my beard and spit in my face.' With these words he went away.

'Surely,' thought the syndic, 'Samsam, whose whole life is one riot of lewdness, ought to know all about these hardening medicines. I will put my trust in Allāh and in him.' He at once returned home and made it up with his wife; and, as they both loved each other, each apologised for their passing anger and told the other how sad it had been to stay estranged for a whole night.

Shams al-Dīn scrupulously followed Samsam's diet for three days and then ate the paste, which he found delicious. Soon he noticed that his blood was boiling, as it had when he was a boy and made bets on certain matters with lads of his own age. He went to his wife and mounted her; she met him half-way, and they were both astonished with the resulting hardness, repetition, heat, jet, intensity and thickness. That night the syndic's wife well and truly conceived; as she herself made certain, when three months passed without flow of blood.

Her pregnancy followed a normal course and, at the end of nine months to a day, she underwent a happy but intensely difficult labour; for the child, when he was born, was as big as if he was already one year old. After the usual invocations, the midwife declared that never before had she seen so big and beautiful a boy; nor is that to be wondered at when we consider the excellent paste.

The midwife washed the child while she invoked the names of Allāh, Muhammad and Alī, and whispered the act of Faith into the baby's ear; then she swaddled him and returned him to the mother, who gave him the breast until he fell asleep. The old woman stayed by the wife for three days to see that all went well; and at the end of that time the usual sweetmeats were distributed among the neighbours.

On the seventh day salt was thrown into the room, and then the syndic entered to congratulate his wife. 'Where is Allāh's gift?' he asked, and, when she held out the child, he marvelled at the beauty of his son, who had the figure of a full year and a face brighter than the rising moon. 'What would you like to call him?' he asked, and the wife replied: 'If it had been a girl, I would have found a name; but as it is a boy you have the right of choice.'

Just at that moment one of the girl slaves, who was swathing the infant, burst into tears of passionate pleasure on seeing a fair brown mole, like a grain of musk, which lay bright upon the small left thigh. Because of this discovery and also because his son had on both cheeks two much smaller beauty-spots of velvet blackness, the good syndic cried: 'We will call him Alā al-Dīn Abū Shāmāt!'

So the boy was called Alā al-Dīn Abū Shāmāt, but soon this name was found too long and he was called simply Abū Shāmāt. For four years he was given the breast by two nurses and by his mother, so that he became as strong as a young lion, while the white of him remained the white of jasmine and the rose the rose of rose. He was so handsome that all the little girls of the neighbourhood adored him to idolatry; he accepted their homage, but would never allow himself to be kissed by one of them, scratching them cruelly when they came too close; so the little girls, and even the big girls, used to take advantage of his sleep to cover him with kisses and rejoice in his fresh beauty.

When his father and mother saw how much Abū Shāmāt was admired and petted, they feared the evil-eye for him and resolved to protect him from its influence. They did not act like so many other parents, who leave their babies' faces to be covered by flies and filth so that they shall seem less beautiful; but at once shut their child in a cellar, built below the house, and had him brought up away from every indiscreet eye. Abū Shāmāt grew without anyone knowing of him, though he was surrounded by the incessant care of slaves and eunuchs. When he became older, he was given learned masters, who taught him fair writing, the Koran, and many sciences. Though he soon became as learned as he was handsome and strong, his parents resolved not to let him leave the cellar until his beard sprouted.

At this point Shahrazād saw the approach of morning and discreetly fell silent.

But when the two-hundred-and-fifty-third night had come

SHE SAID:

One day a slave, who had brought Abū Shāmāt his meal, forgot to shut the cellar door; seeing this opening, which he had never noticed before owing to the great size of the cellar and to the fact that it had many curtains and hangings, the boy hastened through it and ran upstairs into the presence of his mother, who was surrounded by certain high-born women upon a visit.

At that time Abū Shāmāt was a fair child of fourteen, as handsome as a drunken angel; his cheeks were downed like fruit and the twin moles shone on either side of his mouth. I say nothing of the one which might not be seen. When the women saw this unknown youth bound into their midst, they veiled their faces in fright and said to the wife of Shams al-Dīn: 'By Allāh, what shame is this, that you allow a strange young man to see us? Do you not know that modesty is one of the essential dogmas of faith?'

Abū Shāmāt's mother answered: 'Call on the name of Allāh! O guests, this is my dearly-loved son, the fruit of my bowels, off-spring of the syndic of the merchants of Cairo. He has been brought up at the breasts of nurses with a generous milk, in the arms of beautiful slaves, on the shoulders of chosen virgins, in the purest and noblest laps; he is his mother's eye and his father's pride; he is Abū Shāmāt! Call on the name of Allāh, O my guests.'

'The name of Allāh be upon him and about him!' answered the amīrs' and rich merchants' wives. 'But tell us why you have never shown your son to us before.'

Shams al-Dīn's wife rose and, kissing her son upon the eyes, sent him away that he might no longer embarrass her friends; then she said: 'His father has had him brought up in the cellar of our house to protect him from the evil-eye; he is determined not to show him until his beard sprouts, in case his beauty should attract danger and wrong influences. His escape just now must be the fault of some eunuch who forgot to close the door.' Before they left, her guests congratulated the syndic's wife on the beauty of her son and called down the blessings of Allāh upon his head.

Abū Shāmāt returned to his mother and, seeing the slaves harnessing a mule, asked her what the animal was for. 'To fetch your father from the market,' she said, and he continued: 'What is my father's business?' 'My dear,' she replied, 'your father is a great merchant and syndic of all the other merchants in Cairo. He furnishes the Sultān of Arabia and all the Mussulmān Kings. To give you an idea of his importance: buyers never go to him direct, save for transactions which involve over a thousand dīnārs; if a trivial nine hundred and ninety-nine dīnārs are in question, people go to your father's underlings and not to himself. No merchandise can go in or out of Cairo without your father being told of it and consulted about it. Allāh has given your father incalculable riches, my child; therefore be grateful to Him.'

'I thank Him that He created me the son of a syndic,' answered Abū Shāmāt. 'But I do not want to pass all my life shut away from my fellow men; to-morrow I will go to the market with my father.' 'May Allāh hear you, my son,' answered his mother. 'As soon as your father returns this evening, I will speak to him about it.'

When Shams al-Dīn came in, his wife told him all that had passed, adding: 'It is really time that you took your son to the market with you.' 'O mother of Abū Shāmāt,' replied the syndic, 'do you not know that the evil-eye is a very real thing, not a subject for jests? Have you forgotten what happened to the sons of our neighbour so-and-so and our neighbour such-and-such and a host of others, killed by the evil-eye? Half the graves of time are filled with victims of the evil-eye.'

'Father of Abū Shāmāt,' objected his wife, 'every man carries his Destiny about his neck and cannot escape it. What is written cannot be cancelled, and sons will follow their fathers through life and the doors of death. That which is to-day, to-morrow is not! How terrible it would be if our son were to suffer through your fault; for some day—after a long and entirely fortunate life, I hope—you will die and no one will recognise our boy as the legitimate heir to all your riches, since no one knows of his existence. The Treasury will take your goods and cheat your son out of his inheritance. If I called the old men as witnesses, they would only be able to say: "We never heard of son or daughter being born to the syndic Shams al-Dīn."'

These shrewd words made the syndic reflect; after a little while he answered: 'As Allāh lives, I think you are right! To-morrow I will take Abū Shāmāt with me, and teach him the arts of buying and selling and all the secrets of my business.' Turning to his son, who was jumping for joy, he continued: 'I know you will be delighted to come with me, and that is very well; but you must remember that, in the market, one has to be very serious and keep one's eyes lowered modestly. I hope that you will remember to practise the wise precepts which your masters have taught you.'

At this point Shahrazād saw the approach of morning and discreetly fell silent.

But when the two-hundred-and-fifty-fourth night had come

SHE SAID:

Next morning, Shams al-Dīn took his son to the hammām and, after he had bathed, dressed him in a robe of very soft satin, the finest which he had in his shop, and bound his brow with a light turban of striped material, sewn with delicate gold silk. They ate a morsel together and drank a glass of sherbert to refresh themselves before leaving the hammām; then the syndic mounted his white mule and took Abū Shāmāt up behind him, who shone so fresh and fair that he would have seduced the angels themselves. They rode to the market among a group of slaves, who wore new dresses for the occasion; and all the merchants fell to marvelling and saying to each other: 'Yā Allāh! look at the boy! Surely that is the moon a fortnight old!' Others added: 'Who can the delicious child be? We have never seen him before.'

As they were all exclaiming at the passage of the white mule, the broker Samsam passed also and perceived the boy. Now, owing to his excessive debauchery, to his fabulous consumption of hashīsh and opium, Samsam had completely lost his memory, and had therefore quite forgotten the cure which he had worked upon the syndic with his miraculous paste of male roe, musk, cubebs, and the rest.

Therefore, as soon as he saw his old friend accompanied by a youth, he grinned and began to make crapulous jokes to himself, and say to various of the merchants: 'Look at the old man! Is he not like a leek, white-haired but green in body?' With that he went from one to another, repeating his jests and epigrams, until no one in the market doubted that the syndic Shams al-Dīn had installed a young minion in his shop.

When this rumour came to the ears of the principal merchants, they formed an assembly of the oldest and most respected among them to judge the matter; and Samsam appeared before them, making wide gestures of indignation and saying: 'We do not wish to have at our head as syndic a lewd old man, who rubs himself against young boys in public. I suggest that we abstain this morning from going to read before him the seven holy verses as is our custom, and that during the day we choose another syndic who is a little less partial to youth.' The merchants found nothing to say against Samsam's plan, which was unanimously adopted.

When the worthy Shams al-Dīn saw the hour pass on which the merchants and brokers usually came to recite before him the ritual verses of the Fātihah, or opening of the Koran, he did not know what to make of this breach of tradition; therefore, seeing the dissolute Samsam watching him out of the corner of his eyes, he beckoned him to approach. The broker had been waiting for this, so he stepped forward, moving slowly and negligently, with knowing glances at the shop-keepers to right and left, that he might be the centre of all eyes and be considered as the latest posted in this scandal.

As he leaned against the front of the shop, Shams al-Dīn said to him: 'How is it, my good Samsam, that the merchants and their chief have not come to recite their holy verses before me?' The broker answered with a cough: 'Hm! Hm! I really could not say. There are rumours running about the market, rumours, just rumours. This I can tell you, though: a party has been formed among the chief oldsters to deprive you of your office and elect another syndic.'

The worthy merchant lost colour at this, but he asked calmly: 'Can you tell me the reason for this decision?' Samsam winked and undulated his hips, saying: 'Do not be coy with me, old friend; you ought to know better than anyone else. That boy in your shop now; I take it he is not there to kill the flies. Mind you, I strongly under-took your defence, I only among the whole of them. I told them that, if you had been a lover of boys, I should have been the first to know of it, because I always seem to make friends with those who have a taste for green fruit. I told them that the lad must be some relation to your wife or to one of your friends in Tantah or Bagh-dād; but they turned against me and insisted on your replacement. Allāh is great, old friend; and you have one consolation, that truly delightful boy, on whom I heartily congratulate you.'

At this point Shahrazād saw the approach of morning and discreetly fell silent.

But when the two-hundred-and-fifty-fifth night had come

SHE SAID:

Shams al-Dīn could no longer contain his indignation and interrupted Samsam, crying: 'Be quiet, O most corrupt of evil-livers! Do you not know that that is my son? Where is your memory, O hashīsh eater?' 'Since when have you had a son?' asked Samsam. 'Was he fourteen years carried in the belly of his mother?' 'But, ridiculous Samsam,' exclaimed the merchant, 'do you not remember that you yourself prepared that miraculous paste for me fourteen years ago, which so thickened my eggs and concentrated their sap? Working through its means, Allāh gave me a son; but you never came to ask news of your prescription. I have brought the boy up in the great cellar of our house for fear of the evil-eye, and this is the first day that he has been out with me. I had meant to keep him from the sight of all until he could hold his beard in his fingers, but his mother persuaded me to liberate him and teach him my business . . . I am glad to have the opportunity of paying my debt to you, O Samsam. Here are a thousand dīnārs for that paste of yours.'

The broker no longer doubted the truth of Shams al-Dīn's statement, so he hastened to the rest of the merchants and told them of their mistake; thereupon all the chiefs of the market hurried to the syndic to congratulate him and to apologise for not having come to recite their ceremonial verses before him, an omission which they hastened to repair. 'O venerable syndic,' said Samsam in the name of all, 'may Allāh preserve in our affection both the tree and the branches, and may the branches in their turn give odorous and gilded fruit to a starved world! It is the custom, even among the poor, to make a birth the occasion of a distribution of sweetmeats to friends and neighbours, and we have not yet sweetened our lips with butter and honey asīdah to the good health of your first-born. Is there any chance of a great cauldron of asīdah making its appearance?'

'I ask for nothing better,' answered Shams al-Dīn. 'Only I do not offer you a cauldron of asīdah simply, but a great feast at my country house among the gardens. I invite all of you, my friends, to come to my garden to-morrow morning, and there we will make up, if Allāh wills, for lost time.'

The excellent syndic returned home at once and made great preparations for the morrow. He sent sheep, which had been fattened for six months on green leaves, to be roasted at the ovens, with well-buttered lambs, a multitude of pastries, and other pleasant things; he overwhelmed with work those among his slaves who were skilled in the making of sweetmeats and all the confectioners of Zainī Street.

Early on the following morning he took Abū Shāmāt with him to his garden and caused the slaves to spread two enormous cloths in two different parts of it. He said to his son: 'One of these cloths is for the men, and the other for the boys who will come with their fathers. I will entertain the bearded and you must look after the comfort of the beardless.' 'Why this separation?' asked Abū Shāmāt in surprise. 'Surely it is only usual when there is a question of men and women? Boys like myself have nothing to fear from bearded men.' 'My son,' answered the syndic, 'the lads will feel freer and have a more amusing time without their fathers.' And Abū Shāmāt, who was naturally innocent, contented himself with this reply.

When the guests came, Shams al-Dīn received the men, and Abū Shāmāt the boys. They ate and drank and sang, gaiety and delight shone from every face, incense and aromatic woods were burnt in braziers. When the feast was finished, slaves handed round cups of sherbert and snow; and the grown men chatted agreeably together while the boys played games.

Now among the guests there was a certain merchant, perhaps the syndic's best customer, a famous pederast, whose exploits had spared none of the pretty boys in the quarter in which he lived. His name was Mahmūd, but he was never known under any other title than that of Bilateral.

At this point Shahrazād saw the approach of morning and discreetly fell silent.

But when the two-hundred-and-fifty-sixth night had come

SHE SAID:

When Mahmūd Bilateral heard the sweet shouts of the boys at play, he was stirred to his depths and thought to himself: 'Surely there may be some windfall to be picked up over there.' He rose and, pretending that he had a pressing need, stole through the trees until he came all amongst the boys. He halted in appreciation of their lithe movements and handsome faces; it was not long before he decided that by far the most exquisite was Abū Shāmāt. He revolved a thousand plans for speaking to the lad and taking him apart, and was muttering: 'Yā Allāh! if only he would move a little away from his comrades!' when Destiny played into his hands.

Abū Shāmāt, excited by the game, his cheeks blowing with healthy roses, felt the need to piss and, being well brought up, did not wish to squat down in front of his guests. Therefore he went aside among the trees. Seeing this, Bilateral said to himself: 'If I approach him now, I will frighten him. I must adopt some other plan.' He walked out from behind the tree and was at once recognised by the boys, who began to hoot at him and run between his legs. He smiled happily at them, and at last said: 'Listen, my children, each of you shall have to-morrow a new robe and enough money for all his foolishness, if you can succeed in determining Abū Shāmāt to travel and vagabond away from Cairo.' 'That will be easy, Bilateral,' answered the boys; so Mahmūd left them and returned to the other company.

When Abū Shāmāt came back to his place, his comrades winked at each other and the most eloquent said: 'While you were away, we were talking of the marvels of travel and of wonderful far countries, of Damascus and Aleppo and Baghdād. Your father is so rich that you must surely have been many journeys with him among the caravans. Tell us a few of the wonders you have seen.' 'I?' answered Abū Shāmāt. 'Do you not know that I was brought up in a cellar and only came out yesterday? One cannot see much of the world in a cellar. It was hard enough to persuade my father to take me to the shop.'

'Poor Abū Shāmāt! You have been deprived of the most delightful joys in all the world. My friend, if you only knew what a wonderful thing is travel, you would not stay another day in your father's house. All the poets have sung the delights of wandering. One of them said:

> Sing the joys of vagabonding,
> All that's beautiful travels far;
> Even the moon-coloured pearl
> Must forsake the deep green levels,
> Leave the ancient ocean's bonding,
> And be drawn across the beaches
> Where the waiting merchants are,
> Ere it shows and glows and reaches
> To a crown's immortal bevels
> Or the white neck of a girl.'

When he heard this poem, Abū Shāmāt answered: 'You may be right; but a quiet home has its charm also.' One of the boys began to laugh, saying to the others: 'Poor Abū Shāmāt is like the fish who cannot live out of water.' Another improved on this, saying: 'He is afraid of spoiling the roses of his cheeks.' 'He is like a woman,' added a third, 'no woman can go a step alone.' A fourth exclaimed: 'O Abū Shāmāt, are you not ashamed of being such a girl?'

The poor boy was so mortified that he at once left his guests and, mounting his mule, galloped back to the city. He ran to his mother, with rage in his heart and tears in his eyes, so that the woman was frightened by his appearance. He repeated the mocking jests which had been made at his expense and declared his intention of setting out at once, for no matter what place, so long as he could set out. 'You see this knife,' he added, 'I shall thrust it into my breast if I am not allowed to travel.'

His mother could only weep and acquiesce. 'I promise to help you in every way I can,' she said. 'As I am sure your father will refuse his consent, I will give you an outfit of merchandise at my own expense.' 'Then we must act before my father's return,' said Abū Shāmāt.

Shams al-Dīn's wife got the slaves to open one of the reserve stocks of her husband's goods, and made enough of them into bales to load ten camels.

As soon as his guests had gone, the syndic hunted for his son in the garden and at last learned from the slaves that he had set out for home. Fearing lest some misfortune had happened to him by the way, Shams al-Dìn rode his mule at full gallop and came breathless to the courtyard of his house, where he was relieved to hear from the gate-keeper that his son had returned in safety. Nevertheless he was greatly surprised to see bale after bale standing ready in the court, all ticketed to such destinations as Aleppo, Damascus and Baghdàd.

At this point Shahrazàd saw the approach of morning and discreetly fell silent.

But when the two-hundred-and-fifty-seventh night had come

SHE SAID:

He hurried to his wife, who told him all that had passed and insisted that it would be dangerous to thwart the boy. 'Nevertheless I will try to dissuade him,' said the syndic, and, calling Abù Shàmàt to him, he addressed him thus: 'My child, may Allàh lighten your understanding and turn you from your fatal project! Our Prophet (upon whom be prayer and peace!) has said: "Happy is the man who lives on the fruits of the earth and finds contentment for his whole lifetime upon the spot where he was born." The ancients had this saying: "Do not enter upon a journey, even for one mile." After these two wise counsels, do you still persist in your resolution?'

'Dear father,' answered Abù Shàmàt, 'it would grieve me very much to disobey you, but, if you refuse to let me leave, I will throw off my costly clothes, dress in the rags of a darwìsh, and wander on foot through all the countries of the world.'

Seeing that his son was determined, the syndic said: 'Very well, my child, I will give you forty more loads, so that you will have fifty camels altogether. You will find goods appropriate for each of the towns which you enter; for you must not try to sell at Aleppo the fabrics which are popular in Damascus. That would be a bad speculation. Go, my son, and may Allàh protect you and flatten the road before you. Above all, take great care when you go through the Valley of Dogs, which is in the Desert of the Lion. Notorious bandits haunt there, under the leadership of a Badawì known as

Quick.' 'Evil and good alike lie in the hand of Allāh,' answered Abū Shāmāt. 'Whatever I do I shall only receive that which is due to me.'

As these sentiments were unanswerable, the syndic did not reply; but his wife could not be satisfied until she had made a thousand exclamatory prayers, promised a hundred sheep to various holy men, and again and again placed her son under the protection of Abd al-Kādir Jīlānī, saint of wayfarers.

While Abū Shāmāt was escaping with difficulty from the farewells of his weeping mother, Shams al-Dīn took aside the old intendant of the camel-drivers, one Kamāl, and said: 'Worthy intendant, I confide my child to you, the apple of my eye; I trust him to your guardianship and the protection of Allāh. . . . Remember, my son, that this is your father while you are away. Obey him, and never do anything without his advice.' Then he gave a thousand golden dīnārs to Abū Shāmāt, saying as a last recommendation: 'I give you these that you may live on them while waiting for the ripe and advantageous moment on which to sell your goods. Do not offer for sale that which others are offering at the same time; keep it till the stocks of your rivals are exhausted and the price rules high.' After last farewells the caravan started and was soon outside the gates of Cairo.

As soon as Mahmūd Bilateral heard of Abū Shāmāt's departure, he hurried forth and overtook him at two leagues from Cairo, with a troop of mules, camels, and saddle horses. 'O Mahmūd,' he said to himself, 'here in the desert there is no one to denounce you, no one to spy upon you; you can enjoy this child with a tranquil mind.'

At the first halt, Bilateral had his tents pitched beside those of Abū Shāmāt and, telling the child's cook not to trouble to light a fire, invited the object of his desire to feed in his own tent.

Abū Shāmāt came, but he was accompanied by old Kamāl, the intendant of the camel-drivers, so that Bilateral had only his trouble for his pains. The same thing happened on each succeeding day, until both caravans reached Damascus.

At this point Shahrazād saw the approach of morning and discreetly fell silent.

But when the two-hundred-and-fifty-eighth night had come

SHE SAID:

At this city, as at Cairo, Aleppo and Baghdād, Bilateral had a house where he was accustomed to entertain his friends; so he sent a slave to Abū Shāmāt, who remained in his tents at the entrance of the city, inviting him to come alone to visit him. 'Wait till I have asked old Kamāl's advice,' answered Abū Shāmāt; but the worthy camel-driver frowned at the invitation, and said: 'No, my son, you must decline.' Therefore Abū Shāmāt sent a message of polite refusal.

Neither caravan stayed long at Damascus; when both reached Aleppo, Bilateral sent the same invitation to Abū Shāmāt, and Kamāl again advised him to refuse. Although he did not understand why the intendant insisted so, the boy refused again; and Bilateral was still without any reward for his journey.

As soon as Aleppo was left behind, Bilateral swore that he would be thwarted no longer; at the first halt on the road to Baghdād, he prepared a wonderful feast and went himself to invite Abū Shāmāt. This time the youth was obliged to accept, as he had no serious excuse.

As he was dressing himself suitably in his tent, Kamāl came to him, saying: 'You are very imprudent, O Abū Shāmāt. Do you not understand Mahmūd's intentions? Do you not know why he is called Bilateral? At least you should have asked the advice of this old man, of whom a poet has written:

> As an old man I walked bent
> Because my youth was spilt and spent
> Upon the ground;
> I stooped to look for it and take it thence
> When lo! I found
> The fardel of experience
> So heavily upon my back had lain
> I could not straighten it again.'

But Abū Shāmāt answered: 'It would have been very rude to refuse the invitation, whatever reason people have for calling our friend Bilateral. Besides, he cannot eat me.' 'Can he not? He has already eaten many others,' answered the intendant sharply.

Abū Shāmāt laughed and hastened to rejoin Bilateral, who was waiting anxiously for him. They entered the tent where the feast was spread, and the boy saw that his host had spared no pains to receive him with all that might charm the eye or flatter the senses. The meal was gay and animated; both ate heavily and drank from the same cup until they were satisfied. When the wine had well mounted to their heads and the slaves had discreetly withdrawn, Bilateral leaned over Abū Shāmāt and, taking his two cheeks in his hands, tried to kiss them; but the boy, whose mind was troubled by this, instinctively lifted his hand, so that the kiss fell upon its palm. Next Mahmūd threw one arm round his guest's neck and drew him to him with the other. 'What do you wish to do?' cried Abū Shāmāt, and Bilateral answered: 'Simply to expound by practice these verses of the poet:

> Are not this child's eyes all fire?
> O desire,
> Feel the first flush of the eggs
> Between his legs!
> Dearest, seize what you can seize,
> If you please;
> Fill your boyish fist with me
> And then see
> Will it go a little way,
> Just in play?'

Having said these verses in a certain fashion, Bilateral would explain them practically to the boy; but Abū Shāmāt, without very well understanding, felt uncomfortable and wished to depart. Mahmūd held him back, however, and at last made all clear to him.

At this point Shahrazād saw the approach of morning and discreetly fell silent.

But when the two-hundred-and-fifty-ninth night had come

SHE SAID:
When Abū Shāmāt understood Bilateral's intentions and had well considered his request, he rose, saying: 'As Allāh lives, I do not sell that kind of goods. The only consolation I can give you is the assurance that, if ever I sell it to others, I will give it to you for nothing.' Then, in spite of his host's prayers, he left the tent and hurried back to his own camp, where the intendant was anxiously awaiting him. 'Tell me, in Allāh's name, what has passed?' said Kamāl, noticing the boy's strange looks. 'Nothing happened,' answered Abū Shāmāt. 'Only we must certainly strike camp at once and journey to Baghdād, as I do not want to travel longer with Bilateral. His pretensions are exaggerated and troublesome.' 'Did

I not tell you so?' cried the camel-driver. 'But praise be to Allāh that nothing happened! I think it would be very dangerous for us to go on alone; it would be better for us to stay as we are, a single caravan, for mutual protection against the Badawī cut-throats who haunt these ways.' But Abū Shāmāt would not be convinced, and the little caravan set out alone and journeyed forward, until one day at sunset it was only a few leagues from the gates of Baghdād. Kamāl came to Abū Shāmāt, saying: 'My son, we had better push on to Baghdād to-night instead of camping in this place, which is the most dangerous of all our journey and is called the Valley of Dogs. If we were to pass the night here, we would almost certainly be attacked. Let us hurry forward and reach the city before the gates are shut; for you must know that the Khalīfah has them strictly closed at night, lest the wandering fanatics should enter his city by stealth and throw all the books of science and literary manuscripts into the Tigris.'

Abū Shāmāt was not at all pleased with this plan, and answered: 'As Allāh lives, I do not want to enter the city by night. I want to enjoy the sight of the sunrise over Baghdād. We will pass the night here, for I am in no hurry; as you know, I am not journeying for business, but for the simple pleasure, and to see what I have never seen before.' The old intendant could only give way, although he had dark forebodings of the result.

Abū Shāmāt ate a light meal and then, when the slaves had lain down to sleep, left his tent and, walking up the valley for a little way, sat down under a tree in the moonlight. He called to mind books which he had read with his masters in the cellar and, inspired to reverie, began to sing this song:

> With delicate pleasures
> O queen of Irāk,
> O Baghdād, city of poets,
> So long have I dreamed of you:
> O calm . . .

He was interrupted by a terrible clamour on his left, by a galloping of horses, and wild cries from a hundred throats. He turned and saw his camp overwhelmed by a large band of Badawī, who seemed to spring from the earth. A sight so strange kept him, as it were, nailed to the ground, and, in spite of himself, he saw the wholesale massacre of the caravan and the plundering of his goods. When the Badawī outlaws saw that no one was left upon his feet, they drove off the camels and mules, and disappeared with incredible swiftness.

As soon as his stupefaction had a little decreased, the boy hurried to the place where his camp had been and looked upon the bodies of his dead; even old Kamāl's grey hairs had not been spared, he lay with his breast riddled by lances. Abū Shāmāt could not bear to look upon these things, he fled precipitately without daring to glance behind him.

So as not to excite the greed of some other band of robbers, he took off his rich clothes and threw them away from him, keeping only his shirt. After running all night, he entered Baghdād half-naked at the break of day.

As he was broken by fatigue and could no longer stand, he stopped before the first public fountain at the entrance of the city. After he had washed his hands, face and feet, he climbed to the platform overlooking the water and, lying down upon it, fell fast asleep.

Mahmūd Bilateral had also journeyed forward the night before, but he had taken a short cut and so escaped the bandits. He arrived at the gates of Baghdād within a few minutes of Abū Shāmāt. As he passed the fountain, he rode near the stone trough to water his tired horse, but the animal saw the shadow of the boy upon the water and started back. Thus it was that Bilateral lifted his eyes to the platform and nearly fell out of the saddle on recognising the half-naked sleeper as Abū Shāmāt.

At this point Shahrazād saw the approach of morning and discreetly fell silent.

But when the two-hundred-and-sixtieth night had come

SHE SAID:

He jumped from his horse and, climbing up to the platform, stood still in admiration before the delightful picture which the boy made, his head resting on one of his arms in the abandonment of sleep. For the first time Bilateral was able to enjoy the naked per-fections of this young and crystal body, starred by that adornment which had given the child his name. As he revolved the mystery of chance which had led him to find the purpose of all his journey asleep above a public fountain, he feasted his eyes upon the round beauty-spot upon the left thigh before him. 'What must I do?' he said to himself. 'Wake him? Set him on my horse and fly with him to the desert? Wait till he wakes, speak to him tenderly, persuade him to come to my house in Baghdād?'

He finally decided on the last course, and therefore sat down at the boy's feet to wait his waking, enjoying the rose stains which the sun dropped upon that childish body.

When Abū Shāmāt had had his fill of sleep, he moved his limbs and half-opened his eyes; at once Mahmūd took him by the hand, saying in a voice which he knew very well how to make sweet: 'Have no fear, my child. You are safe with me. I beg you to tell me what has happened.'

Abū Shāmāt sat up and, although he was a little troubled to find himself in the presence of his admirer, told Mahmūd the whole story. 'Give praise to Allāh, my young friend,' cried the merchant, 'for though he has taken away your fortune, he has spared your life. A poet has said:

> My gold is lost, my life is spared;
>   That is to say
> My finger nails are pared,
>   A thing of every day.

Also your fortune is not lost, for what is mine is yours. Come to my house for a bath and new raiment; from now on I beg you to consider all Mahmūd's riches your own; even Mahmūd's life, if you require it.' He went on speaking to the boy like a good father, until he persuaded him to his will; then he climbed down and helped the boy into the saddle behind him. As he rode towards his house, he shivered with pleasure to feel the lad's warm bare body straddled against him.

He led Abū Shāmāt to the hammām and bathed him himself, without the help of any rubber or slave; then he dressed him in a most expensive robe and led him to the hall where he was used to receive his friends. This hall was a delicious place of cool shadows, lighted only by the blue-tinted reflections of enamel and frail porcelain, elusive stars falling through the half light. The odour of a rare incense carried the soul to dream gardens of camphor and cinnamon; a fountain sang low in the middle of the floor; rest and ecstasy made one in the serene air.

As the two sat down on carpets, Mahmūd set a cushion for Abū Shāmāt's elbow; they ate daintily and drank choicely together, until at last Bilateral could contain himself no longer, and cried aloud the words of a poet:

> Lust is not content with blushes,
> Kisses taken from pure lips,
> Not content with wedded glances:
> Lust must have a thing which dances,
> Lust must have a thing which gushes,
> Lust must have a thing which drips.

Abū Shāmāt had become accustomed to Bilateral's verses, so he easily understood the drift of this rather obscure poem. He jumped to his feet, saying to his host: 'I cannot understand why you so harp upon this one string. I can only repeat that, on the day I sell this thing, I will give it to you for nothing.' With that he ran out of the hall and out of the house.

He wandered about the city in the falling night and, being a stranger ignorant of Baghdād, determined to pass the night in a mosque which he found. He entered the court and was about to take off his sandals before going further, when he saw two men coming towards him attended by slaves with lighted lanterns. He stepped to one side to let them pass, but the elder paused before him and looked at him closely, saying: 'Peace be with you!' Abū Shāmāt returned his greeting, and the other continued: 'Are you a stranger to the city, my child?' 'I come from Cairo,' answered Abū Shāmāt, 'my father is Shams al-Dīn, syndic of merchants in that place.'

The old man turned to his companion, saying: 'Allāh has prospered our research! We did not think to find our stranger so quickly.'

At this point Shahrazād saw the approach of morning and discreetly fell silent.

But when the two-hundred-and-sixty-first night had come

SHE SAID:

The old man took Abū Shāmāt aside, saying: 'I thank Allāh who has placed you in our way! We wish to ask you a favour for which we will pay you five thousand dīnārs, with goods for a thousand, and a horse worth another thousand.

'You must know, my son, that our law decrees the following: when a Mussulmān puts away his wife once, he may take her back at the end of three months and ten days without any formality; if he puts her away a second time, he may again take her back after the legal interval; but if he puts her away a third time, or if, without ever having put her away before, he says: 'I put you away three times,' or 'I swear by the third divorce that you are none of mine,' he may not take her back until another man has legally married her, lain with her one night, and himself divorced her.

'Now a few days ago this young man who is with me lost his temper with my daughter, his wife, and shouted at her: 'Get out of my house! I know you not! I put you away by the Three!' My daughter covered her face with her veil in the presence of her husband, who was then a stranger, took back her dowry, and returned to my house. But now her husband is very anxious to have her again; he has begged me to undertake the reconciliation. In brief, I offer you the position of Unbinder; you are a stranger, therefore no one need know anything about the matter, except the parties concerned and the kādī.'

Poverty compelled Abū Shāmāt to accept this offer. 'I shall have five thousand dīnārs, goods for a thousand, a horse worth a thousand, and a whole night of coupling,' he said to himself, and then turned to the two men, crying: 'I accept the office of Unbinder.'

'You are helping us out of a great difficulty,' said the husband, who had not yet spoken. 'I love my wife to distraction. My one fear is that to-morrow morning you may find her to your liking and not wish to give her back; in that case the law would be on your side; therefore I shall require you to make an engagement before the kādī to forfeit ten thousand dīnārs to me if you do not consent to the divorce when to-morrow comes.' Abū Shāmāt accepted this condition, as he had quite made up his mind only to lie with the woman for one night.

All three went to the kādī and made the two contracts in his presence. While the legal formalities were being complied with, the kādī looked often at Abū Shāmāt and learned to love him with consuming passion. We shall hear of the kādī during the course of our narrative.

When the contracts had been signed, the father of the divorced woman led Abū Shāmāt to his house and begged him to wait in the vestibule, while he himself hurried to his daughter, saying: 'My dear child, I have found an excellently well-built youth, whom I hope will please you. I recommend him to you with all my heart; have a fine night with him, and deny yourself nothing! It is not every night that one can have so delicious a boy within one's arms.' This good parent then returned to Abū Shāmāt and made him much the same recommendation, begging him to wait for a short time until his daughter should be ready to receive him.

Now the original husband was very jealous, so he lost no time in seeking out a very cunning old woman who had brought him up. 'Good mother,' he said to her, 'I beg you to find some means to prevent this Unbinder from lying with my wife.' 'On your life, that is easy enough,' answered the old woman.

At this point Shahrazād saw the approach of morning and discreetly fell silent.

But when the two-hundred-and-sixty-second night had come

SHE SAID:

Wrapping herself in her veil, she went to the house of the divorced woman and sidled up to the youth, whom she found in the vestibule, saying: 'Can you tell me where I can find the girl who was recently divorced? I come here every day to rub her body with my pomades, although I hardly expect to cure her leprosy, poor thing.' 'Allāh preserve me!' exclaimed Abū Shāmāt, 'is she a leper, good mother? I have to lie with her to-night; I am the Unbinder chosen by her husband.' 'Allāh keep whole your youth, my son!' she answered. 'You had better not lie with a person like that.' She left him in a state of the uttermost confusion and, going to the bride, told her the same tale about the Unbinder, advising her not to risk the contamination of his body.

Abū Shāmāt waited a long time for the girl to call him, but he saw no one except the slave who brought him food and drink. When he had finished his supper, he recited from the Koran to pass the time, and then began gently to sing over some lyric verses in a voice more beautiful than that of David before Saul.

The young woman heard his voice and said to herself: 'What did that wicked old woman mean? A leper could not have so beautiful a voice! As Allāh lives, I will call him and see for myself that the old trot has lied.' She took an Indian lute and sang in a voice to draw birds from the sky:

> I love a fawn with eyes of languishment;
> If you would know the forest way he went,
>> Watch what young branches still are practising
> Their just-learned lesson of the way he bent.

As soon as Abū Shāmāt heard the first notes of this song, he ceased his own and listened with charmed attention. 'By Allāh, that old salve-concocter lied!' he said to himself. 'A leper could not have so beautiful a voice.' Taking his key from the last note of the song, he answered in tones which would have made a rock dance:

> I send my voice to catch the quick gazelle
>   Who still eludes the chase,
> That it may wanton where the roses dwell
>   In the garden of her face.

The accent of this improvisation was so ravishing that the young woman ran to lift the curtains which separated her from the singer, and showed herself to him suddenly, like a moon unrobing from her clouds. Signing to him to enter her own apartment, she showed him the way with such a movement of the hips as would have set upright any impotent old man. As Abū Shāmāt hesitated between rapture at her beautiful youth and fear of leprous contagion, the girl took off her chemise and drawers and, throwing them far from her, appeared as naked and clean as virgin silver, as firm and slim as a palm branch.

Abū Shāmāt felt the heritage of his fathers move within him, the charming child he bore between his thighs. Feeling the infant's need to be pressing, he wished to give him to the woman, who surely would know what to do with him, but she cried out: 'Do not come near! I am afraid that I will catch your leprosy!'

Abū Shāmāt answered this by taking off all his clothes and appearing in his fair nakedness, as pure as a spring of water among rocks, as virgin as a baby's eye.

The girl saw in a flash her husband's villainy and, running to the Unbinder, dragged him to the bed and rolled upon it with him. Panting with desire, she said: 'Prove yourself, old Zacharias, prove yourself, sinewy father!'

At this explicit appeal, Abū Shāmāt seized the girl by the thighs and aimed a great stick of conserve in the direction of the gate of triumphs; then, riding towards the crystal corridor, he halted at the gate of victories. After that he left the main road and spurred vigorously by a short cut to the mounter's door; but, as the nerve failed a little before the narrowness of this wicket, he turned then and, staving in the lid, found himself as much at home as if the architect had built on the actual measures of both. He continued his pleasant expedition, slowly visiting Monday market, the shops about Tuesday, Wednesday counter, and the stall of Thursday; then, when he had loosened all there was to loosen, he halted, like a good Mussulmān, at the beginning of Friday. Such was the voyage of discovery which Abū Shāmāt and his little boy made in the garden of girlhood.

At this point Shahrazād saw the approach of morning and discreetly fell silent.

But when the two-hundred-and-sixty-third night had come

SHE SAID:

Feeling that his child was safely cradled in delight among the girl's pillaged flower beds, he clasped her tenderly, and all three slept together till morning.

At dawn Abū Shāmāt asked his transitory wife her name. 'Zubaidah,' she answered, and he continued: 'Dear Zubaidah, I infinitely regret that I have got to leave you.' 'And why have you got to leave me?' she asked. 'Have you forgotten that I am only the Unbinder?' he questioned. 'As Allāh lives, I had forgotten!' she cried. 'I thought, in my happiness, that you were some marvellous gift which my father had given me to take the place of the other.' 'No, charming Zubaidah, I am only the Unbinder,' he was forced to reply, 'and I have signed a contract in front of the kādī to forfeit ten thousand dīnārs if I do not abandon you. As I have only one dirham in my pocket, it is parting either way; for if I keep you, I shall go to prison.'

Zubaidah reflected for a while and then, kissing the youth's eyes, asked him his name. 'I am called Abū Shāmāt,' he answered, and she went on: 'Yā Allāh, you are well named. Dear Abū Shāmāt, as I prefer the white delicious stick of conserve which sweetened my garden to all the sugar candies in the world, I swear that I will find some way of never leaving you; for I would die if I belonged to another after this.' 'But what can we do?' he asked. 'It is quite simple,' she answered. 'My father will soon come to take you to the kādī to fulfil the formalities of your contract. You must take the kādī apart and whisper in his ear: "I do not want a divorce." "What?" he will ask, "do you refuse five thousand dīnārs, goods to the value of a thousand, and a horse worth a thousand, for the sake of a woman?" "Each of her hairs is worth ten thousand dīnārs," you must answer; then the kādī will say: "The law is on your side, but you must pay the husband ten thousand dīnārs as compensation."

'Now, my dear, listen carefully. The old kādī, though a man of excellent character in every other way, is madly enamoured of young boys, and I am quite sure that you have already made a considerable impression on him.'

'Do you think that the kādī is also bilateral?' cried Abū Shāmāt, and Zubaidah burst out laughing, as she answered: 'Assuredly. Is there anything very astonishing about that?' Said the youth: 'Surely it is written that Abū Shāmāt must spend his life in going from one bilateral to another! I pray you to continue, O clever Zubaidah. But first, surely you are not going to advise me to sell my goods to the old kādī?'

Zubaidah continued: 'Wait and see. When the kādī tells you that you must pay ten thousand dīnārs, you will look at him like this, making your hips move gently up and down, not too much, but enough to melt him with emotion upon his carpet. When you have done this, he will give you time in which to pay your debt; and after that Allāh will provide.'

'The thing is possible,' answered Abū Shāmāt.

Just at this moment a slave entered, saying: 'Mistress Zubaidah, your father waits for this youth outside.' Abū Shāmāt dressed in haste and, joining the father and the husband, went with them to the kādī.

Zubaidah's expectations were fulfilled to the letter. The kādī, being almost done to death by the sidelong glances of the youth, gave him not only three days in which to pay, as Abū Shāmāt modestly requested, but ten days, adding: 'Neither religious nor civil law obliges anyone to divorce. The four orthodox rituals are in accord upon this point. We give the Unbinder ten days in which to pay.'

Abū Shāmāt kissed the hand of the old man, who was saying to himself: 'As Allāh lives, the boy himself is well worth ten thousand. I would willingly lend him the money myself.' When all was completed, the youth said farewell in his most winning manner and hurried to rejoin his wife.

At this point Shahrazād saw the approach of morning and discreetly fell silent.

But when the two-hundred-and-sixty-fourth night had come

SHE SAID:

Zubaidah received his news with transports of joy and gave him a hundred dīnārs to prepare a feast for the two of them, which should last all night. Abū Shāmāt bought all that was necessary, and the lovers ate and drank until they were satisfied; then they coupled long and slowly and, at last, that they might rest themselves, went down to the reception hall, lit all the lamps, and held a concert just for themselves alone, which would have made rocks dance and drawn birds from the sky.

Suddenly Zubaidah heard a knocking on the outer door, and at her suggestion Abū Shāmāt went to open.

That night the Khalīfah Hārūn al-Rashīd, feeling himself distempered, had said to his wazīr Jafar, to his sword-bearer Masrūr, and to his favourite poet, the delicious Abū Nuwās: 'I feel my breast heavy to-night. Let us walk a little in the streets of Baghdād to find some relief for our humours.' The four disguised themselves as Persian darwīshes and set forth. As they wandered through the streets in search of some amusing adventure, they heard the sound of playing and singing in the house of Zubaidah. Faithful to their character of darwīshes, they at once knocked at the door.

When Abū Shāmāt saw them, he received them cordially and led them into the vestibule, for he was in excellent spirits and by nature hospitable. He brought food, but they said: 'As Allāh lives, sensitive spirits have no need of food but only of music. The fair sounds which we heard outside have ceased. What professional singer was discoursing such excellent melody?' 'It was my wife,' answered Abū Shāmāt, and he told them the whole of his story from beginning to end; but nothing would be gained by repeating it here.

The leader of the darwīshes, who was no other than the Khalīfah, felt himself stirred by a sudden affection for Abū Shāmāt, so he said to him: 'My son, take no care for the matter of the ten thousand dīnārs. I am chief of the convent of darwīshes in Baghdād; there are forty of us and we are, thanks to Allāh, in fairly comfortable circumstances; we shall certainly not miss ten thousand dīnārs. I promise to let you have the sum before the ten days are out. Now, if you please, beg your wife to sing us something from behind the curtain, that our souls may be exalted. Music, my son, is a dinner for some, a cure for others, and a fan for others; for us it is all three.'

Zubaidah sang for the darwīshes, and they all passed a night filled with delights, listening with all their ears and applauding with all their lungs, or laughing at the witty improvisations of Abū Nuwās, who was more than half drunk with the beauty of his host.

In the morning the darwīshes rose to go, after the Khalīfah had slipped under his cushion a purse containing a hundred golden dīnārs, all the money he had with him; they thanked their host through the mouth of Abū Nuwās, who invented exquisite stanzas of farewell, privately promising himself at the same time not to lose sight of so delectable a boy.

Towards noon Abū Shāmāt wished to go out to the market to purchase certain necessaries with the money which the Khalīfah had left. On opening the door, he saw before the house fifty mules loaded with bales of precious stuffs, and a fifty-first mule richly harnessed, carrying upon its back a young Abyssinian slave, brown-bodied and as pretty as a dream, who held a letter in his hand.

As soon as he saw Abū Shāmāt, the tender boy jumped to the ground and, kissing the earth between his hands, gave him the letter, saying: 'O Abū Shāmāt, I have been sent from Cairo by your father, my master Shams al-Dīn, to bring you fifty thousand dīnārs' worth of costly merchandise and a present for your wife, the lady Zubaidah, consisting of a jewelled ewer and a basin of wrought gold.'

At this point Shahrazād saw the approach of morning and discreetly fell silent.

But when the two-hundred-and-sixty-fifth night had come

SHE SAID:

Abū Shāmāt was both surprised and delighted at this seemingly miraculous happening. He opened the letter and read:

'*After the fullest possible wishes for his happiness and health from Shams al-Dīn to his son Alā al-Dīn Abū Shāmāt!*

'My dear son, I have heard of the disaster which overtook your caravan and of the loss of all your goods; therefore I have prepared a new lading for fifty mules, worth fifty thousand dīnārs. Your mother sends you a fair robe which she has embroidered herself, together with a ewer and basin destined for your wife. She hopes they will suit her.

'We were a little surprised to hear that you had acted as

Unbinder in a divorce, but feel that you were quite right to keep the woman when you found, by trial, that she pleased you. The goods which I send by little Sālim, the Abyssinian, will much more than pay the ten thousand dīnārs which you owe the former husband.

'Your mother and all of us are well and happy; we hope that you will soon return, and send you affectionate greetings and much love.

'May your life be happy!'

Abū Shāmāt was so pleased with this letter and the rich gift that he did not stop to think how unlikely the whole happening was, but went in at once to tell his wife. He had hardly finished explaining, when Zubaidah's father and first husband entered. 'I pray you have pity on my son-in-law, for he loves his wife to distraction,' said the father to Abū Shāmāt. 'Allāh has sent you riches, so that you may buy the fairest slaves in the market or marry the daughter of some amīr. If you give back this poor man's wife, he will be your slave.' 'Allāh has sent me riches in order that I may richly compensate my predecessor,' corrected Abū Shāmāt. 'I freely give him the fifty mules with their merchandise and also Sālim, the pretty Abyssinian slave. Nevertheless, if Zubaidah consents to return to her former husband, I will give her her freedom.' The older man went to find his daughter and said to her: 'Will you return to your former husband?' Zubaidah answered with exaggerated gestures: 'Yā Allāh! Yā Allāh! He never knew the worth of the flower beds in my garden. He always stopped half-way up the path! As Allāh lives, I will stay with the youth who has wandered in it everywhere.'

When the first husband realised that hope had passed for him, his liver burst upon the spot and he died. So much for him.

Abū Shāmāt lived pleasantly with his delightful wife, and each evening, after feasting and every manner of coupling, they held a concert which would have made rocks dance and drawn birds from the sky.

On the tenth day after his marriage Abū Shāmāt remembered the promise which the darwīsh chief had made to him, so he said to his wife: 'Chief of liars, more like! If I had waited for his help, I would have died in prison. If ever I meet him again, I will tell him what I think of him.'

As evening fell he illuminated the hall, and the concert was about to begin when a knocking was heard on the door. Abū Shāmāt was not surprised, on opening, to see the darwīshes; he laughed in their faces, saying: 'Welcome, O liars! Welcome, gentlemen of bad faith! But come in, come in; for Allāh has freed me from any need of your services. Besides, though you are liars and hypocrites, you are charming and well-bred.' He led them into the hall and prayed Zubaidah to sing them something from behind the curtain. She obeyed him in a fashion to steal away the reason, to make rocks dance, and to draw birds out of the sky.

In the course of time the darwīsh chief rose and departed to satisfy a need; taking advantage of his absence, the poet Abū Nuwās whispered in the ear of his host . . .

At this point Shahrazād saw the approach of morning and discreetly fell silent.

But when the two-hundred-and-sixty-sixth night had come

SHE SAID:

'Charming host, may I ask you a question? How could you believe for a moment in your father's present of fifty mules? How long does it take to come from Cairo to Baghdād?' 'Forty-five days,' answered Abū Shāmāt, and the poet continued: 'And to return?' 'The same,' the youth admitted. Then Abū Nuwās burst out laughing and said: 'How could you expect your father to hear of the loss of your caravan in less than ten days?' 'By Allāh,' cried Abū Shāmāt, 'my joy was so great that I never thought of the matter at all! Tell me, O darwīsh, who wrote the letter, and who sent the gifts?' 'Dear Abū Shāmāt,' replied the poet, 'if you were as clever as you are handsome, you would long ago have divined under these garments the presence of the Khalīfah himself, Hārūn al-Rashīd, Defender of the Faith: Jafar al-Barmaki, his wise wazīr: Masrūr, the sworder: and a simple poet, your devoted slave and admirer, Abū Nuwās.'

Abū Shāmāt was thrown into astonished confusion. 'O great poet,' he asked timidly, 'can you tell me what merit of mine attracts such great kindness from the Khalīfah?' Abū Nuwās answered with a smile: 'Your beauty. In the King's eyes to be young and sympathetic and handsome is the first of virtues; he considers that one cannot pay too high a price for the privilege of looking upon a lovely face.'

As soon as the Khalīfah returned to his place upon the carpet, Abū Shāmāt bowed before him, saying: 'O Prince of Believers, may

Allāh continue you in our love and never deny you great returns for all your kindness.' The Khalīfah smiled and caressed him lightly on the cheek, saying: 'I will expect you to-morrow at the palace.' Then he rose and departed, followed by Jafar, Masrūr, and Abū Nuwās, who strongly urged his host not to forget the appointment.

Next morning Abū Shāmāt chose out the most precious from those things which had been sent him and packed them in a handsome chest which he confided to little Sālim; then, when his wife had dressed and arranged him with great care, he made his way to the Khalīfah's dīwān, taking the slave with him. Laying the chest before the throne, he made a compliment in well-constructed verse, and added: 'Commander of the Faithful, our blessed Prophet (upon whom be prayer and peace!) used to accept gifts in order not to offend their givers. Think of your slave's delight if you would deign to receive this little box as a mark of his eternal gratitude.' The Khalīfah was charmed by this attention. 'It is too much, O Abū Shāmāt,' he said. 'You yourself, without any box, are a gift for kings. Welcome to my palace, for from to-day I give you high employment.' Straightway he deprived of his office the chief syndic of the merchants and gave it to Abū Shāmāt, proclaiming the appointment by a firmān which was cried through all the streets and markets of Baghdād.

From that time the Khalīfah would not let a day pass without seeing Abū Shāmāt; therefore, as the youth had no opportunity himself to sell his merchandise, he opened a handsome shop and installed the small brown slave, who showed great aptitude for delicate business in it.

Two or three days after Abū Shāmāt had become syndic, the death was announced to Hārūn al-Rashīd of his chief cup-bearer. At once he gave the post to Abū Shāmāt, together with the appropriate robe of honour and sumptuous revenues.

Next day, as the youth stood beside the Khalīfah, the chamberlain entered and kissed the earth before the throne, saying: 'Allāh preserve the King's days and make them longer than those of the poor chief Officer of the palace! He has just died.' 'Allāh have him in His holy keeping!' cried the Khalīfah, and at once raised Abū Shāmāt to the high position of the dead man, according him a still more sumptuous allowance. When the new appointment had been announced, Hārūn al-Rashīd waved his handkerchief as a sign that the dīwan was ended.

At this point Shahrazād saw the approach of morning and discreetly fell silent.

But when the two-hundred-and-sixty-seventh night had come

SHE SAID:

Abū Shāmāt spent all his days at the palace, and only returned at night to lie joyfully with his wife, after telling her the happenings at the Court. The Khalīfah's love increased for him each day, and at last he would have sacrificed all he possessed to satisfy the young man's least desire.

For instance, Hārūn al-Rashīd gave a concert at which Jafar, Masrūr, Abū Nuwās, and Abū Shāmāt were present; and the favourite herself, the fairest and most accomplished of his concubines, sang from behind a curtain. Suddenly the Khalīfah looked hard at Abū Shāmāt, saying: 'My friend, I read in your eyes that this favourite of mine pleases you.' 'What pleases the master ought to please the slave,' replied the youth, but the Khalīfah cried: 'I swear by my head and by the tomb of my ancestors that she belongs to you!' He called his chief eunuch, saying: 'Have all the belongings of my favourite, Delight-of-Hearts, together with her forty slaves, taken to the Officer's house; then return and conduct the lady herself to that place in a litter.' But Abū Shāmāt objected: 'I beg you very humbly, O Commander of the Faithful, to spare your unworthy slave the impiety of touching what belongs to his master.' Hārūn al-Rashīd understood and answered: 'Perhaps you are right. It is likely that your wife would be jealous of a woman whose lot has been so royal. Let her remain in my palace.' Then, turning to his wazīr Jafar, he said: 'You must go down to the slave market at once and buy for ten thousand dīnārs the most beautiful slave at present offered for sale. Send her, without delay, to Abū Shāmāt's house.'

Jafar did as he was bid, but took Abū Shāmāt with him to choose for himself.

Now it so happened that the amīr Khālid, who was walī of the city, had also gone down to the market that day to buy a slave for his son, who had just reached the age of puberty. This son was so ugly that he might easily have made any woman miscarry. He was deformed and stinking, with squint eyes, a mouth as large as the sex of an old cow, and unpleasant breath. He went by the name of Big-Bloat.

The night before, Big-Bloat had reached his fourteenth year and his mother had grieved because she had been expecting for some time past to see signs of virility in her son. Her fears were put at rest in the morning by certain unequivocal stains on the mattress, which proved that Big-Bloat had at least learned how to couple in his dreams. In an ecstasy of delight the mother had run to her husband with the good news, and had persuaded him to take the boy down to the market and buy him a beautiful slave.

Thus Destiny, which lies between the hands of Allāh, caused all four to meet in the market and to stay together while the brokers led white, brown, and black slaves before them. They looked at a prodigious quantity of Greek girls, Chinese, Abyssinians and Persians; and were about to go away without having made up their minds, when the chief broker himself walked past, leading a girl more beautiful than the full moon in Ramadān. When he saw her, Big-Bloat began to snuffle with desire, and said to his father: 'That is the one I want.' At the same time Jafar asked Abū Shāmāt: 'Will this one do? and the other answered: 'She will.'

'What is your name, gentle slave?' asked Jafar, and the girl replied: 'O my master, it is Yāsamīn.' The wazīr asked Yāsamīn's price, and the broker answered: 'Five thousand dīnārs, my masters.' At once Big-Bloat cried: 'I will give six!' When Abū Shāmāt murmured: 'I will give eight,' Big-Bloat snorted with rage and shouted: 'Eight thousand and one!' 'Nine thousand and one!' said Jafar, but Abū Shāmāt corrected him, calling out: 'Ten thousand dīnārs!'

'Going, going, gone, at ten thousand dīnārs, the slave Yāsamīn!' said the broker quickly, and he handed over the girl to Abū Shāmāt.

Big-Bloat fell to the ground, beating the air with his hands and feet, much to the chagrin of the amīr Khālid, who hated his son for his ugliness and idiocy, and had only brought him to the market because he made a habit of obeying his wife.

Abū Shāmāt, after cordially thanking Jafar, led Yāsamīn to his own house—for he already loved her and she loved him—and introduced her to his wife, who found her sympathetic and gave her a great friendship. Charmed by Zubaidah's approval, Abū Shāmāt took Yāsamīn as his second wife and slept with her that same night. And she conceived, as the sequel of this tale will show.

When his father had succeeded, with promises and cajoleries, in taking Big-Bloat home, the boy threw himself upon his bed and refused to rise for food or drink; he had almost lost his reason. While the women of the house were crowding round his mother and commiserating with her, an old woman entered, whose son was a very famous thief, called Ahmad-the-Moth.

Now Ahmad-the-Moth, though he was at present serving a life sentence, was so exquisite a robber that, merely for pastime, he would steal a door in the presence of the door-keeper and dispose of it so quickly that it looked as if he had swallowed it; he would dig through walls under their owner's eye, while pretending to piss against them; he could cut off a man's eyelashes while talking to him and never be even suspected, or remove the kohl from a woman's eyes as she complimented him upon his honesty.

Big-Bloat's mother greeted the mother of Ahmad-the-Moth and, when she asked why she was so sad and what illness the boy was suffering, did not hesitate to confide in her. 'O my mistress,' cried the old woman, 'only my son could help you in this matter. Try to obtain his freedom and he will find a way to transfer the beautiful Yāsamīn to our young master. You must know that my poor boy lies chained hand and foot in prison, with an iron collar about his neck on which are engraved the words: "For ever!" And all for a little matter of coining!'

Big-Bloat's mother promised to do what she could; when the walī returned that evening, she went to him after supper, scented and tricked out with excessive care, wearing a practised promising smile, so that the excellent Khālid could not resist the fires which her appearance lit within his heart. He wished to take her, but she resisted, saying: 'First swear by divorce that you will grant me what I ask.' He swore, and the woman at once told him a pitiable tale of the robber and his poor old mother. When he promised the man's release, she allowed him to mount her.

Next morning the amīr went to the prison where Ahmad-the-Moth was confined and asked him whether he repented. 'I bitterly repent,' answered the other. 'I am prepared to proclaim the fact aloud.' So the walī took him from prison and led him before the Khalīfah, who was astonished to see him still alive. 'Are you not dead yet, O thief?' cried Hārūn al-Rashīd, and the man replied: 'As Allāh lives, O Prince of Believers, the wicked are very hard to kill.' The Khalīfah laughed heartily, saying: 'Send for a blacksmith to remove his irons. I know your exploits well, my man. As I wish to keep you in the path of repentance and as none knows better than you all the robbers which there are in my city of Baghdād, I name you chief of police.' So Ahmad-the-Moth, chief of police

kissed the Khalīfah's hand and entered at once upon his new
duties.

To begin with, as a double celebration, he went to a tavern kept
by one Ibrāhīm, a Jew, an old accomplice of his, and emptied
several flagons of his favourite drink, a certain excellent Ionian wine.
There his mother found him a little drunk, pulling the Jew about
the chamber by his beard, a liberty which the old man was forced
to allow to so great and inconvenient an acquaintance. With some
difficulty she managed to take him aside and tell him the whole story
of his deliverance, adding that the least return he could make for it
was to find some way of stealing the slave from Abū Shāmāt. 'It
shall be done to-night. There is nothing very difficult about that,'
answered Ahmad-the-Moth, and straightway began to prepare for
the enterprise.

At this point Shahrazād saw the approach of morning and
discreetly fell silent.

But when the two-hundred-and-sixty-eighth night had come

SHE SAID:

Now you must know that on that night, which was the first of the
month, the Khalīfah had gone, as was his custom, to visit his wife, in
order to talk with her of the affairs of the time and take her advice
on many subjects. He had great confidence in her, loving her for her
wisdom and for a beauty which never seemed to fade. Always,
before entering the chamber of his queen, he would place upon a
special stand in the vestibule his chaplet of alternate amber and
turquoise beads, his sabre which had a jade hilt incrusted with rubies
as big as pigeons' eggs, his royal seal, and a little gold lamp studded
with precious stones which used to light his secret midnight inspec-
tions of the palace.

These details were known to Ahmad-the-Moth and he used them
for his own ends. Waiting till all the slaves were asleep in the dead
of night, he climbed the wall of the pavilion by means of a rope-
ladder and, entering the vestibule as silently as a shadow, took the
four precious objects and went back by the way he had come.

He ran to Abū Shāmāt's house and, noiselessly breaking into the
courtyard, lifted one of the squares of marble which paved it, rapidly
dug a shallow trench, and there hid three of the stolen objects,
keeping the little gold lamp as his commission. Then, when he had

removed all traces of his visit, he returned to continue his carouse at Ibrāhīm's tavern.

Great was the Khalīfah's surprise when he went out in the morning and found none of his possessions on the stand. He questioned the eunuchs, who fell on their faces before him protesting ignorance, and then entered into an anger so formidable that he hurried at once to put on his terrible robe of rage. This was of red silk, and, when the Khalīfah wore it, all who came in his way might be certain of calamity.

Flaming in this deadly garment, Hārūn al-Rashīd seated himself upon his throne in solitude. All his chamberlains and wazīrs came in one by one and lay down on their bellies before him, while Jafar, with a colourless face, stood upright, fixing his eyes upon the Sultān's feet.

After an hour of awful silence the King said to Jafar: 'The cup boils.' 'Allāh prevent evil!' answered Jafar.

Just at that moment the walī entered with Ahmad-the-Moth. 'Come here, O amīr Khālid,' said the King. 'How goes the public peace in my city of Baghdād?' 'Prince of Believers, it goes well,' answered Big-Bloat's father, and the Khalīfah answered: 'You lie!' The walī began to stammer excuses and Jafar was just whispering to him an account of the theft, when the Khalīfah continued: 'If that lost property, which is dearer to me than all my kingdom, is not recovered by to-night, your head shall be hung on the palace gate.'

The walī kissed the earth between the hands of the Khalīfah, crying: 'Prince of Believers, the thief must surely be someone of the palace, for souring wine carries its own ferment. If I may be allowed to speak, the chief of police, who knows every thief in Baghdād, is more responsible than myself. If the stolen things are not recovered, his death should follow and not mine.'

Hearing this, Ahmad-the-Moth came forward, saying: 'Commander of the Faithful, the thief shall be discovered. I beg your majesty to give me a firmān, authorising me to search the houses of all who have employment about the palace, even the kādī, even Jafar, even Abū Shāmāt.' Hārūn al-Rashīd wrote him the firmān, saying: 'Someone's head must be cut off for this; it is for you to choose whether it be the robber's or your own. I swear by my life and by the tomb of my ancestors that even if my own son, the heir to my throne, were guilty, he should be publicly hanged.'

Ahmad took with him his authorisation, two of the kādī's guards, and two of the walī's guards, and began his perquisition. He went to Jafar's house, to the walī's house, to the kādī's house, and came at last to the house of Abū Shāmāt, who had not as yet heard anything of the theft.

Ahmad entered the vestibule, carrying his firmān in one hand and a heavy brass rod in the other, and told Abū Shāmāt all that had happened, adding: 'I shall not dream of carrying out a real search in the house of the Khalīfah's most faithful confidant. Allow me to take the perquisition for granted and retire.' 'On the contrary, O chief of police, duty must be done,' answered Abū Shāmāt. So Ahmad, murmuring: 'For form's sake only,' walked out carelessly into the courtyard and began to strike the marble slabs with his brass rod.

When he came to the slab about which we have already heard, it gave forth a hollow sound, and he exclaimed: 'Dear my lord, there must be some disused vault below this place; I should not be surprised if we had hit upon a buried treasure.' Then said Abū Shāmāt to the four guards: 'Try to lift the slab, that we may see what is beneath it.' They inserted the points of their lances at the sides of the marble and lifted. Then all could see the sword, the seal, and the chaplet which had been stolen.

'In the name of Allāh!' cried Abū Shāmāt and fainted away, while Ahmad sent at once for the walī, the kādī, and witnesses, who wrote out and sealed a full account of the discovery.

Then, while the kādī was hurrying with this to the Khalīfah, the guards took the swooning body of Abū Shāmāt into custody.

When the Khalīfah received damning proof of the treachery of his greatest friend, he sat for an hour without speaking and then turned to his captain of guards, saying 'Let him hang!'

The captain had this sentence cried through all the streets of Baghdād, and then went to the house of Abū Shāmāt and confiscated his goods and his two wives. The money was placed in the public treasure and the wives were about to be cried for sale, when Big-Bloat's father took possession of Yāsamīn, as was his right, and the captain himself led Zubaidah to his own house.

Now this captain of the guards was Abū Shāmāt's great friend and loved him as a father, with a faith which could not lie. Though he executed the Khalīfah's terrible orders in public, he swore to save the life of his adopted son, and began his benevolent work by giving a safe refuge to one of his wives.

That night Abū Shāmāt was doomed to be taken from his prison to the scaffold, so the captain lost no time in going to the governor of the prison and demanding to see the forty or so prisoners who were to be hanged in the evening. He carefully scrutinised each one and, at last, chose out a man who looked very like Abū Shāmāt, saying to the governor: 'This fellow shall serve me, as the ram served the patriarch in place of his son.'

When the hour of execution came, he fixed the rope about the neck of the false Abū Shāmāt and launched him into space, in the presence of a mighty crowd; afterwards he waited till midnight and then secretly removed Abū Shāmāt from the prison to his own house. He told the youth what he had done for him, adding: 'Tell me in Allāh's name, my son, why you allowed yourself to be tempted by those things.'

At this implied accusation Abū Shāmāt fell again into a swoon; when he came to himself, he cried: 'I swear, my father, by Allāh and by the Prophet, that I know nothing of this theft.' The captain of the guard believed him, saying: 'Sooner or later, my son, the guilty person will be discovered. For the moment our concern is rather with your safety, for you cannot stay in this city now that you have a king for enemy. We must leave your wife in my house and hide you somewhere far from Baghdād, until Allāh, in His infinite wisdom, chooses to bring the truth to light. We will cross the salt sea to Alexandria, which is a delightful place to live in, surrounded as it is by green and fertile country.'

They departed, without even leaving time for Abū Shāmāt to say farewell to Zubaidah, and soon left Baghdād behind them. Being without horses, they went slowly; but, in the course of time, met two rich Jews riding upon mules, money-changers of substance in the city. The captain of the guard considered that it would be fatal if these men reported to the Khalīfah that they had seen Abū Shāmāt, so he cried to them: 'Come down from your mules!' When the Jews abjectly obeyed, he cut off their heads, took their money and, mounting one of the animals, gave the other to Abū Shāmāt.

Being now mounted, they soon arrived at the port; there they left their beasts at the inn and set out in search of a boat sailing for Alexandria. Without much difficulty they found a vessel about to up-anchor for that city; so the captain gave Abū Shānāt all the gold he had taken from the Jews and counselled him to wait quietly in Alexandria for any news that he could send him. Promising that he himself would come to fetch him when times were better, he said farewell with tears in his eyes and watched the vessel depart.

He returned to Baghdād and this is what he learned:

The morning after the hanging of the false Abū Shāmāt, the Khalīfah, who was still troubled in his mind, called Jafar, saying: 'O my wazīr, you have seen the way in which this Abū Shāmāt requited all my goodness and abused the great confidence which I had in him; tell me, how could so beautiful a body hide so ugly a soul?' Jafar, though he was very wise, had not been able to conceive a motive for the theft, so he answered: 'Commander of the Faithful, surprising actions are no longer surprising when we know the motives of them. In this sad case we can only judge the effect, the death of the unfortunate boy. Yet Abū Shāmāt the Egyptian had such spiritual fairness shining in his face that, though I have seen the thing, I am inclined not to believe it.'

The Khalīfah reflected for an hour, and then replied: 'Since he was guilty, I wish to see his body swinging in the air.'

The two disguised themselves and went forth to the scaffold. The body was covered with a shroud, but Jatar removed this, and the Khalīfah recoiled in astonishment, crying: 'That is not Abū Shāmāt!' Jafar looked at the body and saw at once that what the King said was true. Nevertheless he asked: 'What can possibly tell you that it is not Abū Shāmāt?' 'He was short and this man is tall,' said the King. 'That is no proof,' answered Jafar, 'hanging stretches out a man.' Then said the Khalīfah: 'My lost friend had two moles upon his cheeks; this man has none.' 'Death plays strange tricks,' answered the wazīr, 'she can disorder the fairest face.' 'That may be,' cried Hārūn al-Rashīd, 'but look at the soles of this fellow's feet; here are tattooed the names of the two great Sheikhs, after the manner of the schismatics of Alī. Abū Shāmāt was not a Shiite but a Sunnite.' Jafar's only answer to this was: 'Allāh alone may see into the heart of a mystery.' The two returned to the palace, having given orders that the body should be buried; and from that day Hārūn al-Rashīd banished all memory of Abū Shāmāt from his heart.

We have heard that the condemned man's second wife, she who had been the slave Yāsamīn, was taken home by the amīr Khālid for the pleasure of his son Big-Bloat. As soon as this lumpish lad saw her, he rose snorting from his bed and would have taken her in his arms, but the beautiful girl, being disgusted at the appearance of the half-wit, drew a knife from her belt and held it at arm's length, saying: 'Keep off, or I will slay you first and myself after!' Big-Bloat's mother ran forward, screaming: 'How do you dare resist my son's desire, insolent baggage?' 'O lawless one,' replied Yāsamīn, 'how can a woman belong to two men at once? How can a dog pasture in a lion's den?'

'If that is your attitude,' snarled Big-Bloat's mother, 'I will teach you what it is to live hard while you are here.' When the girl answered: 'I would rather die than soil my love for my master, be he living or dead,' the walī's wife undressed her and, taking her beautiful silk robes and all her jewels, put on her the goat's-hair rags of a kitchen slut and bade her begone to the cooks, saying: 'Your work will be to peel onions, light fires, squash tomatoes, and knead dough.' 'I would much rather do that than look upon the face of your son,' answered Yāsamīn, as she retired to the kitchen, where she soon won the affection of all the slaves. These good people would not allow her to work, but parted her duties among them.

Big-Bloat, you will be glad to hear, took to his bed for good and all, and never rose from it again.

You must remember that Yāsamīn had been got with child by Abū Shāmāt; a few months after she came to the walī's house, she bore a son as beautiful as the moon, whom she called Aslān, weeping hot tears the while because his father was not there to choose a name for him.

Little Aslān drank his mother's milk for two years and thus became exceptionally strong and beautiful, and could walk by himself. One day, when his mother was busy, he stoutly clambered up the kitchen stairs and marched into the room where the amīr Khālid sat telling his amber chaplet. The walī felt tears come into his eyes when he saw a little fellow looking so like Abū Shāmāt. He took the infant upon his knees and began to caress him, saying: 'Blessed be He who makes beauty and then inspires it with life!'

A little later Yāsamīn noticed her son's absence and, after seeking him everywhere else, dared to enter the amīr's own chamber. Aslān was amusing himself by thrusting his little fingers into the walī's venerable beard, but, when he saw his mother, he stretched out his arms and would have gone to her. Khālid held him back, saying kindly to the woman: 'Is this your son, O slave?' 'Master, he is the fruit of my heart,' she answered. 'And who is the father,' said the amīr, 'one of my servants?' Yāsamīn burst into tears as she answered:

'His father was my husband, Abū Shāmāt, but now, O master, the child is your son.' Moved to the bottom of his heart, the walī exclaimed: 'By Allāh, you are right! He is now my son.' He adopted the child from that hour, saying to the mother: 'After to-day he shall be my son indeed. You must never let him know that he had another father.' 'I hear and I obey,' said Yāsamīn.

Khālid brought up Aslān as if he had really been the fruit of his own marriage; he gave him a careful education at the hands of a most learned professor, an unrivalled calligraphist, who instructed the boy in fair writing, the Koran, geometry and poetry. When he was a little older, the walī himself taught him to ride, to tilt with the lance, to fight in tournament, and to practise with every weapon known to man. When Aslān became fourteen he was already a most accomplished cavalier, and the Khalīfah named him amīr, even as his father was.

One day fate willed that young Aslān and Ahmad-the-Moth should meet outside the door of Ibrāhīm's tavern. Ahmad asked the lad to come in and have a drink, and, as they sat together, the chief of police soon became quite drunk. Taking a little gold lamp from his pocket, he lit it to dispel the coming darkness of night. 'Yā, Ahmad, give me that beautiful lamp!' cried Aslān. 'Allāh preserve me from such generosity!' said the chief of police. 'How could I give you a thing which has cost so many lives? My dear lad, this lamp killed a certain Egyptian named Abū Shāmāt, who was no other than the Officer of the royal palace.' Aslān was deeply interested and begged to be told the story; so Ahmad-the-Moth gave him a true account of the stealing of the lamp, glorifying himself in his drunkenness for having made so clever a stroke.

When Aslān returned home, he informed his mother of all which Ahmad had told him and added that the chief of police still kept the lamp about his person. Much to his surprise, Yāsamīn uttered a great cry and fell swooning to the ground.

At this point Shahrazād saw the approach of morning and discreetly fell silent.

But when the two-hundred-and-sixty-ninth night had come

SHE SAID:

When she came to herself, she clung sobbing to her son's neck, and said: 'My child, Allāh has brought the truth to light; I can keep the secret no longer. Dear son, the amīr Khālid is only your adopted father; your real father was my husband, Abū Shāmāt, who was punished in place of the thief. You must go at once and find your father's old friend, the captain of the guard, and tell him what you have discovered; also you must swear before him to take vengeance on your father's murderer.'

When the captain of the guard heard Aslān's story, he rejoiced exceedingly, saying: 'Glory to Allāh Who throws light into dark places and tears down the veils of mystery! He Himself will undertake your vengeance; be sure of that, my son.'

The old man was right; for on that very day the Khalīfah was holding a tournament of which one of the spectacles was a game of polo. Young Aslān was one of the players; he rode onto the ground, mounted upon one of Khālid's most wonderful horses, dressed in his shining coat of mail, and looked so knightly thus that the Khalīfah was charmed and wished him to play upon his own side.

The game began and all the players showed marvellous skill, following the ball at full gallop and hitting it with great address. Suddenly one of the players of the opposite side hit the ball so strongly in the direction of Hārūn al-Rashīd that it would infallibly have put out one of his eyes, or even have killed him, had not Aslān intercepted it with his stick, when it was within a few feet of the royal face, and returned it so heartily that it broke the back of the man who had hit it first.

The Khalīfah looked at the youth, saying: 'A delightful shot, O son of Khālid.' With that he dismounted and, putting a stop to the game, assembled his amīrs and all the players. Calling Aslān into this assembly, he said: 'O valorous offspring of the walī of Baghdād, I wish you to name your own reward.' The boy kissed the earth between the Khalīfah's hands, answering: 'I beg for vengeance, O Commander of the Faithful! The blood of my father still cries from the ground, and his slayer lives!'

The Khalīfah called out in great astonishment: 'What is this that you say of avenging your father? Your father stands here at my side in excellent health, and I thank Allāh for it.' 'Prince of Believers,' answered Aslān, 'the amīr Khālid is only the best adopted father a boy ever had. My real father is Abū Shāmāt, the late Officer of all your palace.'

Hārūn al-Rashīd saw the light turn to darkness before his eyes, and he answered in a changed voice: 'My son, do you not know that your father betrayed his Sultān?' 'Allāh preserve his memory from such a stain!' exclaimed Aslān. 'The traitor stands even now at your left hand, he is Ahmad-the-Moth, chief of police. Have him searched, for he carries the proof in his pocket.'

The Khalīfah became as yellow as saffron and called the captain of his guard in a terrible voice, saying: 'Search this man in my presence!' Abū Shāmāt's old friend went up to Ahmad and, going through his pockets, immediately brought to light the stolen lamp.

'Come here, you! Say how you became possessed of this lamp!' cried Hārūn al-Rashīd. 'Commander of the Faithful, I bought it,' answered Ahmad. Then cried the Khalīfah: 'Beat him until he confesses!' And, when his body had been stripped naked and sieved out with blows, the chief of police confessed all and told the whole story of his treachery.

The Khalīfah turned to Aslān, saying: 'It is now your turn; hang him with your own hand!' The guards quickly erected a gallows in the midst of the polo ground, and little Aslān and the captain, pulling on the rope together, hoisted Ahmad-the-Moth into the forgiveness of Allāh.

When justice had been done, the Khalīfah again requested Aslān to name his own reward, and he answered: 'I beg you to give me back my father, O Prince of Believers!'

Hārūn al-Rashīd wept, saying: 'My son, do you not know that your poor father was unjustly hanged? He is almost certainly dead; though I admit that there was some doubt as to the identity of the corpse. Since a flicker of hope remains to us, I swear by my ancestors that no favour will be too great for him who tells me that your father is alive.'

At this the captain of the guard came forward, saying: 'Give me the word of safety!' 'Your safety is certain. Speak!' replied the Khalīfah, and the old man cried aloud: 'I bring good news, Commander of the Faithful! Abū Shāmāt, your friend and loving servant, still lives!'

'What is that you say?' cried the King, and the captain continued: 'I swear by my life that the thing is true. I myself saved Abū Shāmāt by having a common criminal hanged in his stead. He now abides safely in Alexandria and probably has taken a shop there.'

Hārūn al-Rashīd rejoiced, saying: 'Depart at once and bring him back to me without a moment's delay!' He gave the captain ten thousand dīnārs for his voyage and despatched him at once to Alexandria, where, if Allāh wills, we shall hear of him again.

To return to Abū Shāmāt: the ship which carried him made an excellent voyage to Alexandria, and the young man was delighted by the appearance of the city, which, although he was a native of Cairo, he had not visited before. He went at once to the market and found that a shop, the owner of which had just died, was being offered for sale as it stood. Abū Shāmāt bought it and found it well equipped for the marine trade. There was a plentiful stock of sails, ropes, packthread, stout chests, sacks for private cargo, weapons of every kind and price; and above all there were great heaps of scrap-iron and old lumber, which are very popular among sea captains, who can sell such stuff to the peoples of the West. The men of those lands are passionately fond of any refuse out of the past; they will exchange their wives and daughters for a bit of rotten wood, a talismanic stone, or a rusty sword. It is not to be wondered at, then, that Abū Shāmāt, in the long years of his exile, did very well in business and gained ten dīnārs for every one of his capital. For there is no more lucrative traffic than the sale for ten dīnārs of antiques which one buys for a dirham.

Having at last got rid of all his stock, Abū Shāmāt determined to sell his shop; he was looking over the empty shelves of it, when he saw some red and shining object at the back of one of them. Taking it up, he was surprised to find that he held a large talisman, cut into six faces and fastened to a thin chain of old gold. On each square were graven unknown characters, which looked like ants and other insects. Abū Shāmāt was carefully examining his trove, when he noticed that a ship's captain had stopped in front of the shop and was craning his neck to look at the talisman.

Seeing that he was noticed, the man said: 'Master, may I have that stone, or is it not for sale?' 'Everything is for sale, even the shop,' answered Abū Shāmāt. 'Will you take eighty thousand dīnārs for the thing?' asked the captain.

'By Allāh,' thought Abū Shāmāt, 'this trinket must be extraordinarily valuable. I will make difficulties.' So he answered: 'An excellent jest, my good sir. Why, I paid a hundred thousand for the thing myself.' 'Then will you sell it for that price?' asked the other, and Abū Shāmāt replied: 'I will, to oblige you.' The captain thanked him, saying: 'I have not all that money about me; it would be dangerous to carry so much among the thieves of Alexandria. If you will come on board with me, I will pay you and throw into the bargain two pieces of cloth, two pieces of velvet, and two pieces of satin.'

Abū Shāmāt shut up his shop and followed the captain into his ship; begging him to wait on deck, the sailor went below to fetch the money; but he did not appear again, and suddenly all the sails were set and the boat plunged out to sea like a gull. Seeing himself a prisoner upon the waters, Abū Shāmāt was overwhelmed by consternation. But he was unable to appeal to any for help, because no sailors were visible upon the ship and she seemed to move across the sea on some invisible impulsion.

He looked up from his perplexity to see the captain regarding him with a mocking smile, one hand twined in his beard. At last his captor said: 'You are the Mussulmān Abū Shāmāt, son of Shams al-Dīn of Cairo, at one time employed about the palace of the Khalīfah at Baghdād. In a few days we shall land at Christian Genoa, and then we will see what fate awaits you.' With that the strange mariner again disappeared.

Soon the ship dropped anchor in the port of Genoa, a city of the western Christians. At once an old woman came aboard, accompanied by two men, and asked for Abū Shāmāt, who did not know what to think of these extraordinary happenings. Submissively he followed the old woman through the city and came at last to a church which belonged to a monastery.

At the door of this sacred building the old woman turned to Abū Shāmāt, saying: 'From this time forth consider yourself the servant of this church and of the monastery. Listen carefully to your duties: you will rise at dawn and go to the forest to cut wood; when you return, you will wash the pavement of the church and of the monastery, shake the mats, sweep the two buildings, husk corn, grind it, make it into dough, and cook it in the oven; after that you will grind and cook a measure of lentils and fill three hundred and seventy trenchers with them, take one of these trenchers to each of the three hundred and seventy good monks, empty the three hundred and seventy pots of ordure which you will find in the cells, and then finish by watering the garden, filling the four fountain basins and all the water-butts along the wall. These duties you should have finished every day by noon. You will spend your afternoons outside the church, compelling passers by to enter and listen to the preaching. If they refuse, here is a heavy mace, surmounted by an iron cross, with which the King authorises you to stun them.

In that way there shall remain in our city only fervent Christians
who will come here to be blessed by the monks. You may begin
your work at once; be careful not to forget anything.'

With that the old woman winked at him and departed.

Abū Shāmāt said to himself: 'As Allāh lives, this is a strange
business.' Not knowing what to resolve, he entered the church and
sat down upon a bench to puzzle out, if so he might, the reason for
all that had happened to him.

At the end of an hour he heard a woman's voice coming to him
between the pillars, and it was so beautiful that he forgot all his cares
while listening to it. It caused all the birds of his soul to start singing;
it fell upon his heart with that blessed relief which only lonely music
can give. When he rose to find the singer, the voice ceased; but he
saw the veiled figure of a girl coming towards him. When she
reached him, she said in a trembling voice: 'Dear Abū Shāmāt, it is
long and long that I have dreamed of you. I give thanks to Heaven
that we have met at last, for now we can be married.'

'There is no other God but Allāh!' exclaimed Abū Shāmāt.
'This is a dream, and I shall soon wake up in my shop at Alexandria.'
'No, all this is real, my dear,' answered the girl. 'You are in Genoa;
I had you brought hither by the sea captain who commands all the
ships of my father the King. I am the Princess Husn Maryam; I
learned sorcery when I was young, and it revealed to me both your
existence and your beauty, so that I fell in love with you at first sight.
See, here about my neck is the talisman which the captain himself
placed in your shop to entice you aboard his ship. Very soon you
shall have proof of its miraculous powers, but first let us get married.
After that I will satisfy any desire which you may express.' 'O
princess,' cried Abū Shāmāt, 'will you promise that I may return to
Alexandria?' 'That will be easy,' answered the girl; and at once a
priest appeared and married them.

'You wish to return at once to Alexandria?' asked Princess
Maryam when the ceremony was over. 'As Allāh lives I do!' he
answered; therefore she took the carnelian talisman and turned
towards the sky that one of its faces on which a bed was engraved.
She rubbed this representation with her thumb, saying: 'In the name
of Sulaimān, O carnelian, I order you to bring me a travelling bed!'

Hardly had the words been spoken when there appeared before
them a travelling bed, all complete with coverlets and cushions.
They mounted upon it and lay down at their ease, while the princess

turned upwards another face of her carnelian, one on which was engraved the figure of a bird, saying: 'Carnelian, O carnelian, I conjure you, in the name of Sulaimān, to carry us safe to Alexandria, by the direct way!'

At once the bed rose in the air, without any jolting, and, going out by the great window in the dome, began to sail through the air more quickly than a bird, but with an easy and riding motion. In less time than it takes to piss, it came to earth in Alexandria.

At the very moment when they stepped from the bed, they saw coming towards them a man dressed in the garments of Baghdād, whom Abū Shāmāt at once recognised as the captain of the guard. He had only just reached the city. They threw themselves into each other's arms, and the captain, announcing the discovery of the thief to Abū Shāmāt, told him all that had happened in Baghdād during the fourteen years of his exile. He reserved to the last the exquisite tidings of the birth of Aslān, who was now the most accomplished cavalier in all the lands of the Khalīfah.

Abū Shāmāt also told the whole of his remarkable story to the captain, who was enormously surprised by what he heard. 'The Prince of Believers wishes to see you as soon as possible,' he said, and Abū Shāmāt replied: 'Allow me first to go to Cairo, to kiss the hands of my father and mother and persuade them to return with me to the city of the Khalīfah.'

The captain of the guard mounted on the bed with them, and all three were transported in the twinkling of an eye to that street in Cairo which is called Yellow, where stood the house of Shams al-Dīn. They knocked at the door, and the syndic's wife opened it herself, saying: 'Who is there?' 'It is I, your son Abū Shāmāt,' came the answer. Then the old woman, who had worn mourning for her son during long years, fainted in his arms for joy, and the elderly Shams al-Dīn ran out and fell upon his neck.

All five rested for three days at the house and then got together upon the magic bed, which transported them to Baghdād, where the Khalīfah kissed Abū Shāmāt, as if he had been his own son, and overwhelmed all three generations, Shams al-Dīn, Abū Shāmāt and Aslān, with honours and lofty employments.

Abū Shāmāt remembered that the prime cause of all his fortune was Mahmūd Bilateral, who had not only ingeniously made him travel in the first place, but had also succoured him when he lay destitute upon the platform above the fountain. He set out to look for him and at last found him, seated in a garden, singing and drinking with a company of young boys. He invited him to the palace, and had him appointed chief of police in the place of Ahmad-the-Moth.

When this obligation had been fulfilled, Abū Shāmāt thanked Allāh for all His favours, and especially for the gift of a son as valiant and as handsome as little Aslān. He lived in Baghdād for many years in more than mortal happiness with his three wives, Zubaidah, Yāsamīn, and the Princess Maryam, until the Destroyer of Delights, the Ravisher of Friends, broke in upon his joy. Let us give praise to that Unalterable towards Whom the lives of all created things converge!

When Shahrazād had finished this story, she felt a little weary and became silent.

Then King Shahryār, who had listened with motionless attention, cried: 'O Shahrazād, this tale of Abū Shāmāt is indeed a remarkable one. Mahmūd Bilateral and the broker Samsam, with his recipe for heating cold eggs, delighted me in the extreme. But I must admit that I was surprised at the paucity of poems in the story, for you have accustomed me to magnificent verses. Also some of the movements and desires of Bilateral seemed to me a little obscure; I should be charmed to hear any clearer explanations which you would care to give.'

Shahrazād smiled slightly and looked at little Dunyazād, who appeared extremely amused, before she answered: 'Seeing that this little one can hear everything, I would rather, O auspicious King, recount to you one or two of the Adventures of the Poet Abū Nuwās, the most delicious, the most charming, and the most spiritual of all the singers who have ever been in Irāk and Arabia.'

Little Dunyazād rose from the carpet where she had been crouching and threw herself upon her sister's neck, crying: 'O please begin at once, Shahrazād! Please, delightful sister!' Shahrazād answered: 'With all my heart and as in duty bound to this most polished King.'

But at this point she saw the approach of morning and therefore discreetly postponed her tale until the following night.

The Tale of Sympathy the Learned

But when the two-hundred-and-seventieth night had come

LITTLE DUNYAZĀD waited until Shahrazād had finished her act with the King, and then raised her head, crying: 'O sister, why do you not start at once the anecdotes which you promised us concerning that delightful poet Abū Nuwās, the Khalīfah's friend, the sweetest singer of Irāk and Arabia?' Shahrazād smiled at her sister, saying: 'I only wait the King's permission before telling you some of the adventures of Abū Nuwās, who was not only an exquisite poet but a notorious evil-liver.'

Dunyazād ran to her sister and embraced her, saying: 'What did he do? Tell us at once, if you please.'

But King Shahryār turned to Shahrazād and said: 'O Shahrazād, it would give me great pleasure to hear one or two of these adventures, for I am sure that they are most entertaining; but to-night my mind is more inclined to higher things and would rather hear words of wisdom from you. If you know some tale which can fortify our souls with moral precepts and help us to profit by the experience of the wise, do not scruple to begin at once. Afterwards, if my patience be not exhausted, you may recount the adventures of Abū Nuwās.'

Shahrazād hastened to reply: 'By chance I have been thinking all day, O auspicious King, of a story which concerns a girl who was called Sympathy, a slave unequalled both in beauty and learning; I am ready to tell you all that I have heard of what she did and what she knew.'

'As Allāh lives,' cried King Shahryār, 'you may begin at once; for nothing pleases me more than to learn wisdom from the lips of beauty. I hope that the tale will satisfy and profit me with an example of that learning which becomes a faithful Mussulmān woman.'

Shahrazād reflected for a short time and then raised her finger, saying:

It is related—but Allāh is all-wise and all-knowing—that there was once a very rich merchant in Baghdād, who had honour and privilege of every kind, but whom Allāh had deprived of one happiness. He had no child, not even a daughter. He grew old in sorrow, seeing his bones becoming more and more transparent, his back more and more arched, without being able to obtain any consoling result from his numerous wives. One day, however, after he had distributed a great alms, visited saints, fasted and prayed fervently, he lay with his youngest wife and, by Allāh's grace, got her with child.

At the end of nine months to a day she bore him a man-child as fair as a fragment of the moon; therefore the merchant in gratitude to Allāh entertained the poor, the widow, and the orphan for seven whole days, and then named his son Abū al-Husn.

The child was carried in the arms of nurses and beautiful slaves, cared for like some jewel of price by all the women, until he reached the age when he might begin to learn. Then wise masters were given to him, who taught him the wonderful words of the Koran, beautiful writing, poetry, arithmetic, and especially the science of shooting with the bow.

Not only was his education finer than that of any other child then living, but his beauty was almost a magic thing. His boyish graces, the fresh colour of his cheeks, the flowers of his lips, and the young down of his face were thus celebrated by a poet:

> Though spring has passed already over the rose trees,
>> Here are some buds not fully opened yet,
>>> In this sweet garden ignorant of weather:
>>>> See, the down feather
>>> Of the violet
>> Under those trees!

Young Abū al-Husn was his father's joy and the light of his eyes, during the old man's remaining term upon this earth. When he felt that his debt was about to be paid to Allāh, he called his son to him, saying: 'My child, quittance nears and I have nothing left to do but prepare myself to stand before the Master. I leave you great riches, money and goods, rich fields and farms, which should last your lifetime and the lifetime of your children's children. Enjoy your property without excess, thanking the Giver and being mindful of Him all your days.' With that the old merchant died, and his son shut himself in with grief, after superintending his father's funeral.

Soon, however, his friends led him away from his sorrow and persuaded him to go to the hammām and change his garments, saying: 'He who is born again in a son like yourself does not die. Have done with tears; make the most of your riches and your youth.'

So Abū al-Husn little by little forgot the counsels of his father and learnt to look upon happiness and gold as inexhaustible. He satisfied every caprice of his nature, frequenting singers and musicians, eating enormous quantities of chicken every day (for he was very fond of chicken), unsealing old jars of strong wine, and hearing ever about him the noise of chinking goblets. He exhausted all that he could exhaust and spent all that he could spend, until he woke one morning to find that there remained of all his possessions only a single slave girl.

But here you must pause to admire the workings of Fate, who had decreed that this one remaining slave should be the supreme marvel of Western and Eastern women. She was called Sympathy; and never had a name been better given. She was as upright as the letter alif, and her figure was so slim that she might defy the sun to cast a shadow by her; the colouring of her young face was wonderful, and its expression was both fortunate and filled with blessing. Her mouth seemed to have been sealed with the seal of Sulaimān to guard the pearls within; the two pomegranates of her breasts were separated by a valley of shadows and delights; and her navel was carved so deep that it would have held an ounce of nutmeg butter. Her reed-like waist ended in so heavy a croup that she left deep prints of it in every sofa and mattress which she used. A certain poet had her in mind when he wrote:

> If you can call the sun and the moon and the rose tree
> Sad-coloured,
> Call her sad-coloured also.

> Hearts beat the advance as she advances,
> And the retreat when she retreats.

> The river of life flows through the meadows of Eden,
> And the meadows of Eden are below her garment,
> The moon is beneath her mantle.

> Her body is a song of colours:
> Carnation of roses answers to silver,
> Black ripe berries
> And new-cut sandal-wood
> Are one note.

> The man who takes her is more blessed
> Than the God who gives her;
> And He is continually called blessed.

Such was the slave Sympathy, the last possession of the prodigal Abū al-Husn of Baghdād.

At this point Shahrazād saw the approach of morning and discreetly fell silent.

But when the two-hundred-and-seventy-first night had come

SHE SAID:

Seeing that he was ruined for ever, Abū al-Husn fell into a desolation which robbed him of both hunger and sleep; for three days and three nights he refused food and drink and sleep, so that the slave Sympathy thought he was on the point of dying and determined to save him at any cost to herself.

She put on the rest of her jewels and those robes which remained most fit to be seen; then she went to her master and said with an encouraging smile: 'Allāh will put an end to your misfortunes by my help. You have only to take me with you to the Commander of the Faithful, Hārūn al-Rashīd, fifth of the line of Abbās, and offer me to him for ten thousand dīnārs. If he objects that the price is too high, you must say: "Prince of Believers, this girl is worth more; as you will discover if you put her to the proof. You will find that she is without equal or near equal, and worthy to serve the Khalīfah." ' She finished by recommending that he should not bate his price on any consideration.

Abū al-Husn had neglected, in his careless way, to notice the supreme gifts of his beautiful slave; therefore he merely thought that the idea was not a bad one and held some chances of success. He led Sympathy into the presence of the Khalīfah without delay, and repeated the offer which she had recommended to him.

The Khalīfah turned towards her, asking: 'What is your name?' 'I am called Sympathy,' she answered, and he continued: 'O Sympathy, are you indeed learned, and can you tell me the various branches of knowledge in which you excel?' 'My master,' she answered, 'I have studied syntax, poetry, civil and canon law, music, astronomy, geometry, arithmetic, the law concerning inheritance, the art of elucidating grimoires and reading ancient inscriptions. I know the Sublime Book by heart and can read it in seven different ways; I know the exact number of its chapters, verses, divisions, parts, and combinations; how many lines, words, consonants, and vowels there are in it; I know which are the inspired chapters written at Mecca and those which were dictated at Madinah. I know both laws and dogmas, and can determine the degrees of authenticity among them from the point of tradition; I am acquainted with architecture, logic, and philosophy; with eloquence, language, rhetoric, and the rules of versification. I know every artifice by which words can be ordered into musical lines. I am equally at home in the construction of simply flowing verses and very complicated examples suited for subtle palates alone; if I introduce an occasional obscurity into my compositions, it is to hold the attention and to delight such minds as can disentangle a fragile thread. I have learnt many things and remembered all I have learnt. I can sing perfectly, dance like a bird, play the lute and the flute, and perform in fifty different ways on every stringed instrument. When I dance and sing, those who see and hear me are damned by my beauty; when I walk in my perfumed clothing, balanced upon my feet, I kill; when I move my bottom, I overthrow; when I wink, I pierce; when I shake my bracelets, I make blind; I give life with a touch, and death by going away; I am skilful in all the arts and have carried my education so far that only those who have worn out their life in study may see it, as it were, upon the far horizon.'

Hārūn al-Rashīd was delighted and astonished to find so much eloquence and beauty in the child who stood before him with lowered eyes. He turned to Abū al-Husn, saying: 'I shall send at once for all the masters of art and science in my kingdõm, to put the knowledge of your slave to public proof. If she comes victorious from the trial, I will not give you ten thousand dīnārs but cover you with honours for having brought so great a marvel to me. If she fail in her examination, she shall remain your property.'

The Khalīfah straightway sent for the most learned man of that time, Ibrāhīm ibn Siyyār, a sage who had gone to the depths of all human knowledge; and he also commanded the presence of the chief poets, grammarians, theologians, doctors, philosophers, astronomers and lawyers of his kingdom. They hastened to the palace and assembled in the great hall, without knowing why they had been summoned. They seated themselves in a circle upon carpets about the Khalīfah's golden chair, while Sympathy stood meekly in their presence, smiling upon them through her light veil.

At this point Shahrazād saw the approach of morning and discreetly fell silent.

But when the two-hundred-and-seventy-second night had come

SHE SAID:

When a silence had fallen upon this assembly so deep that the far-off fall of a needle upon the ground might have been heard, Sympathy made a graceful and dignified bow to those present and said to the Khalīfah in a melodious voice:

'Prince of Believers, it is for you to order and for me to obey; I stand ready to answer any question posed to me by these venerable sages, these readers of the Koran, lawyers, doctors, architects, astronomers, geometrists, grammarians, philosophers and poets.'

Hārūn al-Rashīd turned to those who were about him, saying: 'I have called you hither that you may examine the learning of this girl in all directions and to any depth; it is for you to spare no pains in exhibiting your own scholarship and erudition.' All the sages bowed to the earth, carrying their hands to their eyes and foreheads, and answering: 'Obedience and obeisance to Allāh and to you, O Prince of Believers!'

The slave Sympathy stood for some moments in thought with lowered head; then she looked up, saying: 'Tell me, my masters, which of you is the most learned in the Koran and the traditions of our Prophet (upon whom be prayer and peace!).' All fingers were pointed to one of the doctors, who rose, saying: 'I am that man.' Then said Sympathy: 'Ask me what you will of your own subject.' So the learned reader of the Koran said:

'O young girl, since you have studied the sacred Book of Allāh, you must know the number of the chapters, words, and letters in it; and also the precepts of our faith. Tell me first who is your Lord, who is your Prophet, who is your Imām, what is your orientation, what is your rule of life, what is your guide, and who are your brothers?'

She answered: 'Allāh is my Lord, Muhammad (upon whom be prayer and peace!) is my Prophet; the Koran is my law and therefore my Imām; that Kaabah, the house of Allāh builded by Abraham at Mecca, is my orientation; the example of our holy Prophet is my rule of life; the Sunnah, the collection of traditions, is my guide; and all Believers are my brothers.'

While the Khalīfah marvelled to hear such precise answers from such lovely lips, the sage said:

'Tell me, how do you know that there is a God?'

She answered: 'By reason.'

'What is reason?'

'Reason is a double gift: it is both innate and acquired. Innate wisdom is that which Allāh has placed in the hearts of His chosen servants that they may walk in the way of truth. Acquired wisdom is the fruit of education and labour in an intelligent man.'

'That is an excellent answer. But can you tell me, where is the seat of reason?'

'In the heart, whence inspirations rise to the brain.'

'That is so. How have you learnt to know the Prophet (upon whom be prayer and peace!)?'

'By reading the Book of Allāh, by the phrases contained therein, by the proofs and witnessings of His divine mission.'

'What are the indispensable duties of our religion?'

'The indispensable duties of our religion are five: the profession of Faith: "There is no God but Allāh and Muhammad is the messenger of Allāh!", prayer, alms, fasting during the month of Ramadān, and pilgrimage to Mecca when that is possible.'

'What are the most praiseworthy acts of piety?'

'They are six in number: prayer, alms, fasting, pilgrimage, fighting bad instincts and forbidden things, to take part in a holy war.'

'What is the aim of prayer?'

'To offer the homage of my virtue to the Lord, to celebrate His praises, and to lift my soul towards the calm places.'

'Yā Allāh! That is an excellent reply. Does not prayer necessitate certain indispensable preparations?'

"Certainly it does. It is necessary to purify the whole body by ritual ablutions, to put on garments which have no stain of dirt, to choose a clean place in which to pray, to protect that part of the body which lies between the navel and the knees, to have pure intent, and to turn towards the Kaabah, in the direction of holy Mecca.'

'What is the value of prayer?'

'It sustains faith, of which it is the foundation.'

'What is the fruit or utility of prayer?'

'True prayer has no terrestrial use; it should be regarded only as a spiritual tie between the creature and his Lord. It can produce ten immaterial results: it lights the heart, it brightens the face, it pleases the Compassionate, it infuriates the devil, it attracts pity, it repels evil, it preserves from ill, it protects against enemies, it fortifies the wavering spirit, and brings the slave nearer to his Master.'

'What is the key of prayer? And what is the key of that key?'

'The key of prayer is ablution and the key of ablution is the preparatory formula: "In the name of Allāh, the Merciful, the Compassionate." '

'What are the prescribed usages of ablution?'

'According to the orthodox rite of the Imām Muhammad ibn Idrīs al-Shafii, there are six: the fixed intention to purify oneself in order to be agreeable to the Creator; first washing the face, washing the hands to the elbows, rubbing part of the head, washing the feet from nails to heels, and a strict regard to the order in which these things are done. That order demands the observance of twelve clear conditions: to pronounce the preparatory formula: 'In the name of Allāh!', to wash the palms of the hands before plunging them into the basin, to rinse the mouth, to wash the nostrils by snuffing up water from the hand, to rub all the head, to clean the outside and inside of the ears with new lots of water, to comb the beard with the fingers, to twist the fingers and toes until they crack, to place the right foot before the left, to repeat each ablution three times, to pronounce the act of faith after each ablution and, when the whole ablution is finished, to recite this pious formula: "O God, number me among the pure, the repentant, and the faithful! Praise be to God! I testify that there is no God but You! You are my refuge, and it is from You that I sincerely beg pardon for my sins. Amen." It was this formula that the Prophet (upon whom be prayer and peace!) recommended us to recite, saying: "For him who uses this prayer I will open the eight gates of Eden, and he may enter by which he pleases." '

'That is truly an admirable reply. But can you tell me what the angels and devils are doing while a man is practising ablution?'

'When a man prepares to make ablution, the angels come to stand on his right side and the devils on his left; but as soon as he pronounces the preparatory formula: "In the name of Allāh!" the devils take flight and the angels come nearer, holding a square pavilion of light above his head by the four corners, singing praises to Allāh, and interceding for the remission of the man's sins. If he forgets to pronounce the name of Allāh, or omits it in the course of his ablution, the devils crowd back upon him and do their best to trouble his soul, to suggest doubts, and to cool the fervour of his spirit.'

At this point Shahrazād saw the approach of morning and discreetly fell silent.

But when the two-hundred-and-seventy-third night had come

SHE SAID:

Sympathy continued: 'It is obligatory for the man to let the water run all over his body, over all his hairs, seen or hidden, and over his sexual parts. To rub all parts of the body well, and not to wash the feet till last.'

'That is well answered. Now can you tell me what usages are to be observed in the ablution which is called Tayammum?'

'Tayammum is purification with sand and dust. It is practised on seven occasions decreed by the usages of the Prophet, and following four specific indications of the Book itself. These seven occasions are: lack of water, fear of exhausting the water, need of the water for drinking, fear of losing some of the water while carrying it, diseases which make the use of water dangerous, fractures which demand a reclining position, and wounds which must not be touched. The four necessary conditions are these: to be of good faith, to take the sand or dust in the hand, make as if to rub the face with it, to imitate the action of rubbing the arm as far as the elbow, and to wipe the hands. Two practices are recommended as they conform to the Sunnah: to begin the ablution with the formula: "In the name of Allāh!" and to make ablution of all the right parts of the body before the left.'

'That is quite correct. Let us return for a moment to prayer; how should it be made and what acts are suitable for it?'

'The acts requisite for prayer are the columns which bear it up. The columns of prayer are: the formula of the Takbīr, which consists in pronouncing the words: "Allāh is the Greatest!"; recitation of the Fātihah, the opening chapter of the Koran; prostration with the face against the earth; to rise; to make the profession of faith; to sit upon the heels; to pray for the Prophet, saying: "Upon him be the prayer and peace of Allāh!"; to remain ever in a pure intent. Other conditions of good prayer are taken from the Sunnah, and consist in lifting the two arms with the palms upwards in the direction of Mecca, reciting the Fātihah a second time, reciting another chapter of the Koran, for instance that of the Cow, pronouncing certain other pious formulæ, and finishing with further prayers for our Prophet Muhammad (upon whom be prayer and peace!).'

'You have given a perfect answer. Now can you tell me in what various ways one may pay the tithe of alms?'

'It may be paid in fourteen ways: in gold, silver, camels, cows, sheep, corn, barley, millet, maize, beans, chickpeas, rice, raisins, and dates. If one has less than twenty dirhams of Mecca gold there is nothing to be paid; above that sum the rate is three per centum. The same proportion obtains with silver. A sheep is paid for every five camels; a camel for every twenty-five camels, and so on. One in forty is paid of sheep and lambs, and the same of all other commodities which I have named.'

'Speak to me now of fasting.'

'To fast is to abstain from eating, drinking and sexual enjoyment until sunset on every day of Ramadān, till the new moon is seen. It is excellent during a fast to abstain from all trifling discourse and from all reading not of the Koran.'

'Are there not certain things which seem at first sight to vitiate a fast, but which the Book tells us do not vitiate it?'

'Those things which do not break a fast are: pomades, balms and unguents, kohl and collyrium for the eyes, dust of the road, swallowing the spittle, involuntary ejaculation of semen by day or by night, glances cast at a woman who is not a Mussulmān, blood-letting and cupping. None of these things vitiate a fast.'

'How would you define spiritual retreat?'

'Spiritual retreat is long dwelling in a mosque, without leaving it for any purpose save evacuation, abstention from women and from speech. It is recommended by the Sunnah but is not an obligation of dogma.'

'Speak now of pilgrimage.'

'Pilgrimage to Mecca is a duty which every Mussulmān should accomplish at least once in his life after he has attained the age of reason. Certain conditions must be observed: to wear the pilgrim's garment, to avoid all commerce with women, to shave the hairs, to cut the nails, and to cover the head and the face. The Sunnah also prescribes certain other observances.'

'Now let us pass to the subject of holy wars.'

'A holy war is that undertaken against the Infidels when Islām is in danger. It may only be fought for defensive purposes, never offensive; when the Believer is in arms, he must march straightforward and never retreat.'

'Can you give me some details of buying and selling?'

'In buying and selling both sides must be free and, in cases of sufficient importance, should draw up an act of consent and acceptation.'

At this point Shahrazād saw the approach of morning and discreetly fell silent.

But when the two-hundred-and-seventy-fourth night had come

SHE SAID:

Sympathy continued: 'The Sunnah prohibits the sale of certain things. For example: it is expressly considered unlawful to exchange dry dates for fresh dates, dry figs for fresh figs, salt meat for fresh meat, salt buttèr for fresh butter, and, generally speaking, the fresh and new of any commodity for the old, salt, and dried of the same.'

When the learned commentator of the Book heard Sympathy's answers, he could not but admit to himself that she knew as much as he did; but, being unwilling to confess his inability to catch her out, he asked her the following subtle question: 'What is the linguistic meaning of the word *ablution*?'

'To get rid of all internal or external impurity by washing.'

'What is the meaning of the word to *fast*?'

'To abstain.'

'What is the meaning of the word to *give*?'

'To enrich oneself.'

'To go on a *pilgrimage*?'

'To attain the end.'

'To make *war*?'

'To defend oneself.'

The sage rose up, crying: 'In truth I am short of questions and arguments. This slave astonishes me with her knowledge and the clearness of her exposition, O Commander of the Faithful!'

Sympathy smiled slightly, saying: 'I would like, in my turn, to ask you one question: can you tell me what are the foundations of Islām?'

He reflected for a moment, and then replied: 'They are four in number: faith illuminated by sane reason; righteousness; knowledge of duty and equity, together with discretion; and the fulfilment of all promises.'

Sympathy said again: 'Allow me to ask you a further question.

If you cannot answer it, it will be my right to take away the distinctive garment which you wear as a learned reader of the Book.'

'I accept,' he answered, 'put your question, O slave.'

'What are the branches of Islām?' she asked.

After a long time spent in reflection, the wise man could not answer, so the Khalīfah said to Sympathy: 'If you can give us the answer yourself, the gown belongs to you.'

Sympathy bowed and answered: 'The branches of Islām are twenty: strict observance of the Book's teaching, conformation with the traditions and oral instructions of the Prophet, the avoidance of injustice, eating permitted food, never to eat unpermitted food, to punish evil doers that vice may not increase owing to the exaggerated clemency of the virtuous, repentance, profound study of religion, to do good to enemies, to be modest, to succour the servants of Allāh, to avoid all innovation and change, to show courage in adversity and strength in time of trial, to pardon when one is strong, to be patient in misfortune, to know Allāh, to know His Prophet (upon whom be prayer and peace!), to resist the suggestions of the Evil One, to fight against the passions and wicked instincts of the soul, to be wholly vowed in confidence and submission to the service of Allāh.'

When the Khalīfah Hārūn al-Rashīd heard this answer, he ordered the sage's gown to be stripped from him and given to Sympathy; this was immediately done, and the learned man left the hall in confusion, with his head bowed.

Then a second theologian, famous for his subtlety, to whom all eyes voted the honour of next questioning the girl, rose and turned towards Sympathy, saying: 'I will only ask you a few short questions, O slave. What duties are to be observed while eating?'

'In eating a man must first wash his hands and invoke the name of Allāh. He must sit upon the left haunch, and use only the thumb and two first fingers in conveying the food to his mouth. He must take small mouthfuls, masticate each piece of food thoroughly, and not look at his neighbour for fear of embarrassing him and spoiling his appetite.'

'Can you tell me what is something, what is half something, and what is less than something?'

'A Believer is something, a hypocrite is half something, and an infidel is less than something.'

'That is correct. Now can you tell me where faith is found?'

'Faith abides in four places: in the heart, in the head, in the tongue, and in the members. The strength of the heart consists in joy, the strength of the head in knowledge of the truth, the strength of the tongue in sincerity, and the strength of the members in submission.'

'How many hearts are there?'

'There are several: the heart of the Believer is a pure and healthy heart, the heart of an Infidel is exactly the opposite . . .'

At this point Shahrazād saw the approach of morning and discreetly fell silent.

But when the two-hundred-and-seventy-sixth night had come

SHE SAID:

'There is a heart attached to the things of this world, and a heart attached to spiritual joys; there is a heart mastered by the passions, by hate or avarice; there is a slack heart, a heart burning with love, a heart puffed with pride; there is a lighted heart like that of the companions of our holy Prophet; and there is the heart of the Prophet himself, which is the heart of the Chosen.'

When the learned theologian heard this answer, he cried: 'You have won my approbation, O slave!'

Sympathy looked at the Khalīfah, saying: 'O Commander of the Faithful, allow me to ask one question of my examiner and to take his gown if he cannot answer.' Hārūn al-Rashīd gave his permission, and she asked:

'Can you tell me what duty must be fulfilled before all other duties, however important those may be?'

The wise man did not know what to say, so the girl took his gown from him and herself answered the question:

'The duty of ablution; for we are bidden to purify ourselves before fulfilling the least of religious duties or any of those acts prescribed by the Book or the Sunnah.'

Sympathy cast a glance round the assembly, and this was answered by one of the most celebrated men of the century, supposed without equal in a knowledge of the Koran. He rose and said:

'Since you know the Book of Allāh, O girl full of the sweet perfume of the spirit, can you give me a sample of your study?'

'The Koran is composed of a hundred and fourteen chapters,

seventy of which were dictated at Mecca and forty-four at Madinah. It is divided into six hundred and twenty-one divisions, called decades, and into six thousand two hundred and thirty-six verses. It contains seventy-nine thousand, four hundred and thirty-nine words, and three hundred and twenty-three thousand, six hundred and seventy letters, to each of which attach ten special virtues. The names of twenty-five prophets are mentioned: Adam, Noah, Ishmael, Isaac, Jacob, Joseph, Elisha, Jonah, Lot, Sālih, Hūd, Shuaib, David, Solomon, Dhūl-kafl, Idrīs, Elias, Yahyā, Zacharias, Job, Moses, Aaron, Jesus, and Muhammad (upon all these be prayer and peace!). Nine birds or winged beasts are mentioned: the gnat, the bee, the fly, the hoopoe, the crow, the grasshopper, the ant, the bulbul, and the bird of Jesus (upon whom be prayer and peace!), which is none other than the bat.'

'You are marvellously exact. Now can you tell me in what verse our holy Prophet judges the Unbelievers?'

'In this verse: "The Jews say that the Christians are wrong and the Christians say that the Jews are wrong; to this extent both are right!" '

'How did the Koran come from Heaven to earth? Did it descend complete in its present form, copied from tablets which are kept in Heaven? Or did it descend on different occasions?'

'The angel Gabriel, commanded by the Master of the Universe, carried it to our prophet Muhammad, the prince of the messengers of God, a few verses at a time, according to circumstances, through-out the space of twenty years.'

'What companions of the Prophet were careful to assemble all the scattered verses of the Koran?'

'Four of them: Ubai ibn Kaab, Zaid ibn Thābit, Abū Ubaidah ibn al-Jarrāh, and Uthmān ibn Affān (Allāh have all four in His keeping!).'

'Who were those who handed down and taught the true way of reading the Koran?'

'There were four of them: Abdallāh ibn Masūd, Ubai ibn Kaab, Maādh ibn Jabal, and Sālim ibn Abdallāh.'

'On what occasion did the following verse descend from Heaven: "O Believers, do not deprive yourselves of earthly joys in all their fullness"?'

'When certain of the companions wished to push asceticism too far and had resolved to geld themselves and wear hair-shirts.'

At this point Shahrazād saw the approach of morning and discreetly fell silent.

But when the two-hundred-and-seventy-eighth night had come

SHE SAID:

The learned questioner could contain himself no longer, but cried out: 'I bear witness, O Prince of Believers, that this young girl is unequalled in knowledge!'

Sympathy demanded leave to ask a question in her turn, and said:

'Can you tell me which verse of the Koran contains the letter kāf twenty-three times, which contains the letter mīm sixteen times, and which contains the letter ain forty times?'

The sage stayed with his mouth open, unable to make the least attempt at an answer; so Sympathy first took away his gown and then herself indicated the required verses to the general stupefaction of all.

Next, a learned doctor of medicine rose in the assembly, one famous for the studies he had made and the books he had written, and said:

'You have spoken excellently of the things of the spirit; now it is time that we turn our attention to the body. I require you, O beautiful slave, to give us some information about the body of man, its composition, its nerves, its bones, its vertebræ, and why Adam was called Adam?'

'The name of Adam comes from the Arabic word adīm, which signifies the surface of the earth; it was given to the first man because he was created from earth taken from different parts of the world. His head was made from the soil of the East, his breast from the soil of the Kaabah, and his feet from the soil of the West. Allāh made seven entrances and two exits for the body: the two eyes, the two ears, the two nostrils, and the mouth for entrances, and for exits, one before and one behind. Then the Creator united in Adam four elements to give him a nature: water, earth, fire and air; so that a bilious temperament is of the nature of fire, which is hot and dry; a nervous temperament is of the nature of earth, which is dry; a lymphatic temperament is of the nature of water, which is cold and moist; and a sanguine temperament is of the nature of air, which is warm and dry. After this Allāh assembled the human body. He placed within it three hundred and sixty ducts and two hundred and forty bones. He gave it three instincts: of life, reproduction, and appetite. He gave it a heart, a spleen, lungs, six intestines, a liver, two kidneys, a brain, two eggs, a member, and a skin. He dowered it with five senses, guided by seven vital spirits. As for the position of the organs, he placed the heart upon the left of the breast, and the stomach below it, the lungs to act as fans for the heart, the liver on the right to guard the heart, and, for the same purpose, he placed the interlacing intestines and the articulation of the ribs. The head is composed of forty-eight bones, the chest of twenty-four ribs and twenty-five in a woman; this extra rib is on the right, and is useful to fasten the child in the belly of its mother and to support it, as it were, by an arm.'

'Can you tell us anything concerning the symptoms of diseases?'

'The symptoms of diseases may be divided into exterior and interior; they show not only the kind but the gravity of the illness. A man skilled in his art can divine what is the matter by simply feeling the hand of his patient and determining its degree of dryness, heat, stiffness, cold, or moisture. A man whose eyes are yellow is suffering from a disease of the liver; and a man whose back is bent has serious inflammation of the lungs. Interior symptoms which guide a doctor in his diagnosis are: vomiting, pains, swellings, excrements, and the urine.'

'What causes illness in the head?'

'Illness in the head is due principally to diet, to filling the stomach again before the previous meal is digested, and to eating when the patient is not hungry. Gluttony is the cause of every disease which afflicts the world. He who would live long should practise sobriety, should get up early, should avoid late nights and excess with women, and not abuse the practices of blood-letting and cupping. Above all he should set a watch upon his belly. To do this it is necessary to divide the belly into three parts, to fill one with food, one with water, and one with nothing at all; this third part should be left free for breathing and as a lodging for the soul. The same division should be made with the intestine, which is eighteen spans long.'

'What are the symptoms of icterus?'

'Icterus, that is to say feverish jaundice, is characterised by yellow colouring, bitterness in the mouth, vertigo, quick pulse, vomiting and indifference to women. A man who has this disease is in grave danger of intestinal ulcers, pleurisy, dropsy, swellings, and acute melancholia, which, by weakening the body, may bring on cancer and leprosy.'

'That is perfectly answered. How would you divide medicine?'

'I would divide medicine into two parts: the study of diseases and the study of remedies.'

'What would you say was the best water?'

'Fresh pure water contained in a jar of porous clay, which has been rubbed with some healthy perfume, or simply scented with incense smoke. One should never drink until well after a meal. One may avoid all kinds of illness by this abstention and also put into practice this precept of the Prophet (upon whom be prayer and peace!): "The stomach is the cradle of all disease, constipation is the cause of all disease, and cleanliness is the principle of all cures." '

'What meats are especially excellent?'

'Those which are prepared by a woman, which do not cost you much, and are eaten with a quiet heart. That food which is called tharīd, meat and bread sopped in broth, is certainly the most delicious of all sustenance; for the Prophet (upon whom be prayer and peace!) has said: "Tharīd is the best of meats as Āishah is the most virtuous of women." '

'What do you think of fruit?'

'Fruit and mutton are the healthiest foods. But the former should not be eaten after its season.'

'Speak to us of wine.'

At this point Shahrazād saw the approach of morning and discreetly fell silent.

But when the two-hundred-and-eightieth night had come

SHE SAID:

Sympathy answered: 'How can you ask me about wine when the Book is so explicit on the subject? It is forbidden in spite of its many virtues because it troubles the reason and heats the humours of the body. Wine and games of chance are two things which the Believer should avoid under pain of serious calamity.'

'That is a wise answer. Can you speak to us now of blood-letting?'

'Bleeding is necessary for all who have too much blood. It should be performed fasting on a cloudless Spring day when there is neither rain nor wind. If practised on a Friday, especially when that day falls on the seventeenth of the month, it produces the best results. It advantages the head, the eyes, and the blood; but it is harmful when practised during great heat or great cold, while eating salted or acid things, or on a Wednesday or Saturday.'

'So far there has been nothing lacking in your answers. Now I wish to ask you a question of capital importance, which will show if you have a true knowledge of the facts of life. Can you give us a clear account of copulation?'

On hearing this question the young girl blushed and lowered her head, so that the Khalīfah thought that she was unable to answer: but she turned towards him, saying: 'As Allāh lives, O Commander of the Faithful, my silence is not due to ignorance; for the answer is upon the tip of my tongue, but refuses to leave my lips because of my respect for the Khalīfah.' Hārūn al-Rashīd answered: 'It would give me very great pleasure to hear such an answer from your mouth. Speak freely, explicitly, and without fear.' So the learned Sympathy spoke as follows:

'Copulation is that act which unites the sexes of man and woman. It is an excellent thing, having many virtues and conferring many benefits: it lightens the body and relieves the soul, it cures melancholy, tempers the heat of passion, attracts love, contents the heart, consoles in absence, and cures insomnia. These are its effects when a man couples with a young woman: it is far otherwise when he has to do with an old one. Connection with an old woman exposes a man to many maladies, among others disease of the eyes, disease of the kidneys, disease of the thighs, and disease of the back. In a word, it is a terrible thing, to be avoided as one would avoid a deadly poison. Best of all is to choose a woman expert in the art, one who understands a wink, who can speak with her feet and hands, and spare her owner the necessity of keeping a garden and flower beds.

'All complete copulation is followed by moisture. In the woman this moisture is produced by the emotion felt in her honourable parts; in the man, by the running of that sap which is secreted by the two eggs. This sap follows a complicated road; man possesses one large vein which gives birth to all the other veins; the blood which fortifies these three hundred and sixty smaller veins runs at last into a tube which debouches in the left egg; in this egg the blood turns about, clarifies, and changes into a white liquid which thickens because of the heat of the egg, and smells like palm milk.'

At this point Shahrazād saw the approach of morning and discreetly fell silent.

But when the two-hundred-and-eighty-second night had come

SHE SAID:

'You have answered wisely!' cried the sage. 'I have only two more questions to ask. Can you tell me what thing lives always in prison and dies when it breathes the free air? Also, what are the best fruits?'

'The first is a fish; and the second, citrons and pomegranates.'

When the doctor heard the wonderful replies of Sympathy, he confessed himself incapable of making her stumble and would have returned to his place, but Sympathy signed to him to remain, saying: 'I will now ask you a question. Can you tell me what is round like the earth, and lives in an eye, sometimes going through that eye, and sometimes separated from it, copulating without an organ, leaving its companion for the night, and embracing her again during the day, choosing its habitation upon the edge of things?'

The learned man cudgelled his brains for an answer but could find none, so Sympathy took away his gown and gave the answer herself: 'The button and the button-loop.'

After this an astronomer rose from among the old men and came to face the smiling eyes of Sympathy, which were brighter and more confusing than all the stars of night. He sat by her and said:

'Where does the sun rise and where does he set?'

'He rises from the rivers of the East and sets among the rivers of the West: there are a hundred and forty-four of these rivers. The sun is lord of the day and the moon is lady of the night. Allāh said in the Book: 'I gave the sun his life and the moon her brightness, and fixed them in ordered places so that my people might calculate the days and years. I have marked a limit for the courses of the stars, forbidding the moon to attain to the sun, and the night to pass the day. Day and night, shadow and light, are complementary to each other for ever, but may never mingle!'

'That is an astonishingly exact reply. Can you speak to us of other stars, their good or evil influences?'

'If I spoke of all the other stars, we would need to sit here for more than one day. I will, therefore, answer briefly. Besides the sun and the moon, there are five planets: Mercury, Venus, Mars, Jupiter, and Saturn. The moon is cold and moist, exerting a good influence; she has Cancer for her house, the Bull for her apogee, the Scorpion for her descendant, and Capricorn for her perigee. The planet

Saturn is cold and dry, exerting an evil influence; he has Capricorn
and Aquarius for his house, the Scales for his apogee, the Ram for
his descendant, and Capricorn and the Lion for his perigee. Jupiter
is warm and moist, exerting a good influence; he has the Fishes and
the Collar for his house, Cancer for his apogee, Capricorn for his
descendant, the Twins and the Lion for his perigee. Venus is tem-
perate, exerting a good influence; she has the Bull for her house, the
Fishes for her apogee, the Scales for her descendant, the Ram and
the Scorpion for her perigee. Mercury has sometimes a good and
sometimes a bad influence; his house is the Twins, his apogee Virgo,
his descendant the Fishes, and his perigee the Bull. Last of all, Mars
is hot and moist, wielding a malign influence; he has the Ram for his
house, Capricorn for his apogee, Cancer for his descendant, and the
Scales for his perigee.'

Hearing this answer, the astronomer admired the depth of
Sympathy's knowledge; therefore, wishing to trouble her with a
more difficult question, he asked:

'O slave, do you think that we shall have rain this month?'

Sympathy hung her head and reflected for a long time; so that the
Khalīfah thought that she was unable 'to answer. At length she
raised her head, saying: 'O Commander of the Faithful, I will not
speak unless I have your special permission to reveal all my thought.'
'You have that permission!' cried the astonished Khalīfah, and she
continued: 'Then, O Prince of Believers, I beg you to lend me your
sword for a moment that I may cut off the head of this astronomer,
who is an agnostic and an unbeliever.'

At these words the Khalīfah and all the sages burst out laughing,
and Sympathy went on: 'I must teach you, O astronomer, that there
are five things which only Allāh knows: the hour of death, the fall of
rain, the sex of a child in its mother's womb, what will happen to-
morrow, and the place of death.'

The astronomer answered smiling: 'My question was asked to
test you. Now, as we do not wish to prolong the discussion of this
subject unduly, can you tell me the influence of the stars upon the
days of the week?'

'Sunday is consecrated to the sun. When it begins the year, it is
a sign that the people will suffer great tyranny and vexation from
their sultāns, kings and governors; that there will be much drought
in the land, that there will be hardly any lentils, that the vines will
rot, and that ferocious wars will break out between kings. But Allāh

is all-wise. Monday is consecrated to the moon. When the year begins with a Monday, it is a good sign. There will be abundant rains with a sufficiency of corn and grapes; but there will also be pestilence; the cotton will be bad and flax will hardly grow at all; half of the cattle will die from disease. Tuesday is consecrated to Mars; if it begins the year, many of those great and powerful in the land will die, the price of all grains will rise, there will be little rain and small catches of fish. Honey will be expensive and lentils sell for nothing. Flax-seed will be very dear indeed, but there will be an excellent barley harvest. Much blood will be spilled, and a disease will break out among the donkeys, so that they will become worth a great deal of money. But Allāh is all-knowing. Wednesday is the day of Mercury; when it begins the year, there will be great slaughters by sea, with many storms and much lightning, grains will be dear, while radishes and onions will fetch almost any money. There will also be a disease among little children. But Allāh is all-powerful. Thursday is consecrated to Jupiter: if it begins the year, that is a sign of concord among the people, of justice on the part of governors and wazīrs, of integrity in the doings of kādīs, and general benefit for the human race; with abundance of rains, fruits, cereals, flax, cotton, honey, grapes and fish. But Allāh is all-knowing. Friday is the day of Venus; when Friday begins the year, there will be abundant dew and a beautiful Spring, but there will also be born an enormous number of children of both sexes; there will be many cucumbers, water-melons, pumpkins, tomatoes, and artichokes of both kinds. But Allāh is all-knowing. Saturday is sacred to Saturn. Woe upon that year which begins with a Saturday! Woe upon that year! Heaven shall be greedy and earth shall be greedy; famine shall succeed to war, disease to famine; and the people of Egypt and of Syria shall utter great cries under the oppression and tyranny of their governors. But Allāh is all-wise.'

'That is a clear and comprehensive answer! Now can you tell us in what part or level of the sky the planets are hung?'

'The planet Saturn is hung in the seventh heaven, Jupiter in the sixth, Mars in the fifth, the Sun in the fourth, Venus in the third, Mercury in the second, and the Moon in the first heaven.'

At this point Shahrazād saw the approach of morning and discreetly fell silent.

But when the two-hundred-and-eighty-fourth night had come

SHE SAID:

'Now it is my turn to ask you a question,' continued Sympathy. 'What are the three classes of stars?'

The sage reflected for a long time with his eyes fixed upon the sky, but he could not save himself. Sympathy therefore possessed herself of his gown and answered her own question as follows:

'The stars are divided into three classes, according to their destined uses; some are fixed like torches in the celestial vault that they may light the earth, others are invisibly suspended in the air that they may illuminate the sea, and the third class of stars move at will between the fingers of Allāh; we see them passing through the air at night, they are used to stone and punish all devils who would disobey the orders of the Highest.'

When the astronomer confessed himself inferior to the charming slave and left the hall, the Khalifah ordered a philosopher to take his place; this man confronted Sympathy, saying:

'Can you tell us the nature of infidelity and whether or no it is born with man?'

'I will answer in the very words of our Prophet (upon whom be prayer and peace!): Infidelity circulates among the children of Adam as blood circulates in the veins; so that they blaspheme against the earth, against the fruits of the earth, and against the hours of the earth. The greatest of all crimes is to blaspheme against time and the world; for time is God and the world was made by God.'

'Your answer is both sublime and correct. Now tell me the five creatures of Allāh who ate and drank before they had ever defecated or made water?'

'These five creatures were: Adam, Simeon, Sālih's dromedary, Ishmael's ram, and the bird which holy Abū Bakr saw in the cave.'

'Tell me what five creatures rest in Paradise, being neither man, Jinnī, nor angel?'

'The five are: Jacob's wolf, the dog of the seven sleepers, the ass of Esdras, Sālih's dromedary, and Dhul-kafl, the mule of our sacred Prophet (upon whom be prayer and peace!).'

'What man prayed when he was neither on earth nor in Heaven?'

'Sulaimān prayed upon a carpet hanging in mid-air between heaven and earth.'

'Explain the following: a man looked upon a woman slave in the morning and the act was unlawful; he looked upon her at noon, and it was lawful; he looked upon her in the afternoon and it was again unlawful; he looked upon her at sunset and it was lawful; he looked upon her at night and it was unlawful; he looked upon her next morning and it was lawful. Can you explain how such differing states could succeed each other so quickly, in a day and a night?'

'The explanation is easy: the man looked upon the slave in the morning when she was not his, and therefore, according to the Book, to do so was not lawful; he bought her at noon and therefore could look at her as much as he liked; in the afternoon he gave her her freedom and therefore it was not lawful for him to look upon her; at sunset he married her and to look upon her became lawful, that and other things; in the night he thought fit to divorce her and therefore it was unlawful for him to come near her; in the morning he married her again with the usual ceremonial, and it was lawful for him to resume his relations with her.'

'Can you tell me what tomb moved about with its contents?'

'The whale which took down the Prophet Jonah into its belly.'

'What valley is it upon which the sun shone once and will not shine again until the Resurrection?'

'The valley made in the waters of the sea by the staff of Moses, that his people might escape.'

'What was the first skirt trailed upon the earth?'

'The skirt of the robe of Hagar, Mother of Ishmael, when she swept the earth before Sarah.'

'What thing breathes and yet is lifeless?'

'The morning, for the Book says: "When morning breathes . . ." '

'Solve the following problem if you can: a flock of pigeons alighted upon a tree, some perching upon the upper branches and some upon the lower; those upon the upper branches said to those upon the lower: "If one of you flies up to us our number will be double yours; if one of us flies down to you, our numbers will be equal." '

'There were twelve pigeons in all, seven upon the upper branches and five upon the lower branches. If one of the lower ones joined the higher, there would be eight above, which would be the double of four; but if one of the seven flew down to the lower ones, there would be six in each position. But Allāh is all-knowing.'

When the philosopher heard these various answers, he feared that the girl would ask him something in her turn; therefore, as he was attached to his gown, he hastened from the hall.

Then rose the most learned man of all that century, Ibrāhīm ibn Siyyār, and said to the fair Sympathy: 'I am ready to hear you confess yourself vanquished and that it is unnecessary to question you further.'

'O venerable sage,' replied the girl, 'I advise you to send for other garments than those which you have on, for in a few minutes I will have taken the latter from you.'

'That remains to be seen. What are the five things which the All-Highest made before he created Adam?'

'Water, earth, light, darkness, and fire.'

'The All-powerful made everything by a simple output of His will, except certain things which He made with His own hands. What were those things?'

'The Throne, the Tree of Paradise, Eden, and Adam. These four things He made with His own hands, and the rest by saying: "Let them be!" and they were.'

'Who is your father in Islām and who is the father of that father?'

'My father in Islām is Muhammad (upon whom be prayer and peace!), and the father of Muhammad is Abraham, the friend of God.'

'In what does the faith of Islām consist?'

'In the simple profession of faith: "There is no God but Allāh, and Muhammad is the Prophet of Allāh."'

'What thing began by being wood and ended by having life?'

'The staff of Moses which he threw to the ground and it became a serpent. This same staff could, according to circumstances, become a fruit tree, or a great leafy tree to protect Moses from the heat of the sun, or a huge dog to watch the flock by night.'

'Can you tell me what woman was engendered by man without having a mother? And what man was engendered by woman without having a father?'

'Eve who was born of Adam; and Jesus who was born of Mary.'

'Tell me now of the different sorts of fire.'

At this point Shahrazād saw the approach of morning and discreetly fell silent.

But when the two-hundred-and-eighty-sixth night had come

SHE SAID:

'There is the fire of the world, which eats and does not drink; there is the fire of hell, which both eats and drinks; there is the fire of the sun, which drinks but does not eat; and there is the fire of the moon, which neither eats nor drinks.'

'What is the answer to this riddle: When I drink, eloquence issues from my lips; I walk and I speak in silence; I am never honoured in my lifetime and after my death I am not regretted?'

'The answer is: a pen.'

'And the answer to this riddle: I am a bird, and yet I have neither flesh, blood, feathers, nor down; I am eaten roast, boiled, or as I am; it is hard to say whether I am alive or dead; my colour is silver and gold.'

'You have taken too many words to signify a simple egg. Ask me something more difficult.'

'Exactly how many words did Allāh say to Moses?'

'He said exactly one thousand five hundred and fifteen words.'

'What is the origin of creation?'

'Allāh made Adam from mud, mud from foam, foam from the sea, sea from the darkness, darkness from the light, light from a fish, the fish from a ruby, the ruby from a rock, the rock from water, and the water He made by saying: "Let it be!"'

'Here is another riddle: I have neither mouth nor belly, and yet I eat. I devour trees and animals; food keeps me alive, but if I drink I die?'

'The answer is fire.'

'Give me the answer to this riddle: There are two friends who have never enjoyed each other though they lie every night in each other's arms; they are the guardians of the house and only separate in the morning?'

'They are the two leaves of a door.'

'Explain this: I drag long tails behind me; I have an eye but cannot see; I make many garments which I may not wear.'

'That is a needle.'

'What is the length and breadth of the bridge Sirat?'

'The bridge Sirat, over which all men must pass at the Resurrection, is three thousand years long, a thousand to climb, a thousand to cross, and a thousand to descend on the other side. It is sharper than a knife and narrower than a hair.'

'How often may the Prophet (upon whom be prayer and peace!) intercede for a Believer?'

'Three times, neither more nor less.'

'Who was the first to embrace the faith of Islam?'

'Abū Bakr.'

'Then do you not believe that Alī was a Mussulmān before Abū Bakr?'

'By the grace of the Highest, Alī was never an idolater; at the age of seven Allāh led him into the true way and lightened his heart with the gift of the faith of Muhammad (upon whom be prayer and peace!).'

'Excellent. . . . Now tell me, whom do you consider the more meritorious, Alī or Abbās?'

Sympathy perceived that the learned man wished to compromise her with this insidious question; for if she gave pre-eminence to Alī, the son-in-law of the Prophet, she would displease the Khalīfah, who was himself descended from Abbās, the uncle of Muhammad (upon whom be prayer and peace!). First she blushed, then she grew pale and, after a moment's reflection, answered: 'There can be no question of pre-eminence between two persons of perfect merit.'

When the Khalīfah heard this answer, he rose enthusiastically to his feet, crying: 'By the Lord of the Kaabah, that is an admirable answer!'

The learned man continued: 'Tell me the answer to this riddle: She is slim, tender, and of a delicate taste; she is as straight as a lance but has not a lance's sharpness; her sweetness is useful on an evening of Ramadān?'

'That is sugar-cane.'

'I will ask you a series of questions quickly. Therefore answer shortly: What is sweeter than honey, what is sharper than a sword, what is quicker than poison, what is the joy of the moment, what is the good fortune which lasts three days, what is the happiest day, what is the joy of a week, what is the debt which even the wicked cannot escape paying, what pain follows us to the grave, what is the joy of the heart, what is the sorrow of the soul, what is the desolation of life, what is the ill without remedy, what is the shame which cannot be wiped out, what animal lives in desert places far from cities, avoiding man and uniting in itself the form and nature of seven beasts?'

'Before I answer, I demand your gown from you.'

Then said Hārūn al-Rashīd to Sympathy: 'Your demand is just; but perhaps it would be better, having regard to his great age, to answer his questions first.'

So she answered: 'The love of children is sweeter than honey. The tongue is sharper than a sword. The evil-eye is quicker than poison. The joy of love lasts but for a moment. The joy of three days is the husband's rest during the monthly periods of his wife. The happiest day is that on which one gets the best of a bargain. The joy of a week is the joy of marriage. The debt which all must pay is death. The evil behaviour of our children follows us to the grave. Heart's joy is a woman submissive to her husband. A bad servant is the sorrow of the soul. Poverty is the desolation of life. Bad character is the evil without remedy. The dishonour of a daughter is a shame which cannot be wiped out. And the animal is the grasshopper, which has the head of a horse, the neck of a bull, the wings of an eagle, the feet of a camel, the tail of a serpent, the belly of a scorpion, and the horns of a gazelle.'

Hārūn al-Rashīd was edified in the extreme by so much knowledge and wisdom, and ordered the learned Ibrāhīm ibn Siyyār to give his own gown to the girl. The sage did so and then, lifting his right hand, witnessed publicly that the slave had surpassed him in scholarship and was the marvel of the age.

'Can you play upon instruments of music and accompany yourself while you sing?' asked the Khalīfah, and, when Sympathy replied that she could, had a lute brought to her, which was contained in a red satin case with a tassel of saffron coloured silk and a gold clasp. Sympathy drew the lute from its covering and found carved about it, in interlaced and flowering character, the following verses:

> I was the green branch of a tree
> Birds loved and taught their songs to.
>   Haply the teaching lingers,
> For, when I lie on beauty's knee,
>   Remember under beauty's fingers,
>   The woodland song I sing belongs to
> The birds who sang to me.

She leaned over the lute as a mother over her nursling and, drawing twelve different harmonies from the strings, sang in a voice that echoed long after in all hearts and brought tears of emotion to every eye.

When she had finished, the Khalīfah rose up, crying: 'May Allāh increase your gifts within you, O Sympathy, and have in His benign keeping those who taught you and those who gave you birth!' So saying, he had ten thousand golden dīnārs, in a hundred sacks, given to Abū al-Husn and then turned to Sympathy, saying: 'Tell me, O child of marvel, would you rather enter my harīm and have a palace and retinue for yourself, or return home with this young man?'

At this point Shahrazād saw the approach of morning and discreetly fell silent.

But when the two-hundred-and-eighty-seventh night had come

SHE SAID:

Sympathy kissed the earth between the Khalīfah's hands and answered: 'May Allāh continue to shower His blessings upon our master! Your slave would prefer to return to the house of him who brought her here.'

Instead of being offended by this answer, the Khalīfah immediately gave Sympathy a further five thousand dīnārs, saying: 'May you be found as expert in love as you are in answering questions!' After this he put the crown upon his generosity by raising Abū al-Husn to high employment and numbering him among his intimate favourites.

The two young people left the hall, one staggering under all the gowns of the sages, and the other under all the sacks of gold. As they went, they were followed by the whole marvelling assembly, who lifted their arms, crying: 'Was ever in the world a liberality like that of the descendants of Abbās?'

Such, O auspicious King, continued Shahrazād, were the answers given by Sympathy before the assembly of sages and handed down in the royal annals to be an instruction to every woman of the Faith.

Then Shahrazād, seeing that King Shahryār was still frowning and racking his brains, began at once upon the Adventures of the Poet Abū Nuwās.

Little Dunyazād, who had been half asleep, woke up suddenly on hearing the name of Abū Nuwās and, large-eyed with attention, made ready to listen with all her ears.

An Adventure of the Poet Abū Nuwās

IT is related—but Allāh is all-wise and all-knowing—that the Khalīfah Hārūn al-Rashīd was afflicted one night with lack of sleep and a preoccupation of spirit, so he went out alone from his palace and walked in the gardens to distract his weariness. He came at last to a pavilion the door of which was open, but guarded by a black eunuch who slept across the sill. The Khalīfah stepped over the body of the slave and, entering the single hall of the pavilion, saw a bed with lowered curtains, which was lighted on the right and left by tall torches. Beside the bed stood a little table holding a jar of wine topped by an inverted cup.

Hārūn al-Rashīd was astonished to find these things of which no one had informed him, so he lifted the curtains of the bed and stood stock-still with amazement at the sleeping beauty of a slave who lay there, as fair as the full moon, covered for sole garment with her fallen hair. He took the cup and filled it; then he drank slowly, saying beneath his breath: 'To the roses in your cheeks, O child!' Setting down the cup, he leaned over the youthful face and dropped a kiss upon a little black mole which smiled to the left of the parted lips. Though this kiss was light as air, it woke the girl, who recognised the Prince of Believers and jumped up in the bed. The Khalīfah calmed her fright, saying: 'O young slave, there is a lute beside you which I am sure you can play charmingly. Give me a taste of your skill, for I am determined to pass the night with you although I do not know you, and wish, as a preliminary, to hear your voice.'

The girl took the lute and played upon it in twenty-one different modes, so that the Khalīfah was exalted with delight. Seeing the good impression that she had made, the young woman determined to profit by it, and said: 'O Prince of Believers, I suffer from the assaults of Destiny.' 'How is that?' asked the Khalīfah, and she continued: 'Your son al-Amīn bought me a few days ago for ten thousand dīnārs, intending to give me as a present to your majesty; but your wife, the lady Zubaidah, heard of his intention and, paying him back the money he had spent, gave me to a black eunuch with instructions to keep me a prisoner in this isolated pavilion.'

The Khalīfah was annoyed when he heard this; therefore, after promising to give the girl a palace and a train worthy of her beauty on the morrow, he hastened to waken the sleeping eunuch and ordered him to go at once to command the poet Abū Nuwās to present himself at the palace. For you must know that Hārūn al-Rashīd was always wont to send for the poet when he was in an evil humour, in order to distract himself with the improvised poems and rhymed adventures of that remarkable man.

The eunuch went to Abū's house and, not discovering him there, searched throughout all the public places in Baghdād until he found him in a disreputable tavern at the lower end of the quarter of the Green Gate. He went up to him, saying: 'O Abū Nuwās, our master the Khalīfah sends for you.' The poet laughed as he answered: 'O father of whiteness, how am I going to leave this place when I am in pawn for a young boy?' 'Where is he and who is he?' asked the eunuch, and Abū Nuwās replied: 'He is slender, beardless and pretty. I promised him a thousand dirhams; as I have not the money about me, I can hardly go away.'

'In Allāh's name,' cried the eunuch, 'show me this boy and, if he is as delightful as you say, you shall be excused and more than excused.'

As they were talking in this way, the pretty pet put his head round the door, and Abū Nuwās exclaimed: 'If the branch wavers so pleasantly, will not the song of the birds be beautiful?'

At this point Shahrazād saw the approach of morning and discreetly fell silent.

But when the two-hundred-and-eighty-eighth night had come

SHE SAID:

On this the boy came right into the room of the tavern; and indeed his beauty was wonderful; also he was dressed in three tunics, one on top of the other, white and red and black.

Seeing him all in white, Abū Nuwās felt the fire of inspiration sparkle in his soul and he improvised these verses:

> His robe was white like milk,
> His eyes love-heavy underneath blue lids,
> His cheeks the shadow of wine-coloured silk
> Thrown upon snow.
> > 'What modesty forbids?
> > Why do you pass me so?
> > I am as patient for your hand
> > As a white lamb is patient for the priest.'

'You sing three whites and I have four at least:
A destiny which would be white without you,
A body white and bland,
A face of white,
A garment blanched and exquisite.
You did not count my white aright
And so I flout you.'

Hearing these lines the boy smiled and, taking off his white tunic, appeared all in brilliant red; so that Abū Nuwās was again inspired and sang without a pause:

His tunic was as red as cruelties.
'O child, you boasted white;
What is the meaning of this sight,
Two cheeks dyed in our broken hearts,
A garment stolen from anemones?'
'The dawn has lent me her attire,
The evening sun has put his clouds apart
And given me his fire,
Red are my cheeks' embroideries,
And red the veils which cling about my thighs,
Red is the wine which painted
Red lips where souls have fainted.
So you have missed the addition of my red,'
He said.

Delighted with this song, the minion threw aside his red garment and appeared in a black tunic, which clung to his skin and outlined a charming waist girt in by a silken belt. Seeing him, Abū Nuwās was exalted beyond reason, and sang again:

He would not look at me.
His tunic was as black as night
By no intrusive moon beguiled;
Therefore I said:
'Now I will get it right;
After the white and red,
After the red and white,
Black is the garden of your hair,
Black is your tunic everywhere,
Black are your eyes and black my destiny.

My computation shows no lack;
There's black and black and black on black.'
He smiled.

When the eunuch had considered the beauty of these poems and
of the boy who inspired them, he forgave Abū Nuwās in his mind
and returned straightway to the palace, where he informed the
Khalīfah that Abū was held in pawn at a tavern because he could not
pay what he had promised to a delightful youth. The Khalīfah, who
was both amused and annoyed, sent back the eunuch with the sum
of money required, bidding him bring the poet without delay.

The man hastened to the tavern and brought away the poet, who
staggered a little from drink. When Abū Nuwās had been supported
into the presence of the Khalīfah, Hārūn al-Rashīd lectured him in a
voice which he strove to make furious; but, seeing that the poet
burst out laughing, he took him by the hand and led him to the
pavilion which the young girl occupied.

As soon as Abū Nuwās saw her, seated upon the bed, dressed all
in blue and veiled with a light blue veil, smiling at him with great
dark eyes, the fumes of wine left him and the fumes of inspiration
took their place, so that he improvised this poem:

> I pray the blue veil of this girl:
>> By the white
>> Passing jasmine
>> You hide,
>> By the smile
>> Paling pearl
>> You hide,
>> (Ah, what can the lass mean
>> Inside?
>> Ah, why is the nightwhile
>> Alight?)
>> To requite
>> All the guile
>> And the spite
>> Of that gossiping churl
>> With disdain,
>> Thus again and again
>> In my pain
> I pray the blue veil of this girl.

The young woman gave wine to the Khalīfah, who invited the poet to empty the great cup himself. Abū Nuwās took it off at a single draught and soon felt the effects of the heavy vintage. As he reeled where he stood, the Khalīfah rose in jest and fell upon him sword in hand, making as if to cut off his head. The poet ran hither and thither about the hall with great cries of terror, and Hārūn al-Rashīd pursued him into all the corners, pricking him with the blade. At last the Khalīfah cried: 'Enough! return and drink another cup.' At the same time he signed to the girl to hide the vessel. She immediately concealed it beneath her robe, but Abū Nuwās saw the movement in spite of his drunkenness and sang:

> Even as I desire the cup
> The cup desires
> Lips secret and more pleasant,
> And has gone up
> Within her garments hollow,
> Whither the cup aspires
> Nuwās would follow,
> If only Hārūn were not present.

The Khalīfah laughed consumedly and, as a further jest, said to the poet: 'As Allāh lives, I must raise you to some high employment. From this time forth, I appoint you accredited chief of all the pimps in Baghdād.' 'In that case, O Commander of the Faithful,' retorted Abū Nuwās with a grin, 'what may I have the pleasure of doing for you to-night?'

Hārūn al-Rashīd flew into a rage and commanded the eunuch to call for Masrūr the sword-bearer, his executioner of justice.

At this point Shahrazād saw the approach of morning and discreetly fell silent.

But when the two hundred-and-ninetieth night had come

SHE SAID:
The Khalīfah ordered Masrūr to strip Abū Nuwās of all his clothes, to saddle him with an ass's pack-saddle, to pass an ass's halter round his neck, and to thrust a spur up his fundament. When this had been done, the unfortunate poet was led up and down before all the pavilions of the King's favourites, that they might laugh at him; and Masrūr had instructions, when this exhibition had been

completed, to take Abū Nuwās to the gate of the city, to cut off his head in the presence of the people, and to bring it back upon a dish.

The despairing poet was paraded before each of the three hundred and sixty-five palaces, and, when their inhabitants heard of the death he was about to die, they grieved for him because they loved his wit, and as a sign of their sympathy threw gold and jewels before his path. Then they came out of their dwellings and followed him with words of encouragement, so that the wazīr Jafar al-Barmakī, who was passing on his way to the palace, halted before the weeping man and said: 'Is that you, O Abū Nuwās? What crime have you committed to have earned so grave a punishment?' 'As Allāh lives,' answered Abū Nuwās, 'I have not committed even the suspicion of a crime. On the contrary I recited some of my most exquisite poems before the Khalīfah, and he has rewarded me by giving me his own robe of honour.'

The Khalīfah, who was hiding behind a curtain of the nearest pavilion, heard this answer and burst into a hearty laugh. He not only pardoned Abū Nuwās, but gave him a real robe of honour and a large sum of money; also he continued to make him the inseparable companion of his black hours, as heretofore.

When Shahrazād had finished this tale of the poet Abū Nuwās, little Dunyazād, who had been endeavouring to stifle her silent laughter in the carpet, ran to her sister, crying: 'As Allāh lives, dear Shahrazād, that is a funny tale! I should have liked to see Abū Nuwās disguised as an ass! Will you tell us some more stories about him?'

But King Shahryār cried: 'I do not like this Abū Nuwās at all. If you are quite determined to have your head cut off, you have but to continue telling me his adventures. If, on the other hand, you would save yourself and make the night pass pleasantly, tell me some story of travel; for, since I journeyed into far countries with my brother Shahzamān, after cutting off the head of my wicked wife, I have taken great pleasure in the subject of voyages. If you know some delightful tale of this kind, begin at once; for my insomnia is very bad to-night.'

The wily Shahrazād cried: 'I agree that tales of travel are both more astonishing and more entertaining than all the stories which I have yet told. This you may judge for yourself, O auspicious King, for there is no tale in all the books comparable with that of Sindbād the Sailor, and I am about to begin his adventures, if you will give me leave.'

Thus it was that Shahrazād told:

The Tale of Sindbād the Sailor

IT is related, O auspicious King, that there lived in Baghdād, during the reign of the Khalīfah Hārūn al-Rashīd, a poor man called Sindbād the Porter, who earned his living by carrying loads upon his head. One day, as he was sweating and staggering in the great heat under a more than usually heavy burden, he passed the door of a house which seemed to him to belong to some rich merchant, as the ground about it was well swept and refreshed with rose-water. The breeze blew soft and cool there and a bench stood near the door for tired wayfarers, so Sindbād set his load upon the ground and sat down on the bench to breathe the scented air. He heard the concerted playing and singing of lutes and voices skilled in the craft of song, and the mingled jargonning of doves, nightingales, blackbirds, bulbuls, pigeons and tame partridges, praising Allāh in sweet modes. He marvelled in his soul and, for very pleasure, passed his head through the opening of the door; then he saw a great garden, filled with a press of slaves, servants and guests, and furnished as only are furnished the gardens of kings.

The smell of admirable meats came to him, mingled with wafts of open wine; so that he could not help sighing and crying: 'Glory be to the Creator and Giver of all things, who parts His gifts as it pleases Him! O my God, if I cry to You it is not to call Your justice and Your generosity in question, for the creature may not criticise the Master, but simply to witness what I have seen. Glory be to Him who makes men high and lowly, for He has a reason, though we may not see it. The master of this house is very happy, living in a delight of odours and meats and more than exquisite wines. He is joyous and calm, and there are others like him; while I am hot and tired and poor and miserable!'

Stirred to his depth by such thoughts, the porter made up these stanzas and sang them at the top of his voice:

> I have heard of poor men waking
> In the shadow of a palace,
> But the solace

Of such waking
  Is not for me.

I have seen the rich man's burden,
  Heavy gold on gold increasing;
  But the blessing
Of that burden
  Is not for me.

Though more heavy than those others
  Is the load which makes me weary,
  What I carry
Is for others,
  Is not for me.

Yet when I have heard complaining
  Of the equity of Allāh,
  I thank Allāh
Such complaining
  Is not for me!

When Sindbād the Porter had finished singing, he rose and was about to take up his burden again when the door of the palace opened and a kind-faced little slave, having an exquisite body sumptuously dressed, came up to him and took him by the hand, saying: 'My master wishes to see you. Follow me.' The porter was afraid at this invitation and vainly tried to find some excuse for not going. At length he was constrained to leave his load with the door-keeper and follow the child into the interior of the building.

He saw a wonderful house, filled with grave and noble people, and, when he was led into the great central hall, came upon an honourable company of well-born guests. There were flowers of all kinds, perfumes of every sweetness, great selection of dry conserves, sweetmeats, almond paste, and rare fruits; there were innumerable dishes loaded with roast lambs and other delicate meat, and jars past counting full of wine from a chosen grape. There were fair slaves ranged in due order, bending over lutes. And, in the middle among the guests, sat a tall and dignified old man, with a white beard, a kind and handsome face, and an expression of calm nobility.

At this point Shahrazād saw the approach of morning and discreetly fell silent.

But when the two-hundred-and-ninety-first night had come

SHE SAID:

The porter stood stock still in his amazement, saying to himself: 'As Allāh lives, this must be the palace of some Jinnī or some very mighty king!' He hastened to adopt the attitude demanded by polite breeding and, after wishing peace to all and calling down blessings upon them, stood modestly with lowered head.

The old man begged him to approach and sit down by his side; after a courteous speech of welcome, he had food and drink brought, and not until his new guest had eaten, thanked Allāh and washed his hands, did he allow himself to put a question to him:

'Be very welcome! Be at your ease! Be happy upon this day! Will you allow me to ask your name and your trade?' 'O master,' replied the other, 'I am called Sindbād the Porter, and I carry heavy loads for light payment.' The master of the house smiled, saying: 'O porter, your name is the same as mine; for I am called Sindbād the Sailor. . . . I requested you to come to me because I wished you to sing again those delightful stanzas which I heard when you were sitting outside my door.'

The porter was confused at this and hastened to say: 'In the name of Allāh, do not blame me too much for my inconsiderate singing, for grief, weariness and misery may give birth to rudeness, foolishness and insolence in the best of us.' 'Do not be at all ashamed to have sung in such a manner,' said Sindbād the Sailor to Sindbād the Porter, 'be perfectly at ease here, for you are my brother. I pray you to sing your verses again, for they surprised me by their beauty.'

The porter sang the song which you have already heard, and Sindbād the Sailor turned in delight to the singer, saying: 'My Destiny also makes a strange tale, which I will tell you. When you have heard all my adventures, you will understand what trials and vicissitudes I have had to undergo to reach the felicity of this palace; you will realise that I have had to purchase the wealth which sustains my age with strange and terrible labours, with calamities, misfortunes and hardships that are scarcely credible. I have accomplished seven extraordinary voyages, and the narrative of each one is enough to stupefy listeners with an excess of marvel. And yet all that I tell you had been written for me by Destiny: for all things so written must inevitably come to pass.'

The First Voyage of Sindbād the Sailor

You must know, my noble guests, and you, O honourable porter who bear the same name as myself, that my father was a great merchant. He gave wisely to the poor, and, on his death, left me a considerable fortune in money, land and villages.

These things came into my disposition when I reached manhood, and straightway I set myself to eat strange meats and drink unusual wines, to frequent the youth of my own age, to wear each day a fortune upon my back in clothes, and to cultivate the art of friendship. For a long time I lived in this way, thinking that nothing could abate my patrimony; until one morning I suddenly recovered my senses, on finding that I had practically nothing left. I grew afraid lest I should have to pass my old age in poverty, and called to mind certain words of our master, Sulaimān ibn Dāūd (on whom be prayer and peace!), which my dead father was fond of repeating: *The day of death is better than the day of birth, a living dog is better than a dead lion, and the grave is better than poverty.*

Therefore I rose up and, collecting the little which remained to me of furniture and garments, sold it at auction together with the small holdings and few acres which I had not spent. Thus I gained the sum of three thousand dirhams.

At this point Shahrazād saw the approach of morning and discreetly fell silent.

But when the two-hundred-and-ninety-second night had come

SHE SAID:

With this sum I determined to travel, for I remembered the words of the poet:

> What is success?
> The deathless daughter
> Of your weariness.
> It is to dive in deeper, deeper water,
> And ever deeper, layer on layer
> Of cold green mystery,
> For an ever rosier, ever whiter, ever greyer
> Pearl of the sea.

I ran to the market and bought myself a lading of varied merchandise, which I had carried on board a ship just starting from Baghdād with other merchants. Being determined to put to sea, I rejoiced to feel the boat dropping down stream from Baghdād to the port of Basrah.

From Basrah we sailed, day after day, night after night, over the sea, visiting island after island and land after land, selling or bartering our goods at each.

One day, after some weeks of sailing out of sight of land, we saw an island in the sea with such fair greenery that it appeared like one of the gardens of Eden. At once the captain made towards this delectable land and, when the anchor had been cast and the ladder lowered, allowed his passengers to disembark.

All of us merchants landed, carrying food and cooking utensils with us. Some lit fires and prepared a meal, others washed their linen, and others again contented themselves with resting or walking. I was among the last and, without neglecting either food or drink, found time to wander among the trees and take pleasure in the strange vegetation.

We were all occupied in these various ways, when the island suddenly shook throughout its length so violently that we were thrown to the ground. While we lay dazed, we saw the captain appear in the bows of his ship and heard him cry in an agonized voice with wild gesturings: 'Save yourselves! Come aboard for your lives! That is no island but a gigantic whale! She has lived in the middle of this sea since time was young, and the trees have grown in the sea sand upon her back. You have troubled her repose by lighting fires upon her; now she is moving! Come aboard for your lives, before she sinks in the water and destroys you all!'

Hearing these cries of the captain, the merchants left all they had of clothes, cooking pots and ovens, and rushed towards the ship, which was already weighing anchor. Some of them reached her in time, others did not; for the whale, after bounding terrifically two or three times, sank like lead in the water and involved those who were still upon her back beneath monstrous waves.

I was one of these last, but Allāh saved me from drowning by guiding a piece of hollow wood towards me, a kind of large trough in which some of the passengers had been washing their linen. I clung to it; then, by those more than human efforts which danger and the dear love of life made possible for me, I managed to get astride it. When I was well fixed, I began to beat the water with my feet as if they had been sculls, and made some progress, though my frail craft was canted to right and left by the force of the waves.

By this time the captain was making off with all sails set, leaving those to perish who had not been able to reach the vessel. I rowed as hard as I could with my feet after the disappearing ship; when at last she dropped below the horizon and night fell, I gave myself up for lost. All that night and the next I fought against the sea, and at last wind and wave brought me to the coast of a steep island, covered with climbing plants which fell sheer down the face of the cliffs and trailed in the water. With immense labour of feet and hands I managed to climb up the branches and ropes of these plants, until I reached the top of the cliff.

Being now certain of my safety, I examined the state of my body and found that not only was it covered with wounds and bruises, but that my feet were swelled and marred by bites of fishes, who had filled their bellies with all of me which they could reach. Previous to this examination I had felt no pain, being rendered numb with fatigue and danger, but now I threw myself down on the earth of the island and was soon plunged in a deep swoon.

I remained thus without motion or consciousness until, on the second day, I was wakened by the sun beating down upon my face. I tried to rise, but my feet would not bear me and I fell back upon the ground. I felt in woeful case, but managed to drag myself, sometimes upon my feet and hands, sometimes walking with my knees, until I came at last to a plain covered with fruit trees and watered by pure streams.

There I rested for many days, eating and drinking, until my soul grew stronger and the pains of my body easier. At last I was able to move about with the help of a pair of wooden crutches which I made for myself; and I would spend my time hobbling among the trees, musing, eating fruit and admiring the handiwork of All-Powerful Allāh.

One day, as I went along the shore, I saw far off some thing which I took at first for a savage beast or a monster of the sea. Its appearance so interested me that, although I was in two minds whether it would be safe to do so, I went forward towards it. At last I could see that the animal was a mare of marvellous breed, fastened to a stake upon the shore. She was so excellent a mount that I was on the point of going up quite close to her, when a sudden cry halted me where I was, and a man sprang, as it were, from the earth and ran towards me, crying: 'Who are you? Where do you come from? What led you to venture into this place?'

'Good master,' I answered, 'I am a stranger who was voyaging on a ship and was cast into the sea with certain other passengers. Allāh saved me by means of a wooden trough and I was thrown by the waves upon your shore.'

The man took my hand, saying: 'Follow me.' So I followed him, and he led me down into a cave below the earth which contained a great hall, where he caused me to sit in a place of honour and gave me food. I ate till I was satisfied; when my spirits were a little calmer, the man asked me for my story, and I told it from beginning to end, to his great and unfeigned astonishment. 'In the name of Allāh, my master,' I added, 'do not blame me if I, who have told you the whole truth, now ask you why you dwell in this underground cave and why that mare is fastened all alone on the sea shore.'

At this point Shahrazād saw the approach of morning and discreetly fell silent.

But when the two-hundred-and-ninety-third night had come

SHE SAID:

The man answered: 'There are many of us in this island, posted in different spots to look after the horses of King Mihrjān. Every month, at the new moon, we each take a virgin blood-mare down to the shore and, after fastening her securely, hide in our caves. We have not long to wait before a sea-horse, attracted by the odour of the female, comes up out of the water and, after looking to left and right to see that no one is by, goes up to the mare and covers her. When he has finished he gets off her back and tries to lead her away with him; when she cannot follow him, he whinnies loudly and strikes her with his head and hoofs; this noise is a signal for us that he has finished covering her, so we rush out and converge towards him, uttering loud cries which drive him back into the sea. The mare becomes pregnant and, in course of time, drops a foal worth all of a king's treasure. The sea-horse is due to-day; as soon as his work is over, I will present you to King Mihrjān and show you our country. Blessed be Allāh who caused us to meet, for without me you would have perished of grief in this desert place and never have seen your native land again!'

I heartily thanked the groom, and was still talking to him when suddenly the sea-horse came out of the water, threw himself upon the mare, and covered her. When he had finished, he would have taken her away with him, but she could only rear, neighing all round the circle of her picket. My friend leapt from the cave and, calling his companions, led them towards the sea-horse with loud cries and a clashing of swords against shields, so that the frightened beast plunged like a buffalo into the sea and disappeared.

The other grooms crowded round me and greeted me amiably, offering me food and drink and a good horse to ride on. I accepted their invitation, and we all set off together towards the King's palace. When we reached the city, my companions went first into the royal presence to announce my arrival, and later, when an interview had been granted to me, I was led before King Mihrjān and wished him peace.

He returned my greeting, welcomed me kindly, and asked to hear my story from my own lips. I told him every detail of my adventures, so that he marvelled, saying: 'My son, as Allāh lives, you would certainly not have survived such terrible trials if a long life had not been written for you. Praise be to Allāh for your deliverance!' He reassured me with further benevolent words, admitted me into the number of his friends and, as a proof of his regard, appointed me inspector of ports and bays and registrar of shipping.

My new duties were not so arduous as to prevent my seeing the King every day; he soon came to prefer me above all his friends and to load me with daily gifts. I had so much influence over him that eventually every affair of the kingdom passed through my hands, to the general good of the people.

But, amid all these honours and duties, I did not forget my own country or quite lose hope of some day returning to it. I used to ask each passenger and sailor if he knew in what direction lay the city of Baghdād; but none could answer me or say with truth that they had heard of the place. Therefore, the longer I stayed in this foreign land, the sadder I became for my home and the greater grew my surprise that none of the sea-captains could show me a way of return.

While I lived in that isle, I had occasion to hear and see many astonishing things. I will tell you a few of them:

One day, while I was in the presence of King Mihrjān, I was introduced to certain Indians, who willingly answered the questions which I put to them. They informed me that in their country, which is called India, there are a great number of castes, of which the two most important are Kshatriya and Brahman. The first is composed of well-born and equitable men, who are never guilty of sin or oppression; and the second of pure and holy people who never drink wine and yet are friends of joy, of good manners, of horses, of pageantry and beauty. The learned Indians also told me that these castes are divided into seventy-two lesser castes, whose traditions are separate in every way. This astonished me a great deal. Also I had occasion to visit a neighbouring island belonging to my King, which was called Kābil. This place resounds with the beating of drums and cymbals on every night of the year, and yet I found that the inhabitants were of logical mind and given to beautiful thoughts. In those far seas I once saw a fish more than a hundred cubits long and observed other lesser fish with the heads of owls. Many and strange were the prodigies which I saw there, but it would be wearisome to multiply them in my story. Suffice it to say that I lived long enough in that island to learn many things and to become very rich through judicious bargaining.

One day, as I was standing by the shore, leaning upon my stick and watching for vessels as my duty was, I saw a great ship enter the bay. I waited till she had cast anchor and lowered her ladder and then, going aboard, interviewed the captain to take an inventory of his cargo. The sailors unloaded her in my presence, while I listed the various merchandise; and, when their work was over, I asked the captain if he had anything more aboard. 'My master,' he answered, 'I have still a quantity of merchandise in the hold, but it is in storage, as the owner who came with us was drowned during the voyage. When opportunity serves, I shall sell his property and take the money back to his relations in Baghdād, the City of Peace.'

'O captain, what was the name of that merchant?' I cried with a fast-beating heart. 'Sindbād the Sailor,' he answered. I looked more closely at the man and saw that he was indeed the captain who had had to abandon us upon the whale. 'I am Sindbād the Sailor!' I cried at the top of my voice, and then continued: 'When the whale moved under the fires which were lighted on her back, I was thrown into the water, but, thanks to a wooden trough which some of the merchants had used for washing their clothes, was able to ride upon the sea and paddle with my feet. After that there happened that which Allāh permitted to happen.' Straightway I told the captain how I had been saved and through the course of what trials I had risen to the post of marine registrar under King Mihrjān.

At this point Shahrazād saw the approach of morning and discreetly fell silent.

But when the two-hundred-and-ninety-fourth night had come

SHE SAID:

When the captain heard my words, he cried: 'There is no power or might save in Allāh! In none of his creatures have I ever found honesty or an upright heart. How do you dare, O wily registrar, to pretend to be Sindbād the Sailor, when we all saw him drowned with our own eyes? Are you not ashamed of such an impudent lie?'

'Indeed, good captain,' I answered, 'lies are the weapon of the deceitful. Listen, for I will give you proofs that I am indeed that drowned Sindbād of whom you speak.' Then I reminded him of certain details, known only to myself and him, of that calamity which I have already described to you. At last he could doubt no longer, so he called together the other merchants, and they all congratulated me on my safety, saying: 'As Allāh lives, we could hardly believe at first that you had not been drowned. Surely He has given you a second life!'

The captain delivered all my merchandise to me, and after examining it, to see that nothing was missing and that my name and seal on each bale had not been falsified, I had it carried to the market and sold the greater part of it at a profit of a hundred for one, reserving only certain rich pieces as a present for King Mihrjān. When the King heard of the ship's arrival, he raised his hands in astonishment; as he loved me much, he refused to be outdone in generosity and made me presents of great price. I hastened to sell these for a considerable fortune in money, which I caused to be carried on board the very ship in which I had first set out.

When all my preparations were made, I thanked the King for his protection and great generosity. He gave me leave to depart in many sad and touching words, and made me further costly presents, which I did not sell and which you can see about you in this hall, O honourable guests. As a final cargo I sent aboard a great supply of those perfumes which you can smell even at this moment, aloe-wood, camphor, incense and sandal, in which that far isle abounded.

We set sail, and Allāh sent us favourable breezes, so that after many nights and days we arrived in sight of Basrah and, without delaying long at that port, continued up stream and joyfully cast anchor at Baghdād, the City of Peace, the place of my birth.

I soon came, loaded with riches and ready with great presents, to my own house in my own street, and found the folk of my family in excellent health. I hastened to buy many slaves of both sexes, mamlūks, beautiful veiled women, negroes, lands, houses and other property, more in number than I had inherited on the death of my father.

In this new life I forgot the sorrows, hardships and dangers which I had undergone, the sadness of exile and the fatigues of voyaging. I made charming friends and lived a life of calm joy for many months, feasting my mind with pleasure, eating delicately and drinking rare wines.

Such was the first of my voyages.

To-morrow, if Allāh wills, I shall give you all an account of the second of my seven voyages. I can assure you that it is much more extraordinary than the first.

Sindbād the Sailor asked Sindbād the Porter to dine with him, and at last sent him away with a hundred pieces of gold, begging him to return on the morrow and saying: 'I shall look forward to further acquaintance with your urbanity and charming manners.' 'Be it upon my head and before my eye!' answered the porter. 'I beg respectfully to accept. I pray that joy may be everlasting in your house, my master!'

With that he returned home, marvelling and rejoicing, and dreamed all night of what he had heard and experienced in the house of Sindbād the Sailor.

At this point Shahrazād saw the approach of morning and discreetly fell silent.

But when the two-hundred-and-ninety-fifth night had come

SHE SAID:

In the morning the porter returned to the house of Sindbād the Sailor, who received him affably, saying: 'May you find friendship easy in this house and be altogether at home with me.' The porter wished to kiss his host's hand and, when Sindbād the Sailor would not permit this, cried: 'May Allāh whiten your days and establish His blessing about you for ever!' When the other guests arrived, all sat down about a loaded cloth, rich with roast lambs and golden with fowls, which lay among bowls of delicious stuffing and pistachio paste, and were flanked by abundance of nuts and grapes. They ate and drank and bathed their spirits in the melody of skilful lute players.

When the feasting was over, the guests fell silent and Sindbād spoke to them of:

The Second Voyage of Sindbād the Sailor

I was living a life of unexampled pleasure when, one day, the old desire entered my head to visit far countries and strange people, to voyage among the isles and curiously regard things hitherto unknown to me; also the trading habit rose in me again. I went to the market and spent a great deal of money on suitable merchandise, which I had solidly packed and taken to the quay. There I soon found a fair new ship, equipped with excellent sails, having every sort of marine mechanism aboard and a stout crew of excellent sailors. I fell in love with this vessel, and caused all my goods to be taken aboard and placed with those of other merchants, who were known to me and with whom I was very pleased to journey.

We set sail the same day and made excellent time across the sea, visiting from island to island and ocean to ocean for many weeks, making ourselves known to the notables and chief merchants at each port of call, and both selling and exchanging our goods to great advantage. Fate willed that we should touch at an island of great natural beauty, covered with tall trees, rich in fruits and flowers, filled with the singing of birds, watered by cool streams, but utterly uninhabited.

The captain willingly fell in with our wish to spend a few hours in this place, so we cast anchor and, going on shore, began to walk up and down, breathing the good air of the shady and bird-haunted meadows. Taking a little food with me, I went and sat down by the side of a clear stream, shadowed from the sun by thick leafage, and took great pleasure in eating and drinking in such surroundings. A small breeze whispered an invitation to perfect rest, so I lay upon the grass and let sleep and the cool and scented air overcome my eye lids.

When I woke, I saw none of my fellow-travellers and soon

discovered that the ship had left without anyone noticing my absence. I looked to right and left, before and behind, and could see no moving thing save the white sail dipping far out to sea.

So great was my grief and stupefaction that I felt my bile duct on the point of bursting. What would become of me on this desert island, seeing that all I possessed was being swiftly carried away from me by the ship? A prey to desolate thoughts, I cried aloud: 'All is lost, O Sindbād the Sailor! If a kind Destiny saved you on your first voyage, you cannot expect it to do the same again. The cup which falls a second time is sure to break.'

I wept and groaned, I uttered great cries to break the despair which seemed to be closing round my heart. I beat my head with my hand, crying: 'O miserable fool, why did you so rashly tempt the sea again, when you were living in all delight at Baghdād? Was not your meat, your drink, your clothing all that could be desired? Was there any happiness which you lacked? Was it as if your first voyage had been unsuccessful? . . . We belong to Allāh and all return to Him at last.' With that, I threw myself upon the earth and all but went mad.

At length, realising that my regrets were useless and my repentance a thought too late, I rose to my feet and, after wandering aimlessly for some time, climbed to the top of a tree, to avoid any deadly meeting with wild beasts or unknown enemy. From that perch I looked long to left and right, but could see nothing save the sky, the earth, the sea, the birds, the sands and the rocks. Happening, however, to look in a different direction, I noticed on the far horizon the appearance of something white and enormous. I climbed down from my tree; but, being a little frightened, it was only slowly and very carefully that I made my way towards the strange thing which I had noticed. At length I drew near enough to see that it was a gigantic dome of shining white, with a broad base and yet taller than it was broad. I walked all round it but could find no door of any sort; then I tried to climb up the side of it, but it was so polished and slippery that I could make no progress. At last I had to content myself with measuring the thing. Taking a mark by my footsteps in the sand, I walked round it again and found that it had a diameter of exactly a hundred and fifty paces.

While I was racking my brains to think of some way by which I could enter this dome, I suddenly saw the sun disappear and the day about me change to night. At first I thought that a great cloud had passed before the sun, although such a thing would have been impossible in midsummer; therefore I lifted my head to examine so unseasonable a portent and observed an enormous bird, with formidable wings, flying in the eye of the sun.

I could not believe my eyes until I recalled that travellers and sailors had told me in my youth that there existed, in a far island, a bird of terrifying size called the rūkh, a bird which could lift an elephant. I concluded then that this must be a rūkh, and that the white dome, at whose foot I found myself, was none other than one of its eggs. I was soon proved right in my supposition, for the bird came to earth over the egg, covering it completely, stretching its great wings on either side and letting its two feet touch the earth to left and right. In this attitude it went to sleep. (Blessed be He who sleeps not throughout eternity!)

At this point Shahrazād saw the approach of morning and discreetly fell silent.

But when the two-hundred-and-ninety-sixth night had come

SHE SAID:

I had been lying flat on my belly upon the earth, and now found myself below one of the bird's feet. Seen thus close, it seemed larger than the trunk of an old tree. Rising swiftly, I undid the stuff of my turban and, after having doubled it and twisted it into a strong rope, tied it in a firm knot about my waist and about one of the toes of the rūkh. For I thought to myself: 'This monstrous bird will sometime fly away. When he does so, I will be carried into some place where I can see others of my kind again. Wherever I am set down will be better than a desert island.'

In spite of my movements, the bird took no more notice of me than if I had been a trivial fly or modest crawling ant.

I remained as I was all night, not daring to close my eyes lest the bird should fly away with me while I slept; but it was not till morning that it stepped from the egg, uttered a terrible cry, and soared into the air. It rose and rose until I thought that I was about to touch the vault of Heaven, then suddenly it dropped, so swiftly that I could not feel my own weight, and came to earth with me. It lighted upon a jut of rock, and at once, with trembling fingers, I untied my turban, fearing that the bird might rise with me again before I could free myself. As soon as I was clear of the claw, I shook myself and arranged my garments. I was hurrying to place myself out of reach of my unconscious liberator, when it took the air again, this time carrying in its talons a vast black thing, a very great serpent of detestable appearance. Soon it disappeared in the direction of the sea.

I looked round this new region, and terror fixed me to the spot on which I stood. I was in a wide and deep valley, compassed on all sides by mountains so high that, when I looked at their tops, my turban fell off behind. They were so precipitous that to climb them would have been impossible, and I saw that nothing was to be gained by making the attempt.

My despair was complete, and I cried: 'Oh, how much better it would have been to stay in that deserted island than to come to this barren place, where there is neither food nor water. There at least I had the advantage of fruit trees and the delightful streams, but here are nothing save unfriendly rocks, among which I shall die of hunger and thirst. There is no power or might save in Allāh! I escape from one evil, to fall into a greater and more certain!'

I walked about to take stock of the valley, and found that its rocks were all of diamond. The earth about me was littered with diamonds, great and small, which had fallen from the mountains and, in some places, made heaps as high as a man's head.

I was just beginning to take an interest in these stones when I saw a sight more fearful than all the horrors I had already experienced. The guardians of the diamond rocks were moving about their treasure, innumerable black snakes, thicker and longer than palm-trees, each one of which could have swallowed a large elephant. They were beginning to go back into their dens, for by day they hid themselves from their enemy the rūkh, and only moved about at night.

With infinite precaution I began to move away from the place where they seemed thickest, examining every inch of the ground before I set my foot on it, and saying to myself: 'This is what you get for abusing the patience of Destiny, O Sindbād, O man with empty and insatiable eyes!' In a state of pitiable fear I continued to move up and down the valley, resting from time to time in the most sheltered places I could find until the fall of night.

I had forgotten all about food and drink, and had no other thought than to save my life from the serpents; at last I found a narrow-mouthed cave near the place where I had been set down by the rūkh. I crawled through the entrance and then rolled a stone against it on the inside. I crawled forward, with my fear somewhat abated, looking for a comfortable place to sleep, and thinking: 'To-morrow at dawn I will go out and see what Destiny has in store for me.'

I was about to lie down when I noticed that what I had taken for a large black rock in the middle of the cave was a terrible snake, rolled about her eggs; my skin shrivelled like a dead leaf and I fell senseless to the ground, where I remained until morning.

Coming to myself and finding that I had not been devoured in the night, I found strength to roll away the stone and totter like a drunken man into the open air; I was so worn out with lack of sleep and food that my legs could hardly bear me up. I was looking about me when suddenly I saw a great joint of meat flatten itself with a noisy slap upon the rocks beside me; I started and lifted my eyes to see who bombarded me in this fashion, but could perceive no one. Then a memory flashed across my mind of something I had heard from merchant-adventurers and explorers who had visited the diamond mountains. It seemed that men, who wished to take diamonds from this inaccessible valley, followed the curious practice of cutting sheep into quarters and throwing them from the top of the mountain, so that the diamonds on which they fell pierced them and became fixed in them. Soon rūkhs and mighty eagles would swoop upon this provision and carry it from the valley in their claws, to their nests in the high hills. Then the jewellers would throw themselves upon the birds, with great cries and beatings of their arms, so that they were obliged to let fall their prizes and fly away. After that the men had only to explore the quarters of meat and pick out the diamonds.

With this memory, a plan came to me which might just succeed in saving me from the living tomb of the valley. First I selected a great quantity of diamonds, choosing always the largest and most valuable, and hid them about me everywhere. I filled my pockets with them, let them fall down between my robe and my shirt, stuffed my turban and my drawers with them, and pressed them into the lining of my garments.

At this point Shahrazād saw the approach of morning and discreetly fell silent.

But when the two-hundred-and-ninety-seventh night had come

SHE SAID:

After that I unrolled the stuff of my turban as I had done before and, lying down below the quarter of mutton, bound it solidly to my chest. I had not lain long in this position when I felt myself lifted like a feather by the formidable talons of a rūkh which had fastened upon the meat. In the twinkling of an eye I was lifted out of the valley and set down in the nest which my captor had built high in the mountains. Here the bird began to rip up the meat and my own flesh, in order to feed her young with it. Happily for me a great clamour arose almost at once and the bird flew away, so that I was able to unfasten myself and stand upright, though with my face and clothes all bloody.

I saw a merchant hurrying to the spot, whose face fell and became afraid as he saw me; however, when I did not move or make any hostile demonstration, he hurriedly bent over the meat and examined it, without finding any diamonds. Then he lifted his arms to the sky, crying: 'O loss, O disillusion! There is no power save in Allāh! I take refuge in Allāh against the Evil One!' With that he clapped his hands together in an ecstasy of despair.

I wished him peace; but, instead of returning my greeting, he gave me a furious glance and said: 'Who are you? And by what right have you come here to steal my goods?' 'Do not be afraid, worthy merchant,' I answered. 'I am not a thief, and I have not touched your goods. Also I am a human being and not an evil Jinnī as you appear to believe; I may even claim to be a very honest man, a merchant by profession, a man of strange adventures. As for my being here, it is a wonderful tale which I have to tell you. But first I wish to prove my benevolence towards you by asking you to accept some of these diamonds, which I myself picked up in that valley no human has ever visited before.'

I took some excellent stones from my belt and gave them to the man, saying: 'Here is such profit as you have never dared to hope for in all your life.' Then the owner of the quarter of mutton was filled with joy and loaded me with a thousand effusive thanks, saying: 'A blessing be upon you, O my master. A single one of these diamonds would be enough to make me rich until extreme old age, for never in my life have I seen the like even at the courts of kings.' After further thanks he called to other merchants, who were among the neighbouring peaks, and they crowded round me, wishing me peace and welcome. I told them the whole tale of my strange adventures from beginning to end, but it would be useless to repeat it here.

When the good merchants had a little recovered from their surprise, they congratulated me upon my safety, saying: 'As Allāh lives, your destiny has drawn you alive out of an abyss from which no one before you has escaped.' Then, seeing that I was dropping from hunger, thirst and weariness, they gave me a plenitude of food and drink and, leading me to the tent which they occupied, watched over my sleep for a day and a night. On the second morning they led me down to the sea shore, and I rejoiced with exceeding joy over my two remarkable escapes. After a short voyage we came to a pleasant island, covered with trees so great and shady that a hundred men could have escaped from the sun beneath one of them. From these trees is extracted that white substance of warm and agreeable odour which is called camphor. The tops of the trees are pierced, and the sap, which is as it were the honey of the tree, falls drop by drop like gum into vessels which are placed underneath to catch it.

In that island I also saw a terrible animal, which goes by the name of karkaddan or rhinoceros. It pastures upon the meadows as a cow or buffalo, but is taller than a camel and carries a horn ten cubits long upon its snout. Upon this horn is engraved a human figure and it is so strong that with it the karkaddan fights and conquers the elephant, and at last spits and lifts it from the earth until it is dead. But the fat of the elephant runs down into the eyes of the karkaddan, blinding it and causing it to fall where it stands; then the terrible rūkh swoops down upon both animals from the high air, and carries them to its nest to feed its young. Also I saw many different kinds of buffalo in that island.

We stayed there for some time, rejoicing in the excellent air, and I had time to exchange a portion of my diamonds for a treasure in gold and silver too large to be contained in the hold of a single ship. At length we departed and, voyaging from island to island and from country to country and from city to city, at each of which we admired the beautiful works of God and made advantageous sales and exchanges, came at last to Basrah in the blessed land, and thence up the river to Baghdād, the home of peace. I hastened to my own house in my own street, loaded with much golden money and the finest of my diamonds. After being greeted rapturously by my friends and the folk of my family, I distributed wealth to all, without forgetting the least of my acquaintances.

From that time forth I used life joyously, eating prime meats, drinking delicately, lying soft and dressing rich, and not denying myself the constant society of pleasant persons.

Every day important people came to hear me speak of my adventures and to learn how things went in far-off lands; and I rejoiced to entertain and teach them in the way they wished. They would never leave without first congratulating me on my escape from such terrible dangers and expressing a pleasant surprise at all I told them. Such was my second voyage.

But to-morrow, my friends, if Allāh wills, I shall tell you the strange circumstances of my third periplus, and you will find them far more interesting and breathless than those of my first two.

At this point Shahrazād saw the approach of morning and discreetly fell silent.

But when the two-hundred-and-ninety-eighth night had come

SHE SAID:

Sindbād the Sailor fell silent, and slaves hastened to set food and drink before his astonished guests. Finally Sindbād the Sailor gave a hundred gold pieces to Sindbād the Landsman, who took them with polite thanks and many blessings; he came to his own house, his head turning with all the wonders which he had heard. In the morning the porter rose and, after making his prayer, returned, as he had been invited, to the house of the rich traveller. There he was welcomed cordially and bidden to take part in the daily feast and entertainment, which lasted till nightfall. Then, when the guests fell silent and attentive, Sindbād the Sailor told them of:

The Third Voyage of Sindbād the Sailor

YOU must know, my friends—but Allāh has a greater knowledge than any of His creatures—that the comfortable life which I led after my return speedily made me forget all the dangers I had run and the misfortunes I had undergone, so that I began to grow tired of the monotonous laziness of my existence in Baghdād. My soul longed for change and the delights of travel, and I was tempted anew

by the love of skilful trading. Ambition is the cause of all misfortune, as I was soon to prove in a most terrible fashion. I bought a
quantity of rich merchandise and took it from Baghdād to Basrah,
where I found a great ship already filled with honest, good-hearted
merchants of the kind who can live contentedly together and render
aid when aid is needed. I embarked with them in this vessel, and we
at once set sail, with the blessing of Allāh upon our voyage.

The happiest omens attended our setting forth and, in all the
lands at which we touched, we both traded to advantage and learnt
many new things, so that nothing was lacking to complete our
happiness.

One day, when we were in mid-ocean far from any Mussulmān
country, we saw our captain, who had been closely examining the
horizon, suddenly beat himself about the face, wrench out the
hairs of his beard, tear his garments, and throw his turban to the
deck.

We surrounded him, as he stood there weeping and lamenting,
and cried out: 'What is it, captain?' 'O passengers of peace,' he
answered, 'the contrary wind has beaten us and thrown us from our
course into a sinister sea. We are lost, for fate is driving us upon
that island which you see before you, and no man who ever touched
there has returned alive to tell the tale. It is the Isle of Apes, and
I feel deep in my soul that we are lost for ever.'

As the captain was speaking, we saw our ship surrounded by a
multitude of beings who were hairy like monkeys but more in
number than an army of grasshoppers; while others, staying upon
the beach, uttered howls which curdled our blood. We did not dare
to attack these besiegers or try to repulse them, for fear lest they
should rush upon us and kill us to a man, by the force of their
numbers; for numbers in the end can overcome the most valorous.
We made no movement while the apes climbed aboard and began to
lay hands upon our belongings. They were more ugly than the most
ugly of such ugly things as I have seen in my life, being covered with
hairs, having yellow eyes in black faces, and little bodies no more
than three spans in height. Their grimaces and cries were more
terrible than the mind of man could have imagined. It was clear that
they spoke to us and cursed us, grinding their jaws the while; but
we could not understand their language, although we listened with
our hearts in our mouths. As we stood helpless, they climbed up the
masts and unfastened the sails, cutting the ropes with their teeth,

and at last took possession of the helm. Guided by them and driven by the wind, our vessel soon beached herself; and then the apes took us one by one and carried us to shore. Leaving us there, they climbed on board in a mass and, pushing off, were soon lost to sight in the open sea.

Our only means of transport being gone, we judged it useless to stay upon the sand, gazing upon the ocean; therefore we walked towards the middle of the island, where we found some fruit-trees and a running stream, which would be sufficient to stave off death for many days.

While we were eating, we saw far off among the trees a great building which seemed to have been deserted by man.

At this point Shahrazād saw the approach of morning and discreetly fell silent.

But when the two-hundred-and-ninety-ninth night had come

SHE SAID:

We walked towards this building and found that it was a tall square palace, surrounded by solid walls in which a double door of ebony stood open. As no doorkeeper stood there, we entered and found ourselves in a hall as large as most courtyards, furnished only with kitchen utensils of unusual size and great iron spits. The floor was heaped with mounds of bones, some of which were already white and others still fresh and juicy. A foul odour sickened our nostrils, but, as we were worn out with weariness and fear, we threw ourselves down and slept.

The sun had hardly set when a noise like thunder woke us, and we saw the figure of an enormous black man stepping down through the ceiling. He was taller than any palm-tree and uglier than all the apes put together. His eyes were red like two flaming ovens, his front teeth were long and curling like a boar's tusks, his mouth was as big as the mouth of a well, his lips lolled upon his breast, his ears fell over his shoulders like those of an elephant, and the ends of his fingers were taloned with lion's claws.

First we were convulsed with terror and then stayed very still. The giant sat down on a bench beside the wall and examined us silently one by one. Finally he came up to us and, choosing me from among the others, seized me by the skin of my neck, as if I had been a small parcel of cloth, and turned me this way and that, feeling me as a butcher feels a sheep's head. He apparently found me not to his liking, as I was sweaty with terror and yet little more than skin and bone because of the fatigues of my voyage. He threw me to the ground and treated my neighbour in the same way, only to put him aside and take up another. All of us were examined in this way, until at last it came to the captain's turn.

Now the captain was a fat and fleshy man, as well as being the tallest and strongest person aboard; therefore the giant preferred him to all others and, taking him between his fingers as a slaughterman takes a lamb, broke his neck beneath his foot, spitted him on one of the great spits from mouth to anus, and, lighting a great wood fire in the oven, turned him before it slowly until he was cooked to a nicety. After this the ogre pulled him to pieces with his finger-nails as if he had been a chicken, and swallowed him in a few mouthfuls. Then he sucked and cracked the bones, throwing them to the floor as they were finished.

As soon as his meal was over, the giant stretched himself along the bench to digest it, and was soon snoring like a buffalo. He slept thus till morning and then went away as he had come, leaving us half-dead with fear.

When we were certain that he had really gone, we came out of the terrified silence which we had maintained all night, and began sobbing and lamenting to each other over our evil plight.

'It would have been better,' we cried, 'had we been drowned in the sea or eaten by the apes, than roasted upon a spit. As Allāh lives, that is a filthy kind of death! But what can we do? Allāh's will must run its course! There is no power save in Allāh!'

We left the building and wandered all day about the island, searching for some cave or hiding place; but we found none, because the island was quite flat and bare. When evening fell, it seemed to us the lesser of two evils to return to the palace.

We had not been there long when the black man announced his coming by a noise as of thunder. In the same way as the night before he chose out one of the merchants, whom he spitted, roasted, and ate; then he again snored like a gorged animal until the morning. At dawn he went forth again, grumbling horribly to himself and taking no notice of us at all.

By this time, we had well thought over our deadly situation; therefore, as soon as we were alone, we cried out: 'Let us drown ourselves in the sea rather than be cooked and eaten!' We were about to put this desperate plan into execution when one of us rose, saying: 'Listen to me, comrades. Would it not be better for us to kill this black man than to kill ourselves?' Then I rose in my turn and said to my friends: 'If we determine to kill this giant, we must begin by constructing a raft out of the wood which litters the seashore, so that we can escape from this cursed island as soon as we have destroyed him. We can make our way to some other island and there wait for a ship which will take us back to our own country. Even if the raft capsizes and we are drowned, we will have escaped roasting and avoided the unlawful act of suicide. Our death will be a martyrdom and count as such upon the Judgment Day.'

At this point Shahrazād saw the approach of morning and discreetly fell silent.

But when the three-hundredth night had come

SHE SAID:

'As Allāh lives,' cried all the other merchants, 'that is an excellent plan!'

We went down to the beach and, after making our raft, loaded it with fruits and edible herbs; then we returned to the palace and waited fearfully for the coming of the black ogre.

He came with his customary thunder-clap, baying like a great mad dog, and we had to submit to the loss of the plumpest of our companions before we could put our purpose into execution. At last, when the monster was asleep and snoring like an earthquake, we took two of the iron spits and, making them red-hot in the fire, laid hold of them by the cool ends and staggered with them, many to each one, towards tne sleeper. With all our strength we plunged these terrible weapons into the frightful eyes of the black man and weighed upon them with our bodies until there was no doubt as to his blindness.

His pain must have been atrocious, for he gave vent to a fearful cry, which cast us all many yards away on to the floor. He bounded from the beach and lumbered about blindly with outstretched hands, yelling and attempting to find us; but we were easily able to dodge him. His gropings met no more than the empty air; he soon felt his way to the door and disappeared with moans of suffering.

Feeling certain that the ogre would die of his wounds, we made our way light-heartedly towards the beach, and, after perfecting our raft, pushed it off from the shore and rowed out to sea. We were only a few yards from the shingle when we saw the blind giant running towards us, guided by a woman of his own species, in every way more disgusting than himself. When they came to the beach, they stood howling at us for a little while; then, seizing upon vast lumps of rock, they bombarded the raft with them. Some of the hits told, and all my companions save two were drowned; but we three who survived soon managed to paddle our craft beyond the range of these great missiles.

As soon as we reached the open sea the wind took us and, carrying us for two days and nights, threw us upon another island, just in time to save ourselves from death by taking fruit and water, and then to climb up into a tall tree before the fall of night.

The first thing which we saw when we opened our eyes in the morning was a vile snake, as large as the tree in which we were hiding, which darted towards us with burning eyes, opening jaws at us as great as an oven. Suddenly the beast rose up so that his head was on a level with the tree top and, seizing one of my companions in his teeth, swallowed him with one movement to the shoulders and, with a second, made him disappear entirely. We heard the bones of the unfortunate man cracking in the snake's belly and thought to ourselves: 'As Allāh lives, each new death which we come upon seems more detestable than the others. Our joy at escaping the black man's spit must needs change to the fear of something worse! There is no help save in Allāh!'

Although half unconscious with fear, we were able to climb down from the tree to eat some fruit and satisfy our thirst at a nearby stream. Afterwards we went all over the island, hunting for some more secure shelter than that of the night before, and at last found a tree so high that its upper branches appeared to be out of reach of any serpent in the world. At nightfall we climbed into the top of this and made ourselves as comfortable as we could, drawing quiet breath for the first time in many days. All at once, however, we heard a monstrous hissing and a noise of breaking branches. Before we could make a movement, the snake had seized my companion, who was sitting a little lower than I was, and had engulfed the first three-quarters of him at a single swallow. It was my lot to see the huge creature wrap itself round the tree and crack all the bones of my last comrade, before swallowing him whole.

Though the snake now retired, I stayed in the tree without daring to move until the sun brought me warmth and confidence. My first thought was to cast myself into the sea and thus put an end to a life in which terror accumulated upon the head of terror; but, when I was half-way to the beach, my soul revolted, because the spirit of man is a precious thing, and also because I had conceived a plan which I thought would finally protect me against the snake.

Having collected a large quantity of wood, I stretched myself on the ground and fixed a broad plank of it below the soles of my feet. A second and a third I secured to the outside of my thighs, a fourth in front of my belly, and a fifth and largest over my head. Thus I was surrounded on all sides by wooden bulwarks, which would prove an obstacle to the snake in whatever direction he attacked me. When I had made my preparations, I stayed where I was, lying upon the ground, and delivered myself into the hands of Destiny.

At nightfall the snake came; as soon as it saw me, it threw itself upon me, but could not swallow me down into its belly because of my wooden protections. Therefore it turned round me, jumping up and down, to find an unguarded part; yet, although it pulled me about and plagued me, it could not eat me. All night I fought, feeling its stinking breath in my face; at dawn the terrible beast shook itself in fury and disappeared among the trees.

At this point Shahrazād saw the approach of morning and discreetly fell silent.

But when the three-hundred-and-first night had come

SHE SAID:

When I was quite sure that the snake had gone, I undid the knots which bound the planks to me and lay on the ground for many hours, suffering so throughout all my limbs that I feared that I would never recover the use of them. At last, however, I found that I could stand, and began painfully to cross the island. As soon as I reached the other side and looked out to sea, I saw a ship passing swiftly with all sails set.

At sight of her I waved my arms and cried out like a madman; then I undid the stuff of my turban and, fastening it to the branch of a tree, waved it above my head as a signal of distress. Destiny willed that my despair should not pass unnoticed; the ship turned from her course and made towards the island, and in a very short time I was rescued by the captain and his crew.

As soon as I was on board, I was given clothes to cover my nakedness, and food which I devoured ravenously; but my greatest joy
was a certain store of cool fresh water, from which I was allowed to
drink until I was satisfied. Little by little my heart grew calm, and I
felt rest fall like balm upon my weary body.

I began to live again, after having looked so long upon the face
of death, and thanked Allāh for His mercy. Soon I became so like
my old self that I looked upon my trials and misfortunes as so many
bad dreams.

We made an excellent voyage before a favouring wind and came
at last to the island of Salāhitah, where we cast anchor and the
merchants went ashore to trade. As soon as they had left the ship, the
captain came up to me, saying: 'Listen now to what I have to say to
you! You are a poor man and a stranger; also, by your own account,
you have suffered much; therefore I wish to aid you and help you
to return to your own country, so that, when you think of me, it
may be with pleasure and prayer.' 'O captain,' I answered, 'I will
certainly call down blessings upon you with all my heart.' 'That is
well,' continued the good man. 'Some years ago we had a passenger
who was left behind on an island at which we touched. Since then
there has been no news of him and we do not know whether he is
dead or alive. All his goods are still in the hold, and I intend to hand
them over to you. Then you may sell them and, keeping a commission for yourself, give me the price to carry back to the unfortunate man's family in Baghdād.' 'Let it be as you say, my
master,' I answered. 'I shall ever feel gratitude to you for enabling
me to earn such honest money.'

The captain ordered the sailors to take the merchandise from the
hold, and called the ship's clerk to count and enter it, bale by bale.
'To whom do these goods belong?' asked the man. 'In whose name
shall I write them down?' 'The owner's name was Sindbād the
Sailor,' answered the captain, 'but now you must enter it in the
name of this poor passenger. Therefore ask him what that is.'

'But I am Sindbād the Sailor!' I cried out in astonishment. Then,
looking more closely at the captain, I recognised him for the man
who had forgotten me when I fell asleep on the island at the beginning of my second voyage.

Trembling with emotion, I continued: 'O captain, do you not
recognise me? I am indeed Sindbād the Sailor, a merchant of Baghdād. Listen to my tale! Do you not remember that it was I who

went ashore upon that island many years ago, and did not rejoin the ship? I ate beside a delightful stream and fell asleep, only waking to see your vessel far off upon the ocean. Many merchants in the Mountain of Diamonds saw me and will bear witness that I am indeed Sindbād.'

I had not finished my explanations when one of the merchants came aboard to make a further selection of his goods and, coming up to me, looked closely in my face. When I paused for breath, he clapped his hands together in surprise, saying: 'As Allāh lives, none of you would believe me when I told you of the strange adventure which happened to me one day on the Mountain of Diamonds, when I saw a man lifted from the valley to the peaks by a rūkh, which had pounced upon a quarter of mutton to which the adventurer was attached. Well, this is the man! He is Sindbād the Sailor, that very generous merchant who made me a present of wonderful diamonds.' So saying, my old friend embraced me as if I had been a long-lost brother.

Then the captain also looked more closely at me and suddenly recognised me as Sindbād. He took me in his arms, as if I had been his son, and congratulated me on being alive, saying: 'As Allāh lives, my master, your adventure has been a prodigious one! Praise be to Him who has allowed us to meet again and permitted the recovery of all your goods!' With that he had the bales carried for me on to the quay, and I sold them at such enormous profit that I more than made up for the time that I had lost since I purchased them.

After this we left the island of Salāhitah and came to the land of Sind, where all the ship's company bought and sold. In those far seas I saw so many incredible prodigies that a detailed account of them would be impossible. I saw a fish which looked like a cow and another closely resembling an ass, also a bird which is born from a sea shell, whose little ones live ever upon the surface of the waters and do not fly over the earth.

We sailed on and on until, by the permission of Allāh, we came to Basrah and, staying there only a few days, hastened up-stream to Baghdād.

I went to my own house in my own street and, greeting my old companions and the folk of my family, gave great alms to the widow and orphan, because I had returned richer from my last adventure than ever before.

To-morrow, my friends, if Allāh wills, I shall tell you the tale of my fourth voyage, and you will find it more interesting than the other three.

Then Sindbād the Sailor gave Sindbād the Porter a hundred pieces of gold, as he had done on the days which went before, and invited him to return next morning.

At this point Shahrazād saw the approach of morning and discreetly fell silent.

But when the three-hundred-and-second night had come

SHE SAID:

Next day the porter returned and, when the usual feast was finished, heard Sindbād the Sailor tell of:

The Fourth Voyage of Sindbād the Sailor

THE delightful pleasures of my life in Baghdād could not make me forget my voyages, though my memories did not dwell upon the hardships and the dangers which had been my lot. My traitor soul only showed me the advantageous side of travelling in far countries, so that at last I could resist her whisperings no longer and, leaving my house and great possessions, provided myself with a greater quantity of precious merchandise than I had ever carried before and had it conveyed to Basrah. There I embarked upon a great ship, in company with some of the best known merchants of the city.

We made excellent time across the seas, trading to great profit from island to island and from land to land, until one day, when we were in mid-ocean, the captain suddenly gave the order to anchor, crying: 'We are lost beyond all hope!' A great wind raised all the sea about us and, hurling heavy waves against the ship, broke it to pieces and washed all who were aboard into the gulfs of the water.

Thanks to Allāh, I found a plank in the depths and, clinging to it with hands and feet, tossed hither and thither for half a day with certain other of the merchants who had managed to reach it also. Rowing with our hands and feet and helped by wind and current, we were thrown, more dead than alive with cold and terror, upon the beach of an island.

We lay as we were upon the sand all night, but in the morning were able to rise and make our way into the interior, where we saw a building among the trees.

As we drew nearer, a crowd of naked black men streamed from the door of this building; without saying a word, they surrounded us and led us into a mighty hall, where a king was sitting upon a high throne.

This monarch bade us be seated, and then had trays brought, covered with such meats as we had never seen in our lives before. Their appearance did not excite my appetite, but my companions ate greedily because of the hunger which we had suffered since our shipwreck. Though I did not know it at the time, my abstention saved my life.

After the first few mouthfuls, the other merchants were seized with such a fit of gluttony that they went on swallowing for many hours all that was put before them, with mad gestures and strange snuffling sounds. While they still continued to guzzle, the naked men fetched a vase filled with a kind of ointment, with which they anointed the bodies of all the guests who were feeding heartily. The effect upon the bellies of my friends was extraordinary; I saw them, little by little, grow larger in all directions, until each was swollen to the size of a great waterskin. Their owners' appetites increased in proportion, so that they went on eating; and I was aghast to see that they were never filled.

The sight was so terrifying that I would touch nothing and refused to be anointed; this sobriety on my part was a lucky thing, for I soon discovered that these naked men were eaters of human flesh and used these strange ways of fattening those who fell into their hands and making their flesh more tender and juicy. The King was an ogre who ate every day a roasted stranger, prepared by the method which I have described; but the naked men preferred their abominable diet raw, just as it was, without cooking or seasoning of any kind.

At this terrible discovery my fear for myself and my friends knew no bounds, especially when I noticed that the more their bellies swelled the less their intelligence became, until they ate themselves at last into a state of mere brutishness. When they had become in no way different from slaughter cattle, they were put in charge of a herdsman, who took them out every day to feed upon the meadows.

I myself was worn to a shadow with hunger and fear, and the

flesh became dry upon my bones, so that the natives took no notice of me and forgot all about me, realising that I was unworthy to be roasted or even grilled for their King.

As the black islanders did not watch me, I was able one day to leave the building in which they lived and make off across the island. As I went, I met the herdsman in charge of my unfortunate friends and hastened to hide myself in the tall grass, dodging from tuft to tuft until I had passed them, in order not to be tortured by a sight of their distressing condition.

I walked straight ahead all night, fear of these cannibals having driven away all desire for sleep; and, with only such delays as were necessary to take an occasional meal of herbs, I journeyed on towards the unknown for six whole days and nights.

At this point Shahrazād saw the approach of morning and discreetly fell silent.

But when the three-hundred-and-third night had come

SHE SAID:

On the morning of the eighth day I came to the opposite side of the island and saw men like myself, white and clothed, gathering pepper from the trees which covered that spot. When they saw me, they crowded round me, speaking my own language, which I had not heard for so long. In answer to their questions, I told them that I was a poor stranger, and related the story of my misfortunes. They were exceedingly astonished by what they heard and, after congratulating me on my escape, offered me food and drink, allowed me to sleep for an hour, and then took me down with them into their ship, that they might carry me over and present me to their King, who lived in a neighbouring island.

I found the capital, when we came to it, largely populated, abounding in the excellent things of life, rich in markets and good shops, and transpierced by beautiful roads where a multitude of horsemen galloped up and down, with neither saddle nor spurs, upon horses of a wonderful breed. When I was presented to the King, I did not omit, after respectful greetings, to tell him of my astonishment at seeing men ride bare-backed. 'O my master and lord,' I said, 'why do people not use saddles here? They are excellent things and make a man much more the master of his horse.'

The King was astonished and asked me: 'What thing is this

saddle? We have never seen one in all our life.' I answered: 'Will you allow me to make you one, that you may find out how comfortable and useful a thing it is?'

The King accepted my offer, so I found out a clever carpenter and made him prepare, under my own eyes, a wooden saddle according to my specification. As soon as it was finished, I provided the wooden basis with a padding of linen and leather, ornamenting it all about with gold embroidery and tassels of different colours. Then I taught a certain blacksmith how to make a bit and a pair of spurs; and, because I did not leave him for a moment, he performed his task admirably.

When all was perfect, I chose out the handsomest horse from the King's stables, saddled and bridled it, and equipped it splendidly with such ornaments as long skirts, tassels of silk and gold, and blue tufts about the collar. Then I led it to the presence of the King, who had been impatiently waiting the result of my labour for several days.

The King mounted at once, and felt himself so satisfied with the easy mastery which he now had over his horse that he gave me sumptuous presents and large sums of money.

No sooner had the wazīr seen my saddle and realised what an improvement it was upon the old way of riding, than he begged me to make him one like it. I hastened to oblige him. Then all the notables and high dignitaries of the kingdom asked and received saddles in their turn, rewarding me with such presents that I soon became the richest and most respected man in the city.

I was soon a fast friend of the King, and one day, while I was with him, he turned to me, saying: 'You know that I love you, Sindbād. You have become like one of my own people in my palace, so that I cannot do without you or tolerate the idea that you will some day leave us. Therefore I wish to ask you a favour, which I hope you will not refuse.' 'You have but to order, O King,' I answered. 'Your power over me is made strong by gratitude for all the benefits I have received since my arrival in your pleasant kingdom.' 'Then,' continued the King, 'I wish you to marry a very beautiful woman of the court. She is both rich and talented, and I trust she will be able to persuade you to stay in our city and our palace until the end of your days. Do not refuse me this, O Sindbād.'

I lowered my eyes in confusion and did not know what to answer. 'Why do you not speak, my child?' asked the King, and then I stammered out: 'O Prince of time, the matter is in your hands. I am your slave.' At once he sent for the kādī and witnesses, and married me in that same hour to a noble woman of distinguished family. She was extremely rich, owning goods, buildings, and lands, beside her own considerable beauty. The King also gave me a furnished palace with servants, with men slaves and women slaves, and a following which was truly royal.

I lived in the calmness of supreme joy for many months after my marriage, and ever nourished the secret hope of escaping from that city and returning to Baghdād with my wife; for we loved each other, and the accord between us was marvellous. But, when Destiny proposes a thing, no human power can turn that thing aside. Also what man may know the future? Alas, I was soon to learn yet again that all our projects are but child's play in the eyes of Fate.

One day my neighbour's wife died, for Allāh had willed it so, and, as he was my friend, I went to him and tried to console him, saying: 'Do not grieve more than is lawful, O my neighbour. Allāh will soon make up to you for your loss by giving you an even better wife. May He prolong your days, my friend!' The man seemed stupefied by my words; he raised his head, saying: 'How can you wish me a long life, when you know that I have but an hour to live?' Astounded in my turn, I said: 'Why do you speak in that way? What gloomy presentiments are these? Thanks be to Allāh, you are in perfect health and nothing threatens you; surely you do not mean that you are going to kill yourself?' He answered: 'Ah, now I see that you do not know the customs of our country. It is a rule here that every husband must be buried alive with his dead wife and every wife buried alive with her dead husband. The law is inviolable; in an hour's time I shall be committed to the earth with the body of my wife. Every man, and even the King, must conform to this custom of our ancestors.'

At these words I cried: 'As Allāh lives, the custom is detestable. I never could find it in my heart to abide by it.'

While we were speaking, the friends and relations of my neighbour came in and began to console him as best they might for his own and his wife's death. Then the funeral went forward. The woman's body was placed in an open coffin, dressed in her most beautiful garments and wearing the chief of her jewels; a procession was formed with the husband at the head, walking behind the coffin; and we all proceeded with slow steps towards the place of burial.

We came outside the city to a mountain overlooking the sea;

in a certain part of it I saw a kind of immense well, the stone cover of which was speedily lifted. First the coffin was let down and then my friend was seized; without offering any resistance, he allowed himself to be lowered into the well by a long rope, to which was also attached a large jar of water and seven loaves. Then the stone cover was replaced upon the well, and we all returned whence we had come.

I had assisted at this ceremony, sick with fear and thinking: 'This is more terrible than anything I have yet seen.' No sooner did I reach the palace than I ran to the King, saying: 'My master, I have travelled through many lands, but I have never heard of so barbarous an institution as your custom of burying a husband alive with his dead wife. I should like to know, O King of time, if a stranger is equally amenable to this law.' 'Certainly he is,' answered the King, 'he must be buried alive with his wife.'

At this answer I felt as if my gall-bladder would break against my liver; half mad with terror, I ran to my own house, fearing lest my wife might have died in my absence. When I found her in the best of health, I tried to console myself, saying: 'Do not be afraid, O Sindbād. You are certain to be the first to die; therefore you will never be buried alive.' But this consolation was vain; for in a short while my wife fell ill and, after lying upon her bed for certain days, rendered her soul to Allāh, in spite of all the cares with which I surrounded her.

My grief and horror knew no bounds, for I considered it as bad to be buried alive as to be eaten by cannibals. I could have no doubt about my fate when the King came to visit me and condoled with me over my approaching end. He was so fond of me that he insisted on being present with all his court at my burial, and himself walked beside me when I headed the procession behind the coffin in which my dead wife lay, covered with jewels and ornaments.

When we came to the mountain which overlooked the sea, the well was opened and the body of my wife let down; then all who had come with me clustered round to say farewell. I tried to move the heart of the King by weeping and crying: 'I am a stranger, and it is not just that I should have to suffer by your law. I have a living wife in my own country, and children who have need of me.'

The people took no notice of my sobs and lamentations, but fixed ropes under my arms and, tying a jar of water and the seven customary loaves to my back, lowered me into the well. When I had reached the bottom of it, they cried down to me: 'Unfasten yourself, that we may pull up the ropes!' This I was unwilling to do, but rather kept on pulling upon the cord as a sign that they should haul me up again. Therefore they let go of the ropes, reclosed the mouth of the well with the great stone and went their way, followed by my pitiable cries.

At this point Shahrazād saw the approach of morning and discreetly fell silent.

But when the three-hundred-and-fourth night had come

SHE SAID:

At once the stench of this fearful underground place made me stop my nose, but it did not prevent me from using the light which filtered from above to inspect the mortuary cave, which I found to be filled with old and new bodies. It was very high and stretched further than my eye could reach. I fell to the earth, weeping and crying: 'You deserve this fate, O Sindbād of the unfilled soul! What need was there for you to marry in this city? Why did you not die in the valley of diamonds? Why did you not perish at the teeth of the cannibals? Would that it had pleased Allāh to drown you in one of your shipwrecks rather than reserve you for so terrible a death!' I beat myself in the face and the stomach with my fists; but at last, feeling the effects of both hunger and thirst, and being determined not to die out of hand, I unfastened the loaves and the water from the rope and ate and drank sparingly.

I lived in this way for several days, growing gradually used to the foul odour of the cave and sleeping at night upon a space of earth which I had taken care to clear of bones. The time came when I had neither bread nor water. I had just recited the act of Faith in absolute despair and had shut my eyes before the approach of death when the cover was removed above my head and a dead man was let down in his coffin, accompanied by his wife with seven loaves and a jar of water.

I waited until the men above had covered the opening again and then, noiselessly possessing myself of a great bone from one of the dead, threw myself upon the woman and brought my weapon down upon her head; I gave her a second and a third blow to make sure that she was dead, and then took the seven loaves and the water jar, which kept me alive for several further days.

At the end of that time the covering was again removed and a dead woman was let down with her husband. Life is dear, so I killed the man and took his bread and water. In this way I lived for a long time, killing each new person who was buried, and stealing their provisions.

One day, as I was sleeping in my ordinary place, I was aroused by an unaccustomed noise, as of living breath and hurrying feet. I rose and, taking my bone, followed the noise until I could just distinguish some heavily breathing object fleeing away from me. I followed this escaping shadow for a long time, running behind it in the dark, stumbling over the bones of the dead, until suddenly I saw in front of me something like a luminous star, which shone and faded out by turns. As I went on towards it, this light grew larger; yet I dared not believe that it portended any way of escape, but thought rather that it was a second shaft by which the dead and living were let down. All at once, however, the form in front of me, which I could now see to belong to some animal, bounded through the light and disappeared; then, to my great joy, I realised that I had come upon a hole burrowed by savage beasts, attracted by the bodies in the cave. I followed where the animal had gone before, and soon found myself in the open air, beneath the sky of heaven.

I fell upon my knees and thanked the Highest with all my heart for my salvation, and by my prayers brought peace to my soul. Then I looked about me and saw that I was at the foot of a mountain beside the sea, and that this mountain was so steep and jagged that there could be no communication between the place I was in and the city. Not wishing to die of hunger, I returned to the cave and brought out food and water, which I ate and drank in the sunlight with better appetite than I had ever used in the charnel cavern.

I went on living in this way, returning every day to the cave for food and water, which I obtained by dashing out the brains of those who were buried alive. Also the idea came to me of collecting from the dead all their jewellery, diamonds, bracelets, collars, pearls, rubies, engraved metals, rich garments, and ornaments of gold and silver. These things I hoarded on the sea-shore, in the hope that some day I might be able to escape with them. Indeed, that all should be ready, I made them up into strong bundles with the help of the garments of the men and women in the cavern.

I was sitting one day, lost in dreams of my adventures and my present state, when I saw a ship passing near in. I rose hastily and, undoing the stuff of my turban, made vigorous signs with it, as I ran up and down the sand. Thanks be to Allāh, the men in the ship saw my signal and sent ashore a boat, which took me and all my packages aboard.

When I came on deck, the captain approached me, saying: 'Who are you, and how did you come upon that mountain on which, during all the years that I have sailed these seas, I have never seen anything but savage beasts and birds of prey?' 'O master,' I answered, 'I am a poor merchant, stranger to these lands. The great ship in which I voyaged was lost with all her company except myself, who by courage and endurance succeeded in reaching this coast, with all my merchandise, on a large plank which I gripped as the boat went down. As you see, Allāh saved me from dying of hunger and thirst.' This I said to the captain, being very careful not to tell him of my marriage and burial, lest there should be some aboard who belonged to that barbarous city.

When I had finished explaining myself to the captain, I took a rich jewel from one of my bales and offered it to him, that he might be propitious to me during the voyage. To my great surprise, however, he showed a most rare disinterestedness and refused my payment, saying kindly: 'It is not my custom to ask for payment when I do a good deed. You are not the first whom I have taken up alive out of the sea; I have served many a wrecked mariner and carried him to his own country for Allāh's sake, giving him food, water and clothes, and also a little something for the expenses of his further journey. For Allāh's sake men should behave to men as men.'

I thanked the captain and wished him a long life; after which he set all sail and proceeded with his voyage.

We had fair weather from island to island and from sea to sea, so that I could lie pleasantly for hours together, recalling my adventures and asking myself whether all my dangers and escapes had not been dreams. Sometimes, however, a memory of my sojourn underground with my dead wife came back to me and I would go half mad.

At last, by the grace of Allāh, we came safely to Basrah, where we stayed a few days, and then proceeded up the river to Baghdād.

I hurried to my own house in my own street, loaded with riches, and presented myself before my friends and the men and women of my family, who rejoiced over my return with great festivity and congratulated me on my safety. When I had given bounteous alms to the poor, the widow and the orphan, and large presents to my friends and acquaintances, I shut my treasure in presses and gave myself up to every kind of pleasure and diversion in the company of gracious people.

But all that I have told you is nothing to that which I will tell you to-morrow, if Allāh wills.

So spoke Sindbād on that day, and afterwards gave a hundred pieces of gold to the porter and invited him to dine that night in company with the great folk who were present. When the feast was over, all the guests returned marvelling to their own homes.

At this point Shahrazād saw the approach of morning and discreetly fell silent.

But when the three-hundred-and-sixth night had come

SHE SAID:

Sindbād the Porter went back to his own home, where he dreamed all night of the story he had heard. When he returned to the house of Sindbād the Sailor, his soul was still sick with the thought of how his friend had been buried alive. Yet, as the cloth was already laid, he took his place with the others to eat and drink and thank Allāh therefor. At length silence fell upon all, and Sindbād the Sailor related:

The Fifth Voyage of Sindbād the Sailor

AFTER my fourth voyage I lived so pleasantly, so joyfully, that I soon forgot my past sufferings and remembered only the great profit which my extraordinary adventures had gained for me. You will not be surprised, then, to hear that I soon obeyed the promptings of my soul, when she incited me to further travel among the lands of men.

I bought a quantity of that merchandise which I knew by experience would meet with a ready sale at high prices and, after it had been packed in bales, took it downstream with me to Basrah.

Walking on the quay there, I saw a newly-built ship of great size, which pleased me so much that I bought her out of hand. I hired an experienced captain and a sturdy crew; then I had my bales of merchandise carried on board by the slaves whom I was taking with me to serve me on the voyage; lastly I accepted as passengers certain honest merchants who paid their money upon the spot. Being this time master of the ship, I felt that I would be able to assist the captain with my knowledge of the sea.

We set sail light-heartedly from Basrah and met favourable winds and a calm sea. After buying and selling at various ports of call, we came one day to an uninhabited island, whose sole building appeared to be a large white dome. This I recognised as a rūkh's egg, but unfortunately I said nothing about it to my passengers; therefore, when they went ashore, they found no better employment than to throw great stones at the shell of the egg. When the surface was broken, a liquid substance flowed forth and this, to their great surprise, was followed by one of the legs of the small rūkh. The merchants went on with their work of destruction and, after killing the young bird, cut it in pieces and returned on board to tell me of their adventure. I was stricken with fear on hearing what they had done, and cried: 'We are lost! The father and mother will be here soon, and they will destroy us; we must get away as quickly as we can!' I gave immediate orders for the sails to be set, and we made for the open sea.

As we hurried away from the island, the merchants set to work to cook the pieces of the bird; but they had hardly begun to eat when we perceived two great clouds hiding the sun. These drew nearer, and we saw that they were two gigantic rūkhs; we heard the beating of their wings and their cries which were more terrible than thunder. When they were high above our heads, we saw that each carried in its talons a rock larger than our vessel.

Realising the kind of vengeance which they meant to take, we gave ourselves up for lost. Soon one of the birds let its missile fall directly above the boat; but our captain, with a dexterous turn of the tiller, threw us from our course. The mighty stone just missed us and made so great a well in the ocean that we could see the bottom. We were tossed up and down like a cork upon the consequent waves. Before these had subsided, the second bird let fall its rock, which struck our stern and, breaking the tiller into twenty pieces, swamped half of the vessel in the sea. Those of us who were not crushed to pieces were thrown into the water and dragged down by the waves.

I was able to rise to the surface through the desperate efforts which I made to save my life, and by good luck I managed to clamber on to one of the timbers of the lost ship. Sitting astride this, I paddled with my feet and, by the aid of wind and current, reached an island just as I was about to render my last breath to its Giver, from weariness, hunger and thirst. I threw myself upon the beach and lay there for an hour, until my heart had ceased its inordinate beating and strength had a little returned to me. Then I rose and began to make an examination of the island.

This time I did not have to go far, for Fate had carried me to a very garden of Paradise. On all sides before my delighted eyes were trees with golden fruit, cold silver streams, a thousand wings of birds, and close carpets of scented flowers.

I did not delay to eat the fruits, drink the water, and breathe in the refreshment of the flowers.

At this point Shahrazād saw the approach of morning and discreetly fell silent.

But when the three-hundred-and-seventh night had come

SHE SAID:

I stayed where I was, resting from my exertions until the evening; but, when night fell and I knew myself alone upon the island among those trees, I became suddenly afraid, although beauty and peace surrounded me on every side. Therefore I could hardly sleep and, when I dozed, was visited by fearful nightmares. Dawn brought me a certain measure of tranquillity, so I rose and began to extend my exploration of the island. I soon came to a large pool into which dropped the waters of a fall, and saw, sitting upon its edge, an old man, clothed in a great cloak of sewn leaves. 'This is some shipwrecked sailor like myself,' I thought.

I went up to the old man and wished him peace; but he only answered by signs. 'How come you to be in this place, O venerable sheikh?' I asked, but he only shook his head sadly and signed with his hand, as much as to say: 'I beg you take me upon your shoulders and carry me across the stream, for I would pluck the fruits upon the other side.' 'Sindbād,' I said to myself, 'if you help this old man you will be doing a good deed.' So I bent down and took him upon my shoulders, crossing his legs upon my chest, while he clasped my neck with his thighs and my head with his arms. I carried him across the stream to the spot which he had indicated and then bent down again, saying: 'Alight gently, O venerable stranger.' But he did not move, rather he pressed his thighs more tightly round my neck and weighed down upon my shoulders with all his weight.

I was surprised at this and looked more carefully at his legs, which I then saw to be black and rough and furry like the skin of a buffalo. A great fear took me, and I tried to throw the old man to the earth, but he replied by pressing my throat, until I was half strangled and dark shadows began to appear before my eyes. I made a last effort to dislodge my persecutor and then fell senseless to the ground.

When I came to myself, I found the old man still crouched on my shoulders, with this difference only, that he had slightly opened his legs to let the air return to my body. As soon as he saw that I was again breathing, he kicked me in the stomach until I got up, and then hunched down further upon my neck and signed to me, with one of his hands, to walk beneath the trees. When I did so, he leisurely plucked the fine fruits and ate them; each time I stopped against his will or went too fast, he kicked me violently until I did as he wished. All that day he stayed upon my shoulders, and I was no better than a beast of burden; at night he made me lie down with him, so that he could sleep without leaving his position. In the morning he woke me with a kick in the belly and made me carry him as before.

For the whole of the next day and night he stayed immovable upon my back, doing all his liquid and solid needs upon me, and urging me to my work with fist and feet.

I had never suffered such humiliation of spirit or discomfort of body as I experienced in the service of that ancient. He was as strong as a youth and as cruel as a donkey-driver, and I could find no way to get rid of him. I trudged up and down, cursing the virtuous impulse which had led me to help the sinister old man, and begging for death rather than a continuance of this slavery.

One day, after weeks of servitude, I was carrying my rider under certain trees below which lay great gourds, and the idea came to me to use a gourd as a receptacle for wine. Picking up one of the largest, which was quite dry, I thoroughly emptied and cleaned it. Then I squeezed the grapes of a prolific vine into it and, carefully stopping the opening which I had cut, left it in the sun; therefore in a few days it was filled with pure wine. When the fermentation had ceased, I drank enough to increase my strength and help me to bear the weight of my burden, but not enough to make me drunk. Yet I felt a new man and very gay; I began to jump from side to side with my rider, whose weight I did not feel, and went dancing and singing through the trees. I even clapped my hands in praise of my own dancing and made the glades re-echo with my peals of laughter.

When the old man saw me in this unaccustomed state and realised that my strength was doubled so that I carried him without fatigue, he signed to me to pass him the gourd. I did not wish to comply with this request, but my fear of the old man was too great for me to refuse. He took the gourd from my hand and, carrying it to his lips, took first a tentative taste and then drank it down to the last drop and threw the gourd far off among the trees.

Soon the wine began to work in his brain, for he had taken quite enough to make him drunk; first he danced and jigged on my shoulders, and then half collapsed with slack muscles, bending over to right and left and keeping his seat with difficulty.

Feeling that I was not clasped as strongly as usual, I unfastened his legs from my neck with a rapid movement and then, by an urge of my shoulders, threw the old man to the ground some feet away from me, where he lay without movement. Without more ado I picked up a great rock from among the trees and, throwing myself upon my tormentor, smashed his skull to pieces and mingled his blood with his flesh. Thus he died. May Allāh have no compassion upon his soul!

At this point Shahrazād saw the approach of morning and discreetly fell silent.

But when the three-hundred-and-eighth night had come

SHE SAID:

When I saw the corpse, my spirit grew as light as my body and I ran joyfully down to the seashore, where Destiny willed I should find a party of sailors who had disembarked from an anchored ship to hunt for water and fruit. They were astonished to see me and clustered round, asking questions. I told them what had happened to me both on sea and land: that is to say, that I had been wrecked and afterwards reduced to bestial servitude by the old man whom I had eventually killed.

On hearing my tale, the sailors cried: 'It is a matter of marvel that you escaped from that old man. He is known to all mariners as the Old Man of the Sea, and you are the first whom he has not strangled with his thighs. Praise be to Allāh that He has delivered you!'

They took me to their ship, where the captain received me kindly and gave me clothes to cover my nakedness. When he had heard my story, he also congratulated me, and then set sail.

After many days and nights at sea we entered the port of a well-built city upon a certain coast. I soon learned that it was called the City of Apes, because of the prodigious quantity of these beasts living in the trees which surrounded it.

I disembarked with one of the merchants who was on board, wishing to see if I could find some employment in the city. As we were walking away from the harbour, the merchant, who had become very friendly towards me, gave me a linen bag, saying: 'Fill this with pebbles and go join the crowd of people whom you will see issuing from the gates. Act in every way as they act and you will earn more than enough money for your livelihood.'

Following his instructions, I filled the bag with pebbles and joined myself to a troop which I saw come out from the city gates, each carrying a bag similar to my own. My friend, the merchant, recommended me in the highest terms to these people, saying: 'Here is a poor stranger; if you will teach him to earn his daily bread, Allāh will reward you.'

After walking for some time, we came to a deep valley, covered with trees so tall that no man might essay to climb them. And the branches of these were heavy with apes and a large thick-skinned fruit called cocoa-nuts.

We halted below the trees, and my companions, setting their bags on the ground, began to bombard the apes with pebbles; and I did the like. The animals were excited to fury and answered each stone by throwing down a cocoa-nut, so that we gathered a vast quantity of this fruit and put it into our bags. When they were full, we put them on our shoulders and returned to the city, where my friend the merchant took back the sack which he had given me and gave me the value of its contents in silver. I went out every day with the cocoa-nut hunters and sold my booty in the city; thus, before long, I saved a considerable sum of money, which I increased by shrewd sale and exchange, till it became enough to pay my passage to the Sea of Pearls.

I took a great quantity of cocoa-nuts with me, which I exchanged among the islands for pepper and cinnamon; these last two commodities I sold so advantageously during the rest of my journey that, when at last I came to the Sea of Pearls, I was able to take divers into my service.

My luck never once deserted me in the pearl fishing, and it was not long before I had collected an immense fortune. Then, being unwilling to put off my return any longer, I bought a quantity of the best aloe-wood, such as abounds in those idolatrous seas, and took a boat which brought me safely to Basrah. When I reached Baghdād, I ran to my own house in my own street, where I was joyfully received by my friends and relations.

As I had returned richer than I had ever been before, I spread fortunate ease about me by making judicious presents to those who needed them. I myself settled down to a life of perfect peace and happiness.

Dine with me to-night, my friend, and to-morrow you shall hear of my sixth voyage, which turned out so astonishing that, in the hearing of it, you will forget all the adventures I have yet told you.

When Sindbād the Sailor had made an end of the account of his fifth journey, he gave a hundred gold pieces to the porter, who, after feasting, departed with the other marvelling guests. Next day Sindbād told the same company the tale of:

The Sixth Voyage of Sindbād the Sailor

COMPANIONS and dear guests, I was sitting one day taking the air before my door and feeling as happy as I had ever felt, when I saw a group of merchants passing in the street, who had every appearance of returned travellers. This sight recalled to me how joyful a thing it is to return from journeying, to see the birth land after far voyage, and the thought made me long to travel again. I equipped myself with merchandise of price, suitable for the sea, and left the city of Baghdād for Basrah. There I found a great ship filled with merchants and notables as well provided with goods for trading as myself, so I had my bales carried on board, and soon we peacefully set sail from Basrah.

At this point Shahrazād saw the approach of morning and discreetly fell silent.

But when the three-hundred-and-ninth night had come

SHE SAID:

We sailed from place to place and from city to city, buying and selling and rejoicing in the new sights which met our gaze. But one day, as we were lying on the deck with a feeling of perfect safety, we heard despairing cries and, looking up, saw that they were uttered by the captain, who also threw his turban far from him and, beating himself in the face, pulled out handfuls of his beard.

We clustered round him, asking what the matter was, and he answered: 'All good folk here assembled, learn that we have been driven from the seas we knew into an unknown ocean, where we shall surely perish unless Allāh sends something to save us. Let us pray to Him!'

So saying, the captain climbed the mast and was about to trim his sails, when a great wind rose and, striking us full in the face, broke our rudder to pieces, just as we were passing a high mountain. The captain swarmed down the mast, crying: 'There is no power or might save in Allāh! None can arrest the force of Destiny! My friends, we are altogether lost!'

While the passengers were weeping and saying farewell to each other, the sea rose in her fury and broke our vessel into fragments against the mountain of which I have spoken. We were all thrown into the water, where some were drowned and others, among whom was myself, were able to save themselves by clinging to the lower crags.

Now this mountain rose straight up from the strand of a large island, the beaches of which were covered with the remains of wrecked ships and every kind of jetsam. The place where we landed was strewn with a multitude of bales from which rich merchandise and costly ornaments had escaped.

I walked among these scattered treasures and soon found a little river of fresh water which, instead of flowing into the sea, as do all other rivers, came from a cleft in the mountain and, running inland, at last plunged into a cave at the foot of it, and disappeared.

Nor was that all; the banks of this stream were thick underfoot with rubies and other coloured precious stones, and all crumbling with diamonds and pieces of gold and silver. Also its bed was littered with gems beyond price, instead of pebbles; and the whole region beneath and beside the water blazed with the reflected light of so much riches that the eyes of the beholder were dazzled. Chinese and

Comarin aloes of the first quality grew above the water. In this island there was a stream of raw liquid amber, of the colour of tar, which flowed down to the sea shore, being melted to the consistency of boiling wax by the rays of the sun. Great fish would come out of the sea and drink greedily of this substance, which heated their bellies, so that after a certain time they would vomit it upon the face of the water. There it became hard and changed both its nature and colour; at last it was carried back to the beach in the form of amber-gris, which scented the whole island. The liquid amber, which the fish did not swallow, also spread a perfume of musk about the shore.

All these riches were useless to man, because none might touch upon that island and leave it alive, seeing that every ship which came near was dashed to pieces by the force of the waves.

Those of us who had been saved remained in sorrowful case upon the beach, desolate in the middle of great wealth and starving among the material for many feasts. Such food as we had we scrupulously divided; but my companions, who were not used like myself to the horrors of starvation, ate their shares in one or two meals and began to die off in a few days. I was more careful, eating sparsely and only once a day. Also I had found a separate supply of provision, of which I said nothing to my friends.

We who lived washed those who died and, wrapping them in shrouds made up of the rich fabrics which strewed the shore, buried them in the sand. To add to the hardship of the survivors, a sickness of the belly broke out among us, caused by the moist air of the sea. All but myself of those who had not starved died of it, and I dug with my own hands a grave for the last of my companions.

In spite of my prudent abstention very little of my food remained, so, seeing that death was not far off, I wept and cried aloud: 'Ah, why did you not die while there remained comrades who would have washed you and given you to the earth? There is no power or might save in Allāh!' Then I began to bite the hands of my despair.

At this point Shahrazād saw the approach of morning and discreetly fell silent.

But when the three-hundred-and-tenth night had come

SHE SAID:

I rose and dug a deep grave for myself, saying: 'When I feel that my last moment is at hand, I will drag myself here and die in my

grave; for surely the wind will bury me with sand.' As I was engaged
in this work I cursed myself bitterly for my foolishness in voyaging
again after having learned five times that death lies in wait for the
wanderer. 'How many times did you repent and begin again?' I said
to myself. 'Had you not enough riches laid by in Baghdād to suffice
for the most reckless expenditure throughout two lifetimes?'

To these thoughts succeeded a more practical one, suggested by
the appearance of the river. 'As Allāh lives,' I thought, 'this stream
must have both a beginning and an end. Now I see the beginning,
but the end is hidden from me. The water flows below the mountain,
therefore I will wager that it comes out the other side in one fashion
or another. If that is so my only hope of escape is to construct some
kind of a vessel which will bear me down the current of the stream
and through its subterranean course. If such be my destiny, I will
find a way of safety beyond; if I die, it will be no worse than the
starvation which waits me here.'

A little cheered by this desperate chance, I rose and began to put
my plan into execution. I collected the larger branches of the
Chinese and Comarin aloes, and bound them together with cords.
Using this as a foundation, I built a raft with ship's planks and
furnishings, which was nearly but not quite as broad as the river.
Then I loaded the raft with some large sacks of emeralds, pearls, and
other stones, choosing always the biggest from the heaps which
surrounded me. I also placed on board some bales of chosen amber-
gris, and the rest of my provisions. When the craft balanced well, I
went on board, carrying two planks by way of oars, and confided
myself to Allāh, remembering these words of the poet:

> Out of the country of oppression
>   Depart and save your spirit whole;
>   There are a thousand lands and but one soul,
> So leave the land and keep the soul's possession.
>
> Nothing unwritten shall surprise you,
>   Nothing which has not been for ages;
>   So hurry not for counsel to the sages,
> But stay at home and let your soul advise you.

My raft was hurried by the current under the arch of the cave,
and at once began to bang against the sides violently, while my head
often came into contact with a rocky roof, which I could not see

because of the sudden darkness. Very soon I wished that I could return to the sands of my starvation, but the current grew stronger and stronger as I descended that underground river and the course of it went sometimes wide and sometimes narrow, so that the moving shadows thickened about me and confused my eyes. Leaving go of my useless oars, I threw myself flat down upon the raft to save my head from being crushed by any projection and, worn out by fear and exertion, fell into a deep sleep.

This sleep or swoon of mine seemed to last for more than a year; when I came to myself, I was in full daylight and, opening my eyes, saw that I was lying upon the grass in a vast tract of meadow land and that my raft was fastened by the side of a river. About me were many Indians and Abyssinians.

When these men saw that I was awake, they began to speak to me, but I did not understand their language and so could not answer them. I thought I was in a dream, until a man came towards me who wished me peace in pure Arabic, saying: 'Who are you and where have you come from, and why have you journeyed to our country? We are farmers who, arriving to water our fields and plantations in this place, saw you come down stream asleep upon a raft. We stopped it and fastened it here by the bank, while we laid you upon the grass to have your slumber out. We wished you to wake yourself, so that you should not be afraid. Tell us by what strange adventure you have come to this place.' 'As Allāh lives, my master,' I answered, 'first give me something to eat, for I am starving. Then ask me as many questions as you like.' The man hastened to bring me food, and I ate until I was satisfied and strengthened. Feeling my soul come back to its body, I thanked Allāh and congratulated myself upon my escape from the underground river. Then I told the men who surrounded me the whole story of my adventures on the island.

They marvelled much at what they heard and began talking together in their unknown tongue, and he who spoke Arabic translated their thoughts to me as he had translated my tale to them. It appeared that they wished to conduct me to their King, that he might hear my adventures for himself. When I gladly consented, they formed a procession and led me to the city, carrying with them my raft, just as it was, loaded with ambergris and sacks of jewels.

The King received me kindly, and at his request I gave a complete recital of all that had happened to me, without omitting a single detail. But it would be useless to repeat it in this place.

The King of Sarandīb, for such was the name of the island, congratulated me heartily upon having come alive out of such perils. In return I hastened to open my bales and sacks in his presence, that he might see that there was profit attached to strange and fantastic voyaging.

The King admired my collection, for he was very learned in the matter of precious stones. Also he was pleased to accept samples which I offered him of every kind of jewel, together with a few large pearls and pure ingots of gold and silver. In recognition of my generosity, he loaded me with honours and gave me lodging in his own palace, so that from that day I was his friend and the friend of the chief nobles in the island. They asked me about my own country, and I described it to them; then I questioned them about theirs, and received some interesting answers. I learned that the island of Sarandib was twenty-four parasangs long by twenty-four wide, that it held the highest mountain in the whole world, on which our father Adam had lived for certain of his days, and that it was rich in pearls and precious stones (though not so fine as mine) and many cocoa-nut palms.

At this point Shahrazād saw the approach of morning and discreetly fell silent.

But when the three-hundred-and-eleventh night had come

SHE SAID:

One day the King of Sarandīb questioned me concerning the internal affairs of Baghdād and the government of the Khalīfah Hārūn al-Rashīd. I told him how just and benevolent our ruler was, and laid considerable stress upon his virtues and excellent qualities. The King of Sarandīb marvelled at what I told him, and said: 'I see that the Khalīfah is versed in wisdom and the true art of government. I have conceived an affection for him through the account which you have given me; therefore I am very anxious to send him some present worthy of himself, and I appoint you the bearer of it.' 'I am entirely at your orders, my master,' I answered. 'I swear that I will faithfully remit your gift to the Khalīfah, and that he will be enchanted by it. I will also tell him that you are a good friend and that he may count on your alliance.'

Without delay the King gave orders to his chamberlains. The present which he sent by me to Hārūn al-Rashīd consisted of a large jar, half a foot high and a finger thick, carved from a single ruby of perfect colour, filled with round white pearls as large as nuts; a carpet made from the skin of a gigantic serpent with scales each as large as a dīnār, and having this virtue, that whatsoever sick man lay down upon it should be healed; two hundred balls of camphor in its purest state, each as large as a pistachio; two elephant's tusks, twelve cubits long and two cubits round the base; and lastly a beautiful girl of Sarandīb, smothered in rich jewellery.

At the same time the King gave me a letter for the Commander of the Faithful, saying: 'Make my excuses to the Khalīfah for sending so small a present and tell him that I love him with all my heart. . . . Yet, Sindbād, if you would rather stay in our kingdom, you shall be in everything our favourite and we will send another messenger to Baghdād instead of you.' 'As Allāh lives, O King of time,' I cried, 'your generosity is a royal generosity; my spirit bows beneath your gifts; but there is a boat just starting for Basrah and I am very anxious to go aboard her and to see my friends, my children and my native land once more.'

The King, who did not wish to constrain me against my will, at once sent for the captain of the ship and the merchants who would sail with me, and gave me into their safe keeping with a thousand recommendations, paying my passage money himself, and presenting me with many precious gifts, which I still keep in memory of him.

After saying farewell to the King and to all the friends whom I had made in that delightful island, I set sail and at last came, through the mercy of Allāh, safely to Basrah and thence to Baghdād. The first thing I did on landing was to hasten to the palace, where I was granted a reception by the Prince of Believers. I kissed the earth between his hands and, giving him the letter and present with which I had been intrusted, told him all my adventures from beginning to end.

When the Khalīfah had read the letter from the King of Sarandīb and examined the presents, he asked me if the monarch who had sent them was really as rich as these things seemed to imply. 'O Commander of the Faithful,' I answered, 'I can witness that the King of Sarandīb does not exaggerate, and further that he adds to his wealth both justice and wise government. He is the sole kādī in his kingdom, and the people are so contented that there is never friction between them and their ruler. Indeed he is worthy of your friendship, O King.'

'What you have told me and the letter which I have just read,' returned the Khalífah, 'prove to me that the King of Sarandíb is a good man, f.lled with wisdom and worldly knowledge. Happy are the people whom he governs, say I!' Then the Khalífah presented me with a robe of honour and rich gifts, and, after rewarding me with privileges, commanded the cleverest scribes of his palace to write down all my story, that it might be treasured among the papers of his reign.

I hastened to my own house in my own street, and lived there, surrounded by riches and respect, among my friends and relations, quite forgetting my past troubles and having no other care than to squeeze from this life all the joys of which it is capable.

Such is the story of my sixth voyage. To-morrow, dear guests, if Allāh wills, I shall tell you the tale of my seventh voyage, which is fuller of astonishing prodigies than the other six put together.

Then Sindbād the Sailor feasted his guests and dismissed them, giving a further hundred gold pieces to Sindbād the Porter, who returned home marvelling at all he had heard.

Next morning Sindbād the Landsman made his prayer and returned, as he had been asked to do, to the palace of the other Sindbād.

When all the guests were assembled and had eaten, drunken, chatted, laughed, and listened to fair music, they ranged themselves in a silent circle round their host, who described to them:

The Seventh and Last Voyage of Sindbād the Sailor

I must tell you, my dear friends, that after my return from my sixth voyage I put aside all thoughts of making any further journey; for my age was beginning to be against prolonged absences, and I had no further desire for new adventures after the dangers which I had already run. I was the richest man in all Baghdād, and the Khalífah would often send for me to hear me tell of the strange things which I had seen during my voyages.

One day, when Hārūn al-Rashīd had called me into his presence, I was on the point of beginning a recital of my travels, when he said: 'Sindbād, you must carry my answer and my present to the King of Sarandīb; none knows the way to his kingdom better than you, and he will doubtless be delighted to see you again. Make ready to start to-day, for it would be little worthy of us to keep the King of that island waiting for our answer.'

The world darkened before my eyes and I was in the limit of perplexity, yet I hid my feelings in order not to displease the Khalīfah and, although I had sworn never again to leave Baghdād, kissed the earth between his hands and told him that I was ready. He gave me ten thousand dīnārs for the expenses of my journey and intrusted me with a letter written in his own hand and the presents he intended for the King of Sarandīb. These presents were: a magnificent bed of scarlet velvet, worth an unbelievable sum of money, two other beds of different colours, a hundred robes of Kūfah and Alexandrian silk, fifty robes sewn in Baghdād, a vase of white carnelian dating from old time and enriched with the presentment of a bowman aiming at a lion, a pair of wonderful Arab horses, and other things too numerous to mention.

At this point Shahrazād saw the approach of morning and discreetly fell silent.

But when the three-hundred-and-twelfth night had come

SHE SAID:

I left Baghdād much against my will, and embarked at Basrah on board a ship which was about to set sail. At the end of two months we arrived safely at Sarandīb, and I hastened to lay the letter and the presents before the King. Seeing me again and appreciating the courtesy of the Khalīfah, that kindly monarch rejoiced and wished to keep me with him for a long while; but I would only consent to stay for a few days' rest; then, taking leave of him, I re-embarked in my ship for Basrah, loaded with further presents.

The wind favoured us, and we voyaged along pleasantly, talking among ourselves of many things; but one day, when we were a week out from the island of Sīn, where the merchants on board had traded, a terrible storm broke over our heads and heavy rain fell upon us. We hastened to cover our merchandise with canvas as a protection from the wet, and then prayed to Allāh against the dangers of our journey. While we were doing so, the captain girt up his robe and, climbing the mast, looked for a long time to right and left. He descended very yellow about the cheeks and, looking upon us with an expression of despair, silently beat himself in the face and snatched at his beard. We ran to him, asking what was the matter, and he answered: 'Pray to Allāh that He may lift us from the gulf into which we have fallen; or rather weep and say your farewells, for the current has driven us from our path and thrown us into the last seas of the world.'

Then the captain opened his sea-chest and took from it a linen bag, containing a powder not unlike crushed ashes. He wetted this substance with water and, after waiting a little, sniffed some of it up his nose; then he took a small book from the chest, intoned a few pages of it, and finally turned to us, saying: 'My magic book confirms my gravest fears. That land which you see upon the horizon is the Clime of Kings, where our lord Sulaimān lies buried (upon whom be prayer and peace!). Monsters and terrible serpents inhabit that coast, and the sea is full of gigantic fishes who can swallow down a whole ship at a single mouthful. Now you know the worst! Farewell!'

We remained frozen to the decks with horror, expectant of some fearful end. Suddenly the whole boat was lifted up and then cast down again among the waves, while a cry more terrible than thunder rose from the sea. The ocean boiled beside us, and we saw a marine monster, as great as a mountain, plunging towards us, followed by a second greater still, and a third larger than the first two put together. This last creature leaped suddenly from the gulf of the sea and, opening a mouth like a valley between two hills, swallowed our ship to three-quarters of its length, with all that was in it. I had just time to run to the top of the slanting deck and leap thence into the sea, before the monster drew the whole vessel down into its belly and disappeared into the depths with its two companions.

I succeeded in clambering upon one of the planks which had started from the ship under the monster's jaws and, after some hours of tossing to and fro, was thrown on an island, covered with fruit trees and watered by a clear and pleasant river. As I wished to regain my own country, and as I saw that the river ran very fast indeed, making a noise which could be heard far off, the idea came to me to construct a raft, as I had done on the island of jewels, and to let myself be carried down by the current. 'If I save myself in that way,'

I thought, 'all will be for the best; and I swear never again in all my life to allow the word *voyage* upon my tongue. If I perish in the attempt, still all will be for the best, as I shall be quit of danger and privation for ever.' After I had eaten a little fruit, I collected a great quantity of the larger branches of a tree which I did not know, but which turned out afterwards to be sandal-wood of the very finest quality. As I had no ropes, I bound these together with the flexible stems of certain climbing plants and thus constructed a very large raft, which I loaded with fruit for my journey. I embarked, crying: 'If I am saved, it will be by Allāh!' and had hardly pushed my craft from off the bank when it was hurried down stream at a prodigious rate, so that I fell, powerless with vertigo like a drunken fowl, on to the heaps of fruit.

When I came to myself, I looked about me and was dazed with a noise as of thunder; the river was one gallop of boiling foam, borne more quickly than the wind towards a yawning precipice, which I heard rather than saw.

Giving myself up for lost, I clung with all my strength to the branches of the raft and, shutting my eyes so as not to see the mangling of my own body, prayed to Allāh before my death. Suddenly, as I was over the very lip of the abyss, I felt the raft halted upon the water and opened my eyes to see that my craft had been caught in an immense net thrown by men from the bank. I was dragged towards the shore and lifted from the meshes of the net more dead than alive, while my raft was pulled up upon dry land.

As I lay shivering upon the ground, an old man with a white beard advanced towards me and, giving me courteous welcome, covered me with warm garments which comforted me very much.

At this point Shahrazād saw the approach of morning and discreetly fell silent.

But when the three-hundred-and-thirteenth night had come

SHE SAID:

My strength came back under the solicitous rubbing of the old man, so that I was able to sit up, although I could not speak. My saviour supported me on his arm and led me slowly to a hammām, where I was given a bath which quite restored my spirit, and exquisite perfumes to smell and pour upon my body. Then the old man conducted me to his own house, where his family rejoiced at my coming and received me in all friendship. I was seated upon a couch in the reception hall and served with excellent food and a fresh drink of water scented with flowers. Incense was burnt about me and slaves brought warm perfumed water for my hands and napkins hemmed with silk for my beard and lips. When I was well restored by all their attentions, my host took me to a well-furnished chamber and discreetly left me alone, providing me with slaves who visited me from time to time to see that I lacked nothing.

I was entertained in this way, without being asked any question, for three whole days, until my strength had completely returned to me and my heart become quiet; then the old man sat down beside me and greeted me courteously, saying: 'O guest, may your sojourn among us be calm and pleasurable. I give thanks to Allāh that He placed me upon your path to save you from the precipice. Now will you tell me who you are and whence you come?' I confounded myself in thanks to the old man for having saved my life and for his subsequent entertainment of me, and then said: 'I am called Sindbād the Sailor, because of the many voyages I have made upon the sea. Those strange things which I have seen would serve as a lesson for the attentive reader even were they written with a needle upon the corner of an eye.' With that I told the old man the story of my life from beginning to end, without omitting a single detail.

For a full hour he sat silent from astonishment, but at length raised his head, saying: 'Now, dear guest, I advise you to sell your merchandise without further delay, for, apart from its excellent quality, it is a great rarity here.'

I was astonished at these words and had no idea what they meant, since I had been cast naked among these people; yet, being unwilling to let slip any opportunity, I put on a knowing air as I answered: 'That may well be.' 'Take no care for your goods, my child,' continued my host, 'you have but to come down with me to the market and I will do the rest. If a suitable bid is made, we will accept it; if not, we will keep your valuables in my storehouses until we can get a better price.'

I did not let my perplexity appear, but answered: 'O venerable uncle, whatever seems good to you is right in my eyes. After all you have done for me, I have no thought which is not yours.' With that I rose and went with him to the market.

When we arrived, I received the greatest surprise of my life; for there was my raft, surrounded by brokers and merchants who were respectfully examining it with many wise nods. On all sides I heard such expressions as : 'Yā Allāh, it is a marvellous quality of sandal! Never have we seen so fine a wood.' Then at last I understood in what my merchandise consisted, and thought it fitting to assume a proud and reserved expression.

Soon my venerable host bade the chief broker begin the auction, which he did, opening the bidding at a thousand dīnārs. 'This raft of sandal-wood for a thousand dīnārs!' he cried, and my friend exclaimed: 'Two thousand!' and another cried: 'Three thousand!' When ten thousand was bid, the broker looked at me, saying: 'There is no advance upon ten thousand.' 'I will not sell for that,' I answered.

'My child,' said the old man to me, 'our market is not very prosperous just now and all goods have fallen in value. You had better accept this price. Or, if you like, I will add a hundred dīnārs and buy the lot for ten thousand one hundred.' 'As Allāh lives, I answered, 'for you and for you alone, good uncle, I consent to sell.' At once my host ordered his slaves to carry all the wood to his storehouses, and conducted me back to his house, where he paid me the money agreed upon and fastened it for me in a strong locked box, thanking me all the while for my benevolence.

Later a cloth was spread for us and we ate and drank with merry conversation. When we had washed our hands, the old man said: 'My child, there is a favour which I beg you to grant me.' 'Any favour were easy from me to you, uncle,' I answered, and he continued: 'My child, I am a very old man and have no son; yet I have a beautiful young daughter who will be extremely rich when I die. If you will promise to remain with us, I will gladly marry you to this girl, and then you can be master of all I possess and all I direct in the city; you will inherit both my authority and my wealth.'

I lowered my head and remained silent, so that he continued: 'Do what I ask and you shall not lose by it. If you will, I modify my condition and only stipulate that you remain here during my lifetime; after my death you shall be free to take my daughter with you to your own country.' 'As Allāh lives, venerable father,' I replied, 'I have no opinion other than your opinion, and am more than willing for you to direct my Destiny, since every time I have tried to do so myself evil has followed. I gladly consent to this marriage.'

At this point Shahrazād saw the approach of morning and discreetly fell silent.

But when the three-hundred-and-fourteenth night had come

SHE SAID:

The old man rejoiced exceedingly at my consent and sent for the kādī and witnesses, who married me to the daughter of my host. A great feast was held, and at last I was conducted into the presence of my bride, whose face I had not yet seen. I found her admirable both in disposition and beauty, and was delighted to discover that she wore jewels, ornaments, silks and brocades, worth thousands and thousands of gold pieces. We learned to love each other and lived together for a long time with sport and joy.

At length my father-in-law passed into the peace and mercy of Allāh, and we gave him a sumptuous funeral. I inherited all his possessions; his slaves became my slaves and his goods my goods, and all the merchants of the city named me their chief in place of the dead, so that I had occasion to observe the customs and manners of the place more closely than I had done before.

One day it came to my notice that the people of the city suffered a change every year in Spring: this physical process lasted for a day, and at the end of it the men of the place had wings upon their shoulders and could fly high up into the vault of the air. During the time which this change lasted they were never out of the sky and left only their women and children in the city, because these did not grow wings. Though this circumstance was astonishing enough, I soon got used to it; but in course of time I began to feel shame to be the only wingless man in the city and to have to stay down with the women and children. I tried to find out how to grow wings on my shoulders, but my fellows either could not or would not tell me. I knew dark hours of mortification that I, Sindbād the Sailor, should not be known also as Sindbād the Airman.

One day I took aside a certain merchant, whom I had helped in different ways, and begged him to allow me to cling to him when he next went aloft and thus to experience a new kind of voyage. At first the man would not listen to me, but at length I cajoled him into consenting and, after joyfully telling my wife what I was about to do, took hold of his waist and was carried into the air by the oarage of his wings.

At first and for a long time we went straight up and mounted so high that I could hear the angels singing their holy songs under the vault of Heaven. This wonderful music roused so great a religious emotion in me that I cried: 'Praise be to Allāh in the deep of the skies! Let all creatures glorify and adore Him!'

Hardly had I pronounced these words when the winged man fell through the air like a thunderbolt, with frightful cursing, and descended so rapidly that I fainted away. I should infallibly have been dashed to pieces if we had not fallen upon the top of a mountain, where my carrier left me, with a devilish glance, and disappeared in the air upon his wings. Left alone upon this deserted peak, I knew not what to do nor how to return to my wife; therefore I cried: 'There is no might nor power save in Allāh! Each time I escape from one misfortune, I stumble upon a greater. Surely I deserve all that happens to me!' I sat down sadly upon a rock, trying to think of some escape from my present dilemma, and presently I saw two young boys approaching me, whose beauty was more than human. Each held a wand of red gold in his hand and leaned upon it as he walked.

I rose to my feet with alacrity and, walking towards them, wished them peace. They answered my greeting kindly, so that I was encouraged to continue: 'The blessings of Allāh be upon you, O marvellous youths! Tell me who you are and what you are doing.' 'We are lovers of the true God,' they answered, and then, without further words, one of them pointed out a certain direction to me and, leaving me his gold wand, disappeared hand in hand with his companion.

I took the wand and began walking in the way which had been shown to me, thinking all the time of the surpassing beauty of my guides. Suddenly, on turning the corner of a rock, I saw a gigantic serpent holding in its mouth a man, of whom it had already swallowed three-quarters. The victim's head cried out to me: 'O passer-by, save me from the maw of this serpent, and you shall never repent of your goodness!' I ran up behind the snake and dealt him so well aimed a blow with the red gold wand that he lay dead upon the ground. Then I stretched forth my hand and helped the man out of the belly which had swallowed him.

Looking closely at the man I had rescued, I recognised him for the flyer who had so nearly dashed me to pieces by hurling himself from the vault of the sky to the top of the mountain. Unwilling to bear malice, I said gently: 'Is it thus that friends behave to friends?' 'First I must thank you for saving me,' he answered, 'and then I will tell you something which you do not know. My fall from the sky was occasioned by your unfortunate mention of the Name. The Name has that effect upon all of us, and we never speak it.' 'Do not blame me for my perfectly innocent words,' I answered. 'I promise not to mention the Name if only you will consent to take me back to my own house.' Without answering, the flyer took me upon his back and, in the twinkling of an eye, set me down upon the terrace of my own house.

When my wife saw me again after so long an absence, she thanked Allāh for my safety, and then said: 'We must no longer dwell among these people, for they are the brothers of devils.' 'How then did your father live with them?' I asked, and she answered: 'My father was not of them; he did not behave as they behave, and he did not lead their life. As he is dead, I suggest that we should leave this wicked city, after selling such property and houses as we have in it.'

At this point Shahrazād saw the approach of morning and discreetly fell silent.

But when the three-hundred-and-fifteenth night had come

SHE SAID:

'You must gain much money, so that we can buy fair merchandise and depart to see your family and friends in Baghdād, where we can live in peace, safety, and submission to Allāh.'

Using all the ability which experience had given me, I sold my property bit by bit and realised a hundred for one on each gold piece which the things had cost my dead father-in-law. I bought merchandise and, hiring a vessel for myself and my wife, made a good trading voyage to Basrah. Thence we went up stream and soon entered Baghdād, the City of Peace.

At once I took my wife with me to my own house in my own street, where we were both received with cordial expressions of joy. I put my affairs in order, distributed my remaining merchandise among various shops, and could at last sit down calmly to receive the congratulations of my friends; they informed me that this last and longest of my voyages had kept me away from home for twenty-seven years. I told all those who gathered round me the story of my adventures and vowed that I would never leave Baghdād again; an oath which, as you may see for yourselves, I have scrupulously kept. You must not think that I omitted to give long thanks to Allāh for having saved me from so many and so great dangers, in spite of the numerous occasions on which I had tempted His providence, and brought me back to my family and friends.

Such, dear guests, was my seventh and last voyage, which definitely cured me of any further desire for travel.

When Sindbād the Sailor had finished his tale, amid a hushed and attentive audience, he turned to Sindbād the Porter, saying: 'Now, my friend, consider the labours which I have accomplished and the difficulties which I have overcome, and tell me if your estate of porter has not made for a more tranquil life than that which Destiny reserved for me. It is true that you have remained poor while I have become fabulously rich, but has not each of us been rewarded according to his efforts?' Sindbād the Porter kissed his host's hands, saying: 'As Allāh is with you, my master, excuse the ill-timed inconsequence of my song!'

Sindbād the Sailor gave a feast to his guests, which lasted thirty nights, and then appointed Sindbād the Porter to be his major-domo. The two lived together in perfect friendship and joy until they were visited by That which breathes upon delight, which snaps the links of friendship, which destroys palaces and raises tombs where once they stood: by bitter Death. Glory be to the Living who dies not!

When Shahrazād, the wazīr's daughter, had finished the tale of Sindbād the Sailor, she saw the approach of morning and fell silent for very weariness.

Little Dunyazād, who had listened to all the astonishing narrative with wide-open eyes, jumped up from her carpet and threw her arms about her sister's neck, crying: 'O Shahrazād, how sweet and tender, how pure and delicious, how fresh and savoury have been all your words! What a bold, wonderful, and terrible man Sindbād the Sailor must have been!'

Shahrazād smiled at her sister, saying: 'The whole story is as nothing to that which I would tell you to-morrow night, if Allāh and the good pleasure of the King should spare my life.'

Then King Shahryār, who had found the voyages of Sindbād much longer than the one which he had made with his brother Shahzamān, when the Jinnī appeared to them with his box in the grassland beside the sea, turned to Shahrazād, saying: 'In truth I do not see what further tale you can tell me. I should like one well-stuffed with poems, such as you have already promised me. If you do not care to fulfil that promise, your head shall join the others which have gone before it.' 'Strangely enough,' answered Shahrazād, 'I have been holding in reserve for you, O auspicious King, a tale which will satisfy you completely. It is infinitely more delicious than any of the others which I have told you. You may judge for yourself by hearing the title: The Tale of Zumurrud the Beautiful, and Alī Shār, Son of Glory.'

'I will not kill her until after that one,' thought King Shahryār. Then he took her in his arms and passed the rest of the night with her.

In the morning he rose and went down to his hall of justice, where the dīwān was filled with a crowd of wazīrs, amīrs, chamberlains, and people of the palace. Among them stood Shahrazād's father, the grand wazīr, who held his daughter's shroud over his arm and made no doubt that she was already dead. But the King said nothing upon this subject; instead he continued to judge, to raise folk to employment, to take away office, and to govern the kingdom until nightfall. Then, when the dīwān rose, he re-entered his palace, leaving the grand wazīr still in a state of great perplexity.

King Shahryār went to the apartment of Shahrazād, and they did together that which was usual for them.

But when the three-hundred-and-sixteenth-night had come

LITTLE DUNYAZĀD waited till the act was finished and then cried from her carpet:

'O sister, why do you not begin the tale of Zumurrud the Beautiful, and Alī Shār, Son of Glory?'

Shahrazād answered smiling: 'I only wait for the permission of our charming King.'

'You may begin!' cried Shahryār.

And Shahrazād said:

The Tale of Zumurrud the Beautiful, and of Alī Shār, Son of Glory

IT is related, O auspicious King, that there was once, in the antiquity of time and the passage of the age and of the moment, a rich merchant in the land of Khurāsān, called Glory, who had a son more beautiful than the full moon, whose name was Alī Shār.

One day the merchant Glory, who was far advanced in age, felt threatened by the sickness of death; so he called his son to him, saying: 'My son, the end of my Destiny is in sight and I wish to make a recommendation to you.' 'What recommendation is that, my father?' answered Alī Shār in a sorrowful voice, and Glory continued: 'I advise you never to bind yourself in any relation or have to do at all with the world which I am leaving; for the world is like a forge: if it does not burn you with its fire, or put out your eyes with its sparks, it will certainly suffocate you with its smoke. A poet has said of it:

> On the black road of life think not to find
> Either a friend or lover to your mind;
>   If you must love, oh, then, love solitude,
> For solitude alone is true and kind.

Another said:

> The picture of this world for all to see,
> Is painted on both sides? That well may be.
>   Hypocrisy and lies are on the front
> And on the back lies and hypocrisy.

Another has said:

> Preposterous futility
>   Is the world's wear,
>   Its very coat.
>   If Allāh sends
>   One or two friends
>   When the world's bare,
>   Then use them sparingly
>   As antidote
> For the world's care.'

When young Alī Shār heard these words of his dying father, he said: 'O father, I will in all things obey you. Have you any further advice to give me?' Then said the merchant Glory: 'Do good when you can, but do not expect to be paid either with gratitude or good in return for your good. Also remember, my child, that an occasion for doing good does not arise every day.' 'I will obey you,' said Alī Shār. 'Are these all your recommendations?' The merchant continued: 'Do not riot away the riches I leave you, for a man's only claim to consideration is his money. A poet has said:

> Those who abused my open hand of old,
> Now it is closed are still abusing it;
> I have made enemies in making gold,
> But many more by losing it.'

Then the old man went on: 'Do not neglect the advice of those with more experience than yourself, and never think it time lost when you go out of your way to seek counsel of the wise. A poet has said:

> If you your face would find,
> One glass will do;
> But you need two
> To see yourself behind.

And my last word is this: beware of wine. It is the root of all evil, it steals away the brain and makes the drinker a thing for laughter and derision. Such is my advice to you, given from the ultimate threshold, my dear son. Follow these precepts and my blessing shall follow you.'

The venerable merchant Glory shut his eyes for a moment and gathered together all his strength. Then he lifted his index finger to the level of his glance and recited his act of Faith, on the wings of which his spirit passed into the infinite mercy of Allāh.

After the son and all the folk of the house had wept bitterly, the rich and the poor, the great and the small followed the funeral of the old man. And, when his body had been laid in the earth, these words were written upon the stone of his tomb:

> When I was alive
> I was dust which was,
> But now I am dust in dust
> I am dust which never was.

So much for the merchant Glory.

After his father's death Alī Shār went on trading in the principal shop of the market and scrupulously followed the advice which had been given him, especially in so far as it concerned his relations with his kind, for a whole year; but at the end of that time he allowed himself to be led away by lewd lads, sons of harlots, shameless bastards. He took to the company of these with frenzy and knew their mothers and their sisters, who were wanton wretches, daughters of dogs; he plunged up to the neck in debauchery, swimming in wine and a wicked expense of gold, in the opposite way from salvation. As his mind was not healthy, he argued to himself that it was necessary for him to use the riches which his father had left him if he did not wish, in his turn, to leave them to others.

He followed this line of thought so consistently, joining night to day at both ends with excess, that he soon found it necessary to sell his shop, his house, his furniture and all his garments. And a time came when he wore all his worldly goods upon his back.

Then he was able to see his folly clearly and understand the excellence of his father's advice; for the friends, whom he had sumptuously entertained and at whose doors he now knocked, one by one made some excuse to show him out. One day, when he had no food left, he was obliged to go forth from the miserable khān at which he lodged and to beg his way from house to house. His mendicant round took him past the market, and there he saw a crowd collected in a circle. He went towards these people to see what was happening and saw, in the centre of a group of brokers, merchants and purchasers, a young white slave of elegant and delightful appearance.

At this point Shahrazād saw the approach of morning and discreetly fell silent.

But when the three-hundred-and-seventeenth night had come

SHE SAID:

She was five feet high and had roses instead of cheeks, well-placed breasts and, ah! a croup! You could apply to her, without fear of exaggeration, these words of the poet:

> That her hair is dusk,
> That her breath is musk,
>   Have I found to say;
> That pearls in dew
> Were melted, too,
>   In a secret way
> To cause her breasts,
> Where an argentine
> Pale moonlight rests,
> To move and shine
>   Have I found to say.

> These things were not
> Too fair for speech,
> I have sung of each.
> Of her bottom, what
>   Have I found to say?

When Alī Shăr cast a glance upon the beauties of this child, he
marvelled at them and in his marvel stood stock-still, forgetting for
a little time his misery. He mingled with the crowd of merchants, and
they supposed that he would acquire the slave with the riches left
by the merchant Glory; for as yet they knew nothing of his ruin.

The chief broker took his place by the side of the slave and cried
across the sea of craning heads: 'Come, my masters, merchants all,
urbane citizens, free traders of the desert! Here is the queen of moons,
the pearl of pearls, the noble and modest virgin Zumurrud, the
excitation of desires, the garden of all flowers! Open the auction! Let
no one be afraid to open the auction! You have before you the queen
of moons, the shy and virgin Zumurrud, the garden of all flowers!'

'I open at five hundred dīnārs!' cried one merchant. 'And ten!'
cried another. A deformed and hideous old man with bleary blue
eyes, whose name was Rashīd al-Dīn, squeaked: 'And a hundred!' But
when a voice said: 'And ten!' he raised the bid to a thousand dīnārs.

The other purchasers kept silent, so the broker turned to the
slave's owner and asked if the old man's offer would suit. 'It suits
me,' answered the owner, 'but I have sworn not to let this slave be
bought by any to whom she will not herself consent to be sold. Ask
her consent, O broker.' 'O queen of moons,' said the broker to
Zumurrud, 'do you want to belong to this admirable old man, this
venerable Rashīd al-Dīn?' Zumurrud the Beautiful glanced at the
man who was pointed out to her, whose ugliness I have tried to
paint for you, and turned away with a gesture of disgust, crying: 'O
broker, do you not know that an old poet, who was yet by no means
as hideous as this Rashīd al-Dīn, once said:

> I prayed to kiss her scarlet mouth;
>   She did not take offence,
>   But only showed indifference.
> The corner of her scarlet mouth
>   Dropped this sole answer to my prayer:
>   "I do not love white hair
> Or wet white cotton in my scarlet mouth"?'

'As Allāh lives,' said the broker to Zumurrud, 'you are right to refuse. A thousand dīnārs is no price at all. You are worth at least ten thousand in my opinion.' He turned towards the crowd of purchasers and asked if anyone wished to buy the slave at the price already offered. 'I do!' cried a voice. Zumurrud looked at the owner of this voice and saw that, though he was not so terribly ugly as Rashīd al-Dīn and had eyes which were neither blue nor bleary, his beard had been dyed red to make him look younger than he really was. 'O shame,' she cried, 'to paint pictures upon the face of eld!' And straightway she extemporised these lines:

> I might have taken you, I might
> Have given you respect
> As to an elderly religious saint,
> If you had let your beard stay white;
> But now that it is decked
> With scarlet paint,
> You have become a horror absolute
> That would make any woman drop her fruit.

Hearing these verses, the broker said to Zumurrud: 'As Allāh lives, you have truth on your side!'

As soon as the second proposition had been refused, a third merchant offered to buy for the same price; but Zumurrud looked at the bidder and, finding that he was blind of one eye, burst out laughing and said: 'Do you not know the rhymed riddle about the one-eyed man? Listen:

> Tell me the difference if you can
> Between a liar and a one-eyed man.
> You cannot? Yet I shall not call you dense,
> Because there is not any difference.'

Then the broker showed her a fourth bidder; but, seeing that he was a small man with a beard which fell down to his navel, she said: 'As for this hairy little fellow, my opinion of him is summed up in these words of the poet:

> He had a mighty beard to left and right . . .
> She was as sad as a cold winter night.'

When the broker saw that she would not accept any of those who wished to buy her, he said to Zumurrud: 'Dear mistress, look over all these merchants and noble purchasers and see if there are any who may have the luck to please you, so that I may offer you to them.'

The delightful child closely regarded all the members of the crowd, one by one, and, when her gaze fell upon Alī Shār, a violent love for him was lighted in her heart; for he was indeed of extraordinary beauty, and none might look upon him except passionately. Zumurrud quickly pointed him out to the broker, saying: 'That is the purchaser I want, that youth with the gentle face and swaying body; for I find that he is much to my taste, that his blood mingles already with mine, and that he is lighter than a breeze from the north. It was of him the poet said:

> We who are young, they who are old,
> Have looked upon your grace,
> O youth.
> Behold,
> In selfish ruth,
> A thousand victims bring a thousand veils
> To hide your face.

Another said of him:

> Will you not understand, my lord?
> Beauty like yours is not to hoard,
> But to be thrown adrift, a golden joy,
>   My lord, my gentle boy.
> Your thighs are heavy and your waist is small:
> Do you not feel the need for love at all,
>   My lord, my gentle boy?
> To have your buttocks press upon my knee
> Is heavy ecstasy,
> And when you rise I do not feel relief,
> But heavier grief,
>   My lord, my gentle boy.
> God says to feed the hungry in their need,
> And murder is not praised by any creed,
>   My lord, my gentle boy.

Another has said:

> His cheeks are carmine silk,
> His spittle a sweet milk
>   To cure the heart;

His eyes' black honey puzzles those
Who build a tale in prose;
His eyes' black honey puzzles worse,
    Strange wistful race apart,
The men who carve an ecstasy in verse;
And then the limbs which these have decked
Can make the greatest architect
    Mistrustful of his art.

Another has said:

I sipped wine from his tongue
And I thought the world was young
    And I played the very devil for his curls' sake.
Oh, the camphor of his teeth
And the amber of his breath . . .
    They turned him out of heaven for the girls' sake.

Another has said:

Gross fools with heavy wits,
May they be blasted soon
With all their censuring!
Dare to accuse him of a fault at times;
As if the moon
Were not a perfect thing
Because she shines and flits
In different parts of heaven's vault at times.

Another has said:

This fawn with curling hair
And cheeks of sunset rose,
I swear
Promised to meet me.
Yet he shut his eyes as he said yes;
It is after the hour, and I confess
I think that he will cheat me. . . .
But suppose. . . .

And yet another said of him:

To-day
My friends object:
"How can you love a cheek with so strong down?"

"When ruddy Eden apples grow there,
Can you expect
The shady clusters not to show there,
From which they're grown?"
I say.'

The broker was astonished to find so much talent in a slave so
young. This he admitted to the slave's owner, and the latter said to
him: 'I can understand your surprise at so much beauty and so much
wit; but I would have you know that this miraculous maiden, who
shames the stars and sun, is not only conversant with all the most
delicate and complicated stanzas of the poets, but is an excellent
poetess herself. Also she can write with seven pens, the seven
separate characters, and her hands are more precious than a guarded
treasure. She knows the whole art of embroidery and silk weaving,
so that each carpet or curtain which she makes sells in the market for
fifty dīnārs. Note, also, that she only takes eight days to make the
most beautiful of carpets or the most sumptuous curtain, so that he
who buys her will certainly recoup all his expense in a few months.'

The broker lifted his arms in admiration, crying: 'How happy the
man who shall take this pearl to his home and guard her as his secret
treasure!' Then he went up to Alī Shār and, bowing almost to the
earth before him, kissed his hand and said . . .

At this point Shahrazād saw the approach of morning and
discreetly fell silent.

But when the three-hundred-and-nineteenth night had come

SHE SAID:

'My master, it is great luck for you to be able to buy this treasure
at a hundredth part of her true worth. I see that the Giver has not
been niggardly in blessing you. May the girl bring you happiness
and good fortune!'

Alī Shār lowered his head, laughing to himself at the irony of
Destiny, and whispering, as it were, in his own ear: 'As Allāh lives,
they think that I am rich enough to buy this slave when I cannot
enter into negotiation for a crust of bread! I will say neither yes nor
no, lest I be covered with shame before all these merchants.' So he
cast down his eyes and did not speak.

Zumurrud sent him a glance of encouragement and then, as he

did not see it, said to the broker: 'Lead me to him by the hand, for I wish to speak to him myself and persuade him to buy me. I am determined to belong to him and to no other.'

When the broker did as she requested, the maiden stood before the young man in all her living beauty, and said to him: 'O master of my love, O youth who has lit a fire within my body, why do you not offer the price? Why do you not offer more, if you think that I am worth it? Or less? I wish to be your slave at any price.' Alī Shār sadly shook his head, saying: 'There is no obligation to buy, just as there is no obligation to sell.' 'Master of my love,' answered Zumurrud, 'I see that you find the price of a thousand dīnārs too high; offer nine hundred and I shall belong to you.' Then, when he continued to shake his head and say nothing, she continued: 'Buy me for eight hundred,' and then: 'Buy me for seven hundred,' and at last: 'Buy me for one hundred.' Said Alī Shār: 'I have not quite that round sum in my pocket.' 'How much do you need to make it up?' she asked, laughing. 'If you cannot find the whole hundred to-day, you may pay later.' 'My mistress,' he replied, 'I have not a hundred dīnārs; I have not one dīnār. As Allāh lives, I have no more a white piece than a red piece, a dirham of silver than a dīnār of gold. You lose your time with me; go, find another buyer.'

When Zumurrud understood that the young man was without funds, she said: 'Buy me all the same. Strike me upon the arm, wrap me in your mantle, and pass one of your arms about my waist; for those are the actions of acceptance.' Alī Shār hastened to do these things, and, while his arm was passing about her waist, she slipped a purse from her pocket into his hands, saying: 'Here are a thousand dīnārs. Offer nine hundred of them to my master and keep a hundred of them to satisfy our more pressing needs.' So Alī Shār paid nine hundred dīnārs to the merchant and took the slave with him to his lodging.

Zumurrud showed no surprise at finding that her master lived in a miserable little room, furnished only with a wretched, torn and ancient mat; instead she handed him a further thousand dīnārs in a second purse, saying: 'Run to the market and buy the finest furniture and carpets, the most delicate food and drink, and also bring me back a large square of Damascus silk of the rarest quality, garnet in tint, with reels of gold thread, silver thread, and silks of seven different colours. Also, do not forget large needles and a gold thimble for my middle finger.'

When Alī Shār brought back these things to her, she spread the carpets on the floor, arranged the mattresses and couches, tidied the chamber, and then set the cloth, after having lighted torches.

They sat down together and ate and drank and were happy. Then they lay down upon the new bed and satisfied each other, lying all night close clasped in each other's arms, until morning brought an end to their pure delights and gay actions. Their love grew greater by proof, the words of it bit deeply into the heart of each.

When full morning had come, the diligent Zumurrud lost no time in setting to work. She took the garnet Damascus silk and, in a few days, had made a curtain of it, on which were presented with infinite art the forms of birds and beasts. There was no animal in the world, great or small, which she had not drawn with cunning silk upon that curtain. So lifelike was the embroidery that the footed beasts seemed to move and the birds to sing. In the middle of the curtain were great trees, loaded with their fruits, and the shadows of them were so faithfully shown that the eye of the beholder rested suddenly on delightful freshness. All this was achieved in eight days, neither more nor less! Glory be to Him who has given such dexterity to the fingers of His creatures!

As soon as the curtain was finished, Zumurrud glazed it, polished it, folded it, and gave it to Alī Shār, saying: 'Carry this to the market and sell it at any shop for not less than fifty dīnārs. Only be prepared not to give it up to any chance wayfarer who is not known in the market, otherwise a cruel separation will come upon us. We have enemies who lie in wait for us; therefore beware of the stranger.' Alī Shār approved her condition and, going to the market, sold the marvellous curtain for fifty dīnārs to a merchant who was known to him.

At this point Shahrazād saw the approach of morning and discreetly fell silent.

But when the three-hundred-and-twentieth night had come

SHE SAID:

Again he bought enough silk and gold thread and silver thread to make a new curtain or some fair carpet, and carried all to Zumurrud, who set to work with so much will that, at the end of eight days, she had completed a carpet even more beautiful than the first, which also fetched the sum of fifty dīnārs. For a whole year the two lived in this way, eating and drinking and not forgetting to satisfy their love, which grew greater and greater every day.

One morning Alī Shār left the house, carrying a packet in which was a carpet made by Zumurrud, and walked to the market to offer his ware to the merchants. He handed it to the broker, and the latter was crying it for sale in front of the shops when a Christian passed that way: one of those folk who swarm at the gates of markets and importune buyers and sellers with offers of assistance.

This Christian came up to Alī Shār and the broker, and offered sixty dīnārs for the carpet, but Alī Shār, who hated and mistrusted his tribe and also recalled the advice of Zumurrud, said that he would not sell. Then the Christian offered a hundred dīnārs, and the broker whispered in Alī Shār's ear not to let so excellent a chance escape. The broker had already been bribed with ten dīnārs by the Christian to give this advice; he worked so well upon Alī Shār that the latter at last consented to sell for a hundred dīnārs, took the money with a certain apprehension, and left the market.

On his way home he looked round and saw that the Christian was following him; therefore he stopped and asked: 'What are you doing in this district where people of your kind do not come, O Christian?'

'Excuse me, my master,' answered the other, 'but I have an errand to do at the end of this street. Allāh preserve you!' Alī Shār continued on his way, but, happening to look round as he reached the door of his lodging, he saw that the Christian had followed him by a side-street and was coming towards him. 'Why are you following me in this way, evil Christian?' he cried angrily. 'O my master,' said the other, 'it is quite by chance that I am here. But now I beg you to give me a mouthful of water, for I am burning with thirst. Allāh will reward you!' Thinking to himself: 'As Allāh lives, it shall never be said that a Mussulmān refused a drink to a mad dog!', Alī Shār entered the house, took up a water-jar, and was about to return to the Christian when Zumurrud, who had heard the door opening, came out to meet him, much moved by his long absence. As she kissed him, she said: 'Why are you so late in coming back to-day? Tell me, have you sold the carpet, and was it to some reputed merchant, or to a stranger?' Visibly troubled, Alī Shār made answer: 'I am a little late because the market was very full, but I managed to sell the carpet to a merchant of my acquaintance.' 'As Allāh lives,' said Zumurrud doubtfully, 'my heart is not easy. Why are you carrying that jar?' 'I am going to give a drink to the broker, who came back with me,' answered Alī Shār; but this reply did not satisfy the slave, so that, when he had gone out, she anxiously intoned these lines:

> Poor silly heart,
> You think a kiss is deathless;
> Do you not see eclipse
> Standing a little apart,
> Breathless,
> Finger to lips?

On returning to the Christian, Alī Shār found that he had come into the vestibule by the open door. The world darkened before his eyes, and he cried: 'What are you doing there, dog and son of a dog? How did you dare enter the house without my leave?' 'Excuse me, master,' answered the Christian, 'I was forced to cross the threshold, being worn out with walking and unable to stand upright. Besides, there is no great difference between the door and the vestibule. As soon as I have taken breath I will go away. Do not thrust me forth and Allāh will not thrust you forth!' With that he took the jar from Alī Shār's hands, drank what he needed, and returned it to his host, who remained standing until the unwelcome guest should choose to depart. But when an hour passed without the Christian offering to move, Alī Shār cried out in a rage: 'Will you be gone now?' 'Master,' said the Christian, 'I see that you are not of those who delight in doing a good deed to one who will remember it all his life; not one of those whom the poet mourned when he wrote:

> Gone are the givers
> Whose hands were rivers,
> Refreshed like rivers before you could think;
> Now the world is a miser
> Who says: "Who must buy, sir,"
> When a broken-down wayfarer asks for a drink.

I have quenched my thirst with the water of your house, but hunger so tortures me at this moment that I would be very content with the scraps of your last meal, even if they turned out only to be a crust of dry bread and an onion.' 'Not another word!' cried Alī Shār, more furious than ever. 'Be gone! There is nothing left in the house!' Without moving, the other answered: 'Pardon me, my lord, but if there is nothing left in the house, you still have the hundred dīnārs which you received for your carpet; I conjure you, in Allāh's name, to buy me a simple cheese-cake at the nearest market, that it may not be said that I left your house without there being bread and salt between us.'

'Past doubt this evil Christian is extravagantly mad,' thought Alī Shār. 'I will throw him out of doors and set the dogs of the street upon him.' As he was about to take hold of him, the Christian said: 'I only want a single piece of bread and a single onion to appease my hunger; you must not go to any great expense for me, since the wise man is content with little. As the poet said:

> A crust of dry bread is enough for the wise,
> But a city's supplies
> Of stuffed golden mutton
> Cannot feed the desire of a glutton.'

Alī Shār saw that he would have to comply; therefore, telling the Christian to wait where he was without moving, he left the house, locking the door after him and taking away the key in his pocket. At the market he bought cheese roast with honey, cucumbers, bananas, pastries and bread fresh from the oven, and carried them back to the Christian, saying: 'Eat!' But this unpleasant guest excused himself, saying: 'What generosity, my lord! You have brought enough for ten persons; it is too much. Honour me by sharing my repast.' 'I am not hungry; eat alone,' answered Alī Shār, but the Christian answered: 'The wisdom of nations teaches us that he who refuses to eat with his guest is undoubtedly an ill-born bastard.'

At this point Shahrazād saw the approach of morning and discreetly fell silent.

But when the three-hundred-and-twenty-first night had come

SHE SAID:

When he heard this unanswerable remark, Alī Shār dared refuse no longer; so he sat down by the Christian's side and began to eat with him, letting his mind run the while upon other matters. The Christian profited by his host's inattention to peel a banana and, after splitting it, to slip between the two halves a dose of pure banj mixed with extract of opium, sufficient to send an elephant to sleep for a year. This banana he dipped in the white honey sauce of the excellent roast cheese and offered it to Alī Shār, saying: 'For the truth of your Faith, my lord, accept this succulent banana which I have prepared for you.' Alī Shār, wishing to be done with the matter, took the fruit and swallowed it, but hardly had the mouthful reached his stomach than he fell back senseless. The Christian leaped to his feet like a flayed wolf and bounded into the street, where certain men waited in hiding with a mule. Beside the animal stood old Rashīd al-Dīn, the lecher with blue and bleary eyes whom Zumurrud had spurned and who had sworn to take her by force whatever happened. You must know that he was a base Christian, who only professed the faith of Islām to obtain equal privileges in the market with the other merchants; the Christian who had just drugged Alī Shār was the brother of Rashīd, and his name was Barsūm.

Barsūm hastened to inform his brother of the success of their plan, and the two Christians, followed by the other men, entered Alī Shār's lodging and rushed into the chamber at the side, which the young man had hired as a harīm for Zumurrud. In less time than it takes to tell they gagged the beautiful girl and, throwing her body across the mule, set off so swiftly that in a few minutes they reached old Rashīd's house.

The senile villain had Zumurrud carried into the most retired room and, when her gag had been removed, sat down beside her, saying: 'You are now in my power, beautiful Zumurrud, and it will take more than a rascal like Alī Shār to get you back again. Before you lie down in my arms and prove my valiance in the fight of love, I require you to abjure your evil faith and become a Christian even as I am. By Christ and by the Virgin, if you do not at once accede to my double desire, I will torture you until you are more wretched than a sick dog!'

The girl's eyes filled with tears, which fell down her cheeks; her lips trembled as she cried: 'As Allāh lives, O white-bearded monster, you may cut me in pieces before I will renounce my Faith; you may take my body by force, as a rutting he-goat takes an unformed female, but my soul shall never partake of the impurity of yours. Allāh will know how to reward you for your infamy!'

When the old man saw that his words would not persuade the girl, he called his slaves, saying: 'Turn her over and hold her flat on her belly!' This was done, and the old Christian cruelly beat the round parts of her with a whip, so that each lash left a long red weal on the white of her behind. At each stroke Zumurrud cried: 'There is no God but Allāh and Muhammad is the prophet of Allāh!' And this although Rashīd did not leave from beating her until he could raise his hand no more. At last he ordered his slaves to throw her into the kitchen with the other slaves and to deprive her of all food and drink.

Alī Shār lay unconscious in the vestibule of his house until the following day. When the drunkenness of banj and the fumes of opium had dissipated from his brain, he sat up, crying: 'O Zumurrud!' As no one answered him, he got to his feet and anxiously entered the other room, which he found silent and empty, with the veils and scarfings of Zumurrud scattered upon the floor. At this sight he remembered the Christian and, realising that his dearly loved Zumurrud had been carried away, threw himself upon the ground, beating his head and sobbing, tearing his garments and weeping all the tears of desolation. At the height of his despair he rushed from his house and, gathering up from the road two great stones, one in each hand, ran about the streets, beating his breast with them and crying: 'O Zumurrud, Zumurrud!' A large crowd of children soon surrounded and followed him, yelling: 'A madman! A madman!', while the people who knew him looked at him with compassion and wept for the loss of his reason, saying: 'That is the son of Glory, poor Alī Shār!'

He wandered extravagantly in this sort, loudly beating his breast with stones, until he met an excellent old woman, who said to him: 'My child, may safety and sanity attend you! When did you become mad?' Alī Shār answered with these lines:

> My sickness is love-lack;
> O doctor, do not probe and ask,
> But give her back,
> Who is a silver salve in a gold flask.

Hearing these lines and looking closely at Alī Shār, the old woman understood that here was only a lover suffering from the extremity of love, so she said to him: 'My son, do not fear to tell me of your unhappiness, for perhaps Allāh has placed me on your path to help you.' Alī Shār told her his adventure with Barsūm the Christian, and the good old woman, after reflecting for an hour with bent head, raised her eyes to him, saying: 'Go as quickly as you can and buy me a pedlar's basket; then hurry to the market and fill it with bracelets of coloured glass, rings of silvered copper, eardrops, and such trinkets as old women sell from door to door among the servants of great houses. I will put the basket on my head and visit all the homes of the city in turn, until I glean some news which will put us on the right track and, if it pleases Allāh, bring the lady Zumurrud back to us.'

At this point Shahrazād saw the approach of morning and discreetly fell silent.

But when the three-hundred-and-twenty-second night had come

SHE SAID:

Alī Shār wept for joy and, kissing the good old woman's hand, hastened to buy her what she needed. In the meanwhile his helper entered her own house to dress herself for her undertaking. She veiled her face with a brown honey-coloured veil, covered her head with a Kashmir shawl, and wrapped herself in a great veil of black silk. Then, balancing the basket upon her head, and sustaining her venerable years with a stick, she made a slow tour of the harīms belonging to merchants and important persons in the different districts of the city. In this way she came at last to the house of old Rashīd al-Dīn, the miserable Christian, whom may Allāh confound and burn in the fires of His hell and torture until the end of time. Amen!

She came to the house just as the unfortunate girl had been thrown into the middle of the slaves and servants of the kitchen and lay half dead upon a shabby mat, groaning from the blows which she had received.

The old woman knocked at the door and, when one of the slaves had opened to her and greeted her in a friendly manner, she said: 'My child, I have some very pretty things to sell; is there any one within who cares to buy?' 'I think so,' answered the slave, and at once introduced the newcomer into the kitchen, where she was immediately surrounded by all the servants. She made no difficulty about her prices and sold bracelets, rings, eardrops and other trinkets so cheaply that she soon won the hearts and confidence of all—by this, and also by the unctuous sweetness of her address.

Looking round, she saw Zumurrud lying upon her mat and learned from the slaves all that they knew about her presence there. Being certain that this was the girl whom she sought, she went up to

her, saying: 'My child, Allāh avert all evil from you! He sends me to
your rescue! You are Zumurrud, the well-loved slave of Alī Shār,
son of Glory.' Then she told her the reason of her own presence
there, disguised as a pedlar, and added: 'To-morrow evening make
ready to be rescued. Stay by the kitchen window which looks out
upon the road and, when you hear a whistle from someone hidden
in the shadows, answer with another whistle and climb out fearlessly. Alī Shār will be there himself.' Zumurrud kissed the hands
of the old woman, who hastened to leave that house and tell Alī
Shār all that had happened. 'You must be under the kitchen window
to-morrow evening and do such and such,' she said.

Alī Shār thanked her for her good offices and would have made
her a present; but she refused and went her own way, with many
wishes for the success of the enterprise, leaving Alī Shār to murmur
over verses dealing with the bitterness of separation.

On the following evening Alī Shār took his way to the house
which the excellent old woman had described to him and, when he
found it, sat down in the shadow of the wall to wait for the hour.
But, as he had passed two nights without sleep, it was not long
before slumber overcame him and he knew no more. Glory be to
Him who sleeps not!

On that same night Fate had decreed that a certain expert and
audacious robber should have come to examine the house in the
hope of being able to break into it. During his tour of inspection
he came to the place where Alī Shār slept and, being tempted by the
richness of his clothes, dexterously stole from him his beautiful
turban and his mantle. The thief had hardly muffled himself in
his spoil when he heard someone open the window and whistle.
Looking up, he saw a woman beckoning to him. Without understanding what this might mean, the robber answered her whistle,
and at once Zumurrud climbed out of the window into the street
by means of a cord. The robber, who was a rascal of considerable
strength, received her upon his back and made off with the speed
of light.

When Zumurrud felt herself carried with so much strength, she
was astonished and said: 'Dear Alī Shār, the old woman told me
that you could hardly walk, being so weakened by your grief and
fear, but I find you stronger than a horse.' The thief's only answer
was to gallop more quickly, so Zumurrud passed her hand over his
face and, finding it spiked with hair harder than a hammām broom,

so that one might have thought that here was a pig which had half-swallowed a fowl, was seized with terror and hit the face with her fists, crying: 'Who are you? What are you?' As, by this time, they were in the open country, far from all houses, surrounded by night and solitude, the thief halted and lifted the girl to the ground, crying: 'I am Jawān the Kurd, the stoutest and wickedest of all Ahmad al-Danaf's band. There are forty of us brave fellows, and we have been deprived of fresh meat for a long time; but to-morrow night will be the most blessed of your life, for we shall all mount you, one by one, dabble in your belly, wallow naughtily between your thighs, and roll your button till the morning.'

Zumurrud understood the full horror of her situation and, beating her face, wept for the mistake which had thrown her into the hands of the forty. Then, realising that evil Destiny was for the moment ascendant in her life and that it was useless to struggle, she let herself be carried on again by her ravisher and contented herself with sighing: 'There is no God but Allāh! In Him I put my trust! Each of us carries his fate about his neck, and it may not be removed!'

At this point Shahrazād saw the approach of morning and discreetly fell silent.

But when the three-hundred-and-twenty-third night had come

SHE SAID:

Jawān, the terrible Kurd, ran on until he came to a cave hidden among the rocks, which was the headquarters of the forty thieves and their captain.

Jawān's mother, an old woman who kept house and cooked for the robbers, heard his signal and came out of the cave to greet her son. The Kurd handed Zumurrud over to the dame, saying: 'Take good care of this gazelle until I come back, for I am going to fetch the rest of the band that they may mount her with me. We cannot be here before to-morrow at midday, as there are certain thefts arranged for to-night; so feed the girl well, that she may be able to support our love-making.'

When he had gone, the old woman came up to Zumurrud with a bowl of water, saying: 'My child, what a happiness for you to be pierced by forty young and lusty men, to say nothing of the captain who, in his own person, is more solid than all of them! As Allāh lives, you are fortunate to be young and desirable!' Zumurrud did not answer, but, wrapping her head in her veil, lay sleepless upon the ground until the morning.

The night brought both reflection and courage, so that at dawn she said to herself: 'Surely it is wicked to do nothing in such a pass! Must I patiently wait for these forty lusty thieves to come and pierce me and fill me as full as a sinking ship? No, by Allāh, I will save my soul and body at the same time!' With this determination she rose and, going to the old woman, kissed her hand and said: 'Good Mother, the night has well rested me and I now feel very ready to honour my guests. What shall we do to pass the hours of waiting? Would you like to come out with me into the sunlight and let me comb your hair and search for lice in it?' 'As Allāh lives, that is an excellent idea!' said the old woman. 'Since I have been in this cave I have not been able to wash my head, so that it now serves as a guest-chamber for every kind of louse ever known upon men or animals. At night they come out and march in armies over my body; there are white ones and black ones, big ones and little ones, and even one with a very long tail which walks backwards; also some of them smell worse than old farts. If you will rid me of these unpleasant beasts, I promise to treat you very well while you remain with us.' She went out of the cave with Zumurrud and, squatting down in the sunlight, took off her head covering. Then the girl was able to see that indeed the old dame harboured every known variety of louse, and even some that were hitherto unknown. Plucking up her courage, she lifted them and threw them away by handfuls, combing the hairs to the roots with sturdy thorns; then, when only a normal quantity of lice remained, she sought for them with her agile fingers and popped them between her nails in the ordinary way. After this, she soothed and smoothed the hair so slowly and pleasantly that the old woman was charmed into a profound sleep.

Without losing a moment, Zumurrud ran to the cavern and, dressing herself in men's clothes which she found there, covered her head with a costly stolen turban. Then she saddled and bridled a stolen horse, which was grazing near by with hobbled legs, and, mounting astride, set off at full gallop, with a prayer to the Master of all rescues.

She rode without a halt till nightfall; she started again on the following morning at dawn, not pausing throughout the second day except to eat a few roots, which she plucked up from the ground, and to let her horse graze. She went on in this way for ten days and nights.

On the morning of the eleventh day she left the desert which she had been crossing and entered a grass country of surpassing green, where fair waters ran and the eye was rejoiced with great trees, with shadows, and with roses and flowers which the eternal Spring of that place brought out in multitudes. The birds of creation fluttered there, herds of gazelles passed through it, and the most graceful of Allāh's beasts dwelt there.

Zumurrud rested for an hour in this delightful place and then, remounting her horse, continued along a beautiful road between fresh thickets, which led to a great city whose minarets shone far off under the sunlight.

When she was near the walls and gate of this city, she became aware of a great crowd which uttered delirious cries of joy and triumph as she approached. The gates opened, and amīrs, nobles and captains rode out to meet her. When they reached her, they bowed and kissed the earth before her with such marks of submission as people render to their King, while, from the intoxicated crowd on every hand, rose this mighty cry: 'Allāh give victory to our Sultān! O King of the earth, may your coming bring benediction to the people of the Faith! Allāh make strong your reign, O our King!' At the same time thousands of warriors on horseback made a double hedge to keep the crowd back, and a herald, riding upon a richly-harnessed camel, proclaimed to the people in a loud voice the happy arrival of their King.

The disguised Zumurrud could find no meaning in all this, so she asked the chiefs of the city, who were leading her horse by the bridle: 'Great lords, what is happening in your city and what do you wish with me?' By way of answer, the chamberlain came forward and bowed to the ground, saying: 'O master, the Giver of all things has been in no wise niggardly in sending you to us. Praise be to Him! He has led you by the hand to place you upon the throne of this kingdom, and I thank Him that He has chosen so young and fair a King, a child of a noble Turkish family, a Sultān with a shining face. I thank Him, I say, for if he had sent us some beggar or unimportant person, yet would we still have had to accept him as our King and render homage to him. . . .'

At this point Shahrazād saw the approach of morning and discreetly fell silent.

But when the three-hundred-and-twenty-fourth night had come

SHE SAID:

'For you must know that it is the custom in our city to come out upon this road if our King dies without male issue, and to wait for the arrival of the first comer whom Destiny sends us, that we may make him our new King and salute him as such. To-day it has been our good fortune to meet you, O most beautiful of all the Kings of the earth, O unique in our time and all times!'

Zumurrud, who had a head on her shoulders and was fertile in plans, did not allow her face to betray any confusion at this strange news, but said to the chamberlain and the other worthies: 'O faithful subjects of mine, do not think for a moment that I am a Turk of obscure birth or a son of common people; learn rather that I come of a noble Turkish family and have left my native land in search of adventures, after having quarrelled with the people of my house. As Destiny has presented me with such a chance of experiencing some new thing, I consent to mount your throne.' With that she put herself at the head of the procession and entered the city in triumph, cheered to the echo by all her new subjects. When she halted her horse before the door of the main palace, the amīrs and chamberlains dismounted and, holding her under the arms, lifted her down and carried her into the great reception hall. When they had clad her in royal garments, they set her upon the gold throne of the old Kings and fell down before her, kissing the earth between her hands and reciting the oath of submission.

Zumurrud began her reign by opening the royal treasures, which had accumulated throughout the ages, and distributing large sums to the soldiers and to the poor, so that the people loved her and prayed that she might long reign over them. Also she gave great quantities of robes of honour to the officers of the palace and distributed her favours among the amīrs and chamberlains and among their wives and among all the women of the harīm. She abolished taxes, imposts and town dues, freed the prisoners in the gaol, and redressed all abuses. In this way she drew to her the love of both great and small. Also, thinking that she was a man, the people marvelled at her chastity when they learned that she never went into the harīm or lay with any of her women. As a matter of fact she chose for night duty two delightful little eunuchs, who had to sleep across her door.

Far from being happy, however, Zumurrud never left off thinking of Alī Shār, whom all the enquiries which she made in secret failed to find. She wept and prayed and fasted in order to bring down the blessing of Allāh upon her lover and obtain that she might some day find him, and stayed thus for a whole year, so that all the women of the palace lifted their arms in despair, crying: 'O misfortune, that our King is so devout and continent!'

At the end of a year Zumurrud had an idea which she wished at once to put into execution; she called her wazīrs and chamberlains, and gave orders that her architects and engineers should smooth out a vast enclosure, a parasang long by a parasang broad, and build in the middle of it a magnificent domed pavilion, richly carpeted and containing a throne and seats for the chiefs of the kingdom. These orders were executed in a very short time: the space was traced out, the pavilion built, and the seats disposed in hierarchic order. Then Zumurrud called together all the nobles of the city and of the palace, and gave them a feast which might not be paralleled in the memory of the oldest of her subjects. When they had well eaten and drunken, she turned to her guests, saying: 'During my reign I will call you all together in this pavilion at the beginning of each month, and you shall take your places upon your seats, while every man in my kingdom eats and drinks before you in one party and gives thanks to the Giver of all things. Heralds shall call my people to their feast and warn any who refuses to come that he will be hanged.'

At the beginning of the next month heralds went throughout the streets of the city, crying: 'O buyers and sellers, rich and poor, hungry and full, the King, your master, summons you to his pavilion. There you shall eat and drink and give thanks to Allāh. He who refuses shall be hanged. Shut your shops and come! Cease from buying and come! He who refuses shall be hanged!'

The crowd ran eagerly at this invitation and poured into the pavilion in close waves, to find the King sitting upon his throne and all the great ones of the kingdom ranged in hierarchic order upon their seats about him. The crowd fell to on many excellent things, on roast sheep, on buttered rice, and especially on that delightful dish, made with crushed corn and fermented milk, which is called kasak. While they ate, the King carefully examined them one after the other and so attentively that each said to his neighbour: 'As Allāh lives, I do not know why the King is looking at me!' The nobles from their seats encouraged the people all the time, saying: 'Eat without shame and take your fill, for you cannot please the King better than by showing a good appetite.' Also they said to each other: 'As Allāh lives, we have never in all our lives seen a King who so loved his people and so wished them well.'

Now among the most greedy who ate with a fiery swiftness, making plate after plate of the excellent food disappear, the greediest of all was Barsūm, the miserable Christian who had drugged Alī Shār and stolen Zumurrud for Rashīd al-Dīn. When he had finished with the meat and with all things cooked in butter or fat, he noticed a dish, which was out of his reach, full of an excellent rice-cream sprinkled with cinnamon and sugar. Therefore he shouldered aside his neighbours and, reaching the plate, drew it towards him and, taking an enormous handful from it, stuffed his mouth full.

At this point Shahrazād saw the approach of morning and discreetly fell silent.

But when the three-hundred-and-twenty-fifth night had come

SHE SAID:

One of those who were sitting near said in a shocked voice: 'Are you not ashamed to have so long an arm and to keep a great dish all to yourself? Do you not know that the code of true politeness teaches us only to eat what is put before us?' Another added: 'May the stuff weigh upon your belly and upset your tripes!' An amusing fellow, a great eater of hashīsh, said: 'In Allāh's name, let us share! Come here by me and I will take a mouthful or two.' But Barsūm looked at him disdainfully and said: 'O wicked hashīsh-eater, these noble meats were not intended for your jaws. They are for delicate fellows like myself.' He was getting ready to plunge his hand into this delicious paste again when Zumurrud, who had been watching him for some time, recognised him and sent four of her guards to him with these instructions: 'Take hold of that man who is eating rice-cream and bring him to me.' The four threw themselves upon Barsūm and, snatching from his fingers the mouthful which he was about to swallow, threw him face downwards upon the earth and dragged him towards the King. The other guests were so astonished that they stopped eating and began to whisper among themselves: 'See what comes of being greedy and taking the nourishment away from other people!' The hashīsh-eater said to those who were near him: 'As Allāh lives, it was a good thing that I could not persuade him to share that cinnamon-rice with me! What punishment will he get, think you?' With that all the guests watched closely to see what would happen.

Zumurrud's eyes blazed with fury, but she concealed this and said to the man: 'Tell me, fellow with bad blue eyes, what is your name, what your trade, and why have you come into our country?' The miserable Christian, who wore a white turban, which is not lawful save for Mussulmāns, made answer: 'O King, my name is Alī, and I am a lace-maker by trade. I came into your country to carry on that trade and to earn my bread with the work of my hands.'

Zumurrud said to one of her little eunuchs: 'Go quickly and fetch me my table of divining sand and geomantic copper pen.' When this order had been executed, she spread the sand carefully over the surface of the table and with the copper pen traced the appearance of an ape and certain lines in an unknown character. For some minutes she regarded these lines absorbedly and then, suddenly lifting her head, cried out in so terrible a voice that it was heard by all the guests: 'O dog, how do you dare to lie to Kings? Are you not a Christian and is your name not Barsūm? Did you not come to this country to search for a female slave whom you had stolen? Dog and devil, you now shall confess the truth which has been revealed to me so clearly by my magic sand!'

The terrified Christian crawled along the ground towards the King with clasped hands, saying: 'Mercy, mercy, O King of time! I will not deceive you! Allāh preserve you from all evil! I am indeed an ignoble Christian and came here with the intention of raping away a Mussulmān woman, whom I had stolen and who fled from our house.'

Amid murmurs of admiration from all her people, who could not help crying: 'Allāh, Allāh, never in all the world was there a geomancer, a sand reader, like our King!' Zumurrud called her executioner and his assistants, saying to them: 'Take this miserable dog beyond the city, flay him alive and, after stuffing his skin with rotten straw, return and nail it to the gate of the enclosure. Burn his body on a fire of dry dung and throw what is left into the drain.' The executioner and his men at once took out the Christian and inflicted upon him this punishment, while all the people who remained in the hall said that the sentence was both just and wise.

Those who had been the neighbours of Barsūm at table exchanged their impressions of this happening. One of them said: 'As Allāh lives, I shall never again allow myself in all my life to be tempted by rice-cream, although I love it very much.' The hashīsh-eater, holding his belly for a colic of sheer fear, cried: 'It was my good angel who kept me from that wicked rice!' And all swore that they would not pronounce the word *rice-cream* as long as they lived.

When the next month came and the people gathered together to feast before their King, a great space was left about the dish of rice-cream and no one would even look in its direction; yet all, to please the King who was examining each of them by turn, ate, drank and rejoiced exceedingly. It was noticeable, however, that no one touched anything which was not directly before him.

During the course of the feast a man of terrifying appearance walked quickly into the pavilion, thrusting aside all those who came in his way and, seeing every place taken except one by the rice-cream dish, squatted down before that dish and, amid general consternation, stretched out his hand towards its contents.

At once Zumurrud recognised this fellow as Jawān, the terrible Kurd, one of the forty thieves led by Ahmad al-Danaf. He had come to that city to seek Zumurrud, for her flight had mightily enraged him when he had come back with all his companions and was ready to mount her. He had bitten the hand of despair and sworn to bring her back, though she were at the other side of Mount Caucasus or hidden somewhere like a pistachio in its shell. His search had led him at last to the city ruled over by Zumurrud, and, in order to escape being hanged, he had entered the pavilion with the others.

At this point Shahrazād saw the approach of morning and discreetly fell silent.

But when the three-hundred-and-twenty-sixth night had come

SHE SAID:

He sat down before the dish of rice-cream and plunged his whole hand into the very middle of it. From every side cries greeted this action: 'What are you doing?' 'Take care!' 'You will be flayed alive!' Do not touch that ill-omened dish!' But the man rolled frightful eyes about him, crying: 'Be quiet! I will fill my belly with this rice-cream, for it is a thing I love.' His neighbours cried again: 'You will be flayed and hanged!' But, for all answer, he drew the dish nearer to him by the hand which was plunged in it, and leaned over the succulent confection. The hashīsh-eater, who sat nearest him and was now quite cleared from the fumes of his drug, fled precipitately further off, as a sign that he had no lot or part in what was going to happen.

After Jawān the Kurd had plunged his hand, which was black as a crow's foot, into the dish, he brought it out as big and heavy as the foot of a camel. Rounding the great mass which he had lifted in his palm, he made a ball of it as large as a citron and threw it with one movement to the bottom of his throat, where it was swallowed with a noise like thunder mingled with the sound of a torrent in a reverberating cave, so that the dome of the pavilion re-echoed again and again. The place where he had taken out his handful was so deep that the bottom of the mighty dish could be seen of all men.

The hashīsh-eater raised his arms, crying: 'Allāh protect us all, he has engulfed the whole dish in one mouthful! Thanks be to Allāh who did not create me in the form of rice-cream! Let the rest of us eat at our ease, for I see on that man's forehead the image of a flayed skin. O horrible gulf, may your digestion turn on you and smother you!' The Kurd took no notice of what was said about him, but thrust his bludgeon-like fingers a second time into the tender mass, which opened with a dull quaking sound, and brought them back, holding a lump as big as a pumpkin. He was already turning this in his hands before swallowing it, when Zumurrud said to her guards: 'Bring me that man before he swallows his mouthful.' The men threw themselves upon Jawān, who did not see their approach because he was bent over the dish, and, after turning him and binding his hands in one dexterous movement, dragged him before the King. 'It is his own fault,' cried the guests. 'We advised him not to touch that terrible rice-cream.'

'What is your name?' asked Zumurrud of the man. 'What is your trade, and why have you come into our city?' 'My name is Uthmān, and I am a gardener,' answered the other. 'I came into this city to look for work.' 'Bring me my sand table and copper pen!' cried Zumurrud. When these objects were set before her, she traced forms and figures in the sand and seemed to reflect and calculate for an hour, before she raised her head and said: 'Woe betide you, miserable liar! My calculations tell me that your real name is Jawān the Kurd, and that your real trade is theft and murder. O pig, O son of a thousand whores! Admit the truth at once if you do not want the stick to aid your memory!'

Jawān, who did not suspect for a minute that this King was the girl whom he had stolen, became suddenly yellow; his jaws chattered together and his lips retracted from his teeth so that these appeared like the fangs of a wolf. Thinking that the truth would save his head, he said: 'You are right, O King! But I repent before your face from this very moment and will walk in the straight way for ever after.' But Zumurrud cried: 'It is not lawful to allow an evil beast to live in the path of Mussulmāns. Take him out and skin him alive, stuff his skin and nail it to the door of the pavilion, and do with his body as you did with the body of the Christian.'

When the hashīsh-eater saw the guards taking the man out, he rose and turned his behind to the dish of rice-cream, saying: 'O rice-cream, O sugared and cinnamoned thing, I turn my back upon you! Unhappy confection, you are not worthy of my regard, scarcely of my bottom! I spit upon you and hate you.'

At this point Shahrazād saw the approach of morning and discreetly fell silent.

But when the three-hundred-and-twenty-seventh night had come

SHE SAID:

When the day came for the third feast, all happened as before: the King sat with his nobles and the common people began to eat, drink and make merry, filling every part of the pavilion save that immediately about the plate of rice-cream. Suddenly there entered a man with a white beard, who, seeing a place by the great vacant dish, walked to it and sat down, in order that he might not be hanged. Zumurrud looked at him and recognised old Rashīd al-Dīn, the miserable Christian who had contrived her capture with his brother.

This is what had happened. After Rashīd had waited for a month for the return of his brother, whom he had sent to look for the escaped girl, he resolved to set out on the quest himself, and, in course of time, Fate had led him into the pavilion and into that seat in front of the rice-cream.

'As Allāh lives,' said Zumurrud to herself, 'this rice-cream is an excellent dish, for it attracts all the malefactors I have ever known. I think I should make it the obligatory food of all my people and hang those who do not grow to love it. In the meantime I must deal with this senile wretch.' So she cried to her guards: 'Bring me the man at the rice!' And they brought him to her, dragging him along the ground by his beard. 'What is your name, what is your trade, and why have you come into our city?' she asked, and the old man answered: 'O auspicious King, my name is Rustam, and I have no trade save poverty, for I am a darwīsh.' 'The sand and the pen!' cried Zumurrud. When these things were brought, she made marks and figures on the surface of the sand and pondered over them for an hour. Then she raised her head, saying: 'O evil dog, you have lied to the King! Your name is Rashīd al-Dīn; your trade is the ravishing and prisoning of Mussulmān women; outwardly you profess the faith of Islām, but within you are a miserable Christian decayed with vices. Admit the truth, or your head shall drop before your feet even now!' Rashīd confessed all his crimes and faults, thinking to save his head, but Zumurrud said to the guards: 'Turn him over and give him a thousand strokes on the sole of each foot!' When this had been done, she continued: 'Take him out and skin him, stuff his hide with rotten hay and nail it at the entrance of the pavilion. Then let his body go to join those of the other two dogs.'

While this sentence was being carried out, the rest of the guests settled down to eat again, marvelling at the wisdom and justice of their King.

When the feast was finished, Zumurrud went back to her palace; but she was not happy. 'Thanks be to Allāh who has given my heart the relief of vengeance!' she said to herself. 'But this does not bring me back my Alī Shār. Yet the Highest is also the All-Powerful. If He wills, He can do this and more also for those who adore Him.' Stirred to the depths by memories of her lover, she shed abundant tears all through that night and then shut herself in with her grief until the beginning of the following month.

As soon as the King and his nobles had taken their place for the fourth feast and all the people were eating and drinking, Zumurrud made this prayer within her soul: 'O You who gave back Joseph to his old father and cured the terrible sores of holy Job, of Your great goodness return my lover Alī Shār to me! O Master of the Universe Who turns the strayed creature back into the right and pleasant way and benevolently hears the voices which rise towards You, send Alī Shār to your poor slave!' Hardly had Zumurrud murmured this prayer to herself when a young man came into the enclosure, bending his slim waist as he walked, just as the branch of a willow bends before the wind. He was as beautiful as the light is beautiful, but seemed pale and weary. Finding no other seat vacant, he sat down by the plate of rice-cream, while horrified glances followed his every movement.

Zumurrud recognised him at the first glance and with difficulty strangled a cry of joy upon her lips. As she did not wish to betray herself before her people, she waited for the agitation of her bowels and the clamour of her heart to still themselves before she dared to send for Alī Shār.

At this point Shahrazād saw the approach of morning and discreetly fell silent.

But when the three-hundred-and-twenty-eighth night had come

SHE SAID:

Now you must know that Alī Shār had wakened at daybreak, when the merchants began to open their shops. Surprised at first to find himself lying in that street, he carried his hand to his forehead and thus discovered that his turban was missing. When he saw that his mantle had also gone, he began to understand the truth of the matter and ran sorrowfully to tell his misadventure to the old woman, whom he begged to return to the house and ask for news. When she came back to him at the end of an hour, her face was altered with grief, her hair was undone, for she had heard of the disappearance of Zumurrud. 'My child,' she said, 'I think you must now give up all hopes of ever finding your mistress. In grief there is no power or might save with Allāh. All that has happened to you is your own fault.'

Alī Shār saw the light change to darkness before his eyes, he wished for death, and fell weeping and sobbing into the arms of the good old woman. Then he fainted. Thanks to her attentions, he recovered consciousness, but had to go to bed at once. He lay there stricken by an illness which deprived him of all sleep and would have led him straight to the doors of the tomb had not his venerable friend tendered him, loved him, and encouraged him. For a whole year he lay thus, and the old woman did not leave him for a moment. She gave him syrups, and chicken broth to strengthen him, and fortifying perfumes to smell, while he, in his languor and weakness, let her do what she would, and said over a thousand poems of separation. This was one of them:

This fever and this fever
Wears down the eyes with water,
Wears out the heart with fire,
And cuts the red thread shorter
With the hot sword of desire,
While the spirit breaks
Because it wakes
For ever and for ever.

Alī Shār stayed without hope of cure because he was without hope of finding Zumurrud, so that at last the old woman, not knowing how to lift him from the stupor which held him, said: 'My child, you will never find your love by lying here; rise up now, and be strong. Make pilgrimage throughout all cities and all lands; for no one knows the road by which comes safety.' She kept on speaking to him in this way, goading him and encouraging him, until at last he was persuaded to rise, to go to the hammām where she bathed him herself, to drink sherberts and eat chickens which she prepared for him. After a month of this treatment he was strong enough to travel; he said farewell to the old woman, and began his journey. Thus it was that he ended in the city where Zumurrud was King, seated before the dish of rice-cream powdered with sugar and cinnamon.

As he was hungry, he raised his sleeves to the elbows and, after repeating the preparatory formula, began to eat. His neighbours, sorrowful to see what they took to be his danger, advised him not to touch the contents of the dish, and, as he persisted, the hashīsh-eater said: 'Be careful! You will surely be flayed and hanged.' 'Death would be a blessed thing, a deliverer,' answered Alī Shār. 'Also I intend to eat this rice-cream.' With that he stretched out his right hand and began to eat heartily of the pleasant food.

Zumurrud watched him, saying to herself: 'I will let him eat his fill before I summon him.' When she saw his lips moving in the grace: 'Thanks be to Allāh!' she said to her guards: 'Go to that young man who is sitting before the dish of rice-cream and beg him, gently and politely, to come and speak with me.' The guards went up to the youth and, bowing before him, said: 'Master, our lord the King wishes to put a question to you.' 'I hear and I obey!' answered Alī Shār, as he rose and moved towards the King. Seeing this, the guests hazarded a thousand conjectures. Some said: 'Woe, woe upon his youth! Who knows what will happen?' Others said: 'If ill were

intended, the King would not have let him eat his fill; he would
have stopped him at the second mouthful.' And yet others said:
'The guards have not dragged him along by his feet; they have gone
with him, following at a respectful distance!'

Ali Shār kissed the earth between the King's hands, while
Zumurrud asked in a gentle and trembling voice: 'What is your
name, O gentle youth, what is your trade, and what has brought
you into our city?' 'O auspicious King,' answered the other, 'I am
called Ali Shār, son of Glory. My father was a merchant in the land
of Khurāsān. My trade was the same as his, but calamity long since
made me leave it . . .'

At this point Shahrazād saw the approach of morning and
discreetly fell silent.

But when the three-hundred-and-twenty-ninth night had come

SHE SAID:

Ali Shār continued: 'I came into this land to look for a dearly
loved woman whom I have lost; she is sweeter to me than light and
hearing and my own soul. Since she was taken from me, I have
walked like one in an evil sleep. Such is my lamentable tale.' With
that he burst into tears and was rocked by such a storm of sobs that
he fell down in a swoon.

Zumurrud ordered her two little eunuchs to sprinkle his face with
rose-water, and on smelling the rose-water he came to himself.
Then said Zumurrud: 'Bring me my sand table and my copper pen!'
She traced figures and hieroglyphics, over which she brooded for an
hour before she raised her head and said in a sweet voice, but one
loud enough to be heard by all the guests: 'O Ali Shār, son of
Glory, the sand confirms your story, you have spoken the truth.
I predict that Allāh will soon bring your lover back to you. Therefore be of good cheer!' Proclaiming the feast at an end, she ordered
the little slaves to conduct Ali Shār to the hammām and, after
providing him with a robe of honour from the royal cupboards
and a steed from the royal stables, to bring him back to her at
nightfall.

The people, having seen these things and heard these orders,
said to each other: 'What secret reason can the King have for treating
this young man with so much honour and consideration?' 'As Allāh
lives,' returned those more knowing than the rest, 'the boy is

beautiful. What other reason do you want?' But yet others of them
said: 'We knew exactly what would happen directly we saw the
King allow him to finish his meal of rice-cream. By Allāh, we did not
know that rice-cream could cause so powerful and so different
results.' With that the guests trooped away, still buzzing with
opinions and aphorisms.

Zumurrud waited with indescribable impatience for nightfall,
when she might be alone again with the dear one of her heart. No
sooner had the sun disappeared and the muezzin begun to call the
folk to prayer than she undressed and lay down upon her couch,
clothed only in a silk chemise. She lowered the curtains that she
might be in shadow and ordered the two little eunuchs to introduce
Alī Shār.

In the meanwhile the chamberlains and officers of the palace,
seeing Alī Shār treated in this unusual way, said to each other: 'It
seems certain that the King has fallen in love with this young man.
To-morrow, after they have passed a night together, he will surely
be appointed chamberlain, or perhaps general of the army.' So much
for them.

When Alī Shār was led in, he kissed the earth between the King's
hands and, after offering up prayers for his safety, waited to be
questioned. 'I will not reveal myself to him all at once,' thought
Zumurrud, 'for, if he recognised me suddenly, he might die of
emotion.' So she turned to him and said: 'Gentle youth, come a little
nearer to me. Have you been to the hammām?' 'Yes, my lord,' he
answered, and she continued: 'Were you washed and perfumed and
refreshed all over?' 'Yes, my lord,' answered Alī Shār, and Zumurrud
went on: 'Did not the bath give you an appetite? See, here is a dish
of chicken and pastries to your hand. I pray you eat a little.' When
Alī Shār had eaten and was content, 'Now you must be thirsty,' said
Zumurrud, 'see, here are drinks. Allay your thirst and then come
nearer to me still.' Alī Shār drank a glass from each jar of wine and
somewhat timidly approached the couch.

The King took him by the hand, saying: 'You please me very
much, O youth. Your face is beautiful, and I love beautiful faces.
I pray you, bend down and rub my feet.' Alī Shār rolled up his
sleeves and, stooping, began to rub the feet of the King, who after a
few moments said to him: 'Now rub my legs and my thighs.'

While Alī Shār rubbed the legs and the thighs of the King, he was
astonished to find them unbelievably tender and white; so he said to

himself: 'As Allāh lives, Kings' thighs are not like those of other men! They are quite white and hairless.'

'Sweet youth,' said Zumurrud, 'your hands are most expert in the art of rubbing. Go up a little higher now, towards my navel.' Alī Shār stopped suddenly in his work and said with a frightened accent: 'Excuse me, my lord, but I do not know how to rub higher than the thighs. I have now finished all that I know.'

At this point Shahrazād saw the approach of morning and discreetly fell silent.

But when the three-hundred-and-thirtieth night had come

SHE SAID:

At this answer Zumurrud assumed an angry voice and cried: 'Do you dare to disobey me? As Allāh lives, if you hesitate any longer, this night shall be a fatal one to your head! Bend down, now, and satisfy my desire. In return, I will make you my lover of lovers, and appoint you my amīr of amīrs, my captain of captains.' 'But, O King, I do not understand exactly what you wish,' said Alī Shār. 'What must I do to obey you?' 'Undo your drawers and lie down on your face,' answered the King, and Alī Shār exclaimed: 'That is a thing which I have never done before in all my life. If you force me to it, I will hold you accountable on the Day of Resurrection. Let me go out of here and leave this country.' But Zumurrud answered in a yet more furious voice: 'I order you to take down your drawers and lie upon your face. Otherwise I will have your head cut off. Be reasonable, sweet youth, and lie with me. You will never repent it.'

Alī Shār was forced to obey: he undid his drawers and lay down on his face; Zumurrud took him in her arms and, mounting upon him, lay all along his back. Feeling the King mount him so impetuously, Alī Shār said to himself: 'Now shall I be destroyed!' But then, feeling some soft thing lightly caressing him with a touch as of silk or velvet, something round and gentle at the same time, something firm and moist at once, he said: 'As Allāh lives, this King has a flesh which I prefer to that of any woman!' And he waited for the critical moment. But after lying for an hour in this way, without feeling any terrible perforation, he suddenly saw the King rise from his back and stretch himself on his own back. 'Glory and thanks be to Allāh,' thought Alī Shār, 'his zabb has not risen! In what a sorry

state would I have been if it had done so!' He was beginning to
breathe more freely when the King said: 'You must know, dear Ali
Shār, that my zabb will only rise when it is manipulated with the
fingers. If you do not now handle it, you are a dead man. Give me
your hand.' So saying, Zumurrud, who lay still upon her back, took
Ali Shār's hand and placed it gently upon the curved part of her
story. Ali Shār felt something round and as high as a throne, as fat
as a chicken, warmer than the throat of a pigeon, hotter than a loving
heart; and this round thing was smooth and white, melting and
enormous. Suddenly it reared up like a mule between his fingers;
like a mule pricked in the nostril or an ass stabbed in the back.

'Surely this King has an entrance!' thought Ali Shār in astonishment. 'This is the most prodigious thing I ever heard of.' And,
emboldened beyond all its hesitations by this discovery, his own
zabb rose in a moment to the extreme limit of erection.

This was the time for which Zumurrud had been waiting: she
burst out laughing so heartily that she would infallibly have fallen
over on her back if she had not been there already. To Ali Shār she
murmured through her laughter: 'Do you not recognise your slave,
dear master?' And when Ali Shār, who understood nothing of all
this, asked: 'What slave and what master, O King of time?' she
answered: 'O Ali Shār, I am Zumurrud. Do you not know me?'

Ali Shār looked closely at the King and recognised his well-
beloved. He took her in his arms and embraced her with transports
of joy which are more easily imagined than told to you. 'Will you
resist any longer?' asked Zumurrud, and Ali Shār, for sole response,
leapt upon her like a lion upon a sheep. Remembering the road, he
thrust his shepherd's staff into the food-bag and went straight on
without regarding the narrowness of the way. Coming to the end of
the path, he stood up straight and still for a long time, at once the
porter and Imām of that gate.

On her side, Zumurrud did not leave him for an inch; she lifted
with him, knelt with him, rolled and rose with him, panting and
following his every movement. Game answered game and thrust
answered thrust, amid a hundred charming flirtations of the two
bodies. Cry called forth sigh, sigh called forth cry, until the noise of
them attracted the little eunuchs, who lifted the curtain to see if the
King had not need of their services. Before their frightened eyes
appeared the spectacle of their King stretched out on his back,
intimately covered by the young man, adopting quick poses, giving

snort for snort, thrust for assault, inlay for scissor work, and for every shiver a pleasant trembling.

At this point Shahrazād saw the approach of morning and discreetly fell silent.

But when the three-hundred-and-thirty-first night had come

SHE SAID:

Seeing these things, the two little eunuchs stole silently away, saying: 'Our King's behaviour is hardly that of a man. He is more like a woman and a mad one at that.' But they kept the secret carefully to themselves.

When morning came, Zumurrud dressed herself again in her royal robes and called together, into the courtyard of her palace, all her amīrs, chamberlains, captains, wazīrs, counsellors and nobles. To these she said: 'O faithful subjects, to-day I permit you to go out into the road where you first met me and to find some other man to be your King. For I have resolved to abdicate my throne and depart with this youth into his own country; I have chosen him to be the friend of my life and, as I have given him all my love, would give him all my days also. The peace of Allāh be with you!'

The court answered with hearing and obedience, and the slaves rivalled each other in preparing for the journey, filling chest after chest with food, riches, jewels, robes, gold and silver, and loading them upon the backs of mules and camels. When all was in readiness, Zumurrud and Alī Shār got up into a velvet and brocaded palanquin, carried by a dromedary, and, accompanied only by the two little eunuchs, journeyed to the land of Khurāsān, and came at last to their city and their own house. Alī Shār gave great alms to the poor, the widow and the orphan, and distributed rich presents among his friends and neighbours. The two lived for many years amid a large gift of sons from Allāh; their joy was never diminished until the visit of the Destroyer, the Separator. Glory be to Allāh, who lives untroubled throughout eternity!

But, continued Shahrazād to King Shahryār, do not think for a moment that this story can be compared with the tale of the Six Different Coloured Girls. If the poems in that are not more admirable than any you have already heard, you may cut off my head as soon as you like.

And Shahrazād said:

The Tale of the Six Different Coloured Girls

IT is related, O auspicious King, that the Commander of the Faithful, al-Mamūn, sat one day upon the throne in his palace, surrounded not only by his wazīrs, amīrs and nobles, but by all the poets and pleasant wits with whom he was intimate. His greatest friend among them all was Muhammad of Basrah. It was to this man that the Khalīfah turned, saying: 'O Muhammad, I wish you to tell me some tale which has never been heard here before.' 'That is easy, Prince of Believers,' answered the other. 'Would you like a story which I have heard, or a tale of things which I have myself seen?' 'I wish the most marvellous; it does not matter of which kind,' said al-Mamūn, and straightway Muhammad of Basrah spoke as follows:

O Commander of the Faithful, lately I have become acquainted with a rich man, a native of Yaman, who left his own country and came to live in our city of Baghdād, in order to eat the fruits of joy and calm. This Alī al-Yaman, finding the conditions of life in Baghdād very much to his taste, ended by transferring all his belongings from Yaman, including his harīm of six young slaves, each more beautiful than any moon.

The first was white, the second brown, the third fat, the fourth thin, the fifth blond, and the sixth black; but all were perfect in beauty, in the knowledge of literature, in the art of dancing and playing upon instruments of music.

At this point Shahrazād saw the approach of morning and discreetly fell silent.

But when the three-hundred-and-thirty-second night had come

SHE SAID:

The white girl was called Moonlight; the brown, Incense-Flame; the fat, Full-Moon; the thin Girl-of-Paradise; the blond, Sunlight; the black, Dark-of-the-Eye.

Now one day, when Alī al-Yaman felt in better spirits than usual, owing to the delectable peace which he experienced in our city, he invited his six slaves to come together to keep him company, to drink, to talk, and to sing with him. The six came, and the hours passed pleasantly in every kind of game and joyful amusement.

As they were all laughing together, Alī took a cup, filled it with wine, and turned towards Moonlight, saying: 'O sweet white slave,

271

O Moonlight, let us hear the delicate harmony of your perfect voice.'
Moonlight, the white slave, took a lute and, after drawing from it a
low prelude which would have charmed the very stones to rise up
and dance, made this song and sang it to her own accompaniment:

> With burning dyes
> Love has painted my beloved upon my eyes
> And stained the picture of my beloved upon my breasts
> Beneath my saffron vests;
> Therefore should he depart
> I turn into a heart,
> And when he is by
> I change into an eye.

The master of Moonlight was moved with pleasure at this song
and, after moistening his lips at the cup, offered it to the girl, who
drank it down. He filled the cup a second time and, holding it in his
hand, turned to the brown slave, saying: 'O Incense-Flame, O
remedy of souls, let me hear the accents of your voice; sing something that you love.' Incense-Flame took the lute and, after playing
a melody which would have charmed all hearts to dancing, sang this:

> O brightest carving of God's hand,
> You found a way between His fingers and
> Now upon earth keep gentle school
> To teach all beauty to the beautiful.

The master of Incense-Flame was moved with pleasure at this
song and, after moistening his lips at the cup, offered it to the girl,
who drank it down. He filled the cup again and, holding it in his
hand, turned to the fat slave, saying: 'O Full-Moon, O heavy girl
whose blood runs light and sweet, sing us some song with lines as
fair and clear as is your flesh.' The fat girl took the lute and, after
playing a prelude which would have charmed the hardest rocks to
dancing, and humming over a few notes to herself, sang in a voice
of wonderful purity:

> I'd lose the world for a smile
> If I could beguile you.
> The kings of the earth might walk
> If I heard you talking.

> The kings of the earth might talk
> If I saw you walking.
> I'd lie all life at your feet
> If I could entreat you.
> I'd lose the world for a kiss . . .
> If I could dismiss you.

The master of Full-Moon was filled with pleasure at this song and, after moistening his lips at the cup, offered it to the girl, who drank it down. He filled the cup again and, holding it in his hand, turned to the thin slave, saying: 'O slim Girl-of-Paradise, it is now your turn to pluck ecstasy from the lute by the singing of your voice.' The thin slave bent over the instrument, as a mother over her babe, and sang:

> He cares as little as I love much;
> There should be a court to decide on such,
> A judge to fine me all my passion
> And give it the prisoner for my offence
> And then, in regular legal fashion,
> Award the plaintiff indifference.

The master of Girl-of-Paradise was moved with pleasure at this song and, after moistening his lips at the cup, offered it to the girl, who drank it down. He filled the cup again and, holding it in his hand, turned to the blond slave, saying: . . .

At this point Shahrazād saw the approach of morning and discreetly fell silent.

But when the three-hundred-and-thirty-third night had come

SHE SAID:

'O Sunlight, O body of amber and gold, will you embroider us some verses upon the delicate silk of love?' The blond girl bent her golden head over the sounding lute, half shut her dawn-clear eyes, played a chaplet of melodious notes which charmed the body and soul alike to dancing, and sang:

> His eyes shot a black arrow with black art,
> Then I said to my heart:
> 'Poor heart, you suffer from a poisoned wound,
> Where shall a cure be found?'

Yet if heart answered me I could not hear,
    Because heart was not there,
Being still dragged behind love in the dust
    On the bright string of lust.

The master of Sunlight was moved with pleasure at this song and, after moistening his lips at the cup, offered it to the girl, who drank it down. He filled the cup again and, holding it in his hand, turned to the black slave, saying: 'O Dark-of-the-Eye, O black without but very white within, whose body is the colour of grief, but whose face shines with all joy, pluck us some flowers of music as rosy as the sun.'

Dark-of-the-Eye took the lute and, after playing upon it in twenty different ways, returned to her first melody and sang this, which was her favourite song:

Mourn over love's gold fire
Because my lover is pleasant to other women;
But do not tell me to cease from adoring roses.

What shall a heart do
Which is stirred by roses?

Here are twenty cups full of wine
And an old guitar for kisses,
But I have no myrrh.

My roses burn in the gold fire,
But there are others
And it is always spring in paradise.

Pray God, it is not a crime
To love so popular a creature.

The master of Dark-of-the-Eye was moved with pleasure at this song and, after moistening his lips at the cup, offered it to the girl, who drank it down.

After this all six rose together and kissed the earth between their master's hands, begging him to let them know which charmed him most with voice and verse. Alī al-Yaman was perplexed at this request; after looking at them long, admiring their different graces and calling to mind their songs, he found them all equally admirable and therefore said:

'Glory be to Allāh, the Giver of all beauty, Who has allowed me six perfect women to be my solace! I swear that I love you all equally and can find in my soul no point on which to give the palm to any one of you. Come, my lambs, embrace me all together!'

The six girls fell into his arms and caressed him in a thousand ways for an hour together.

Then Alī made them stand in a circle before him and said to them: 'I myself was unwilling to choose a favourite from among you, for it would have been unjust to do so; but you may make the choice yourselves. All of you are deeply read in the Koran and other fair writings; you have studied the annals of old and the histories of our fathers in the Faith; you all are eloquent. Now I wish each one of you to give herself the praises which she thinks that she deserves, pointing out the qualities of her own beauty and deprecating the delights of her rivals. We will have the struggle between pairs: for instance, between the white and the black, the thin and the fat, the blond and the brown; but the weapons must only be beautiful words, well-chosen maxims, citations from the wise, the authority of poets, and the warrant of the Koran.'

At this point Shahrazād saw the approach of morning and discreetly fell silent.

But when the three-hundred-and-thirty-fourth night had come

SHE SAID:

The six girls consented to the test. The white slave, Moonlight, rose and signing to Dark-of-the-Eye to stand before her, said:

'O black girl, the books of the wise tell us that Whiteness spoke in this fashion: "I am the shining light. I am the moon rising above the rim of the world. My tint may be seen of men and my forehead burns with silver. Thus said a poet of me:

> God breathed into a foam of pearl
> And fashioned the beginnings of this girl,
> After, He mingled myrtle with the dew
> And took white roses, too;
> But in the end He had to add to these
> All His bright gardens, all His wavering trees."

'Listen, black girl!

'My colour is the colour of day, of orange-flowers, and the pearl star of morning.

'Allāh said to Moses (upon whom be prayer and peace!) when his hand was covered with leprosy: "Put your hand in your pocket and you will bring it forth white and pure and whole."

'Also it is written in the Book of our Faith: "Those who keep their faces white and stainless shall be chosen by the mercy of Allāh."

'My colour is the queen of colours; my beauty is my perfection, and my perfection is my beauty.

'Rich garments and shining jewels consort best with my colour and show up my bright tint to confound the soul.

'The snow which falls from heaven is always white.

'The Believers have chosen white muslin to be the stuff of their turbans.

'Many excellent and convincing things might be said about my colour; but the truth of them is evident, like a lamp shining before the eyes, and therefore I will praise myself no more. Rather I will speak a little in your dispraise, O black girl, ink-coloured, smoke-coloured, forge filings, crow-face!

'Speaking of black and white, a poet has said:

> They buy a pearl with captive kings,
> But sell a bag of charcoal for a shilling;
> Heaven is white faces and white wings,
> Else it would not be heaven. I am willing,
> If you would have me tell
> The whole truth, to admit
> And so be done with it,
> They use the colour black a lot in Hell.

'The annals of the Just tell us that Noah, the holy man, was sleeping one day with his two sons, Shem and Ham, beside him. A breeze lifted his robe and exposed his hidden members; therefore Ham laughed, for Noah, the second father of men, was rich in rigid glories; but Shem rose without a smile and hastened to replace his father's robe. Noah woke up and, after cursing the laughing face of Ham, blessed the serious face of Shem. Immediately Shem's face became white and Ham's black; and afterwards from the loins of

Shem sprang the prophets, the shepherds of the people, sages and kings; whereas Ham, fleeing from the presence of his father, founded the line of negroes, men of Sūdān. And you know well, O black girl, that not only the wise, but also common men, agree that there can come no sage or lawgiver among the blacks!'

'You may stop now,' said Alī, 'for it is the black one's turn.' Then Dark-of-the-Eye, who had been standing motionless, fixed her eyes upon Moonlight, and said:

'O ignorant white girl, do you not know that, in the Koran, Allāh swears by the dark night and by the shining day, and that, in His oath, He gives preference to the night over the day by naming it first?

'Black hairs and black hair are the sign and ornament of youth, while white is a symbol of age and the end of enjoyment.'

At this point Shahrazād saw the approach of morning and discreetly fell silent.

But when the three-hundred-and-thirty-fifth night had come

SHE SAID:

'If black were not the best of all colours, Allāh would not have made it so dear to the eye and heart. Well advised was the poet who said:

> A black body is filled with fire
> And black flesh tingles with desire,
> Black flesh is young.
> Dear heaven, I beg
> I never have to live on white-of-egg:
> To love on white-of-egg were more
> Distasteful, I should scream aloud.
> It was upon my tongue
> To say I do not love a dead white shroud
> Or those white hairs which are the stage before.

'Another said:

> You frown because I've lost my wits again
> For a black girl? Allow me to explain:
> The doctors always shake their heads and say
> Black thoughts can drive the sanest man insane.

'Another poet wrote:

> I never love at noon,
>   I hate girls sickly white
>   Like rotten flour:
>   They are not worth an hour.
>   Black sweet, were there no night
> How could there be a moon?

'Are not the intimate meetings of friends at night? Do not lovers owe much gratitude to the shadows which cover up their love and hide them from the indiscretion of the scandalous light? Do they not hate the inquisition of the compromising day? That should be enough proof for you, O white girl. But listen again to a poet:

> I love not blank white boys who live on fat,
>   A slim black youth is worth a score of these.
>   What then?
>   Are you surprised at that?
>   I ride a quick black stallion, if you please,
>   And leave white elephants to older men.

'And another poet has this:

> Black night brings kisses
>   And white dawn brings shame;
> If I'd a choice of blisses
>   I'd thank God for the same
> And pray that all these tedious days of white
> Were changed to darkness, deep and exquisite.

'O white girl, if I continued to number the praises of black, I would offend against the maxim: "Brevity is the soul of argument." Therefore I will only point out how pale your charms seem in comparison with mine. You are white, just as a leper is white and stinking. If you compare yourself with snow, do not forget that in hell there is snow to torture the damned, with cold more terrible than any fire. If you compare me with ink, remember that the Book of Allāh was written with black ink and that black musk is the present of kings. Recall these words of the poet for your instruction:

Black musk is best
   But rotten pears are white;
And, for the rest,
   Black girls are my delight.
Take low for lack of high
   If you've a mind. . . .
But one sees with the black of the eye
   And the white is blind.'

When Dark-of-the-Eye had made an end of these words, Alī al-Yaman cried out: 'O black and white, you have excellently well spoken! Now it is the turn of two others.'

While the black and white regained their places, the fat and the thin rose and stood facing each other.

Full-Moon, the fat one, elected to speak first; but before she did so she undressed, showing her wrists and ankles, her arms and thighs, the magnificent folds of her rich belly, her round, deep-shadowed navel, and the opulence of her bottom. These treasures were veiled, but not hidden, by the light tissue of her chemise. After a few lascivious shivers, she turned to her rival, the slim Girl-of-Paradise, and said:

At this point Shahrazād saw the approach of morning and discreetly fell silent.

But when the three-hundred-and-thirty-sixth night had come

SHE SAID:

'Praise be to Allāh who, truth to tell, covered each corner and hill and dell with soft delightful cushions' swell; who stuffed my skin with fats which smell like benzoin and hydromel, and gave me sturdy muscles as well, so that one blow of my fist can fell and make my foe a jelly.

'Thin girl, the wise have said: "The joy of life is in three things: to eat flesh, to mount on flesh, and to put flesh in flesh."

'Who can see gigantic curves of the body without a tremble of delight? Allāh himself praises fat in the Book, when He orders the sacrifice of fat sheep, fat lambs and fat calves.

'My body is an orchard of fruits: my breasts are pomegranates, my cheeks are peaches, and my bottom is water-melons.

'What bird was most regretted by the children of Israel on their flight out of Egypt? Was it not the fat and juicy quail?

'Have you ever seen anyone stop at the butcher's and ask for scraggy meat? Does not the man keep his fattest and fleshiest morsels for his best customers?

'A poet wrote of a fat woman like myself:

> Look at her walking,
> She sways and heaves
> More lusty and more lustful than the littles;
> Look at her resting,
> She sits and leaves
> A deeper, sweeter imprint than the brittles;
> Look at her dancing,
> Her bottom weaves
> A spell and knocks our souls about like skittles.

'Is there anything which you resemble so much as a plucked sparrow? Your legs are like the feet of a crow, your thighs like pokers, and your body is as hard and angled as a gallows-tree. A poet said:

> God grant I never have to mount a thin one
> And bruise my staff upon her stony way,
> Even if I found a little pleasure in one
> I would be black and blue at dawn of day.'

'Now you may stop!' cried Alī al-Yaman. 'It is the turn of Girl-of-Paradise.' The slim child looked smiling at fat Full-Moon, and said:

'Praise be to Allāh, who made my body the swaying branch of a poplar and added thereto the wavering of the cypress, the balancing of the lily!

'I rise lightly and I sit down lightly; because of my lightness I can jest with charm. My breath is perfumed because my soul is pure and has abhorred the touch of fatness.

'I have never heard a lover praise his beloved, saying: "She is enormous as an elephant; she is as fleshy as the hills are high."

'Rather I have ever heard lovers saying when they would paint their mistress: "Her waist is supple and slim; she walks so lightly that the dust may not tell of her passage; light food suffices her and a few bright drops of water; her cheeks and her caresses are discreet; there is the perfection of light lust in her embraces. She is quicker than a sparrow, more lively than a starling, she bends like the bamboo; her smile is light. She is a feather to lift, and delicately bends above me; she lies like a scarf of silk upon my knees."

'O fat girl, it is the slim and fine, such as I, who burn the hearts of men, sending them mad with passion. I am the vine climbing a palm tree, surrounding the stem with effortless kisses. I am the gazelle with moist eyes, nor am I called Girl-of-Paradise for nothing.'

At this point Shahrazād saw the approach of morning and discreetly fell silent.

But when the three-hundred-and-thirty-seventh night had come

SHE SAID:

'Now, O fat girl, I will tell you the truth about yourself.

'O mass of grease and flesh, when you walk, you are a duck; when you eat, you are an elephant. You are insatiable in copulation and unreasonable in repose.

'What member is long enough to reach the cave hidden so deep between three mountains, your belly and two thighs?

'Even if a man wins to it, he is immediately bounced back by your swollen belly.

'You would never be sold by your qualities, but simply by weight to an evil butcher.

'Your soul is as gross as your body; your jokes as heavy as the two put together. Your swagging cheeks destroy the beholder, your laughter fractures the ear-bone.

'If your lover sighs in your arms, you can hardly breathe; if he embraces you, you become one glue of sweat.

'You snore asleep, and breathe like a buffalo awake; you can hardly move from one place to another, and when you rest you are a burden even to yourself. You pass your life in chewing like a cow and urging like a camel.

'If you piss you wet your robes; if you spend, you drown the mattress; if you go to stool, you fall in up to the neck; if you go to the bath, you cannot reach your parts, so that they remain stewing in their juice and tangled with unclean hairs.

'Seen from the front, you look like an elephant; seen from the side, you look like a camel; seen from behind, you look like a full waterskin. The poet was thinking of you when he wrote:

> She is as swollen as a bag of piss;
> She walks about, and there an earthquake is.
> She farts among the nations of the West
> And in the quiet East we hear of this.'

Said Ali al-Yaman: 'Great is your eloquence, O Girl-of-Paradise, and admirable your language, O Full-Moon. Now go back to your places and let the blond and the brown speak.'

Sunlight and Incense-Flame rose and stood facing each other. The blond girl said:

'I am that light colour spoken of at so great length in the Koran. Allāh praised me when He said: "Yellow is the colour which rejoices the eyes." Therefore I am the fairest of all colours.

'My colour is a marvel, my beauty the limit of beauty, and my charm, the end of charm. I give the gold its value and their beauty to the stars and sun.

'I paint apples and peaches and give its delight to saffron. I colour many a precious stone and tint the ripe corn.

'Autumn owes to me the gold of all her jewellery, nor would earth be fair under the carpet of her leaves had I not dyed them with the sun.

'O brown girl, when your colour is found in anything, the value of that thing is lessened. Nothing is more common and ugly than your dye. Buffaloes, asses, wolves, and dogs, all are brown.

'Tell me a single kind of meat in which we rejoice to see your colour. Neither flowers nor gems are brown; but copper is brown when it has not been cleaned.

'Yet you are neither white nor black; therefore you cannot take to yourself any of the praises which have been given to either of these colours.'

Then said her master: 'Now let Incense-Flame speak.'

The brown girl showed the double string of pearls of her smile. Also, as she had, beside her dark honey colour, the advantage of a harmonious body, a curving waist, an excellent proportion of limb, and coal-black hair falling in heavy waves down to her dimpled croup, she allowed these things to be seen for a silent moment before she said to her rival:

'Praise be to Allāh that He did not make me deformed by fatness, or thin by illness, or white like plaster, or yellow like colic, or black like powdered charcoal; but rather mixed in me, with surpassing art, delicate colours and distracting lines!

'All the poets have sung my praises in every tongue; I am the preferred of every age and every sage.

'I have no need to praise myself, but am content to cite a few of the verses written in my favour.'

At this point Shahrazād saw the approach of morning and discreetly fell silent.

But when the three-hundred-and-thirty-eighth night had come

SHE SAID:

'One poet wrote:

> Brown girls, all other kinds of girl above,
> Have love's own secret. This if you would prove,
>   Lie with a brown girl for an hour or so;
> She'd teach the dead in heaven how to love.

'Another said:

> Brown, swift, and slim, it is not everyone
> Has loved a brown swift girl as I have done,
>   A little girl, a little brown, slim girl,
> A branch of tender aloes in the sun.

> Brown is the colour of my dreams.

'O yellow girl, you are faded like cheap mallow-leaves, hard and fibrous, plucked about the Bāb al-Lūk; you are coloured like the sheep's head seller's gravy in an earthen pot.

'You are coloured like the ochre and orpiment used for depilation at the baths; coloured like quitch.

'Your copper face is like the fruit of the tree Zakkūm, which grows in hell and bears the heads of devils.

'It was of you the poet said:

> God gave a yellow woman for my wife
> And a continuous headache all my life.
>   Once I suggested that we ought to part;
> I have no teeth to eat with since that strife.'

When Alī al-Yaman heard these words, he shook with pleasure and so laughed that he fell over on his back; he bade the two girls rejoin the others and, to prove to all six the joy he had had in their discourses, gave them equal presents of fair robes and jewels of the land and sea.

Such, O Prince of Believers, continued Muhammad of Basrah to the Khalīfah al-Mamūn, is the tale of the six girls, who now live together in concord at the house of their master, Alī al-Yaman, in our city of Baghdād.

The Khalīfah was delighted with this story and said: 'Do you know the house of the master of these girls? Can you go and ask him if he will sell them?' 'As far as I know, O Commander of the Faithful,' answered Muhammad, 'he will never consent to be parted from them, because he loves them dearly.' Then said al-Mamūn: 'Take with you ten thousand dīnārs as the price of each; that will be sixty thousand dīnārs; and give them to this Alī al-Yaman, saying that I wish to buy his slaves.'

Muhammad of Basrah took the money and hastened to find Alī, to whom he transmitted the wish of the Khalīfah. The poor man did not dare to refuse; therefore, taking the sixty thousand dīnārs, he handed over the six slaves to Muhammad, who led them at once to al-Mamūn.

The Khalīfah was enchanted at the variety of their colours, the elegance of their manners, their wit and charm. To each he gave a special place in his harīm, and for many days took pleasure in their varied perfections.

During this time Alī al-Yaman felt his solitude weigh heavily upon him and bitterly regretted that he had consented to the demands of the Khalīfah. One day he came to the end of his patience and therefore sent a letter to the Commander of the Faithful. It was filled with his despair and, among other sad phrases, contained these lines:

> My spirit flies and clings
>   On sad moth wings
> To those six tender ones.
>   They were my eyes, my food,
>   My garden solitude,
> My drink, my life, at once.
>
>   I should have closed my eyes
>   Upon that gentle prize
> And let my eyelids hold the six of them. . . .

Remains the oil, desire,
Remains the needful fire,
But there's no light, lacking the wicks of them.

When the Khalifah al-Mamūn, who was great of soul, had read this letter, he hastily called the six girls and, giving each of them ten thousand dīnārs, with marvellous robes and other gifts of price, sent them back to their master.

Ali al-Yaman saw them come to him, more beautiful than ever, richer and happier than they had been; so he rejoiced exceedingly and continued to live with them in all delight and pleasure until the day of final separation.

But, continued Shahrazād, do not believe, O auspicious King, that all these tales which you have heard up to the present are in any way to be compared with The Extraordinary Tale of the City of Brass, which I will tell you to-morrow night if so you wish.

Little Dunyazād cried: 'O Shahrazād, it would be most sweet of you to tell us just the first words of it to-night.'

So Shahrazād smiled and said:

It is related, O auspicious King, that there was once a king—but Allāh is the only King—in the city of . . .

At this point Shahrazād saw the approach of morning and discreetly fell silent.

The Extraordinary Tale of the City of Brass

When the three-hundred-and-thirty-ninth night had come

SHAHRAZAD SAID:
IT is related that there was once, on the throne of the Umayyad Khalifahs in Damascus, a king—but Allāh is the only King—called Abd al-Malik ibn Marwān, who often took pleasure in talking with the wise men of his kingdom concerning our master, Sulaimān ibn Dāūd (upon the two be prayer and peace!) and in discussing his virtue, his wisdom, and his boundless power over the beasts of the desert, the Afārīt of the air, and Jinn of the sea and under earth.

One day, as he was listening with great astonishment and an air of disbelief to a tale which was told him of the old copper jars filled with strange black smoke in devilish forms, Tālib ibn Sahl, the renowned traveller, rose among those who were there and, after confirming what had been said, added: 'O Prince of Believers, it was in those copper jars that the Jinn who rebelled against the orders of Sulaimān were imprisoned in times past; afterwards they were sealed with the powerful seal and thrown to the bottom of the moaning sea in the outermost parts of Maghrib in western Africa. The smoke which escapes from them is, quite simply, the condensed souls of the Afārīt, who, on contact with the air, resume their terrible first forms.'

The wonder and curiosity of the Khalīfah were noticeably increased by these words; he turned to Tālib ibn Sahl and said: 'O Tālib, I am very anxious to see one of those vases filled with the smoke of Afārīt. Do you think the thing possible? If so, I am ready to go on the search myself.' 'O Commander of the Faithful,' answered Tālib, 'you can have the thing brought to you here, without trouble or fatigue to your sacred person. You have only to send a letter to the amīr Mūsa, your viceroy in the lands of Maghrib; for the mountain, at whose foot lies the sea which holds the jars, is joined with Maghrib by a tongue of land which may be crossed dryshod. When the amīr Mūsa receives your letter, he will not fail to execute the orders of his Khalīfah.'

Convinced by these words, Abd al-Malik said to Tālib: 'And who more fitting than you, O Tālib, to journey quickly to Maghrib and carry the letter to my amīr Mūsa? I authorise you to draw on my treasure for all that you think necessary for the journey and to take as many men as you need. Above all, hasten, O Tālib.' The Khalīfah wrote a letter with his own hand to Mūsa, sealed it, and gave it to Tālib, who kissed the earth between his hands and set out upon the hour for Maghrib, where he eventually arrived without accident.

The amir Mūsa joyfully and honourably received him and, after taking and reading the letter, carried it to his lips and forehead, saying: 'I hear and I obey!' Then he commanded the sheikh Abd al-Samad to appear before him: a man who had journeyed over all the habitable earth and was spending the days of his old age in noting down, for the instruction of posterity, the observations which he had made during his countless voyages. When the sheikh arrived, the amīr Mūsa saluted him respectfully, saying: 'O Abd al-Samad, the Commander of the Faithful has sent me a command to set out in search of certain old copper jars in which the rebel Jinn were imprisoned by our master, Sulaimān ibn Dāūd. They lie at the

bottom of a sea which surges about the foot of a mountain; and it
seems that this mountain stands in the furthest confines of Maghrib.
Although I have known the whole country for a long time, I have
never heard tell of this sea or the road which leads to it; but you,
who have wandered over the whole earth, cannot be ignorant of the
place of that mountain and that sea.'

The old man reflected for an hour, and then said: 'O Mūsa ibn
Nusair, I have memories of that mountain and that sea, but at this
late day I cannot go there alone, much as I would wish to; the road
is a very difficult one because of the lack of water in the wells; it
would take two years and some months to go and longer to return.
If a return, that is, were possible from a land whose people have
never given a sign of their existence and live in a city perched on the
top of that mountain, a city which no stranger has ever entered and
which is called the City of Brass.'

So saying, the old man fell silent and reflected again, before continuing: 'I must not hide from you, O amīr, that the road is sown
with dangers and even with terrors. There is a desert to cross,
peopled by the Afārīt and the Jinn who guard such lands as have
since the beginnings of time been innocent of human habitation.
For you must know, O son of Nusair, that the places in the extreme
west of Africa are forbidden to the sons of men; two men only have
been able to pass over them, Sulaimān ibn Dāūd and Alexander of
the Double Horn. Since their time silence has been untroubled
master of those vast deserts. If, disdaining the mystery of those perils
and difficulties, you insist upon carrying out the orders of the
Khalīfah and undertaking a journey through that pathless land with
no other guide than myself, you must load a thousand camels with
full waterskins and a further thousand with provisions, and take
with you the smallest possible number of soldiers; for no human aid
could avail us against the anger of those dark powers whose homes
we are about to penetrate, and it would be dangerous to affront them
by a display of useless arms. When all is ready, make your will, O
amīr Mūsa, and let us start.'

At this point Shahrazād saw the approach of morning and
discreetly fell silent.

But when the three-hundred-and-fortieth night had come

SHE SAID:

The amīr Mūsa, governor of Maghrib, called upon the name of Allāh and did not hesitate; he assembled the captains of his armies and the chiefs of his kingdom and, making his will in their presence, appointed his son, Hārūn, to govern in his stead. Then he made the preparation which Abd al-Samad had suggested and, taking with him, beside Tālib ibn Sahl, only that old man and a few chosen warriors, journeyed out into the desert. For days and months the caravan went slowly through flat and unpeopled lands, as empty of all life as is the surface of the sea. It continued in an infinite silence until, one day, the travellers saw something afar off on the horizon which looked like a shining cloud, and made their way towards it. Soon they distinguished a building, high-walled with Chinese steel, and supported by four rows of gold columns four thousand paces round. The dome of this palace was of lead and served as a resting place for countless crows, who were the only living things in sight. Upon the great wall, in which opened the principal door made all of massive ebony plated with gold, a vast tablet of red metal bore certain words in Ionian character. These the sheikh Abd al-Samad deciphered and translated to the amīr Mūsa thus:

> Enter and learn the story of the rulers,
> They rested a little in the shadows of my towers
> And then they passed.
> They were dispersed like those shadows
> When the sun goes down;
> They were driven like straws
> Before the wind of death.

The amīr Mūsa was moved to sorrow by these words and murmured: 'There is no other God but Allāh!' Then he crossed the threshold with his companions and entered the palace.

There rose up before them, in the midst of a silent flight of large black birds, a high tower of naked granite whose top was lost to view and about whose foot were clustered four circles of a hundred sepulchres, which surrounded a bright crystal tomb. Encompassing the tomb, this inscription was graved in Ionian character, the letters filled with gold and diversified by precious stones:

The drunkenness of youth has passed like a fever,
And yet I saw many things,
Seeing my glory in the days of my glory.
The feet of my war-horse
Drummed upon the cities of the world;
I sacked great towns like a hot wind
And fell like thunder upon far lands.
The kings of the earth were dragged behind my chariot
And the people of the earth behind my laws;
But now
The drunkenness of youth has passed like a fever,
Like foam upon sand.
Death took me in a net:
My armies warred against him in vain,
My courtiers flattered him in vain.
Listen, O wayfarer, to the words of my death,
For they were not the words of my life:
Save up your soul
And taste the beautiful wine of peace,
For to-morrow the earth shall answer:
He is with me,
My jealous breast holds him for ever.

The amīr Mūsa and his companions, hearing these words translated to them by the old man, could not but weep. They stood for a long time before the tomb and the sepulchres, saying the mournful sentences over to themselves. Then they went towards the tower, which was shut by a double door of ebony on which these words were picked out in jewels and in the same character:

In the name of the Eternal,
In the name of the Master of Strength,
In the name of Him who moves not!
Wayfarer in this place,
Look not upon the glass of appearance,
For a breath may shatter it
And illusion is a pit for the feet of men.
I speak of my power:
I had ten thousand horses
Groomed by captive kings,
I had a thousand virgins of royal blood

To serve my pleasure
And a thousand excellent virgins
With moon-coloured breasts,
Chosen from all the world.
They brought forth little princes in my chambers
And the little princes were as brave as lions.
I had peculiar treasures
And the West and the East were two heads
Bowing before me.
I thought my power eternal
And the days of my life
Fixed surely in the years;
But a whisper came to me
From Him Who dies not.
I called my captains and my strong riders,
Thousands upon thousands
With swords and lances;
I called my tributary kings together
And those who were proud rulers under me.
I opened the boxes of my treasures to them, saying:
'Take hills of gold, mountains of silver,
And give me one more day upon the earth.'
But they stood silent,
Looking upon the ground;
So that I died
And death came to sit upon my throne.
I was Kūsh ibn Shaddād ibn Ad,
Surnamed the Great.

Hearing these sublime truths, the amīr Mūsa and his companions
burst into sobs and wept for a long time. Then they went into the
tower and began to move through the vast halls, filled with empti-
ness and silence. They came at last to one larger than all the others,
vaulted with a dome and furnished alone of all. The plenishing of
this room was a gigantic table of wonderfully carved sandal wood,
upon which this inscription was interlaced in fair character as before:

About this table
Sat many hawk-eyed kings
With many one-eyed kings
To bear them company;

> But now all sit in the dark and none are able,
> None are able to see.

The amīr Mūsa was astonished before the mystery of what he saw; not being able to find any clue in the inscription, he copied the words upon his parchment; then he left the palace with his companions in sorrowful mood and continued his journey towards the City of Brass.

At this point Shahrazād saw the approach of morning and discreetly fell silent.

But when the three-hundred-and-forty-first night had come

SHE SAID:

They went on for three days until they saw, outlined against the red rays of the setting sun, the appearance of a motionless rider, set upon a high pedestal, brandishing a mighty iron lance which glowed like a flame by reason of the fiery star upon the horizon. When they came close, they could distinguish that the rider, his horse, and his pedestal were all of brass and that, upon the iron of the lance, were graved these words in fiery character:

> If you know not where to go
> In this forbidden place,
> Turn me about with all your strength
> And I will show
> Your path by the direction which at length
> I face.

The amīr Mūsa approached this statue and pushed it with his hand; at once, with the quickness of light, the rider turned and halted with his face towards a point of the compass directly opposed to that which the travellers had been following, so that Abd al-Samad knew that he had been mistaken and that the new direction was the right one. Turning upon its tracks, the caravan went for many days in the way which had been shown, and came at last, at the fall of a certain night, to a column of black stone to which a strange being was chained, one half of whose body was visible and the other half deeply hidden in the ground. The upper half seemed to be that of some monstrous birth imprisoned there by infernal powers. It was as black and large as the trunk of an old and naked palm-tree;

it had two great black wings and four hands, of which two were like the taloned feet of lions. A shaggy covering of rude onager-tail hairs moved savagely upon the terrible head, while under the roofs of the sockets flamed two red eyes, and a third shone, immovably green like that of a tiger or a panther, between the twin horns of the bull-like brow. Seeing the travellers, the body waved its arms despairingly, as if to break the chain which bound it to the black column, and gave forth such mournful cries that the whole party were stricken motionless.

The amīr Mūsa turned towards old Abd al-Samad, saying: 'O venerable, can you tell us what this thing is?' 'As Allāh lives,' answered the sheikh, 'it passes my knowledge.' 'Go nearer and question it,' said Mūsa, 'perhaps it will be able to tell us itself.' Abd al-Samad did not wish to show a moment's hesitation, so he went up to the monster, crying: 'In the name of the Master who holds beneath His hand all things visible and invisible, I conjure you to answer me! Tell me who you are, how long you have been here, and why you have suffered so strange a punishment.'

The body bayed like a dog and then addressed these words to the amīr Mūsa, the sheikh Abd al-Samad, and their companions:

I am Dāhish ibn al-Aamash, an Ifrīt of the line of Iblīs, father of the Jinn, chained here by the Invisible Strength until the death of time.

Once, in this land governed by the King of the Sea, there was an idol of red agate, which protected the City of Brass, and I was at once the guardian of and the dweller in this idol. All the people of the land came in crowds to consult Destiny through me and to listen to my oracles and prophecies.

The King of the Sea, whose vassal I was, held supreme command over all the armies of such Jinn as were rebellious to the orders of Sulaimān ibn Dāūd, and had named me chief of this army in the event of a war breaking out between himself and the Master of the Jinn. Eventually such a war did break out, and in this way:

The King of the Sea had a daughter, whose beauty was so great that it came even to the ears of Sulaimān, and he, being desirous to add her to the number of his wives, sent a messenger to her father to ask her in marriage and at the same time to command him to break the agate idol and affirm that there was no other God but Allāh and that Sulaimān was the prophet of Allāh. Also he threatened him with his vengeance if he did not comply with these commands.

The King of the Sea called together his wazīrs and the chief of the Jinn, saying: 'Sulaimān threatens me with every sort of calamity if I do not give him my daughter and break the idol in which your chief Dāhish ibn al-Aamash dwells. What say you: shall I obey or disobey?'

'Why should you fear the power of Sulaimān, O king?' answered the wazīrs. 'Our forces are as strong as his.' Then they turned to me and asked my advice. I said: 'Let our answer to Sulaimān be a good beating to his messenger.' My advice was carried out, and then the man was sent away with instructions to tell his master what had happened to him.

When Sulaimān learned the treatment which his envoy had undergone, he grew mightily indignant and at once assembled all his forces, of Jinn, of men, of birds and of animals. To Āsaf ibn Barakhyā he gave the command of his human soldiers; to Dimiryāt, King of the Afārīt, the leadership of all the forces of the Jinn to the number of sixty millions and also of the troops of animals and birds of prey which he had assembled from earth and sky and sea. Heading the combined forces himself, Sulaimān entered the lands of my master and drew his army up into battle array.

He set the animals on the two wings in ranks of four abreast, and posted the great birds of prey in the air above them to act as sentinels and spies upon our movements and to hurl themselves upon our men when an opportunity served for tearing out their eyes. He put his human soldiers in the vanguard and the army of the Jinn in the rear; he placed the wazīr Āsaf ibn Barakhyā on his right and Dimiryāt, King of the Afārīt of the air, upon his left. He himself stayed in the centre, sitting upon a throne of porphyry and gold, held up by four elephants, and gave the signal for attack.

At once a terrible noise was heard which increased every minute with the galloping of the soldiers, the tumultuous flight of the Jinn and the birds of prey, the leaping and charging of the men and the wild beasts; the surface of the earth resounded with the tread of a million feet, the air with the beating of a million wings, with howls and yells and cries.

I was in command of the vanguard of the rebel Jinn who owned allegiance to the King of the Sea. I gave the signal to my troops and, leading them myself, threw them upon the opposing Jinn, commanded by King Dimiryāt.

At this point Shahrazād saw the approach of morning and discreetly fell silent.

But when the three-hundred-and-forty-second night had come

SHE SAID:

I sought out the King to attack him myself, when suddenly he changed to a bursting mountain, vomiting fire and striving to lay me low and smother me under the hurtling coals which he poured in solid waves upon my people. For long I rallied my followers, defended myself, and attacked hardily; it was only when I saw that the number of my foes would surely overwhelm me that I gave the signal of retreat and myself fled away through the air with all the strength of my wings. By the orders of Sulaimān we were pursued and hemmed in on all sides by Afārīt and men, by the beasts and the birds; some of us were stricken to death, others crushed beneath the feet of the great animals, and others hurled from the high air by the birds of prey, with eyes plucked out and flesh torn into ribbons. When I myself was taken, after a flight of three months, I was condemned to be fastened to the black pillar until the death of time; while my followers were changed into smoke and imprisoned in copper jars, which were then sealed with the seal of Sulaimān and thrown into the sea which bathes the walls of the City of Brass.

Chained here, as I have been, since the ruin of our power, I cannot well tell you what has happened to the people of this country; but if you journey to the City of Brass perhaps you will see traces of them and learn something of their story.

When the body had finished speaking, it began to shake itself so desperately that the amīr Mūsa and his companions, fearing lest it should get free or oblige them in some way to free it, hastened away on their journey towards the City, which they now saw afar off with the light of evening hanging red upon its towers and walls.

Although they were not far from the City when night fell, the surrounding country seemed so menacing that they preferred to wait till morning before approaching its gates; therefore they pitched their tents and slept, being worn out by the fatigues of their journey.

As soon as the first light of dawn came upon the eastern mountain tops, the amīr Mūsa woke his companions and set out with them in order to reach one of the gates as soon as possible. Soon they saw, rising formidably before them in the clear light of morning, the brass walls, which were so polished that they seemed to have come newly out of moulds. They were so high that they had the appearance of being but the lowest range of the gigantic mountains which surrounded them, in whose flanks they were so firmly fixed that they might have been hewn out of the original metal of the hills.

For some time the party halted in motionless silence before this wonder, while their eyes searched for some door by which to enter the city. This they could not find, so they began to walk round the walls, always hoping to discover some entrance. For many hours they continued their search, without seeing any door or breach whatsoever, or person coming towards the city or going from it. Though the day was far advanced, they heard no noise either within or without the walls and could remark no movement either on the walls or at their feet. The amīr Mūsa, without losing hope, encouraged his companions to go on walking; so they journeyed till evening, seeing nothing but the inflexible line of the brass walls stretching out before them, following the movement of the earth, the valley, and the peaks, and seeming to rise from the bosom of the world itself.

The amīr Mūsa ordered his companions to halt for food and sleep; and he himself sat down to ponder a course of action. When he was rested, he ordered his soldiers to watch over the encampment until his return, and himself, with the sheikh Abd al-Samad and Tālib ibn Sahl, climbed a high mountain in order to inspect the surrounding country and more clearly to see this city, which offered so stubborn a resistance to human visitors.

At this point Shahrazād saw the approach of morning and discreetly fell silent.

But when the three-hundred-and-forty-third night had come

SHE SAID:

At first they could distinguish nothing in the darkness, for night had already spread her shadows over the plain; but suddenly the light in the east grew greater and the splendid moon swam from behind the top of a mountain and lighted earth and sky at once with the sparkling of her eyes. Then at their feet unrolled a sight which made them hold their breath.

They were looking down upon a city of dream.

Under the white radiance falling from on high, as far as the eye might reach towards the horizon which was still bathed in night, spread out the domes of palaces, the terraces of houses, calm gardens levelled in the living brass, moon-bright canals making a thousand wanderings in and out of the shadows of trees, and, lowest of all, a metal sea holding in its cold breast the drowned fires of the sky: so that the brass of the walls, the lighted jewels of the domes, the white terraces, the canals, and all the sea, together with the shadows which lay towards the west, mingled in the night breeze because of the witchcraft of the moon.

This vast prospect was buried in silence as in a tomb; no trace of human life might be found there; but tall figures of brass on monumental bases, mighty riders hewn from marble, winged animals in motionless flight, all showed with the same frustrate gesture of movement; and, in the sky above the buildings, turned, the sole moving things in all the motionless perspective, thousands of enormous vampires, whose flight was accompanied by the lamentations of invisible owls, calling from the dead palaces and sleeping towers.

When the amīr Mūsa and his companions had filled their eyes with this strange sight, they descended from the mountain in a state of great astonishment (for they had seen no sign of human habitation within the walls) and came to the lower level at a part of the brass battlements where were four inscriptions carved in Ionian character. These the sheikh Abd al-Samad deciphered and translated to the amīr.

The first said:

> O sons of men,
> You add the future to the future
> But your sum is spoiled
> By the grey cipher of death.
> There is a Master
> Who breathes upon armies,
> Building a narrow and dark house for kings.
> These wake above their dust
> In a black commonwealth.

At those words, the amīr Mūsa cried: 'O sublime truth! O waking of the soul in the equality of earth! That strikes one to the heart!' When he had copied the words upon his parchment, the sheikh translated to him the second inscription, which said:

> O sons of men,
> Why do you put your hands before your eyes
> And play in this road as if for ever,
> Which is a short passing to another place?
> Where are the kings
> Whose loins jetted empires,
> Where are the very strong men,
> Masters of Irāk?
> Where are the lords of Isfahān,
> O sons of men?

The amīr Mūsa copied this inscription and, sore at heart, listened to the old man as he translated the third:

> O sons of men,
> You see a stranger upon the road,
> You call to him and he does not stop.
> He is your life
> Walking towards time,
> Hurrying to meet the kings of India and China,
> Hurrying to greet the sultāns of Sina and Nubia,
> Who were blown over the mountain crest
> By a certain breath,
> Even as he.

The amīr Mūsa cried: 'Where are the sultāns of Sina and Nubia? They are cast over into nothing!' The fourth inscription said:

> O sons of men,
> Lean death perches upon your shoulder
> Looking down into your cup of wine,
> Looking down on the breasts of your lady.
> You are caught in the web of the world
> And the spider Nothing waits behind it.
> Where are the men with towering hopes?
> They have changed places with owls,
> Owls that lived in tombs
> And now inhabit a palace.

The amīr Mūsa could no longer contain his emotion but wept, holding his brow in his hands and saying to himself: 'O mystery of birth and death! Why is a man born if he must die? Why live, if death brings forgetfulness of life? But Allāh alone understands the purpose of our Destiny; it is for us to bow before Him in silent obedience.' After these reflections he went on with his friends towards the camp, and ordered his soldiers to set to work at once on the construction of a long and solid ladder, which would reach to the top of the walls and might be used as a means of descent into the gateless city.

At once the soldiers collected wood and the large dry branches of trees, cut and shaped these as well as they were able with their swords and knives, and bound them together with their turbans and belts, with the halters of the camels, and the leather of the equipments, until they had constructed a ladder tall enough to reach the top of the walls. They carried it to the most favourable position, propped it on all sides with large stones, and then, after invoking the name of Allāh, began to climb slowly, with the amīr Mūsa leading them.

At this point Shahrazād saw the approach of morning and discreetly fell silent.

But when the three-hundred-and-forty-fourth night had come

SHE SAID:

The amīr Mūsa, with his two companions and such of his soldiers as he had not left below to guard the camp, walked along the top of the wall for some time and at last came to two towers joined by a double door of brass so perfectly made that even the point of a needle could not have passed into the crack of it. On this door a golden rider was engraved in relief, with stretched arm and open hand: upon the palm of the hand were to be seen some words traced in Ionian character, which the sheikh Abd al-Samad deciphered and translated thus: 'Twelve times rub the nail in my navel.'

Surprised by these words, the amīr Mūsa went up to the picture of the rider and saw that there was indeed a golden nail fixed in the very centre of his navel. Stretching up his hand, he began to rub this nail and, when his finger had passed over it the twelfth time, the two halves of the door opened fully, showing behind them a winding stair of red granite, which led downwards. Without hesitation, Mūsa and his party walked down this stair, which eventually led them into a hall, giving, at its own level, upon a street, where were stationed sentinels, armed with bows and swords. 'Let us go speak with them, that they may not interfere with us,' said the amīr Mūsa.

They went up to these guards, some of whom stood to attention with their shields upon their arms and their naked swords in their hands, and others of whom sat or lay at ease, and Mūsa, addressing himself to one who seemed to be a captain among them, courteously wished him peace. The man did not move or answer the greeting; the other sentinels remained motionless with fixed eyes, paying no attention at all to the new-comers.

Thinking that these soldiers did not understand Arabic, Mūsa said to Abd al-Samad: 'O sheikh, speak to them in all the languages which you know.' The old man spoke to them first in Greek and then, seeing that this was useless, in the language of Hind, and afterwards in Hebrew, Persian, Ethiopic, and Sudanese. But none answered to these tongues or made any sign. Then said Mūsa: 'Perhaps these soldiers are offended that you have not greeted them with the peculiar salute of their country. Try the gestures of greeting of all the countries which you know.' The venerable Abd al-Samad at once tried over all the polite movements used in the greetings of the peoples of all the lands which he had known; but none of the soldiers moved even for that.

In his astonishment, the amīr Mūsa tried no further, but, bidding his companions follow him, walked along the street, puzzling his brains for the meaning of this dumbness. 'As Allāh lives,' said Abd al-Samad to himself, 'never in all my travels have I met with so extraordinary a circumstance!'

At last the travellers came to the entrance of the market and, finding all the doors open, walked into it. The place was filled with folk buying and selling and the fronts of the shops were marvellously filled with merchandise; but the buyers and the sellers and all others in the market seemed, by common accord, to have halted in their movements as soon as they were seen, and appeared to be waiting for the departure of the strangers before going on with their business. They paid no attention to the new-comers and only expressed their displeasure at this intrusion by ignoring them. Amid a disdainful silence, the travellers walked on until they came to a great enclosed and vaulted market, where their footsteps echoed with a great noise because of the lack of all other sound. They walked through this building without exciting either welcoming or hostile movements or smiles; and in the same way visited the markets of the jewellers, silk-merchants, saddlers, cloth-merchants, cobblers, and sellers of spices and aromatic woods.

When they had passed through this last market, they came suddenly upon a great square of brass where the sun blinded their eyes, which had before been soothed by the half-lights of the markets. At the other end of this square, between brass columns of prodigious height surmounted by golden animals with spread wings, rose a marble palace, flanked by brass towers and ringed round with armed, immovable guards, whose lances and swords burned everlastingly. A gate of gold gave entrance to the palace, and through this the amīr Mūsa ventured with his friends.

At first they saw a gallery supported by prophyry columns which ran the whole length of the building and enclosed a court refreshed with basins of coloured marble. This gallery seemed to be an arsenal, for there were fastened to all the columns and all the walls and to the ceiling admirable weapons of war, marvellously enriched with precious stones, and taken from all the countries of the earth. Resting on ebony benches, wonderfully inlaid with gold and silver, sat or lay a host of warriors in their parade dresses; but not one of them made a movement to bar the progress of the new-comers or to prevent them from continuing their astonished exploration.

At this point Shahrazād saw the approach of morning and discreetly fell silent.

But when the three-hundred-and-forty-fifth night had come

SHE SAID:

Following this gallery, they saw that the higher part of it was ornamented with a heavily carved cornice, on the blue ground of which was engraved in letters of gold an inscription in the Ionian tongue, which the sheikh Abd al-Samad faithfully translated thus:

> O sons of men,
> Turn quickly and you will see death
> Behind your shoulder.
> Adam saw him,
> Nimrod saw him
> Who wound his horn in the forest,
> The masters of Persia saw him.
> Alexander, who wrestled with the world
> And threw the world,
> Turned quickly and saw death

Behind his shoulder.
Hamūn and Kārān,
Shaddād the son of Ad,
Turned and beheld him.
They were ordered to leave their places
And answer a question,
Which the world could not ask.
O sons of men,
When you give yourselves to the sweet trap of life
Leave one limb free for God.
The fear of death is the beginning of wisdom
And the fair things you do
Shall blow and smell like flowers
On the red and fiery day.

When they had written this moving inscription on their parchments, they opened a large door in the middle of the gallery and went through into a hall where a fountain of transparent marble threw its jet of water into the air. Above this fountain there spread out, as a ceiling of pleasing colour, a pavilion of silk and gold, whose shades were married with a perfect art. To come to the fountain basin, the water followed four canals, hollowed in the floor of the hall, with calculated meanderings. Each canal had a bed of different colour: the waters of the first flowed over a bed of rose porphyry, of the second over topazes, of the third over emeralds, and of the fourth over turquoises; so that the water in each case took the colour of its bed and, stricken by the altered light filtering through the silks above, threw on all things about its course and upon the walls of marble the fair appearance of the sea.

They went through a second door and entered a second hall, filled with old gold and silver monies, with jewels and pearls, with rubies and every precious stone, heaped into so frequent mounds that they had difficulty in walking across the place and attaining a third hall which lay beyond.

This last was filled with warlike arms constructed of precious metals: gold shields bossed with deep-coloured jewels, antique helmets, Indian swords, lances, javelins, and mail of the time of Dāūd and of Sulaimān. All these weapons were in such a state of preservation that one would have said that they had come but the day before from the hands of their smiths.

They found a fourth hall filled with presses and shelves of rare woods, on which were carefully ordered rich clothes and sumptuous robes of costly silk and admirably-worked brocade. Crossing this hall, they came into a fifth, which held from floor to ceiling nothing but vases and other utensils for eating, drinking and ablution: there were gold and silver jars, basins of rock crystal, cups hollowed each from a single precious stone, with dishes of solid jade or different coloured agate.

When they had filled the admiration of their eyes with these things and were thinking of returning by the way they had come, it occurred to them to lift a mighty curtain of gold and silk which covered one of the walls of this last hall. Behind it they found a larger door than all, worked with fine inlay of ivory and ebony and fastened by locks of solid silver with no trace of room for a key. The sheikh Abd al-Samad set to work to study the mechanism of these locks and at last found a hidden spring which gave beneath his pressure. Then the door opened of itself and gave free way to the travellers into a miraculous chamber hollowed inside a polished marble dome, which had the appearance of a steel mirror. By a trellis of emeralds and diamonds across the windows of this place a shining white and green light filtered, which painted everything with its splendour. In the middle of the room, lifted on little gold pillars each surmounted by a bird with emerald feathers and a ruby beak, was a platform, spread with fabrics of silk and gold, which fell from it down an ivory decline and on the floor mingled with a magnificently coloured carpet, where cunning looms had caused odourless flowers to flourish among sapless grass and had created all the lifeless life of a forest filled with birds and beasts caught in the exact beauty of their nature and of their rigorous lines.

The amīr Mūsa and his friend climbed to this platform and were there stricken still in amazement. Under a velvet canopy starred with diamonds, there lay, on a large bed of silken carpets, a girl of flower-like colouring, her lids languid with sleep below curved brows. Her magic beauty was heightened by the gold crown which checked the play of her hair and by a moist collar of pearls which kissed her golden skin. To right and left of the bed stood two slaves, one white and the other black, armed each with a naked sword and a steel pike. At the foot of the bed was to be seen a strip of marble on which these words were engraved:

I am Tadmūrah, Princess of the Amalekites. This city is my city. O you who have come so far, take all which pleases you; but ah, beware! if my beauty and your lust draw you to lay a violating hand on me!

When the amīr Mūsa had recovered from the emotion caused in him by the sleeping girl, he said to his companions: 'It is time now that we left these places, for we have seen all astonishing things, and it is our duty to go towards the sea to find those copper jars. You may take from this palace anything which attracts you, but beware of setting hand to this king's daughter or touching even so much as her garment.'

At this point Shahrazād saw the approach of morning and discreetly fell silent.

But when the three-hundred-and-forty-sixth night had come

SHE SAID:

Then said Tālib ibn Sahl: 'O amīr, nothing in this palace can compare for beauty with this young girl. It would be a pity not to take her to Damascus and offer her to the Khalīfah. He would prefer such a gift to all the jars of Afārīt in the world.' 'We must not touch the princess,' answered Mūsa. 'To touch her would be to offend her and to draw down calamities upon ourselves.' But Tālib answered: 'O amīr, princesses do not mind that sort of violence, whether they are awake or asleep.' So saying, he approached the girl and would have lifted her in his arms; but he fell dead, pierced by the swords and pikes of the two slaves, through the heart and through the head.

Seeing this, the amīr Mūsa would not stay for a moment longer in that palace; but, leaving the city with his companions, hastened along the road towards the sea. When they came to the shore, they saw a great many black men occupied in drying their nets, and these men answered their greetings in Arabic, according to Mussulmān usage. The amīr Mūsa said to the eldest among them, who appeared to be their chief: 'Venerable old man, we come on behalf of our master the Khalīfah, Abd al-Malik ibn Marwān, to search this sea for jars containing Afārīt of the time of the prophet Sulaimān. Can you help us in our quest and explain to us the mystery of the city where all the people are motionless?' The old man answered: 'My son, all we fishermen upon this shore are Believers in the word of Allāh and of His Prophet (upon whom be prayer and peace!). But the in-habitants of the City of Brass have been enchanted since old time and will stay as they are until the Judgment Day. Nothing is easier than for you to gain possession of those jars of Afārīt, for we have a great number of them, which we use for cooking our fish once they have been unsealed. We can give you as many as you like; only I warn you that it is necessary to slap the jars with your hand before unsealing them and to extract an oath from those within that they will acknowledge the truth of the mission of our Prophet, Muham-mad, to atone for their first fault and rebellion against the supremacy of Sulaimān ibn Dāūd. . . . We shall also be pleased to give you, as a proof of our fidelity to the master of all, the Commander of the Faithful, two Daughters of the Sea, whom we have caught to-day and who are more beautiful than all human women.'

So saying, the old man handed over to the amīr Mūsa twelve copper jars, lead-sealed with the seal of Sulaimān, and the two Daughters of the Sea, miraculous creatures, with long hair combing like waves, with faces of moonlight, and round breasts as hard as the pebbles of ocean. From their navels down they lacked the fleshy beauties which are so attractive in the daughters of men, but had instead fish bodies, which they moved to right and left as other women move their thighs when they see that men are watching their walking. Their voices were sweet and their smiles most pleasing, but they could neither speak nor understand any known language, and answered all questions put to them with the laughter of their eyes.

The amīr Mūsa and his companions thanked the old man for his generosity and invited him, with all the other fishermen, to leave that country and journey with the caravan to Damascus, city of flowers, of fruits and of sweet waters. The fishermen accepted this offer, and the whole party first visited the City of Brass, where they possessed themselves of all which they could carry of gold, jewels, and things light to lift but of heavy price. Thus burdened, they came down from the brass walls, filled their sacks and provision cases with their booty, and took the road to Damascus, where they arrived after a long and uneventful journey.

The Khalīfah, Abd al-Malik, marvelled delightedly at the story which the amīr Mūsa told him. When he had heard it, he cried: 'I regret that I was not with you in the City of Brass, but, with the leave of Allāh, I will go there myself soon, to see these marvels and try to unravel the mystery of that enchantment.' After that he opened the twelve copper jars with his own hand, and, each time, a thick smoke welled out, which changed into a terrible Ifrīt, who threw himself at thé feet of the Khalīfah, crying: 'I ask pardon for my rebellion, from Allāh and from you, O Sulaimān, Master!' and then disappeared through the ceiling, to the great surprise of all who were present.

The Khalīfah marvelled no less at the beauty of the two Daughters of the Sea: their smiles, their voices, and their unknown tongue touched his heart and moved him to generosity. He placed them in a fountain basin, where they lived for some time and then died of consumption and the excessive heat.

The amīr Mūsa obtained leave from the Khalīfah to retire to holy Jerusalem, there to pass the rest of his days in meditation upon the ancient inscriptions which he had copied so carefully on his parchments. He died in that city, after having lived as an object of veneration to all Believers; they still go to visit the tomb where he rests in the peace and benediction of Allāh.

Such, O auspicious King, continued Shahrazād, is the Tale of the City of Brass.

'A truly extraordinary tale, O Shahrazād!' said King Shahryār. 'I think so, O King,' she continued, 'but I should not like this night to pass without telling you an altogether charming adventure which happened to Ibn al-Mansūr.' 'Who is Ibn al-Mansūr? I do not know him,' cried the astonished King. Then Shahrazād with a smile said: 'Listen!'

The Tale of Ibn al-Mansūr and the Two Girls

YOU have already heard, O auspicious King, that the Khalīfah, Hārūn al-Rashīd, used to suffer from a frequent lack of sleep caused by the cares of his kingdom. One night, as he turned from side to side upon his bed and could not fall asleep, he grew weary of the useless trying and therefore kicked his coverings away and, clapping his hands for Masrūr, the sword-bearer, who watched each night at his door, said to him: 'Masrūr, find me some distraction, for I cannot sleep.' 'My lord,' answered Masrūr, 'there is nothing like walking in the night for calming the spirit and making a man drowsy.

Outside the night is beautiful in the garden; let us go down among the trees, among the flowers; we will look at the stars in their magnificent incrustation, and admire the fairness of the moon as she advances among them and comes down to bathe herself in the waters of the river.' 'Masrūr,' said the Khalīfah, 'I do not wish to see these things to-night.' 'My lord,' continued the sword-bearer, 'you have in the palace three hundred secret women, each owning a pavilion of her own. Let me go and warn them to be ready; then you can come behind the curtains of each pavilion and, without betraying your presence, admire the simple nakedness of each.' 'Masrūr,' said the Khalīfah, 'this palace is my palace, and these young women are mine, but to-night my soul has no desire for them.' 'My lord,' went on the other, 'let me assemble before you the learned men, the sages, the poets of Baghdād: the sages will rejoice you with their polished sentences, the learned with the discoveries which they have lately made in the annals, and the poets with the genius of their rhythmed verse.' 'Masrūr,' said the Kahlīfah, 'to-night my soul wishes for none of these things.' 'My lord,' continued Masrūr, 'there are delightful cupbearers and charming youths within the palace; shall I order them to bear you company?' 'Masrūr,' said the Khalīfah, 'my soul will have none of them.' Then said Masrūr: 'My lord, why not cut off my head? Perhaps that is the only way by which you can be cured of your melancholy.'

At this point Shahrazād saw the approach of morning and discreetly fell silent.

But when the three-hundred-and-forty-seventh night had come

SHE SAID:

Al-Rashīd laughed heartily at this, and then said: 'Well, Masrūr, perhaps it will come to that some day; but, for the present, go into the entrance hall and see if anyone remains there whom it would be pleasant for me to see and hear.'

Masrūr went out, and presently returned, saying: 'O Commander of the Faithful, I can find no one except that old rascal, Ibn al-Mansūr.' 'What Ibn al-Mansūr?' asked the Khalīfah. 'Do you mean Ibn al-Mansūr of Damascus?' 'Indeed, it is that malicious old man, my lord,' answered the chief eunuch. 'Bring him in quickly!' said al-Rashīd, and at once Masrūr introduced al-Mansūr, who cried: 'A blessing be upon you, O Commander of the Faithful!' The

Khalīfah returned his greeting, saying: 'O Ibn al-Mansūr, let me hear one of your adventures.' 'Prince of Believers,' answered the other, 'shall I tell of a thing which I have seen myself or one of which I have merely heard?' 'If you have yourself seen some very astonishing thing,' said the Khalīfah, 'tell me of it forthwith; for things seen are more interesting than things heard.' 'Then, O Commander of the Faithful,' said al-Mansūr, 'give me your ear and a sympathetic hearing.' 'Ibn al-Mansūr, I have a ready ear, a ready eye, and a ready heart,' answered the Khalīfah. So Ibn al-Mansūr said:

Prince of Believers, you must know that every year I go to Basrah, to pass a few days with the amīr Muhammad al-Hashamī, your lieutenant in that city. One year, on arriving at the palace, I saw the amīr about to mount his horse to go out upon a hunt. When he saw me, he welcomed me and invited me to go with him; but I said: 'Excuse me, my lord, but the very sight of a horse interferes with my digestion, and it is all I can do to remain upon an ass. I could hardly go hunting upon an ass.' Accepting my excuse, the amīr Muhammad put his palace at my disposal and commanded his officers to treat me with all honour and see that I lacked for nothing until his return; instructions which they carried out to the letter.

When he had gone, I said to myself: 'As Allāh lives, Ibn al-Mansūr, year after year you have come regularly to Basrah, and until to-day you have been content to go from the palace to the garden and from the garden to the palace, without seeing any more of the city. You will never learn anything of the place in this way; come now, while you have such leisure, try to find something interesting in the streets of Basrah. The walking will help your digestion, and it needs helping; you are getting fat and swelling like a waterskin.' I obeyed this despairing cry of my soul, which was like to be smothered under so much grease, and, putting on my most costly robes, left the palace and wandered here and there at haphazard.

Now you must know, Prince of Believers, that in Basrah there are seventy distinct streets, and that each street is seventy Irāk parasangs in length. It is not surprising then that, after a short time, I found myself quite lost among so many streets, and in my perplexity began to move more and more quickly, not daring to ask my way for fear of being made a laughing-stock. I sweated wonderfully, I grew very thirsty indeed, and I became certain that the terrible sun would melt every atom of fat about my body.

I dived down the first side-street I came to, searching for a little shade, and soon found myself in a blind alley, stopped by the entrance of a very great and beautiful house. This entrance, which was half hidden by a red silk curtain, gave upon a large garden lying in front of the house; on each side of it stood a marble bench, shaded by the leaves of a climbing vine; and on one of these I sat down to get my breath.

As I wiped my forehead and puffed in the heat, I heard the voice of a woman in the garden singing these words to a plaintive air:

> When the wild deer fled from the cave of my heart,
> Sorrow crept into the vacant lair;
> Why should he leave me, why reprove me?
> I used no art
> Of lips or hair
> To make the maidens love me.

The voice was so beautiful and the words so mysterious, that I said to myself: 'If the woman is as beautiful as her song leads me to believe, she must be indeed a marvellous creature!' I rose and, approaching the entrance, gently lifted the curtain a little way, so that I might see without being seen. In the middle of the garden I beheld two girls of extraordinary beauty, one evidently the mistress and one the slave. It was the mistress who sang and she was the more beautiful; the slave accompanied her upon a lute. I might have been excused for thinking that I saw the moon upon her four-teenth night coming down into the garden. I recalled these lines of the poet:

> A miniature wicked city of Babylon
> Burns in each of her eyes,
> The lights and swords and flowers of Babylon.

> Over her neck of jasmine ivory
> Falls her hair's ebonies,
> Night come visiting jasmine ivory.

> Are they breasts of white flesh tenderly rounded
> Or hand-soft ivories
> Or fruit like white flesh tenderly rounded?

> White sand moving or moving thighs?

And also these lines:

> Two petals of narcissus close her eyes,
> Yet they are large enough
> To hold the dawn.
> Also, the lips I love
> Are sealed with molten
> Rose rubies and her dress
> Is wavering and golden.
> Below it
> Half withdrawn
> A garden plot of paradise
> Wind-nods for ever. Poet,
> You languishing through the hours,
> You cannot guess
> The colour of the flowers.
> I know it.

Prince of Believers, I could not prevent myself from exclaiming: 'Yā Allāh, Yā Allāh!' and stood stock-still, eating and drinking with my eyes. The girl, turning her head in my direction, saw me and quickly lowered the little veil before her face; then, with every sign of indignation, she sent the small slave, the lute player, running towards me, who said to me: 'O sheikh, are you not ashamed to look so at women in their own house? Do not your great age and your white beard counsel you to observe the proprieties?' I answered in a loud voice, so that the seated girl might hear me: 'To a certain extent you are right, my mistress. My great age is a byword, but as for my shame, that is another matter.'

At this point Shahrazād saw the approach of morning and discreetly fell silent.

But when the three-hundred-and-forty-eighth night had come

SHE SAID:

When the girl heard my answer, she rose and, coming over to her slave who stood by me, said angrily: 'Could there be a greater shame upon your white hairs, O sheikh, than the impudence of stopping at the door of a harīm which is not your harīm, and of a house which is not your house?' I bowed and answered: 'As Allāh lives, my mistress, the shame upon my beard is not very great, for my intrusion has its excuse.' 'And what excuse is that?' she asked. I answered: 'I am a stranger, driven almost to death by excessive thirst.' 'As Allāh lives, we accept your excuse; for it is a good one,' answered the girl, and with that she turned to the slave, murmuring: 'Gentle one, run and bring him something to drink.'

The child departed and returned in a moment, bearing a gold cup upon a platter and a little green silk napkin; she offered me the cup, which was full of clear water, agreeably perfumed with fresh musk, and, taking it, I began to drink very slowly, at the same time sending sidelong glances of admiration at the mistress and open grateful looks at both. After some time of this play, I handed the cup back to the young girl, who then gave me the napkin and invited me to wipe my mouth with it. It was deliciously perfumed with sandal; I used it, returned it, and stayed where I was, without offering to depart.

When the beautiful girl considered that my stay had passed the bounds of propriety, she said in a troubled voice: 'O sheikh, why do you not seek your way upon the road of Allāh?' 'Mistress,' I answered in a dreamy voice, 'there are thoughts which occupy my soul and reflections encompassing it which I cannot make clear to myself.' 'What reflections are those?' she asked, and I replied: 'My mistress, I am reflecting upon the other side of things and the march of those happenings which are the fruit of time.' 'Indeed, those are heavy thoughts,' she said. 'We all have to bewail some evil trick of time; but tell me, O sheikh, what has caused you to ponder in this fashion at the entrance of our house?' 'I was thinking of the master of the house,' I answered. 'Now I remember him well. He used to tell me that he lived in this by-street, in a house standing alone in its garden. As Allāh lives, the owner of this house used to be my best friend.' 'Then you ought to be able to remember the name of your friend,' she said. 'I do,' I replied, 'he was called Alī ibn Muhammad, and he was the greatly-respected syndic of all the jewellers in Basrah. It is years since I lost sight of him and I fear that he must now have passed into the mercy of Allāh. Allow me to ask you if he left any children?'

The girl's eyes filled with tears at my words, and she said: 'The peace and love of Allāh be upon the syndic Alī ibn Muhammad! Since you were his friend, I will tell you, O sheikh, that he left one daughter called Budūr and that she is the sole heir to his great riches.' 'As Allāh lives,' I cried, 'the daughter of my old friend could be none other than yourself!' 'You have guessed right,' she answered with a smile, and I said: 'May Allāh multiply His blessings upon you, O daughter of Alī ibn Muhammad! Now it seems to me, as far as I can see through the silken heaviness of your veil, O moon, that your face is very sad. Do not fear to tell me the reason of your grief, for perhaps Allāh has sent me to you to remove the sorrow which sits so heavily upon your beauty.' 'But how can I tell you of such intimate things,' she asked, 'when I know neither your name nor your quality?' I bowed and answered: 'Your slave, mistress, is Ibn al-Mansūr of Damascus, one whom your master, the Khalīfah Hārūn al-Rashīd, honours with his friendship and delights to call companion.'

Hardly had I pronounced these words, O Prince of Believers, when the lady Budūr said: 'Be very welcome to my house, Ibn al-Mansūr. I beg you to use our hospitality largely and as a friend.' With that she invited me to accompany her, and made me sit down in the reception hall.

When we were all three seated in this hall, which lay at the bottom of the garden, and had partaken of the usual refreshments, which were of an exquisite quality, Budūr said to me: 'Since you wish to know the reason of the grief which you have discovered in my face, first faithfully promise to keep that which I have to say a secret.' 'Mistress,' I answered, 'a secret in my heart is as good as enclosed in a steel box whose key is lost.' 'Then listen to my tale,' she said. And, when the delightful little slave had offered me a further spoonful of rose jam, Budūr began:

'I am in love and my lover is far from me. That is the whole story!'

With that Budūr sighed and fell silent, and I said: 'You have been given perfect beauty, and therefore the man you love must surely have perfect beauty also. What is his name?' 'As you have said, Ibn al-Mansūr,' she answered, 'my lover has perfect beauty; he is the amīr Jubair ibn Umair, transcendently the fairest youth in all Basrah and Irāk.' 'He could hardly be otherwise, my mistress,' said I. 'Come, tell me, was your love together in words only, or had it gone as far as long rich intimate proofs?' 'Indeed, the proofs were long enough,' she said, 'if length of time could fasten hearts together. But the amīr Jubair was unfaithful to me, simply on suspicion.'

At these words, O Commander of the Faithful, I cried out: 'Alas, who dares suspect the lily of loving the mud because the breeze bends her towards the earth? Even if his suspicions had been well founded, your beauty would be excuse enough for all.' She smiled and continued: 'Even if it had been the question of some man! But the amīr accused me of loving a girl, this sweet and gentle little thing whom you can see for yourself.' 'I ask Allāh's pardon for the amīr!' I cried. 'May the Devil be confounded! How can two women love each other? At least tell me on what the amīr founded his suspicions.' She answered:

'One day, when I had taken my bath in the hammām of the house and was stretched on my couch under the hands of this faithful slave, who was attending to the cares of my toilet and combing my hair, the heat was so great that the child, to give me cool, slipped the great towels from my shoulders and my breast and began to arrange my tresses. When she had finished, she looked at me and, finding me beautiful, threw her arms about my neck and kissed me upon the cheek, saying: "O mistress, I wish I were a man that I could love you even more than I do now!" Then the pleasant child tried to amuse me with a thousand loving games. In the middle of these, the amīr entered; he threw a strange look towards both of us and precipitately retired, sending me, a few minutes later, a note on which these words were written: "Only that love which is not shared can bring us happiness." Since that time I have not seen him, and he has never sent me news of himself, O Ibn al-Mansūr.'

'Were you bound by a marriage-contract?' I asked, and she replied: 'What was a contract to us? We were bound together by our wills, without the meddling of any kādī or witnesses.' 'Then, if you will allow me,' I said, 'I shall be pleased to attempt to reunite you, simply for the pleasure of knowing that two fine creatures have come together again.' 'Blessed be Allāh, who set you in our way, old man of so auspicious face!' she cried. 'Do not think that you are doing this favour to one who is forgetful of kindness. I will at once write a letter with my own hand to the amīr Jubair, and you can give it to him with such words of your own as may make him listen to reason.' Then to her favourite she said: 'Gentle one, bring me ink and a sheet of paper.' When these were brought, the lady Budūr wrote:

Beloved, why is our separation for so long time? Grief has driven the sleep from my eyes and when your face appears to me in dreams I hardly recognise it, for it is so changed.

'Tell me, why have you left the door open to those who speak evil of me? Rise up, shake off the dust of suspicion, and come back to me! Oh, how will that day which sees us reconciled be white and blessed before our eyes for ever!'

At this point Shahrazād saw the approach of morning and discreetly fell silent.

But when the three-hundred-and-fiftieth night had come

SHE SAID:

When she had finished this letter, she folded, sealed, and gave it me, at the same time slipping into my pocket a purse of a thousand golden dīnārs, without giving me a chance of preventing her. This last I decided to keep in memory of the good offices I had performed in other days towards her dead father, the worthy syndic, and also as a provision for the future. I took leave of the lady Budūr and went at once to the house of Jubair ibn Umair, whose dead father I had also known.

When I arrived at his palace, they told me that he was out hunting, and I sat down to wait his return. In a short time he came back and, when he had learnt my name and condition, begged me to accept his hospitality and sent word to say that I must consider his dwelling as my own. Presently, too, he came to welcome me in person.

O Commander of the Faithful, when I saw the finished beauty of this young man, I was stricken dumb and felt my reason finally forsake her throne. Noticing that I did not move, he thought that I was held back by timidity, so he came towards me smiling and embraced me: I embraced him and felt as I did so that I was clasping the sun, the moon, and the whole universe with all which it contains. As it was time for a meal, the amīr Jubair took me by the arm and made me sit beside him upon a mattress, while slaves spread a cloth before us.

This was covered with gold and silver plate of Khurāsān, and the plate, in turn, with every kind of fried or roasted meat which the palate, the nose, and the eyes could appreciate or desire. Among other excellent things, there were birds stuffed with pistachios and grapes, tender fishes couched upon hot breads, and, more especially, a purslane salad which filled my mouth with greedy water. I shall say nothing of the rest, and yet I must just mention a marvellous rice with buffalo cream, into which I would willingly have plunged my arm up to the elbow, and a carrot jam with nuts, a confection I adore. Oh, one of these days it will be the death of me! Also there were fruits and drinks.

And yet I swear by the nobility of your ancestors, O Commander of the Faithful, that I repressed the solicitations of my soul and did not eat a mouthful. Instead, I waited for my host to invite me to stretch out my hand, and then I said: 'As Allāh lives, I have made a vow not to touch any of the meats of your hospitality, O amīr Jubair, until you have granted me the prayer which I came here to make.' 'O guest,' he answered, 'at least let me know what the prayer is before I engage myself in a matter so grave that it might result in your renouncing my hospitality.' For answer, I took the letter from my bosom and handed it to him.

He received it, opened it and read it; then he tore it up, threw the pieces upon the ground, and stamped on them; finally he said: 'O Ibn al-Mansūr, ask what you will and it shall be granted upon the instant; but do not speak about this letter, for I have no answer to give either to it or to you.'

I rose and wished to depart, but he held me back by the garments, begging me to remain and saying: 'O guest, if you knew the reason of my refusal you would insist no further. Do not believe that you are the first who has been sent upon this mission. If you wish, I will tell you the exact words which she charged you to repeat to me.' With that he reproduced the very sentences, as if he had been present when they had been spoken. 'Take my advice,' he said, 'and do not concern yourself in this matter, but stay and rest in my house for as long as your soul desires.'

These words decided me to remain; I passed the rest of the day and all the evening in eating, drinking, and talking with the amīr Jubair. All that time, I was astonished to hear no sound of singing or of music, though these things are the accepted accompaniment of every feast. At last I decided to give expression to my surprise; when I had done so, I saw the young man's face grow dark and his whole aspect become uncomfortable. 'For a long time I have suppressed all singing and music at my feasts,' he said, 'but if you desire such things, you shall have them.' At once he commanded, and one of his slaves came forward with an Indian lute wrapped in a satin case. She sat before us and, after preluding in twenty-one different tones, sang the following:

The moaning daughters of fate
Weep with troubled hair
Over the fountain, the roses, and the wine,
Over the roasted meats and the narcissus budding and breaking.
When will the poppied cate
Of the year's making
Beguile
This heart of mine
To smile
Over the ordered rare
Fountain, roses and wine,
Roasted meats and narcissus budding and breaking?

Then, to a more mournful melody, she sang:

> There is a drink of honey and aloes,
>   Have you not sipped it yet?
> There is a torture which pleases,
>   Have you not felt it?
> A mouth which refreshes and teases,
>   Have you not lipped it?
> And a rose which burns in the darkness.
>   Have you not smelt it yet?

Hardly had the singer let the last words of this complaint die upon the air than I saw my young host fall back fainting with an unhappy cry. 'This is your fault, O sheikh,' the slave said to me. 'For a long time now we have avoided singing before him because of the agitation and emotion which every love song causes him.' I bitterly regretted bringing this trouble upon my host and, at the slave's invitation, retired to my own room that I might disturb him no more with my presence.

Next day, just as I was getting ready to leave and was begging one of the slaves to carry my thanks to his master, a servant came to me bearing a purse of a thousand dīnārs from the amīr, with a message of farewell, and a prayer that I should accept the purse for the inconvenience to which I had been put. Thus, although I had not succeeded in my part of ambassador, I left the dwelling of Jubair and returned to her who had sent me.

Coming to the garden, I found the lady Budūr waiting for me at the door; without giving me time to open my mouth, she said: 'O

Ibn al-Mansūr, I know that you have not succeeded in your mission.'
Then she gave me so exact an account, word for word, of all which
had passed between myself and the amīr Jubair, that I could not
help thinking that she must have spies in her pay to inform her of
anything which happened at all concerning her. 'How is it that you
know these things so well?' I asked. 'Were you hidden somewhere
when I spoke to him?' 'O al-Mansūr,' she replied, 'the hearts of
lovers are eyes which see that which is hidden. The refusal which
you met was my Destiny and not your fault.' Then, lifting her eyes
to heaven, she continued: 'O Master of hearts, Lord of souls, make
me to be loved without loving! Turn all the love which stays in this
heart for Jubair into his own heart to torment him! Make him return
to me a suppliant and I not heed him!' After that she thanked me for
my good intentions and dismissed me. I returned to the palace of the
amīr Muhammad, and thence to Baghdād.

The following year I went again to Basrah on business, as was
my custom; for I must tell you, O Commander of the Faithful, that
the amīr Muhammad was in my debt and only by these regular
visits could I make him pay. On the morning after my arrival I said
to myself: 'As Allāh lives, I must learn what has happened in the
story of those two lovers.' With this object I walked at once to the
lady Budūr's house.

I found the door of the garden shut and a silence everywhere
which weighed upon my soul. Looking through the grill of the door,
I saw a tomb of new marble beneath the branches of a weeping
willow in the middle of one of the alleys; but I was too far off to be
able to read the inscription upon it. 'She is no more,' I said to myself. 'Her youth has been cut away. Alas, that such beauty should be
for ever lost! Surely grief crushed her down and broke her heart!'

At this point Shahrazād saw the approach of morning and
discreetly fell silent.

But when the three-hundred-and-fifty-first night had come

SHE SAID:

Stricken with an agony of sorrow, I made my way to the palace
of the amīr Jubair, where an even sadder sight met my eyes. All was
deserted, the walls had fallen into ruin, the garden was dry and un-
cared for, the door was unguarded, and no living soul seemed to
remain to tell me of the fate of those who had lived there. Thinking

to myself: 'He also is dead.' I sat down at the door and improvised these lines:

> Even the threshold brought tears to my eyes.
>> Where is the Prince of Hospitalities,
>> Where are the joyful guests who sat with him?
> The spider questions and the wind replies.

As I was thus giving expression to my grief, a black slave appeared before me, and said violently: 'Be silent, old man! May you die suddenly! Why do you say such lamentable things at our door?' 'I was simply improvising some lines to the memory of one of my friends,' I answered. 'He used to live in this house and his name was Jubair ibn Umair.' Then said the slave: 'Allāh's name be upon him and about him! Pray for the Prophet, old man! Why do you say that the amīr Jubair is dead, when, thanks be to Allāh, he still lives, rich and honoured among us?' 'Then why this desolation of the house and garden?' I cried. 'Because of love,' he answered. 'The amīr Jubair is alive, it is true; but he is little better than one dead, for he lies motionless upon his bed. When he hungers, he does not say: "Bring me food!" and when he thirsts, he does not say: "Bring me drink!"'

When the negro said this, I exclaimed: 'In Allāh's name, go quickly, white auspicious face, and tell him that I wish to see him! Say that Ibn al-Mansūr waits at his door.' The slave departed and returned in a short time to say that there was no difficulty in my seeing his master. As I was going in with him, he whispered to me: 'I warn you that he will hear nothing of what you say unless you know some word or words to touch him.'

I found the amīr Jubair stretched upon his couch, his face thin, pale, and hardly recognisable; his glance lost in vacancy. I greeted him, but he did not return my greeting; I spoke to him, but he did not answer. 'He understands nothing but verse,' whispered the slave in my ear. I asked for no better, and, after a moment's reflection, improvised this stanza in a distinct voice:

> Still Budūr puts your tortured soul to school,
> Or have your waking eyes forgot her rule,
>> Or are your nights still full of sleeplessness,
> Sweet fool, sweet fool, but none the less a fool?

Hearing these lines, he opened his eyes, saying: 'Be welcome, Ibn al-Mansūr. Things have taken a serious turn with me.' 'Can I be of any use to you, my lord?' I asked, and he answered: 'You alone can save me. I would send a letter by you to the lady Budūr, for you alone can persuade her to answer me.' 'Upon my head be it!' I returned, and at once, regaining his strength, the amīr sat up, spread a sheet of paper upon the palm of his hand and, taking a pen, wrote the following:

'*Hard love, I have gone mad, I am drowned deep in despair. I used to think love a foolish, light and easy thing; but now, alas, wrecked on his waves, I own him to be a most terrible sea. I come back to you with a wounded heart, begging pardon for the past. Have pity upon me, and remember that once we loved. If you wish my death, you have but to be ungenerous.*'

He sealed this letter and gave it to me. Although I was ignorant of what had happened to the lady Budūr, I did not hesitate to take it. Walking to the garden, I crossed the court and entered the reception hall without announcement.

Picture my surprise when I saw ten young white slaves sitting upon carpets and, in the midst of them, the lady Budūr like a pure sun, in full life and health, but clothed in mourning garments. I bowed before her, wishing her peace, and she, who had smiled on me as soon as I came in, answered my salute, saying: 'Be welcome, Ibn al-Mansūr! Sit down, the house is yours!' Then said I: 'May all misfortune be far from this place, my mistress! Why do you wear a mourning garment?' 'Do not ask me, Ibn al-Mansūr,' she replied. 'My gentle one is dead; you can see the tomb where she sleeps in the garden.' With that she burst into tears, and the slaves about her tried to comfort her.

At first I thought it my duty to keep silence; but at last I said: 'May Allāh sustain her in His mercy! May all of life which was owed to that young girl, that sweet favourite for whom you weep, be added to your share, my lady, for it is she who is dead.' 'It is she, poor thing,' said the lady Budūr.

Taking advantage of the woman's softened state, I drew the letter from my belt and gave it to her, saying: 'Life or death hangs upon your answer; for the hope of a reply is all which binds the poor young man to life.' After she had read the letter with a smile, she said: 'Is he now so far gone in passion, who would not even read my letters of last year? I knew it would be sufficient to keep silence and employ disdain, if I wanted him to come back hotter than ever in his love for me!'

At this point Shahrazād saw the approach of morning and discreetly fell silent.

But when the three-hundred-and-fifty-second night had come

SHE SAID:

'You are right,' I answered. 'And you would even be justified in speaking more bitterly of him; but still forgiveness is an ornament of the soul. What would you do alone in this palace with grief, now that your gentle and consoling friend is dead?' I saw her eyes fill with tears when I said this; for a whole hour she sat dreaming before she answered: 'I think that you are right, al-Mansūr. I will send a reply to him.'

Then, Commander of the Faithful, she took paper and wrote a letter which the finest scribes in your palace could not have equalled for moving eloquence. I do not remember the exact terms of it, but this was the substance:

O lover, I never could understand the reason of our separation, though I wished to do so. It is possible that I was guilty in the past, but the past is now no longer and jealousy should die with the dead.

Let me have you beneath my eyelids to rest my eyes more sweetly than sleep.

We will drink that cup again which cures all thirst. And, if we get drunk, there shall be none to blame us.

When she had sealed it, I received this letter from her hands, and said to her: 'As Allāh lives, this will quench his thirst and cure his evil!' I was about to take my leave and carry the good news to him who was waiting it, when she stopped me for a moment, saying: 'Ibn al-Mansūr, you may also say that to-night will be a night from paradise.' Full of joy, I ran to the amīr's palace and found him with his eyes fixed on the door by which he knew I would enter.

When he had read the letter and taken in its meaning, he uttered a great joyful cry and fainted. Soon he came to himself and anxiously asked me if the lady Budūr had written the letter with her own hand. 'As Allāh lives, she does not do that sort of thing with her foot!' I answered.

Hardly had I spoken these words, O Commander of the Faithful, when we heard from behind the door a clinking of bracelets, a tinkling of bells, and a rustling of silk; a moment afterwards the girl stood before us.

My words could not paint such an excess of joy worthily, and therefore I will not try. I will only say that the two lovers ran towards each other and embraced long and long with mouth to silent mouth.

When they came out a little from their ecstasy, the lady Budūr refused to sit down, although her lover begged her to do so. This astonished me and I asked the reason. 'I will only sit down when our compact has been made,' she said. 'What compact is that?' I asked, and she answered: 'One which concerns lovers only.' So saying, she leaned down and whispered in her lover's ear. To whatever it was she said, he answered: 'I hear and I obey!' Then, calling one of his slaves, he gave him an order and dismissed him.

Soon afterwards I saw the kādī enter the chamber with witnesses; they drew up the marriage-contract of these two young people and then departed, with a present of a thousand dīnārs which the lady Budūr gave to them. I also would have retired, but the amīr prevented me, saying: 'It shall never be said that you shared our griefs and did not share our happiness.' They entertained me with a feast till dawn and then allowed me to retire to the room which they had set apart for me.

In the morning a little slave brought me a basin and ewer. After I had made my ablutions and my prayer, I sat in the reception hall, and presently the married couple came to me, fresh from the hammām after their loves. I wished them a happy morning and complimented them upon their joys, adding: 'I am delighted to have had a certain part in your reunion. But, as Allāh lives, if you wish, O amīr Jubair, to show me a kindness for what I have done, explain to me what it was which angered you so in time past that you separated yourself from the lady Budūr. She has told me of the occasion when the little slave embraced and played with her after combing her hair, but I cannot imagine that that would have been enough to move you so, if you had not had some other reason for suspicion.'

The amīr Jubair smiled, saying: 'You are very wise, O Ibn al-Mansūr. Now that the lady Budūr's favourite is dead, my resentment is dead also, and I can tell you the beginnings of our misunder-

standing. The whole thing started with a jest which was reported to
me, as having been said between the two of them, by a boatman who
once took them for a river trip. "My lord," he said to me, "how can
you bear to have a wife who mocks you with a favourite slave
whom she loves? When they were in my boat, they sat in each
other's arms and sang most disturbing things about the love of men.
They even sang this:

> All that I have of hot
> > Grows cold,
> For he is not
> > That which he was of old.
> These days, however oft
> > I use my art,
> > There is a change from part to part,
> His heart is hard, his other thing is soft."

'When the boatman said this, the world turned dark before my
eyes; I hurried to the lady Budūr's house and there I saw that which
I saw. Thus were my suspicions confirmed. But, thanks be to Allāh,
all that is now forgotten!'

At this point Shahrazād saw the approach of morning and
discreetly fell silent.

But when the three-hundred-and-fifty-third night had come

SHE SAID:

He begged me to accept three thousand dīnārs as a proof of his
gratitude for my happy intervention. I multiplied my good
wishes. . . .

Here Ibn al-Mansūr suddenly halted in his story, interrupted by a
snore. The Khalīfah was sleeping deeply, wooed by the drowsiness
which the tale had heaped upon him. Fearing to wake him, Ibn al-
Mansūr slipped quietly away by the door which the chief eunuch
even more quietly opened for him.

Shahrazād fell silent for a moment and then looked at King
Shahryār, saying: 'In truth, O auspicious King, I am astonished that
the tale has not brought you sleep also.' Then said King Shahryār:
'Not at all. You are quite mistaken, Shahrazād. I did not wish to
sleep to-night. And have a care, for, if you do not at once tell me

some instructive tale, I will remember al-Rashīd's threat to Masrūr. Now could you not say a few words, for instance, concerning suitable cures for women who torment their husbands with fleshly desire and thus open the door of the tomb for them?'

Shahrazād reflected for a moment, and then said: 'O auspicious King, one of the tales which I remember best happens to deal with that very subject. I will tell it to you at once.'

And Shahrazād told:

The Tale of Wardān the Butcher and the Wazīr's Daughter

AMONG other relations it is told that there was once in Cairo a man named Wardān, who was by profession a mutton butcher. Every day a girl of magnificent face and form, but with very tired eyes and pale complexion, would come to his shop, followed by a porter charged with a basket, and, after choosing a portion of the choicest meat that he had and also some ram's eggs, would pay for them with a piece of gold weighing more than two dīnārs. When the meat was stowed in the basket, she would go in turn to all the other shops in the market, buying something from each of the merchants. She continued this daily practice for so long that at last Wardān, the butcher, having become very curious concerning the appearance and silence and habits of this youthful purchaser, resolved to search out the mystery and thus leave his mind free for other speculations.

He found the opportunity for which he was looking when the young woman's porter passed the shop alone. Wardān called him in, placed a prime sheep's head in his hand, and said: 'O porter, tell the cook not to overdo this head or it will lose its savour. . . . I am very perplexed concerning the girl who employs you every day. Who is she? Where does she come from? What does she do with the ram's eggs? Why are her eyes and face always so tired?' 'As Allāh lives,' replied the other, 'I am as anxious as you are to know the answers to these questions. But what little I know I will tell you, as you stretch forth so generous a hand towards the poor. . . . As soon as all her other purchases are made, my mistress goes to the Christian merchant at the corner and buys a dīnār's worth or more of rare old wine; then she leads me up to the entrance of the wazīr's gardens. There she binds my eyes with her veil, takes me by the hand, and leads me to some stair; we go down this together, and my basket is taken from my head. I am given a half-dīnār and an empty basket in place of the full one, then, still with my eyes bandaged, I am led back to the gate of the garden and dismissed until the next day. I have never been able to find out what she does with all the meat and fruit, almonds, candles and the like, which she makes me carry to the bottom of that subterranean stair.' 'You have but added to my perplexity, O porter,' said Wardān, and then, as other customers were approaching the shop, he dismissed the porter and began to serve them.

When, next day, after a night passed in consideration of the problem, he saw the girl and the porter coming to his shop at their usual hour, he said to himself: 'As Allāh lives, whatever happens I must know what I wish to know to-day!' As soon as the girl had passed by with her purchases, he left his boy in charge of the shop, and began secretly to follow her in such a way that he could not be noticed. He walked after her to the entrance of the wazīr's gardens, and hid behind the trees there until he saw the porter returning with bandaged eyes, being led by the hand through the alleys. When the man had been dismissed and had moved out of sight, Wardān rose from his hiding-place and followed the girl with naked feet, using all available cover of the trees. Thus he was able to observe her pause before a slab of rock, push it in a certain way so that it turned upon itself, and disappear by a stairway which led down into the earth. Waiting for a few moments to give her time to descend, he went up to the rock and, manipulating it as she had done, succeeded in making it open. Then he descended the stairs, after having pushed the rock back into its place, and this, in his own words, is what he saw:

At first I could distinguish nothing because of the darkness, but at length I saw light filter from some opening at the end of a corridor; holding my breath, and walking on tiptoe, I went towards the light and came to a door, from behind which I could hear a storm of laughter and grunting. Putting my eye to the crack by which the light was admitted into the corridor, I saw embraced upon a couch, rolling in every lascivious contortion, the girl I had been following and an enormous ape with an almost human face. After a moment or so, the girl disengaged herself and, standing upright, took off all her clothes; then she stretched herself again upon the couch, and the ape leapt upon her nakedness, clasping her in his arms and covering her. When he had done his act, he rose and rested for an instant; then he took her again and covered her. He rose again, rested again, only to hurl himself upon her a third time; and this continued until he had given ten assaults, while she had answered him as finely and delicately as if he had been a man. At last the two fell back, worn out to the point of unconsciousness, and lay without movement.

At this point Shahrazād saw the approach of morning and discreetly fell silent.

But when the three-hundred-and-fifty-fourth night had come

SHE SAID:

Even in my stupefaction, I said to myself: 'Now or never is my chance!' So, breaking in the door with a blow of my shoulder, I leapt into the room, brandishing my butcher's knife, which was so sharp that it reached the bone before the flesh.

Throwing myself strongly upon the enormous, motionless ape, I cut off his head with one blow, so that the vital force left him with a great noise, rattling and convulsion; and the girl, suddenly opening her eyes, saw me standing above her with my bloody knife. Her cry of terror was so loud that I feared to see her fall dead; but at last, seeing that I did not wish her ill, she little by little recovered her senses and recognised me. Then she said: 'O Wardān, is it thus that you reward a faithful customer?' 'O enemy to your own salvation,' I answered, 'are men not strong enough that you have to indulge in such substitutes?' 'O Wardān,' she replied, 'listen while I tell you the cause of all this, and then perhaps you will forgive me.

'I am the only daughter of the wazīr. Until the age of fifteen I lived quietly in my father's palace; but one day a black slave taught me that which I had to learn and took from me that which I had to give. Perhaps you know that there is nothing like a negro for inflaming the insides of us women, especially when the assuaging of this black dung is the first the garden feels. If so, you will not be surprised to hear that my garden became so famished that it needed the negro to give it a dressing every hour.

'After some time the negro died at his work, and I told my misfortune to an old woman of the palace, who had known me from infancy. She shook her head, saying: "The only thing which can replace a negro is an ape, my daughter. Apes are most marvellous in this act."

'I allowed myself to be persuaded by the old woman, and one day, seeing the master of certain performing apes pass by the palace windows with his troupe, I quickly uncovered my face before the largest of them, which happened to be looking in my direction. At once the animal broke its chain and, before its master could stop it, fled by side streets, made a great circle through the gardens, and came back to the palace. There, it ran straight to my chamber and, taking me in its arms, did that which it did ten times without stopping.

'At last my father heard of my relations with the ape, and, upon that day, he nearly killed me. As I was not able to do without my lover, I had this subterranean chamber prepared in secret, and shut my ape inside to save his life. Every day I have brought him food and drink, but to-day, alas, alas! Fate led you to my secret and you have killed my dear! What will become of me?'

I tried to console the girl, saying: 'One thing is certain, dear mistress, I can excellently replace the ape myself. You must judge for yourself, as I have some reputation as a rider.' Thus it came about that I mounted her on that day and on following days, and my strength was greater than that of the dead ape or the dead negro.

Things, however, could not go on long in this way. At the end of a few weeks I was lost, as it were, in a bottomless gulf, while the girl seemed to become more desirous day by day and more plagued by an internal fire.

In this troublesome situation I had recourse to the learning of an old woman whom I knew to be without equal in the art of compounding filtres and of preparing cures for the most deep-rooted ills of the body. I told her my story from beginning to end, adding: 'I wish to know, good aunt, if you can make me up some remedy which will quench the desires of this woman and calm her nature.' 'Nothing is easier,' said the old woman, and I exclaimed: 'I rely entirely on your wisdom.'

At once she took an earthen jar, in which she placed an ounce of Egyptian lupin seed, an ounce of virgin vinegar, two ounces of hops, and some leaves of digitalis. These she boiled for over two hours and then strained off the liquor, saying: 'The cure is ready.' I begged her to accompany me to the underground chamber, and, when we had arrived there, she said: 'First you must ride her until she falls back quite worn out.' With that she withdrew into the corridor to wait until I had followed her advice.

I did as she had suggested so well that the girl fainted quite away; then the old woman came in and, after reheating the mixture, poured it into a little copper basin and placed that between the thighs of my mistress. The resulting fumigations must have penetrated deeply and had a powerful effect, for suddenly I saw two things fall, one after another, from between the open thighs, and lie there wriggling. Looking close at them, I saw that they were two eels, one yellow and the other black.

At this point Shahrazād saw the approach of morning and discreetly fell silent.

But when the three-hundred-and-fifty-fifth night had come

SHE SAID:

Seeing the two eels, the old woman cried out joyfully: 'My son, give thanks to Allāh, the cure has worked! These two eels were the cause of the insatiable appetite of which you complain. One of them was born of the couplings of the negro and the other of the couplings of the ape; now that they have come out, the girl will take her pleasures in moderation and not show herself inordinate in her desires.'

She spoke the truth, for, as soon as the girl came to herself, I found her so calm that I did not hesitate to ask for her hand in marriage. Having become used to me, she consented; and, since then, we have lived together the sweetest and most delicious life. Also we have taken care to add to our household the old woman who accomplished this marvellous cure and taught us the remedy for immoderate desires.

Glory be to the Living, Who dies not and holds all empires and all kingdoms beneath His hand!

That, O auspicious King, continued Shahrazād, is all that I know of cures which may be worked on women who demand too much.

Then said King Shahryār: 'Indeed, I wish that I had known of that prescription last year, that I might have fumigated the wicked woman whom I surprised in the garden with that black slave. Now, Shahrazād, I wish you to abandon tales of science for the time being and tell me to-night, if you can, a story more wonderful than any which I have heard. For to-night I am sadder than usual.' 'I can,' said Shahrazād, and she told:

The Tale of Yamlika, Queen of the Serpents

IT is related, O auspicious King, that there was once, in the antiquity of time and the passage of the age and of the moment, a Greek sage called Daniel. He had many disciples who listened respectfully to his teaching and profited by his knowledge, but he had not been blessed with a son to inherit his books and manuscripts. Knowing no other way to attain this object, he prayed to the Master of All, and the Highest, at the door of Whose generosity there is no doorkeeper, heard his prayer and made the wise man's wife with child at that same hour.

During the months of his wife's pregnancy, the sage, seeing that he was very old, said to himself: 'Death is near, and I have no assurance that the son, whom perhaps I shall have, will find my books and manuscripts intact when he should need them.' Urged by this consideration, he passed all his time in compressing the know-ledge which was to be found in his many writings into a few sheets; employing a fine script, he distilled the quintessence of his wisdom and of the five thousand manuscripts which he possessed, upon five sheets of paper. When these were finished, he reread them and, reflecting for a long time, discovered that there were things upon the five sheets which might be compressed still further. He pondered for a whole month and then wrote out all that was really necessary of the five sheets on to a single sheet, which was also five times smaller than they.

When he had finished his work, he felt that his end was near, so he threw all his manuscripts into the sea, that no other might possess them, and kept only the little bit of paper. To his pregnant wife, he said: 'My time is finished. I shall never see the child which Heaven has given us. It is not allowed to me to bring him up myself. As an inheritance I leave him this little bit of paper, which you must only give him on that day when he demands his share of his father's goods. If he can read and understand what he reads, he will be the wisest man of his time. I wish him to be called Hāsib.' So saying, the sage Daniel rendered his last breath into the peace of Allāh.

All his disciples and the inhabitants of the city walked at his funeral, and there were abundant tears and grief for him.

A few days after this Daniel's wife bore a man child, who was called Hāsib in accordance with his father's wish. She at once summoned the astrologers, who with calculation and observation of the stars cast the child's horoscope, saying: 'O woman, your son will live for many years if he escapes a danger which hangs above his youth. Also, if he avoids that danger, he will attain great knowledge and wealth.' Then they went their way.

When the boy was five years old, his mother put him to school to learn something; but he learnt nothing. She took him from school and would have had him enter some profession, but he insisted on passing the years in doing nothing, and reached the age of fifteen without having learnt anything or contributed in any way to the expenses of his mother's life. The woman wept, and the neighbours said to her: 'Only marriage can give him a taste for work; he will see that, when one has a wife, one has to work for her support.' Hearing this advice, his mother looked among the daughters of her acquaintances and, finding a suitable girl, married her to Hāsib. The young man suited his bride and certainly did not neglect her; but he continued to do nothing and would not work.

Now among their neighbours were certain woodcutters who, one day, said to the older woman: 'Buy an ass, some ropes, and an axe for your son, and let him go with us to cut wood upon the mountain. We will share the profit with him, and thus he will be able to help in your support and that of his wife.'

Joyfully Hāsib's mother bought him an ass, some ropes, and an axe, and eloquently confided her son to the woodcutters, who answered: 'Have no fear, for he is the son of our master Daniel; we will protect him and watch over him.' They took Hāsib with them to the mountain and taught him to cut wood and load it upon an ass. And in a short time he became very fond of his employment, since it allowed him to wander as he pleased in the open air and yet to support his wife and mother.

One day, as the whole party were cutting wood on the mountain side, they were surprised by a storm of rain and thunder which caused them to hide in a nearby cave. There they lit a fire to warm themselves and had young Hāsib, the son of Daniel, chop faggots to feed the flames.

While Hāsib was splitting wood at the back of the cave, he heard his axe strike the ground so sonorously that it seemed certain there must be a hollow below the earth in that place. At once he began digging with his feet and soon laid bare a slab of antique marble, in the middle of which was a copper ring.

At this point Shahrazād saw the approach of morning and discreetly fell silent.

But when the three-hundred-and-fifty-sixth night had come

SHE SAID:

Hāsib hailed his companions, who ran up and, helping him to lift the slab, discovered a deep, wide opening in the earth, where innumerable ancient and carefully sealed jars were ranged in rows. Immediately they let Hāsib down with ropes into the hollow, to see what the jars might contain and to fasten them to the ropes that they might be drawn up into the cave.

When he reached the ground, Hāsib knocked off the neck of one of the earthen jars with his axe and at once saw prime yellow honey escaping from it. He told the woodcutters of his discovery and, though they were a little dashed at finding honey where they expected ancient treasures, they were not displeased to think of the profit which they would make by selling all the jars and their contents. As fast as Hāsib fastened the jars to the ropes, they pulled them up and loaded them upon their asses; but, at the end, instead of pulling up their companion, they made off towards the city, saying to each other: 'If we had hoisted him up out of the pit, we would have had to share the profit with him. He is a good-for-nothing and is better dead.'

They drove their beasts to the market and then sent one of their number to Hāsib's mother, who said to her: 'While we were on the mountain your poor son's ass was frightened by the storm so that it ran away. Your son hurried after it, while the rest of us hid in a cave. Suddenly, as evil fortune would have it, a wolf leapt from the forest and, killing Hāsib, ate him and his ass together. A little blood and a few bones are all that we could find of them.'

Hāsib's mother and wife beat their faces and, after weeping all the tears of despair, covered their heads with dust. So much for them.

The woodcutters sold the jars of honey at a high price and made such profit that each was able to buy a shop and set up as a merchant. They stinted themselves for nothing, eating and drinking of the best on every occasion. So much for them.

When Hāsib saw that they did not draw him up out of the pit, he called and begged in vain, and then tried to dig holes in the side of the pit for his feet and hands; but the walls were of granite and resisted the steel of his axe. His despair knew no bounds, and he had thrown himself down on the floor of the pit to die, when suddenly he saw a great scorpion come out of a crack in the granite wall and dart forward to sting him. He crushed the beast with a blow of his axe and, examining the fissure from which it had come, saw light beyond. Thrusting in the head of his axe and pulling strongly, he found to his great surprise that he was lifting a sliding door, which soon rose high enough to admit the passage of a man's body.

Without hesitating, Hāsib crawled through the opening and found himself in a long subterranean gallery lighted at the far end. This gallery he followed for a whole hour and came at last to a vast door of black steel with a silver lock and a gold key. He opened the door and passed through, to find himself suddenly in the open air, on the border of a lake at the foot of a hill of solid emerald. At the side of the lake he saw a gold throne, splendid with sparkling stones, and all about it, delightfully reflected in the water, chairs of gold and silver, of emerald and crystal, of steel, of ebony and of white sandal-wood. These chairs he counted and found them to number twelve thousand, neither more nor less. When he had made his count and admired the beauties of all about him and of the water which reflected those beauties, he sat down on the throne to enjoy the prospect of the lake and the mountain more at his ease.

He had not long been seated on the gold throne when he heard a music of cymbals and gongs, and saw, advancing from behind the flanks of the emerald hill and moving towards the lake, a procession of beings who glided rather than walked. But he could not see of what form they were because they were yet far off. When they came nearer, he distinguished that they were women of ravishing beauty, but having their lower parts long and limbless and ramping like those of serpents. Their voices were sweet, and they sang Greek praises of a queen whom he could not yet see. Presently, though, four of these snake-women came from behind the hill, gliding in a square and carrying, upon arms upraised above their heads, a vast basin of gold, in which was seated their beautiful smiling Queen. The four women came up to the throne, which Hāsib had hastily vacated, and, setting their Queen upon it, smoothed the folds of her veils and ranged themselves behind her, while the other serpents slipped each towards one of the costly chairs disposed about the lake. The Queen addressed them in Greek, with a most pleasant-sounding voice, and then, at a signal given by the cymbals, all the doubtful beings sang a Greek hymn in her honour and sat down upon the chairs.

When the hymn was ended, the Queen, who had noticed Hāsib's presence, turned her head kindly towards him and signed to him to approach. Though somewhat frightened, he walked towards the throne, and straightway the Queen invited him to sit down, saying: 'Be welcome to my kingdom under earth, O youth, whose happy fortune has led him hither. Lay aside all fear and tell me your name. I am Queen Yamlika: these serpent-women are my subjects. Speak now, and tell me who you are and how you come to this lake, which is my Winter dwelling and for which, at a certain season of the year, I leave my Summer home, Mount Kāf.'

Young Hāsib kissed the earth between the hands of Yamlika and sat down on an emerald seat at her right hand, saying: 'My name is Hāsib, son of Daniel, the wise man who is dead. Although I could be a merchant or even a great sage, I am content with the trade of woodcutter, as it allows me to breathe the free air of the woods and mountains. I always say to myself that it will be time enough after death to be shut between four walls.' Then he told her in detail his adventure with the other woodcutters and how, by chance, he had reached her subterranean kingdom.

Hāsib's tale delighted Queen Yamlika. 'Hāsib,' she said to him, 'you must be very hungry and thirsty after all the time that you were shut in that pit.' So saying, she signed to one of her women, who glided towards the young man bearing on her head a gold dish filled with grapes, pomegranates, apples, pistachios, nuts, fresh figs and bananas. When he had eaten and appeased his hunger, he drank a delicious sherbert in a cup hollowed out of a single ruby. At length the woman took away the dish, and Queen Yamlika said to Hāsib: 'You may rest assured that, while you stay in my kingdom, nothing unpleasant will happen to you. If you would like to spend a week or so with us beside our lake and in the shadow of our mountains, I will pass the time for you by telling you a tale which will be of use to you when you return to the land of men.'

Thus it was that Queen Yamlika, sovereign under earth, told this tale in Greek to the twelve thousand serpent-women, sitting upon their chairs of emerald and gold, and to young Hāsib, son of Daniel the sage:

The Tale of Bulūkiya

THERE was once, in the kingdom of Banū Isrāil, a very wise King who, as he lay upon his deathbed, called his son, the heir to his throne, and said to him: 'Bulūkiya, my son, when you gain possession of my power, I advise you to make a personal inventory of everything in the palace and to let nothing pass without the most careful scrutiny.'

Young Bulūkiya's first care, when he became King, was to examine all the goods and treasures of his father, and to walk through the various halls which had been used to store the accumulated wealth of the palace. In so doing he came at last to a far and hidden room, where he saw a little chest of ebony, supported by a white marble column rising in the middle of the floor. Opening this, he found inside it a gold box and inside the gold box a roll of parchment, which he spread out before his eyes. It contained this, written in Greek:

He who would become the master and lord of men, of Jinn, of birds and beasts, need but find the ring which the prophet Sulaimān wears upon his finger in the Isle of the Seven Seas where he lies buried. It is the magic ring which Adam, father of men, wore upon his finger in Paradise before his fall. It was taken from him by the angel Gabriel, who later gave it to Sulaimān the Wise. But to cross those seas and to reach that Isle beyond the Seventh Sea no ship avails; he only may succeed who finds the plant with magic juice which, rubbed upon the soles of the feet, makes men capable of walking on the surface of the sea. That plant grows in the subterranean kingdom of Queen Yamlika, only she knows where; for she understands the language of all plants and flowers, with the virtue and property of each. Therefore, he who would find the ring must go first to the subterranean kingdom of Queen Yamlika. If he at last succeeds in taking the ring, not only will he be the lord of all created beings but may journey into the Land of Darkness and drink there the Fountain of Life, which gives beauty, youth, wisdom and immortality.

At this point Shahrazād saw the approach of morning and discreetly fell silent.

But when the three-hundred-and-fifty-eighth night had come

SHE SAID:

When Prince Bulūkiya had read this parchment, he called together all the priests, magicians and sages of Banū Isrāil and asked if there was one among them who could show him the road to the subterranean kingdom of Queen Yamlika. All pointed to the wise Affān, a worthy old man deeply versed in all knowledge, in the mysteries of magic, the keys of astronomy and geometry, and the arcana of alchemy and sorcery. He rose and stood before the young King, who said to him: 'O Affān, are you truly able to guide me to the kingdom of this hidden Queen?' 'I am,' answered Affān.

Young Bulūkiya gave his wazīr power to direct the affairs of state during his absence and, putting off his royal robe, dressed himself in a pilgrim's mantle and shoes of travel. Then, followed by the learned Affān, he left the city and journeyed into the desert.

Only when they had gone some way did Affān say to him: 'Here is the propitious place for those conjurations which will show us our way.' They halted; Affān drew a magic circle about him in the sand and, after performing certain rituals, brought to light the spot which was the entrance, on that side, to my subterranean kingdom. After he had performed other ceremonial, the earth opened and left a free way for the two of them to this lake which you now see, O Hāsib.

I received them with the courtesy which I always extend to visitors and, when they told me the object of their coming, had myself raised up in my gold basin upon the heads of my carriers and conducted my guests towards the top of this emerald hill. As I went along, the plants and the flowers all began to speak in their own language, left or right, low or high, boasting their various powers. Among the concerted voices of musical and perfumed sap, we came to a cluster of a certain plant which sang from the red mouths of all ts flowers in harmony with the breeze which bent them: 'He who rubs his feet with my marvellous juice may walk unwetted over all the seas of God.'

'This is the plant for which you are looking,' I said to my visitors, and at once Affān plucked as many of the blossoms as he wished and, crushing the shoots, collected the sap in a large flask which I had given him.

Wishing to question Affān, I said to him: 'O wise old man, will you tell me why you both wish to cross the seas?' 'O Queen,' he answered, 'it is because we wish to reach the Isle of the Seven Seas and there to find the magic seal of Sulaimān, who was master of men and Jinn, beasts and birds.' 'Do you not know,' I said, 'that it is impossible for anyone since Sulaimān to own that ring? Believe me, Affān! Listen to me, young King Bulūkiya! Leave this rash project, this mad undertaking, and pluck rather this other plant which gives eternal youth to those who eat it.' But they would not listen to me; they bade me farewell and disappeared by the way they had come.

Here Queen Yamlika paused and, peeling a banana for young Hāsib, ate a fig herself, and said: 'O Hāsib, before I go on with the tale of Bulūkiya and describe his journey across the Seven Seas and the other adventures which befell him, would you not like to know exactly where my kingdom lies at the foot of Kāf, which surrounds the earth as with a belt, and to hear something of its size, its neighbourhood, its living and talking plants, its Jinn, and its snake-women of whom Allāh alone can tell the number? Would you not wish me to describe how Kāf lies all along on a marvellous rock of emerald, al-Sakar, whose reflection gives their colour to the skies? I could tell you the exact place in Kāf where is Jinnistān, which is the capital of the Jinn ruled over by King Jān ibn Jān, and reveal to you the place where the rūkhs live in the Valley of Diamonds, and point out to you the battlefields which yet sing the exploits of old heroes.'

Young Hāsib answered: 'O Queen Yamlika, I would much rather hear the rest of the adventures of King Bulūkiya.'

So the princess of under earth went on:

When Bulūkiya and the wise Affān left me to make their way to the island at the other end of the Seven Seas, where lies the body of Sulaimān, they came presently to the shore of the First Sea and, sitting down, began to rub the soles and ankles of their feet with plant juice from the flask. This done, they rose and began to walk very cautiously upon the water; but, when they found that they could walk more easily upon the sea than upon dry land, and without any fear of drowning, they grew bolder and began to walk faster, so as to lose no time. For three days and three nights they walked over that sea and, on the morning of the fourth day, came to an island which they thought to be Paradise because it was so beautiful.

At this point Shahrazād saw the approach of morning and discreetly fell silent.

But when the three-hundred-and-fifty-ninth night had come

SHE SAID:

The sand was of gilded saffron and the rocks of jade and ruby; the meadow spread out into gardens of bright flowers scenting the breeze which wandered there; the smiles of roses married with the tender glances of narcissus; lilies and carnations, violet, anemone and camomile, lived in one scented friendship together, while the light gazelles leaped and ran between hedges white with jasmine. Forests of aloes and trees with large shining flowers murmured through their branches as the doves leaned from them to answer the water streams. There the nightingales told of their martyred love to the roses in voices of silver pain, while the roses listened. Melodious rivers hid among clumps of sugar-cane, their only reeds; and the natural earth showed forth at ease her rich youth, breathing of all her thousand Springs.

Bulūkiya and Affān walked in this beauty till evening, shaded by the groves and filling their souls with happiness. Then, as night fell, they climbed up into a tree to sleep and were about to close their eyes when suddenly the island began to ring with a lowing which made it tremble to its foundation. There came up out of the waves of the sea a monstrous beast, holding a luminous stone in its jaws as if it had been a torch, and, directly behind it, a multitude of other sea-monsters, each holding a like stone in a like manner. When these lighted jewels had made the island as bright as day, there came down from the interior so many lions, tigers and leopards, that Allāh alone might have counted them. The land beasts met the sea beasts on the shore and there they talked and chatted together until the morning. With the first light, the sea-monsters returned into their element and the wild beasts went back to the fores   Then Bulūkiya and Affān, who for very fear had not slept a wink all night, came down hastily from their tree and, running to the shore, made haste to rub their feet with the juice of the magic plant.

They walked across the Second Sea for days and nights, until at last they came to the foot of a chain of mountains in the middle of which opened a marvellous valley. In it every pebble and every rock was magnetic, and there was no trace of wild beast or any dangerous animal. They journeyed through the valley all day at haphazard, sustaining themselves with dried fish, and at evening sat down on the sea shore to watch the setting of the sun. Suddenly a terrible screaming came to their ears and, turning quickly, they saw a tiger springing towards them. They had just time before it sprang to rub their feet with the sap and to run out to sea beyond the creature's reach.

This was the Third Sea. The night was very black and the waves were high because of the wind, so that walking upon it became most tiring to travellers who were already worn with want of sleep. Happily, at dawn, they came to an island and there lay down to sleep. When they woke, they walked inland and discovered that the isle was filled with fruit trees which differed from other trees in this marvellous particular, that the fruit grew upon them already preserved in sugar. The two travellers enjoyed themselves very much in this island, especially Bulūkiya who was extremely fond of crystallised fruits and all sweet things. He passed the rest of the day in eating and persuaded Affān to stay there for ten further days in order that he might have time to take full advantage of the delicious fruits. At the end of the tenth day, however, he had so abused the sweet trove that he had a bellyache; therefore he and Affān anointed their soles and ankles once more and walked out on to the Fourth Sea.

They went forward upon it for four days and four nights and then landed at an island, which was nothing more than a strip of very fine white sand in which every kind of reptile known to man lay hid, after having placed their eggs to be hatched in the sun. As there was no tree or blade of grass to be seen, the travellers only stayed long enough upon this sand to give their feet a fresh coating from the flask.

They had but to walk for one day and one night across the Fifth Sea before they came, at dawn, to a little island whose mountains were of crystal with great veins of gold, and which was covered with astonishing trees whose flowers were bright yellow. At night these flowers shone like stars and their light, reflected by the crystal rocks, lit up the island so that it shone more even than in the daytime. Said Affān to Bulūkiya: 'This is the Isle of Gold Flowers; when these blossoms fall from the trees and dry, they run to powder and become gold. The Isle of Gold Flowers is a piece of the sun which fell to earth in times gone by.'

They passed a night of great splendour upon that island, and in the morning, after rubbing their feet with the precious fluid, ventured out upon the Sixth Sea.

At this point Shahrazād saw the approach of morning and discreetly fell silent.

But when the three-hundred-and-sixtieth night had come

SHE SAID:

They walked over the Sixth Sea for long enough to feel great pleasure when they came to an island thickly and beautifully wooded. They rested upon the shore until they were refreshed, then began to walk among the trees; but, to their horror, they soon noticed that these bore human heads on stalks of hair instead of fruit. These human clusters had different expressions: some smiled, others wept or laughed, and those which fell from the trees rolled about in the dust until they became globes of fire which lighted the forest and paled the sunlight. Thinking upon the strangeness of the forest, the two companions dared not approach the fruits more closely, but returned to the sea shore. They were sitting behind a rock, as evening fell, when suddenly they saw twelve sea-girls, of surpassing beauty and wearing chains of pearl about their necks, come up out of the water and dance around upon the sand, leaping and playing a thousand pretty games for an hour together. After that they sang in the moonlight, and then swam out to sea. Though Bulūkiya and Affān were delighted by the beauty and the singing and the dancing of these sea-girls, they did not care to stay any longer in that island because of the terrible growth upon the trees; therefore they rubbed their feet and ankles with more sap from the flask and ventured out upon the Seventh Sea.

Their journey was long over this Seventh Sea; they walked day and night for two months without spying any land, and in order that they might not die of hunger were obliged to catch fish, which came sometimes to the surface, and to eat them raw. It was not long before they realised the wisdom of the advice which had been given to them, and heartily wished that they had followed it; yet, at length, they came to an island which they rightly supposed to be the Isle of the Seven Seas, where was the body of Sulaimān and the magic ring upon his finger.

They found the Isle of the Seven Seas covered with fruit trees and watered by many streams. As they were hungry and dry in the throat after their long diet of raw fish, they joyfully approached a large apple tree, burdened with ripe fruit. Bulūkiya stretched out his hand and would have plucked one, when a terrible voice was heard crying from inside the tree: 'If you touch this fruit you will be cut into two bits!' At the same moment an enormous giant, forty cubits high, appeared before them, to whom the terrified Bulūkiya said: 'O chief of the giants, we are dying of hunger and do not know why you should forbid us to touch these apples.' 'How can you pretend to be ignorant of the reason?' asked the giant. 'Have you forgotten, O sons of men, that Adam, the father of your race, rebelled against Allāh and ate forbidden fruit? Since then it has been my duty to stand guard over this tree and to kill all who would touch its clusters. Depart and find your food in some other place.'

Bulūkiya and Affān hastened to leave that spot and, after refreshing themselves with other fruit in the interior of the island, began their search for the burial place of Sulaimān.

After wandering for a day and a night about the island, they came to a hill whose rocks were of musk and yellow amber and in whose sides opened a magnificent cave with roof and walls of solid diamond. Since it was thus lighted more brightly than by the sun, they ventured further in, finding the light grow greater and the roof higher as they advanced. They walked on and on, marvelling all the time, and suddenly, just as they had begun to wonder whether the cave had any end, turned into a vast hall hewn from the solid diamond, having in its centre a great bed of heavy gold on which lay Sulaimān ibn Dāūd in the green mantle sewn with mighty pearls which he wore in life. The magic ring circled the fingers of his right hand and shot out fires which paled the splendours of the diamond; the hand which wore it rested upon his breast, the other stretched out beside him, holding a gold sceptre eyed with emeralds.

At first Bulūkiya and Affān felt so much respect for the illustrious dead that they dared not advance; but at last Affān said to Bulūkiya: 'We have faced so many dangers upon our weary journey, we must not recoil now that we have attained our end. I will go alone up to the throne where the Prophet sleeps, while you pronounce the conjurations which I have taught you, to cause the ring to slip from the rigid finger.'

Bulūkiya began the magic formula while Affān went up to the throne and stretched forth his hand to take the ring; but the young man, in his emotion, pronounced the words of power backwards and this mistake was fatal to the sage; for, from the bright ceiling, there fell a drop of liquid diamond which set him all on fire and, in the twinkling of an eye, reduced him to a handful of dust at the foot of the throne of Sulaimān.

When Bulūkiya saw the punishment which had fallen upon Affān for his sacrilegious attempt, he rushed through the cave and, leaving its entrance, hastened directly down to the sea. There he would have rubbed his feet and left the island, but he remembered that he could not, since the flask and its miraculous contents had been burned up with Affān.

At this point Shahrazād saw the approach of morning and discreetly fell silent.

But when the three-hundred-and-sixty-first night had come

SHE SAID:

Sadly at length he understood all I had meant when I warned him of the misfortunes which he was certain to encounter upon his desperate quest. He walked at random about the isle, alone, friendless, and without a guide, not knowing at all what he should do.

As he wandered thus, he saw a great cloud of dust from which issued a tumult more deafening than thunder; he heard within it the shock of lances and swords, with a confused sound of galloping and cries of things inhuman. Suddenly the dust fell and from it appeared a whole army of Afārīt, Jinn, Marids and Ghouls, with every other spirit of air and sea and ocean, of wood and stream and sand.

Being too terrified to run away, he waited till the chief of this fabulous army came towards him, saying: 'Who are you? How did you come to this isle which we visit every year to watch over the cave where our master Sulaimān ibn Dāūd sleeps?' 'O mighty captain,' answered Bulūkiya, 'I am Bulūkiya, King of the Banū Isrāīl. I was lost at sea, and that is why I am here. May I ask in my turn who you are, and who are all these warriors?' 'We are those of the Jinn who claim descendence from Jān ibn Jān,' replied the other. 'We have just come from the land where dwells Sakhr, our mighty King. He is the master of the White Land, reigned over in times past by Shaddād, son of Ād.' 'Where is that White Land where the great Sakhr lives?' asked Bulūkiya, and the other answered: 'Behind Mount Kāf, which is seventy-five months' journey from here by human reckoning. But we can cover the distance in the twinkling of an eye. As you are a King's son, we will, if you like, take you and

present you to our master.' The young prince hastened to accept
this offer, and was immediately transported by the Jinn to the
dwelling of King Sakhr.

He found this to be a magnificent plain, seamed with canals
having gold and silver beds. The floor of it was covered with musk
and saffron and it was shaded with artificial trees whose leaves were
emeralds and their fruit rubies. The whole space was covered with
proud tents of green silk, held up by thin poles of jewelled gold.
In the centre was a pavilion higher than all the rest, made out of red
and blue silk, supported by alternate columns of ruby and emerald.
Within it, on a throne of wrought gold, sat King Sakhr, with his
vassal kings on his right hand, and on his left, his wazīrs, lieutenants,
nobles and chamberlains.

Bulūkiya kissed the earth between the King's hands and made him
a compliment. Then Sakhr kindly invited him to sit on a gold seat
by his side and asked him his story. When the young man told all
that had happened to him from beginning to end, without omitting
a single detail, the King and all with him were mightily astonished.
The cloth was set for a feast, and servant Jinn brought dishes and
plates of porcelain to the company. Those dishes which were of gold
contained fifty young boiled camels and fifty roasted ones, while the
silver dishes held fifty sheep's heads, and the porcelain plates a
careful arrangement of marvellously big fruit. When all was ready,
the Jinn and their guest ate and drank abundantly, until not a trace
remained of any of the food which had been set before them.

Then, and only then, King Sakhr said to Bulūkiya: 'You are
doubtless ignorant of our story and our origin. I will tell you of
them in a few words, so that, when you return among the sons of
men, you may hand down to future ages the truth of matters which
otherwise would be dark and doubtful to them.'

At this point Shahrazād saw the approach of morning and
discreetly fell silent.

But when the three-hundred-and-sixty-second night had come

SHE SAID:
'In the beginning Allāh created the Fire and shut it within seven
different regions of the Globe, placed one above the other, but a
thousand years apart. He called the first region of the Fire Jahannam
and in His wisdom set it apart for rebel creatures who would not

repent. He called the second region Lazā, because it was dug in the form of a gulf, and set it apart for those who, after the future coming of Muhammad the Prophet (upon whom be prayer and peace!), should remain in the darkness of their error and refuse to believe. The third region he formed as a boiling cauldron, calling it Jahīm, and appointed it for Gog and Magog. The fourth region He called Saīr, and appointed it for the place of Iblīs, commander of the rebel angels, who had refused to recognise and humble himself before Adam, thus disobeying the strict command of the Almighty. He fixed the bounds of the fifth region, calling it Sakhr and appointing it for the impious, the lying and the proud. Then He dug an immense cavern and, filling it with sultry and pestilential air, called it Hitmah, and appointed it for the tortures of Jews and Christians. The seventh, Hāwiyah, He placed in reserve, to contain the overflow of Jews and Christians and those who made a show of belief. These two last regions are by far the worst, while the first region is easily supportable. Their structure is much the same in each case. The first, Jahannam, has seventy thousand mountains on fire, each mountain encloses seventy thousand valleys, each valley holds seventy thousand cities, each city, seventy thousand towers, each tower, seventy thousand houses, and each house, seventy thousand benches. On each of these benches, whose number you can reckon out for yourself, there are seventy thousand separate kinds of torture and punishment, whose infinite variety is known to God alone. As this first region is the mildest of the seven, you may form some idea of the torments which wait in the six others.

'I have given you this sketch and explanation of the Fire because we, the Jinn, are the sons of Fire.

'The first two creatures which Allāh created from Fire were the two Jinn, whom He appointed to be His own particular guard, calling them Khalīt and Malīt. To one He gave the form of a lion and to the other the body of a wolf; the lion He equipped with masculine organs and the wolf with feminine. The yard of the lion Khalīt is twenty years long and the passage of Malīt, the wolf, is formed like a tortoise and made in proportion to Khalīt's yard. One is black and white, the other white and rose. It came to pass that Allāh joined Khalīt and Malīt together and, from their copulation, were born serpents, dragons and scorpions and all beasts that stink, so that the seven regions might be stocked for the torment of the damned. Then Allāh commanded Khalīt and Malīt to couple a second time, and from that coupling were born seven males and seven females who grew up in obedience. When they were full grown, one of them, who gave the brightest hopes, was specially chosen out by the Highest and given command of those increasing cohorts which sprang from the incessant business of Khalīt and Malīt. This chief was named Iblīs. Later, because of his disobedience to Allāh, Who had ordered him to bow down before Adam, he was hurled into the fourth region with all those who had joined him in his rebellion. From Iblīs and his seed are sprung all the male and female devils with which the hells are peopled. As for the six other youths and the females, who had remained obedient, they came together and from them are sprung the Jinn to whom we belong. There you have our genealogy in a few words. You must not be astonished to see us eat so much, for, as you now know, we are sprung, in the first place, from a lion and a wolf. To give you an idea of the capacity of our bellies: each of us every day eats ten camels and twenty sheep and drinks forty ladles full of soup, each ladle being as big as a cauldron.

'Now, O Bulūkiya, that you may be all-wise when you return among the sons of men, learn that the earth on which we live is ever refreshed by snows from that Mount Kāf which circles it like a girdle; otherwise no one could live upon the earth because of the fires beneath it. Earth herself is also formed in seven layers, which rest upon the shoulders of an exceedingly powerful Jinnī. This Jinnī stands upon a rock and the rock upon the back of a bull; the bull is held up by an enormous fish, and the fish swims in the Sea of Eternity.

'The bed of the Sea of Eternity is the roof of Hell, which, with its seven regions, is held in the jaws of a gigantic serpent, who shall stay still until the Judgment Day. Then he shall vomit up Hell and its people into the presence of God, Who will then pass His final judgment upon all things.'

At this point Shahrazād saw the approach of morning and discreetly fell silent.

But when the three-hundred-and-sixty-third night had come

SHE SAID:

'There, rapidly resumed, is the story of our making and of the making of the world.

'That your instruction may be perfect, I must also tell you that our age never changes; we never grow old, though the earth about us, with its nature and the men and beasts upon it, hurries unceasingly towards decrepitude. This eternity of youth we owe to the Fountain of Life which Khidr guards in the land of shadows and of which we have drunk. It is holy Khidr who equalises the seasons, recrowns the trees with royal green, unbinds the fleeing streams, spreads out grass carpets on the meadows, and hangs his light green mantle in the evening air to colour the skies after the sun has set.

'Now, Bulūkiya, since you have listened to me with great attention, I will, if you wish it, reward you by having you carried from here to the confines of your own country.' The prince heartily thanked the King of the Jinn for his hospitality, for his instruction, and for his last offer. He took leave of the wazīrs and other Afārīt and, mounting astride the shoulders of a very strong Jinnī, was carried in a flash of time through space and set down gently upon earth he knew, near the frontier of his own country.

Bulūkiya had determined which road to follow and was about to step forth in it towards his capital, when he saw, between two tombs, a youth sitting and weeping bitterly. The stranger's beauty was ravishing, but his face was pale and very sad. Going up to him, the young King greeted him in friendly fashion, saying: 'Fair youth, why do you thus sit weeping between two tombs? Tell me the reason of your sadness and I will try to comfort you.' The young man lifted his sad eyes to Bulūkiya, and answered weeping: 'O traveller, why do you thus stop upon your way? Let my tears fall in solitude upon these stones of my grief.' But Bulūkiya said: 'Unfortunate brother, I have a compassionate heart and am ready to listen; you can tell me the cause of your sadness without fear.' So saying, he sat down on the marble and, taking the youth's two hands, encouraged him to speak by telling him his own story from beginning to end. 'And now, brother,' he said when he had finished, 'what tale is yours? Hasten to tell me, for I feel that it will touch me infinitely.'

The youth with the sweet sad face, who wept between the two tombs, said to young King Bulūkiya:

The Tale of the Fair Sad Youth

BROTHER, I also am a King's son, and my story is so strange and extraordinary that if it were written with needles in the corner of an eye yet it would serve as an improving lesson to whomso read it sympathetically. Therefore I will not delay in telling it to you.

(He remained silent for a few minutes, wiping away his tears and leaning his forehead upon his hand, then he began the following remarkable story:)

I was born in the land of Kābul, where my father, King Tīghmūs, rules over the Banū Shahlān and over Afghanistan. My father, who is a very great and just King, has seven tributary kings beneath him, each the master of a hundred cities and a hundred fortresses. He commands a hundred thousand brave riders and a hundred thousand mighty warriors. My mother is the daughter of King Bahrwān, lord of Khurāsān. My name is Jānshāh.

From earliest childhood, my father had me trained in knowledge, art and bodily exercise, so that by the time I was fifteen I was considered one of the most accomplished cavaliers in all the kingdom and would lead every hunt or race upon my deer-swift horse.

One day, during a hunt at which the King, my father, and all his officers were present, when we had been out for three days in the forest and had killed much game, I saw, just as the sun was setting, a fine gazelle spring up near the place where I was resting with seven of my mamlūks. Seeing us, she turned tail and lightly leaped away. For many hours I followed with my mamlūks, and we came at last to a broad deep river where we hoped to be able to corner the animal and capture her. But, after a moment's hesitation, she sprang into the river and swam powerfully towards the opposite shore. We jumped off our horses and, leaving one to guard them, leapt into a fishing boat, which was stranded thereabouts, and rowed quickly after the gazelle. By the time we had reached the centre of the stream, however, we were no longer master of our craft; the wind and current bore us out of our course in the growing darkness, and, in spite of all our efforts to return to safety, we were hurried along all night at a terrifying speed, expecting to be destroyed each moment against some rock or other obstacle. All next day and through the second night we were borne helplessly, but without accident; it was only on the morning of the second day that the current swept us to land and enabled us to disembark.

During this time my father, King Tīghmūs, having learnt of our disappearance in the river from the mamlūk whom we had left to guard the horses, was thrown into such a state of despair that he burst into sobs, threw his crown from him, bit the hands of grief, and hastened to send messengers into all parts to look for us. My mother, hearing that I was lost, gave herself violent blows in the face, tore her garments, bruised her breast, pulled out her hair, and put on mourning robes.

When we landed, we found a fair stream flowing between the trees and a man sitting quietly by the side of it, refreshing his feet in the water. We greeted him courteously and asked him where we were; but he, without returning our greeting, answered in a shrill voice, like the cry of a bird of prey.

At this point Shahrazād saw the approach of morning and discreetly fell silent.

But when the three-hundred-and-sixty-fourth night had come

SHE SAID:

Then he rose with a bound and split in two at the waist; his body rushed upon us while his lower half made off in another direction. At once, from all parts of the forest, appeared other men like him, who, running down to the stream, there divided themselves in half with a backward jerk, and came bounding towards us with their bodies only. They flung themselves upon the three of my mamlūks who were nearest and began to eat them alive. I and the other three threw ourselves in terror into our boat, preferring a thousand times to be swallowed by the water than by these monsters. Pushing out from the bank, we allowed ourselves to be carried down stream. We saw all the legs and thighs rushing along the bank and trying to reach us, while the bodies remained to finish eating the three unhappy mamlūks. This horrid pursuit was kept up until we were well out of reach; therefore we were astonished by the terrible appetites of these bodies with divided belly and, while we mourned our unfortunate companions, asked each other how such a thing might be.

We were carried on by the current until the following morning, when we grounded again upon a spit of land covered with fruit trees and large gardens of delightful flowers. Not wishing to land myself, I bade my three mamlūks go on shore to inspect the country. They returned after half a day, telling me that they had gone far to right and left without beholding any suspicious thing. Eventually they had seen a palace of white marble, whose pavilions were of crystal, built round a splendid garden with a fair lake. They had entered the palace and seen a vast hall in which ivory chairs were ranged about a throne of jewelled gold; but neither in the garden nor the palace had they found trace of any living thing.

Reassured by this report, I decided to leave the boat. On our way through the gardens we refreshed ourselves with ripe fruit plucked from the trees, and then entered the palace to rest. I sat on the gold throne, while my mamlūks seated themselves on the ivory chairs. In this royal situation I remembered the King, my father, and my mother and the throne which I had lost, and I wept until my followers wept for sympathy.

While we were plunged in these sad memories, we heard a great noise like the tumult of the sea and saw a procession entering the hall made up of what seemed to be wazīrs, amīrs, chamberlains and nobles, but who were, nevertheless, all apes. They were a great host, some small, some large; and we thought that this time our death had surely come. But the wazīr of the apes, a beast of enormous stature, came and bowed before me with signs of evident respect and, speaking with a human tongue, told me that he and his people acknowledged me as their King and my three mamlūks as the commanders of their army. After regaling us with roast gazelle, he invited me to review the army of the apes, my subjects, who were all prepared for immediate battle with their ancient foes, the Ghouls, their nearest neighbours.

Being worn with fatigue, I dismissed the wazīr and the others, keeping only my three mamlūks. We discussed our situation for an hour and decided to leave that palace and that land as quickly as possible. We therefore made our way down to the river; but there we discovered that our boat had disappeared and were therefore obliged to return to the palace, where we slept till morning.

When we woke, the wazīr of my new subjects came to salute me and told me that all was ready for the battle against the Ghouls. At the same time other important people brought round to the palace four great dogs which should serve for riding animals for myself and my mamlūks. We had no choice left but to mount these dogs, which were bridled with steel chains, and take our place at the head of the army, while numberless cohorts of apes, led by the wazīr, followed us with howls and terrible cries.

After marching for a day and a night, we came opposite a high black mountain riddled with lairs of the Ghouls. The enemy soon showed themselves. They were of different kinds, each more horrid than the other: some had the heads of bulls on the bodies of camels, others were like hyenas, and yet more had an indescribably base appearance and could be compared with nothing known to man.

When the Ghouls saw us, they rushed down from the mountain and, halting at its foot, began to trouble us with a rain of stones. My followers answered with the same missiles, and soon the fight was terrible and general on both sides. My mamlūks and I, armed with our bows, killed a great quantity of the Ghouls with our arrows, to the vast joy of my followers. At last we gained the victory and set out in pursuit of the fleeing Ghouls.

We four resolved to take advantage of the disorder of the pursuit to escape from the apes through the speed of our dogs; therefore we turned and made off in the opposite direction, without attracting attention, and disappeared at full gallop from sight of the two armies.

After we had ridden for a long time, we halted to breathe our dogs, and in that place where we stopped we saw a big smooth rock on which this inscription was engraved in Hebrew:

O captive, whom Fate has cast into this place to be a king of Apes, if you would renounce that royalty in flight, two roads are open for your salvation: the shorter which lies to the right will lead you to the bank of that sea which goes all round the earth; but the way leads through savage deserts filled with monsters and the evil Jinn; the other, to the left, is four months long and makes through a great valley which is called the Valley of the Ants. If you take this second road and manage to escape the ants, you will come to a mountain of fire at the foot of which is built the City of the Jews. I, Sulaimān ibn Dāūd, have written this for your salvation.

When we had read this inscription marvelling, we hastened along the road to the left, which should lead us to the City of the Jews by way of the Valley of the Ants.

At this point Shahrazād saw the approach of morning and discreetly fell silent.

But when the three-hundred-and-sixty-fifth night had come

SHE SAID:

We had not journeyed for more than a day when we felt the ground tremble beneath our feet and presently saw behind us all my subject apes, with the wazīr at their head, advancing towards us at great speed. When they reached us, they surrounded us on all sides with howls of joy at having found us again, and the wazīr, making himself their spokesman, made us a speech of congratulation upon our safety.

This meeting annoyed us very much, but we took care to hide our feelings and were about to turn round and go back to the palace, with the people of my new kingdom, when, from the other end of the valley which we were crossing, there burst an army of ants each as big as a dog. In the twinkling of an eye a terrible skirmish took place between my subjects and the ants, the latter taking the apes in their pincers and cutting them in two with one movement, and the apes throwing themselves by ten and ten on an ant and pulling it to pieces.

We wished to take advantage of this unexpected battle to fly upon our dogs, but unhappily I was the only one who was able to escape, for my three mamlūks were seen by the ants and rent in pieces with their terrible pincers. Mourning for the fate of my lost companions, I came at last to a river which I crossed by swimming, having left my dog upon the nearer bank. Landing in safety, I dried my clothes and fell into a deep sleep until morning, feeling certain that I need not fear pursuit as I had placed the river between myself and the combined danger of the apes and the ants.

When I woke, I started on foot upon a journey which lasted for days and days, during which I had no sustenance but plants and roots. In the end, however, I came to the mountain of fire, at the foot of which I found the City of the Jews, even as I had been told in the inscription. But the writing on the rock had not informed me of one thing, which I noticed later and which astonished me very much: a river which I was able to cross dryfoot to reach the city on that particular day, was filled with water for all the rest of the week. Afterwards I learnt that this abundant flood did not flow on Saturday, which is a feast day with the Jews.

I entered the city, but saw no one in the streets; therefore I went up to the first building which I saw and, opening the door, walked into it. I found myself in a hall where a great number of venerable men were seated in a circle. Encouraged by their appearance, I went up to them and, after saluting them respectfully, said: 'I am Jānshāh, son of King Tīghmūs, master of Kābul and lord of the Banū Shahlān. I beg you to tell me, my masters, how far I am from my own country and what road I must take to get there. Also I am hungry.' The seated men looked at me without answering, and he who seemed to be their chief signed to me without uttering a word: 'Eat and drink, but do not talk.' He showed me a dish of astonishing meats, such as I had never seen before and which seemed, to judge by the smell, to be all composed on a basis of oil. I ate and drank and kept silence.

When I had finished, the leader of the Jews came up to me and asked me, also by signs: 'Who? Whence? Whither?' I asked him by signs if I were allowed to answer; to which he replied by another sign which seemed to say: 'Only use three words.' Then said I: 'Caravan, Kābul, when?' 'Not know,' he answered by a sign, and then signalled to me to depart as I had finished my meal.

I saluted him and the rest, and then went out marvelling at these strange manners. Once in the street, I was looking about for someone who would help me in my difficulty, when I heard the public crier calling in a loud voice: 'He who would earn a thousand gold pieces and gain possession of a young slave, whose beauty is without equal, has but to follow me and do an hour's work!' Being utterly destitute, I went up to the man and said: 'I accept the work and also the thousand dīnārs and the young slave.' He took me by the hand and led me to a richly furnished house, where an old Jew was sitting upon a seat of ebony. The crier bowed before him, saying: 'Here is a young stranger. He is the only one who has answered my invitation during the three months that I have cried it.'

As soon as he heard this, the old Jew made me sit down at his side and with great kindness offered me food and drink of excellent quality. When I had feasted, he gave me a purse containing a thousand gold pieces, which were not counterfeit, and, at the same time, ordered his slaves to clothe me in a silk robe and conduct me into the presence of the young girl. For he gave me her in advance in consideration of the unknown work which I had to do.

At this point Shahrazād saw the approach of morning and discreetly fell silent.

But when the three-hundred-and-sixty-sixth night had come

SHE SAID:

After putting the silk robe upon me, they led me into the room where the young girl waited for me. I saw at once that she was very beautiful and, when I was left alone to pass the night with her, found that she was also a virgin as the old Jew had described. I stayed with her for three days and three nights, eating, drinking, and doing that which I had to do; but on the morning of the fourth day the old man called me to him, saying: 'Are you now ready to do the work for which you have been paid?' Although I did not know what this work was, I had to answer that I was ready.

Then, at the old Jew's order, slaves brought round two harnessed mules; their master mounted one of them and bade me mount the other and follow him. We set off at a good pace and rode till we came to the foot of a high mountain, up whose sides was no path by which man or beast might climb. We dismounted and the old Jew handed me a knife, saying: 'Thrust this into the belly of your mule. The time has come for work.' I thrust the knife into the belly of my mule, which died at once, and then, under the direction of my master, skinned the beast and roughly cleaned the hide. When this was done, he said: 'Now lie down upon the skin while I sew you up in it.' I obeyed and, when I was well stretched upon the skin, the old man sewed it over me carefully. 'Listen,' he said, 'very soon a great bird will pounce upon you and carry you up to its nest at the top of this inaccessible mountain. Be very careful not to move when you feel yourself in the air, for if you do the bird may let go of you and you will be dashed to pieces; but when he sets you down upon the mountain you must rip up the skin with your knife and come out of your concealment. The bird will be terrified and let you be. Then all you have to do is to pick up the precious stones which are strewn on that high peak and throw them down to me. After that you can come down and rejoin me.'

Hardly had the old Jew finished speaking when I felt myself lifted into the air and then, at the end of a few further moments, set down again. Slitting up the skin with my knife, I thrust forth my head, which so terrified the monstrous bird that it flew away as fast as its wings would carry it. I set to work and speedily gathered a considerable quantity of rubies, emeralds and other precious stones, which I threw down to the old Jew. But, when I would have gone down myself, I realised that there was no foothold. And, even while I was looking for one, I saw the old Jew galloping away upon his mule, which he had loaded with the jewels.

Despairing utterly, I wept over my fate and found nothing better to do than to walk straight before my face at haphazard for two long months, until I came, by Allāh's grace, to the end of that chain of mountains and found there a wonderful valley, where the streams, the trees and flowers glorified Him among the jargoning of countless birds. I saw a mighty palace rising high into the air, and made my way towards it. Coming to the gate, I beheld, seated upon a bench in the entrance, an old man whose face was shone about with light. He held a ruby sceptre in his hand and on his head there was a crown of diamonds; therefore I bowed low before him. He greeted me kindly, saying: 'Sit down beside me, my son,' and, when I was seated, he continued: 'Whence have you come into this land which never before a human foot has visited? And whither have you in your mind to go?' For sole answer I burst into tears, strangling myself with sobs; so that the old man said to me: 'Do not weep in this way, my son, it cuts me to the heart. Be of good courage and, before you tell me anything, strengthen yourself with food and drink.' He led me into a high hall and fed me until he saw that I was in better case; then he asked me to tell him my story. I did so and afterwards asked him in my turn to whom the palace might belong; he answered: 'My son, this palace was built of old time by our master Sulaimān, whose lieutenant of the birds I am. Each year all the birds of the world come to do me homage. If you wish to return to your own country, I will give you into the care of the first who return to take my orders and they will carry you whither you will. To pass the time until they come, you may move freely about this immense building and enter all its halls, except that one that is opened with the gold key which you see among all these other keys.' Then the old man, the lieutenant of the birds, gave me the keys and left me to follow my own inclination.

I began by visiting the halls which gave upon the main court of the palace, and then examined the inner rooms, which were all fitted up to serve as lodgings for the birds. In the end, I came to the door which was opened by the gold key and stood looking at it for a long time, not daring even to touch it with my hand, because of the command which the old man had given me.

At this point Shahrazād saw the approach of morning and discreetly fell silent.

But when the three-hundred-and-sixty-seventh night had come

SHE SAID:

In the end, however, not being able to resist the curiosity with which my soul was filled, I placed the key in the lock and, opening the door, entered the forbidden place, trembling with expectation.

Far from my eyes being greeted by some frightful spectacle, I saw, in the middle of a pavilion whose floor was formed with a mosaic of many coloured jewels, a silver fountain basin surrounded by birds made of gold, from whose mouths the water jetted with so sweet a noise that it seemed as if the living voices of those creatures which the fountain copied were echoing back from the silver walls in forest music. In ravishing variety, all round the basin, were beds of softly-perfumed flowers, marrying their colours with those of the fruits which hung down from trees coolly shadowing the water. The sand yielding to my feet was powder of emeralds and powder of diamonds; it stretched in a soft path up to the steps of a throne which overlooked the water. This throne was hewn out of a single ruby, whose faces cast red rays across the garden into the water.

I halted in ecstasy before this simple union of the pure elements. Then, climbing on to the throne, which was shaded by a red silk canopy, I shut my eyes to let the refreshment of this vision penetrate my spirit.

When I opened my eyes, I saw three beautiful doves coming down to the basin to take their bath, ruffling their white plumes. They hopped gracefully upon the broad rim of the silver basin and then, before my marvelling eyes, when they had embraced and given each other a thousand charming caresses, each one threw from her her virgin mantle of feathers and, coming out of it, appeared in jasmine nakedness as a young girl fairer than the moon. They plunged into the water and there gave themselves up to sweet and foolish games, sometimes diving from sight, then reappearing in a sparkle of ripples, then sinking again, with pretty laughter, until only their hair showed spread out, as bright as flame upon the water.

At this sight, O Bulūkiya, my brother, I felt my reason swimming about my mind and trying to escape. Not being able to contain myself, I ran madly towards the basin side, crying: 'O young girls, O moons, O queens!'

When the maidens saw me, each gave a cry of fright and, coming up quickly out of the water, ran and covered her nakedness with her robe of feathers. Then all three flew up into the highest of those trees which fringed the basin and looked down upon me laughing.

I went up to the tree and lifted my eyes, saying: 'O royal ladies, I pray you tell me who you are. I am Jānshāh, son of King Tīghmūs, master of Kābul and lord of the Banū Shahlān.' Then the youngest of the three, whose charms had moved me most, answered: 'We are the daughters of King Nasr, who lives in the palace of diamonds; we but came here to bathe and for our amusement.' Then said I: 'In that case, have compassion upon me, my mistress, come down and finish the game with me.' 'O Jānshāh,' she answered, 'since when have young girls been able to play with young men? If you are determined to know me better, you have but to follow me to my father's palace.' So saying, she gave me a glance which pierced my very liver and flew away with her two sisters.

Seeing them disappear, I gave a despairing cry and fell in a swoon beneath the tree.

I do not know how long I lay there; when I came to myself, the old man, the lieutenant of the birds, sat at my side sprinkling my face with water of flowers. As soon as he saw me open my eyes, he said: 'Behold, my child, the fruit of disobedience! Did I not forbid you to open the door of this pavilion?' For sole answer, I burst into tears and improvised these lines:

> Rubies in a queen's hair,
>   Roses on a tree,
> Hide their reds, hide their heads
>   Before her lips.
> The moon's light is not white
>   Before her hips,
> And all the girls of India
>   They die of jealousy.

When I had made an end of this verse, the old man said: 'I understand what has happened to you; you have seen the young girls dressed like doves who sometimes come to take their bath here.' 'I have indeed seen them, my father,' I cried, 'and I beg you to tell me the way to the palace of diamonds where they live with their father, King Nasr.' 'You must not even think of going there, my son,' he answered. 'King Nasr is one of the most powerful leaders of the Jinn, and I am very sure that he would not give you one of his daughters in marriage. Rather busy yourself with preparations for your journey; for I myself will help your return by recommending you to the birds who will soon be coming to give me their homage.' 'I thank you, my father,' I said, 'but I renounce all thought of returning to my people if I cannot see again that girl who spoke with me!' So saying, I threw myself weeping at the old man's feet and begged him to find some way by which I might find again those white-plumed maidens.

At this point Shahrazād saw the approach of morning and discreetly fell silent.

But when the three-hundred-and-sixty-eighth night had come

SHE SAID:

The old man took me by the hand and lifted me to my feet, saying: 'I see that your heart burns with passion for the girl, and therefore I will show you a way of beholding her again. You must hide behind the trees and wait patiently for the return of those doves. Allow them to undress and go down into the water; then suddenly run to their feather mantles and gain possession of them. The girls will soften their language towards you; they will come up to you and try to flatter you, with a thousand caresses and honeyed words, into giving back their plumes. If they can persuade you, you will never see them again; therefore sternly refuse to give back the robes, and say: "I cannot let you have them until the sheikh returns." Treat them gallantly while you are waiting for me and, when I come, I will find means of turning matters in the way you wish.'

I thanked the venerable lieutenant of the birds and ran to hide myself behind the trees, while he retired into his pavilion to receive his subjects.

After I had waited a long time, I heard a beating of wings and laughter in the air, and saw the three doves alight on the rim of the basin and cast bright glances to left and right to see that they were unobserved. The one who had before spoken to me turned to the others, saying: 'My sisters, do you not think that some one is hidden in the garden? What has become of the young man whom we saw here before?' 'Oh, Shamsah,' answered the two, 'do not worry

yourself about that, but come and bathe.' Then all three cast off their
feathers and dived into the water, where they played so sweetly that
I seemed to see three naked moons of virgin silver reflected in the
fountain.

I waited until they had swum well out of the centre of the basin
and then, darting forward more quickly than light itself, took
possession of the mantle of the girl I loved. My movement of depre-
dation was answered by three frightened cries, and I saw the girls,
ashamed at being overlooked in their pleasantry, dive so that only
their heads appeared above the water and hurry towards me with
imploring looks. This time, sure of the mastery, I laughed, drawing
back from the rim and victoriously waving the feathered garment in
the air. Seeing this, Shamsah, the young girl who had first spoken to
me, said: 'O young man, how dare you take what does not belong to
you?' 'My dove,' I answered, 'come up out of the basin and talk to
me.' 'I would like to talk to you, fair youth,' she said, 'but I am quite
naked and cannot come out of the water. Give me my mantle and I
will then come up and speak to you; I will even let you caress me
and embrace me as much as you wish.' 'O light of my heart, mistress,
queen of beauty, fruit of my life,' I answered, 'if I gave you back
your cloak, I would be stabbing myself with my own hand. I certainly cannot do so until my friend, the venerable lieutenant of the
birds, comes to this place.' Then said she: 'Since it was only my
mantle which you took, go a little further off and turn away your
head, so that my sisters can come up out of the basin and clothe
themselves. Then they will lend me some of their feathers to hide
what is most necessary.' 'That I can do,' I answered, and hid myself
behind the ruby throne.

The two older girls left the water and quickly put on their
mantles; then they pulled out some of their most downy feathers
and made them into a little apron with which they hid the essential
parts of their young sister. 'Now you may come!' they cried. At
once I ran to them and, throwing myself down before my dear
Shamsah, kissed her feet again and again, being careful to keep firm
hold of her garment all the time. She lifted me to my feet and, with
a thousand gentle words and pleasant caresses, tried to persuade me
to return her covering; but, instead of doing so, I managed to pull
her towards the ruby throne, where I sat down and took her upon
my knees.

Seeing that she could not escape, she answered to my desires and, throwing her arms about my neck, gave me kiss for kiss and clasp for clasp, while the sisters smiled upon us and kept guard that we might not be surprised.

In a short time the old man, my protector, opened the door and came in; we rose in his honour and, going forward to meet him, kissed his hands respectfully. Begging us to seat ourselves again, he said to Shamsah: 'My daughter, I am delighted that you have chosen this young man who adores you so. He is of illustrious origin, his father is King Tīghmūs, lord of Afghanistan. You will do well to accept the alliance and to persuade your father, King Nasr, to give his consent to it.' 'I hear and I obey,' she said, and the old man continued: 'If you truly accept this youth, swear to me to be faithful to your husband and never to abandon him.' The beautiful Shamsah rose then and made her oath between the hands of the old man, who said to us: 'Let us thank the Highest for your union, my children. I call down blessings upon you both! May you be happy! Now you may love each other freely and Jānshāh can give back the mantle, for Shamsah will never leave him.' So saying, the sheikh led us into a hall where there were mattresses covered with carpets, and dishes filled with select fruit and exquisite refreshments. Begging her sisters to go before and announce to their father her marriage and speedy return, Shamsah with great sweetness of manner prepared the fruits and shared them with me. After that we lay down together in each other's arms with an excess of joy.

At this point Shahrazād saw the approach of morning and discreetly fell silent.

But when the three-hundred-and-sixty-ninth night had come

SHE SAID:

Shamsah was first afoot next morning. She put on her feather mantle and then woke me with a kiss between the eyes, saying: 'Dress yourself quickly, for it is time that we went to the palace of diamonds to see my father, King Nasr.' I did as she had told me, and, after we had presented ourselves before the lieutenant of the birds and kissed his hands with abundant thanks, Shamsah said: 'Now climb upon my shoulders and hold tightly, for the journey is rather long and I mean to go with all possible swiftness.' When I was well fixed on her shoulders, she carried me through the air with the speed of light and, in a short time, set me down near the entrance to the palace of diamonds. Then we walked slowly towards the dwelling, while servant Jinn, who had been placed on the look out, ran forward to announce our arrival.

King Nasr, Shamsah's father and master of the Jinn, was delighted to see me. He took me in his arms and pressed me to his bosom; then he ordered me to be clothed in a magnificent robe of honour, put upon my head a crown wrought out of a single diamond, and introduced me to his queen, the mother of my wife, who congratulated her daughter on the choice which she had made. She gave Shamsah a vast quantity of diamonds and led both of us to the hammām, where we were washed and perfumed with rose and musk, amber and scented oils. Finally feasts, which lasted three days and three nights, were given in our honour.

When I desired to take my wife and show her to my father and mother, the King and queen approved my wish, though they were sad indeed to be parted from their daughter and made me promise to return for a part of each year to visit them. The King had made for us a throne so vast that two hundred male Jinn and two hundred females might stand upon the steps of it. When all was completed, we sat upon the throne and, after four hundred picked attendants had ranged themselves upon the steps, a whole army of the Jinn lifted up the throne and carried it through the air so quickly that in two days we had covered a two years' foot journey and reached the palace of my father in Kābul.

When my father and mother saw me arrive, after so long an absence that hope had died in it, and had seen my wife and learnt who she was and how I had come to marry her, they wept for joy, embracing us both over and over again. My poor mother was even so moved that she fell down in a swoon and was only recovered by the use of rose-water, of which my wife happened to have a large flask.

After all the feasts of rejoicing which attended our arrival and marriage were well finished, my father asked Shamsah what he could do to please her, and because her tastes were modest she answered: 'O auspicious King, I wish only that we may have a pavilion in the middle of a garden watered by streams.' The King gave orders and, in a very short time, we were installed in such a pavilion as my wife desired, and lived there in perfect happiness.

At the end of a year, passed as it were upon a summer sea of all delight, my wife wished to see her father and mother again in the palace of diamonds, and reminded me of my promise that we should visit them every year. Loving her as I did, I had nothing to say against this project, but alas! alas! it was an evil journey which we undertook.

We mounted our throne, and our porter Jinn carried us swiftly through the air, so that we passed over a month's journey every day. At night we did not travel, but had ourselves set down to rest by some watercourse or in the shadow of trees. One evening we halted in such a place, and Shamsah wished to bathe in the waters of a river which flowed near. I tried to dissuade her, telling her that the evening was too cold and that illness would come of it; but she did not wish to hear me and took certain of her slaves to bathe with her. They undressed upon the bank and went down into the water, where Shamsah seemed like the rising moon among a train of stars. They played happily together, until suddenly my wife cried out and fell back into the arms of her slaves, who hastened to lift her from the water and carry her up on to the bank. I spoke to her and would have cared for her, but she was dead. The women showed me the bite of a water-snake upon her heel.

I fell down in a faint and stayed so long without consciousness that they thought me also dead. But, alas! I was fated to live on and to mourn for Shamsah and to build this tomb for her. This other tomb is my own. I have built it beside the resting-place of my beloved and here I try to pass away the cruel time in tears and memories until I may at last sleep by Shamsah, far from the kingdom which I have renounced, far from the desert of the world.

When the fair sad youth had finished telling this tale to Bulūkiya, he hid his face in his hands and wept. Then said the other young King: 'As Allāh lives, my brother, your story is so strange and wonderful that it has made me forget my own adventures which, so short a time ago, I thought were marvellous. May He sustain you in your grief, my brother, and as the years go by enrich your spirit with forgetfulness.'

At this point Shahrazād saw the approach of morning and discreetly fell silent.

But when the three-hundred-and-seventieth night had come

SHE SAID:

He stayed with the mourner for a further hour, trying in vain to persuade him to come with him to his kingdom. Then he took leave

of him, for fear of seeming importunate, and, after having kissed
him with words of consolation, followed the road to his capital,
which he reached without accident after having been absent for five
years.

Since then I have had no news of young King Bulūkiya. Now that
you are here, O Hāsib, I quite forget him and the hope which I
once had that he would return to me. You at least will not leave me
so quickly, and I trust to enjoy your company for many years. You
may be sure that I will not let you lack for anything; also I know
many other extraordinary tales to tell you which will make those of
King Bulūkiya and the Fair Sad Youth seem simple everyday affairs.
As a proof that you have pleased me by listening so well, my
women will now serve us a feast and charm us with their singing
until the morning.

When Queen Yamlika of under earth had finished telling the
tales of Bulūkiya and the Fair Sad Youth to young Hāsib, son of
Daniel the sage, and when the feasting and the singing and the
dancing of the serpent-women were ended, preparations were made
for the whole assembly to return to the Summer residence of the
Queen. But Hāsib, who dearly loved his mother and his wife, said:
'O Queen, I am only a poor woodcutter and yet, though you offer
me a life of delights with you, I have a wife and a mother in my house
at home. As Allāh lives, I cannot leave them longer in the anxiety
and despair which they must feel. Therefore let me return to them
before they die of grief. One thing I can say with certainty: all my
life I will regret not having heard the other tales with which you
had meant to charm my stay!'

Queen Yamlika realised that Hāsib's determination was virtuous,
so she said to him: 'O Hāsib, I am willing to let you return to your
mother and wife, although it will cost me pain to part from so
excellent a listener as yourself. But I exact an oath from you and, if
you do not swear it, I shall not let you go. You must promise me
never to take a bath in a hammām during all the remainder of your
life. If you break your promise you will infallibly be lost. For the
moment I cannot tell you more.'

Though Hāsib was astonished at this condition, he took the oath
because he did not wish to go against the wishes of the Queen.
When he had done so, she said farewell to him and sent one of her
snake-women to lead him to that way out of her kingdom which

was hidden by a ruined house and which lay in the opposite direction from the honey-pit by which he had come in.

The sun was yellowing in the east when Hāsib knocked at the door of his house. His mother opened the door, recognised him and, uttering a great cry, threw herself into his arms, weeping for joy. His wife, hearing the cries and happy sobs of the older woman, ran also to the door and respectfully kissed her husband's hands. All three went back into the house and abandoned themselves to transports of the liveliest joy.

When they became calmer, Hāsib asked news of the woodcutters, his old comrades who had left him in the honey-hole. His mother told him that, after they had informed her of his death at the teeth of a wolf, they had become rich merchants, owners of large and beautiful shops, and had seen the world widening before their gaze as the days passed over them.

Hāsib reflected for a little and then said to his mother: 'To-morrow you must go to the market and, calling them all together, tell them of my return and inform them that I shall be pleased to see them.' On the next day Hāsib's mother did this thing, and the woodcutters, after changing colour, answered that they would be delighted to visit Hāsib and welcome him back among them. Then they planned together and, in order to put the best possible face on his return, loaded Hāsib's mother with the rarest silks and brocades which they had in their shops and, on their way to the house, agreed that each should give Hāsib a share of their riches, slaves and houses. They saluted the young man and kissed his hands, begging him to accept their offer and forget the wrong which they had done him. Not wishing to bear malice, Hāsib accepted their gifts and said: 'The past is past, and what happened must have been fated to happen.' They took leave of him with many expressions of gratitude and, from that day, Hāsib was a rich man. He opened a merchant's shop in the market, which in the course of time became the most elegant building in the city.

One day, as he was walking to his shop, he passed by the hammām which stood at the entrance to the market. The owner of the bath was taking the air in front of his door; seeing Hāsib, he saluted him and said: 'Honour me by entering my bath, for I have never had the pleasure of a visit from you. To-day I wish to entertain you for my own pleasure; the rubbers shall rub you with a new hair glove and soap you with fibres of loofah which never have been used before.' 'As Allāh lives, I cannot accept your offer,' answered Hāsib, remembering his oath, 'for I have made a vow never to enter the hammām.'

At this point Shahrazād saw the approach of morning and discreetly fell silent.

But when the three-hundred-and-seventy-first night had come

SHE SAID:

The master of the hammām, not believing that anyone could have taken such an oath, since at the risk of death itself no man may omit to bathe before he approaches his wife sexually, cried out: 'O master, why do you refuse me? As Allāh lives, I swear in my turn that, if you will not be persuaded, I shall at once divorce my three wives. I swear it three times by divorce!' In spite of this most serious undertaking, Hāsib would not accept; therefore the master of the bath threw himself down before the young man, begging him not to make the performance of the oath necessary. He kissed his feet, weeping and saying: 'I take upon myself the responsibility and consequences of your act.' Then all the passers, who had crowded round them on hearing what was toward, also began to beg Hāsib not to bring down unmerited misfortune on a man who offered him a free bath. Soon, seeing the uselessness of their prayers, they determined to employ force. In spite of his terrified cries, they bore Hāsib into the hammām, pulled off all his clothes, and poured twenty or thirty basins of water over his body; rubbed him, soaped him, dried him and, wrapping him about with hot towels, enveloped his head in a large embroidered covering. The owner of the bath, rejoicing to see himself quit of his oath, brought Hāsib a cup of sherbert perfumed with amber, and said to him: 'May the bath be light and healthful upon you! May this drink refresh you as much as you have refreshed me!' Hāsib, who was more and more terrified as time went on, did not know whether to accept or refuse this last invitation. He was about to answer when the hammām was suddenly filled with the King's guards, who threw themselves upon him, took him up, covered just as he was from the bath, and, in spite of all protestation and resistance, carried him to the King's palace, where they left him in the hands of the wazīr who was impatiently awaiting them at the door.

When he saw Hāsib, the wazīr rejoiced exceedingly and, greeting him with singular marks of respect, begged him to go with him to the King. Hāsib, who was now resolved to let his Destiny run its course, followed the wazīr into the hall, where were ranged, in hierarchic order, two thousand governors of provinces, two thousand chief officers, and two thousand executioners with swords, who waited but a sign to send heads flying. The King himself lay upon a large gold bed, his head and face covered with silk, and seemed to sleep.

Terrified at these strange sights, Hāsib thought that he would die. Falling at the foot of the bed, he publicly protested his innocence, though he did not know of what he was accused. The wazīr hastened to lift him up most respectfully, and said to him: 'O son of Daniel, we wait for you to save our King, mighty Karazdān. A mortal leprosy covers his face and body; we have determined that you shall cure him, as you are the son of Daniel the sage.' At this all the governors, chamberlains, officers and executioners, cried out with one voice: 'By you alone shall King Karazdān be saved!'

'As Allāh lives,' said the terrified Hāsib to himself, 'they take me for a sage!' Then he continued aloud to the wazīr: 'It is true that I am the son of Daniel, but I am very ignorant. They put me to school, but I learnt nothing; they tried to teach me medicine, but, at the end of a month, I gave it up because my instructor was not a good one. At length my mother bought me an ass and some ropes, and made a woodcutter of me. That is all the learning I have.' But the wazīr answered: 'O son of Daniel, it is useless to hide your knowledge any further. We know perfectly well that, if we searched east and west, we would not find your equal as a practitioner of medicine.' 'But, O wisest of wazīrs,' cried poor Hāsib, 'how can I cure the King when I know nothing of either disease or remedy?' 'These denials are useless, young man,' retorted the wazīr, 'we know that the King's cure lies in your hands.' 'How so?' exclaimed Hāsib, lifting his arms to the sky, and then the wazīr said: 'You can obtain the cure because you are acquainted with Queen Yamlika, princess of under earth, whose virgin milk, taken fasting or used as a balm, can cure incurable disease.'

At this point Shahrazād saw the approach of morning and discreetly fell silent.

But when the three-hundred-and-seventy-second night had come

SHE SAID:

Hāsib then understood that his entrance into the hammām had betrayed him; in an attempt to deny the fault, he cried: 'I have never seen this milk, my master; I have never heard the name of Yamlika before; I do not know who she is.' 'Since you insist,' answered the wazīr smiling, 'I will explain why your denial is useless. I know that you have been in the presence of Queen Yamlika; for all who have visited her since ancient time have returned with black skin upon their bellies; but the skin does not become black until the visitor of Queen Yamlika has entered the hammām. This I know from a learned book. Now the spies, whom I had posted in the hammām to examine the bellies of all the bathers, came to me a short time ago and told me that your belly turned black while you were having a bath. Do not palter with me any further.'

'Even so,' Hāsib insisted, 'as Allāh lives, I never saw this princess!' At once the wazīr came up to him and, baring his belly of the towels, showed that it was black as that of a buffalo.

Hāsib nearly fainted at this exposure; but, wishing to try one last expedient, he said: 'I must confess that I was born with a black belly.' 'It was not black when you entered the hammām,' cried the wazīr with a laugh, 'my spies assured me of that!' At length, as Hāsib would not betray the Queen by telling where she lived and continued to swear that he had never seen her, the wazīr signed to two of the executioners, who immediately stretched out Hāsib upon the ground, naked as he was, and rained blows upon the soles of his feet so violently that he would have died if he had not cried for mercy and promised to tell the truth.

At once the wazīr raised him up and ordered the towels to be replaced by a magnificent robe of honour; then he himself led the young man into the courtyard and, providing him with the finest horse in the royal stable, mounted his own charger. The two set forth, followed by a troop of attendants, and made their way to the ruined house through which Hāsib had left the kingdom of Queen Yamlika.

There the wazīr, who had learned the art of magic from books, burned certain perfumes and pronounced conjurations at the doors, while Hāsib, acting under orders, besought the Queen to show herself. Suddenly a trembling seized the earth, which threw most of those who were there to the ground, and a hole opened through which appeared, borne in her gold basin by four snakes with human heads breathing out fire, Queen Yamlika herself, her face shining like gold. She looked reproachfully at Hāsib, saying: 'Is it thus that you keep the oath you swore to me?' 'As Allāh lives, O Queen,' cried Hāsib, 'the fault lies with the wazīr, who had me nearly killed with blows.' 'I know it,' she answered, 'and that is why I will not punish you. You were forced to come here and I myself was forced to appear, because it is necessary to cure the King. You come to ask me for milk with which to perform that cure; I will give it to you in memory of my hospitality and the excellent attention which you paid to my tales. Here are two flasks of my milk; I will tell you how to use them if you come near to me.' Hāsib approached, and the Queen said to him in a voice so low that no one else might hear: 'One of the flasks, which is marked with a red spot, will cure the King; the other is for the wazīr who had you beaten. When he sees that the King is cured, he will wish to drink my milk himself, in order to be immune from all disease. Then you must give him the second flask.' When she had said this, Queen Yamlika handed the two flasks to Hāsib and at once disappeared, the earth closing over her and her attendants.

As soon as Hāsib came to the palace, he did exactly as the Queen had told him. He went up to the King and made him drink of the first flask. No sooner had the sick man tasted the milk than all his body began to sweat and, in a few moments, the leprous skin started to fall away in flakes and, in its place, there grew a skin as new and pure as silver. Then the wazīr, wishing to drink the milk also, took the second flask and emptied it at a draught. Immediately he began to swell, and when, little by little, he had expanded until he was as large as an elephant, he suddenly burst in all directions and died upon the spot. The remains were taken out and buried.

When the King saw that he was really cured, he made Hāsib sit by his side and, after overwhelming him with thanks, appointed him wazīr in the place of him who had died. A robe of honour heavy with diamonds was put upon him, and his appointment was cried throughout all the palace. Then he was given three hundred mamlūks, three hundred girls for secret women, and three princesses of royal blood; so that he had four wives. Also he was presented with three hundred thousand dīnārs of gold, three hundred mules, three hundred camels, and vast herds of buffaloes, oxen and sheep.

At an order from the King, who said: 'Who honours me will honour him!' all the officers, chamberlains and nobles came up to Hāsib and kissed his hand, assuring him of their submission and respect. Without delay the young man took possession of the dead wazīr's palace, and lived there with his mother, his wives and his favourites, for many rich and honoured years, during which he had the leisure to learn to read and write.

As soon as he had mastered these two arts, he recalled that his father Daniel had been a very learned man and, more from curiosity than anything else, asked his mother if there was no legacy awaiting him of books and manuscripts. 'My son,' his mother answered, 'before he died your father destroyed all his papers and all his manuscripts, leaving as your sole inheritance a little sheet of paper which he commanded me to give you when you asked for it.' 'I wish very much to see it,' exclaimed Hāsib, 'for now I am eager for learning that I may better direct the affairs of the kingdom.'

At this point Shahrazād saw the approach of morning and discreetly fell silent.

But when the three-hundred-and-seventy-third night had come

SHE SAID:

Hāsib's mother hastened to take the small piece of paper from a box where she had hidden it with her jewels. Returning with the legacy left by Daniel the wise, she gave it to Hāsib, who took it and unrolled it on the spot. This is what he read: 'All learning is vain; for the times are now at hand when the Elect of Allāh shall show the fountain of all Wisdom to His people. His name shall be called Muhammad! Upon him, upon his companions, and upon all Believers be blessing and peace until the death of time!'

Such, O auspicious King, continued Shahrazād, is the tale of Hāsib, son of Daniel, and of Queen Yamlika, princess under earth. But Allāh knows more!

When Shahrazād had finished the telling of this strange tale, King Shahryār suddenly cried: 'I feel a great weariness of spirit, O Shahrazād. Be very careful! If this state of things continues, I verily believe that tomorrow morning your head will fall one way and your body another!' Terrified at these words, little Dunyazād hid herself still further among her carpets, but Shahrazād calmly answered: 'In that case, O auspicious King, I will now tell you one or two little stories to pass the rest of the night. As for the morrow, Allāh knows all!' Then said King Shahryār: 'How can you possibly find for me a tale which is at once short and amusing?' 'O auspicious King,' answered Shahrazād with a smile, 'that is the kind of tale which I know best. I will begin at once to repeat a few anecdotes drawn from the Flowering Terrace of Wit and from the Garden of Gallantry. After that I am willing to have my head cut off.'

At once she continued:

THE FLOWERING TERRACE OF WIT AND GARDEN OF GALLANTRY

Al-Rashīd and the Fart

IT is related, O auspicious King, that the Khalīfah Hārūn al-Rashīd, being once taken with weariness and finding himself in the same state of spirit which your majesty suffers at this moment, walked out upon the road which leads from Baghdād to Basrah, taking with him his wazīr Jafar al-Barmakī, his favourite musician Abū Ishāk, and Abū Nuwās the poet.

As the Khalīfah went along with sombre eyes and compressed lips, an old man passed by mounted upon an ass. Hārūn al-Rashīd turned to Jafar, saying: 'Ask that old man where he is going.' The wazīr, who up to that moment had been cudgelling his brains in vain for some distraction which might please the Khalīfah, resolved to amuse him at the expense of the aged traveller, who was jogging along with the cord loose upon his donkey's neck. Therefore he went up to him and asked: 'Whither away, old man?' 'I journey from Basrah to Baghdād,' the other answered. 'Why have you undertaken so long a journey?' demanded Jafar, and the traveller replied: 'As Allāh lives, I wish to find some learned doctor in Baghdād who will give me a collyrium for my eyes.' Then said Jafar: 'Chance and cure are in the hands of Allāh, O sheikh. What will you give me if I save you expense and time by myself prescribing a remedy which will cure your eyes in one night?' 'Allāh alone could reward such kindness,' murmured the old man. Hearing this, Jafar turned to the Khalīfah and Abū Nuwās with a wink, and then said to the traveller: 'Since that is so, good uncle, carefully remember the following simple prescription: Take three ounces of the breath of the wind, three ounces of sun rays, three ounces of moon rays, and three ounces of lamp rays; mix them carefully in a bottomless mortar and expose them to the air for three months. For a further three months pound the mixture, and then pour it into a porringer with holes in the bottom and leave it in the sun for another three months. By that time the cure will be ready, and you have only to apply it three hundred times to your eyes on the first night using three large pinches of it each time, to wake in the morning absolutely cured, if Allāh wills.'

Hearing these words, the old man bent over flat on his belly on the ass in front of Jafar, in sign of gratitude and respect, and suddenly let a detestable fart, followed by two long funks, saying at the same time: 'Be quick and gather them up, O learned doctor, before they float away, for they are the sole payment which I have about me for your windy remedy. Be sure, however, that, when I return to my own country, I will at once send you a female slave, with a bottom as ruddled as a ripe fig, who will give you such delight that you will die of it. Her grief, also, will be so great that, as she weeps over you, she will piss on your cold face and water your dry beard.'

Then the old man touched up his ass and went on his way, while the Khalīfah fell over on his backside and strangled with laughter, as he looked at the expression of his wazīr, standing there surprised, embarrassed and without an answer. As for Abū Nuwās, he made extravagant signs of congratulation, as a father would proudly commend the cleverness of a child.

As soon as he heard this anecdote, King Shahryār's sombre face broke into smiles, and he said to Shahrazād: 'O Shahrazād, tell me another tale at least as amusing as the last!' 'O Shahrazād,' cried little Dunyazād, 'how sweet and savoury are your words, my sister!' So after a short silence Shahrazād said:

The Youth and his Master

IT is related that the wazîr Badr al-Dîn, governor of Yaman, had a young brother, whose beauty was so incomparable that both men and women would stop and turn when he passed them and stand bathing their eyes in the charm of his appearance. The wazîr, who feared that some untimely adventure might come to so fair a being, kept him far from the regard of men and prevented him from companionship with lads of his own age. Not wishing to send him to school, where he might not be sufficiently watched, he had a venerable and pious old man, whose manners were notoriously chaste, come to the house as tutor. This old man visited every day and was shut up for many hours together with the pupil in a room which the wazîr had set aside for the lessons.

It was not long before the beauty and seduction of the boy had their usual effect; after a few days the old man was so violently in love with his young charge that he heard all the birds singing again in his soul and, at their singing, something woke which had long slept.

Knowing no other way to master this feeling, he opened his heart to the boy and assured him that he could no longer live without him. 'Alas,' said the youth, who was deeply touched by the emotion of his teacher, 'my hands are tied, and every minute of my time is watched over by my brother.' The old man sighed and said: 'How I long to pass an evening alone with you!' 'You may well say so,' retorted the other. 'If my days are so well guarded, what do you think is done about my nights?' 'I know, I know,' said the old man, 'but the terrace of my house joins the terrace of this; it should be easy, when your brother is asleep, to climb up noiselessly on to your terrace. There I will meet you and lead you over the little barrier wall on to my terrace. No one can spy on us there.'

At this point Shahrazâd saw the approach of morning and discreetly fell silent.

Said King Shahryâr to himself: 'I will not kill her until I know what passed between the youth and his master!'

THE YOUTH AND HIS MASTER

So when the three-hundred-and-seventy-fifth night had come

SHAHRAZĀD SAID:

The youth accepted the invitation. He pretended to go to sleep that night, but, as soon as his brother the wazīr had retired, climbed on to the terrace, where the old man was waiting for him. The sage led him by the hand over the boundary wall on to his own terrace, where fruits and filled wine cups were arranged for his entertainment. They sat down on a white mat in the moonlight and began to drink and sing together, the clear night aiding and inspiring them and the stars' soft rays lighting them on to ecstasy.

As the time was thus passing pleasantly, the wazīr Badr al-Dīn took it into his head to visit his young brother, before lying down himself to sleep, and was mightily astonished not to find him. After searching the whole house, he went up on to the terrace and, approaching the boundary wall, saw his brother and the old man sitting side by side with wine cups in their hands. As good luck would have it, the old man had, on his side, noticed the approach of the wazīr and, being possessed of a ready tact, he broke off the song on which he was engaged and improvised a stanza so adroitly that it appeared to belong to the original:

> His mouth graced the cup with his spittle
>   Before it met mine,
> And the shame of his cheek dimmed a little
>   The red of the wine. . . .
>
> His excellent brother, the Full Moon of Duty,
>   Can hardly object
> If I call this sweet other the Full Moon of Beauty
>   Serene and unflecked.

When the wazīr Badr al-Dīn heard this delicate allusion, being a discreet and very gallant man, and also seeing nothing improper between the two, he retired, saying to himself: 'As Allāh lives, I will not trouble their festivity.' So the couple continued their evening in perfect happiness.

Having told this anecdote, Shahrazād paused for a moment, and then said:

369

The Wonderful Bag

IT is related that one night, when the Khalīfah Hārūn al-Rashīd was plagued with sleeplessness, he called to him Jafar his wazīr, saying: 'O Jafar, to-night my breast is heavy for lack of sleep. I charge you with the lightening of it.' 'Commander of the Faithful,' answered Jafar, 'I have a friend called Alī the Persian, who has in his scrip many delicious tales which are sovereign remedies for the blackest humours and annoyances.' 'Bring him to me at once,' said al-Rashīd, and when Jafar had obeyed and the man was seated in the presence, he continued: 'Listen, Alī, I am told that you know stories which can dissipate weariness and bring sleep to the sleepless. I require one of them now.' 'I hear and I obey, O Prince of Believers,' answered Alī the Persian. 'I pray you tell me whether you wish a story of things heard or a tale of things seen with my own eyes?' 'One in which you have taken part yourself,' said Hārūn al-Rashīd. So Alī the Persian began:

I was sitting one day in my shop when a Kurd came up and began bargaining with me for certain of my goods; suddenly he took up a little bag and, without attempting to hide it, tried most openly to walk off with it, as if it had belonged to him ever since he was born. I jumped out into the street and, stopping him by the skirts of his robe, told him to give me back my bag. He only shrugged his shoulders, saying: 'That bag, and all that is in it, belongs to me.' In rising anger, I cried out: 'O Mussulmāns, save my goods from this wretched unbeliever!' At once all who were in the market crowded round us, and my fellow merchants advised me to lay a complaint before the kādī without further delay. I agreed to this, and immediately willing hands helped me to drag the Kurd who had stolen my bag into the presence of the kādī. As we all stood respectfully before him, he asked: 'Which of you is the plaintiff and which the defendant?' Without giving me time to open my mouth, the Kurd stepped forward, crying: 'Allāh increase the power of our master the kādī! This bag is my bag, and all that it contains belongs to me! I lost it and then found it again on this man's counter.' 'When did you lose it?' asked the kādī. 'I lost it yesterday,' answered the impudent fellow, 'and I could not sleep all night for thinking of it.' 'In that case,' said the judge, 'give me a list of its contents.' Without a moment's hesitation, the Kurd answered: 'O kādī, there are in my bag two crystal flasks filled with kohl, two silver sticks for putting on kohl, a handkerchief, two lemonade glasses with gilded rims, two torches, two ladles, a cushion, two carpets for gaming tables, two water-pots, two basins, one dish, one cook-pot, one earthen water-jar, one kitchen dipper, one large knitting-needle, two provision sacks, a pregnant cat, two bitches, a rice-jar, two donkeys, two bedroom sets for women, a linen garment, two pelisses, a cow, two calves, a sheep with two lambs, a camel with two little camels, two racing dromedaries with their females, a buffalo and two oxen, a lioness and two lions, a female bear, two foxes, one couch, two beds, a palace with two reception halls, two green tents, two canopies, a kitchen with two doors, and an assembly of Kurds of my own kind all ready to swear that the bag is my bag.'

At this point Shahrazād saw the approach of morning and discreetly fell silent.

But when the three-hundred-and-seventy-sixth night had come

SHE SAID:

Then the kādī turned to me, saying: 'What answer have you to this?'

I was so astonished by what the Kurd had said, O Commander of the Faithful, that it was a little time before I was able to advance and answer: 'May Allāh lift up and honour our master the kādī! I know that, in my sack, there are only a ruined pavilion, a house without a kitchen, a large dog-kennel, a boys' school, some jolly young fellows playing dice, a brigand's lair, an army with captains, the city of Basrah and the city of Baghdād, the ancient palace of the amīr Shaddād son of Ād, a smith's furnace, a fishing net, a shepherd's crook, five pretty boys, twelve untouched girls, and a thousand leaders of caravans all ready to bear witness that this bag is my bag.'

When the Kurd had heard my answer, he burst into tears and cried between his sobs: 'O our master the kādī, my bag is known and well known; it is universally acknowledged to be my property. Beside those things which I mentioned before, it contains two fortified cities and ten towns, two alchemical alembics, four chess players, a mare and two foals, a stallion and two geldings, two long lances, two hares, a buggered boy and two pimps, a blind man and two far-seeing men, a lame man and two paralytics, a sea captain, a ship with sailors, a Christian priest and two deacons, a patriarch and two monks, and a kādī and two witnesses ready to swear that this bag is my bag.' Then the kādī turned to me again, and said: 'What answer have you to all that?'

Being filled with hot rage, even to my nose, O Commander of the Faithful, I advanced and replied as calmly as I could: 'Allāh lighten and make strong the judgment of our master the kādī! I ought to add that there are in the bag, beside the things which I have already mentioned, headache cures, filtres and enchantments, coats of mail and armouries filled with arms, a thousand rams trained for fighting, a deer park, men who love women, boy fanciers, gardens filled with trees and flowers, vines loaded with grapes, apples and figs, shades and phantoms, flasks and cups, new married couples with all their marriage fresh about them, cries and jokes, twelve disgraceful farts and as many odourless funks, friends sitting in a meadow, banners and flags, a bride coming out of the bath, twenty singers, five fair Abyssinian slaves, three Indian women, four Greek women, fifty Turkish women, seventy Persian women, forty women from Kashmir, eighty Kurdish women, as many Chinese women, ninety women from Georgia, the land of Irāk, the Earthly Paradise, two stables, a mosque, many hammāms, a hundred merchants, a plank, a nail, a black man playing on the clarinet, a thousand dīnārs, twenty chests full of stuffs, twenty dancers, fifty storehouses, the city of Kūfah, the city of Gaza, Damietta, al-Sawan, the palace of Khusran Ānūshīrwān, the palace of Sulaimān, all the lands between Balkh and Isfahān, the Indies and Sūdān, Baghdād and Khurāsān, and—may Allāh preserve the days of our master the kādī—a shroud, a coffin, and a razor for the beard of the kādī if the kādī does not recognise my rights and say that this bag is my bag!'

When he had heard all this, the kādī looked at us and said: 'As Allāh lives, either you are two rascals mocking at the law and its representatives, or else this bag is a bottomless abyss or the Valley of the Day of Judgment itself.'

Finally, to see which of us had spoken the truth, the kādī opened the bag before his witnesses and found in it a little orange peel and some olive stones.

At once I told the flabbergasted kādī that the bag must belong to the Kurd and that mine had disappeared. Then I went my way.

When the Khalīfah Hārūn al-Rashīd heard this tale, he was knocked over on his backside by the explosive force of his laughter.

He gave a magnificent present to Alī the Persian, and that night slept soundly until the morning.

But do not believe, O auspicious King, added Shahrazād, that this little tale is more delicious than one in which al-Rashīd finds himself in an embarrassing predicament because of love. 'I do not know that tale. What is it?' cried King Shahryār, so Shahrazād said:

Al-Rashīd Judges of Love

IT is related that one night Hārūn al-Rashīd, lying between two fair girls whom he loved equally and of whom one was from Madinah and the other from Kūfah, did not wish to decide with whom he should finish, especially since if one gained the other would have to lose.

Therefore he decided that the prize should go to her who should win it. At once the slave from Madinah clasped his hands and began to caress them gently, while the one from Kūfah, lying lower, rubbed his feet and took advantage of her position to slip up her hand from time to time and dandle the principal merchandise. Under the influence of these delicate touches the merchandise suddenly began to increase considerably in weight; then the girl from Kūfah laid open hold of it and, pulling it towards her, shut it all up in the hollow of her hand. On this the Madinah woman exclaimed: 'You are keeping the capital for yourself and you will not even let me have any of the interest.' Then with a quick movement she pushed her rival away and, taking hold of the capital herself, shut it carefully in her hands. The cheated slave, who was deeply learned in the traditions of the Prophet, said to the other: 'I have a right to the capital, according to these words of the Prophet (upon whom be prayer and peace!): He who makes the dead earth live again shall own it for himself!' But the slave from Madinah, who was no less versed in the Book than her rival, kept hold of the merchandise and answered: 'The capital belongs to me, according to these words of the Prophet (on whom be prayer and peace!): Game shall belong, not to him who starts it, but to him who kills it.'

When the Khalīfah heard these quotations, he considered them so much to the point that he satisfied both the girls on that one night.

But, O auspicious King, continued Shahrazād, none of these short tales is so excellent as that of the two women who argued as to whether a youth or a ripe man were better for the deed of love.

Which is the Better, a Youth or a Ripe Man?

THE following anecdote is told by Abū al-Ainah, who says:
One evening I went up on to my terrace to take the air and heard a conversation between women on the adjoining terrace. Those who spoke were my neighbours' two wives, each of whom had a lover to console her for the coldness of the impotent old man. One loved a fair youth, tender, rosy, and smooth; and the other a ripe and hairy man with a very thick beard. Not dreaming that they could be overheard, the two women were discussing the respective merits of their lovers.

At this point Shahrazād saw the approach of morning and discreetly fell silent.

But when the three-hundred-and-seventy-seventh night had come

SHE SAID:
Said one of them: 'Sister, how can you bear the roughness of your lover's beard when you kiss him? Surely it must scratch your breasts, and the points of his moustaches stick into your lips and cheeks? How can you prevent yourself being cruelly cut to pieces each time? Take my advice, change lovers and do as I do; find some boy whose cheeks are downy and desirable as a fruit, whose delicate flesh melts in the mouth under your kisses! As Allāh lives, you will discover many savoury things about him to console you for the beard.'

The other answered: 'My sister, you are a fool; you have neither intelligence nor taste. Do you not know that a tree is only beautiful when it has leaves, and a cucumber only savoury when it is coarse and pimpled on the outside? Is there anything more ugly in the world than a man beardless and bald as an artichoke? A beard and moustaches are to a man what long hair is to a woman. This is a fact so evident that Allāh (glorify Him!) appointed one angel in Heaven with no other work than to praise the Creator for having given beards to men and long hair to women. And yet you tell me to choose a beardless boy for my lover! Do you think that I would ever stretch myself out for love below a youth who, hardly mounted, thinks of dismounting; who, hardly stretched, thinks of relaxing; who, hardly knotted, thinks of unknotting; who, hardly arrived, thinks of going away; who, hardly stiffened, thinks of melting; who, hardly risen, thinks of falling; who, hardly laced, thinks of unlacing; who, hardly stuck, thinks of unsticking; and who, as soon as he has fired, thinks of retiring? Undeceive yourself, poor sister! I will never leave a man who enlaces as soon as he sniffs, who stays when he is in, who fills himself when he is empty, who begins again when he has finished, whose moving is an excellence, whose jerking is a gift, who is generous when he gives, and, when he pushes, pierces!'

Hearing such wisdom, the lover of the beardless boy exclaimed: 'By the Master of the holy Kaabah, my sister, you make me inclined to taste a bearded man!'

After a short silence Shahrazād continued:

The Price of Cucumbers

ONE day, while the amīr Muīn ibn Zaid was out hunting, he met an Arab mounted upon an ass, coming across the desert. He rode up and saluted him, saying: 'Where are you going, O brother Arab, and what is it that you carry so carefully rolled up in that little sack?' 'I go to find the amīr Muīn,' answered the Arab, 'to carry him some cucumbers which have come up before their time on my land and are its first fruits. He is the most generous man in the kingdom and I am sure he will pay me a worthy price for my cucumbers.' The amīr, whom the Arab had never seen before, asked him how much he expected to be paid for the cucumbers and the other answered: 'At least a thousand dīnārs of gold.'

'And if the amīr says that is too much?'
'I will only ask five hundred.'
'And if he says that is too much?'
'I will only ask three hundred.'
'And if he says that is too much?'
'One hundred.'
'And if he says that is too much?'
'Fifty.'

'And if he says that is too much?'

'Thirty.'

'And if he says that is still too much?'

'I will drive my ass into his harîm and run away.'

Muîn laughed heartily at this and, spurring his horse, rejoined his followers. Then, without a moment's delay, he returned to his palace and ordered his chamberlain to admit the Arab when he should come with the cucumbers.

An hour later the man arrived with his bag, and the chamberlain led him at once into the reception hall, where the amîr Muîn waited him in the midst of all the majesty of his court and surrounded by guards with naked swords. The Arab, who did not at all recognise, among so much grandeur, the horseman whom he had met upon his way, stood with the sack of cucumbers in his hand, waiting to be questioned. 'What do you bring me in that sack, O brother Arab?' the amîr enquired, and the man replied: 'Trusting in the liberality of our master the amîr, I have brought him the first young cucumbers which grew in my field.'

'An excellent idea! And what do you think my liberality is worth?'

'A thousand dînârs.'

'That is a little too much.'

'Five hundred.'

'Too much.'

'Three hundred.'

'Too much.'

'One hundred.'

'Too much.'

'Fifty.'

'Too much.'

'Thirty, then.'

'Still too much.'

Then cried the Arab: 'As Allâh lives, it was an unlucky meeting I had in the desert with that foul-faced man! O amîr, I cannot let my cucumbers go at less than thirty dînârs!'

The amîr smiled and did not answer; therefore the Arab looked at him more closely and, recognising him as the man he had met in the desert, exclaimed: 'As Allâh lives, my master, let the thirty dînârs be brought, for my ass is fastened just outside the door.' The amîr was taken with such a gust of laughing that he fell over on his backside; when he was a little recovered, he called his intendant, saying: 'Count out immediately to this our brother, the Arab, first a thousand dīnārs, then five hundred, then three hundred, then one hundred, then fifty, and finally thirty, to induce him to leave his ass tied up where it is.' I need not say that the Arab was stupefied at receiving one thousand, nine hundred and eighty dīnārs for a little sack of cucumbers. Such was the liberality of the amīr Muīn. May the mercy of Allāh be upon all concerned for ever!

Then Shahrazād said:

White Hair

ABU SUWAID TELLS THIS STORY:

ONE day I went into an orchard to buy fruit and saw, far off, a woman sitting in the shade of an apricot tree and combing her hair. Going nearer I perceived that she was old and had white hair, though her face was beautiful and her complexion fresh and young. Although she saw me approaching, she made no movement to veil her face or cover her head, but went on arranging her hair with her ivory comb. I stopped before her and greeted her, saying: 'O woman old in years but young of face, why do you not dye your hair and look altogether like a girl? Surely there is no reason why you should not do so?'

At this point Shahrazād saw the approach of morning and discreetly fell silent.

But when the three-hundred-and-seventy-eighth night had come

SHE SAID:

She lifted her head and, looking at me with her great eyes, answered by these lines:

> I used to dye my hair
> But time undyed it.
> Now I am sage,
> I show my bottom bare
> Which does not age.
> (I used to hide it.)

Shahrazād continued:

A Difficulty Resolved

IT is related that the wazīr Jafar received the Khalīfah Hārūn al-Rashīd at his house one night and spared no pains to entertain him pleasantly. As the feast proceeded, the Khalīfah said suddenly: 'Now I remember, Jafar, that you have bought a very beautiful slave for yourself and that, having seen her, I want to buy her from you. I wish you to give her up to me at any price which suits you.' 'I have no intention of selling her, Commander of the Faithful,' answered Jafar. 'Give her to me, then,' said Hārūn, but Jafar replied: 'I have no intention of doing that either, Commander of the Faithful.' Al-Rashīd drew his brows together and cried: 'I swear by the three oaths that I will instantly divorce my wife, the lady Zubaidah, if you do not consent either to sell or give me the slave!' Then Jafar cried: 'And I swear by the three oaths that I will instantly divorce my wife, the mother of my children, before I will do either!' When they had both sworn, they suddenly realised that, bemused by the mist of wine, they had gone a great deal too far and, by common consent, began to search for a way out of their difficulty. After a few moments of perplexity, al-Rashīd said: 'I see no way out of such an embarrassing situation, unless we are guided by the wisdom of the kādī Abū Yūsuf, who knows all that there is to be known of the law concerning divorce.' At once they sent for this man, and Abū Yūsuf thought to himself: 'If the Khalīfah demands my presence in the middle of the night, some serious difficulty must have arisen in Islām.' He went out quickly and mounted his mule, saying to the slave who was to follow the animal: 'Take his forage bag with you, for he has not yet finished his meal, and do not forget to fasten it to his head when we arrive.'

When he entered the chamber where the Khalīfah and Jafar were waiting him, Hārūn al-Rashīd rose in his honour and made him sit down by his side, a privilege which he never accorded to anyone but Abū Yūsuf. 'I have called you on a very grave and delicate affair,' he said and then explained the case. 'Commander of the Faithful,' said Abū, 'the solution is the simplest thing in the world,' and, turning to Jafar, he continued: 'All that you have to do is to sell the Khalīfah one half of the slave and give him the other half.'

This solution delighted the Khalīfah because of its admirable subtlety, which not only got them both out of their difficulty, but brought it about that he should have the slave. The girl was at once sent for, and the Khalīfah said: 'I cannot wait for the legal time to pass when her freeing will be complete and I can take her. Therefore, O Abū Yūsuf, you must also find us some way by which this freeing can be instantly completed.' 'That is easier still. Bring in some young mamlūk!' said Abū Yūsuf, and, when a mamlūk was brought, continued: 'For this immediate freeing to be lawful, the slave must be legally married. I will give her in marriage to this mamlūk together with a sum of money, on condition that he divorces her without touching her. Then she can be your concubine at once, Commander of the Faithful.' To the mamlūk, he said: 'Do you accept this slave as your lawful wife?' The mamlūk answered: 'I accept her.' 'Then,' proclaimed the kādī, 'you are married! Here are a thousand dīnārs! Now divorce her!' But the mamlūk exclaimed: 'Now that I am legally married to her, I shall stay married, for the girl pleases me.'

On this the Khalīfah drew down his brows in anger, saying to the kādī: 'By the honour of my ancestors, this wisdom of yours will carry you to the gallows!' But Abū Yūsuf only answered calmly: 'Let not our master concern himself with the mamlūk's refusal, for now things are even easier than they were before. Only grant me permission to use this mamlūk as if he were my slave.' 'I allow it,' answered Hārūn. 'He is your slave and your property.' At once Abū Yūsuf turned to the girl, saying: 'I give you this mamlūk as a present, as a purchased slave! Do you accept him as such?' 'I accept him,' she answered, and the kādī cried: 'In that case his marriage with you is null and void; you are free from him! Such is the law! I have given my judgment!'

In an ecstasy of admiration, Hārūn al-Rashīd leapt to his feet, crying: 'O Abū Yūsuf, there is not your equal in all Islām!' At once he had brought in a great dish filled with gold, and asked the kādī to accept it. Yūsuf thanked him profusely, but was at a loss how to carry so much gold until he remembered the mule's bag. Having had the bag brought to him, he emptied all the gold into it and went his way.

This little tale is a proof that the study of jurisprudence leads to honour and riches. May the mercy of Allāh be upon all concerned in it!

Then Shahrazād said:

Abū Nuwās and Zubaidah's Bath

IT is related that the Khalīfah Hārūn al-Rashīd loved his wife and cousin, Zubaidah, so well that he made, for her sole use and in her own garden, a great fountain basin of water, hidden among leafy trees, where she might bathe, safe from the eyes of men and the sun's rays. On one day of great heat the lady Zubaidah came alone into the grove and, undressing completely by the side of the fountain, stepped into the water. She did not, however, go in above her knees, fearing the shiver of water when the body is plunged into it entire and also being unable to swim. Instead she poured water over her shoulders in little waves out of a cup which she had brought with her, shivering at its cool and silver kisses.

The Khalīfah, who had seen her going towards the fountain, followed her softly, deadening the sound of his footsteps, and arrived when she was already naked. Hidden by the leaves, he set himself to admire the white rareness of her against the water; but, as he was leaning with his hand against a branch, it suddenly cracked beneath his fingers.

At this point Shahrazād saw the approach of morning and discreetly fell silent.

But when the three-hundred-and-seventy-ninth night had come

SHE SAID:

In a sudden fright Zubaidah turned towards the sound, instinctively carrying her two hands to her affair in order to hide it from any indiscreet eye. Now Zubaidah's affair was so remarkable a thing that two hands could hardly have hidden the half of it; also it was so sleek and slippery that she could not hold it at all. It glided between her fingers, and appeared in all its glory to the delighted Khalīfah.

Al-Rashīd, who had never before had the opportunity of seeing his cousin's beauty by daylight and in the open air, was pleasantly astonished at its sumptuous size, and hastened to slip away as he had come. That which he had seen inspired him, and he tried in vain to write a poem. He achieved this line:

I saw silver in the fountain . . .

but, however much he tortured his soul in the attempt, he could not find a rhyme, or at all go on with the stanza. He wandered about, feeling himself very unhappy, and sweating as he repeated over and over: *I saw silver in the fountain. . . .* At last, knowing that the difficulty was too much for him, he called the poet Abū Nuwās, saying: 'Let us see if you can make a short poem beginning with this line: *I saw silver in the fountain. . . .*' At once Abū Nuwās, who had also been carrying out investigations near the bathing pool and had seen all that had happened, answered: 'I hear and I obey!' and, to the Khalīfah's surprise, instantly improvised these lines:

> I saw silver in the fountain,
>   Still the picture lingers,
> When the pale girl's little mountain
>   Slipped between her fingers,
> Sleek and prominent and hairless.
>   If I had my wish
> I'd be water, I'd be careless,
>   I would be a fish.

The Khalīfah did not probe to find out how Abū Nuwās was able to make so relevant a poem, but instead expressed his admiration with a large gift.

But do not think, O auspicious King, added Shahrazād, that this example of the poet's quick subtlety is in any way more admirable than that given by his charming improvisation in the following tale:

Abū Nuwās Improvises

ONE night the Khalīfah Hārūn al-Rashīd, being in the grip of stark sleeplessness, was walking alone in the galleries of his palace when he saw one of his women slaves, whom he greatly loved, hastening in the direction of the pavilion which he had reserved for her. He followed and, walking behind her into the place, took her in his arms and began to caress her and play with her until the veil which covered her fell away and the tunic slipped from her shoulders.

Desire flamed up in the Khalīfah's heart and he would have possessed the beautiful slave there and then, if she had not excused herself, saying: 'O Commander of the Faithful, I beg you to put the thing off till to-morrow, for to-night I had not expected the honour

of a visit and am not well prepared. To-morrow, if Allāh wills, you
shall find me scented, with all my jasmines sweetening the couch.'
So al-Rashīd insisted no further, but returned to his lonely walking.

Next day he sent Masrūr, his chief eunuch, to announce his visit
to the girl; but the slave, who had felt tired since dawn and less
disposed than ever, answered Masrūr, when he reminded her of her
promise, by quoting this proverb: 'Words of a night to bring the
day!'

While Masrūr was repeating this answer to the Khalīfah, the poets
Abū Nuwās, al-Rakkāshi and Abū Musab entered the presence. At
once the Khalīfah turned to them, saying: 'Let each of you immediately improvise a poem introducing the sense of this phrase: "Words
of a night to bring the day." '

Without pause al-Rakkāshi said:

> Beware, my heart, the heartless child
>   Who'll neither visit nor receive,
> Her promises are sweet and wild,
>   Then, laughing in her sleeve:
> 'Words of a night to bring the day,'
>   She'll say.

Next Abū Musab came forward and said:

> The quicker my heart turns
>   The better the toy for her,
> The fiercer my heart burns
>   The better her joy;
> She breaks in the light time
>   The promise night gave for her
> With: 'Words of the night time
>   To bring in the day.'

Lastly Abū Nuwās came forward and said:

> Beautiful, troubled, and gay,
> Sweetly resisting,
> When the bold drunken breeze
> In the black midnight trees
> Would sway, tenderly sway,
> The waist and its fruit;
> O over-light silk, you are misting

The white lighter fruit
Which is budded,
The other is budless;
Now, I am full-blooded
If others are bloodless,
I slip the bright vest
From the pearl of the crest
Of her shoulder.
The dim torches show her
With not angry brows;
I grow bolder,
For darkness allows,
And the vest tumbles lower.
I whisper: 'The rest!'
But she smiles and says: 'Wait!'
It will not be too late
On the morrow!'
Ah, sorrow, my sorrow!
Next morning I pray
But she turns it away
In a laughing despite
With: 'Words of the night
For the day!'

When he had heard these improvisations, al-Rashīd gave large sums of money to the first two poets, but condemned Abū Nuwās to instant death, crying: 'As Allāh lives, there must be something between you and the girl. If not, how could you have made so exact a description of things which happened when I was alone with her?' Abū Nuwās burst out laughing and answered: 'Our master the Khalīfah forgets that a true poet can guess at what is hidden. The Prophet (upon whom be prayer and peace!) painted us well enough, when he said: "Poets follow all roads as if they were mad. Inspiration guides them, or it may be the devil. They write excellent things but do not do them."'

Hearing this excuse, the Khalīfah, instead of seeking to plumb the mystery any further, pardoned Abū Nuwās and gave him double the amount which he had given to the other two poets.

When King Shahryār had heard this story, he cried: 'As Allāh lives, I would not have pardoned Abū Nuwās! I would have solved the mystery and cut off the rascal's head. Once and for all, Shahrazād, I forbid you to tell me any more of this crapulous poet, who had no respect for Khalīfahs or laws.' Then said Shahrazād: 'Since that is your wish, O auspicious King, I will now tell you the tale about the ass.'

The Ass

ONE day a jolly fellow, who belonged to that class which is always being taken in, was walking through the market leading an ass behind him by a simple cord. A clever robber saw him and, wishing to steal the beast, expressed his desire to one of his companions, who asked: 'How can you do it without the man noticing you?' 'Follow me and you shall see,' answered the other.

At this point Shahrazād saw the approach of morning and discreetly fell silent.

But when the three-hundred-and-eightieth night had come

SHE SAID:

He went up behind the man and, softly untying the halter from the ass, put it round his own neck, without the exchange being noticed; then he walked along like a beast of burden, while his companion made off with the ass.

When the thief knew that the stolen animal was out of sight, he halted abruptly so that the man in front, without turning, tried to pull him forward. Finding that he could not do this, the victim looked over his shoulder to curse the ass and saw the robber at the end of the halter, regarding him with humble and imploring eyes. In his stupefaction he stood stock-still in front of the unexpected changeling, and it was some time before he could summon breath to ask: 'What thing are you?' Filling his voice with tears, the robber cried: 'I am your ass, my master; but my tale is a strange one. In my youth I was a bad lad, given to all sorts of disgraceful vice. One day I returned home in a disgusting state of drunkenness, and my mother, who could not contain her anger, heaped reproaches upon me and would have turned me out of the house. I pushed her away and even struck her in my intoxicated frenzy; therefore she cursed me and, because of that curse, I was changed into an ass.

You, my master, bought me in the market for five dīnārs and, ever since then, while I have served you as a beast of burden, you have continually pricked my bottom when I was worn out and could not walk, and have subjected me to a thousand oaths which I would not dare to repeat. I could not complain, because my voice had been taken away from me; the very most I could do, and that on the rarest occasions, was to fart instead of speaking. But to-day my poor mother must certainly have remembered me kindly and, in the pity of her heart, prayed mercy on me from the Highest; and this mercy has undoubtedly changed me back into my original form.'

Hearing this, the poor man cried aloud: 'O fellow human, for Allāh's sake forgive me the injuries which I have done you and forget the harsh treatment which you have undergone. There is no help, save in Allāh!' So crying, he undid the halter from the robber's neck and returned, bitterly repenting, to his own house, where remorse prevented him from closing his eyes all night.

A few days after the victim of this trick went to the ass market to buy another animal, and was mightily surprised to see his old donkey in its original form being put up for sale. Thinking to himself: 'This rascal must have committed some other heinous act!' he went up to the ass, which brayed with delight on seeing him, and, bending down to its ear, cried into it as loud as he could: 'O incorrigible young man, you have been beating your mother again! As Allāh lives, I will not buy you a second time!' He spat furiously in the donkey's face and then, passing on, bought himself another animal, which was notorious as being descended from the father and mother of all asses.

That same night Shahrazād also said:

Zubaidah Caught in the Act

IT is related that the Commander of the Faithful, Hārūn al-Rashīd, went to rest one noon in the bedchamber of his queen, Zubaidah, and was stretching himself on the bed when he noticed in the middle of it a large and quite fresh stain, concerning the origin of which there could be no mistake. The world darkened before his eyes; tottering with indignation, he sought out Zubaidah and, with eyes on fire and trembling beard, cried out to her: 'What is this stain on our bed?' The queen bent her head over the stain and sniffed it, saying: 'It is man's semen, O Commander of the Faithful.' Holding back his wrath with difficulty, the Khalīfah demanded: 'And can you explain the presence of such stuff, still quite warm, upon the bed where I have not lain with you for more than a week?' 'Faith be upon me and about me, Prince of Believers!' cried Zubaidah in great emotion. 'Can you possibly suspect me of fornication?' 'I so suspect you,' said al-Rashīd, 'that I am going to send for the kādī, Abū Yūsuf, to give an expert opinion on the stain, and by the honour of my ancestors, O daughter of my uncle, I shall stick at nothing if the kādī says that you are guilty!'

When the kādī arrived, al-Rashīd said to him: 'O Abū Yūsuf, tell me what this stain may be?' The kādī went up to the bed, placed his finger in the middle of the stain, carried it to his eye and his nose, and then said: 'Commander of the Faithful, it is man's semen.'

At this point Shahrazād saw the approach of morning and discreetly fell silent.

But when the three-hundred-and-eighty-first night had come

SHE SAID:

'And the immediate origin of it?' asked the Khalīfah. Now here the kādī was placed in a very awkward position. Being unwilling to bring down upon himself the enmity of Zubaidah, he cast up his eyes to the ceiling, as if in reflection, in order to gain time and, in doing so, saw the wing of a bat extruding from a hole in which it was sleeping. With a sudden inspiration, he said: 'Give me a lance, O Prince of Believers.' The Khalīfah handed him a lance, and Abū Yūsuf at once stabbed the bat so that it fell heavily to the floor. Then he said: 'Commander of the Faithful, the books of medicine teach us that the bat's semen closely resembles that of a man. The mess was certainly made by this bat while he looked upon the lady Zubaidah in her sleep. You see that I have punished his temerity with death.'

This explanation entirely satisfied the Khalīfah who, being re-assured as to the innocence of his wife, gratefully loaded the kādī with gifts. Zubaidah herself was delighted and therefore not only added to the Khalīfah's gifts, but invited Abū Yūsuf to eat some early fruit with herself and al-Rashīd. The kādī sat down upon carpets between the Khalīfah and his queen, and Zubaidah, peeling a banana, handed it to him with these words: 'I have in my garden other fruits which are very rare at this season; would you prefer them to the banana?' 'Mistress,' he answered, 'I make it a rule never to give judgment by default. I must see those early fruits and compare them with these early fruits before expressing a preference.' Zubaidah had the other rare dainties of her garden plucked and brought in. When the kādī had tasted them, she said: 'Which do you prefer now?' Abū Yūsuf smiled knowingly and, looking at the Khalīfah and Zubaidah in turn, replied: 'As Allāh lives, the answer is not easy. If I preferred one of these fruits, I would be disparaging the other and run the risk of an indigestion!' When they heard this answer, al-Rashīd and Zubaidah laughed so greatly that they fell over on their backsides.

Here Shahrazād, seeing certain indications that King Shahryār would rather that Zubaidah had been condemned without mercy, hastened to distract his attention by telling him the following tale.

Male or Female?

AMONG other tales of the great Khusrau, King of Persia, it is told that he was very fond of fish. One day, as he was sitting on his terrace with his wife the beautiful Shīrīn, a fisherman brought him a fish of great size and distinction. The King was delighted and ordered the fisherman to be given four thousand dirhams, but Shīrīn, who never approved of the generous prodigality of her husband, waited until the man had gone, and then said: 'You must not be so spendthrift as to give four thousand dirhams for a single fish; you must get the money back, for otherwise, in the future, anyone who brings you anything will start his hope of reward at four thousand dirhams, and you will never be able to keep pace with such pretensions.' 'It would be a deep shame for a King to take what he had given,' answered Khusrau. 'Let us forget the matter.' But Shīrīn exclaimed: 'It is impossible to leave the thing as it is. Besides, there is a way of getting back the money from the fisherman without incurring any criticism at all. All you have to do is to call the man back and ask him whether the fish he brought is male or female. Then, if he says it is a male, give it back and say that you wanted a female; and if he says it is a female, give it back and say that you wanted a male.'

The King, who loved his wife with consuming passion and did

not wish to displease her, regretfully had the man recalled. But the fisherman had been gifted with ready wit and, when Khusrau said to him: 'Is the fish male or female?', he kissed the earth and answered: 'The fish, O King, is an hermaphrodite.'

Khusrau was overjoyed at these words and, in the midst of his laughter, ordered the intendant to give the fisherman eight thousand dirhams instead of four thousand. When the money had been counted out and put in the fish bag, the man joyfully went on his way.

While he was crossing the courtyard of the palace he accidentally let fall one silver dirham from the bag. At once he set his burden down and searched diligently until he found the coin, which he replaced with many expressions of satisfaction.

Khusrau and Shīrīn were watching from the terrace and saw all that passed; the queen, not wishing to let slip so good an opportunity, exclaimed:

At this point Shahrazād saw the approach of morning and discreetly fell silent.

But when the three-hundred-and-eighty-second night had come

SHE SAID:

'What a shameful fellow! He drops a dirham and, instead of leaving it to be picked up by one poorer than himself, is vile enough to recover it and cheat the necessitous.' Khusrau was impressed by this remark, so he recalled the fisherman and said to him: 'O abject being, your soul is so small that you cannot even be called a man! Avarice is your ruin. You set down a bag filled with money in order to pick up a single dirham which has fallen to be a good fortune to the poor.' The fisherman kissed the earth and answered: 'May Allāh prolong the life of my King! If I picked up the dirham, it was not because it was worth much money to me, but because it had a great and other value in my eyes. Does it not bear on one of its sides the image of the King, and on the other the name of the King? I did not wish to leave it lying where it might be shamed by the feet of some passer. Also, in hastening to pick it up, I was following the example of my King who picked up out of the dust a poor fisherman not worth a dirham in his eyes.'

This answer so pleased King Khusrau that he gave the man another four thousand dirhams and ordered heralds to proclaim publicly all through his empire: 'Never let yourselves be guided by

the advice of women. If you listen to them, you will commit two
faults in avoiding a half fault!'

King Shahryār, on hearing this tale, exclaimed: 'I highly approve
Khusrau's conduct and also his mistrust of women. They are the
cause of many calamities.' But already Shahrazād was beginning to
relate with a smile:

The Share

ONE night the Khalīfah, Hārūn al-Rashīd, was complaining of
his insomnia to his wazīr Jafar and Masrūr, his sword-bearer,
when suddenly Masrūr burst out laughing. The Khalīfah looked at him
with frowning brows and said: 'What are you laughing at? Are you
mad or are you merely impertinent?' 'As Allāh lives, Commander of
the Faithful,' answered Masrūr, 'I swear, by your blood kinship
with the Prophet, that I laughed from neither of these causes, but
just because I remembered the jests of a certain Ibn al-Karībī,
about whom listeners were making quite a circle yesterday on the
banks of the Tigris.' Then said the Khalīfah: 'If that is the case, go
quickly and fetch this Ibn al-Karībī; perhaps he will succeed in
distracting me from my sleeplessness.'

At once Masrūr ran off in search of the humorous Ibn al-Karībī
and, having met him, said: 'I have spoken of you to the Khalīfah;
he wishes you to come and make him laugh.' 'I hear and I obey!' said
the man, and Masrūr continued: 'I am very willing to conduct you
to the Khalīfah, but it must be on condition that you give me three-
quarters of any reward he makes you.' 'That is too much,' answered
Ibn al-Karībī. 'I will give you two-thirds as commission.'

After making a few more difficulties for form's sake, Masrūr
accepted the bargain and conducted the man into the presence of
the Khalīfah.

On seeing him enter, al-Rashīd said: 'They tell me that you say
very amusing things. Let us have a sample of your quality; but I
must warn you that, if you do not make me laugh, the stick awaits
you.'

This threat effectually froze all Ibn al-Karībī's wit and he could
think of nothing but disastrous commonplaces; therefore al-Rashīd,
instead of laughing, grew more and more irritable and at last cried
out: 'Give him a hundred blows on the soles of his feet to bring

down the blood which is obstructing his brain!' At once the man was stretched out on the ground and the soles of his feet soundly beaten; but suddenly, when the number of strokes had passed thirty, the victim cried out: 'The rest are for Masrūr, because we agreed that he should have two-thirds of all I got!' Hearing this, the Khalīfah made a sign and the guards stretched Masrūr out in the other's place and began to make his feet feel the rhythm of the stick. After the first few blows, however, the eunuch cried out: 'As Allāh lives, it was unjust of me to ask more than a quarter! I forfeit the rest of my share.'

Straightway the Khalīfah so laughed that he fell over on his backside and, after, gave each of the sufferers a thousand dīnārs.

Being unwilling to let the night pass without beginning the following tale, Shahrazād went on without pause:

The Schoolmaster

A VAGABOND, whose trade was living upon other people, once had the idea, although he could not read or write, of becoming a schoolmaster, since that was the only profession in which he could make money by doing nothing. For it is notorious that anyone can be a schoolmaster, although he be completely ignorant of the rules and elementary principles of language. It is only necessary to be cunning enough to make others believe that one is a great grammarian; and that is not difficult, since really great grammarians are usually poor men with narrow, mean and disparaging intellects, impotent and incomplete.

Our vagabond turned himself into a schoolmaster by the simple process of increasing the folds and size of his turban and opening a little room at the bottom of a street, which he decorated with pictures of writing and the like baits.

He had not long to wait for clients, because, at the sight of his imposing turban, all the people of the quarter felt convinced of his great learning and hastened to send their children to him.

At this point Shahrazād saw the approach of morning and discreetly fell silent.

THE SCHOOLMASTER

But when the three-hundred-and-eighty-third night had come

As he could not read or write, he invented the following ingenious way of conducting his school: he made the children who knew a little teach those who knew nothing, while he pretended to overlook the lesson and approve or disapprove. In this way the school flourished and the master began to put by money. One day, as he sat with his stick in his hand, frowning with terrible eyes upon the unfortunate little children who fearfully regarded him, a woman came in, holding a letter in her hand, and begged the master to read it to her, as is the custom of women who cannot read. The schoolmaster did not know how to avoid this direct proof, so he rose and made as if to go out hastily; but the woman held him back, begging him to read the letter before he went. 'I cannot stay just now,' he answered. 'The muezzin has announced midday prayer and I must go to the mosque.' 'Allāh be with you!' cried the importunate woman. 'This letter is from my husband who has been away for five years, and you alone in all the quarter can read it to me.' With that she thrust the letter into his hand.

The schoolmaster was thus forced to take it, but all he could then do, in his embarrassment, was to hold it upside down and, as he looked at the writing, beat his brow, thrust aside his turban, and sweat at every pore.

Seeing this, the poor woman thought: 'There can be no doubt of it; if it agitates the schoolmaster so much, it must contain bad news. Alas the day! Perhaps my husband is dead!' Anxiously she asked the master: 'Is he dead? For pity's sake hide nothing from me!' When the man shook his head vaguely and kept silence, she cried again: 'O woe upon my head, must I tear my garments?' He answered: 'Tear!' 'Must I beat and claw my cheeks?' she sobbed, and he answered: 'Beat and claw!'

Maddened with grief, the unfortunate woman ran from the school and filled her own house with cries of desolation. While all her neighbours, who had run in, were vainly trying to console her, one of her relations entered and, having taken up and read the letter, said to the woman: 'Who told you your husband is dead? There is nothing about it in the letter. This is all it says: *Greeting and salutation, O daughter of my uncle! I am in excellent health and hope to be with you in a fortnight. In the meanwhile I send you a linen sheet wrapped up in a cover. Allāh be with you!'*

On this the woman took the letter and returned to the school, meaning to reproach the master for having led her so far astray. She found him sitting at his door, and said to him: 'Are you not ashamed of so deceiving a poor woman and telling her that her husband is dead, when all that he has written is that he will be home soon, and sends me a sheet and a cover?' 'My poor woman,' answered the schoolmaster, 'you are quite right to reproach me, but I hope you will forgive me if I tell you that I was deeply occupied with other matters when I had your letter in my hand. Reading it quickly and the wrong way up, I thought it said that they were sending the remains of your husband back to you covered in a linen sheet.'

Then Shahrazād said:

Inscription on a Chemise

IT is related that al-Amīn, brother of the Khalīfah al-Mamūn, on going one day to visit his uncle al-Mahdī, saw a very beautiful young slave playing the lute, and fell in love with her. Al-Mahdī noticed the impression which the child had made upon his nephew and, wishing to give him an agreeable present, waited until he had gone and then sent the slave after him, loaded with jewels and very richly dressed. But al-Amīn, knowing that his uncle had a great reputation as a lover of still unripe fruit, imagined that he had had first use of the slave; therefore he did not wish to accept her and sent her back with a letter, saying that apples which the gardener had bitten before they were ripe were not popular in the market.

Al-Mahdī at once undressed the girl, placed a lute in her hand, and sent her back again to al-Amīn, dressed only in a silk chemise over which ran this inscription in letters of gold:

> No hand has been allowed to touch
> The rose I hide,
> Though eyes have looked upon it and desired it.
> Surely the thought of all this foiled desire
> Should feed your fire

And fan your pride
And raise the value of the bud, as such,
If it required it!

On seeing the girl's charms displayed by this delightful garment and on reading the inscription, al-Amīn accepted the gift as one of the most pleasant he had ever had.

On that same night, Shahrazād said:

Inscription on a Cup

ONE day the Khalīfah, al-Mutawakkil, fell sick and his doctor, Yuhannā, prescribed excellent remedies which dissipated the illness, so that convalescence came. Then from all sides there poured in gifts of congratulation upon the Khalīfah. Al-Fath ibn Kahkān sent him an untouched girl, whose breasts were the form and example for the breasts of all the women of that time. Beyond her own beauty, she carried and brought to him a fair crystal jar filled with choice wine, from which she poured a draught into a gold cup, having this inscription picked out in rubies upon it:

Some wise electuary or balm,
Some learned knife,
May cure particular complaints;
But when the whole soul faints
Here is the old, the calm,
The purple remedy for life.

Yuhannā, who was present, read the inscription laughing and said to the Khalīfah: 'As Allāh lives, O Commander of the Faithful, this girl and her medicine will bring back your strength better than all the cures of ancient or modern art.'

Then without pause Shahrazād began the following tale:

The Khalīfah in the Basket

THIS story was told by the famous singer, Ishāk of Mosul, who said:

One night, when I had left after feasting late with the Khalīfah al-Mamūn, I was suffering so greatly from a long continence of urine that I made my way down the first unlighted side-street and, going near the wall—but not too near, as I did not wish to receive a jet of my own water in my face—squatted down politely and pissed my fill. It was a great relief. I had hardly finished and was shaking myself, when I felt something fall on my head in the darkness. Springing up in a fright, I took hold of the thing and discovered, by feeling it, that it was a large basket, fastened at the corner with four cords which led up to the house under which I stood. Carrying my investigations further, I found that it was lined with silk and contained two delightfully scented cushions.

Now I had drunk a little more than usual and my uplifted fancy suggested that I should sit down in the basket and rest. No sooner had I given rein to this inclination than I felt myself rapidly pulled up to the terrace above, where I was met by four young silent girls, who led me into the house and invited me to follow them. One of them walked in front of me, torch in hand, and the three others came behind, while I passed down a marble stair and entered a hall, so magnificent that it could only be compared with that in the Khalīfah's palace. 'They must mistake me for someone else,' I said to myself. 'Allāh will unwind the adventure as He thinks fit!'

A vast silk curtain, which hid one part of the hall, now rose, and I saw ten ravishing women walking towards me, tripping and swaying exquisitely, carrying torches and gold censers, in which the best of nard and aloes burned sweetly. Among them was a girl, most like the moon, who could have tortured all the stars with jealousy. As she walked she balanced on her little feet and looked tenderly sideways, so that the grossest and heaviest soul would have flown upwards at the sight. I leapt to my feet and bowed towards her, while she looked at me smiling and said: 'Welcome, O stranger!' Then she sat down and continued in a delightful voice: 'Rest yourself, my lord.' I sank on to a cushion, quite sobered from the wine but already drunken with a fiercer drink. 'How was it, my lord, that you came into our street and sat in the basket?' said the girl, and I answered: 'O mistress, it was the anguish of my urine which led me into the street, the wine which led me into the basket, your generosity which led me into this hall, your charms which led away the wine and led me into stronger intoxication.' The girl was visibly pleased with my reply and asked me what my trade might be. Feeling that I could hardly tell her that I was the Khalīfah's singer and musician, I answered: 'I am a weaver from the weavers' market in Baghdad.' 'Your manners are exquisite and you are a credit to the weavers' market!' she exclaimed. 'If you added a knowledge of poetry, we should never regret having received you among us. Do you know anything of verse?' 'A little,' I said; but, when she begged me to repeat some stanzas, I answered: 'O my mistress, a guest is always somewhat put out of countenance by his reception. I beg you to encourage me by saying some of your favourite poems first.' 'Willingly,' she answered, and straightway began to recite well-chosen passages, from the older poets such as Imru al-Kais, Zuhair, Antar, Nābighah, Amir ibn Kulthūm, and Tarafah; and from the moderns, such as Abū Nuwās, al-Rakkāshī, and Abū Musab. I was marvelling at the purity of her diction when she said to me: 'I hope that your shyness has now passed.' 'As Allāh lives, it has!' I answered and, in my turn, chose out all the most delicate of the verses I knew and recited them with considerable feeling. When I had finished, she said to me: 'By Allāh, I did not know that there were such cultivated people in the weavers' market!'

At this point Shahrazād saw the approach of morning and discreetly fell silent.

But when the three-hundred-and-eighty-fifth night had come

SHE SAID:

A feast was brought in which there was no dearth of fruit or flowers, and the girl served me herself with the choicest morsels. Then, when the cloth was lifted, wine and cups were brought and she filled for me, saying: 'Now is the best part of our meeting. Do you know any beautiful tales?' I bowed and started at once to tell her many amusing details of the life of kings and courts; but suddenly she stopped me, saying: 'Truly, I am more than ordinarily surprised that a weaver should know so much about the inner life of Khalīfahs.' 'There is nothing astonishing in that,' I replied. 'I have a delightful friend who is much about the palace and, in his leisure, he often charms me with reminiscences.' 'In that case,' she said, 'I can only admire the excellence of your memory.'

All this time, as I inhaled the perfumes of nard and aloes and looked upon this beauty, understanding the language of her lips and eyes, I felt that I had never been so happy and said to myself: 'What would the Khalīfah do if he could see me? Surely he would sprout wings and fly here instantly!'

Soon the girl said to me: 'You are a most distinguished man; your wit has been polished with pleasant knowledge and your manners are of great refinement. I have only one further thing to ask of you: will you accompany yourself upon the lute and sing us something?' Being a professional musician, I did not care to sing, so I answered: 'Once I tried to learn singing, but nothing came of it; therefore I gave it up. I would perform with the greatest pleasure if I could; but, as it is, my ignorance must be my excuse. On the other hand, everything about you leads me to suppose that you have a voice of perfect beauty. If you would sing me something, the happiness of our night would be crowned with happiness.'

She had a lute brought and sang to me; never in all my life have I heard a fuller, clearer, or better-controlled voice than hers, or a greater knowledge of the truly subtle effects in music. Seeing my astonishment, she said: 'Do you know who wrote the words or the music?' Although I could hardly plead ignorance, I answered: 'I do not know at all.' Then she cried: 'Is it possible that anyone in the world should not know that song? The words are by Abū Nuwās and the music, which is really great, is by the famous Ishāk of Mosul.' Without moving a muscle, I exclaimed: 'As Allāh lives, Ishāk is nothing compared with you.' 'Bak, bak,' she cried, 'you must not say such things! Ishāk has not his equal in the world. One can see that you have not heard of him.' Then she went on singing, interrupting herself from time to time to see that I lacked for nothing, and we continued in this pleasant way until the dawn.

With the first light an old woman, who must have been her nurse, came to warn her that the time for departure had come. Before leaving me, the girl said: 'Is it necessary to recommend discretion? Intimate parties are like a pledge which one leaves at the door before retiring.' 'Such a recommendation is not necessary,' I answered bowing, and then, taking leave of her, allowed myself to be placed in the basket and lowered into the street.

I returned home and, after making my morning prayer, retired to bed and slept until the evening. When I woke, I dressed hastily and went to the palace, where the chamberlains told me that the Khalīfah had gone out and bade me wait his return, as he had need of me that night to sing at one of his feasts.

I waited for a long time and then, as the Khalīfah did not return, told myself that I was a fool to miss another evening of so joyous a sort. I ran to the street and found the basket hanging as before;

getting inside, I was again hauled up and soon found myself in the presence of the girl.

When she saw me, she laughed, saying: 'As Allāh lives, I believe that you mean to take up your permanent abode among us!' I bowed and answered: 'Surely a very natural wish. Only you know, my mistress, that the rights of hospitality last for three days, and this is but the second. If I come back after the third, you have a right to shed my blood!'

We passed the night in joyous fashion, chatting, telling tales, saying verses, and singing as before. As I was about to be let down in the basket, I thought of the anger of the Khalīfah and said to myself: 'He will not accept any excuse unless I tell him of this adventure, and he will never believe the adventure unless he tests my story with his own presence.' Therefore I turned to the girl, saying: 'O mistress, it is evident that you love singing and good voices. Now I have a cousin who is much better looking than I am, better mannered, cleverer, and knowing every song which Ishāk of Mosul ever wrote. Will you allow me to bring him with me to-morrow, on the third and last day of your charming hospitality?'

At this point Shahrazād saw the approach of morning and discreetly fell silent.

But when the three-hundred-and-eighty-sixth night had come

SHE SAID:

'See, you are already becoming indiscreet!' she answered. 'But, as your cousin is such a pleasant fellow, you may bring him.' Delighted with this permission, I thanked her and went my way.

When I got home, I found the Khalīfah's guards waiting for me, who treated me with plentiful bad words, arrested me, and dragged me into the presence of al-Mamūn. I saw him seated upon his throne with terrible flaming eyes, as in the worst days of his anger. As soon as he saw me, he cried out: 'Son of a dog, have you dared to disobey me?' 'No, no, Commander of the Faithful,' I answered, 'I had a very good reason.' 'What is that?' he asked, and I answered: 'It is a secret for your ear alone.' At once he ordered everyone to retire and bade me speak. Then I told him my adventure in all its details, and added: 'To-night the girl expects us both. I have promised her.'

Al-Mamūn was all smiles at once and said: 'You are right; it was a very good reason. I am glad you were inspired to think of me.' He could hardly wait till nightfall; but I filled in the time by continually recommending him not to betray himself by calling me 'Ishāk' in front of the girl. He gave me a formal promise and, when the suitable time had come, disguised himself as a merchant and accompanied me to the little street.

We found two baskets instead of one, and took our places in them. Without delay we were pulled up and led down from the terrace into the magnificent hall which I have already described, where we were soon joined by the girl.

She was more beautiful that night than she had ever been, and I saw that the Khalīfah fell violently in love with her. When she sang, he became almost delirious, for the notes of her voice acted like wine upon the wine which she had already given us. With gay enthusiasm, al-Mamūn cried out: 'Come, come, Ishāk, why do you not sing some new song of yours in answer to this charming one?' I was obliged to answer: 'I hear and I obey, Commander of the Faithful.'

The girl looked at us for a moment and then ran from the room to cover her face, as a woman must in the presence of the Khalīfah. Grieved that she had left us owing to his carelessness, al-Mamūn told me to find out at once who was the master of the house. I called the old nurse and, under fear of the Khalīfah, she answered: 'O calamity, O shame upon our heads! My lady is the daughter of the Khalīfah's wazīr, Hasan ibn Sahl!' 'The wazīr to me instantly!' cried al-Mamūn, and in a few moments the trembling old woman introduced a most astonished wazīr into the presence of the Khalīfah.

Seeing his blank expression, al-Mamūn burst out laughing and said: 'Have you a daughter?' 'I have, Commander of the Faithful,' answered the old man. 'What is her name?' asked the Khalīfah. 'Khadījah,' was the reply. Then said the Khalīfah: 'Is she married or a virgin?' 'A virgin, Commander of the Faithful,' returned ibn Sahl. On hearing this, al-Mamūn exclaimed: 'I wish you to give her to me as lawful wife.' 'My daughter and I are the slaves of the Prince of Believers!' cried the wazīr, and the Khalīfah continued: 'I will give her a hundred thousand dīnārs as dowry. You can come for the money to-morrow morning to the palace. In the meanwhile, conduct your daughter to her future home with all the magnificence which such a marriage demands. You may divide among the folk of the bride's train a thousand villages and a thousand farms as a gift from me.'

With that the Khalīfah rose, and I followed him; as we were going out, this time by the main door, he said to me: 'Be very careful not to speak of this adventure to anyone, Ishāk. Your head answers for your discretion.'

I kept the secret until the death of the Khalīfah and of the lady Khadījah, who was without doubt the most beautiful woman I ever saw. But Allāh knows more!

When Shahrazād had made an end of this tale, little Dunyazād cried from her carpet: 'O sister, how sweet, savoury, and tender are your words!' 'You may well say so, when you have heard the Tale of the Tripe-Cleaner,' answered Shahrazād smiling, and at once continued:

The Tripe-Cleaner

ONE day at Mecca, during the annual pilgrimage, just when the crowd of pilgrims were making their seven circles round the sacred Kaabah, a man came out from among them and, going up to the wall of the Kaabah, took hold of the sacred veil which covers it with both his hands. Then he put himself into the attitude of prayer and cried with an accent of heartfelt sincerity: 'O Allāh, make the woman angry with her husband again, so that I can lie with her!'

When the pilgrims heard this strange prayer said in such a holy place, they were so scandalised that they threw themselves upon the man and, casting him to the ground, rained blows upon him. Then they dragged him before the amīr of the pilgrims, whose authority is absolute over all of them, saying: 'O amīr, we heard this man offering up impious words while he held the veil of the Kaabah!' Then they repeated the words, and the amīr of the pilgrims said: 'Let him hang!'

At this point Shahrazād saw the approach of morning and discreetly fell silent.

But when the three-hundred-and-eighty-seventh night had come

SHE SAID:
But the man threw himself at the amīr's feet, crying: 'I conjure you by the virtues of the Messenger of Allāh (upon whom be prayer

and peace!) to hear my story before you judge me!' The amīr nodded assent, and he who was condemned to be hanged continued:

O amīr, I have two trades: to collect the unpleasantness of the street and to clean sheep's tripes for sale and livelihood. One day I was walking quietly behind my donkey, which was loaded with full tripes which I had fetched from the slaughter-house, when I met a large quantity of frightened persons, fleeing in all directions or hiding in doorways. Looking behind them, I saw a troop of slaves armed with long sticks driving these foot passengers before them. I asked what was the matter and was told that the harīm of some great man was about to use that street, and it was therefore being cleared of people. Knowing that I might be exposed to great danger if I continued on my way, I halted my ass and dragged him with me into the corner of a wall, where I hid as well as I could, turning my face so that I should not be tempted to look at the great man's women. Soon I heard the harīm passing and was beginning to think of continuing my journey when I felt myself rudely seized in the two arms of a negro and saw my ass being carried off by another. In my fright I turned my head and perceived thirty girls all looking at me; in the midst of them was a young woman with the languishing glances of a gazelle which thirst has tamed, and a waist as slim and supple as a banana palm. With my hands tied behind my back, I was dragged along by other black eunuchs, in spite of my protestations and the protests of passers-by, who had seen me with my face to the wall and said to my persecutors: 'He has done nothing! This poor man is an honest collector of unpleasantness and cleaner of tripes. It is unlawful in the sight of Allāh to arrest and bind an innocent man!' But my captors, without taking any notice, went on dragging me behind the harīm.

All this time I was thinking to myself: 'What crime have I committed? Perhaps the nasty smell of the tripes offended the lady's nose; she may be pregnant and have felt something go wrong inside because of them. That must be the reason; or perhaps it is my own disgusting appearance and the holes in my rags which show the less respectable parts of me. There is no help save in Allāh!'

I was dragged along, amid the pitying cries of the people, until we all came to the door of a great house, where I was forced into a forecourt, the magnificence of which I cannot describe to you. 'This is the place of my punishment,' I thought. 'I shall be put to death, and none of my family will ever know the reason of my disappearance.' In my last moments I began to think of my poor ass, which had always been so ready and careful, which had never upset the tripes or the baskets of unpleasantness. I was startled out of these afflicting reflections by the arrival of a pretty little boy slave, who gently begged me to follow him. He led me to a hammām, where I was received by three fair women slaves, who said: 'Swiftly take off your rags.' When I had done as I was told, they took me into the hot room and bathed me with their own hands, one taking charge of my head, one of my limbs, and one of my belly. They rubbed me, perfumed me, and then dried me. Lastly, they brought magnificent robes and begged me to put them on. At this point I was greatly perplexed, for I did not know by which end to take them and had not the slightest idea how to arrange them, having never seen such things in all my life. 'As Allāh lives, my mistresses,' I said, 'I shall have to remain naked, for I can never dress in these extraordinary clothes by myself!' Then the slaves came up to me laughing and helped me to dress, tickling and pinching me the while and hefting the weight of my merchandise in their hands, a matter which they seemed to find unusual in size and quality.

At this point Shahrazād saw the approach of morning and discreetly fell silent.

But when the three-hundred-and-eighty-eighth night had come

SHE SAID:

When they had finished dressing me and had sprinkled me with rose-water, they took me by the arm, as if I had been a bridegroom, and led me into a hall which was furnished so elegantly that I may not describe it and ornamented with paintings of coloured lines pleasantly interlaced. There I saw the woman of whom I have spoken, lying at ease on a bed of bamboo and ivory, dressed in a light robe of Mosul silk, with a few slaves about her. She signed to me to approach and, when I had done so, made me sit down; then she ordered the slaves to bring food, and we were served with astonishing meats whose names I do not know and the like of which I had never seen before. I ate a few platefuls to satisfy my hunger and then, after washing my hands, set to upon the fruit. Next, jars of various wines were brought and little censers of perfume; after we had been well smoked with incense and benzoin, the woman poured wine for me with her own hands, and we drank out of the same cup until we were both drunk. Finally she signed to her slaves, who left us alone, and, pulling me towards her, threw her arms about me. I served her with jam so that she was delighted, sometimes giving her stiff slices of the fruit and again feeding her with the jelly. Each time that I pressed her against me, I grew drunk with the musk and amber of her body and thought that I was either dreaming or dead in the arms of a paradisal hūrī. We stayed embraced until the morning, and then, when she told me that it was time to go, she informed herself of my address, saying that she would send for me should occasion serve. At parting she gave me a handkerchief embroidered with gold and silver, into which something was knotted at the corner. 'Buy food for your ass,' she said, and dismissed me as if I had been a bad angel and she Paradise.

When I got to the tripe-shop in which I lodged, I began to unknot the handkerchief, saying to myself: 'This feels like five coppers; it would be enough to buy something for dinner.' Picture my surprise when I found fifty mithkāls of gold. Digging a hole, I hid them away against hard times and then, buying myself some bread and an onion, ate at the door of the shop, dreaming of my adventure.

At nightfall a little slave came from her I loved and led me back to the same hall and there she was waiting for me. I would have kissed the earth between her hands, but she raised me up and, stretching herself with me on the ivory and bamboo bed, gave me as blessed a night as the one before. In the morning, when dismissing me, she gave me another handkerchief containing a further fifty mithkāls. For eight whole days and nights this adventure was repeated; each time a feast of dry conserve and wet conserve, and fifty gold pieces for me.

One evening, when I had gone there and was already on the bed in act to unload my merchandise, a slave entered suddenly and, whispering some words in her mistress's ear, led me swiftly out of the hall and locked me into a room on the floor above. From that place I heard a great noise of horses in the street and saw, through a window which looked on to the courtyard, a young man, as handsome as the full moon, enter the house with a numerous train of guards and slaves. He went into the room where my lady was and passed all the night with her, in charges, assaults, and other games. I was able to hear all they did and to count on my fingers the number of nails they drove, because of the astonishing noise which they made in doing it. 'As Allāh lives,' I thought, 'they must have built a blacksmith's forge on the bed! The iron bar must be very hot to make the anvil groan so much!'

At this point Shahrazād saw the approach of morning and discreetly fell silent.

But when the three-hundred-and-eighty-ninth night had come

SHE SAID:

The noise ceased with morning, and I saw the owner of the sounding hammer go out by the great door. Hardly had he disappeared when the woman came to me, saying: 'You saw the young man who has just gone out? He is my husband. I will tell you what has passed between us in order that you may know why I chose you for my lover. One day I was sitting beside him in the garden when he left me and walked away in the direction of the kitchen. At first I thought that he had gone to satisfy some pressing need; but, when he had been absent for an hour, I went and looked for him where I thought he would be, and could not find him. At last I made my way towards the kitchen, to ask news from the servants, and on entering saw him lying on a mat with the dish cleaner, the filthiest slave of them all. I retired hastily, swearing to myself that I would no more receive him in my bed until I had revenged myself by taking a lover from among the lowest and ugliest of the people. Daily I walked about the streets looking for such a man, but it was only on the fifth day that I met you and gave you the palm, on account of your unusual dirtiness and filthy smell. Now I have accomplished my oath and am reconciled with my husband. You can retire with the assurance that, if my husband again lies with any of the slaves, I will send for you at once.' She gave me a further four hundred mithkāls and dismissed me. I came to this place to implore Allāh to drive the husband into that slave's arms, so that the wife may call me back to her. Such is my story, O amīr of the pilgrims.

After hearing him, the amīr of the pilgrims said: 'We must pardon this man for his thoughtless words in presence of the Kaabah, for his circumstances seem to justify them.'

Then Shahrazād said:

The Girl Cool-of-the-Eyes

ONE day Abu Īsā, son of Hārūn al-Rashīd, saw at the house of his cousin, Alī ibn Hishām, a young slave called Cool-of-the-Eyes, and ardently loved her. Abū Īsā took great care to hide the secret of his love and, at the same time, tried hard by indirect hints to persuade Alī to sell him the slave. Seeing at last that his efforts were useless, he decided to change his tactics; therefore he sought his brother, the Khalīfah al-Mamūn, son of Hārūn al-Rashīd, and begged his company for a surprise visit to Alī. The Khalīfah consented, and the two men rode to Alī's palace.

When Alī saw them, he kissed the earth between the Khalīfah's hands and, having his feast-hall opened, led his two visitors into it. They found it to be a fair place, built with walls and pillars of contrasting marbles, having incrustations in the Greek style which is very pleasant to the eye, and the floor covered with Indian matting surmounted by a single piece of Basrah carpet, which occupied the whole area of the hall. After casting a quick glance of appreciation over floor, walls and ceiling, al-Mamūn said: 'Well, Alī, why do you not give us something to eat?' At once Alī clapped his hands, and a multitude of slaves entered, bearing a thousand kinds of chicken and pigeons and roast birds, hot and cold. There was every sort of liquid and solid meat, but especially there was game stuffed with almonds and raisins; for al-Mamūn was enormously fond of game, and particularly if it were so stuffed. When the eating was finished, an astonishing wine, pressed from grapes chosen globe by globe, matured with perfumed fruits and scented edible nuts, was served in cups of gold and silver and crystal by young beautiful boys. These were dressed in floating Alexandrian draperies with silver borders; they sprinkled the guests with musked rose water from diamond sprays while plying them with the wine.

The Khalīfah was so delighted with all this that he kissed his host, saying: 'As Allāh lives, O Alī, you shall not henceforth be called Alī, but Father-of-Beauty!' Then Alī ibn Hishām, who ever since then was known as Father-of-Beauty, made a sign to his chamberlain. At once a curtain was lifted at the end of the hall and there appeared ten young singers dressed in black silk, as beautiful as a bed of flowers. They came forward and sat on gold chairs, which ten black slaves had circled round the hall. Preluding with absolute mastery upon their stringed instruments, they sang in chorus an ode of love. Al-Mamūn, fixing his eyes upon that one whose beauty had moved him most, asked her her name. 'I am called Harmony, O Commander of the Faithful,' she answered, and he continued: 'You are worthy of your name, O Harmony. I wish to hear you sing alone.' Then Harmony tuned her lute and sang:

> My tenderness
> Has fears
> Of eyes,
> My slenderness
> Distrusts
> Its enemies,
> But when love nears
> I melt
> Into his lusts.
> He goes
> And I have felt,
> Ah, over well,
> What the gazelle
> Among
> Her slaughtered young
> Untimely knows.

Al-Mamūn called out delightedly: 'You have indeed excelled, O girl! Who made that song?' 'It was written by Amr ibn Maadi Karib al-Zubaidī, and the music is by Maabid,' answered the singer, and the Khalīfah emptied the cup which we held, while Abū Īsā and Alī did the same. As they were putting down their empty cups, ten new singers, dressed in blue silk and scarfed with Yaman gold brocade, took the places of the others and skilfully rendered a combined prelude. The Khalīfah fixed his eyes on one of them who was like rock crystal, and asked her name. 'I am called Wild-Roe, O Commander of the Faithful,' she replied. Then he said: 'Sing us something, Wild-Roe.'

At this point Shahrazād saw the approach of morning and discreetly fell silent.

But when the three-hundred-and-ninetieth night had come

SHE SAID:
Then she who was called Wild-Roe tuned her lute and sang:

> Free girls of cheer
> Who smile
> At all affront,
> Wild Mecca deer
> Which man
> Is not allowed to hunt,
> The evil-minded can
> Of wanton guile
> Accuse us
> Because our eyes
> Are weary full,
> But beautiful
> Replies
> Excuse us,
> Though the lewd gests
> Below our vests
> Make righteous men abuse us.

Al-Mamūn, finding this song delicious, asked the girl whom it was by. 'The words are by Jarīr,' she answered, 'and the music by Suraij.' Then the Khalīfah and the two others emptied their cups, while the singers retired and were replaced by ten others, clothed in scarlet silk and girt with scarlet scarves; so that, with heavy hair falling down their backs, they had the appearance of red rocks over-flowed by waves at night. They sat on the gold chairs and sang in chorus, each to her lute. When they had finished, al-Mamūn turned to the fairest of them, asking her name. 'I am called Seduction, O Commander of the Faithful,' she said. 'Let us hear your voice by itself, O Seduction!' said the Khalīfah, and Seduction sang:

> A girl is not afraid
> Of jewels red
> Or white,
> Or silk brocade;
> Each night,
> Each morning on her bed

These dyes
Do stand confessed,
Her lips, her eyes,
Her rest.

'Who wrote that poem, O Seduction?' asked the enraptured
Khalīfah, and she replied: 'Adī ibn Zaid wrote it to a very old air.'
Al-Mamūn and the two others emptied their cups, and ten new
singers, dressed in gold and cinctured with gold, took the place of
the others and sang. The Khalīfah asked the name of the slimmest,
and she answered: 'I am called Sparkle-of-Dew.' 'Sing to us,
Sparkle-of-Dew,' he said, and at once she sang:

I sipped the rose-wine of his cheek
And, having drunken hard
Of so much sweet,
Dressed only in a perfumed shift
Of aromatic nard,
Ran out, oh, mad, to lift
Our love song in the street,
Dressed only in a perfumed shift
Of aromatic nard.

'As Allāh lives, you have excelled, O Sparkle-of-Dew!' cried the
Khalīfah. 'Repeat the last phrase of your song again.' So she sang
with even more feeling:

Ran out, oh, mad, to lift
Our love song in the street,
Dressed only in a perfumed shift
Of aromatic nard.

Then said the Khalīfah: 'Who wrote that song, O Sparkle-of-
Dew?' 'Abū Nuwās wrote it, Commander of the Faithful,' she
answered, 'and the music is by Ishāk of Mosul.'

When these ten slaves had finished their entertainment, the
Khalīfah wished to be gone, but Alī said to him: 'O Commander of
the Faithful, I have still one more slave. She cost me ten thousand
dīnārs, and I would show her to the Khalīfah if he should deign to
stay a few minutes longer. If she pleases him, he will be able to keep
her for his own; if she does not please him, I will alter my thoughts
of her.' 'Show me the girl,' said al-Mamūn, and there appeared a
young woman slave of more than mortal beauty, swaying and slim

as the branch of a palm, with eyes of Babylonian enchantment, brows of a true curve, and a colour borrowed from the jasmine. She had a gold circlet round her forehead, on which these words were picked out in diamonds:

> Who but a Jinn-taught girl would know
> To shoot a shaft from a cordless bow?

The child came forward slowly and sat down smiling on one of the gold chairs; but no sooner had Abū Īsā seen her than he let fall his cup and so violently changed colour that al-Mamūn noticed, and asked: 'What is the matter, my brother?' 'O Commander of the Faithful,' answered Abū Īsā, 'it was but a twinge of the liver pain which I get sometimes.' Then said the Khalīfah: 'Do you by any chance know this girl? Have you seen her before?' 'O Commander of the Faithful,' answered Abū, 'who does not know the moon?' 'What is your name?' asked al-Mamūn of the girl, and she answered: 'Cool-of-the-Eyes, O Commander of the Faithful,' 'Sing us something, Cool-of-the-Eyes,' he said, and she sang:

> O my own,
> O my lad so young,
> With red love on his tongue
> And a heart of stone!
> They say to be near
> Cures love,
> But I fear
> That cure will prove
> As useless as the other they essay,
> To be away.

Marvelling at her voice, the Khalīfah asked her who had written the song. No sooner had she answered that the words were by al-Khuzāi and the air by Zurzūr, than Abū Īsā, in a trembling voice, said to his brother: 'Allow me to answer that song, Commander of the Faithful.' The Khalīfah gave leave, and Abū Īsā sang:

> Beneath these robes of mine
> Hardly a body but rather a weight of love!
> If I'll not let it rise
> Into my eyes
> It is because I would not shame the shine
> Of slim and silver moons above.

When Alī, Father-of-Beauty, heard this answer, he understood that Abū Īsā was lost in love to the slave Cool-of-the-Eyes; therefore he rose and, bowing before Abū Īsā, said: 'Dear guest, a wish shall never be framed, even in thought, within my house, without being satisfied at once. If the Khalīfah will allow me to make an offer in his presence, Cool-of-the-Eyes is yours.' The Khalīfah gave his sanction and Abū Īsā led away the girl.

Such was the extraordinary generosity of Alī and the men of his time! May Allāh have them all in His keeping!

Finally Shahrazād told this tale:

Girls or Boys?

THE SAGE UMAR AL-HUMSĪ RELATES:

THERE came to Hamāh, in the five hundred and sixty-third year of the Flight, the most eloquent and learned woman in all Baghdād, she whom the wise men of Irāk called the Mistress of the Masters; and there flocked to the same place the most diversely erudite men of that time, for the pleasure of hearing her and asking her questions. For I must tell you that this most marvellous of all women used to journey from country to country with her young brother, for the purpose of holding public argument on the most difficult subjects and of asking and answering questions on science and law, theology and literature.

Wishing to hear her, I asked my learned old friend, al-Salihānī, to come with me to the place of that day's argument. We both entered the hall where the lady Dahīa, for that was her name, sat behind a silk curtain so as not to offend the custom of religion, and placed ourselves upon benches, where her brother served us with fruit and other refreshment.

I had my name and titles taken to Dahīa with the suggestion that we should hold an argument in divine jurisprudence and the interpretation of religious law. While we were waiting for an answer, my friend, the venerable al-Salihānī, fell in love with Dahīa's young brother, a lad of most extraordinary beauty, and could not keep his eyes off him. Dahīa noticed my companion's distraction and, looking at him closely, understood what was engaging his attention. She suddenly called his name, saying: 'It seems to me, old man, that you belong to the number of those who prefer boys to girls.'

At this point Shahrazād saw the approach of morning and discreetly fell silent.

But when the three-hundred-and-ninety-first night had come

SHE SAID:

'Certainly,' answered my friend with a smile. 'And why?' she asked. Then said he: 'Because Allāh modelled the bodies of boys into admirable perfection, making them unlike those of women, and my tastes have always led me to prefer the perfect to the imperfect.' She laughed behind her curtain, saying: 'Very well, if you are ready to defend your opinion, I am equally ready to attack it.' Then, when he had accepted the challenge, she continued: 'Attempt to prove that men and boys are preferable to women and girls.' Thereupon my friend said:

'For half of my proof I shall rely on logic, and for the other half on the authority of the Book and the Sunnah.

'The Koran says: "Men surpass women because Allāh has given them superiority." It also says: "A man's share in an inheritance shall be twice that of a woman; the brother shall have double the portion of the sister." These holy words prove once and for all that a woman is only worth half a man.

'The Sunnah teaches us that the Prophet (upon whom be prayer and peace!) assessed the value of a man's sacrifice at double that of a woman's sacrifice.

'From the point of view of pure logic, reason confirms this tradition. Let us ask ourselves simply which takes the first place, activity or passivity? Without a doubt the answer will be in favour of activity. Now man is the active principle in life and woman the passive; therefore, past peradventure, woman is below man and a boy preferable to a girl.'

Dahīa answered:

'Your quotations are correct. I agree that Allāh in His Book preferred men to women in a general sense. But He did not speak specifically. If you seek for perfection, why do you only go to young boys for it? Surely you ought to prefer bearded men, venerable ancients, with wrinkled brows. For such have journeyed much farther along the way of perfection.'

He answered:

'I certainly would prefer them to old women, but that is not the question; for the matter under discussion is the seduction of boys. Surely you will admit that a woman has nothing which can be compared with the beauty of a youth, his supple waist, his fine drawn limbs, the tender mingling of colour in his cheeks, his gentle smile, the charm of his voice? The Prophet himself, in putting us on our guard against so evident a danger, said: "Do not look long upon beardless boys, for their eyes hold more of temptation than the eyes of hūrīs." Remember, too, that the greatest praise that a man can find for the beauty of a girl is to compare it with the beauty of a boy. The poet Abū Nuwās expressed that and more, when he wrote:

> Allāh save her
> In our joy!
> Shout it forth:
> She had thighs
> Like a boy
> And so can waver
> As the palm of the banana
> In the North.

'If the beauty of boys was not noticeably superior to that of girls, why should poets make use of the comparison?

'Also a youth is not content only with his beauty; he can ravish our hearts with his language and the perfection of his manners. And how delicious a thing it is to see young down beginning to shade his lips and cheeks, those marriage-beds of roses! Is anything in the world comparable with that charming period of transition? Abū Nuwās said excellently again:

> "Over-red with the outcome of hairs."
> O what a fault is theirs!
> For now the face shows up
> Like pearls in a bright green cup;
> And as the hairs grow longer
> It's a sign his thighs are stronger.
> Roses swear faith to his cheek,
> His eyelids speak,
> His brows reply.
> Also the down hides from your foolish eye
> That face which gives a poppy to the wine
> And has green shade to make the silver shine.

Another poet said:

> They say I am blind to the hairs on that dear face,
> Loving it still;
> But I could not bear the white of it otherwise.
> I loved the barren garden place;
> How should I take it ill
> When wet Spring paints my garden with surprise?

And another said:

> I loved him when he had but roses;
> Only a fool supposes
> I could forget
> Now he had added myrtle, violet. . . .

And another, one out of a thousand, said:

> His cheeks and eyes compare
> The numbers of their slain,
> His sword is of narcissus,
> Its handle is of myrtle . . .
> Nay, beauty would dismiss us
> And loose her final kirtle
> If she could swear
> She had got back again
> The beauty of her world,
> This child-hair curled.

'Surely I have given you enough proofs that a lad's beauty is greater than female beauty at any age.'

At this point Shahrazād saw the approach of morning and discreetly fell silent.

But when the three-hundred-and-ninety-second night had come

SHE SAID:

Dahīa answered: 'May Allāh pardon you your fallacious arguments, unless, perhaps, you advance them merely as a joke. Be that as it may, the time has come for truth to triumph; therefore do not harden your heart but prepare to admit the verity of what I say.

'Tell me, in Allāh's name, where we may find a youth whose beauty is comparable with that of a young girl? A girl's skin has not only the light and whiteness of silver but the softness of silk. Her waist is a branch of myrtle, her mouth a flowering camomile, her lips two moist anemones. Her cheeks are apples and her breasts are little ivory gourds. Light shines from her forehead and her brows ceaselessly hesitate as to whether they should meet or part. When she speaks, there is a flash as of fine pearls; when she smiles, a river of sunlight flows out of lips sweeter than honey and softer than butter. The seal of beauty has made the dimple of her chin, and her belly is beautiful. The lines of her thighs are excellent, folding one over the other. Her flanks are fashioned all of one ivory and her feet are moulded of almond paste. Her bottom is full and not depressed, the waves of a crystal sea or mountains of the moon. Old man of weak understanding, do you not know that kings, khalīfahs, and all the great of the annals, have bowed themselves to the yoke of women, considering it a glory? Mighty men have knelt before them, leaving riches, land, father and mother, and even kingdoms for their sake. On their account palaces rise to heaven, silks are woven and stuffs brocaded. Because of them amber and musk, which have a sweet smell, are sought over the whole earth. Their beauty has damned the dwellers in Paradise, has overset the earth, and made rivers of blood to spring forth among all nations.

'You have quoted from the Book, but it is more favourable to my contention than to yours. The Book says: "Do not look long upon beardless boys, for their eyes hold more of temptation than the eyes of hūrīs." Now that is direct praise of the hūrīs, who are women and not boys. I have always noticed, too, that you, who love boys and wish to describe them, compare their caresses with those of girls. You are not ashamed of your corrupt tastes; you parade them, you satisfy them in public. You forget the words of the Book: "Why do you seek out male love? Has not Allāh created women for the satisfaction of your desires, that you may enjoy them as you will? But you were ever a stiff-necked people." When you compare girls with boys, you simply flatter your corrupt desire. We know your boy-loving poets well! The greatest of them all, Abū Nuwās, the king of pederasts, spoke thus of a young girl:

> You have no hips
> And you have cut your hair,
> Also there lies a light shade even
> Upon your lips.

> Dear child, by these exceptions and this dearth
> You'll have two kinds of lovers upon earth
> And more in heaven.'

At this point Shahrazād saw the approach of morning and discreetly fell silent.

But when the three-hundred-and-ninety-third night had come

SHE SAID:

'As for the pretended attraction of a beard in young men, a poet has answered that excellently:

> Wise lovers fled at the first ugly hair
> Which charcoal-smutched that chin beyond compare,
>   When the white page is covered with black prose
> Who but a fool would write his lyrics there?

'Give thanks to Allāh for uniting in women every joy of life, and promising to prophets, saints and all believers, marvellous girls for their reward in Paradise. If the All-Good had thought that there could be any pleasant lusts apart from women, He would have reserved them for and promised them to His faithful servants after their death. But Allāh only mentions young boys as being servants of the elect in Heaven; He does not speak of them as having any other function. The Prophet himself (upon whom be prayer and peace!) had no sort of leaning in your direction. In fact he used to say: "Three things have made me love your earth: woman, perfume, and the beauty of a soul in prayer." I cannot recapitulate my argument better than by quoting this verse of the poet:

> Between the bottoms of the young
> (Now I give freedom to my tongue)
> A gulf is fixed.
> To approach some is suave incense,
> But others, a deep brown offence
> Within your garment mixed.
> Who dare
> Compare
> A girl and boy—
> What hardihood!—

For nard he would
Employ
An old sow's dung. . . .
Between the bottoms of the young
A gulf is fixed.

'But I see that this discussion has excited me too much and made me pass those bounds of modesty which no woman should cross in the presence of sages and old men. Therefore I beg pardon of any who have found such criticism to make in what I have said, and I rely on them to use discretion in telling others of this argument. The proverb says: "The hearts of well-born men are tombs." '

When Shahrazād had made an end of this tale, she said: 'That, O auspicious King, is all I can remember of the Flowering Terrace of Wit and the Garden of Gallantry.'

'Indeed, Shahrazād,' answered King Shahryār, 'these little tales have pleased me very much and disposed me to hear another longer story, such as you used to tell me.' 'That is as I had hoped,' said Shahrazād and continued:

The Strange Khalīfah

I T is related that, one night, when the Khalīfah Hārūn al-Rashīd was suffering from sleeplessness, he called his wazīr, Jafar al-Barmakī, to him and said: 'My breast is heavy; I would walk the streets of Baghdād and go as far as the Tigris, to distract myself for the rest of the night.' Jafar at once helped the Khalīfah to dress himself as a merchant, and provided the same disguise for himself and Masrūr, the sword-bearer. They left the palace by the secret door and walked the silent streets of Baghdād until they came to the banks of the river. There they saw an old boatman, about to wrap himself in his coverlet, before going to sleep on board his craft. They went up to him, saying: 'Old man, we would be very much obliged if you would take us on board your boat and row us about for a little upon the river to enjoy the delicacy of the fresh breeze. Here is a dīnār for your trouble.' 'What are you asking, my lords?' answered the old man in a terrified voice. 'Do you not know the order? Do you not see the Khalīfah's boat coming towards us even now?' In their astonishment, they asked: 'Are you sure that boat contains the

Khalīfah himself?' 'As Allāh lives,' replied the other, 'is there anyone in Baghdād who does not know the appearance of the Khalīfah? It is al-Rashīd himself, my lords, with his wazīr Jafar, and Masrūr his sword-bearer. See, there are his mamlūks and singers! Listen to the herald standing in the bows and proclaiming: "It is forbidden to great or small, young or old, noble or simple, to be upon the river! Who disregards this warning shall have his head cut off or be hanged to the mast of his own boat!" '

At this point Shahrazād saw the approach of morning and discreetly fell silent.

But when the three-hundred-and-ninety-fourth night had come

SHE SAID:

Al-Rashīd, who had never given such an order and had not been on the river for more than a year, questioned Jafar with astonished eyes; but the wazīr, who was equally at a loss, turned to the old boatman, saying: 'Here are two dīnārs. Put us off in your boat and row us under one of the sunken arches, that we may see the passing of the Khalīfah and his suite without being seen ourselves.' After some hesitation the boatman consented and, having embarked all three, put in his craft under the arches and covered his passengers with a black cloak, that they might be more invisible. No sooner were they hidden than the boat drew near, lighted by torches and cressets, which little slaves dressed in red satin, their shoulders covered with yellow mantles, their heads turbaned with white muslin, fed, from minute to minute, with aloe-wood. Some stood at the prow, others at the stern, lifting their torches higher and crying the warning into the night. The hidden observers saw two hundred mamlūks ranged on each side of the boat, surrounding a central dais. This was surmounted by a gold throne, where sat a young man dressed in black and gold, flanked, on the right, by a man miraculously like Jafar, and, on the left, by the counterpart of Masrūr, holding a naked sword. Below the dais sat twenty singers and musicians.

'Surely this must be one of our sons, Jafar,' cried al-Rashīd, 'either al-Mamūn or al-Amīn! Those other two are extraordinarily like you and Masrūr; those singers and players much resemble mine; what do you think of all this? I can make nothing of it.' 'As Allāh lives, I can make nothing of it either, Commander of the Faithful!' answered Jafar.

Already the lighted boat had passed beyond their sight. The old boatman, freed from his anxiety, cried out: 'At last we are safe! No one has seen us!' When he had rowed from under the arch and landed his three passengers on the bank, the Khalîfah turned to him, saying: 'Old man, are you sure the Khalîfah goes out in his illuminated boat like this every night?' 'Indeed, my lord, he has done so for the last year,' answered the boatman, and the Khalîfah continued: 'We are strangers on our travels, with a strong taste for interesting and beautiful things. If I give you ten dînars, will you be waiting for us here to-morrow at the same time?' The old man joyfully agreed to this arrangement, and the Khalîfah, taking leave of him, returned with his two companions to the palace, where they talked together of the night's strange happening.

Next day the Khalîfah, after spending the whole day in doing judgment, receiving his wazîrs, chamberlains, amîrs and lieutenants, and forwarding the affairs of state, returned to his apartment at nightfall and again disguised himself as a merchant. When the time came, the three set out as before, and arrived without adventure at the spot where the old boatman expected them. Pushing off without delay, they again sheltered themselves under the arch and waited for the illuminated boat.

Before they had time to become impatient, they heard the sound of music and the whole surface of the water was lighted up by the approach of the boat. Its lading was the same as on the previous night; there were the same mamlûks, the same guests and, on the dais, the same mock Khalîfah between the same Jafar and Masrûr.

'O wazîr,' said al-Rashîd, 'I would never have believed this thing if I had been told of it!' Then, turning to the boatman, he said: 'Here are ten more dînars. Row us in the track of that boat. You need not be afraid, for they cannot see us, since we are in darkness and they in bright light. We wish to enjoy the beautiful illumination for as long as possible.'

At this point Shahrazâd saw the approach of morning and discreetly fell silent.

But when the three-hundred-and-ninety-fifth night had come

SHE SAID:

The boatman accepted the ten dînars and somewhat fearfully began rowing in the wake of the boat, taking care not to venture into the circle of its lights. Soon they came to a park, which sloped down to the river, and saw the boat moored and the strange Khalīfah, with all his suite, disembark and go up into the pleasure grounds to the sound of music.

The old man hid his boat in the gloom and allowed his passengers to disembark. As soon as they were in the park, they mingled with the crowd of torch-bearers and strolled in the wake of the strange Khalīfah.

While they were thus following the procession, some of the mamlūks recognised them as intruders and, seizing them roughly, led them into the presence of the young man. 'How and why have you come here?' he asked, and they answered: 'We are merchants, strangers to this country. We only reached Baghdād to-day and, walking at random, came to this place without knowledge that the garden was forbidden. We were strolling quite quietly when we were seized by your people and brought before you.' 'Since you are strangers to Baghdād you need have no fear,' said the mock Khalīfah. 'If it had been otherwise you would certainly have had your heads cut off. Come with us now and be our guests for the evening.'

The three followed in this strange train and came at last to a palace which could have no rival save in that of the Khalīfah himself. Over the door of it they read this inscription:

> Time used his paints in it
> To decorate this place,
> But now time faints in it.
> Where art has most
> Bequeathed her grace
> The stranger is as welcome as the host.

They entered a magnificent hall carpeted with yellow silk, where the strange Khalīfah, seating himself upon a gold throne, called upon the rest to be seated also. At once a feast was served of which all partook, and afterwards, when the guests had washed their hands, drinks were set out upon the cloth and the cup went round spaciously. But when Hārūn al-Rashīd's turn came, he did not drink; so the mock Khalīfah turned to Jafar and said: 'Why does your friend not drink?' 'It is a long time since he has given up wine,' answered the wazīr. 'In that case he must have something else!'

cried the host, and he ordered one of his mamlūks to carry a flask of apple sherbert to the Khalīfah, which the disguised al-Rashīd accepted and drank with considerable pleasure.

When wine had mingled with their reason, the mock sultān beat three times with a small gold stick and, at this signal, the two leaves of a large door opened at the end of the hall to admit two negroes carrying on their shoulders a small ivory throne, on which sat a young white slave as brilliant as the sun. When they had set the throne down facing the master of the feast and had placed themselves behind it, the slave took up an Indian lute and, after preluding in twenty-four different modes, returned to the first one and sang:

> How could you find a calm
> When I was far and grieving,
> Or any balm
>> When I was near and leaving?

> Ah, empty is the perfumed gloom
>> Our coloured couch above,
> And empty is the marble room
>> Of songs of love.

As soon as the strange Khalīfah had heard this singing, he uttered a loud cry, tore down his fair-diamonded robe, his shirt and other garments, and fell into a swoon. The mamlūks threw a satin cover over him, but not before al-Rashīd, Jafar, and Masrūr had noticed that the young man's body was covered with deep scars as of sticks and whips.

'As Allāh lives,' said the Khalīfah, 'it is a pity that so beautiful a youth should bear such certain signs that he is an escaped criminal.' Before Jafar had time to answer, the mamlūks had dressed their master in a new and richer robe, and he had taken his place again upon the throne as if nothing had happened. Seeing his three guests leaning towards each other, he said: 'Why this air of astonishment and these whispers?' 'My friend was just saying,' answered Jafar, 'that he had journeyed over many lands and seen the fashion of their kings without discovering any as generous as our host. He also expressed his astonishment at seeing you tear a robe which must have been worth at least ten thousand dīnārs. In fact he was just quoting this verse in your honour:

    Gift built this house in your right hand,
       If gift should lose the key
   Your left could find another kind
       Of generosity.'

At this point Shahrazād saw the approach of morning and discreetly fell silent.

But when the three-hundred-and-ninety-sixth night had come

SHE SAID:

The young man was delighted with this compliment and ordered Jafar to be given a thousand dīnārs and a robe as beautiful as the one he had torn. Then the drinking and conversation went on as before; but al-Rashīd, who could think of nothing but the scars which he had seen, said to Jafar: 'Ask him the cause of them.' 'It would be better to be patient and not to seem indiscreet,' answered Jafar, but the Khalīfah exclaimed: 'By my head, and by the tomb of Abbās, if you do not question him at once your soul will go begging for a body when we get back to the palace!'

The young man, who was again looking in their direction, noticed that they were whispering once more. So he called out: 'What is this great secret of yours?' 'Nothing but good,' answered Jafar. Then said the mock Khalīfah: 'I beg you, in Allāh's name, to let me hear what you are saying.' 'My friend,' answered Jafar, 'noticed that your flanks, my lord, had been cut about with rods and whips, a sight which greatly astonished him. He was very anxious to know what terrible adventure had caused our master, the Khalīfah, to receive a chastisement so little sorting with his dignity.' The young man smiled at this and said: 'Be it so! Since you are strangers, I am willing to reveal the whole matter to you. My tale is so prodigious and filled with marvel that, if it were written with needles in the corner of an eye, yet it would serve as a lesson to him who read it with attention.' Then he said:

My lords, I am not the Commander of the Faithful, but simply Muhummad-Alī, son of the syndic of the Baghdād jewellers. When my father died, he left me much gold and silver, countless pearls, rubies and emeralds, with wrought smith's work in precious metals; also he bequeathed to me buildings, lands, orchards, gardens, shops and storehouses, and left me master of this palace, with all its men

and women slaves, its guards and servants, its young boys and
girls.

One day, as I sat in my shop surrounded by slaves ready to do
my bidding, I saw dismount before my door, from a handsomely-
harnessed mule, a girl followed by three attendants of moonlike
beauty. As I rose to do her honour, she came in and sat down, saying: 'Are you not Muhammad-Alī, the jeweller?' 'I am not only
Muhammad-Alī, but your slave,' I answered. 'Have you some really
beautiful trinket that is certain to please me?' she asked, and I
answered: 'I will show you all the most beautiful things in my shop.
If any of them can suit you, I shall be happy beyond description.
If you find nothing worthy, I shall deplore my bad fortune until the
day of my death.'

As I had a hundred jewelled collars of perfect workmanship in
my shop at that time, I showed them all to her and she handled them
and scrutinised them more expertly than I could have done myself.
At last she said: 'I should like something better than those.' Now it
so happened that my father, in the old days, had bought a quite
small collar for a hundred thousand dīnārs and that I had kept it
shut out of sight alone in a precious coffer. Therefore I brought
the coffer and opened it ceremoniously in front of the girl, saying:
'I do not think that any king, great or small, has the like of this.'

The young woman glanced at the collar and then cried out for
joy, saying: 'I have wanted it all my life! How much is it?' 'It cost
my father a hundred thousand dīnārs,' I replied. 'If it pleases you,
I shall be only too happy to offer it to you for nothing.' She gave
me a long look, and then said laughing: 'I will take it at the original
price, plus five thousand dīnārs by way of interest.' 'Dear mistress,'
I answered, 'both the collar and its present owner belong to you. I
have nothing more to add.' 'I have fixed the price,' she answered
with another smile, 'and even at that I shall be in your debt.' So
saying, she sprang to her feet and, running from the shop, mounted
her mule, crying over her shoulder: 'My master, will you carry the
collar for me and come to my house for the money? My day is milk
to me because of you.' Not wishing to insist further that the collar
should be a gift, I ordered my slaves to shut up the shop and
followed the girl on foot to her house.

At this point Shahrazād saw the approach of morning and
discreetly fell silent.

But when the three-hundred-and-ninety-seventh night had come

SHE SAID:

I gave her the collar and she, after begging me to be seated on a bench in the entrance hall to wait for my money to be counted out to me, disappeared into her own apartments.

As I sat in the hall, a young woman came to me, saying: 'My master, be good enough to follow me into the ante-chamber, for the entrance hall is not intended for persons of your quality.' Following her to the ante-chamber, I sat down on a stool covered with green velvet and waited, until another slave came to me, saying: 'My mistress begs you to enter the reception hall and rest yourself there until the money is ready.' Hardly had I reached the reception hall, when a curtain at the end of it was lifted and four young slaves came towards me, bearing a gold throne on which the girl was seated, wearing the collar on the moonlight of her neck. Seeing her thus unveiled, I felt my reason go mad and begin to tear down the fortress of my heart. The lady signed to her slaves to retire, and came towards me, saying: 'Light of my eye, should one who is all-beautiful, as you are, behave so cruelly to one who loves him?' 'All the beauty of the world is yours,' I answered. 'If there is any which you have not absorbed to yourself, I, for one, have not seen it.' Then said she: 'Muhammad-Alī, I love you, and all that I have done to-day has been but a trick to bring you to my house.' She leaned abandonedly over me and drew me to her, bathing me the while in the languor of her eyes. I took her head between my hands and kissed her again and again, while she pressed me against her breasts, which were so hard that I thought they would have entered my heart even as she had done. I knew that this was no time for retreat and wished to do what was right in such a scene; but at the moment when the child, now completely roused, was clamouring lustily for its mother, she said: 'What would you do with that, my master?' 'Put him out of the way,' I answered. Then she said: 'I cannot help you to hide him, because my house is not open; some-one must break down the wall, for I am an untried virgin. If you think you have to do with some unknown woman or wild veil of Baghdād, undeceive yourself; for, such as I am, I am the daughter of Yaḥya ibn Khālid al-Barmakī, sister of the wazīr Jafar.'

On hearing these words, my masters, I suddenly felt the child fall back into a profound sleep, and understood how indecorous it had been in me to pay any attention to his cries and wish to quiet him with the help of so high-born a lady. 'As Allāh lives,' I said, 'it was not my fault that I wished the child to share the hospitality which you showed to its father. You were too generous in letting me see the home fire behind the open door of your hospitality.' 'You have nothing with which to reproach yourself,' she answered. 'You will reach your end, but only by the legal road. With Allāh's help, all may happen as we wish, for I am my own mistress and none may control me. Would you like me to be your wife?' 'Indeed I would!' I answered. At once she sent for the kādī and his witnesses and said to them: 'Here is Muhammad-Alī, son of Alī the late syndic. He asks me in marriage and has given me this collar as a dowry. I accept and consent.' Without a moment's delay our marriage contract was written out and we were left alone. Slaves brought us wine and cups and lutes, and we drank together until our souls shone with the wine. She took a lute and sang:

> Time gave his wine in daily bowls
>> To me,
> Until I could remember our torn souls
>> Not all unhappily;
>> Then in the garden close
> He gave a hundred flowers with each your hue,
>> But, ah, in those
> I could too soberly see
>> You.

When she had finished singing, I took the lute and, after showing that I was master of it, chanted these words of the poet to a whispering accompaniment:

> O prodigal, by what extravagant art
>> Do you join bright water and red fire
>>> In one small face,
>> And in my heart,
>>> That little space,
>> Refresh as water, ravin like desire?

After we had made an end of our singing, it seemed time to dream of the couch; so I lifted my bride in my arms and stretched her on an embroidered bed which the slaves had prepared for us.

At this point Shahrazād saw the approach of morning and discreetly fell silent.

But when the three-hundred-and-ninety-eighth night had come

SHE SAID:

When I had stripped her naked, I saw that she was indeed an un-pierced pearl, a steed untouched of riders; for this reason into that night was concentrated all the joy of my life, and I held her as close until the morning as a hand holds a dove with folded wings.

My happiness in this kind continued, not for a night, but for a whole month, in which I forgot my shop, my business, and my fair house itself. When the first day of the second month came, she said to me: 'I must go away from you for a few hours, to the hammām and back. I beg you not to leave this bed, or to rise up at all until I return. Soon I will be with you again, light and perfumed from the bath.' When she had made me swear solemnly that I would not quit the couch, she departed with two slaves bearing bundles of towels, linen and fresh garments.

Now, my masters, she had scarcely left me for a minute when, as Allāh lives, I saw the door open and an old woman come into the room. She approached me with respectful greetings, saying: 'O Muhammād, the lady Zubaidah, wife of the Commander of the Faithful, has sent me to you to beg you to come to the palace, since she wishes to see and hear you. Many have spoken to her in terms of the greatest admiration of your manners and the beauty of your voice. Therefore she greatly desires to know you.' 'As Allāh lives, good aunt,' I answered, 'the lady Zubaidah does me too much honour, but I cannot leave this house until my wife returns from the hammām.' Then said the old woman: 'My child, I advise you, in your own interest, not to delay for a moment, unless you wish the lady Zubaidah to become your enemy. Her enmity is very danger-ous; so come now and talk with her. Afterwards you can return to your house.'

These last words decided me to break my oath, and I followed the old woman to the palace, where she introduced me into the queen's presence without any difficulty.

The lady Zubaidah smiled upon me and bade me approach, say-ing: 'Light of my eye, are you not the lover of the wazīr's sister?' 'I am your slave,' I answered, and she continued: 'Indeed they did not exaggerate when they painted the charm of your manners and your voice to me. I wished to discover for myself the tastes of Jafar's sister. Now I am satisfied. But my pleasure will not be complete unless you sing me something.' 'Love and honour!' I answered and, taking a lute which a slave handed to me, played a short prelude and sang two or three stanzas about happy love. When I had finished, the lady Zubaidah said: 'May Allah crown His work by giving you added perfection, if that be possible, young man! I thank you for having come to me. Now hasten home before your wife gets back, that she may have no reason for thinking that I wish to rob her of your love.' Taking advantage of this permission, I kissed the earth between her hands and left the palace.

When I got back to the house, I found my wife already sleeping on the bed, and she did not wake when I approached her. But, when I lay down at her feet and began gently to caress them, she suddenly opened her eyes and kicked me so violently in the groin that I rolled off the bed. 'Perjured traitor,' she cried, 'you have broken your vow and gone out to visit the lady Zubaidah! As Allāh lives, if I had no fear of shame and did not loathe to confess my intimacy with you in public, I would go to the queen even now and teach her not to debauch the husbands of other women! As it is, you shall pay for both.' With that she furiously clapped her hands and cried: 'O Sawwāb!' and her chief eunuch ran in, a negro who had always frowned upon me. 'Cut off this traitor's head, this liar's head!' she cried, and Sawwāb, drawing his sword and bandaging my eyes with a strip torn from the skirt of his robe, bade me say my prayers.

At this point Shahrazād saw the approach of morning and discreetly fell silent.

But when the three-hundred-and-ninety-ninth night had come

SHE SAID:

At that moment all the slaves of the house, great and small, young and old, to whom I had always been kind, ran in and cried to their mistress: 'Spare him, for he did not know the gravity of his fault! How was he to suppose that a visit to the lady Zubaidah, your enemy, would anger you more than any other action in the world? He was ignorant of the rivalry between you. Spare him, O mistress!' 'Be it so,' she answered, 'I will spare his life; but he must carry away

an indelible memory of his indiscretion.' Thereupon Sawwāb replaced his sword with a terribly supple stick and beat me cruelly
upon the most sensitive parts of my body. Then, discarding the
stick in its turn, he took up a whip and murderously lashed my
flanks and private parts five hundred times. That, my lord, is the
explanation of the scars which you have seen upon me.

After witnessing my punishment, my wife had me taken up and
thrown into the street like a load of dung.

I struggled to my feet and dragged myself, all bleeding, to my
own house, where I fell down in a swoon in those halls which I had
left so long.

When I came to myself after many hours, I called a learned and
light-handed bone-setter to me, who delicately bound my wounds
and brought about my cure with balms and unguents. After remaining for two months without movement upon my bed, I rose, took a
bath, and visited my shop. There I sold every precious thing that it
held at a sacrifice and, with the money thus realised, bought four
hundred young mamlūks, whom I habited richly, and the boat in
which you saw me to-night. I chose out one of them, who resembled
Jafar, to be my companion upon my right hand and upon my
left hand I set a false Masrūr, to carry my sword of justice. Then,
that I should forget the shame which I had undergone in the relief
of borrowed majesty, I dressed myself as the Khalīfah and rowed
each night upon the river with lights and songs. I have spent a
whole year in this high illusion, to cure the memory of the chastisement which I received at my wife's hands because I had unwittingly
meddled in a womanish dispute. That is my sad tale, good folk.
I have but to thank you for joining us to-night in such a friendly
fashion.

When the Khalīfah Hārūn al-Rashīd had heard this story, he
cried: 'Praise be to Allāh, Who has given a cause for every effect!'
Then he rose and, begging the young man's leave to depart, returned to his own palace with his companions, pondering a way to
right the wrong which the two women had done to his host. At the
same time Jafar grieved that his sister should have been the cause of
such injustice, especially as it was now certain to be made known to
all the palace.

Next morning, as the Khalīfah sat clothed with all his authority
among his amīrs and chamberlains, he said to Jafar: 'Bring me the
young man who entertained us last night.' The wazīr went out and

soon returned with the false Khalīfah, who bowed low before al-Rashīd and made him compliment in verse. Much charmed by this, Hārūn bade him approach and sit by his side, saying: 'O Muhammad-Alī, I have summoned you that I may hear from your own mouth the tale which yesterday you told to three strange merchants. It is both astonishing and full of useful lessons.' Quite abashed, the young man answered: 'O Commander of the Faithful, I cannot speak until you have given me the kerchief of immunity.' The Khalīfah threw him his handkerchief, and then the young man told his tale again without suppressing a single detail. When he had finished, al-Rashīd asked: 'Would you still like your wife to return to you, in spite of the wrong she did?' 'All which came to me from the hānds of the Khalīfah would be welcome,' answered the young man, 'for our master's fingers are the keys of kindness and his actions are not only actions, but jewelled collars about the necks of all.' Then said the Khalīfah to Jafar: 'Bring your sister to me, O wazīr!' Jafar obeyed, and al-Rashīd said to the woman: 'Tell me, O daughter of Yahya, our faithful amīr, do you recognise this man?' 'Commander of the Faithful,' she answered, 'since when have women learned to know strange men?' 'I will tell you his name,' returned the Khalīfah smiling. 'He is called Muhammad-Alī and is the son of the jewellers' late syndic. That which is past is past. In the present I wish to give you to him as a wife.' 'The gifts of our master are ever generous,' she replied.

At once the Khalīfah called the kādī and his witnesses, and had the two young people most strictly married again, that their happiness might be perfect. Also he kept Muhammad-Alī with him as one of his intimate friends until the end of his life. That is how al-Rashīd used his leisure to unite those who were sundered and bring happiness to those whom Destiny had betrayed.

But do not think for a moment, O auspicious King, that this tale, which I only told you as a contrast to the short anecdotes, can equal, or come anywhere near equalling, the marvellous Story of Rose-in-the-Bud and World's-Delight.

The Tale of Rose-in-the-Bud and World's-Delight

AND SHAHRAZĀD SAID TO KING SHAHRYĀR:

IT is related that there was once, in the antiquity of time and the
passing of the ages, a powerful and glorious king who had a wazīr
named Ibrāhīm. Ibrāhīm had a daughter who was the marvel of all
grace and beauty, and added to a perfection of carriage and sweetness of behaviour a most unusual intelligence. She loved the joy of
friends and the gaiety of wine, fair faces, rare verse, and any tales
of wonder. The delicacy of her perfection turned every head and
heart; a poet of that time said of her:

> I also lie in the snare
>   Of this fair huntress of the Turks,
>   Who, being learned in the sages' works,
> Once said, before I was aware:
> 'Although my article is accusative
>   Your verb will not rise up and govern it.'
> What answer could I give
>   To so much wit?
> 'The rules have been revised of late,' I said,
>   'If you consent
>   I'll show you without fail
> That now the head
>   Of my most weighty argument
>   Comes at the finish of my long-drawn tail.'

This sweet and beautiful girl was called Rose-in-the-Bud.

At this point Shahrazād saw the approach of morning and
discreetly fell silent.

But when the four-hundredth night had come

SHE SAID:

The King, who delighted to have her by his side at every feast,
both for her wit and her beauty, was used each year to hold a festival
and to profit by the presence in his palace of the chief persons of his
kingdom to play at ball with them.

One day, as the King's guests were playing at ball and Rose-in-the-Bud was seated at her window watching the game, the contest became suddenly fast and furious, and the wazîr's daughter, observing with more attention, noticed among the players a young man of infinite beauty, with smiling teeth, slim waist, and mighty shoulders. She took such pleasure from the sight of him that she could not prevent herself, but favoured him with long glances. At last she called her nurse, saying: 'Do you know the name of that exquisite and distinguished youth?' 'They are all so beautiful, my child,' answered the nurse. 'I do not see the one you mean.' 'I will point him out,' said Rose-in-the-Bud, and at once, taking up an apple, she threw it at the young man, who thereupon turned round and looked up at the window. He saw Rose-in-the-Bud, smiling and fair like the moon journeying through a dark space of the night, and in that second, even before he could lower his eyes, he fell in love. As he murmured to himself these lines of the poet:

> An arrow's hum,
> Surprise,
> A wound, abasement!
> Bowmen
> Or eyes?
> Or did it come
> From foemen
> Or a casement?

Rose-in-the-Bud turned to her nurse and said: 'Now can you tell me his name?' 'He is called World's-Delight,' answered the nurse. The young girl shook her head with pleasurable emotion at these words and, falling back upon her couch, moaned to herself and improvised these verses:

> Son of a wise father,
> For he called you World's-Delight,
> O rising of the full moon
> Upon our dark!
> God drew the oval of your eyes
> With night
> On His white dawn.
> O strength,
> Reeds in the wind are clumsy
> For I have seen you.

When she had made this poem, Rose-in-the-Bud took a sheet of paper and carefully wrote it; then she folded the paper and placed it in a little bag of embroidered silk which she hid beneath the cushion of her couch.

The old nurse, who had seen these signs of love in the girl, talked to her of one thing and of another until Rose-in-the-Bud fell asleep; not till then did she take the paper from below the cushion, read it and, after determining the depth of her mistress's passion, put it back in the same place. When the girl woke, the old woman said to her: 'My child, I am your best and tenderest adviser; therefore I tell you that the passion of love is a violent passion, melting a heart of steel and bringing sorrow and sickness to the body. But if the sufferer opens her heart to another the hurt is lessened.'

'O nurse,' answered Rose-in-the-Bud, 'do you know the cure for love?' 'I do,' replied the old woman, 'it is to enjoy the lover.' 'How can that enjoyment be obtained?' asked the girl, and the nurse continued: 'The first thing to do is to exchange gentle letters, filled with salutation and compliment; that begins to bring two friends together and is the first step in cutting knots and avoiding complications. If you have anything hidden in your heart, do not fear to tell me; for I can keep a secret, and you will never find anyone more ready to satisfy your least desires with eyes and head, and most discreetly to carry letters.'

At this point Shahrazād saw the approach of morning and discreetly fell silent.

But when the four-hundred-and-first night had come

SHE SAID:

Rose-in-the Bud felt her reason totter for very joy; but she was careful not to betray her feelings. 'No one knows my secret yet,' she said to herself. 'It will be better not to tell this woman until I have had certain proof that he loves me.' But as this thought was passing through her mind, the nurse continued: 'My child, last night a man appeared to me in a dream, saying: "Your young mistress and World's-Delight are in love with each other, and it is fated that you must help them by carrying letters and performing discreet services; otherwise you will miss a great reward." I simply tell you what I saw; it is for you to decide.' 'O nurse,' exclaimed the girl, 'can you really keep a secret?' 'Can you doubt it,' replied the other,

'when I am known to be the essence of the essence of chosen hearts?'
Without further hesitation the girl showed the old woman the paper
on which she had written her verses and gave it her, saying: 'Carry
this to World's-Delight and bring me back an answer.' At once the
nurse departed and, finding World's-Delight in his house, first
kissed his hands, then made him many courteous compliments and,
lastly, gave him the letter.

World's-Delight unfolded the paper and read its contents; when
he understood all the delicious news which it carried, he wrote these
lines upon the back of the note:

> The wings of my heart beat so,
> I cannot hold them;
> He flies abroad and sings.
>
> I say to my friends:
> 'These tears come from a sickness of the eyes,'
> Poor heart.
>
> I slept a free man on my bed,
> I waked
> And love held a silk whip above me.
>
> I come telling a tale of torture
> Written with tears
> On the white sand of your pity.
>
> The moon has woven a veil for you
> And the stars would pierce it;
> The palms did not know how to sway
> Until you passed.
>
> Come to me,
> But that would weary you.
> I send my soul as a present,
> Come to me!

He folded the leaf and kissed it; then he gave it to the nurse, saying: 'Mother, I rely upon you to favour me with your mistress.' 'I
hear and I obey,' she answered and at once hurried back with the
note.

Rose-in-the-Bud carried the letter to her lips and to her brow
before she opened and read it. When she had well understood what

World's-Delight would say, she wrote beneath his poem the following answer:

> Be patient,
> You who have fallen in our nets,
> For we have no proof your heart is torn.
>
> Our heart is torn,
> Also we are afraid.
>
> The night of separation comes down upon us,
> But our heart is a red fire.
>
> Your sleeplessness lies upon our bed,
> Our body moves restlessly
> All through the night.
>
> Silence is best,
> Our veil must not be lifted
> Among your friends.
>
> Ah, but our body cries for you!

At this point Shahrazād saw the approach of morning and discreetly fell silent.

But when the four-hundred-and-second night had come

SHE SAID:

When she had finished writing this, she again folded the paper and gave it to the nurse, who at once left the palace. But Fate willed that she should meet the wazīr's chamberlain and that he should say: 'Where are you going at such an hour?' 'To the hammām,' she answered trembling, and went upon her way; but her trouble had been so great that she had let fall, without noticing it, the note which had been insecurely fastened in a fold of her sash. So much for her.

The note fell to the ground near the palace door, where it was picked up by one of the eunuchs and carried at once to the wazīr, who happened, after a visit to his harīm, to be seated upon a couch in the reception hall. The eunuch interrupted his calm reflection by holding out the note and saying: 'I found this on the ground, my lord, and hastened to bring it to you.' The wazīr opened the paper and, after reading the poems, made sure, by examination, that two of them were in the handwriting of his daughter, Rose-in-the-Bud.

He at once sought out his wife, the girl's mother, with tears coursing down his beard. 'Why do you weep, my master?' cried the woman, and he replied: 'Look at this paper.' She took the note and saw at once that it was a correspondence between Rose-in-the-Bud and World's-Delight. Tears came to her eyes, but she controlled her soul and said to the wazīr: 'My lord, tears are useless in this matter. It were better to think of a way to safeguard your honour and hide our daughter's shame.' After she had comforted her husband for some time, he said: 'I fear this passion for our child! Surely you know that the Sultān is very fond of Rose-in-the-Bud? My concern is a double one: I fear for my daughter because she is my daughter and I fear for her because she is a favourite with the Sultān. What is your thought in this matter?' 'Give me time to make the prayer for guidance,' she answered and, placing herself in the attitude for it, went through the pious practices which the Sunnah recommends in such a case.

When she had finished her prayer, she said: 'In the midst of the sea Bahr al-Kunūz there lies a mountain called the mountain of the Bereaved Mother, where none may land without great difficulty. I advise you to build a home there for our daughter.'

The wazīr, approving of his wife's advice, resolved to have an inaccessible palace built upon this mountain and to confine his daughter there, with provisions for a year, to be renewed during the following years, and a troop of attendants to bear her company. He therefore called together a band of masons, carpenters and architects, and sent them to the mountain, where they built an inaccessible palace such as the eye of man had never seen.

When he received word that this was done, the wazīr provisioned a caravan for the journey and, visiting his daughter in the middle of the night, ordered her to depart. Rose-in-the-Bud was stricken with the violent pangs of separation and shed abundant tears when she reached the outside of the palace and saw that the final preparations had been made. Suddenly the idea came to her to inform World's-Delight of her violent passion, which might have melted the hardest rocks and started streams of tears, by writing the following lines upon the door:

> Here is a perfumed kiss, O house,
> For he will pass in the morning.

I know not where I go
On this swift journey.
To-night the birds will sing among the leaves of pain:
Pity, parting, pity, parting!
But already
I have drunk the aloed cup of Destiny,
And there is memory in the wine.

At this point Shahrazād saw the approach of morning and discreetly fell silent.

But when the four-hundred-and-third night had come

SHE SAID:

When she had traced these lines on the door, she took her place in the palanquin and the caravan started. They crossed sown and desert, hill and plain, and came at last to the sea al-Kunūz, where they pitched their tents and set about constructing a great boat. When it was ready, they put out to sea, taking the young girl and her attendants with them.

As the wazīr had ordered the leaders of the caravan to come back across the sea when they had confined Rose-in-the-Bud in her palace, and then to destroy their boat, they hastened to fulfil his command in every particular and at last came back to him, weeping for what they had done. So much for them.

World's-Delight rose on that morning and, after making his prayer, mounted his horse and rode towards the palace to serve the Sultān. As he passed the wazīr's door, he saw the verses written upon it and nearly lost consciousness. The reading of them lit a quenchless fire in his racked entrails. He returned home, but could not stay in one place because of his wretchedness; when night came, he feared that he would reveal his secret to the folk of his house and therefore went out, all haggard and perplexed, to wander at random in the streets.

He walked all that night and through the next morning, until the great heat and his consequent thirst obliged him to rest a little. He sat down beneath a shady tree beside a little stream and lifted the water in the hollow of his hand to drink. But he found no taste or refreshment in it, for, as he leaned over the water, he saw that his face had become ravaged and yellow in a single day. Also he felt his feet much swollen by his wanderings. He wept abundantly and said these verses, while the tears coursed down his cheeks:

> I am drunken with love,
> But the cup is held to my lips
> And I must drink again.
> Why should I not wander in the ways,
> Forgetting food?
> There is no joy in all these roads,
> For I cannot meet my beloved
> Or one who has known my beloved
> Or one who has known one
> Who has known my beloved.

When he had said these verses, World's-Delight wept until he had made a pool on the earth beside him; then he rose and left that place. As he was wandering in despair through plains and deserts, there appeared suddenly before him a great-maned lion with a mighty neck. Its head was as large as a dome, the stretch of its jaws more than a door, and its teeth had the appearance of elephant's tusks. Seeing this beast, World's-Delight gave himself up for lost; turning towards Mecca, he pronounced his act of Faith and prepared to die. Then he suddenly remembered that he had read in ancient books that a lion is very sensible to flattery and can easily be tamed through its delight in words. Therefore he said to the animal: 'Lion of all the forests, lion of all the deserts, fearless lion, renowned chieftain of the brave, Sultān of beasts, you see before you a poor lover, worn out with separation, whose passion has brought him to the doors of death. Hear me and have compassion upon my grief.'

At this speech, the lion retired a little and, sitting down on its behind, lifted its head towards World's-Delight with pleased movements of its tail and two front paws. Encouraged by these signs, World's-Delight recited the following:

> O brave tumultuous lion,
>> I am no prize
>> For I am thin,
>> My body dies,
> O brave tumultuous lion.
>> Your foes would grin
>> If you ate me

> And say you could
> Not catch for food
> A living enemy.
> But if you have a mind
> To be unkind,
> O brave tumultuous lion,
> My body hates
> Its loneliness,
> And you would hurt me less
> Because your claws are not as sharp as Fate's,
> O brave tumultuous lion.

At this point Shahrazād saw the approach of morning and discreetly fell silent.

But when the four-hundred-and-fourth night had come

SHE SAID:

When the lion heard these lines, his eyes filled with tears. He came gently up to World's-Delight and began to lick his feet and hands. Then he signed to him to follow and set off across the desert. World's-Delight went after his guide for a long time; when they had climbed a high mountain and dropped down the other side, they came upon plain traces of the caravan. The young man hurried forward with his eyes fixed upon the track, while the lion, being assured that his friend was now going in the right direction, returned by the way he had come to mind his own concerns.

World's-Delight followed in the trace of the caravan until he came to a sea moaning with all its waves, and there he lost the tracks upon the sand. Realising that the party which he sought had taken ship from that place, he lost all hope of again seeing his mistress. With abundant tears he said over this poem to himself:

> There are no footsteps on the sea,
> Though all the sea
>   Could not put out my heart;
> And no deep sleep
>   By any art,
> Although the sea is deep.
> Great Euphrates
> My tears' mate is,

I am lord of rain
And the rivers
   Of my pain
Grow to greater rivers.

I throw the worthless coin of life
To play with life,
   But if I win, I cannot win;
For my own love,
   A traitor's sin,
Pulls down the fort above.

Willows growing by the streams
Of my dreams,
   Half a world between us,
Would that gentle death
   Had seen us
In the breast of death.

When he had made an end of these lines, he wept so long that at last unconsciousness came to him and he went into a deep swoon. As soon as he came to himself he looked to left and right and, seeing that he was in a desert, was taken with a sudden fear of savage beasts. He therefore climbed a high mountain, at the top of which he heard the sound of a human voice. Listening attentively, he came to the conclusion that the voice was that of a hermit who had left the world, to live a life of devotion in a cave which could be seen among the rocks. He knocked three times at the door of this cave and then, as no one came forth, sighed deeply and intoned these lines:

How may desire win home,
   How may the soul forget,
When all the chiefs of all the griefs
   About my head have met
   To whiten its young jet?

Harsh flowers fell in the wine
   Until its taste was rude;
I fed the fire of my desire
   With bitter aloe wood
   Which grew in solitude.

I went to find my dear
  And found a verse instead;
It dashed the stuff of all my love
  In ruin round my head
  And left my soul for dead.

Yet, loser of the world,
  If I could have my choice
I'd choose again that life of pain
  Where living girls and boys
  May suffer and rejoice.

As he was finishing these lines, the door of the cavern opened and he heard a voice cry: 'The mercy of Allāh be upon you!'

At this point Shahrazād saw the approach of morning and discreetly fell silent.

But when the four-hundred-and-fifth night had come

SHE SAID:

He entered the cave and wished the hermit peace. 'What is your name?' asked the holy man. 'I am called World's-Delight,' he answered, and at once told his story from beginning to end. When it was finished, the hermit wept, saying: 'O World's-Delight, I have lived in this place for twenty years without beholding a human being until yesterday. I heard the sound of tears and voices and, looking down from this mountain, saw a caravan with tents pitched upon the beach. I watched while a group of men constructed a boat and, going on board, made for the open sea. A short time afterwards some of them returned and, when they had destroyed their boat, went back across the desert. I think that those who went and did not return were the folk for whom you are looking, O World's-Delight. I understand your grief and I excuse it. There was never a lover who was not acquainted with sorrow.' Then the hermit recited these lines:

O World's-Delight, you think that I have passed
Beyond all human sympathy at last,
Not knowing that a touch of passion's hand
Winds and unwinds me like a linen band.
Even as a child I found love's worst and best,
Drinking its fury from my mother's breast;

> I was a known practitioner of love
> When my young comrades were not old enough;
> Seeing my frenzy, older men of wit
> Used my name as a synonym for it.
> And this one thing I learned from passion's page,
> In lusty youth and in my meagre age,
> The single sin in love, for which regret
> Can in no wise atone, is to forget.

The hermit clasped World's-Delight in his arms, and the two wept together until the mountains echoed their grief. Then they both swooned away.

When they recovered consciousness, they swore a mutual oath to be brothers in Allāh (exalted be His name!) and the hermit said: 'I will pray to-night and ask for the guidance of Allāh in your affair.' 'I beg you to do so,' answered World's-Delight. So much for them.

When Rose-in-the-Bud was taken to the mountain of the Bereaved Mother and had entered the palace prepared for her, she examined the place attentively. Finding it both fair and comfortable, she began to weep and say: 'As Allāh lives, O dwelling, you have all delights save one. My lover is not here.' Then as she had seen that there were many birds in the island, she ordered nets to be spread for their capture, and each one, as it was taken, to be placed in a cage within the palace.

As she leaned out of a window and gave herself up to memory, desire rose in her like a flame not to be put out by any tears. The burden of these verses came to her:

> I would out-sing the sorrows of these song-birds
> Because of love,
> But I am afraid.
>
> I am burnt up
> More easily than a wooden twig,
> I am slim tinder.
>
> But he cannot see this.
>
> You need not be ashamed, sun of warm gold,
> To make each ray a kiss
> For my beloved;
> He is more worthy of your light
> Than any moon.

Sun of warm gold,
You have never shone on river reeds
More fair than he.

Impudent roses,
You could feign his right cheek,
Only if you were the roses of his left.

The water of my beloved's mouth
Could put out hell.

He is my suffering and my delight,
He is my beloved.

When night came down with his shadows, Rose-in-the-Bud felt her desire grow hotter and the memory of her woes flame up in agony.

At this point Shahrazād saw the approach of morning and discreetly fell silent.

But when the four-hundred-and-sixth night had come

SHE SAID:
She cried aloud these lines:

With night there beats a white-hot sun
Of memory upon my bed.
Burning,
I lie all fire,
Turning
My maidenhead
To every angle of desire
But one.

I could not say farewell that day;
I charge you, night, to say it now
Seeing
My little sleep.
'Being
All hot to keep
The letter of her vow,'
Oh, say!

Thus Rose-in-the-Bud lamented.

When the hermit had well prayed, he said to World's-Delight: 'Go down into the valley and bring me a load of palm fibres.'

World's-Delight did so, and the hermit wove them into a great net, such as is used for carrying straw. Then he said again: 'In the valley there grow gourds which dry, as soon as they are ripe, and fall from their stems. Go down and fill this net with dry gourds; then throw all into the sea and climb on top; the current will bear you out and carry you to the place where you would be. May good fortune attend you!' World's-Delight bade farewell to his friend and, climbing down into the valley, made the suggested preparations.

When he was well out to sea, floating upon his net of gourds, a violent wind arose and carried him beyond the hermit's sight. For three days and three nights he was the plaything of a terrible sea, buffeted by waves, carried to the top of headlong crests, sunk into mighty gulfs, until at last Fate cast him at the foot of the mountain of the Bereaved Mother. Hungry and thirsty, he crawled up the sand, as giddy as a hen, and came in a short time to a place of running streams and fruit trees sung about by birds. Having eaten and drunken, he made his way inland and soon saw, white against the horizon, a mighty palace with steep unfriendly walls. Finding the door of it shut, he sat down in that place and did not move for three days. At the end of this time the door opened and a eunuch appeared, who asked him whence he came and what chance had brought him to the island. 'I am from Isfahān,' he answered. 'I was sailing the seas with my merchandise when the ship went down and the waves carried me to this shore.' On hearing this, the slave wept and threw his arms about the neck of World's-Delight, saying: 'Allāh preserve you, O face of friendship! Isfahān is my own country. My cousin, the daughter of my uncle, the dear love of my childhood, dwells there still. One day our tribe was attacked by a greater and I was carried off as part of the spoil. Since I was still a child, my eggs were cut off to increase my value and I was sold as a eunuch.' After this the slave, with many expressions of welcome, led World's-Delight into the vast outer court of the palace.

There he saw a wonderful fountain, surrounded by trees from whose slim leafy boughs hung silver cages with gold doors. In these, birds of various kinds were singing agreeable praises to their Creator. Going up to the first cage, World's-Delight saw that it

held a dove, whose cry seemed to say: 'Generous! Generous!'
Hearing the word, the young man fell down in a swoon; at last he
recovered and, with a deep sigh, murmured this song. . . .

At this point Shahrazād saw the approach of morning and
discreetly fell silent.

But when the four-hundred-and-seventh night had come

SHE SAID:

> Though you have felt your heart grow dim,
>   O silver sleepy dove,
>   Be not ashamed of praying,
>   But tune your throat to saying:
> 'O generous one!' to Him,
>   For He is love.
>
> But all your passion is a bird's,
>   No man may surely say
>   Whether the meaning
>   Of your tired keening
> Is: 'Break, my heart, in minor thirds,'
>   Or: 'I am gay.'

As soon as he had said these lines, he wept until he swooned
again. When he recovered consciousness, he went up to the second
cage, which contained a wood-pigeon, who seemed ever to be
singing: 'Glorify Him!' The young man sighed deeply and said:

> The wood-pigeon murmurs: 'Glorify Him!'
> Why should I not murmur: 'Glorify Him!'
> Since I am no sadder than the wood-pigeon?
> And yet the slow honey of the voice of the wood-pigeon
> Comes not from my lips
> And the slow blood of the heart of the wood-pigeon,
> Filling the ruby,
> Is not my heart.
> If I opened the door of his cage
> The wood-pigeon would murmur: 'Glorify Him!'
> Therefore why should I murmur: 'Glorify Him!'?

Then World's-Delight went up to the third cage, in which was a nightingale. Seeing a stranger the bird began to sing, and the young man answered its song, saying:

> Allāh has set aside the nightingale
>> To be our tears.
>>> Each prayer for pity
>>>> Which, being dumb, we could not make
>> In any years,
> Must agonise, make pale
>> His ditty
>>> For our sake.

> Allāh has set aside the nightingale
>> To be our prayer.
>>> The nights, which over-long
>>>> Wore down our passion to a burning thread,
>> He hears not in our tale;
>>> And so leans down instead
>> To this bird's song
> To find them there.

After this he went up to the fourth cage and saw within it a bulbul, which at once began to sing. With a deep sigh, World's-Delight answered the song:

> The dawn which is so pale and sweet
> Makes lovers' hearts to beat
> And the gold of noonday's heat
> Gilds her two wayward feet. . . .
>> The bulbul sings this.

> The scent of rain on garden flowers
> Stabs this desire of ours,
> Dew-watered musk has powers
> Over lovers' hours. . . .
>> The bulbul sings this.

> We cannot find the needed song
> The coloured paths along,
> And the light buds among
> Are silent for love's wrong. . . .
>> The bulbul sings this.

> When she has been away
> And then brings back the day
> Her lovers kneel and say:
> We thank our hearts for May. . . .
>   The bulbul sings this.

World's-Delight went further on until he came to a cage of such remarkable workmanship that it surpassed all the other cages put together.

At this point Shahrazād saw the approach of morning and discreetly fell silent.

But when the four-hundred-and-eighth night had come

SHE SAID:

This cage contained a wild pigeon with a rich collar of pearls about its neck; its plaintive amorous singing, its air of sadness, so affected World's-Delight that he sobbed and said:

> Wild pigeon of the leaves,
> Brother of lovers,
>
> If you have seen an arrow killing
>   From far
> The mild-eyed deer
>   By rills
>   Of summer hills,
>
> If you have heard an arrow singing
>   From far
> And then strike sheer
>   The wings
>   Of airy things,
>
> Wild pigeon of the leaves,
>   You are
> Brother of lovers.

When the pigeon heard this song, it came out of its dream, moaning and moving with so much melancholy that it seemed, in its own language, to be singing this:

Now I remember my free flying
And my songs for
The brave grey breast of my mistress
Bright in the branches.
Men came with flutes to the forest
But I turned to the night songs
Of the brave grey throat of my mistress
Bright in the branches.
Men came with nets to the forest
And I saw no more
The brave grey breast of my mistress
Bright in the branches.

World's-Delight turned to his friend, the eunuch from Isfahān, saying: 'Whose palace is this? Who built it and who lives in it?' 'The wazīr of a certain king built it for his daughter, that she might be free from happening and accident,' answered the eunuch. 'She is confined there with a train of servants, and the inner door is only opened once a year when new provisions come for us.'

'I have reached my goal,' thought World's-Delight, 'but, ah, how long will be the waiting!' So much for him.

Since her coming to the palace, Rose-in-the-Bud had not known the joy of eating and drinking, nor the joy of sleep. As time went by the torment of her heart increased and she would wander through the palace looking in vain for a way of escape. A day came when she could control herself no longer; bursting into tears, she murmured these lines:

They made my torture-chamber a prison
And my prison a torture-chamber.

They heated irons
In the fire of his absence,
And gave me burning drugs
Distilled from my desire.

Who shall break the rack
Built from my sighing,
Or pierce the wall
Raised from my grief,

And I run drunken-footed to my love?

Then Rose-in-the-Bud climbed up to the terrace of the palace and, by means of strong Baalbakk fabrics which she tied carefully together, let herself down the outside of the walls and reached the ground in safety. Dressed just as she was in her fairest robe, and with a collar of great diamonds about her neck, she crossed the flat desert and came to the sea shore.

At this point Shahrazād saw the approach of morning and discreetly fell silent.

But when the four-hundred-and-ninth night had come

SHE SAID:

She saw a fisherman whom the wind had cast upon that coast, seated in his boat and fishing. The man caught sight of her at the same moment and, thinking that she was some appearance from another world, began fearfully to push off from the shore. Rose-in-the-Bud called and signed to him and, when he stayed to listen, spoke to him as follows:

> I am no ghost from the sea mist,
> > Fisherman,
> But a lover burned in fire
> And never kissed.
> Lend me your boat to find desire,
> > Fisherman,
> And I'll give pearls of the sea
> To be your hire.
> He is the absent half of me,
> > Fisherman,
> And I the half on fire:
> So come to me.

Hearing these lines, the fisherman wept, groaned, and lamented the days of his youth, when he had been conquered by love, tormented by passion, tortured by desirous dreams, and burnt in the fires of ecstasy. He answered:

> Tears were the pasture of my youth,
> A broken heart my only wear,
> I bled; I used to tell the fair
> Desire was love and love was truth.

> Then do you wonder I am bold
>   To bring these poor young lovers weal?
>   If they feel half I used to feel
> I ought to get a heap of gold.

When the fisherman had said this, he brought his boat to the shore, exclaiming: 'Come into my boat and I will take you anywhere you wish.' Rose-in-the-Bud accepted this invitation, and the fisherman rowed strongly away from the shore. Soon a high wind rose behind them and urged them forward till land was lost and they could know nothing of their direction. At the end of three days the storm abated, the wind fell, and Allāh (may His name be exalted!) beached their boat beside a city.

As the fisherman's boat came to ground, the King of that city, whose name was Dirbās, was sitting with his son at a window in his palace and looking out to sea. Perceiving in the boat a girl as beautiful as the full moon lying upon night's unclouded breast, wearing a collar of great diamonds and having magnificent rubies in her ears, he imagined that she must be some king's daughter and at once hurried down to the shore through the seaward door of his palace.

By the time he reached the boat it had been moored, and the young girl was calmly sleeping. As the King watched her she opened her eyes and began to weep. Then said he: 'Whence come you? Whose daughter are you? And what is the reason of your journey?' 'I am the daughter of Ibrāhīm, wazīr of King Shāmikh,' she answered. 'The reason of my voyage is strange, my adventure is remarkable.' With that she told the King the whole of her story from beginning to end, and finished by weeping and sighing and saying:

> My lids are rotten with my tears
>   And my love tale's wondrous beyond weeping,
>   For I was never paid
>   As man pays maid
>   And time is keeping
> The arrears,
>   O World's-Delight!

> Your love had been to magic school,
>   Your eyes were art-come-up with olden cantraps,
>   Each whisper was a sin.

> Taught by the Jinn,
> Your lips were mantraps
> For the fool,
> O World's-Delight!

After this she told the King further details of her life and then, bursting into tears, improvised this song:

At this point Shahrazād saw the approach of morning and discreetly fell silent.

But when the four-hundred-and-tenth night had come

SHE SAID:

> Sire, sire,
> Who would have thought this thing,
> That tears could turn to fire,
> O stranger king;
> Who would have thought my mind
> Could change a tear to blood,
> O kingly, kind;
> Or who that the sea would
> A living dead girl bring
> To you, O mild, O good,
> O stranger king?

When the King heard Rose-in-the-Bud's tale, he was convinced of the depth of her love-longing and said compassionately: 'Have no fear, for you have reached your goal. I am ready to help you by bringing you to your lover.' Then the King recited these lines:

> Delightful maid,
> There is no need to be afraid;
> Even to-day I have made
> A merchandise cavalcade
> And bade
> Strong riders, richly paid,
> Carry a brave parade
> Of musk and of brocade
> King Shāmikh to persuade
> To lend his aid
> And be the powerful shade

In which our head is laid,
Therefore there is no need to be afraid,
Delightful maid.

So saying, the King went out to his soldiers and, bidding his
wazīr prepar? innumerable bales of the intended presents, commanded him to set out at once and carry them to King Shāmikh.
'Also,' said he, 'you must bring me back a young man called
World's-Delight. Say to the King: "My master seeks you for an
ally and wishes the alliance to be sealed by a marriage between
Rose-in-the-Bud, daughter of your wazīr, and World's-Delight, a
youth in your own train. Give this young man to me and I will
conduct him to King Dirbās that the contract may be drawn up in
his presence." '

Then King Dirbās wrote a letter to King Shāmikh and gave it to
his wazīr with a repetition of his orders concerning World's-
Delight. 'If you do not bring him back,' he added, 'you shall be
relieved of your high position.' 'I hear and I obey!' answered the wazīr,
and at once set out for the lands of King Shāmikh.

When he arrived, he greeted King Shāmikh from King Dirbās
and gave him the presents and the letter. But to his surprise, King
Shāmikh shed many tears, saying: 'Alas, alas, where is World's-
Delight? He has disappeared and we know not where to seek him.
If you can give him back to me, O wazīr, I will gladly pay double
the worth of the presents which you have brought me.' Then, with
many groans, King Shāmikh said:

Give him to me
And you shall have for fee
Blue burning diamonds from my treasury.

He was the moon
In night's blue burning noon,
Whose simplest words were songs to a low tune,

My prince of palms,
Whose branches in his calms
Bore golden-mannered speeches like gold psalms.

Enough of trees,
My child was more than these,
Himself blue burning noon and the relenting breeze.

Then he turned to the visiting wazīr, who had brought the presents and the letter, saying: 'Return to your master and tell him that World's-Delight has been absent for more than a year and that the King, his master, does not know what has become of him.' 'But, my lord,' the wazīr answered, 'the King, my master, told me that if I did not bring back World's-Delight, I should be cast from my high office and might never again set foot in his city. How dare I return?'

King Shāmikh turned to his own wazīr, Ibrāhīm, father of Rose-in-the-Bud, saying: 'Take a strong escort and accompany this envoy, helping him to seek in every place for World's-Delight.' 'I hear and I obey!' answered Ibrāhīm, and at once set out, accompanied by a troop of guards and the other wazīr, to seek for World's-Delight.

They journeyed for many days, and each time they met with caravans or wandering tribes they asked news of World's-Delight, saying: 'Have you seen a young man of such and such an appearance?' But always the strangers would answer: 'We do not know him.'

At this point Shahrazād saw the approach of morning and discreetly fell silent.

But when the four-hundred-and-eleventh night had come

SHE SAID:

They inquired through cities and villages, and hunted every plain and mountain, until they came to the sea. There they took ship and, in the course of time, saw the mountain of the Bereaved Mother rising above the waves.

Then said the wazīr of King Dirbās to the wazīr of King Shāmikh: 'Why did that mountain receive its name?' 'I will tell you,' answered the other, and he said:

'Of old there was a Jinnīyah, of the race of the Chinese Jinn, who met a mortal in her journeyings and learned to love him. Fearing the anger of the Jinn if the thing became known, and yet being unable to control her passion, she sought for some solitary place where she could hide her lover from the eyes of the Jinn, and at last found this unknown mountain which lay apart from the passage of men and fiends. She brought her lover through the air to this island and lived with him here, only leaving from time to time to make a necessary appearance among the Jinn. Several times she became pregnant by her lover and bore many children on the mountain. Thus it happened that merchants, who chanced to sail along this coast, would hear the children crying; as the sounds seemed very like those of a mother who had lost her young, they would say to each other: "There must be some bereaved woman upon that mountain." Such was the origin of the name.'

This tale and the astonishment of the other wazīr had brought them ashore and to the palace gate. In answer to their knocking, a eunuch came forth and, recognising his master, the wazīr Ibrāhīm, father of Rose-in-the-Bud, kissed his hand and led the two new-comers into the palace.

In the courtyard, Ibrāhīm noticed among the crowd of servants a man of wretched appearance who, though the old man was far from recognising him, was none other than World's-Delight. He asked his people the meaning of the stranger's presence there, and they answered: 'He is a poor merchant who was shipwrecked on the island, after having lost all his goods at sea. There is no harm in him, for he is a saint, bound ever in the ecstasy of prayer.' Without troubling further about the matter, the wazīr entered the palace.

When he did not find his daughter in her apartment, he questioned the young girl slaves who were there, and they replied: 'We do not know how she departed from this place. All we can say is that she did not stay long among us.' Hearing this, the wazīr burst into tears and improvised these lines:

> House, haunted with bird music,
> Of proud thresholds,
>
> Sobbing with desire came the lover,
> Your doors were wide for him;
> We looked in gladness to discover
> Your hidden bride for him.
>
> Chamberlains of luxurious lot
> Grew ruddy there;
> Brocade was everywhere,
> House, haunted with bird music,
> But she was not.

The wazīr Ibrāhīm wept again when he had made an end of these verses. 'None may escape from the decrees of Allāh,' he exclaimed, 'nor trick the fixture of eternity!' So saying, he went up on to the terrace and found the Baalbakk fabrics, fastened by one end to the battlements and hanging down the walls. As he stood there, realising and sorrowing for the manner of his daughter's grief-guided flight, he saw two great birds, one a crow and one an owl, slowly passing the terrace. Taking their appearance for an evil omen, he sobbed and said:

> Late have I come to the home of my dear,
> She is not here
> And, lo!
> Wheeling an owl and a crow.
> Craw, craw,
> You broke love's law,
> Cruel were you.
> To whoo, to whoo,
> To whom?
> To these poor two.
> So, so
> In the gloom
> The owl and the crow.

At this point Shahrazād saw the approach of morning and discreetly fell silent.

But when the four-hundred-and-twelfth night had come

SHE SAID:

He came down weeping from the terrace and ordered the slaves to search the mountain for their mistress. The slaves hunted for many hours but did not find her. So much for them.

When World's-Delight heard for certain of the flight of Rose-in-the Bud, he uttered a great cry and fell senseless to the ground. Seeing him lie there unconscious, the folk of the palace thought that he had been lifted into a divine ectasy and that his soul was drowned in the glorious contemplation of God. So much for him.

As soon as the wazīr of King Dirbās saw that Ibrāhīm had lost all hope of finding his daughter and World's-Delight, and that his heart was very low because of this, he resolved to return to the city of his King, although he had not succeeded in his mission. He made his farewells to the father of Rose-in-the-Bud, saying, as he pointed to the poor young man on the ground: 'I wish to take this saint with me, for perhaps his merits will bring blessing upon me; perhaps Allāh may soften the heart of my master, so that he does not deprive me of my office. Later I will not fail to send the holy man to Isfahān; for that city is not far from our land.' 'Do as seems good to you,' answered Ibrāhīm.

The two wazīrs separated, each taking the road to his own country; and the wazīr of King Dirbās, though far from guessing his identity, took World's-Delight along with him, still in his swoon and mounted on a mule.

The swoon lasted for the first three days of the journey, but on the fourth day World's-Delight, who had before been ignorant of all which passed about him, recovered consciousness, murmuring: 'Where am I?' A slave who was by answered: 'You are travelling with the wazīr of King Dirbās,' and at once ran to inform his master that the holy man had come to himself. The wazīr immediately sent his guest a draught of sugared rose-water, which brought his strength back to him. After that the journey went on and the caravan soon came to the outskirts of the city.

King Dirbās sent a message to his wazīr, saying: 'If World's-Delight is not with you, beware of showing yourself before my face.' The unhappy wazīr did not know what to do, for he was completely ignorant that Rose-in-the-Bud was with the King, and why the King desired to find World's-Delight, and especially that the young man who was always fainting in his company was World's-Delight. Also, you must remember that World's-Delight did not know whither he was being taken or that the wazīr had been sent out in search of him.

Recalling that World's-Delight had recovered consciousness, the wazīr went to him, saying: 'O holy man of Allāh, I wish for your advice in a cruel perplexity. My master the King sent me upon a mission in which I have not succeeded; now that he knows of my return, he has warned me that I may not enter the city if I have failed.' 'What was your mission?' asked the young man and, when the wazīr had told him the whole story, he mastered his emotion and continued: 'Fear nothing! Go to the King and carry me with you. I take it upon myself to bring about the return of World's-Delight.' 'Are you telling the truth?' cried the delighted wazīr, and, when the other replied that he was, the old man mounted with him on horseback and speedily sought the presence of the King.

When they were before the face of Dirbās, the Sultān cried: 'Where is World's-Delight?' For answer, the holy man advanced, saying: 'O great King, I know the hiding-place of World's-Delight.' The King signed to him to approach and, when he had done so, asked in a moved voice: 'Where is that?' 'Very near here,' replied the other. 'But tell me first why you want him, before I hasten to place him in your hands.'

'I will gladly do so,' said the King, 'but we must be alone.' He ordered his people to fall back and, taking the young man with him into an inner chamber, told him the whole story from beginning to end.

Then said World's-Delight: 'Bring me rich robes and, when I have put them on, I will instantly make World's-Delight appear.' The King had a sumptuously ornamented garment brought to him, and World's-Delight, when he had put it on, cried: 'I, even I, am World's-Delight, the desolation of the envious!' Piercing all hearts with the dark glances of his eyes, he improvised these lines. . . .

At this point Shahrazād saw the approach of morning and discreetly fell silent.

But when the four-hundred-and-thirteenth night had come

SHE SAID:

> She was a coloured shadow of delight
> Going before me in the dark of night,
>   Burning my pains away.
> My only water-streams were tears for love,
> But they were cool and sparkling and enough
>   With her to light me. Nay,
> My very self a river washing hell
> But kissing the reed bank of heaven as well
>   With her to light the day.
>
> But heart and head have watched together so,
> My heart, being drained of sleep, is white as snow,
>   My head is like white frost;
> How may I know that the long book of grief
> Is closed at last, without the darling chief
>   Young chapter being lost;
> How can I know that we may find, in truth,
> A golden youth in a gold youth of youth
>   When that sweet gold were most?

When World's-Delight had made an end of this, King Dirbās said: 'As Allāh lives, I see that you each loved the other with the same sincere passion. You are two flashing stars in the sky of beauty. Your tale is a prodigy and your adventures pass the telling!' Then, when King Dirbās had told him the whole tale of Rose-in-the-Bud, the young man asked: 'O King of time, where is she now?' 'She is in my palace,' he answered, and at once sent for the kādī and witnesses, who drew up the marriage contract for the two young people. After that Dirbās loaded World's-Delight with honour and riches, and sent a courier to tell King Shāmikh all that had happened.

King Shāmikh rejoiced exceedingly and sent a letter back to King Dirbās, saying: 'As the contract has already been put in order, I greatly desire that the feast and the consummation of the marriage should take place in my palace.' Also he prepared camels, horses, and a great train of attendants, which he sent to fetch the bride and bridegroom.

When this letter and escort arrived, King Dirbās gave a great present in gold to the lovers and, after adding to their train, bade them farewell.

It was a memorable day when they arrived at Isfahān in their own country; the city had never seen so fair a day. King Shāmikh called together every musician in the confines of his kingdom and gave mighty feasts of rejoicing for three whole days, casting gold to the people and distributing numerous robes of honour.

When the feast was finished on the first night, World's-Delight went into the bridal chamber of Rose-in-the-Bud and, because they had hardly seen each other since they had met again, they threw themselves into each other's arms with a joy that passed the boundary of tears. Rose-in-the-Bud improvised these lines:

> See, the yellow lamp of joy abating
> All the black shades of our waiting
> To the grief of those
> Who were our foes.
>
> Now the little winds of love are cooling
> Us, who had an ardent schooling
> And ate burning fruits . . .
> There are the flutes. . . .

> These are not the salt tears of our grieving,
> But fresh silver waters weaving
> > Nets to drown in joy
> > A girl and boy.

They sprang together and remained close pressed in each other's arms until they fell limp for delight.

At this point Shahrazād saw the approach of morning and discreetly fell silent.

But when the four-hundred-and-fourteenth night had come

SHE SAID:

When they came out of their lethargy, World's-Delight improvised these lines:

> > These are the hours we deemed once,
> > Merged in a bed divine now,
> > Impossible-silver-seamed once.

> > > Our bed is silver hung with sea yellow
> > > But fairer is my bed-fellow
> > > Than it, or anything the sky below.

> > Over us floats God's sign now,
> > These are the hours we dreamed once,
> > Proving that she is mine now.

The two lovers clasped each other again and, throwing themselves upon the bed, crushed pleasure between them. Until they were drowned in love, they tempted his thousand different ways. Their delight, their lust, their happiness, their pleasure, and their joy made seven days and seven nights pass without notice. It was not until they saw the musicians come that they understood that they were at the end of the seventh day of their marriage. In her surprise Rose-in-the-Bud improvised these lines:

> > I won to him in spite of sentinels.
> > On virgin silks, on velvets, he has pressed me,
> > And mattresses of feathers of rare birds.
> > What need had I of wine when he caressed me
> > And, with his words,
> > What need of song?

Present and past are in a poppied dream
And only seem;
Though seven days and nights were long
If spent in else.
Here are the girls to say:
'God make your day
One night
(Why were they sent in else?)
With World's-Delight.'

When she had recited these lines, World's-Delight embraced her
an incalculable number of times and then improvised the following:

I have drunken the perfumed sherbert of her eyes
And gone outside the world.
We have been curled
Below, above, and lover-wise;
Have lain as dead,
Have leapt,
Have slept
But little, I can vouch,
Forgetting on our couch
The bitter nights, which would have frozen us,
In a sweet rhythm of fire,
For God has chosen us
To be desire.

Then the two rose and, going out of their chamber, gave to all
who were in the palace gifts of money and presents of rare robes.
Afterwards Rose-in-the-Bud gave order to her slaves that the hammām of the palace should be cleared for her especial use. 'Cool of
my eyes,' she said to World's-Delight, 'I now so want to see you
in the hammām, where we can be alone and at our ease.' A sudden
wave of happiness came over her and she made up this song:

Boy, without whom I may not go
To any place, I love you so,
Come to the hammām; let your eyes
Make fire in a cool paradise.
We will burn scent of nard and lie
Naked in its blue wizardry,
Dreaming above each other's flesh;

We'll pardon Fate her clumsy mesh
And whisper praise to the Most High
That He has laid us thigh to thigh . . .
Then, when you bathe I'll watch and sing:
Oh, bathe for ever, sweet my king.

When she had said these lines, the two lovers went to the hammām and passed agreeable hours there. Afterwards they returned to the palace and spent their lives in the most intense felicity, until they were visited by the Destroyer of pleasures, the Separator of friends.

Glory be to Him who moves not, the Eternal towards whom all lives and things converge!

But do not think, O auspicious King, continued Shahrazād, that this story is like The Magic Tale of the Ebony Horse.

Then said King Shahryār: 'I have been delighted with the new verses said by these lovers, O Shahrazād. Now I am ready to hear you tell that magic tale. For I have not heard it.'

So Shahrazād said:

The Magic Tale of the Ebony Horse

IT is related, O auspicious King, that there was once, in the antiquity of time and the passage of the ages, a great and powerful King of the Persians whose name was Sābūr. He was not only the richest and wisest monarch of his time, but also the soul of generosity and benevolence, so that his hand was never weary of opening to any who called upon him for help. He had a large hospitality for those who only sought the barest shelter from him, and could comfort the broken-hearted with the sweetness of his discourse and the amenity of his actions. To the poor he was ever charitably disposed; the gates of his palace were always wide to the stranger; but in the severity of his justice the oppressor could find neither grace nor pardon.

King Sābūr had three daughters, three fair moons in the night sky, or three wonderful flowers shining in a well-kept garden; also he had a son who was called Kamar al-Akmār, the moon of moons.

Each year it was the King's custom to give two great festivals to his people; one at the beginning of Spring, which was the feast of

Nau Roz, and the other in Autumn, of Mihrgān. On these two occasions all the gates of his palace were opened, alms were distributed, pardons were called through the streets by heralds, new officers were created, and the lieutenants and chamberlains of the court were advanced in their positions. The people came from all the ends of his vast empire to render homage to their King and to do him pleasure on these two days of festival, by making presents of slaves, eunuchs, and other valuables.

During one of the Spring festivals the King, who had a great love of science, geometry and astronomy, was seated on his throne when three wise men presented themselves before him, masters of secret knowledge and hidden arts, who could mould the images of things with a perfection which confounded the beholder and were deeply versed in those mysteries of which ordinary folk know nothing. They had come to the city from three several countries, and each spoke a different language; the first was Hindi, the second Rūmī, and the third a Persian from the confines of the King's own land.

The Hindi sage kissed the earth between the King's hands and, after having wished him joy and happiness upon that day, offered him a truly royal present: a man of gold incrusted with rare diamonds, who held a golden trumpet in his hand. 'What is the use of this figure. O sage?' asked King Sābūr, and the other answered: 'My lord, his use is in this admirable virtue: if you set him up at the gate of your city he will be a sleepless guardian of it; for, if an enemy approaches, he will divine him from far and, raising the trumpet to his lips, blow a blast which shall paralyse your foe with fear and kill him with terror.' 'As Allāh lives,' cried the King, 'if what you say is true, I promise to realise your every wish and least desire!'

The Rūmī sage kissed the earth between the King's hands and offered him a vast silver basin, in which was a gold peacock surrounded by twenty-four gold peahens. King Sābūr looked with astonishment upon the thing, and then said: 'O sage, what is the use of this peacock and these peahens?' 'My lord,' answered the other, 'each time that an hour passes of the day or night, the peacock pecks one of the twenty-four peahens and mounts her, with a great beating of his wings, thus marking the hours until all the females have been mounted. Further than that, when the month has passed, he will open his mouth and the crescent of the new moon will appear in his throat.' Then cried the King in a marvel: 'As Allāh lives, if what you say is true, you shall want for nothing!' The wise man of Persia then kissed the earth between the King's hands and, after formal compliments and good wishes, offered him a horse made from the blackest and rarest ebony, inlaid with gold and diamonds, and bearing a saddle, bridle and stirrups such as are not seen even upon the horses of Kings. King Sābūr, wondering and quite put out by the beauty and perfections of the horse, asked what its virtues might be. 'My lord,' answered the Persian, 'the prodigious use of this horse is that, when it is mounted, it carries its rider through the air with the speed of light, taking him wheresoever he would go and covering in a day the year's journey of a horse of flesh and blood.' Astounded by these three prodigies appearing to him upon the same day, the King cried to the Persian: 'As Allāh lives, Who created all beings and gave them food and drink upon the earth, if what you boast is proved true, I undertake to satisfy your least desires and realise your most hidden wishes!'

For three days the King put his presents to the proof, making the sages display the qualities of each. And, even as had been promised, the gold man blew his gold trumpet; the gold peacock pecked and mounted his twenty-four gold peahens; and the Persian sage, seated upon the ebony horse, rose in the air and, after describing a vast circle with extraordinary speed, came gently to earth on the spot from which he had risen.

At this point Shahrazād saw the approach of morning and discreetly fell silent.

But when the four-hundred-and-sixteenth night had come

SHE SAID:

At first King Sābūr was stupefied by what he saw; then he so trembled with joy that he nearly fell upon the ground; and lastly he said to the wise men: 'Illustrious sages, now that I have proved the truth of your words it but remains for me to fulfil my promise. Ask all that you desire and it shall be given you upon the instant.'

The three answered: 'Since our master the King is satisfied with us and our presents, and leaves us the choice of recompense, we ask for his three daughters in marriage, for we greatly desire to become his sons-in-law. It is a matter that can in no way trouble the King. Also kings never go back upon their promises.' 'At once I grant what you desire!' answered the King, and forthwith he called the

THE MAGIC TALE OF THE EBONY HORSE

kādī and witnesses to prepare the marriage contracts of his three daughters with the three sages.

It happened that, while they were talking, the King's three daughters were seated behind a curtain in the reception hall and heard what was said. So the youngest looked closely at the sage whom she would have to marry and behold! he was a very, very old man, at least a hundred, if not more. His scanty rests of hair were white with time, he had a wagging head, moth-eaten eyebrows, and split and tumbling ears; his beard and moustaches were dyed and lifeless, his red bleared eyes squinted, his yellow furrowed chaps hung limp beside his face, his nose was like a gross black artichoke, his face was wrinkled as is a cobbler's apron, his teeth jutted like those of a wild pig, and his lips were hanging and trembling like a camel's testicles. In a word, the old sage was a thing of horror, a compost of monstrous uglinesses achieving the supreme deformity of the time and the most plain creature of that age. Beyond those features which I have told, he had nearly toothless gums from which sprang fangs instead of dog-teeth, making the old man look like one of those Afārīt who frighten children in deserted houses or set hens screaming in the hen-roost.

On the other hand, the youngest of the three princesses was the fairest and sweetest of all her century; to look at her more delighted than to behold a young gazelle. She was suaver than the meadow breeze and brighter than the full moon; she was truly formed for the games and works of love. She moved, and the branches were put to confusion in their balancing; she walked, and the roe-deer grew clumsy in its leaping. She surpassed her sisters in white beauty.

When she saw the sage who had been allotted to her, she ran to her room and, falling face downward upon the ground, began to tear her robes and claw her cheeks and sob and sigh exceedingly.

While she was in that state, her brother, Prince Kamar al-Akmār, who loved her dearly and preferred her to his other sisters, returned from hunting and, hearing her cries, sought her in her chamber. 'What has happened?' he asked. 'Tell me quickly; hide nothing from me.' Beating her breasts, she cried: 'O dear and only brother, I will hide nothing from you. I tell you that, even if the palace be straitened before your father, I am ready to go out from it; and if your father be set on committing odious sin, I will leave him and flee away. I ask no provision for the journey from him, for Allāh will provide.'

Then said Prince Kamar al-Akmār: 'But tell me what this means, my sister. What is it that has so troubled the humours of your body?' 'Dear and only brother,' answered the princess, 'my father has promised me in marriage to an old sage, a horrible magician, who brought him an ebony horse as a present. The man has surely bewitched the King and abused him by some perfidy. I am resolved to die rather than give myself to his senile ugliness.'

Her brother began to calm and console her with caresses and pleasant words, until he had reassured her; then he hurried to his father, saying: 'What is this I hear of a sorcerer to whom you have promised my little sister in marriage? What is this present which he has brought you and which can so persuade you to kill my sister with grief? The thing is not just and shall not happen.'

The Persian, who was near by, heard the prince's words and was thrown into a fury of mortification; but the King answered: 'Kamar al-Akmār, my son, if you had seen the horse this wise man has given me you would not be in such a taking.'

At this point Shahrazād saw the approach of morning and discreetly fell silent.

But when the four-hundred-and-seventeenth night had come

SHE SAID:

The King went with his son into the great court of the palace and had his slaves bring out the horse.

When the young prince saw the horse, he was delighted with its beauty and, being an excellent rider, leapt lightly upon its back, thrust his feet into the stirrups, and spurred the wooden sides. As the steed did not move, the King turned to the sage, saying: 'Go and see why it remains motionless; help my son and he will doubtless help you to accomplish your desires.'

The Persian, who hated the prince because he had opposed his sister's marriage, went up to him, where he was seated in the saddle, saying: 'Do you see that gold peg on the right of the pommel? That is the mechanism of ascent; you have but to turn it.'

At once the prince turned the peg, and behold! the horse rose in the air with the quickness of a bird, so high that the King and those who were with him lost sight of it in a few moments.

Seeing his son disappear and not return even at the end of several hours of anxious waiting, King Sābūr was puzzled and alarmed.

'O sage,' he said to the Persian, 'what must we do to bring him back?' 'Master,' answered the other, 'I can do nothing; you will not see your son again until the Resurrection. He would not give me time to explain the use of the left-hand peg, by which a descent is made; but, trusting to his self-sufficient ignorance, went off with the lesson unlearned.'

King Sābūr was filled with a fury of anger. In his rage he ordered his slaves to beat the Persian and throw him into the darkest dungeon of the city; then he himself tore the crown from his head, beat himself in the face, and pulled out handfuls of his beard. Returning to his palace, he caused all the doors to be shut and set himself to sobbing, groaning and lamenting, together with his wife, his three daughters and all the people of his court. Their joy was turned to affliction and their happiness to despair. So much for them.

The horse rose and rose with the prince into the air, until it seemed that he would touch the sun. When he realised his danger and the horrible death that awaited him in those parts of the sky, he bitterly repented his rashness and said within his soul: 'It is certain that the wise man meant to destroy me because I interfered between him and my little sister. What must I do now? There is no power or might save in Allāh! Surely I am lost beyond recall! . . . And yet there must certainly be a second peg, like the other, to bring this thing to earth again.' With that, as he was both intelligent and skilful, he sought all over the horse and at last found, on the left side of the saddle, a very little screw no larger than a pin's head. 'There is no other,' he said, and pressed down upon the screw. At once the upward movement of the horse began to slow, the animal stayed for a moment motionless in the air, and then began to descend as quickly as it had risen. Yet, as it approached the surface of the earth it began to go more slowly and at last alighted without even a shock, allowing its rider to breathe calmly and reassure himself.

As soon as young Kamar al-Akmār well understood the management of the horse and the screw, he rejoiced and thanked Allāh who had delivered him from certain death. Then, turning first the peg and then the screw and pulling the bridle to left and right, he began to exercise the horse forwards and backwards, up and down, sometimes with the quickness of light, sometimes at a walking pace, until he had thoroughly mastered all its movements. When he was quite certain of his power, he rose to a moderate height and journeyed straight forward at an easy pace, so that he could enjoy the prospect which unrolled itself below him upon the earth. Thus he was able to behold at his ease all the marvels of land and sea, and admire countries and cities which he had never seen or known in his life before.

Among the cities which spread themselves beneath his gaze he saw one in which the houses and other buildings were distributed with a charming symmetry, in the midst of a land laughing with rich green, furrowed by many water-courses, and abounding in pastures over which leaped troops of gazelles.

At this point Shahrazād saw the approach of morning and discreetly fell silent.

But when the four-hundred-and-eighteenth night had come

SHE SAID:

As Kamar al-Akmār ever loved to distract himself with new sights, he said to himself: 'I must know the name of this city and the land in which it is.' And he began to circle round the city, pausing in the air over the most beautiful parts of it.

When the sun dipped to the horizon and the day was ended, the prince thought to himself: 'As Allāh lives, I will find no better place than this city in which to pass the night. I will sleep here and to-morrow at daybreak return to my kingdom, to my friends, and the people of my house. I shall be glad to tell my father all that has happened to me, and describe to him what my eyes have seen.' Looking about him to choose a safe spot where he might pass the night and stable his strange horse, his eyes were attracted by a tall palace in the middle of the city, flanked by embattled towers and guarded by forty black slaves in coats of mail, armed with lances, swords and bows. 'This is a good place,' he said and, pressing the screw, guided his horse until it alighted like a tired bird upon the terrace of the palace. 'Praise be to Allāh!' cried the prince as he leapt from the saddle; then, as he looked over and examined his steed, he continued: 'As Allāh lives, he was a master craftsman who fashioned you so perfectly! If the Highest spares my life and brings me back to my father, I will load that learned man with benefits and make him taste of my generosity.'

Already night had fallen, but the prince remained upon the terrace until all the palace should be asleep. When it was late, being tortured with hunger and thirst, for he had not eaten or drunken since he set out, he said to himself: 'A palace like this cannot lack victual.' Leaving his horse upon the terrace, he descended the stair in search of something with which to stay his pangs. Soon he came to a large courtyard paved with white marble and transparent alabaster, which reflected the light of the moon under the night; he marvelled at the beauty of the building of the palace but, look as he might to right and left, he saw no living soul and heard no sound of human voice. After a hesitation of perplexity, he said to himself: 'The best thing I can do for the moment is to climb up again to the terrace and pass the night by the side of my horse. To-morrow, when the day begins to lighten, I will mount again and go my way.' As he was about to put this project into execution, he saw a light in the interior of the palace and, moving towards it, discovered that it came from a lighted torch placed before the harīm door, at the head of a bed on which a black eunuch lay asleep. This slave snored thunderously and looked like an Ifrīt under the orders of Sulaimān or one of the Black Jinn. He was stretched on a mattress across the door, and blocked it better than a tree trunk or a bench; the hilt of his sword sparkled furiously in the torch-light, and, above his head, his bag of food hung from a granite pillar.

At sight of this horrible negro young Kamar al-Akmār murmured in a terrified whisper: 'I put my trust in the power of Allāh! O Master of earth and sky, You who have already saved me from certain death, help me again and be my safety in this palace!' So saying, he lightly detached the black man's bag of provisions and, stealing away, opened it. Finding that it contained food of the finest quality, he began to eat. When he had completely emptied the bag, he went to the fountain basin in the courtyard and stayed his thirst with the pure fresh water which gushed from it. Then he went bach to the eunuch, returned the bag to its place and, unsheathing the slave's sword, took it away with him, while the fellow still lay snoring in his sleep.

At this point Shahrazād saw the approach of morning and discreetly fell silent.

But when the four-hundred-and-nineteenth night had come

SHE SAID:
After this the prince went forward into the palace and came to a second door, covered by a velvet curtain. Passing through that, he

found himself in a hall of marvels, where was a great bed of the whitest ivory, patterned with pearls, rubies and hyacinths, and guarded by four young girls who slept upon the ground. He went up to the bed to see who might be in it, and beheld a young girl lying upon it with her abundant hair for only covering. She was so fair that one would have taken her, not for the moon rising on the eastern rim, but for a second and more marvellous moon come fresh from the hands of God. Her brow was a white rose, her cheeks were two anemones blushing lightly, enriched on either hand by a delicate spot of beauty.

Seeing such grace and charm and elegance, Kamar al-Akmār well-nigh fell swooning or dead; when he might a little master his emotion, he went up, trembling and shaking with desirous pleasure, and kissed the sleeping girl upon the right cheek.

The child woke with a start at the feel of this kiss and, opening wide eyes, saw the prince standing beside her pillow. 'Who are you and whence do you come?' she cried. 'I am your slave and the lover of your eyes,' he answered. Then said she: 'Who led you here?' and he replied: 'Allāh, Fate, and my good fortune.'

Princess Shams al-Nahār, for such was her name, instead of showing fear, said to the young man: 'Are you by chance the King's son of Hind who yesterday asked me in marriage and whom my father would not accept as a son-in-law on account of his ugliness? If you are he, as Allāh lives, you are far from ugly, and your beauty has already subdued me, my lord.' Then, as he stood there as radiant as the shining moon, she drew him to her, and they embraced each other; drunken with beauty and youth, they exchanged a thousand caresses stretched in each other's arms, and said a thousand follies during a thousand games, with a thousand tender or bold speeches in each other's ears.

While they were rejoicing in this way, the handmaidens woke and cried out, seeing the prince with their mistress: 'O lady, who is this young man?' 'I do not know,' she answered. 'I found him at my side when I came out of sleep. I think he must be the youth who yesterday asked my hand in marriage of my father.' But the girls, confounded with emotion, cried out: 'As Allāh lives, this is not the youth who asked for you yesterday, for he was hideous, and this young man is sweetly beautiful and surely of a noble line. The other was not worthy to be your slave.' So saying, the attendants went and woke the eunuch at the door and filled his heart with fear, saying:

'How is it that you, the guardian of the palace and the harīm, let men come into us while we sleep?'

The negro jumped to his feet and would have drawn his sword, but found his scabbard empty. This increased his terror, so that he was trembling all over his body when he lifted the curtain and entered the hall. When he saw the handsome young man on the bed with his mistress, he cried out: 'My lord, are you a man or a Jinnī?' 'Miserable slave and most evilly disposed of black negroes,' answered the prince, 'how dare you confound the sons of the Kings of Persia with Afārīt or Jinn?' So saying, he rose in fury like a wounded lion and seized the sword, exclaiming: 'I am the King's son-in-law. He has married me to his daughter and empowered me to come into her presence.'

'My lord,' answered the eunuch, 'if you are really a man and not a Jinnī, our young mistress is worthy of your beauty and you better deserve her than any other King's son in the world.'

After this the eunuch ran into the presence of the King, uttering loud cries, tearing his garments, and covering his head with dust. Hearing his lamentations, the King exclaimed: 'What calamity is this? Speak quickly and shortly, for you have brought a trembling to my heart.'

At this point Shahrazād saw the approach of morning and discreetly fell silent.

But when the four-hundred-and-twentieth night had come

SHE SAID:

'O King,' answered the negro, 'run to the help of your daughter, for a Jinnī in the body of a King's son is with her and has taken possession of her! Run! Hurry!'

The King fell into a fury and was on the point of killing the eunuch; then, controlling himself, he cried: 'How did you dare to lose sight of my daughter and let this demon go into her, when I had charged you to watch over her day and night?' After that, with every appearance of madness, the King ran to the princess's apartment, and found the girls pale and trembling by the door. 'What has happened to my daughter?' he cried, and they answered: 'O King, we do not know what happened while we were asleep, but when we woke we found what we took to be the full moon in bed with our mistress, a young man of perfect beauty who was talking with her in a manner both delicate and reassuring. We have never seen any-one like this youth. When we asked him who he was, he told us that he had been married to the princess by the King. More than that we do not know, nor can we say for certain whether he is a man or an Ifrīt. Whichever he may be, we can assure you that he is amiable, well-intentioned, modest, highly-born and quite incapable of the least misconduct; for, when one is so handsome, nothing that one does may be called misconduct.' The King's anger cooled at this assurance; gently and with many precautions he lifted the curtain a little and saw a most charming prince, whose face seemed made of moonlight, lying beside his daughter on the bed and whispering to her.

At this sight his paternal jealousy rose again, together with a mighty fear for the honour of his daughter. Leaping through the curtain, he bounded towards the pair, sword in hand, as furious as a Ghoul. When the prince saw him coming, he asked the girl if this was her father and, when she replied that it was, leapt to his feet, seizing the sword, and made so terrible a war-cry in the King's face that he recoiled abashed. Kamar al-Akmār then made as if to run him through, and the King, realising that he was the weaker, re-sheathed his sword and adopted a conciliatory pose. As the young man was almost upon him, he said, in his most courteous and amiable voice: 'O youth, are you a man or a Jinnī?' 'As Allāh lives,' cried the young man, 'if I did not regard you as my equal and think highly of our daughter's honour, I would already have shed your blood. How dare you confound a prince of the royal line of Persia with Jinn or demons? If we had a mind, it would be sport to us to sweep you from your throne as by an earthquake and to level your glory with the dust!'

The King was filled in equal measure with respect for this young man and fear for himself, so he hastened to answer: 'If you are really a King's son, how did you dare to come uninvited into my palace, take my daughter, and destroy my honour, proclaiming that I, even I, who have killed so many kings and princes because they would have forced me to give up my daughter, had married you to her secretly? . . . And who will save you from my might when I order my slaves to put you to the worst of deaths?'

'In truth,' answered Prince Kamar al-Akmār, 'I am astonished that you should be so short-sighted and heavy-witted. Tell me, where will you find a better suitor for your daughter? Have you ever

seen a bolder young fellow or a richer in every way?' 'Possibly not,'
answered the King, 'but if you marry my daughter, it must be before
the kādī and witnesses; for a secret marriage breeds an ill name.'
'You speak truly,' answered the prince, 'but do you not see that, if
you call your guards to me, both your honour and your kingdom
will be lost by the public exposure? There is nothing left for you to
do, O King, except to listen to what I have to say and to follow my
counsel in this matter.' 'Speak then, for I will hear you a little,' said
the King.

At this point Shahrazād saw the approach of morning and
discreetly fell silent.

But when the four-hundred-and-twenty-first night had come

SHE SAID:

Then said Prince Kamar al-Akmār: 'You have the choice of two
ways: either you must engage with me in single combat and, if you
are beaten, cede your throne to me, or else you must leave me all
night with your daughter and in the morning send against me your
whole force of horse and foot and slaves and . . . but first tell me
how many there are.' 'I have forty thousand warriors,' answered the
King, 'without counting my slaves and my slaves' slaves, who are as
many again.' 'That is well,' returned the prince. 'Draw them up in
battle array against me at dawn, and say to them: "This man wishes
my daughter in marriage and I have made it a condition that he shall
fight against you all and overthrow you. This he means to do."
Then leave me to fight against them; if they kill me, your secret will
be safe; if I put them to flight, you will have found a son-in-law to
do honour to any King.'

The King fell in with this plan, though his mind was all abroad
at so much hardihood and assurance. In his heart of hearts he was
certain that the young man would perish in his insane combat and
that thus the honour of the kingdom would be saved. He sent the
eunuch to find his wazīr and order him to assemble all his troops and
hold them under arms. The eunuch carried this message to the
wazīr, who soon had the King's armies drawn up in battle order,
with the chiefs and notables of the kingdom at their head.

Meanwhile the King stayed to talk with the young prince, both
because he was charmed with the excellence of his conversation, his
beauty and his manners, and also because he did not wish to leave

him any longer alone with his daughter. As soon as dawn appeared, the King returned to his palace and, sitting upon his throne, ordered his slaves to bring forth the finest horse from his stables for the prince, to saddle it magnificently, and deck it with all the honourable ornaments of war. Hearing this order, the prince exclaimed: 'I wish no other horse than the one I came upon last night.' 'As you like,' said the King, and he led the young man on to the polo-ground, where the troops were ranged for battle. While the prince was considering their number and quality, the King turned to them, crying: 'O warriors, this man has come to ask me for my daughter's hand in marriage. I have never seen a more handsome or braver cavalier. He claims that he can put you all to rout with his single arm and that he would think little of you even if you were a hundred thousand times as many. When he charges you, do not scruple to receive him on your points, for that will teach him not to meddle in high matters.' Then to the young man he said: 'Be bold, my son, and let us see your prowess.' 'O King,' answered the youth, 'you do not treat me justly; how can I fight against all these horsemen when I am on foot?' 'I offered you a horse and you refused,' said the King. 'You can still choose one, if you have a mind.' Then said Kamar al-Akmār: 'None of your horses please me; I will only ride the one which brought me to your kingdom.' 'Where is it?' asked the King. 'On top of your palace,' answered the prince. 'On top of my palace?' repeated the astonished Sultān. 'Yes, on the terrace,' replied Kamar al-Akmār. The King looked at him closely, crying: 'Extravagant boy, this is the best proof yet of your folly! How could there be a horse on the terrace? Yet I will send to see.' Then, turning to the chief of his armies, he said: 'Run to the palace and bring me back word of what you see there. Also fetch me anything you find on the terrace.'

The people who were by marvelled at the prince's words and said to each other: 'How could a horse possibly go up the stairs to the terrace? This is the most extraordinary thing we have ever heard!'

Meanwhile the King's messenger came to the palace and mounted to the terrace, where he beheld the finest horse that he had ever seen. Going up to look at it more closely, he found that it was made of ebony and ivory; then he and the soldiers he had brought with him burst out laughing and said one to the other:

At this point Shahrazād saw the approach of morning and discreetly fell silent.

But when the four-hundred-and-twenty-second night had come

SHE SAID:

'As Allāh lives, if this is the horse the young man spoke of, he must be mad. Still it were better to get to the truth of the matter, for there may be more in it than meets the eye. The young man may be well-born and have some real merit.' So saying, they lifted the wooden horse and, carrying it in their arms, set it down before the King. At once a crowd collected round it, admiring the beauty of its proportions and the richness of its decoration. The King turned in surprise to Kamar al-Akmār, saying: 'O youth, is this your horse?' 'It is,' replied the prince, 'and I will show you marvels with it.' 'Mount then!' cried the King, but the prince replied: 'I will not mount until all these people have gone further back.'

The King ordered all who were present to retire a bowshot from the horse. 'Look well, O King!' cried Kamar al-Akmār. 'I shall leap on my horse and charge your troops until they give way to right and left; I shall bring great trembling and fear upon them!' 'Do what you wish,' said the King. 'Above all do not spare them, for they certainly will not spare you.'

Immediately Kamar al-Akmār placed a right hand on the horse's neck and leapt upon its back.

Opposed to him, the armies anxiously waited in close formation. Some said: 'When he charges, we will pick him up on our points and then drop him on our blades.' But others said: 'As Allāh lives, it is a great pity! How can we have the heart to kill so elegant, tender, and handsome a youth?' And yet others said: 'As Allāh lives, we must have been mad to think that we could easily vanquish this young man. He would never have gone into such an adventure if he were not certain of succeeding! Whatever happens, he will have shown a high soul and great courage.'

When Kamar al-Akmār felt himself firm in the saddle, he a little moved the rising peg, while all beheld him; at once the horse began to shake, quiver, pant, paw the ground, jig up and down, leap forward, advance and retire; then, with elastic movements, it curvetted sideways with more fire and elegance than any horse in the stables of kings. Suddenly its flanks expanded with the wind and it darted straight up into the sky more quickly than an arrow, carrying its rider with it.

The King nearly fell to the ground in surprise and rage. He cried to his chief warriors: 'Catch him, catch him, ill-omened ones! He is escaping!' But his wazīrs and lieutenants answered: 'O King, can a man catch a bird on the wing? This is not a man like other men but some magician or an Ifrīt or a Marid of the air! Allāh has delivered you from him, and saved us also! Let us thank the Highest who has granted salvation to you and to the army!'

The King returned, in the height of perplexity, to his palace and told his daughter all that had passed on the polo-ground; hearing that the young prince had disappeared, the girl wept and despaired so bitterly that she fell seriously ill and lay upon her bed a prey to fever and black dreams. The King embraced and soothed her, clasping her to his breast and kissing her between the eyes, while he repeated the details of what had happened. 'My daughter,' he said, 'you should rather thank and glorify Allāh that He has delivered us from this sorcerer, this liar, this lecher, this robber, this pig.' He might have spared his pains, for the princess would neither hear nor be comforted; instead she wept and sighed, saying: 'As Allāh lives, I will neither eat nor drink till He reunites me with my charming lover! Until then I shall remain buried in despair and have no art but weeping.' Seeing that he could not persuade his daughter from her affliction, the King beheld the world darken before his eyes and himself fell into a melancholy. So much for him and the Princess Shams al-Nahār.

At this point Shahrazād saw the approach of morning and discreetly fell silent.

But when the four-hundred-and-twenty-third night had come

SHE SAID:

When Prince Kamar al-Akmār had risen in the air, he turned his horse's head towards his native land and, travelling easily, fell to dreaming of the beauty of the princess and revolving schemes for seeing her again. Although he had taken care to discover the name of the city, which was none other than Sanā, the capital of al-Yaman, his mind could hit upon no easy way of returning to it.

It seemed no time at all, thanks to the great speed of the horse and the intensity of his thoughts, before the prince came to his father's city. He made a great circle about it and then alighted on the terrace of the palace. Leaving the animal, he went down into the building, where the general appearance of grief and room after room strewn with ashes led him to believe that some member of the royal house was dead. He went into the King's private chamber and there found his father, mother and sisters dressed in mourning, with yellow sunken cheeks and eyes laden with tears. His father leapt to his feet on beholding him and, having made certain that it was truly his son who had come back, uttered a great cry and fell into a swoon. When the old man came to his senses, he threw himself into his son's arms and hugged him with transports of excessive joy. His mother and sisters devoured him with their kisses and danced about him, the tears still wet upon their cheeks.

When they were a little calmed, they asked what had happened to him, and he told them the whole of his story from beginning to end; but it would be useless to repeat it in this place. Then cried his father: 'Praise be to Allāh for your safety, cool of my eyes, stone of my heart's fruit!' He gave great feasts of rejoicing to the people for seven whole days, distributing gold to the sound of fifes and cymbals, decorating the public ways, and throwing open the prisons and dungeons with a general pardon to all malefactors. Then, with his son riding by his side, he made procession through every quarter of the city, that the people might rejoice their eyes with a sight of the prince whom they had thought lost.

As soon as these rejoicings were finished, Kamar al-Akmār said to his father: 'What has become of the Persian who gave you the horse?' 'Allāh confound the sage!' answered the King. 'May He remove His blessing from him and curse the hour when my eyes first looked on him, for he was the cause of our separation from you. He lies in a dungeon, the sole prisoner in my kingdom whom I have not pardoned.' At his son's entreaty the King then had the old man delivered from his prison and brought into his presence, where he pardoned him, gave him a robe of honour, and liberally heaped riches upon him. Nothing, however, was said of the princess, for the King was fully determined not to marry her to the Persian. On his side, the sage inwardly raged and bitterly repented his imprudence in letting the prince mount the magic horse; for this, as he understood, had led to the discovery of its secret.

The King could not set his mind at rest about the horse, so he said to his son: 'I think it would be better, my child, if you never went near the wretched animal again, and above all never dreamed of getting on its back; for, as like as not, you do not know half the secrets of it, and it certainly is not safe.'

Kamar al-Akmār repeated to his father what had befallen with the King of Sanā and his daughter, and how he had escaped the resentment of that monarch. 'My son,' answered King Sābūr, 'if it were fated that he should kill you, he would have killed you; but your destined hour had not yet come.'

During this while, the prince never for a moment forgot Shams al-Nahār; through all the feasts and rejoicings with which his father continued to celebrate his return, she was always in his thoughts. One day the King, who was possessed of expert singers and lute players, ordered them to sing fair poems before him to the sound of their instruments. One among them took her lute and, bending over it as a mother over the babe at her breast, sang this song among others:

> Your memory will not be dying
> For all the leagues between us twain,
> For love will live though days be dying,
> Though years be dead, and time be slain;
> So in your love I would be dying
> Or in your love would live again.

When the prince heard these lines, the fire of passion flamed up in his vitals, the embers of desire grew red within him, regret and sadness draped his soul with mourning, and love turned his heart over in his breast. He was not able to resist the feeling which drew him to the princess of Sanā, so he rose from his place and climbed on to the terrace, and there, in spite of his father's advice, he leapt upon the ebony horse and turned the peg. At once his steed rose with him like a bird into the air, making for the high regions of the sky.

On the following morning the King searched for him throughout the palace, and not finding him, went up to the terrace. As soon as he saw that the horse was gone, he bit the fingers of repentance that he had not hewn the invention in pieces, saying to himself: 'As Allāh lives, if my son returns again I will destroy the horse, for only so can my heart be free from alarms.' With that he went down again into the palace and fell a second time to mourning and weeping.

Kamar al-Akmār continued his swift aerial flight and came at last to the city of Sanā. Dismounting on the terrace of the palace, he went silently down the stairs and made towards the chamber of the princess. He again found the eunuch sleeping across the door, and did not scruple to step over his body and tiptoe to the second door. Before raising the curtain, he listened attentively and heard his beloved sobbing bitterly and saying over to herself sad verses, while her women tried to console her.

At this point Shahrazād saw the approach of morning and discreetly fell silent.

But when the four-hundred-and-twenty-fourth night had come

SHE SAID:

'Dear mistress,' they were saying, 'why do you weep for one who certainly does not weep for you?' 'What are you saying, O fools?' she answered. 'Do you think the sweet youth I love and for whom I weep could ever forget me?' Then she wept so long and sorely that she swooned, and the prince felt his heart break in pieces for her, his gall bladder like to burst inside his liver. Without delay he lifted the curtain and entered the room, where he found the young girl lying in her bed, covered only with her long hair and her fan of white feathers. As she took no note of his coming, he went up to her and gently caressed her; at once she opened her eyes and saw him standing beside her, bent with an anxious air of questioning, and heard him murmur: 'Why these tears?' Immediately new life came to her; she rose and threw herself all against him, winding her arms about his neck and covering his face with kisses. 'For love of you and because you were gone from me, O light of my eyes!' she said. 'And I,' he answered, 'have lived ever in desolation because of you.' 'I mourned for your absence,' she whispered. 'If you had stayed longer you would have found me dead.' 'Mistress,' he said, 'what think you of my treatment at your father's hands? As Allāh lives, if it had not been for you, seduction of the earth and moon, temptation of heaven and hell, I would have cut his throat and made him a dead example for all living things; but as I love you, I love him also.' 'How could you find it in your heart to leave me?' she asked. 'Did you think that there could be any sweetness in my life without you?' 'Since you love me,' he said, 'will you hear me and follow my advice?' 'You have only to speak,' she answered, 'and I will obey you.' Then said he: 'First let food and drink be brought, for I am hungry and thirsty; after that we will talk.'

The princess ordered her maidens to bring meat and drink, and the two ate and drank together, exchanging sweet confidence until the night was nearly spent. When day threatened, Kamar al-Akmār rose to take leave of the girl before the eunuch should wake; but Shams al-Nahār asked him where he was going. 'To my father's house,' he answered, 'but I swear I will return to see you once every week.' At this she burst into sobbing, and cried: 'I beg you, in Allah's name, to take me with you and carry me where you will, rather than make me taste again the bitter apple of this separation!' 'Are you really willing to come with me?' he asked joyfully, and she answered: 'Yes.' 'Rise then and let us be off!' he cried, helping her to her feet. The princess opened a chest, filled with splendid robes and riches of adornment, and put upon herself all the most precious of the things she owned: collars, rings, bracelets, and a diversity of trinkets set with expensive gems. Then she went out with her beloved, none of her maidens daring to hinder her.

Kamar al-Akmār guided her to the terrace and, mounting his horse, took her up behind him, begging her to hold to him tightly. When he had fastened her to himself with strong swathings, he turned the peg and the horse rose with them into the air.

Seeing this ascent, the maidens uttered piercing cries which brought the King and Queen out of their sleep and on to the terrace, where they were in time to see the magic horse rising on its airy journey with the prince and princess. In his desolation the King found strength to cry to the youth, as he mounted higher and higher: 'O King's son, I conjure you to have compassion on myself and this old woman who is my Queen. Do not take our daughter away from us!' The prince did not answer, but the thought came suddenly to him that the young girl might perhaps regret to leave her father and mother in this way. Therefore he said to her: 'Tell me, O splendour, O ravishment of this age and of my eyes, do you wish me to give you back to your father and mother?'

At this point Shahrazād saw the approach of morning and discreetly fell silent.

But when the four-hundred-and-twenty-fifth night had come

SHE SAID:
'As Allah lives, my master,' she answered, 'I only wish to be with you everywhere and in everything; for my love makes me forget all else, even my father and mother.'

The prince rejoiced at this answer and sent his horse flying at its highest speed, which did not trouble the girl at all. Soon they had covered half their journey, and therefore came to earth for a short rest in a rich meadow watered by running streams. There they ate, drank and rested, and in a short while rose again on the magic horse and sped towards the capital of King Sābūr. By morning they came safely within sight of the city, much to the prince's delight, who rejoiced beforehand at the thought of showing the princess his great possessions and proving to her the power and glory of his father, whom he could not but esteem to be richer and greater than the King of Sanā. He brought the ebony horse to earth in the middle of a fair garden outside the city walls, where the King was accustomed to come to take the air, and led the princess into a domed summer pavilion which the King had built and furnished for himself. 'I will leave you here for a short while and go to my father with an announcement of our coming,' said the prince. 'I have left the ebony horse at the door and I charge you to watch over it while I am away. Soon I will send you a messenger, to bring you to your own palace, which I shall instantly have prepared for you.' The girl understood from this that it was intended for her to enter the city with all the honours and attentions due to her rank, and her heart was beating high with pleasure when she bade the prince adieu.

King Sābūr well-nigh died of joy when he saw the coming of his son: first he embraced him and then scolded him, with tears in his eyes, for having led them all down to the doors of the tomb by his departure. 'Guess whom I have brought with me,' said Kamar al-Akmār, and when his father cried: 'As Allāh lives, I cannot guess!' he continued: 'I have brought the daughter of the King of Sanā, the most accomplished girl in Persia and Arabia. I have left her in our garden outside the city and have come forward to tell you, that you may prepare a grand procession to welcome her and give her a high idea of your power and greatness.' 'As it is to please you, I will do the thing gladly and richly, my son,' answered the King, and at once ordered the city to be decorated and the streets gaily ornamented for her coming. He arranged a procession of unexampled grandeur and, placing himself at the head of his brightly-armoured cavaliers, went out to meet Shams al-Nahār, with banners flying, fifes playing, and drums beating, followed by a close mass of foot soldiers, citizens, women and children.

Prince Kamar al-Akmār opened up the coffers of his treasure and took from them his fairest jewels and greatest marvels, such as the sons of Kings use to display their splendour. He prepared for his bride a vast canopy of red, green and yellow brocade, beneath which was raised a gold throne starry with diamonds. Under the dome of gilded silks which shadowed the throne, he ranged young Indian, Greek and Abyssinian slaves, some seated, some standing, and had four other white slaves to walk by the throne, bearing great fans of rare feathers. The canopy was carried on the shoulders of negroes, naked to the waist, in the train of the King's procession and moved on its way towards the garden through a dense press of people and women shrilling for joy.

Kamar al-Akmār could not stomach the delay of following the procession on foot, so, throwing himself on the back of one of his father's swiftest horses, he took a short cut and came in a minute or so to the pavilion where he had left the princess. To his horror he discovered that both she and the ebony horse had disappeared. In his despair he beat his face, tore his clothes, and ran like a madman through the gardens, crying and calling on his mistress.

When he became a little calmer and reason was returning to his mind, he said to himself: 'How could she have known the secret mechanism of the horse when I have told her nothing of it? Indeed it must be the Persian sage who has come upon her by accident and carried her off out of revenge.'

At this point Shahrazād saw the approach of morning and discreetly fell silent.

But when the four-hundred-and-twenty-sixth night had come

SHE SAID:

He ran to the guardians of the garden, saying: 'Has anyone passed this way? Tell me the truth or your heads shall answer for it!' Terrified by his threat, the guardians answered with one voice: 'As Allāh lives, we have seen no one enter the garden except the Persian sage who came here to cull simples. He has not yet come out.' When he knew for certain that it was the Persian who had stolen his beloved, the prince went back in grief and perplexity to meet the procession and, going up to his father, told him what had happened. 'Take your troops and return with them to the palace,' he said. 'I will never come back until I have got to the bottom of this black business.' The King wept at his son's determination and said, beating his breast: 'My child, have pity on me. Master your anger and grief, and return with me. Whatever King's daughter you desire,

I will give you at once in marriage.' Kamar al-Akmār paid no attention to his father's words, but, bidding him brief adieu, galloped off
on his horse, while the King returned weeping and groaning to the
city. The joy of all his house was turned to sadness, to torture and
consternation. So much for them.

As Destiny had decreed beforehand, the Persian sorcerer, when
he came that day to the garden to pluck simples and aromatic herbs,
smelt a delicious odour of musk and other admirable perfumes.
Putting his nose to the wind, he guided himself towards the sweet
savour, which was none other than the charming scent of the
princess which filled all the garden as with balm. The old man's
acute sense of smell led him in almost a straight line to the pavilion,
at the door of which he found the magic horse, the work of his
hands. It would be impossible to tell the joy which filled his heart
when he knew for certain that he had recovered his masterpiece,
whose loss had taken away his appetite for food and drink and sleep.
Finding the mechanism intact and in good working order, he was
about to leap on the horse's back and fly away, when it occurred to
him to find out whom the prince had brought with him and left in
charge of the animal. He stepped into the pavilion and saw what he
took to be the rising sun in a quiet sky; this was the princess, lying
at ease upon a couch. As soon as he beheld her, he realised that she
must be of noble birth and that the prince had only left her in the
pavilion while he went to prepare a splendid welcome for her.
Therefore he came forward and kissed the earth between her hands,
while she slowly raised her eyes and then quickly shut them, to
escape the sight of so much horrible ugliness. 'Who are you?' she
asked, and he answered: 'Mistress, I am the messenger sent by
Prince Kamar al-Akmār to lead you to another pavilion, finer than
this and nearer to the city. The Queen, my mistress, the prince's
mother, is a little unwell to-day and she therefore wishes you to be
nearer to her, that she may be the first to welcome you, but without
too much fatigue to herself.' 'But where is the prince?' asked Shams
al-Nahār. 'He is with the King in the city,' answered the Persian,
'soon he will come to meet you with a grand procession.' 'Tell me,'
she said, 'could not the prince find some messenger a trifle less ugly
than yourself?' Although he was deeply mortified at this question,
the old man smiled with all the wrinkles of his yellow face, and
answered: 'As Allāh lives, my mistress, there is no more hideous
mamlūk in the palace than myself; but the abominable plainness of

my face must not lead you astray as to my value. One day you will put my capacity to the proof as the prince has done, and then you will praise me. I think the prince chose me as his messenger because of this very hideousness of mine, so that he might have no cause for jealousy; for, believe me, the palace lacks not mamlūks nor young slaves nor handsome negroes nor enticing eunuchs. Thanks be to Allāh, there is no numbering them, and each is more seductive than the others.'

At this point Shahrazād saw the approach of morning and discreetly fell silent.

But when the four-hundred-and-twenty-seventh night had come

SHE SAID:

These words persuaded the princess, so that she rose and gave her hand to the old wizard, saying: 'My father, what have you brought to carry me?' 'Mistress,' he replied, 'you shall mount the horse on which you came.' 'Oh, I could never ride on it alone,' she cried, and the sage smiled for he knew that he had her in his power. 'I will ride with you!' he exclaimed and, leaping into the saddle, took up the girl behind him. When he had securely fastened her, all unsuspecting, to his waist, he turned the peg, and the horse filled its belly with wind and began to leap to and fro like the waves of the sea. Soon it rose like a bird and, in a moment, the city and the gardens were left far behind.

'What are you doing?' cried the girl. 'Why do you not obey your master's orders?' 'My master? Who is my master?' he asked. 'The King's son!' she cried, but, when he demanded of her what King, she could only answer: 'I do not know.' The Persian burst out laughing and said: 'If you are talking of young Kamar al-Akmār, whom may Allāh confound, it is a poor lad, a stupid lubber.' 'Woe upon you, beard of ill omen!' she cried. 'How dare you speak so ill of your master?' 'I tell you, the youth is not my master! Do you know who I am?' retorted the sorcerer. 'I know nothing of you except what you have told me yourself,' answered the princess. Then said he with a smile: 'All that I told you was but a net for the feet of you and the prince. That young blackguard stole my horse from me, the work of my hands, so that I wept and burnt my heart for it. Now I have become master again of my own, and it is his turn to weep and burn the heart. Pluck up your courage, dry and refresh your eyes, for I shall be a greater profit to you than that young idiot. I am generous, powerful and rich; my servants and slaves will obey you as they obey me; I will dress and jewel you beyond kings and satisfy your least desire before you have spoken it.'

Shams al-Nahār beat her face and sobbed. 'O my torture!' she cried. 'I shall lose my beloved, as I have lost my father and mother!' Her tears fell bitterly, because of her evil state, while the Persian headed his horse towards the land of Rūm. After a journey for weary hours at the speed of light, he brought the horse to earth in a green meadow of that country, bright with trees and diversified with water-courses.

Now this meadow lay near the city over which ruled a very powerful King, and on that same day the King had come forth to breathe the country air and to walk there. Seeing the old man with a horse and a young girl beside him, he sent his slaves, who quickly threw themselves upon the Persian and brought him, with his two possessions, into the presence of the King.

The Sultān was astonished at the old man's disgusting ugliness and at the ravishing beauty of the girl. 'O mistress, what sort of a cruel family is yours to have married you to so old and so hideous a man?' he asked. 'She is my cousin and my wife,' the Persian hastened to answer, but the princess gave him the lie, saying: 'O King, as Allāh lives I hardly know this evil-looking ancient; so far from being my husband, he is a wicked sorcerer who has carried me off by fraud and force.'

When he heard this, the King of Rūm ordered his slaves to beat the old man, and they obeyed so heartily that he nearly died under their blows. Then the King had him taken to the city and thrown into a dungeon, while he brought the girl and the ebony horse, the qualities of which he was far from suspecting, to his own palace. So much for the Persian and the princess.

Prince Kamar al-Akmār dressed himself in travelling clothes and, taking a provision of food and money, set out to search for the princess with a very heavy heart. As he passed through land after land and city after city, he asked news of an ebony horse, so that those he questioned were astonished by what he said and considered him altogether extravagant.

At this point Shahrazād saw the approach of morning and discreetly fell silent.

But when the four-hundred-and-twenty-eighth night had come

SHE SAID:

For weary months he went on his way, searching and questioning more and more diligently, without hearing any news of those he sought. He came to the city of Sanā, where ruled the father of Shams al-Nahār, but none there could give him news of the princess. Indeed the people could only add to his despair by telling of the sorry state into which their King had fallen. He continued his journey, making by chance towards the land of Rūm, and asking of every wayfarer and at every halt if anything had been seen of a princess and an ebony horse.

One day he stopped at a khān where a circle of merchants were talking with each other; as he sat down beside them, he heard one of them say: 'My friends, I recently came across a prodigy, the like of which you have never heard.' When the others asked him what that might be, the man continued: 'I took my goods to such and such a city and heard the inhabitants talking of a strange thing. It appears that the King of that place had gone out hunting and had found a very disgusting old man in his territory, standing beside a girl of incomparable beauty and a horse made entirely of ebony and ivory.' The merchant went on to tell all that had happened in that city, but it would be useless to repeat it here.

Kamar al-Akmār did not doubt for a moment that he had found what he was seeking; therefore, after having made himself acquainted with the name and direction of the city, he made all speed towards it. When he would have entered the gates, the guards took him in custody in order to lead him before their King, that he might be questioned according to the custom of the country. As it was already late, the guards postponed the youth's introduction until the following morning and, in the meanwhile, led him to prison, that he might spend the night there. But, when the gaolers found how handsome and well-mannered he was, they could not find it in their hearts to lock him up; instead they begged him to sit among them and share their repast. They began to talk among themselves after they had eaten, and one of them said to the prince: 'From what country do you come, O youth?' 'I come from Persia,' he answered, and all the gaolers burst out laughing. Said one of them: 'O Persian, I wonder if you are as great a liar as your countryman, who is shut up in the dungeon?' Said another: 'In truth I have seen many peoples and heard their talk and the tales they tell, but I have never met such an extravagant old fool as the one we have here!' 'As Allāh lives,' added another, 'I have never seen anyone so disgustingly plain in all my life!' 'What are his lies?' asked the prince, and they answered: 'He pretends that he is a sage and an illustrious doctor. Our King found him when he was out hunting, standing beside a young girl and a marvellous horse of ebony and ivory. The King was much taken with the girl's beauty and would have married her, if she had not suddenly gone mad. Had the old man been the great doctor he claims to be, it would have been worth his while to cure her, for the King has left no stone unturned to make her well, and has in vain spent immense sums of money on physicians and astrologers. The ebony horse is shut in among the King's treasure, and the ugly old man is here in prison, where he groans and moans all night so that we cannot sleep.'

'At last I am in a fair way,' said Kamar al-Akmār to himself. 'I must form some plan.' When the hour for sleep arrived, the gaolers led him into the interior of the prison and locked the door upon him. At once he heard the sage weeping and crying in the Persian tongue: 'Alas, alas, that I did not hatch a better scheme! Now I am lost, without having once satisfied myself upon the girl. Alas, alas, for my ambition and lack of judgment!' Kamar al-Akmār spoke to him in Persian, saying: 'Whence these tears and lamentations? Do you think that you are the only unfortunate in the world?' Encouraged by these words, the old man entered into conversation and, without recognising him in the least, poured into the prince's ears the story of his failure. The two passed the night together in speech, as if they had been friends.

At this point Shahrazād saw the approach of morning and discreetly fell silent.

But when the four-hundred-and-twenty-ninth night had come

SHE SAID:

Next morning the gaolers took Kamar al-Akmār from his prison and led him before the King, saying: 'This young man came to the city late last evening, so that we were not then able to bring him into the King's presence to be questioned.' Then said the King: 'Whence come you? What is your name? What is your trade? And why have you visited my kingdom?' 'My name is Harjah, in the

Persian tongue,' answered the prince. 'Persia is my country, and my profession is that of a wise doctor, especially skilled in curing those who are mad or deranged. I journey through lands and cities to exercise my art and to add to the knowledge which I have already. I practise without the ordinary accoutrement of astrologers and sages. I do not enlarge my turban or increase the number of its folds, I do not prolong my sleeves, I do not carry a great weight of books under my arm, I do not stain my lids with black kohl, I do not carry round my neck a chaplet of a thousand beads; I cure without mysterious mutterings, I do not blow in my patients' faces or bite the lobes of their ears. Such am I, O King.'

'O excellent doctor,' exclaimed the joyful monarch, 'you come when we have most need of your services!' He told the prince the story of the young girl's sufferings, and added: 'If you can cure her of the madness into which the evil Jinn have thrown her, you have but to ask of me and all your desires shall be granted.' 'Allāh rain graces and favours on the King!' answered Kamar al-Akmār. 'First you must tell me all the details you have noticed of this madness, with the time of its endurance and every particular which you can remember of the girl, the old Persian, and the ebony horse.' At once the King told him the whole story from beginning to end, adding: 'As for the old man, I have thrown him into a dungeon.' 'And the horse?' asked the prince. 'It is carefully guarded in one of my pavilions,' answered the King. Then said Kamar al-Akmār to himself: 'Before everything I must see the horse again. If I find it intact, my object is gained; but if anything has gone wrong with the mechanism, I must think of some other way to save my beloved.' Turning to the King, he said aloud: 'I must first see the horse, for it is likely that, by examining it, I may find something which will help me with the cure.' 'Certainly,' said the King, and at once led Kamar al-Akmār to the place where the horse had been deposited. The prince examined it carefully, looking all round, and found to his great joy that it was in working order. 'Allāh favour and exalt the King!' he cried. 'I am now ready to see the girl and diagnose her trouble. I hope, under Allāh's favour, to cure her by my skill, working in co-operation with this wooden horse.' So saying, he recommended the guards to give particular attention to their charge and followed the King to the princess's apartment.

He found her twisting her hands and beating her breasts and tearing her clothes to ribbons as was her custom. He saw at once that her madness was only feigned and that neither man nor spirit had practised upon her reason. Also he understood that she had had recourse to this trick to keep all folk away from her.

Kamar al-Akmār went towards her, saying: 'Enchantress of the three world, may all trouble and torment sit far off from you!' When he addressed her, she looked at him and, in the great joy of her recognition, uttered a loud cry and fainted away. The King took this seizure to be the result of her fear of the doctor, but Kamar al-Akmār, having brought her to herself, leaned over her, saying in a whisper: 'O Shams al-Nahār, O black of my eye, O stone of my heart's fruit, have a care for your life and mine! Be bold and patient for a little longer; our case requires infinite precaution and great prudence if we would win from the hands of this tyrannical King. First I am going to confirm his belief that you are possessed by a Jinnī and that your madness comes from that; then I will assure him that my occult virtue can instantly cure you. This you must prove by talking calmly to him.' 'I hear and I obey!' answered the princess.

The young prince went up to the King, who stood at the further end of the chamber, and said to him, with a hopeful face: 'O auspicious King, thanks to the excellent Destiny which follows you, I can both diagnose and cure this folly; indeed I have done so already. Go up to the girl and speak with her kindly; promise her all you have in your mind to promise, and things shall go as you wish.' Greatly marvelling, the King went up to Shams al-Nahār, who at once rose and kissed the earth between his hands, wishing him welcome and saying: 'Your servant is confused by the honour of this visit.'

At this point Shahrazād saw the approach of morning and discreetly fell silent.

But when the four-hundred-and-thirtieth night had come

SHE SAID:

Seeing so great a change in her, the King nearly swooned for joy; he ordered his servants, his women slaves and his eunuchs to put themselves at her disposition, to lead her to the hammām and to prepare rich robes and ornaments for her. The women bowed before her, and she returned their salute sweetly and gently. Then they habited her in royal robes, hung a collar of diamonds about her neck and led her to the hammām, where they bathed and served her until she appeared like a moon of the fourteenth night.

With heart and soul at ease, the King said to the young prince: 'O sage, O learned doctor, O skilled philosopher, our present great happiness is due entirely to your merit. May Allāh increase His blessings upon your healing breath!' 'O King,' answered Kamar al-Akmār, 'to put a crown upon the cure it is necessary for you to go out with all your train of soldiers and courtiers to the place where you found the girl, taking with you my patient and the ebony horse; for the horse is no other than a Jinnī who has possessed the girl and made her mad. I will make the necessary exorcisms in that place, for otherwise the Jinnī will re-enter into possession of her at the beginning of each month and all the cure will be to do again. Once I have made myself his master, I will prison and kill him.' 'I will certainly do as you say!' cried the King of Rūm, and at once, accompanied by the prince and the young girl and all his following, he left the city for the meadow.

When all had arrived, Kamar al-Akmār ordered the girl to be mounted upon the ebony horse and both to be placed far enough off not to be clearly seen by the King and his people. As soon as this had been carried out to his satisfaction, he said: 'Now, with the permission and goodwill of the King, I shall begin my fumigation and conjuring, so that I may catch this enemy of life and render him powerless to do further evil. I will myself mount upon the ebony-seeming horse and place the girl behind me; soon you will see the animal tremble and move and struggle; then it will gallop towards you and stop between your hands. That will be a proof that we have him altogether in our power. After that you can do as you wish with the girl.'

Leaving the King of Rūm in joyful anticipation, Kamar al-Akmār mounted the horse and fastened the princess securely behind him. Under the gaze of all eyes, he turned the peg and the horse rose straight up into the air and disappeared.

For a long time the King had no suspicion, but stayed with his people in the meadow, waiting half the day for the return of the two. As they did not come back, he decided to wait in his own palace; when hours had passed there without result, he called to mind the ugly old man whom he had imprisoned. At once he had him brought into his presence, and cried: 'O traitor, ape's bottom, how dared you hide from me the mystery of that spell-bound horse and its possession by a Jinnī? Now, alas, it has flown up into the air with the doctor who cured the girl of her madness and the girl herself. Who knows what will happen to them? I hold you responsible for the jewels and valuable treasure with which I ornamented the child when she came from the hammām; therefore your head must part from your body even now.' At a sign from the King the executioner advanced and, with a single turn of his wrist, made two Persians out of one Persian. So much for the people in Rūm.

Prince Kamar al-Akmār and Princess Shams al-Nahār made their swift flight in all tranquillity and came safely to the capital of King Sābūr. This time they would have none of the pavilion in the garden, but came to rest on the terrace of the palace. The prince bestowed his beloved in a sure place and ran to tell his father and mother of the safe return. Going into the chamber where the King, the Queen, and the three princesses remained plunged in despairing tears, he threw himself into their arms and wished them peace. At once the heavy weights of affliction fell from their hearts, and they rejoiced.

To celebrate the return of his prince and the coming of the daughter of the King of Sanā, Sābūr gave long feasts to all the people of his city, and the rejoicing lasted for a whole month. Kamar al-Akmār entered into the marriage-chamber and joyed with the young girl during long nights of blessedness.

King Sābūr assured the future tranquillity of his heart by breaking the ebony horse in pieces and destroying its mechanism with his own hands.

At this point Shahrazād saw the approach of morning and discreetly fell silent.

But when the four-hundred-and-thirty-second night had come

SHE SAID:

Kamar al-Akmār wrote a letter to the King of Sanā, his father-in-law, in which he told him the whole story of his adventures and announced the marriage and perfect happiness of the two concerned in them. The messenger who took this letter was accompanied by slaves bearing magnificent presents of rarity and price. When the King of Sanā in al-Yaman had read the letter, he rejoiced exceedingly and accepted the gifts; also, by the same messenger, he sent back valuable presents to his son-in-law. This relenting especially pleased the handsome prince, for he had been sad to think that the old King might disapprove of his conduct. He made it a rule to send a fresh letter and further presents every year, until the King of Sanā died. His own father, King Sābūr, passed in his turn to the mercy of Allāh, and Kamar al-Akmār began his reign by marrying his youngest and favourite sister to the new King of al-Yaman.

King Kamar al-Akmār governed wisely and justly, and by these means gained supremacy not only over far lands, but over the hearts of the people who dwelt in them. He and his wife Shams al-Nahār lived the most tranquil and delightful of lives together, until there came to them the Destroyer of sweetness, the Separator of friends, the Plunderer of palace and cot, the Builder of tombs, and the Enricher of graveyards.

Now glory to the Only Living, Who does not die and Who holds in His hands the dominion of the Visible and Invisible world!

When Shahrazād, the wazīr's daughter, had finished this story, she fell silent. Then said King Shahryār: 'This is a prodigious tale, Shahrazād. I would give a great deal to understand the extra-ordinary mechanism of that ebony horse.' 'Alas, it was destroyed,' said Shahrazād. 'As Allāh lives, my soul is tormented to think of it!' exclaimed Shahryār, and Shahrazād answered: 'Then I am ready, O auspicious King, if you will allow me, to calm the trouble of your mind with the most entertaining tale I know, in which you shall hear of Delilah-the-Wily and her daughter Zainab-the-Cheat.' 'As Allāh lives,' cried King Shahryār, 'you may tell me that tale, for I do not know it! When it is finished, I will decide about your head.'

So Shahrazād told:

The Tale of the Shifts of Delilah-the-Wily and her Daughter Zainab-the-Cheat, with Ahmad-the-Moth, Hasan-the-Pest, and Alī Quicksilver

IT is related, O auspicious King, that there was in Baghdād, during the reign of the Khalīfah Hārūn al-Rashīd, a man called Ahmad-the-Moth and another known as Hasan-the-Pest. Both were so famous for their prodigious mastery in theft and fraud that the

Khalīfah, who could draw advantage from every sort of talent, called them to him and appointed them the chiefs of his police. He gave each a robe of honour, a salary of a thousand golden dīnārs every month, and a guard of forty horsemen, at the same time putting the safety of the city on land in charge of Ahmad-the-Moth and intrusting its safety by water to Hasan-the-Pest. The two walked ever at the Khalīfah's side, one on the right hand and the other on the left.

On the day of their nomination they went forth with the amīr Khālid, walī of Baghdād, and rode in procession, followed by their forty guards and preceded by a herald who cried this decree of the Khalīfah: 'By order of the King, O all you people of Baghdād! Know that the chief of police upon our right hand is Ahmad-the-Moth and the chief of police upon our left hand is Hasan-the-Pest. See to it that your obedience and respect are ever at their call!'

At that time there lived in Baghdād a redoubtable old woman called Delilah, and known commonly as Delilah-the-Wily. She had two daughters, one married and the mother of a little piece named Mahmūd Miscarriage, the other unmarried and famous under the name of Zainab-the-Cheat. Old Delilah's husband had been a great man in his time, the director of carrier-pigeons for the whole empire, who, for his important services, was dearer to the Khalīfah than his own children. He had had honours and precedence, with a monthly wage of a thousand dīnārs; but now he was dead and forgotten, and the old woman was left upon the world with her two daughters. Delilah had grown old in the arts of theft and trickery, and in clever devices; she could have overreached a snake and left it bare, or taught the Devil useful lessons in deceit.

On the day when the two new chiefs of police were invested with their office, young Zainab heard the herald, and said to her mother: 'You remember that fellow Ahmud-the-Moth, who came here to Baghdād as an outlaw from Egypt? Well, he has shown such high criminal expedients since he arrived that his fame has gone abroad even to the ears of the Khalīfah, and Hārūn al-Rashīd has made him chief of police on his right hand. The other chief of police is Hasan-the-Pest, that bald and scabby man. Each has a cloth laid day and night in the palace, a bodyguard, a monthly thousand dīnārs, and every sort of honour; while we stay unemployed and forgotten in our own house, without any caring what comes of us.' 'As Allāh lives, my daughter, that is so,' said old Delilah with a shake of her head. 'Mother,' continued Zainab, 'I beg you rise up now and find some really evil device or notable fraud which will make us famous and cause the Khalīfah to give us back the appointments and prerogatives of our father.'

At this point Shahrazād saw the approach of morning and discreetly fell silent.

But when the four-hundred-and-thirty-third night had come

SHE SAID:

'By the life of my head,' answered Delilah, 'I promise you, my dear, that I will play such first-class tricks in Baghdād that those of both Ahmad-the-Moth and Hasan-the-Pest will be forgotten!' To make good her boast, she at once set about the following preparations: she covered her face with a veil, dressed herself in a Sūfī's mantle, the sleeves of which swept the ground, and circled her waist with a large linen girdle; then she filled a ewer to the neck with water, placed three dīnārs in the mouth of it and pressed down a plug of palm fibre on top; she put about her shoulders and breast several chaplets of beads, as heavy as a load of firewood, and took in her hand the flag of a Sūfī beggar, made with strips of red, yellow and green material. Thus disguised, she went out of the house, crying: 'Allāh, Allāh!' in a loud voice and praying with her tongue, while her heart galloped along the road of devils and her mind revolved notable and perverse expedients.

She passed through several parts of the city until she came to a blind-alley, paved with marble and carefully swept and watered, at the foot of which rose a great door, corniced with alabaster and guarded by a well-dressed Moorish slave. This door was made of sandalwood ornamented with bronze rings and having locks of silver, as befitted the owner of the house, who was none other than the chief of the Khalīfah's guard, a man rich, respected, and heavily paid for his duties. This man, who was both violent and ill-mannered, was known as Mustafā the Street Scourge, because with him blows came first and words second. He had married a delightful girl and had sworn to her, out of his great love, on the night of the first penetration, never to take a second wife while she was alive and never to sleep away from home. At about this time, however, Mustafā the Street Scourge had noticed that each amīr who went with him to the dīwān had one or more sons; also, on the day of which I am speaking, he had looked in the hammām mirror and seen that the white hairs in his beard greatly outnumbered the black. Therefore he asked himself: 'Shall He who has taken away my father not send me a son?' When he went again into his wife's presence, he sat down on the couch in a very bad humour, without giving her a single look or word, but as soon as she approached and wished him a good evening, he exclaimed: 'Get out of my sight! The day I saw you first I saw nothing good.' 'How is that?' she asked, and he went on: 'The night I penetrated, you made me swear not to take another wife; to-day at the diwān I saw each amīr bringing with him one son or two, and the thought of death came to me. My heart is sore that I have not been given a son or even a daughter; for he who leaves no posterity, leaves no name. That is why I am angry, O barren fool, O stony valley who wasted all my seed!' The girl blushed as she retorted: 'As Allāh lives, it hardly becomes you to talk; the thing is not my fault: I have worn out whole mortars in pounding spices, triturating herbs, and powdering roots against sterility. I tell you the lack is with you; you are a sapless mule with a flat nose; your eggs are filled with water and dead seeds.' 'Very well,' he answered, 'when I return, I will marry another wife.' 'My fate is in the hands of Allāh!' she cried after him as he left the house; but she would have recalled her hardy words as soon as he had departed; and he, on his side, regretted their quarrel as soon as he was in the street. Now you know something of the owner of the house in the blind-alley.

When Delilah-the-Wily had come under the walls of the house, she saw the amīr's young wife sitting at her window, seeming a new-married bride because of the great treasure of jewels which she wore, and shining like a dome of crystal in her white expensive clothes. 'O Delilah,' said the old woman to herself, 'now is the time to open the sack of your inventions. Let us see if you cannot entice this girl from the house and strip her of all those jewels and lovely clothes.' Upon this thought she halted under the window and began to call on the name of Allāh in a loud voice, saying: 'Allāh! Allāh! and you, O walīs, friends of God, make clear my path!' As soon as they saw this holy old woman, dressed as a mendicant Sūfī, and heard her invocations, all the women of that quarter ran to kiss the skirts of her mantle and to demand a blessing. 'Perhaps,' thought the amīr's wife, 'Allāh will send me His grace through this holy mother.' She called her servant to her and said with shining eyes: 'Go down to our doorkeeper, Abū Alī, and kiss his hands, saying: "My mistress Khātūn begs you to allow the holy woman to come up to her, that we may obtain the blessing of Allāh." '

The servant ran down and kissed the porter's hands, saying: 'O Abū Alī, my mistress Kātūn begs you to allow the holy woman to come up to her, that we may obtain the blessing of Allāh. It is likely that all of us will receive the benefit of her benediction.' The porter went up to the old woman and would have kissed her hands, but she started back, exclaiming: 'Away, away! You say your prayers without ablution, as do all servants, and your impure touch would make my cleanliness of no avail. I pray that Allāh may deliver you from this slavery, O Abū Alī, the doorkeeper, for you are in the good graces of His saints.' This wish touched Abū Alī to the heart, for there was three months' pay owing to him from the terrible amīr, Mustafā the Street Scourge, and his mind misdoubted him about the payment. 'O mother,' said he, 'let me drink a little from your ewer, that your blessing may flow with the water.' She took the ewer from her shoulder and shook it in the air, so that the plug of palm fibre fell out and the three golden dīnārs rolled on the ground, as if they had been cast from Heaven. The porter hastened to pick them up, saying to himself: 'Glory be to Allāh! This old beggar is a saint of saints and has all the hidden treasures of God at her disposition. It has been revealed to her that I have wages owing to me and am hard pressed for money; therefore, by her holiness, she has called these three dīnārs from the hollow air.' Stretching out the coins to the old woman, he said aloud: 'Take these three dīnārs, good aunt, for perhaps they fell out of your ewer.' 'What have I to do with money?' she answered. 'I do not occupy myself with the things of this world. Keep the coins, for they will better your circumstance and replace what your master owes you.' 'Glory be to Allāh for His help!' said the porter, raising his arms on high. 'This is nothing less than revelation!'

As soon as this scene was over, the slave girl kissed Delilah's hand and led her into the presence of her mistress.

The old woman was astounded by the beauty of her hostess, and indeed the child looked like a naked treasure whose guardian seal had been loosed to make her visible.

At this point Shahrazād saw the approach of morning and discreetly fell silent.

But when the four-hundred-and-thirty-fourth night had come

SHE SAID:

The beautiful Khātūn threw herself at the old woman's feet and kissed her hands. 'My child,' said Delilah, 'I came because Allāh inspired me with the thought that you had need of my counsels.' Khātūn at once brought food, according to the hospitality which is usually given to holy beggars; but the old woman refused to eat, saying: 'I have no gusto for any but the meats of Paradise; therefore I fast always, except on five days in the year. Now, my child, I see that you are in trouble and am very anxious that you should tell me about it.' 'Good mother,' answered the girl, 'on the day of my penetration I made my husband swear never to take a second wife; but now he sees the sons of others and, wishing for one himself, has called me barren. I answered that he was a sapless mule, and he went out in anger, swearing to marry again when he returned; I fear that he will take a second wife and that she will bear him children; for he is rich in houses and lands, allowances and villages, and, if he has offspring by another, I shall be cheated out of all these goods.' 'My daughter,' said the old woman, 'it is well seen that you know nothing of the virtues of my lord the sheikh Father-of-Thrusts, the powerful Master-of-Bangs, the holy Multiplier-of-Pregnancies. A single visit to this saint turns a poor debtor into a rich creditor and a barren woman into a fruitful barn.' 'Mother,' replied the fair Khātūn, 'I have not once been out of the house since I married, not even for visits of congratulation or condolence.' Then said the old woman: 'I will take you to my lord the Father-of-Thrusts, the Multiplier-of-Pregnancies, and you must not fear to tell him all your trouble. When you return, your husband will lie with you and in coupling make you most certainly with child. Whether it be male or female, you must consecrate it to the service of the Master-of-Bangs.'

Khātūn, all on fire with hope, hastened to put on her fairest robe and richest jewels; then, recommending the house to the care of her servant, she went down to the door with Delilah. When the old Moorish porter asked her whither she would go, she answered: 'I am going to visit the sheikh Multiplier-of-Pregnancies.' Then said the porter: 'My mistress, this holy old woman is a blessing straight from Allāh. She has His treasures in her keeping. Not only did she tell my difficulty without my having spoken of it, but she gave me

three holy blessed dīnārs of red gold. May the virtue of her yearly
fast be a little upon my head!'

As the two set off, Delilah said to Khātūn: 'As Allāh lives, dear
mistress, I trust that, when you visit the Father-of-Thrusts, he will
not only be able to calm your spirit, satisfy your wish, and bring
back your husband's love, but also that he will contrive that there
shall never more be quarrel or high words between you.' 'O
mother,' answered the amīr's wife, 'already I long to see that holy
old man!'

As they went, Delilah-the-Wily was saying to herself: 'How can I
steal the jewels and strip this young fool in such a crowd?' Suddenly she said aloud: 'It will be better if you walk far behind me,
keeping me carefully in sight, for I am an old woman rudely burdened with the loads of others and, all along the street, people meet
me with pious offers for my lord and gifts which I must carry. For
the moment, then, I had better walk alone.' The girl did as she was
bid, and presently the two arrived in this order at the principal
market, which echoed with the golden clinking of the bracelets
about Khātūn's delicate feet, and the cadenced tinkling of the
sequins in her hair, as if to well-played music.

As they passed the shop of one Sīdī Muhsin, that handsome
scarce-bearded young merchant remarked the girl's beauty and sent
her sideway glances which the old woman was not slow to interpret.
She returned to the girl, saying: 'Sit down and rest a little, my
daughter, while I speak with this young merchant on a matter of
business.' Khātūn sat down near the shop, bestowing one glance
upon the youth which came nigh to maddening him. When he was
thus, as it were, cooked to a turn, the old woman bowed before him,
saying: 'Are you not Sīdī Muhsin, the merchant?' 'I am,' he answered, 'but who told you my name?'

At this point Shahrazād saw the approach of morning and
discreetly fell silent.

But when the four-hundred-and-thirty-fifth night had come

SHE SAID:

'Good folk have sent me to you,' she answered. 'That girl whom
you see is my daughter. Her father, who was a great merchant, died
and left her well-off. She has left the house to-day for the first time,
for she has only just become marriageable, as I know by certain

unequivocal signs. I hastened to bring her forth, acting on the advice of the wise, who say: "Offer your daughter soon and your son late." Divine inspiration and a presentiment lead me to offer her to you in marriage. You need have no anxiety in the matter, for, if you are poor, I will give you all her money and you can open two shops in the place of one. Thus Allāh will have gifted you not only with a charming girl, but also with three desirable things beginning in C; cash, comfort, and coupling.'

'Mother,' answered Sīdī Muhsin, 'this is excellent and more than I could wish. I thank you from the bottom of my heart and have no sort of doubt about the first two C's. As regards the third C, I must confess that I will not be reassured until I have seen the territory for myself. For my mother, before she died, said earnestly to me: "My son, I wish I could have married you to some young girl whom I had examined for myself." I swore to her that I would carry out this business on my own account, and she died with a quiet mind.' 'In that case, rise up and follow me,' said the old woman. 'I take it upon myself to show her to you quite naked, if you will walk far behind her and be guided by the way I take.'

The young merchant rose and took up a purse containing a thousand dīnārs, saying to himself: 'One never knows what will happen; it may be as well to have the money for the contract with me.' Then he followed the old whore, who had already gone forward, thinking to herself: 'Now, wise Delilah, how are you going to pillage this young calf?'

As she walked on, followed in order by the girl and the young man, her eyes fell upon the shop of a dyer called Hājj Muhammad, a man famous in all the market for the dual direction of his tastes. He was like the knife of one who sells kolocasia, which cuts through male and female alike; equally he loved the tender fig and the acid pomegranate. Hājj Muhammad lifted his eyes when he heard the clicking of anklets and, seeing the boy and the girl, strongly felt that which he felt. As he was gazing, Delilah came up and said with a bow: 'Surely you are Hājj Muhammad, the dyer?' 'I am,' he answered, 'what do you want?' 'Folk have spoken well of you to me,' she replied. 'Now look at these, my son and daughter, two charming young people whose education has cost me a pretty penny. . . . The house where they live with me is great but very old, so that of late I have had to strengthen it with wooden joists and props. Now the master builder has said that I risk being crushed if I go on living there until the place has been rebuilt. I am therefore on the lookout for some other house, where I can live for the time being with these two children. I was recommended to come to you, and now I beg that you will, of your generosity, allow us to stay in your house until the repairs are finished.'

The dyer felt his heart dancing among his entrails at this speech. 'O Hājj Muhammad,' he said to himself, 'here is butter on a biscuit for your old teeth!' Then aloud to Delilah he continued: 'It is true that I have a house with a very large chamber on the top floor; but, although I myself live below, I have no other place than that in which to receive my guests, the peasants who bring me indigo.' 'My son,' exclaimed the old woman, 'we only wish lodging for a month or two and we know no one in this city. I beg you to divide your upper chamber into two, and let the three of us live in one-half of it. As Allāh lives, your guests, the indigo planters, can be our guests and welcome at that. We are ready to eat with them and sleep with them.' Being reassured on this point, the dyer gave her the three keys of his house, saying: 'The big one is for the front door, the little for the vestibule, and the twisted for the upper chamber. I give you the use of all, good mother.' With profuse thanks Delilah took the keys and went forward, followed as before by the girl and the young merchant, and, coming at length to the street in which the dyer's house was situated, hastened to open the door with the large key.

At this point Shahrazād saw the approach of morning and discreetly fell silent.

But when the four-hundred-and-thirty-sixth night had come

SHE SAID:

She went in first herself, signing to the young man to wait, and then led Khātūn to the upper chamber, saying: 'My daughter, on the ground floor dwells the venerable Father-of-Thrusts. Take off your great veil and wait for me here. I will not be long.' She hurried down and, opening to the young merchant, introduced him into the vestibule, saying: 'Sit down here and wait till I bring my daughter to you; for I wish you to judge about the third C with your own eyes.' Then she ran up to Khātūn, and said: 'We will now visit the Father-of-Thrusts.' 'What joy, my mother!' she cried, but the old woman continued: 'My daughter, I fear for one thing. I have an idiot son below who is the representative and helper of the old man. He knows not heat from cold, and is always naked. When some noble lady like yourself comes to visit my lord, the sigh of her silks and ornaments sends him into a fury, he throws himself upon her and tears her robes to pieces, scattering her jewels and wrenching her earrings from her ears. I think you had better take off your jewels and all your garments here; I will look after them for you until you return from the holy man.' At once the girl took off all her jewels and every garment except a light silk chemise. She gave all these things to Delilah, who said: 'I will go and place them under the holy man's robe that they may acquire virtue.' She left the chamber and, after hiding the rich packet below the stairs, went down to the young merchant, who was impatiently awaiting her. When he asked her where her daughter was, she began to beat her breast and face in silence. 'What is the matter?' asked the young man, and she answered: 'May the devil smite all envious and evil-speaking neighbours. They saw you come in with me and, when I told them that you were to be my daughter's husband, they took the girl aside and said to her, doubtless out of jealousy: "Is your mother so tired of maintaining you that she is ready to marry you to a man with the itch and the leprosy?" What could I do but swear to her, even as you swore to your mother, that she should not marry until she had seen you naked?' 'I call Allāh to witness against these evil-minded slanderers!' cried the young man, and without more ado he hurried off all his clothes and stood up naked, white and spotless like virgin silver. 'You are as pure as you are beautiful. There is nothing to fear,' said Delilah-the-Wily. And then, as he was beginning to fold together his rich marten cloak, his belt, his silver and gold dagger and his purse, she prevented him, saying: 'You must not leave these tempting things in the vestibule; I will put them in a place of safety for you.' She made all his belongings into a bundle and, locking the door on the youth with a promise of speedy return, took the other packet from under the stairs and noiselessly left the house.

As soon as she gained the street, she put her rich takings in the care of a spice merchant of her acquaintance and made for the shop of the libidinous dyer at her best speed. 'Well, my aunt,' he cried as soon as he saw her, 'I hope that the house suits you?' 'It is a blessed house,' she answered, 'and I am more satisfied with it than I can say. Now I am going to hire some porters to carry in our belongings. As I shall be occupied for some little time in this, I beg you to take this dīnār and buy bread-soup and hashed meat for my children, who have not eaten since this morning. Take the food with you and have your meal with them, if you will be so good.' 'Who will look after my shop and my clients' goods?' objected the dyer. 'Your little apprentice,' she said. Then said he: 'Be it so,' and, without loss of time, took a plate and bowl and went out to buy the bread-soup. So much for the dyer. We shall soon return to him.

Delilah-the-Wily retrieved her two bundles from the spice merchant and, returning to the dyer's shop, said to the apprentice: 'Your master wishes you to run at once and meet him at the bread-soup seller's.' 'I hear and I obey!' answered the lad, as he hurried from the shop. Before he was out of sight, the old woman began to gather together all the portable goods in the place. While she was thus employed, she saw a donkey-boy passing the shop with his ass. For a week he had been out of work and he was also a hashīsh-eater. 'Ho, donkey-boy!' cried the old harlot. The man stopped at the door and Delilah said to him: 'Do you know my son, the dyer?' 'As Allāh lives,' he answered, 'no one knows him better than I do, mistress.'

At this point Shahrazād saw the approach of morning and discreetly fell silent.

But when the four-hundred-and-thirty-seventh night had come

SHE SAID:

Then said Delilah-the-Wily: 'Know, good donkey-boy, that my poor son is insolvent; each time that he has been put in prison in the past I have got him free; but to-day I have persuaded him to declare his bankruptcy and make an end. I am now collecting his clients' goods to return them to their owners, and I wish you to hire me your ass to carry them. Here is a dīnār. While you are waiting my return, you may occupy yourself by breaking the shop to pieces and smashing the jars of dye, so that when the kādī sends his men they may find nothing to seize.' 'Be it upon my head and before my eyes!' answered the donkey-boy. 'Your son, the dyer, has been good to me in times past and I owe him gratitude. Therefore I will break up the place and destroy the stock in Allāh's name, and not charge anything for doing it.'

Satisfied by this assurance, the old woman loaded all her thefts upon the ass and led it along by its halter in the direction of her house. Having arrived safely, by the mercy of Allāh, she found her daughter Zainab waiting her return as upon hot coals. 'O mother,' cried the girl, 'my heart has been with you! Have you achieved some brave deception?' 'The first morning,' answered Delilah, 'I have played four excellent tricks on four several persons: a young merchant, the wife of a terrible captain, a libidinous dyer, and a donkey-boy. I bring you all the clothing and ornaments of the first two, the chief goods of the third, and the donkey which used to belong to the fourth.' 'O mother,' cried Zainab, 'now you can no longer go about freely in Baghdād, since all four will be looking for you.' 'Pooh,' answered Delilah, 'I do not bother about them, except perhaps the donkey-boy who knows me.' We will now leave Delilah for the moment.

The dyer bought the bread-soup and hashed meat, gave them to his apprentice to carry, and took the road to his house. His way lay past the shop; when he reached it, he saw the donkey-boy demolishing the fittings and breaking up the great jars. Already he had worked so well that the shop was a mass of ruin and flowed with a kind of blue mud. 'Stop! Stop!' cried the dyer, and at once the donkey-boy ceased from his work, saying: 'My heart has been with you. Praise be to Allāh that you have escaped from prison!' 'What are you saying? What does all this mean?' cried Hājj Muhammad, and the man answered: 'You have been declared bankrupt while you were in prison.' 'Who told you that?' asked the dyer with starting eyes and trembling lips. 'Your mother told me,' replied the other, 'and ordered me, in your interest, to break and destroy everything here, so that the kādī's men should find nothing to seize.' 'Allāh confound the Far-One!' exclaimed the astonished tradesman. 'My mother has been dead for years,' Realising that he had been practised upon, he beat his breast and cried at the top of his voice: 'Alas, alas! My goods are lost, my clients' goods are lost!' And the donkey-boy wept and shouted: 'Alas, my ass is lost! My ass is lost! Dyer of my bum, give me back the ass which your mother has taken!' At this Hājj Muhammad threw himself on the donkey-boy and, seizing him by the neck, began to punch him with his fists, crying: 'Where is she? Where is your old confederate?' 'My ass, where is my ass? Give me back my ass!' yelled the donkey-boy from the bottom of his entrails. A moment more and the two were locked in fight, biting, insulting and buffeting, butting each other in the stomach and trying to get hold of each other's testicles to crush them between the fingers. Soon a crowd sprang up about them, and at last they were separated, not without a shrewd blow or two falling upon the peacemakers. One asked the dyer what the trouble might be, but it was the donkey-boy who answered, crying at the top of his lungs, and adding: 'I did it to oblige the dyer!' Then said another: 'O Hājj Muhammad, surely you must have known the old woman, to leave her thus in charge of your shop?' 'I never saw her until to-day,' he answered, 'but I know that she has gone to live in my house with her son and daughter.' On this another member of the crowd gave his opinion: 'On my conscience, I think that the dyer is responsible for the ass; for, if its owner had not thought that Muhammad had trusted his shop to the old woman, he would not have trusted his animal to her.' 'O Hājj Muhammad,' ventured a third, 'as you have lodged this old woman in your house, you ought to give back the ass or pay its value.' Then, by common consent, the crowd accompanied the two combatants to the dyer's house.

At this point Shahrazād saw the approach of morning and discreetly fell silent.

But when the four-hundred-and-thirty-eighth night had come

SHE SAID:

Now let us return to the young merchant and the girl. While the youth waited in the vestibule to examine his future bride, the young woman waited in the upper chamber until the saintly mother should carry her the idiot assistant's permission to visit Father-of-Thrusts. When the old woman did not come, Khātūn left the room and descended the stairs, dressed only in her light chemise. As she went down, she heard the merchant, who had become aware of the chinking of her anklets, calling up to her: 'Be quick, bring your mother to me that we may be married!' 'My mother is dead,' answered the girl. 'Are you not the idiot, assistant to Father-of-Thrusts?' 'As Allāh lives, light of my eye,' called back the youth, 'I am not altogether an idiot, but I have some reputation as a father of thrusts.' The girl blushed at this reply and, in spite of the merchant's grumbling, remained half-way down the stairs, to wait for the holy mother.

While affairs were in this state, the dyer and the donkey-boy, followed by the crowd, knocked at the door and waited long for it to be opened. When no one answered, they forced the door and, tumbling into the vestibule, found the young merchant quite naked and trying to hide his exposed merchandise with his two hands. 'Son of a bitch, where is your wicked old mother?' cried the dyer. 'My mother has been dead for many years,' he answered. 'The old woman who owns this house is my future mother-in-law.' He told the dyer, the donkey-boy and all the crowd, the story of the offer of marriage, adding: 'The bride, whom I am going to examine, is half-way up the stairs behind the door.' On this the second door was broken down and the frightened girl discovered, trying to pull the chemise as far down as possible over the glory of her thighs. 'Child of adultery, where is your bawd of a mother?' cried the dyer. 'My mother has long been dead,' she answered in her shame. 'The old woman who led me hither is a saint in service of our lord the Multiplier-of-Pregnancies.'

At these ingenuous words all who were there, the dyer in spite of his ruined shop, the donkey-boy in spite of his lost ass, and the merchant in spite of his purse and clothing, laughed so heartily that they fell over on their backsides.

When they had thoroughly understood the tricks which had been played on them, the three victims resolved to have vengeance on Delilah. Their first action was to find clothes for the terrified girl, who dressed herself and hurried back to her husband's house.

The dyer, Hājj Muhammad, and the donkey-boy made up their quarrel and asked each other's pardon; then, taking the merchant with them, they sought the amīr Khālid, walī of the city, and, after telling him their tale, demanded redress for the calamities which Delilah had inflicted on them. 'This is a very strange story, good folk,' said the walī, but they answered: 'As Allāh lives and by the head of the amīr, all that we say is true!' Then said the walī: 'But, good folk, how am I going to find one old woman among all the old women in Baghdād? I cannot send my men among the harīms to unveil every face.' 'Alas! alas!' lamented the three. 'My shop! . . . My ass! . . . My purse! . . .' The walī had pity on them, and continued: 'Good folk, search the city yourselves and, if you can bring the old woman to me, I promise to put her to the torture until she confesses.' Delilah-the-Wily's three victims had to be content with this. As soon as they left the presence, they parted and each went off in a different direction to look for the evil old woman. We will come back to them presently.

Delilah-the-Wily said to her daughter: 'All that is nothing. I must find some bigger thing to do.' 'O mother, I fear for you!'

exclaimed Zainab, but the old woman reassured her, saying: 'Have no fears for me; I am like a bean in its cod, safe from fire and water.'

At this point Shahrazād saw the approach of morning and discreetly fell silent.

But when the four-hundred-and-thirty-ninth night had come

SHE SAID:

Delilah changed her Sūfī's garments for those of a rich man's servant and went out, revolving further outrages upon the folk of Baghdād. It was not long before she came to a side-street, decorated throughout all its length with rich stuffs and coloured lamps. The ground of it was also covered by a thick carpet. She heard the voices of singers and the reverberation of tambourines; at the door of the house from which these sounds came she saw a woman slave bearing on her shoulder a little boy, splendidly dressed in gold and silver velvet, wearing a red tarbūsh round which ran three circles of pearls, having about his neck a gold collar set with diamonds, and a little brocaded mantle on his shoulders. From the guests, who were going in and out, she heard that the house belonged to the syndic of the Baghdād merchants and that the child was his son. By piecing scraps of conversation together she determined that the syndic was that day celebrating the betrothal of his daughter, a marriageable virgin, and that the little boy had been given to the slave to be guarded by her and amused until the guests should have gone, because he was for ever clinging to his mother's skirts and hindering her in her duties as a hostess.

No sooner had old Delilah discovered these things than she said to herself: 'My duty for the moment is to wile away the child from the slave.' She pushed forward among the crowd, crying: 'Shame upon me that I should be so late!' Then going up to the slave, who was something of a fool, she slipped a counterfeit coin into her hand, saying: 'Here is a dīnār for yourself, my child. Go up to your mistress and say: "Your old nurse, Umm al-Khair, rejoices with you in your joy, because of the gratitude which she owes you. On the day of the marriage she will come with her daughters and bring the customary presents for the bride's women." ' 'Good mother,' answered the slave, 'I would willingly take your message, but every time my young master here sees his mother he clings hold of her garments and hinders her.' 'I will look after him for the short time you are gone,' said Delilah, and at once the foolish slave trusted the child to her and went upstairs.

The wily one made off as fast as she could with the child and carried him into a dark lane, where she stripped him of all that he wore of value, saying to herself: 'This is not all; you are too smart to be content with this. Surely there is more money in this adventure if it be handled properly.' Taking up the child again, she hurried to the market of the jewellers and sought out the shop of a certain Jew, a famous dealer in gems. The Jew, who was sitting behind his counter, recognised the child as belonging to the merchants' syndic as soon as the old woman entered. Now, though he was very rich, he was also very jealous and could not abide that any of his neighbours should make a sale unless he himself made a better one. Therefore he rejoiced on seeing Delilah and asked her politely what she wanted. 'Are you not our master, Azariah the Jew?' she asked. 'I am,' he said, and she went on: 'This child's sister, the daughter of the shāhbandar of the merchants, is betrothed to-day and they celebrate the promising even now. You can see, then, that she has immediate need of certain ornaments, notably two pairs of gold anklets, a pair of gold bracelets, a pair of pearl earrings, a carved gold belt, a ruby-sprinkled jade-hilted dagger and a seal ring.' Eagerly the Jew gave her what she asked to the value of at least a thousand dīnārs. 'I will take them on approval,' she said. 'My mistress will choose what pleases her and then I will come back with the money. In the meanwhile will you be so good as to look after the young gentleman?' 'If you wish it,' replied the Jew, 'but I do not need such a guarantee.'

When young Zainab-the-Cheat saw her mother return, she asked her what new exploits she had contrived. 'Quite a little one this time,' answered Delilah. 'I stole and stripped the shāhbandar's little son and then left him in pawn with Azariah the Jew, taking jewels to the value of a thousand dīnārs in exchange!' 'Surely this is the end!' cried her daughter. 'It will no longer be safe for you to venture abroad in Baghdād.' 'Fear not for me, my child,' replied the old woman. 'I have not yet done a thousandth part of what I mean to do.'

Meanwhile the foolish young slave had entered the reception hall, saying: 'My mistress, your old nurse, Umm al-Khair, sends greetings and good wishes. She says that she rejoices with you and that, on the marriage day, she will come with her daughters and act generously towards the bride's women.' 'Where have you left your young master?' cried her mistress, and she replied: 'I left him with the nurse, in case he should get in your way. Here is a gold piece which she gave me for the singers.' The chief singer took the coin and at once discovered that it was made of brass. Then cried the syndic's wife in alarm: 'Run down, you whore, and bring the boy to me!' The slave hurried downstairs and, not finding trace of either the child or the old woman, fell forward on her face, uttering a great cry which brought the other women running from above. Even as their mirth was changed to woe, the syndic himself entered. When he learnt from his despairing wife what had happened, he went out to look for the child, followed by all his guests, who scattered far and wide to assist in the search. After a thousand useless investigations, he found the boy, sitting almost naked on the doorstep of the Jew's shop. Being filled with anger as well as joy, he threw himself upon the Jew, crying: 'Wicked old man, what would you do with my son, and why have you stripped him?' 'As Allāh lives, my master,' answered the frightened and astonished Jew, 'I never asked for such a guarantee; but the old woman insisted on leaving him with me when she took that thousand dīnārs' worth of jewels to your daughter.' At this the wrath of the shāhbandar knew no bounds. 'O blackguard,' he shouted, 'what need has my daughter of your dirty jewels? Give me back my son's clothes and ornaments!' 'Help me! Help me! O Mussulmāns!' cried the Jew in terror, and in answer to his calling there appeared the first three victims, coming by different roads; that is to say, the donkey-boy, the merchant, and the dyer. When they had heard what had happened, they were not long in making up their minds that this was more of the calamitous old woman's handiwork. 'We know her!' they cried. 'She is a swindler who has already nicely pickled us this day.' They told their story to the Jew and the syndic, and in the end the latter was forced reluctantly to say: 'It is something that I have found my child. I shall not concern myself for his lost clothes since they have ransomed him; but one day I shall get the worth of them out of that old woman!' So saying, he hurried back to his house and transported his wife with delight by returning the child to her.

The Jew asked the other three what they thought of doing and, when they told him that they meant to continue their hunt for the old woman, he begged to be allowed to accompany them. 'Is there any one of you,' he asked, 'who knew the woman before her thefts?' 'I did,' answered the donkey-boy, and the Jew continued: 'It would be better for us not to walk together, but to carry out our investigations separately, so as not to give any warning to our quarry.' 'You are right,' said the donkey-boy. 'Let us tryst for noon at the shop of Hājj Masūd, the Moorish barber.' When they had agreed on this meeting-place, they parted and went their several ways.

At this point Shahrazād saw the approach of morning and discreetly fell silent.

But when the four-hundred-and-forty-first night had come

SHE SAID:

It was written that the donkey-boy should be the first to meet the villainous old woman, as she wandered through the city seeking some further mark for her cleverness. He recognised her in spite of her disguise and rushed towards her, crying: 'At last I have you, O decrepit thief, O sere and evil tree!' 'What is the matter, my son?' she asked, and he cried: 'The ass, give me back the ass!' 'My child, talk low,' she whispered, 'and be content to cover up what Allāh has already covered with His veil. Is it your ass that you want or the goods of the others?' 'Only my ass,' he replied, and she went on: 'I know that you are poor and I have no thought to deprive you of your ass. I left him for you in charge of the Moorish barber, Hājj Masūd, whose shop is just over the way. I will go and ask him to return the animal to you; wait here for a moment.' She entered the shop with tears in her eyes and kissed the barber's hand, saying: 'Alas, alas!' 'What is the matter, good aunt?' asked Hājj Masūd. 'Do you not see my son standing outside your shop?' she cried. 'He used to be a donkey-boy, but one day, when he was already ill, he exposed himself to a draught, which corrupted his blood and made him mad. Since then he has done nothing but cry for his ass. When he rises, he calls for it; when he lies down, he calls for it; when he walks, he calls for it. A great doctor whom I consulted, said to me: "Your son's reason is badly dislocated; nothing will cure him and bring him back into the way of sanity except the extraction of his two great molars and a good cauterisation on each temple with the fly cantharides or a hot iron." Here is a dīnār, good barber. You can entice him in by saying: "Your ass is here." '

'I will fast for a year,' cried the barber, 'if I do not most thoroughly give him back his ass!' When he had told one of his two assistants to heat nails red-hot in the fire, he called aloud to the

505

donkey-boy, saying: 'Come here, my son; your ass is in the shop!'

As soon as the poor man entered, the barber led him by the hand into his back shop and there struck him in the belly and tripped him up, so that he fell on his back to the ground and was held motionless by the two assistants. The master-barber at once thrust down his throat an instrument like a blacksmith's tongs, which he used for taming recalcitrant teeth, and, with a single jerk of his arm, pulled out the two molars. Then, in spite of the yells and twistings of his victim, he took up the two red-hot nails in a pair of pincers and liberally cauterised the donkey-boy's temples, calling on Allāh the while.

When the double operation was over, he said: 'As Allāh lives, my lad, your mother will be very pleased with me! I will call her in, that she may judge of my cure.' While the donkey-boy struggled with the two assistants, the barber went back into his shop and behold! . . . the shop was empty, cleaned as if by a mighty wind. There was nothing left. Razors, mother-of-pearl mirrors, scissors, irons, basins, ewers, towels, stools, all had disappeared; not a shadow of any of them remained. Also the old woman herself had vanished; not so much as a smell of her remained. The shop lay there swept and garnished, as if it were being put up for sale.

At the sight of this miraculous theft, the barber rushed furiously into his back shop and shook the donkey-boy violently by the throat, crying: 'Where is that vile old bawd, your mother?' Half-mad with grief and rage, the poor man answered: 'Son of a thousand virtueless ones, my mother is in the peace of Allāh!' The barber shook him again, crying: 'Not so! The ancient whore who brought you here was your mother! She has stolen all my goods!' Before the donkey-boy had time to say anything in reply, the three other victims entered the shop, returning from a fruitless search. The dyer, the merchant and the Jew, seeing the barber, whose eyes were starting out of his head, struggling with their fellow, who displayed burnt and swollen temples, lips foaming with blood, and two molars hanging out of his mouth by their nerves, cried out to know what was the matter. 'Justice against this bugger, O Mussulmāns!' cried the donkey-boy at the top of his voice. He told them what had happened, and they asked the barber why he had done these things. He in his turn told them his side of the story, and they at once understood that the old woman had brought off yet another coup. 'As

Allāh lives,' they cried, 'this can be none other than the work of that wicked old woman!' When mutual explanations had been made and the two adversaries had become reconciled, the barber shut his pillaged shop and joined himself to the other four. They went forth together, the donkey-boy not ceasing to cry aloud: 'Alas, my ass! Alas, my molars!'

At this point Shahrazād saw the approach of morning and discreetly fell silent.

But when the four-hundred-and-forty-second night had come

SHE SAID:

After wandering for a long time through various parts of the city, they turned a certain corner and immediately the donkey-boy again recognised the hurrying form of Delilah. He threw himself upon her, crying: 'Here she is! Now shall she pay for all!'

The five men dragged her to the walī's palace and gave her in charge of the guard, saying: 'We would see the amīr Khālid.' 'He is resting,' answered the soldiers. 'Wait a little until he wakes.' Thus it was that the five complainants waited in the courtyard, while the old woman was handed over to the eunuch, who shut her into a room of the harīm.

By devious ways Delilah reached the apartment of the walī's wife and, after kissing her hand, said to the innocent woman: 'My mistress, I wish to see our master, the amīr.' 'He is sleeping,' answered the other. 'What do you wish with him?' Then said the wily one: 'My husband, who is a slave-merchant, trusted me, before he went away on his last voyage, with five mamlūks to sell for him. Our master, the walī, saw them and I consented to sell them to him for one thousand two hundred dīnārs. I am here to deliver them.' Now, as it happened, the walī had need of slaves and had gone so far, the day before, as to give his wife a thousand dīnārs to buy some. The woman therefore believed Delilah and asked where the slaves might be. 'Under your window,' she answered, 'in the courtyard.' The walī's wife looked out and saw the five victims waiting for justice. 'As Allāh lives,' she exclaimed, 'they are handsome enough men! Each one is worth a thousand dīnārs.' Leaving the window, she handed the money to the old woman, saying: 'Good mother, I still owe you two hundred dīnārs. I beg you to wait for them until the walī wakes.' 'Mistress,' answered Delilah, 'I forgive you a hundred for the excellent glass of syrup which I have just drunk; the other hundred I will collect on my next visit. Now I beg you to let me out by the private door of the harīm, as I do not wish to see my slaves again since they have ceased to be mine.' The walī's wife let her out by the private door, and the Protector brought her safely to her own house.

'What have you done this time, dear mother?' cried Zainab, and Delilah answered: 'My child, I have sold the donkey-boy, the dyer, the Jew, the barber and the young merchant to the walī's wife for a thousand dīnārs. The donkey-boy is the only one who worries me; he was the son of a bitch who recognised me each time.' 'Then do not go out any more,' said the daughter, 'stay in the house and remember the proverb:

> Not every time you drop a cup
> Will it be worth the taking up.'

Thus she tried to persuade her mother not to risk the streets again, but she wasted her breath in all she said.

When the walī woke, his wife said to him: 'May your sleep be sweet upon you! I congratulate you on the purchase of the five slaves.' 'What slaves?' asked the walī. 'Why do you want to hide the matter from me?' said his wife. 'As Allāh lives, I have not bought any slaves,' exclaimed the walī. 'Who told you that I had?' 'The same old woman from whom you had them for twelve hundred dīnārs,' she replied. 'She showed them to me in the courtyard and, I assure you, the clothes of each are worth a thousand dīnārs.' 'You gave her the money?' he asked, and she answered: 'I did.' The walī hurried down into the courtyard, but could see only the donkey-boy, the barber, the Jew, the merchant and the dyer. 'Where are the five slaves which your mistress bought?' he asked the guards. 'Since our lord lay down to rest,' they answered, 'we have only seen these five.' The walī turned to the complainants, saying: 'Your venerable mistress has sold you to me; you may start your work by emptying the cesspools.' For sole answer the dupes cried out: 'If this is your justice, we will appeal against you to the Khalīfah. We are free men, not to be bought and sold. Come with us to the Khalīfah!'

At this point Shahrazād saw the approach of morning and discreetly fell silent.

But when the four-hundred-and-forty-third night had come

SHE SAID:

'If you are not slaves, you are cheats and robbers!' cried the walī. 'You combined this trick with the old woman, but, as Allāh lives, I will sell you separately to strangers for a hundred dīnārs each.'

The walī and witnesses were thus quarrelling when Mustafā the Street Scourge, captain of the palace guards, entered the courtyard to lay complaint concerning the misadventure of his wife. For you must know that when he returned to his house he had found her ill in bed from fright and mortification, and had learnt the whole story from her. 'This would never have happened,' she had added, 'if it had not been for your cruel words which persuaded me to have recourse to the sheikh Father-of-Thrusts.'

As soon as Mustafā saw the walī, he cried: 'I take it that your high office consists in allowing pimping old women to enter the harīms and beguile the wives of amīrs? As Allāh lives, I hold you responsible for the trick which was played upon my wife and the losses she sustained through it!' Then cried the five: 'O amīr, O valiant Captain Scourge, we put our cause into your hands!' 'What have you to complain of?' he cried, and then, when he had heard their story: 'It is plain that you have been tricked also. The walī does not seem to realise his position.'

'O amīr,' said the walī, 'I lay it upon myself to indemnify you for the loss of your wife's effects, and I take the business of the old swindler into my own hands.' Then turning to the five, he asked: 'Which of you would recognise the woman?' Led by the donkey-boy, they answered in chorus: 'We would all recognise her!' 'And I,' continued the donkey-boy for himself, 'would recognise her among a thousand whores by her sharp blue eyes. Give us ten of your guards and we shall catch her.'

As chance would have it, no sooner had the five gone out, followed by the ten guards, than they happened on the old woman, and she ran away from them. They caught her, bound her hands behind her back, and led her before the walī. 'What have you done with the stolen goods?' thundered Khālid, and Delilah answered: 'I have never stolen anything in my life! I do not understand what you are saying.' The walī turned to his chief gaoler and commanded him to throw the prisoner into his dampest dungeon for the night; but the gaoler humbly refused, saying: 'As Allāh lives, I will not take the responsibility, for she is certain to find some way of escaping me.' Then said the walī: 'Perhaps it will be best to guard her in the sight of all and to watch over her through the hours of the night until she is brought to judgment.' In pursuance of this plan, he mounted his horse and set forth, followed by all concerned. They dragged the old woman outside the walls of Baghdād and fastened her by the hair to a post in the open country. Then the walī left the five complainants to watch over her during the night and himself returned to the city.

The five, especially the donkey-boy, began to display their feeling towards the old woman by spattering her with all the names to which they could put their tongues. But everything has an end, even a donkey-boy's sack of abuse, a barber's basin of malice, and a dyer's vat of highly coloured remarks; the five had not slept for three nights and were, besides, worn out with the emotion of their losses; as soon as they had eaten, they fell asleep in a circle round the post.

The night was already far advanced and the five watchers were snoring about their prisoner when two Badawī drew near on horseback, chatting so loudly together that Delilah was able to hear what they said. One asked the other: 'What was the pleasantest thing you did when you were staying in wonderful Baghdād, my brother?'

At this point Shahrazād saw the approach of morning and discreetly fell silent.

But when the four-hundred-and-forty-fourth night had come

SHE SAID:

The other answered after a silence: 'As Allāh lives, I ate my favourite food, delicious fried honey cakes with cream. That was the pleasantest thing I did in Baghdād.' The first speaker sniffed in the air after the imaginary odour of fried cakes bursting with cream and honey, then he cried: 'By the honour of the Arabs, I swear that I will go straight to Baghdād and taste those delightful things!' The Badawī who had already eaten the cakes took leave of his desirous companion and returned by the way he had come, while the other, hastening towards the city, passed by the post and saw Delilah fastened there. 'Who are you and why are you here?' he asked. 'O sheikh of the Arabs,' sobbed old Delilah, 'I put myself under your protection!' 'Allāh is the most powerful Protector,'

answered the other, 'but why are you fastened to this post?' 'O
very honourable stranger,' she said, 'I have an enemy, a merchant-
cook of fried honey cakes with cream, the most reputed in Baghdād
for that confection. The other day, to avenge a sore injury which he
had done me, I went to his counter and spat upon his cakes. He
complained of me to the walī, who condemned me to be fastened
to this post and to stay here without food until I consented to eat
at one meal ten large dishes filled with fried cakes. To-morrow
morning the plates will be brought; but, as Allāh lives, O sheikh of
the Arabs, my soul has a disgust for all sweetmeats, and especially
abhors fried honey cakes with cream. Alas, alas, I shall die of hunger
in this place!' 'By the honour of the Arabs,' answered the Badawī,
'my sole reason for leaving my tribe and visiting Baghdād is to taste
these same fried honey cakes. If you wish, good aunt, I will eat all
of them in your stead.' 'They will not let you do it,' she replied,
'unless you are also fastened to the post instead of me. Yet the thing
is possible, for my face has been ever veiled, and they will not know
the difference if you set me free and make an exchange of clothes.'
Nothing could have pleased the Badawī better; he quickly released
the old woman and, after changing clothes with her, was fastened
to the post himself. Delilah, with a word of farewell, jumped upon
the horse, clad in the man's burnous and bound round the head with
his twisted fillets of black camel's hair, and galloped away towards
Baghdād.

Next morning, as soon as the five opened their eyes, they gave
their prisoner good day by recalling such epithets as they had not
used the night before; but the Badawī said: 'Where are the fried
cakes? My stomach greatly desires them.' 'By Allāh, it is a man!'
cried the five when they heard the voice. 'And he speaks like a
Badawī.' The donkey-boy jumped to his feet and hurried up to the
post, crying: 'What are you doing there? How dared you free the
old woman?' 'Where are the fried cakes?' answered the prisoner. 'I
have not eaten all night, so do not spare the honey. The poor old
woman detested pastries, but with me it is otherwise.'

The five understood that the Badawī also had been tricked by
Delilah and buffeted their faces, crying: 'No man can escape from
Destiny or change a word which has been written by Allāh!' As
they stayed there, uncertain what to do, the walī rode up with his
guards and the Badawī called out to him: 'Where are the fried
honey cakes?' 'What is this?' asked the walī, when he saw the man

fastened to the post. 'It is Fate,' answered the five. 'The old woman fooled the Badawī and escaped. We will hold you responsible before the Khalīfah for her flight, O walī; for, if you had given us some of your guards to watch her, she could not have got away. We are not guards any more than we are slaves to be bought and sold.' The walī asked the Badawī what had happened and the man told his story, larding it with cries of desire and ending: 'Now give me the fried cakes!' At this the walī and his guards burst out laughing, while the five rolled vengeful, bloodshot eyes, crying: 'We will not leave the walī save in the presence of our master, the Prince of Believers!' The Badawī, too, when he realised at length that he had been tricked and that there were no fried honey cakes forthcoming, said: 'I hold you responsible, O amīr, for the loss of my horse and my clothes.' Thus the walī was obliged to take them all with him to Baghdād and to accompany them into the presence of the Khalīfah Hārūn al-Rashīd.

At this point Shahrazād saw the approach of morning and discreetly fell silent.

But when the four-hundred-and-forty-fifth night had come

SHE SAID:

Audience was granted them and they entered the dīwān, where already Captain Scourge had foregone them and stood among the first complainants.

The Khalīfah, who saw to all such business himself, began to interrogate them, beginning with the donkey-boy and ending with the walī, and drew forth the story of each with all its details.

Hārūn al-Rashīd marvelled, saying: 'By the honour of my ancestors, I promise that all which has been stolen shall be restored. The donkey-boy shall have his ass and an indemnity, the barber his furniture and the tools of his trade, the merchant his purse and his clothing, the Jew his gems, the dyer a new shop, and the Badawī his horse and garments with as many dishes of fried honey cakes as his soul desires. But first the old woman must be found. You, amīr Khālid, shall have your dīnārs returned to you, and you, Mustafā, the jewels and clothing of your wife with damages. I charge you two, especially, to find the woman.'

The amīr Khālid shook his garments and lifted his hands on high, crying: 'As Allāh lives, O Commander of the Faithful, I beg you to excuse me! I dare not undertake the task, for, after the way I was fooled in the past, I cannot guarantee that she would not find some other way of escaping and leaving the burden of her evil deeds with me.'

The Khalīfah laughed and said: 'Charge some other with the business then.' 'In that case, O Commander of the Faithful,' replied Khālid, 'give the order to the ablest searcher in Baghdād, Ahmad-the-Moth, chief of police upon your right hand. Up to the present, for all his cleverness and for all his great monthly wage, he has done nothing.' 'Step forward, Ahmad!' called the Khalīfah, and Ahmad-the-Moth advanced, kissing the earth between the Khalīfah's hands and saying: 'At your orders, O Commander of the Faithful!' 'Listen, Ahmad,' said Hārūn, 'there is in this city an old woman who has done such and such. I charge you to find and bring her to me.' 'I answer for her, O Prince of Believers!' replied Ahmad, and at once left the presence followed by his forty archers, leaving the five and the Badawī in the hands of the Khalīfah.

Chief of the archers attendant on Ahmad-the-Moth was a man called Alī Camelback, who was well used to investigations of this kind and was moreover accustomed to speak freely to his captain, the one-time robber. 'Master Ahmad,' said this fellow, 'there is more than one old woman in Baghdād; you may believe my beard that the capture will not be an easy one.' 'Speak what you have in your mind,' said Ahmad, and the other continued: 'There are not enough of us to circumvent so redoubtable a lady, and I suggest that you ask Hasan-the-Pest to come to our assistance with his forty; for he is even better versed than we are in matters of this sort.' Now Ahmad-the-Moth was very unwilling to share any of his glory with his colleague, therefore he answered in a loud voice, so that Hasan-the-Pest, who stood at the great door of the palace, might hear what he said: 'In Allāh's name, O Camelback, since when have we needed help in our business?' Hasan-the-Pest was mortified by this answer, coming on top of the Khalīfah's choice of Ahmad. As the latter passed proudly on his horse, followed by his forty, the second chief of police said to himself: 'By the life of my head they will have need of me yet!'

As soon as the troop had come to the open space before the palace, Ahmad encouraged his men, saying: 'Good fellows, I wish you to divide into four bands and comb out the four quarters of Baghdād. To-morrow at noon I will expect you to report to me in the tavern in Mustafā Street.' The archers split into four companies as they were bid and went to search the city, while Ahmad-the-Moth took up the trail on his own account.

Rumour soon came to the ears of Delilah and her daughter Zainab that the Khalīfah had charged Ahmad-the-Moth with the apprehension of an old woman whose exploits were in the mouth of all. And they were even informed, by one who had overheard it, the name of the tavern which Ahmad had appointed for a meeting with his men. 'My daughter,' said Delilah, 'I am not afraid of these who have been sent against me, as long as Hasan-the-Pest is not with them. He is the only man in Baghdād whose intelligence I respect, and also he knew us in the old days. He could come straight to this place and arrest us; therefore let us thank Allāh that he is not employed in the matter.' 'Dear mother,' answered Zainab, 'this seems an excellent opportunity for playing some striking trick on Ahmad and his forty fools. How pleasant that would be, my mother!' 'Child of my bowels,' said the old woman, 'to-day I am feeling a little unwell; therefore I resign to you the pleasure of overreaching these forty-one rogues. This thing should be easy for so clever a girl.'

At this point Shahrazād saw the approach of morning and discreetly fell silent.

But when the four-hundred-and-forty-sixth night had come

SHE SAID:

Zainab, who was a curved and supple girl, with deep eyes and a delightful face, dressed herself with unusual care and veiled her face with very light silk to heighten the velvet quality of her glances. Rigged out in this way, she kissed her mother, saying: 'I swear by my locked and unpierced treasure that I will make these forty-one my plaything!' Then she left the house and, walking to Mustafā Street, entered the tavern of Hājj Karīm of Mosul.

She greeted him sweetly, so that he was quite charmed and rendered her salute with double courtesy. 'O Hājj Karīm,' she said, 'here are five dīnārs for the hire of your large hall until to-morrow. I have invited some friends and do not wish your ordinary frequenters to have access to them.' 'On your life,' he answered, 'on the life of your eyes, your pretty eyes, you can have the hall for nothing on condition that you do not stint the drink of your guests.' Then said Zainab with a smile: 'My guests are pots whom the potter forgot to breach; all that you have of wine will pass their way, have no fear of that.' She returned to Delilah's house and transported, on the donkey-boy's ass and the Badawi's horse, all that they had of cushions, carpets, stools, cloths, dishes and plates, to the hall which she had hired. After she had carefully arranged these plenishings, spread the cloths, marshalled wine jars, and added food, she took up her position at the tavern door.

It was not long before she saw ten of Ahmad's archers approach, with Camelback at their head, looking very martial. As he led his nine men up to the tavern, he saw the girl who, by a strange chance, had momentarily let slip her veil. 'What are you doing here, my child?' asked Camelback, quite charmed with her bold young beauty. 'I wait my Destiny,' she answered, with a long oblique glance. 'Are you the great captain Ahmad?' 'As Allāh lives, I am not,' he said, 'but I am the leader of these archers, one Alī Camelback, O eye of splendour. There is nothing that Ahmad could do for you which I will not.' 'O archer prince,' she murmured with a smile, 'surely if good manners and exquisite politeness were lacking a home they would not have far to seek. Come in and be very welcome as charming guests.' She led the ten into the hall and, making them sit down in a circle round the wine jars, gave them deep drinks of wine mingled with drowsy banj, so that they fell upon their backs like drunken elephants or muddled buffaloes and dropped into a deep sleep. Zainab dragged them one by one by their feet to the back of the tavern and, piling them on top of each other, covered them carefully and concealed them with a curtain; then she made all neat again in the hall and took up her post by the door.

Soon the second file of ten appeared and suffered the same fate as the first, from the smiling eyes and drugged offerings of the young Zainab. When the third ten and the fourth ten had gone the same way and had been piled up behind the curtain, Zainab again straightened the hall and watched for Ahmad-the-Moth. Soon he rode up on his horse, shooting dangerous fires from his eyes and with the hairs of his beard and moustaches bristling like the coat of a starved hyena. When he had dismounted and tied his horse to an iron ring in the tavern wall, he called out: 'Where are these sons of dogs? I ordered them to wait for me here. Have you seen them, O slut?' Zainab wriggled her hips, smiled with her red mouth and sent two killing glances towards Ahmad, saying: 'Of whom do you speak, my master?' Ahmad felt his entrails moving about his stomach, and a

certain inheritance from his father, with its double interest, beginning to notice the girl. As Zainab stood there in her childish pose,
he said: 'Sweet maid, I am looking for my forty archers.' Zainab
feigned to be struck with a sudden sentiment of respect; she came
forward to Ahmad and kissed his hand, saying: 'O great chief of
police, your forty men begged me to tell you that they saw old
Delilah crossing the bottom of this street and have gone in pursuit
of her. They promise that they will bring her in presently and pray
you to wait in the hall of the tavern, where I myself will be proud to
be your minister.' Ahmad-the-Moth followed the girl into the
tavern, where the wiles of her beauty soon had him drinking of the
doctored cup. As soon as he was overcome, Zainab stripped him of
all his ornaments and clothes, except his vest and drawers. Then she
pillaged the forty in the same way and, loading all the clothes,
together with the plenishing which she had brought to the tavern,
upon the backs of the donkey-boy's ass, the Badawi's horse, and
Ahmad's costly charger, made all speed to her mother's house,
where she was received by Delilah-the-Wily with tears of joy.

At this point Shahrazād saw the approach of morning and
discreetly fell silent.

But when the four-hundred-and-forty-seventh night had come

SHE SAID:

Ahmad-the-Moth and his forty archers slept for two days and
two nights; when they awoke on the third morning, they did not
know where they were; but, as soon as their wits had cleared a little,
they guessed the authorship of their humiliation and cursed aloud.
It was very much against their stomachs to show themselves in the
street in their undergarments, especially as they had so haughtily
refused the services of Hasan-the-Pest, but, as there was no help for
it, Ahmad adventured at last into the street clad only in his vest and
drawers. The forty archers followed him in the same undress, and
the first person they saw was Hasan-the-Pest. At once he understood what had happened and began to sing, as if unconscious of
his colleague's presence:

> Green girls think men are all alike
>   Because each wears a turban;
> But one will be a country tyke
>   And one a knowing urban,

> One be a white and kindling star,
> One murky, lacking culture,
> One a clean feed, as eagles are,
> And one a corpse-fed vulture.

When Hasan had finished his song, he pretended to recognise Ahmad for the first time, and said: 'As Allāh lives, great Ahmad, these mornings are cool upon the Tigris. Is it wise to come out in your vest and drawers?' 'O Hasan,' answered Ahmad, 'I know something colder than these mornings upon the Tigris, and that is your sense of humour. No one escapes his Destiny and I was destined to be fooled by a young girl. Do you know her?' 'I know her as well as I know her mother,' replied Hasan. 'Would you like me to go and capture the two of them?' 'How can that be?' asked Ahmad, and the other replied: 'You have only to appear before the Khalīfah and shake your collar as a sign of incapacity; then you may beg him to transfer the arrest to me.' Acting on this advice, Ahmad proceeded to the dīwān with Hasan, as soon as he had put on fresh clothes. When the Khalīfah asked: 'Where is the old woman, O Ahmad?' he shook his collar and said: 'As Allāh lives, Commander of the Faithful, I do not know. Captain Hasan would do the business better. He not only knows the old woman, but assures me that she has done all this solely in order to be brought to the notice of our master the Khalīfah.' 'Is that true, O Hasan?' asked al-Rashīd. 'You really know the old woman? You believe that she has done all this to win my favour?' 'Indeed, yes, O Prince of Believers,' replied Hasan, and at once the Khalīfah exclaimed: 'By the tomb and honour of my ancestors, if she will give back all that she has taken, I will pardon her!' 'Give me a guarantee of safety for her, my lord,' said Hasan. When the Khalīfah threw down his handkerchief as a guarantee, he took it up and, leaving the dīwān, ran straight to the house of Delilah.

As soon as Zainab opened to him, he asked where her mother might be, and she answered: 'Upstairs.' Then he said: 'Tell her that Hasan, chief of police upon the left hand, has brought her the kerchief of safety from the Khalīfah on condition that she returns what she has stolen. Beg her to descend of her own free will, or I shall be obliged to use force.' Delilah had heard what he said and now cried down: 'Throw me the kerchief and I will go with you to the Khalīfah with all my takings.' The Pest threw her the handkerchief, and she tied it round her neck; then, with her daughter's help, she loaded the ass and the two horses with all her booty. Said Hasan, who had been watching: 'There remain only the clothes of Ahmad and his forty.' 'By the Great Name,' answered Delilah, 'I never took them.' 'That is true,' he replied laughing, 'but I think Zainab here had a hand in it. Very well, keep them.' Then he started out, leading the three animals by a single long trace, and brought Delilah into the presence of the Khalīfah.

At this point Shahrazād saw the approach of morning and discreetly fell silent.

But when the four-hundred-and-forty-eighth night had come

SHE SAID:

When al-Rashīd actually saw the diabolical old woman, the order sprang to his lips unbidden for her to be thrown upon the blood carpet and forthwith beheaded. 'I am under your protection, O Hasan!' she cried, so the Pest kissed the Khalīfah's hands, saying: 'I demand her pardon, O Prince of Believers! Behold, she wears the kerchief of clemency about her neck!' 'That is true,' answered Hārūn. 'I pardon her for your sake.' Then he turned to Delilah, saying: 'Come here, old woman; what is your name?' 'My name is Delilah,' she replied. 'I am the widow of your late master of pigeons.' 'You are not lacking in remarkable expedients,' said the Khalīfah. 'I confirm you in the name of Delilah-the-Wily. Now tell me why you played so many tricks upon these people and raised such a stir in our city?' Delilah threw herself at his feet and answered: 'Not for greed, O Commander of the Faithful, but because, after hearing tell of the one-time shifts and tricks of your two chiefs of police, it occurred to me that, if I could do the like and even perhaps surpass Ahmad and Hasan in their old way of business, our master the Khalīfah might be moved to reinstate me in the positions of my late husband.'

At this point the donkey-boy leapt to his feet, crying: 'Let Allāh judge between me and this old woman! Not content with stealing my ass, she incited the Moorish barber to pluck out my two molars and cauterise my temples with red-hot nails.' Then the Badawī rose and cried: 'Let Allāh judge between me and this old woman! Not content with fastening me to the post in her place and stealing my horse, she roused in me inward-turning desire for fried honey cakes.'

After this the dyer, the barber, the Jew, the young merchant, Captain Scourge and the walī all rose in turn, demanding justice and damages from Allāh. When he had heard them out, the large-minded and open-handed Khalīfah returned each what had been taken from him, with an ample gratuity suiting the particular case. He gave the donkey-boy a thousand golden dīnārs as a composition for his teeth and burns, and also appointed him chief of the corporation of donkey-boys. All the complainants left the dīwān with their troubles already forgotten, congratulating each other on the justice and generosity of the Khalīfah.

'Now, O Delilah,' said Hārūn al-Rashīd, 'you may ask whatever you wish of me.' Delilah kissed the earth between his hands and answered: 'O Commander of the Faithful, I ask only of your benevolence that you give me back the duties and emoluments of my late husband, who was director of your carrier-pigeons. I understand the work; for, when my good man was alive, my daughter and I used to feed the pigeons, clean the lofts, and attach the letters. Also it was I, and not my husband, who looked after the great khān which you had built for the pigeon service, and which is guarded day and night by forty negroes and those forty dogs which you took in battle from the King of the Afghans, who were of the seed of Sulaimān's.' 'Be it so, Delilah,' cried Hārūn. 'I shall write out your appointment at once, charging you with the conduct of the great khān, with powers over the forty negroes and the forty Afghan hounds. Your head shall answer for the loss of one of the pigeons, which are dearer to me than my own children; but I do not doubt your capacity.' Then said Delilah: 'I would also like my daughter, Zainab, to live with me in the khān and help me with its general supervision.'

The Khalīfah readily gave his permission, and Delilah, after kissing his hands, returned to her own house. At once she set to work to transport all her belongings to the great khān and to arrange them in the pavilion at the entrance. That very day she took command of the forty negroes and rode on horseback to the palace, clad in man's garments and wearing a gold helmet, to take her orders and collect any messages which had to be sent into the provinces. When night came, she loosed the forty dogs, sprung from the hounds of the shepherds of Sulaimān, in the great courtyard of the khān. Every day thereafter she made her official call at the palace, wearing her gold helmet surmounted by a silver pigeon, and accompanied by her forty negroes dressed in red-brocaded silk. As a suitable decoration for her new home, she hung about the walls the clothes of Ahmad-the-Moth, Alī Camelback, and the thirty-nine archers.

Thus it was that Delilah-the-Wily and her daughter Zainab-the-Cheat, both of Baghdād, obtained by their remarkable address the honourable command of the royal pigeons and the control of the forty negroes and the forty nocturnal dogs. But Allāh sees more clearly!

Now, O auspicious King, continued Shahrazād, it is time to tell you of Alī Quicksilver and his adventures with Delilah and her daughter Zainab, with Delilah's brother Zuraik the fried fish merchant, and Azariah the Jew magician. The details are infinitely more astonishing than any which you have heard up to the present. 'As Allāh lives,' said King Shahryār to himself, 'I will not kill her until I have heard the adventures of Alī Quicksilver.' At this point Shahrazād saw the approach of morning and discreetly fell silent.

But when the four-hundred-and-forty-ninth night had come

SHE SAID:

It is related, O auspicious King, that there was in Baghdād in the time of Ahmad-the-Moth and Hasan-the-Pest, another robber so subtle and elusive that the police could never put their hand on him. They would think that they had him and then he would slip between their fingers like a bead of mercury; that is why in Cairo, which was his native city, he had been nicknamed Alī Quicksilver.

As I have said, Alī Quicksilver lived in Cairo before he came to Baghdād, and his reasons for changing his city are worth being recorded at the beginning of this tale.

One day he was sitting, sad and idle, among his companions in the cellar which was their headquarters; and, though the men of his band tried to distract him from his black humour, he continued to sit lowering in his corner with a frowning face and bent brows. 'Chief,' said one, 'there is nothing better than a walk through the streets and markets of Cairo to cure a fit of the blues.' So Alī, to have done with this chatter, went out and wandered at random in the city, without his oppression being at all lifted. He came at length to the street called Red, where all the folk made eager way for him out of their great respect.

As he was about to enter a tavern where it was his custom to get drunk, he saw a water-carrier approach him with his goatskin bag upon his back, clinking his two copper cups as he came along. This fellow used to chant many street cries, in some of which his water appeared as honey, and in others as wine. On this day he was singing, to the rhythm of his cups:

> There's nothing like the blood of grapes
> To give escapes
> From care's infesting, festering apes.
> To set the wit upon probation,
> To give an edge to conversation,
> To make a friend of a relation,
> There's nothing like the blood of grapes.

But, when he saw Alī Quicksilver, he banged his cups more loudly and, leaving imagination, chanted:

> Here's cool water for you,
> Here's fresh water!
> Crystal light, my water,
> Joy of throats, my water,
> Diamonds, my water!

'My lord, do you wish a cup?' he asked. Quicksilver nodded, and the man, filling a cup which he had meticulously rinsed, offered it, saying: 'Delight! Delight!' Alī looked at the cup for a moment and then spilled the water on the ground, saying: 'Give me another.' The carrier was offended at this, and cried: 'As Allāh lives, my water is clearer than a bird's eye! Why do you throw it away?' 'It is my humour,' answered Alī. 'Pour me another.' The man filled the cup a second time and handed it, with due observance, to Alī, who again spilled it, saying: 'Pour once more.' 'If you do not want to drink,' exclaimed the porter, as he handed the third cupful, 'let me go about my business.' But this time Alī drained the cup at one draught and handed it back to the carrier with a golden dīnār. Instead of showing himself pleased at such royal payment, the carrier looked Quicksilver up and down and said sardonically: 'Good luck, my boy! Small folk are one thing and great lords are another.' Alī needed but this to make his anger boil over; he seized the carrier by his gaberdine and, while with one hand he rained blows upon him, with the other he banged him and his waterskin against the wall of the public fountain which stands in the street called Red. 'Son of a pimp,' he cried, 'do you find a golden dīnār so little for three cups of water? I have not drunk or wasted more than a pint, and your whole supply is not worth more than three silver pieces.' 'What you say is true, my lord,' gasped the water-carrier. 'Then why did you speak to me like that?' asked Alī. 'Have you ever met with a more generous man in all the world?' 'As Allāh lives, I have,' said the man. 'I have met a more generous man than you; for, as long as women bear, there will be matchless generosity among the great.' 'Who was this man?' asked Quicksilver, and the other answered: 'If you will loose me and sit down on the step of the fountain, I will tell you my story, which is a very strange one.'

At this point Shahrazād saw the approach of morning and discreetly fell silent.

But when the four-hundred-and-fiftieth night had come

SHE SAID:

Alī let go of the man and sat down with him, beside the water-skin, on the marble steps of the fountain. Then the water-carrier said:

O generous master, my father was chief of the corporation of water-carriers in Cairo, not the wholesale folk who supply houses, but the retail, like myself, who cry the precious stuff from street to street. When he died, he left me five camels, a mule, a shop and a house, which was more than enough for my condition. But the poor are never satisfied and, if by chance they attain satisfaction, they die. I thought that I would increase my inheritance by trading, and so, getting as many merchants as I could to trust me with their goods, I set out with my camels and mules to trade at al-Hijāz at the time of the pilgrimage to Mecca. But the poor never get rich and, if by chance they attain riches, they die. I did so bad a trade that, by the time the pilgrimage was finished, I had lost all my belongings and was obliged to sell my camels and my mule to satisfy my most pressing creditors. 'If I go back to Cairo,' I said to myself, 'those to whom I owe money will have me thrown into prison.' Therefore I joined a Syrian caravan and went with it to Damascus, Aleppo and Baghdād. As soon as I got to the last city, I called upon the chief of my corporation there and, after I had recited the opening chapter of the Koran to him in good Mussulmān fashion, I wished him peace. When he had heard my story, he provided me with a carrier's slop, a waterskin and two cups; and I went out on to the road of Allāh, crying my cry in all quarters of the city as we do in Cairo. But the poor will stay poor, for that is their Destiny.

I soon saw that there is a great difference between the people of Baghdād and those of Cairo. In Baghdād they are never thirsty, and those few who need a drink do not pay, because they consider that water is from Allāh. The answers of the first folk whom I addressed showed me that I was in for a bad business. One said: 'Have you given me food that you now offer me drink?' and another: 'Profit on your wares should go to Allāh! Pass on your way in peace!' I did not allow myself to be discouraged, but tried the markets, stopping before the most prosperous-looking shops and clinking my copper cups. Yet no one signed to me to pour and, at noon, I had not earned enough to buy me a crust of bread and a cucumber. The poor are sometimes hungry, but hunger is less hard than humiliation; the rich know humiliation and bear it less easily than the poor. I was offended by the way you behaved towards me, my master, not for my own sake, but because water is an excellent gift from God. Yet, indeed, your treatment concerns yourself alone.

Seeing that my trade in Baghdād had begun so sorrily, I said to myself: 'It would be better for you to die in a prison of your own city than among these strangers who do not wish for water.' While I was thus murmuring to myself in very low spirits, I saw a great movement and running together of people in the market. As my business consists principally in joining every crowd, I ran as fast as I could towards the disturbance, with my waterskin on my back. When I had caught up with the people I saw a splendid procession of men walking in two files, carrying long sticks, wearing pearl-embroidered bonnets and costly silk burnous, and jutting rich swords from their hips. At their head rode a man of angry aspect, before whom all the people bowed. 'What is this procession and who the rider?' I asked of one who stood by me. 'Anyone could tell,' he answered, 'by your Egyptian accent and your ignorance that you do not belong to Baghdād. That noble on the horse is Ahmad-the-Moth, chief of police on the right side of the Khalīfah. It is his duty to keep order in the streets, and he gets a thousand dīnārs a month, as does his colleague Hasan-the-Pest. Each of his men has a hundred dīnārs a month. They have just come from the dīwān and are going to their own place for their midday meal.'

At once I began to give my street cry in the Egyptian manner, accompanying myself by ringing the cups, even as you heard just now. The chief of police heard me, saw me, and rode to my side, saying: 'O Egyptian brother, I well remember your cry. Give me a cup of water.' He took the cup I offered and twice threw the contents on the ground, as just you did, my master, and then, also like you, drank the third filling of the cup at a single draught. 'Long live the people of Cairo, my brother!' he cried in a loud voice. 'Why did you come to this city, where water-carriers are neither paid nor honoured?' When I told him the story of my debts, he welcomed me to Baghdād and gave me five golden dīnārs. Then he turned to his men, saying: 'Because of the love of Allāh, I recommend this countryman of mine to your liberality.' On this hint, each archer of the train took a cup of my water and paid me a dīnār for it, so that I soon had more than a hundred dīnārs in the copper box at my belt. Then said Ahmad-the-Moth: 'This shall be your price each time you pour us drink while you are in Baghdād.' Thus it was that in a few days my box was full and, when I counted the contents, there were over a thousand dīnārs. 'Now is the time to return to my own country,' I said to myself. 'One's native city is best, and I have debts to pay there.' With this project in mind I presented myself at the dīwān, where I was already known and honoured, and began to take leave of my benefactor by reciting this verse:

> A stranger building in a stranger land
> Lays his foundation on the fickle air:
> Against a breeze his palace may not stand
> And the first puff of wind will leave him bare.

At this point Shahrazād saw the approach of morning and discreetly fell silent.

But when the four-hundred-and-fifty-first night had come

SHE SAID:

'A caravan is setting out for Cairo,' I continued, 'and I would join with it in order to return to my own people.' At once Ahmad ordered me to be given a mule and a hundred dīnārs, saying: 'In my turn I would charge you with a confidential mission. Do you know many of the folk in Cairo?' 'I know all who are generous,' I answered. 'Then take this letter,' said he, 'and give it into the hands of

Alī Quicksilver, my old companion. Say to him from me: "Your chief sends you salutation and good wishes. He is at present with the Khalīfah Hārūn al-Rashīd." '

After taking the letter and kissing Captain Ahmad's hand, I left Baghdād and in five days found myself back in Cairo. I sought out my creditors and paid them to the last dirham with the money which Ahmad's generosity had enabled me to earn in Baghdād. Then I put on my slop again and became a water-carrier as before. All the time, as I ply my trade, I am searching for Alī Quicksilver, Ahmad's friend, that I may give him the letter which I carry in the folds of my gaberdine.

Such, good master, is the story of my most generous client.

When the water-carrier had finished his story, Alī Quicksilver embraced him like a brother, saying: 'My friend, forgive me for treating you so ill. The man of whom you have spoken, who is certainly more generous than I am though perhaps the sole human of whom that might be said, is my one-time chief. I am Alī Quicksilver, his old companion. Rejoice, my friend, and brighten your heart and eyes, and give me the letter.'

At once the carrier gave the latter to Alī, who opened and read it. It ran as follows:

'*Greeting from Ahmad, Chief of Police, to the first and most famous of his children, Alī Quicksilver.*

'O ornament upon perfection, I write on a flying leaf. If I were a bird, I would hasten on the wings of desire towards your arms; but how may a bird move when its wings are clipped?

'You must know, my beautiful, that I am now at the head of forty good scoundrels, all old doers like ourselves, masters of a thousand splendid thefts. You may judge of their quality when I tell you that Alī Camelback is one of them. Our master, the Khalīfah, has made me chief of police on his right hand. I am concerned with the city and her streets; I touch a thousand dīnārs every month, without counting the little usual and unusual extras from folk who wish to stand well with me.

'Dearest, if you would have a wider field for your genius and see the door open to riches and honour, come and rejoin your old one in Baghdād. If you can contrive a few exploits of the old kind in this city, I promise to obtain the Khalīfah's favour for you, and that will lead to an appointment worthy of both you and our friendship, with emoluments as great as mine.

'Come, my son, and swell my heart with pleasure.

'The peace and blessing of Allāh be upon you, O Alī!'

As soon as Alī read this letter, he trembled for joy. Brandishing his long stick in one hand and the letter in the other, he executed a fantastic dance on the steps of the fountain, knocking over several beggars and old women. Then he kissed the paper a great many times and, after pouring all the gold which his copper belt contained into the hands of the water-carrier as thanks and commission for the good news, hastened to rejoin his band in the underground chamber.

'My children,' he said to then, 'I recommend each of you to the other.' 'Are you leaving us then?' cried his lieutenant. 'My Destiny waits me in Baghdād at the hands of my old captain, Ahmad-the-Moth,' answered Alī. Then said the robbers: 'Things are not going well for us just now; our larder is empty. What will become of us without you?' 'Even before I get to Baghdād,' answered Alī, after some deliberation, 'in fact, as soon as I reach Damascus, I will find some means of satisfying your necessity. Trust in me, my children.' He took off his clothes and, after ablution, put on a close-fitting robe and a traveller's mantle with wide sleeves; he thrust two daggers and a cutlass into his belt, placed a tarbūsh of extraordinary design upon his head and, taking in his hand a great lance forty-two cubits long made out of collapsible sections of bamboo, mounted his horse and left the city.

At this point Shahrazād saw the approach of morning and discreetly fell silent.

But when the four-hundred-and-fifty-second night had come

SHE SAID:

No sooner had he left Cairo than he saw a caravan bound for Damascus and Baghdād. This he joined, and found that it belonged to the syndic of the Damascus merchants, a very rich man who was returning from Mecca. Alī, who was young, handsome and still unbearded, was very much to the syndic's taste and greatly appealed to the camel-men and muleteers. He succeeded, however, not only in defending himself from certain of their nocturnal enterprises, but also in saving the caravan from cut-throat Badāwī and wandering lions, so that when they reached Damascus each man of the party thanked him with a gift of five dīnārs and the syndic gave him a thousand. At once he remembered his companions and sent back all the money to Cairo, save the bare sum necessary for his journey to Baghdād.

Thus it was that Alī Quicksilver of Cairo left his own country and came to Baghdād, to find his Destiny at the hands of Ahmad-the-Moth, his friend and sometime tutor.

As soon as he entered the city, he asked the direction of his friend's house from many passengers, who either would not or could not enlighten him. In the course of his enquiries he came to the square of al-Nafz, where he saw many little boys playing together under the leadership of the smallest of them, Mahmūd Miscarriage, the nephew of Zainab-the-Cheat. 'O Alī,' thought Quicksilver to himself, 'children know most of the news.' Acting on this thought, he went to the shop of a sweetmeat seller and bought a large lump of halwā, confected of sugar and sesame oil. Then, holding his purchase in his hand, he went up to the children, calling out: 'Who would like some halwā?' Mahmūd Miscarriage prevented the other little boys from coming forward and approached Alī by himself, saying: 'Give me the halwā.' Quicksilver gave him the sweet and at the same time slipped a silver piece into his hand; but, when Miscarriage saw the money, he thought that the man wished to seduce him and therefore cried: 'Go away, for I am not for sale. I do not do those disgraceful things. Ask anyone and they will tell you.'

Alī, who had no thought for such wickedness at such a time, hastened to reassure the obscene child by saying: 'That money is the price of information. I have paid you highly, because bold fellows are always open handed with others of their kind. Can you tell me where I will find the house of Ahmad-the-Moth?' 'If that is all you want, the thing is easy,' answered Miscarriage. 'I will go before you and, when we reach the house, I shall pick up a stone between my toes and cast it sideways at the door. Thus you will know what you want and yet no one will have seen me pointing out the place to you.' Quicksilver followed the boy and, when he saw a stone jerked sideways at a certain door, marvelled at the little scamp's prudence and precocity, caution and skill, malice and quickness. 'O Mahmūd,' he cried, 'when I am named captain of the guard or chief of police, you shall be the first of my braves.'

Mahmūd disappeared, and Alī knocked at Ahmad's door. As soon as the noise was heard within, the Moth leapt joyfully to his feet and cried to Camelback: 'Run and open to the fairest of the sons of men!

He who knocks is my old lieutenant from Cairo, Alī Quicksilver. I recognise his manner of knocking.' Camelback hastened to lead Alī into Ahmad's presence, and the two old friends embraced each other tenderly. After the first effusion of greeting, Ahmad introduced his guest to the forty archers, who welcomed him like a brother; then he fetched out a magnificent robe and put it upon Alī, saying: 'When the Khalīfah appointed me chief of police on his right and gave me uniforms for my men, I put aside this dress for you, feeling that one day or another I should find you.' Alī sat down among them in the place of honour, and a great feast, which lasted all night, was set before them all to celebrate his coming.

On the following morning, when the hour came for Ahmad to present himself before the Khalīfah, he said to his friend: 'O Alī, you must be prudent for your first few days in Baghdād. Be careful not to leave the house, for if you do you will be noticed by the folk of this part, whose eyes are ever sticky with curiosity. Do not think that Baghdād is like Cairo; our city is the Khalīfah's throne, and spies swarm here as do flies in Egypt. Rogues and swindlers multiply in Baghdād as geese and toads in Cairo.' 'My old one,' answered Alī, 'surely I have not come to Baghdād to be shut up between four walls like a virgin.' But Ahmad counselled patience and set out for the dīwān at the head of his archers.

At this point Shahrazād saw the approach of morning and discreetly fell silent.

But when the four-hundred-and-fifty-third night had come

SHE SAID:

Alī Quicksilver abode patiently in the house for three days; but on the fourth his heart was heavy and he asked Ahmad if the time had not come for him to set about those meritorious thefts which were to gain him the favour of the Khalīfah. 'There is a time for everything, my son,' answered Ahmad. 'Leave your case entirely in my hands, and I will slip a word into Hārūn's ear about you, even before you have undertaken any exploits.'

In spite of this advice Quicksilver felt, as soon as Ahmad had gone out, that he could stand his imprisonment no longer. Telling himself that he but meant to take the air for a minute or so, he left the house and began wandering about the streets of Baghdād, stopping occasionally before the counter of a cookshop or confectioner to eat a mouthful of their wares. As he was thus employed he saw coming towards him a band of negroes dressed in red silk, wearing high bonnets of white felt, and armed with great steel cutlasses. They marched orderly, two by two, and behind them rode an old woman on a bedizened mule. Upon her head was a gold helmet topped with a silver pigeon and she glowed in a mail-coat of fine steel.

This was none other than Delilah-the-Wily, officer of the pigeons, who had left the dīwān and was returning to the khān. She did not know Alī Quicksilver, but, as she passed him, she was agreeably surprised by his youth and elegance, and disagreeably by a certain resemblance between his expression and that of Ahmad-the-Moth, her enemy. She whispered a word to one of her negroes, and at once the man left the rank and began to ask secretly among the merchants for the name and condition of the handsome youth. None could give the information, so, as soon as Delilah entered her pavilion, she told Zainab to bring her the table of divining sand. 'My daughter,' she said, 'I saw a young man in the market who is so handsome that beauty herself would choose him for her favourite, but the look in his eyes reminded me of Ahmad-the-Moth, our enemy. I am very much afraid that this unknown has come to Baghdād to play us some evil trick. I wish to consult the sand about him.'

She shook the sand according to cabalistic art, murmuring words and reading backward charms over it; then she constructed a figure with algebraic and alchemical ciphers. 'My daughter,' she cried, 'the handsome young man is one Alī Quicksilver of Cairo, he is a friend of Ahmad-the-Moth, who has called him to Baghdād to plague us, in revenge for the business of the drugged wine and the stolen clothes. The youth lodges even now with Ahmad.' 'Dear mother,' answered the girl, 'why make such a fuss about a beardless boy?' 'Beardless or not,' retorted Delilah, 'the sand tells me that his fate bears strongly upon yours and mine.' 'We shall see,' said Zainab, and at once dressed herself in her finest. When she had added velvet to her look with a stick of kohl and joined her brows with perfumed black paste, she left the house in the hope of meeting the young man.

She walked slowly through the markets of Baghdād, undulating her hips and moving her eyes beneath their little veil; her path was strewn with destructive glances, with smiles for some, silent promises for others, coquetries and temptations, with eye answers and lashes' questioning, murders with the lids, awakening by bracelets, music of anklets and general fire for all. Soon her luck brought her opposite Alī Quicksilver, who leant over a counter of katāif, and she recognised him by his beauty. She struck him with her shoulder as if by accident and made him stumble; then, as if offended, she said: 'Good luck to the blind, O eagle-sighted one!'

Pierced through and through by her glance, Alī contented himself with smiling. 'You are beautiful, my child,' he said. 'To whom do you belong?' 'To anyone handsome and resembling you,' she answered. 'Are you married or a maid?' he asked. 'Married, you will be glad to hear,' she replied. Then he asked: 'Shall it be at your house or mine?' 'Mine,' said she. 'I am a merchant's daughter and married to a merchant. This is the first day I have been able to go abroad. This morning my husband went away for a week, and as soon as he left I determined to enjoy myself. I told my servant to cook some of my favourite dishes and then came out to find some-one as handsome and well-mannered as yourself to share them with me and stay the night. Love came into my heart as soon as I saw you; will you deign to uplift and rejoice my soul by eating a mouthful at my cloth?'

At this point Shahrazād saw the approach of morning and discreetly fell silent.

But when the four-hundred-and-fifty-fourth night had come

SHE SAID:

'A guest so charmingly invited hardly could refuse,' said Alī, and he followed the girl from street to street, keeping a prudent distance behind her. As he walked, he thought to himself: 'Alī, for a stranger in this city you are being very imprudent. Who knows that the husband will not fall upon you while you sleep and cut off the bird and eggs together? A wise man has said: "He who forni-cates when he is a guest in a strange land shall be chastised by the Host of all." It will be safer for me to excuse myself politely.' Taking advantage of a moment when they were crossing an unfrequented square, he caught up with the girl, saying: 'My child, take this dīnār for yourself and let us postpone our meeting till another day.' 'By the Great Name,' she answered, 'you must be my guest to-day, for I have never felt so disposed to multitudinous games of strength.' Hearing this, Alī followed her again until she stopped before a great house, the door of which was locked. Zainab made as if to search for the key in her garments; then she cried in a vexed voice: 'I have lost the key! How can we open the door? Will you not try?' 'How can I open a lock without a key?' objected Alī. 'I do not want to use force.' She answered with a glance from beneath her veil which at least opened all Quicksilver's locks. In spite of what he had said, he set his hand to the door and lo! even before Zainab could murmur the name of the mother of Moses, the door was somehow open.

The girl led Alī into a hall, hung with fine weapons and richly carpeted, where she bade him sit down. She spread a cloth and then, sitting down by his side, ate with him, serving him mouthfuls from her own fingers, and joyfully drank with him, without ever allowing a touch, a kiss, a pinch or a bite to come her way. Each time he leaned over her, she caught his kiss upon her hand, and, when he pressed her, told him that desire grew full only with darkness.

When the meal was finished, they rose and went out into the courtyard to wash their hands. Zainab insisted on raising the bucket from the well herself; while she was doing so, she uttered a cry and leaned far over the brim, beating her breast and stretching down her arm. 'What is the matter, eye of my heart?' asked Quicksilver. 'Alas, my ruby ring!' she answered. 'My husband bought it yester-day for five hundred dīnārs; it was too large for me, so I lessened the opening with wax, but now it has fallen into the well. The water is not deep; I must strip naked and go down to find my husband's gift. Turn your face to the wall and let me undress.' 'It would be shame upon me,' answered Alī, 'to let you go down when I am here. I will find the ring myself.' Without more ado he stripped to the skin and, seizing the fibre rope between his hands, let himself down to the bottom of the well in the bucket. When he came to the surface of the cold black water, he let go the rope and dived after the ring. Immediately Zainab hauled up the bucket, and crying: 'Perhaps Ahmad-the-Moth will help you out!' ran from the house with all Quicksilver's clothes beneath her arm. She shut the door behind her and returned to the khān of pigeons.

The house to which Zainab had taken Alī Quicksilver belonged to an amīr of the dīwān, who was absent on business. When he returned and found the door of his house unfastened, he imagined that a thief had broken in and, calling his groom to him, searched the whole building to see if anyone was there. Finding that nothing had been taken and that there was no trace of any robber (for Zainab had cleared away all signs of the stolen banquet), he thought that he would wash after his journey and told the groom to fetch him fresh water from the well. The man went out and lowered the bucket, but, when he would have raised it again, it was unnaturally heavy. He looked down the well and, seeing a vague black form seated in the bucket, took it for an Ifrīt and, letting go the rope, ran to his master, crying: 'There is an Ifrīt sitting in the bucket of the well!' 'What is he like?' asked his master, and other answered: 'He is black and terrible and grunts like a pig.' Then said the amīr: 'Run and fetch four learned readers of the Koran, that they may recite passages from the Book and exorcise him.'

At this point Shahrazād saw the approach of morning and discreetly fell silent.

But when the four-hundred-and-fifty-fifth night had come

SHE SAID:

The groom hastened out and soon returned with four readers, who ranged themselves round the well and began to recite verses of conjuration, while the master and his man slowly raised the bucket. All of them started back in afright when the Ifrīt jumped to land, crying: 'Allāh akbar!' The amīr was the first to perceive that he had to do with a human being. 'Are you a thief?' he asked. 'No, by Allāh, I am not!' answered Quicksilver. 'I am a poor fisherman. While I was sleeping by the banks of the Tigris, I coupled with the thin air in my dreams and woke to find my belly wet. At once I undressed and went down into the water to cleanse myself; but a whirlpool sucked me to the bottom and an underground current hurried me through what dark ways I know not until I came to your well. I thank both Allāh and you, my lord, for my salvation.' The amīr did not doubt for a moment the truth of this recital, so he gave Alī an old mantle to cover his nakedness and sent him away with many expressions of commiseration.

Quicksilver found Ahmad-the-Moth anxiously awaiting him. When he told his story, he was well mocked by all and especially by Camelback, who said: 'How, in the name of Allāh, can you ever have been the leader of a band in Cairo, when the first girl you meet in Baghdād can fool you and rob you of your clothes?' Also Hasan-the-Pest, who happened to be visiting his colleague, was led to remark: 'O simple Egyptian, do you know the name of the girl who played this trick on you, or whose daughter she is?' 'As Allāh lives,' answered Quicksilver, 'she is a merchant's daughter and a merchant's wife, but I do not know her name.' Hasan gave a mighty laugh at this. 'I will tell you more about her,' said he. 'You take her to be a married woman, but I will swear to her virginity. Her name is Zainab; she is no merchant's daughter, but the worthy child of Delilah-the-Wily, mistress of the pigeons. The two of them turn Baghdād round their little fingers. Why, she was the very girl who stole the clothes from your own captain, Ahmad, and his forty archers. What do you propose to do now?' 'Marry the girl,' answered Alī after consideration. 'Even after what has happened I love her to distraction.' Then said Hasan: 'In that case, my boy, I will furnish the means, for without me you can give up all thought of the girl.' 'Help me with your advice, O Hasan!' cried Quicksilver, and the other continued: 'Gladly, if you will promise afterwards to drink of no palm but mine and walk only under my flag.' 'I will be your lad and your disciple, O Hasan,' agreed Alī. Then said the Pest: 'Strip yourself naked to begin with.'

When Alī Quicksilver had undressed, Hasan took a pot filled with a pitch-coloured liquid and, dipping a feather, blackened the youth's body and face until he looked just like a negro. To complete the resemblance Hasan stained his lips and the circles of his eyes with red kohl. When all was dry, the chief of police covered the old heritage from Alī's father with a loin cloth, saying: 'Now you are a negro. The next step is for you to become a cook. Listen carefully: Delilah's cook, whose business it is to prepare food not only for the old lady and her daughter, but for the forty negroes and the forty hounds, is also a black man. You must contrive to meet him and say, in his own language: "O brother, it is a long time since we have put down beer together and eaten lamb kabābs. What do you say to an orgy?" He will answer that the cares of his kitchen prevent him from accepting, and will invite you instead to eat and drink with him at Delilah's expense. When you are in the khān, you must try to make him drunk and then question him as to the quantity and quality of the food which he cooks for Delilah and her daughter, what sort of rations are given to the forty negroes and the dogs, where are the kitchen and the larder keys, and anything else that you may require to know. He will tell you all, being a babbler in his cups. As soon as you are abreast of his duties, you must drug him with banj, dress yourself in his clothes, stick his kitchen knives in your belt, and go out with his basket to buy meat and vegetables

from the market. On your return to the kitchen, you must take from
the larder all you need of butter, oil, rice and the like, and set about
cooking the meals according to the direction which the real cook
will have given you. You must mix banj with all the food and thus
send the two women, the forty negroes, and the hounds into a
deep sleep. After that you can strip them of their clothes and ornaments, and bring all to me; but, if you wish to obtain Zainab as your
bride, I advise you also to remove the forty carrier-pigeons and
bring them here in a cage.'

At this point Shahrazād saw the approach of morning and
discreetly fell silent.

But when the four-hundred-and-fifty-sixth night had come

SHE SAID:

Alī Quicksilver carried his hand to his forehead for sole answer
and went out without a word to look for the negro cook. He found
him in the market and, after saluting him, invited him to get drunk
on beer; but the cook excused himself because of his duties and asked
Alī to accompany him to the khān. When they arrived, Quicksilver
followed Hasan's instructions to the letter and, as soon as the cook
was drunk, asked him about that day's meals. 'My brother,' answered
the cook, 'every day I prepare five courses, different in form and
colour, for the midday meal of my mistresses, Delilah and Zainab,
and in the evening five more. To-day they have ordered two extra
courses. I am going to give them lentils, peas, a good soup, mutton
stew, and a rose sweet; the extra dishes will be rice with honey and
saffron, and pomegranate pulp prepared with blanched almonds,
sugar and flowers.' 'How do you usually serve your mistresses?'
asked Alī, and the other answered: 'I set a separate cloth for each in
different rooms. I have a deal to do; for the forty guards must have
boiled beans fried in butter with chopped onions, and flagons of
beer; also there are three ounces of meat for each of the dogs, to
supplement the bones from the meal of the two women.'

As soon as Quicksilver had learnt these things, he mingled banj
with the cook's drink, and the man was soon snorting on the floor
like a black buffalo. Alī took the keys from where they hung on a nail
and, recognising the one which opened the kitchen by the feathers
and onion skins which clung to it, and that which gave access to the
larder by its coating of butter and oil, opened the doors of both

these places. Then he went out and bought the necessary provisions. His first care on returning was to follow the cook's cat about, until he knew the whole khān as if he had lived there all his life. When he was sure of his way, he cooked the various courses, mixing banj with all, and served Delilah and Zainab, the negroes and the dogs, without one of them noticing anything strange about the cook or the cooking.

As soon as Alī Quicksilver saw that every living creature in the khān, except the cat, had fallen into a deep sleep, he undressed the old woman and found her body detestable in its ugliness. Possessing himself of the official costume and helmet, he entered Zainab's room and stripped her naked. He found her altogether desirable, clean, cared for, and sweet smelling; but, being a very honest man, he would not open her treasure without permission and contented himself with feeling her all over and imagining his future pleasures. He took stock of the consistence of her flesh, its velvet tenderness and sensibility; in order to be sure of the last quality, he tickled the soles of her feet and was quite satisfied with the violent kick which he received in return. After that, he added the clothes of the negroes to those which he had already taken and then, mounting to the terrace, put all the pigeons into a cage. Laden with his booty, he walked calmly forth, without even bothering to shut the doors. He carried all to Ahmad's house, where the Pest was waiting for him; when he displayed the booty, Hasan marvelled at his skill and promised to help him as far as he was able to win Zainab for a bride.

Delilah-the-Wily was the first to wake from her drugged sleep. It was some time before she completely recovered her wits; but, as soon as she realised that her food had been tampered with, she jumped to her feet and, hurrying into her woman's clothes, ran up to the pigeon loft, which she found entirely empty. Next she descended to the courtyard, where she saw the dogs stretched out as if they were dead, each in his kennel. A hasty visit to the guards' barrack showed her the forty and the cook lying insensible. Lastly, bubbling with anger, she came to Zainab's room and found the girl sleeping naked, with a paper tied round her neck by a thread. On this paper was written: 'I, Alī Quicksilver of Cairo, the brave, the generous, the noble and the skilful, I, and none other, have done this thing.' As soon as she had read, she cried aloud: 'If he should have broken the lock!' and, leaning quickly over her daughter, examined her. When, to her great relief, she discovered that the lock had not been tampered with, she made the girl smell at a counter-banj and, as soon as she came to herself, informed her of what had happened. 'My daughter,' she said, 'you should have some gratitude towards this Quicksilver for not having broken your lock when he could easily have done so. Instead of making your bird bleed, he contented himself with stealing all those belonging to the Khalīfah. But what are we to do now?' She sat in thought for some time and then, telling Zainab that she would not be long gone, hurried to Ahmad's house and knocked at the door.

Hasan-the-Pest cried: 'That is Delilah-the-Wily. I recognise her knock. Go and open the door, Quicksilver.' Ali hastened to let the old woman in, and she entered the hall with a broad smile, bowing to all who were present. Hasan, Ahmad and the rest were seated round a cloth on the ground, eating a meal of roast pigeons, radishes and cucumbers. The Pest and the Moth rose in Delilah's honour, saying: 'O mother of all that is spiritual, sit down and eat pigeons with us. We have left some for you.' Delilah saw the world go black before her eyes, and cried: 'Are you not ashamed to have stolen and roasted those birds which the Khalīfah prefers to his own children?' 'Who has been stealing the Khalīfah's pigeons?' they asked, and she answered: 'That Egyptian yonder, Alī Quicksilver.' At this Alī spoke up, saying: 'O mother of Zainab, when I roasted these pigeons I did not know that they were carriers. Here are some of them back at all events.'' Delilah pulled a wing from one of the roast birds which he handed to her and put it to her lips; but, when she had taken one bite, she cried: 'As Allāh lives, my pigeons are alive, for this is not their flesh! I fed mine on musk-scented grain, and would surely know the smell and taste of them.'

All the feasters burst out laughing, and Hasan said: 'Your pigeons are safe with me, and I am very willing to give them back on one condition.' 'Speak, O Hasan,' answered Delilah. 'I consent to your condition in advance, for I am altogether in your hands.'

At this point Shahrazād saw the approach of morning and discreetly fell silent.

But when the four-hundred-and-fifty-seventh night had come

SHE SAID:

Then said Hasan: 'If you would have back your pigeons, you have only to grant the desire of the first of all our lads, Ali Quicksilver of Cairo, who wishes to marry your daughter Zainab.' 'It would be an honour for me and mine,' she answered, 'but I cannot force my daughter to marry against her will. First give me back my pigeons; for it is rather by gallantry than by sharping that my daughter is to be won.' At a nod from Hasan, Ali gave the cage to Delilah, who thanked him, saying: 'If you really wish to take my daughter in honest marriage, you must not address yourself to me but to my brother, Zuraik the fried fish merchant, who, besides being her uncle, is her legal guardian. Neither of us can do anything without his consent, but I promise that I will speak for you to Zainab and intercede for you with Zuraik.'

Delilah returned laughing to her daughter and told her of Ali's proposal. 'Mother,' answered the girl, 'I am not averse from the match, for Quicksilver is handsome and well-mannered; also he behaved very well in not breaking that which he could have broken while I slept.' 'Nevertheless, my child,' observed Delilah, 'I think that, before he obtains the consent of your uncle Zuraik, he will break an arm or so and a leg or so, and perhaps even lose his life.'

When they were alone, Ali Quicksilver asked Hasan-the-Pest to tell him something of this Zuraik and where his shop might be found. 'My son,' said Hasan, 'now that we know that you have to get the permission of that strange old man, it would be as well for you to renounce all hopes of the fair Zainab. For you must know, Ali, that though Zuraik is now a fried fish seller, he was once a chief in the great trade, known throughout all Irāk for exploits which far surpassed yours and mine and those of our brother Ahmad. He is so subtle a practitioner that, without leaving his seat, he can pierce through mountains, steal the moon out of the sky as if it were a silver coin, and rob the bright eyes of the stars of the nightly kohl which may be supposed to lie about them. There is no one in the world to equal the malice of him or to come near the fertility of his invention. It is true that he is settled down now and has exchanged the leadership of a robber band for a fried fish shop, but not one of his talents has been allowed to rust. To give you an idea of the old rascal's efficiency I have only to tell you of the last scheme he has hit upon to advertise his shop and find a ready sale for his fish. He has hung up by a silk cord in the entrance of his shop a purse containing a thousand dīnārs, which is his whole fortune, and has had this announcement made by public crier throughout the markets: "Give ear, O prigs of Irāk, O Baghdād crooks, O desert cutters, O

Egyptian cracks! Give ear, Afārīt and Jinn of the air and the earth and the sea! Whoever can lift the purse hung in the fried fish shop of Zuraik may keep it and no questions asked!" You can easily understand that, since this announcement, customers have thronged the shop and bought fish while trying to steal the purse, but the cleverest of them has not succeeded, because Zuraik has installed an elaborate mechanism connected with the purse by an invisible thread. The lightest touch upon the purse sets off an astonishing system of bells and rattles, so that even if Zuraik is at the back of his shop or serving a customer, he has plenty of time to prevent the theft. He only has to stoop down and pick up one of a heap of lead buns which are always handy and throw it at the experimenter, who seldom gets off without a broken limb or a cracked head. You can understand now, Alī, why I counselled you not to move in this matter. If you tried to practise against such a man as Zuraik, you would be walking, as it were, to your own funeral. If I were in your place I should forget Zainab, for to forget is the beginning of happiness and a man who has forgotten can live without the thing which he forgets.'

In spite of Hasan's prudent advice, Alī Quicksilver exclaimed: 'No, as Allāh lives, I could never forget that dark-eyed and most sensitive girl! It would be shameful in a man like me. I must try to lift the purse and thus force the old bandit to give consent to my marriage in order to get it back.' Thinking that there was no time like the present, Alī bought a selection of female garments and, when he had dressed himself in them, lengthened his eyes with kohl and put henna on his fingers. When he had modestly wrapped a silk veil about his face, he walked up and down the room experimentally, with such movements of the hips as women use, and succeeded to a marvel in his imitation.

At this point Shahrazād saw the approach of morning and discreetly fell silent.

But when the four-hundred-and-fifty-eighth night had come

SHE SAID:

When Alī felt that he had mastered the intricacies of female deportment, he sent out for a sheep and, when it was brought, cut its throat and collected the blood. Then he filled the stomach with the blood and fastened it over his own belly under the clothes, so that he had the appearance of a pregnant woman. Next he killed two fowls and, filling their gizzards with warm milk, arranged them in his bosom, so that he appeared to have the vast breasts of a woman who is about to bear. To make all perfect, he wetted a considerable number of napkins with starch and wrapped them one after the other about his backside; thus, when they were dry, he had a mountainous and solid bottom, well suiting with the part he had to play. Thus transformed, Alī went out into the street and began to walk slowly towards Zuraik's shop, hearing men cry as he passed them: 'By Allāh, what a bum!'

Before he had gone half way, he found himself greatly inconvenienced by the starched napkins, so he hailed a passing donkey-boy and mounted his ass with a thousand precautions, in order not to burst the bag of blood or the milky gizzards. When he came in front of the shop, he saw the purse hung in the entrance and Zuraik frying fish, with one eye on his task and one on the door. 'O ass-man,' said Quicksilver, 'my nose is sensible of those fried fish and the desire of my pregnancy yearns mightily towards them. Run and buy me one to eat now or I shall certainly miscarry in the open street.' The ass-man at once halted his animal and called to Zuraik: 'Give me a fried fish quickly for this pregnant woman; the smell of the frying has awakened the child in the womb, so that it leaps and threatens to come forth.' 'Wait a little,' answered the old rascal, 'for the fish are not yet cooked to a turn and, if you cannot wait, let me see your back.' 'Give me one of those from the counter,' said the ass-man, but Zuraik answered: 'Those are not for sale.' Then, without paying any more attention to the boy, who helped his passenger to dismount and lean against the counter, he went on turning the fish in his pan and singing:

> Ah, ah, the delicate flesh,
>   Little birds flying under the sea,
> Until they are caught in a mesh, a mesh,
>   And bought and brought to me!
>
> The oil is a lover who gilds them with gold,
>   Amorous is the dish;
> And the lust of my belly can not be told
>   For the crisp, gold, delicate fish!

Even as Zuraik was singing, the pregnant woman uttered a great cry, while a stream of blood poured from beneath her garments and drowned the shop. 'Oh, oh, ah, oh!' she groaned. 'Oh, the fruit of my bowels! Ah, my back is breaking! Oh dear, my thighs! Oh, ah, my little, little child!'

'You calamitous old fool,' cried the ass-man, 'see what you have done! I warned you! Your refusal has made her miscarry; you are responsible to Allāh and to her husband!' Zuraik, who was a little startled by this accident and feared to be polluted by the blood which was pouring from the woman, escaped to the back of the shop, out of sight of the purse. As quick as light, Alī stretched forth his hand; but no sooner had he touched the silk than a deafening discord of rattles, bells and old iron sprang up in every corner of the shop, and Zuraik, running forward, saw Alī's outstretched hand and understood all in a flash. Seizing one of the lead buns, he hurled it at Quicksilver's belly, crying: 'Take that, you gallowsbird!' The heavy lump was cast with such violence that Alī rolled out into the middle of the road, all encumbered with his napkins, and lay half-dead in a mess of blood and milk. He had just strength enough to drag himself to Ahmad's house, while the passers-by collected round Zuraik's shop, crying: 'Are you a merchant or a professional swash-buckler? If you are a fried fish seller conduct your trade less violently. Take down that tempting purse and spare honest folk your malice.' 'Certainly, certainly! And anything else?' answered Zuraik with a grin.

When Alī Quicksilver had recovered from the blow in the belly, he found himself still determined to win Delilah's daughter. After he had washed, he disguised himself as a groom and, taking an empty napkin and five pieces of copper money in his hand, returned to Zuraik's shop to buy fish.

At this point Shahrazād saw the approach of morning and discreetly fell silent.

But when the four-hundred-and-fifty-ninth night had come

SHE SAID:
He handed the five coins to Zuraik, saying: 'Put the fish in my napkin.' 'Certainly, master,' answered Zuraik, and would have served the groom with some of his fish from the counter, but the groom said: 'I want it hot.' 'The fresh is not yet cooked,' replied the merchant, 'wait a little, while I blow up the fire,' and with that he retired to his back shop.

Quicksilver at once stretched out his hand to the purse, but the attempt was greeted by a thunderous concert of bells, rattles, buzzers and old iron. Zuraik leapt with one movement to the front of the shop and, seizing a lead bun, threw it with all his might at the head of the pretended groom, crying: 'Do you think I did not recognise you, you old bugger, you with your napkin and your money?' This time Alī was more wary and, ducking his head, ran from the shop, while the heavy lump of lead landed in the middle of a tray filled with basins of curd which the kādī's slave was carrying on his head. The curds sprayed out and fell all about the face and beard of the kādī, covering his robe and turban, so that the crowd round the shop cried out: 'This time, O Zuraik, the kādī will pay you interest on the money in your purse! And serve you right, you bully!'

When Alī Quicksilver reached Ahmad's house, he told him and the Pest of his second fruitless attempt, and then, since his love for Zainab would not permit him to relinquish the quest, he disguised himself as a snake-charmer and thimble-rigger, and returned to Zuraik's street. Sitting on the ground outside the shop, he drew three large puff-necked tongue-darting snakes from his bag and began to play the flute to them, varying his performance sometimes with feats of sleight of hand. Suddenly he threw the largest snake into the middle of the shop, where it fell at Zuraik's feet and so frightened him that he ran yelling to the back. Quicksilver jumped towards the purse and would have taken it, but Zuraik in spite of his terror was keeping one eye on his possession; with a double movement, the merchant smashed in the snake's head with one of his lead buns and threw a second with all his force at Alī, who again ducked and fled, while the missile fairly caught an old woman who was passing and hurried her into the peace of Allāh. On this the neighbours cried: 'Such conduct is not lawful, O Zuraik! If you do not take down that calamitous purse, we will confiscate it by force. Your evil humour has unfortunate results.' 'I consent,' answered Zuraik and, much against his will, took down the purse and carried it to his own house, where he deemed that it would be safer from Alī Quicksilver.

This Zuraik was married to a negress, one time the slave of Jafar al-Barmakī and afterwards freed by the generosity of that great man. She had borne Zuraik a man-child, whose circumcision was about to be celebrated; therefore, when her husband handed her the purse, she said: 'This is unusual generosity, O father of my son. I shall now be able to celebrate the little one's circumcision in a fitting manner.' 'Do you think I have brought you the purse to empty on celebrations?' said Zuraik. 'As Allāh lives, I had no such intention. Go and hide it under the kitchen floor and then come up to bed.' The negress went down and dug a hole in the kitchen floor; then, after burying the purse, she returned to lie down at Zuraik's feet. The merchant was soon lulled to sleep by the heat of his wife and dreamt that he saw a great bird digging in the kitchen floor with his beak, uncovering the purse, and flying off with it in his talons. He woke with a start, crying: 'O mother of my son, the purse is being stolen! Run to the kitchen!' The negress rose from sleep and ran down to the kitchen with a light, where she saw no bird indeed, but a man disappearing through the open door with the purse in his hand. The thief was none other than Alī Quicksilver, who had followed Zuraik home and, hiding behind the kitchen door, had succeeded at last in bearing off the coveted prize.

When Zuraik heard of the loss, he cried: 'As Allāh lives, I will get it back this very evening!' Then said his wife: 'If you do not recover it, I shall not open the door and you can lie in the street.'

At this point Shahrazād saw the approach of morning and discreetly fell silent.

But when the four-hundred-and-sixtieth night had come

SHE SAID:

Zuraik went swiftly by side-streets and came before Alī to the house of Ahmad, where he knew the thief to lodge. He opened the door with the help of an arsenal of keys which he always carried and, shutting it after him, waited silently behind it. Soon Alī came and gave his customary knock. 'Who is there?' asked Zuraik, counterfeiting the voice of Hasan-the-Pest. When Alī had answered that it was he, Zuraik said through the door: 'Have you got the purse of that old rascal Zuraik?' 'I have,' answered Alī, then said Zuraik: 'Thrust the purse under the door before I open, for I have made a bet with the Moth, of which I will tell you later.' Quicksilver pushed the purse under the door and Zuraik, seizing it, climbed on to the terrace and, passing to the terrace of the next house, ran quietly down the neighbouring stairs, slipped through the door, and set out light-heartedly for his own house.

Alī remained long in the street, but at last, as no one opened to him, he knocked violently on the door and roused everyone in the house. 'It is Alī,' cried Hasan. 'Run, Camelback, and open the door.' 'And the rascal's purse?' asked the Pest ironically, as soon as Alī entered his chamber. 'Do not jest, good chief,' answered Quicksilver. 'You know very well that I passed it to you under the door.' Immediately Hasan fell over on his backside, roaring with laughter. 'O Alī,' he cried, 'your work is all to do again, for certainly Zuraik has taken back his own!' After a moment's reflection, Alī Quicksilver exclaimed: 'As Allāh lives, if I do not bring you back the purse this time, may I be ever held unworthy of my name!' Without an instant's delay, he ran by side-streets to Zuraik's house and, arriving there before its master, gained access by the neighbouring terrace and entered the room where the negress was sleeping with her little boy.

He cast himself upon the woman and, after gagging and binding her upon the bed, turned his attention to the child. He contented himself with gagging the boy and fastening him in a basket filled with hot cakes, which had been prepared for the feast of the circumcision. Then he stationed himself at the window and waited for Zuraik.

As soon as he heard knocking at the door, he cried out in the very tones of the negress: 'Is that you, my dear? Have you recovered the purse?' 'I have it here,' called up Zuraik, and Alī continued in the wife's voice: 'I cannot see it because of the darkness, and I will not open the door to you until I have counted the money. Put the purse in the basket which I am going to send down to you.' So saying, Quicksilver let a basket down from the window and drew it up again with the purse inside. Slipping the purse into his bosom and taking up the basket containing the little boy and the cakes, he escaped by the way he had come and soon delivered his triple booty into Hasan's hands. The Pest congratulated him and was proud of him; soon all the household were eating the cakes and cracking a thousand jokes at Zuraik's expense.

The fried fish merchant waited a long time in the street for his wife to open the door to him; but at last his patience was exhausted and he rained a volley of blows upon the door, which woke all the neighbours and the neighbouring dogs, but elicited no movement from the house. Then he forced the door and, going up to the bedroom, saw what he saw. When he had freed his wife and heard from her what had happened, he beat himself in the face, tore out handfuls of his beard, and ran towards Ahmad's house. It was already morning when he knocked at the door, and all the household was awake. Camelback showed the piteous fishmonger into the hall, where he was greeted with a storm of laughter. He turned towards Quicksilver, saying: 'As Allāh lives, you have fairly earned the purse, but give me back my son.' The Pest answered for Alī, saying: 'My child is ready to give you back your son and even your purse, if you will consent to his marriage with your niece Zainab.' 'Since when has it been the custom to force a consent in matters of this kind?' asked Zuraik. 'Give me back the child and the purse, and then we will talk about marriage.' At a sign from Hasan, Alī returned the child and the money, saying: 'When will the marriage be?' 'Softly, softly,' replied Zuraik with a smile. 'Believe me, O Alī, I cannot dispose of Zainab like a sheep or a bit of my own fish. I will consent to the match if you bring the dowry which the child demands, and not otherwise.' 'I am ready to bring that dowry,' said Quicksilver. 'What is it?' Then said Zuraik: 'Zainab has sworn that she will never have her breasts pressed by any until he has brought her the gold robe, the gold crown, the gold belt and the gold slippers of Kamar, daughter of Azariah the Jew.'

At this point Shahrazād saw the approach of morning and discreetly fell silent.

But when the four-hundred-and-sixty-first night had come

SHE SAID:

'If that is all,' cried Quicksilver, 'I am quite willing to resign all thought of marriage with Zainab if I do not bring you the things this very evening!'

'That may prove to be a sorry oath, Alī,' said Hasan-the-Pest, when Zuraik had departed. 'I fear that you are little better than a dead man. The Jew Azariah is a powerful and malicious sorcerer with all the Jinn and Afārīt of the world at his command. He lives outside the city in a palace, the bricks of which are alternate gold and silver; but the place is only visible when the magician is in residence. As he leaves every day to carry on his usury in the city, the building disappears. Each evening when he returns, the Jew shows himself in the window and, displaying his daughter's gold robe on a gold dish, cries out: "O all ye master criminals of Irāk, Persia and Arabia, steal my daughter's garment if you can, and you shall marry her!" The most expert crooks among us all have tried the adventure, much to their own distress, for the sorcerer has changed them into mules, bears, asses or apes with one motion of his lips. I advise you to give up the enterprise and stay with us.' 'If I renounced my love for the most sensitive Zainab, it would be great shame upon me,' answered Alī. 'As Allāh lives, I will dress her in the gold robe on the night of our marriage; I will crown her with the gold crown, gird her with the gold belt, and set the gold slippers on her little feet.'

He went out to find the shop of Azariah, usurer and magician, and, when he came to it, people pointed out the Jew to him. The old man, who was busy weighing gold in his scales, fastening it in sacks, and loading it upon the back of a mule which stood tethered near the door, was not only ugly but repulsive, and Alī was a little frightened by his face. Nevertheless, he waited until the Jew had completed his work and, after shutting the shop, rode off upon the mule; then he shadowed the animal secretly and came behind it beyond the city walls. Alī was beginning to ask himself if they were never going to stop, when the Jew halted and drew from his mantle a bag from which he took a handful of sand. Then he breathed on the sand and threw it into the air. Immediately there rose in that place a magnificent palace, the bricks of which were alternate gold and silver. It had an immense gate of alabaster and vast marble steps, up which the Jew rode his mule, and disappeared. A few moments afterwards he opened a window and held out from it a gold dish containing a gold robe, a gold crown, a gold belt and gold slippers. 'O all ye master criminals of Irāk, Persia and Arabia,' he cried, 'steal my daughter's garment and these other matters if you can, and you shall marry her!'

Alī Quicksilver, who was not lacking in sense, determined that his best course was to explain to the Jew how matters stood with Zuraik and ask him for the robe and other things as a present. Therefore he held up his finger, crying: 'I, Alī Quicksilver, the first of Ahmad's lads, desire to speak with you.' 'You may come up,' answered the Jew and, when Alī had climbed up into his presence, asked him what he wanted. Alī told his story, adding: 'Now I must have this gold robe and the other things to give to Zainab, daughter of Delilah.'

The Jew laughed, showing his terrible teeth, and proceeded to cast Alī's horoscope at his sand-divining table. 'If life is dear to you,' he said, 'if you do not wish to be lost beyond recall, take my advice and renounce your project. Those who have egged you on to this adventure only wished you to meet the same fate as others who have tried before you. If I had not seen from the sand that your destiny is twined with mine, I would already have cut off your head.' This cold advice set Alī in a flame of anger, so that he drew his sword and placed it against the magician's breast, crying: 'If you do not give me all those things, if you do not abjure your heresies and pronounce the act of Faith at once, you are a dead man!' The Jew stretched out his hand, as if to pronounce the required words, but cried instead: 'May your right hand be withered!' At once Alī's right hand withered and stayed useless in the air, while the sword dropped to the ground. Alī swiftly picked it up with his left hand and menaced the Jew again. 'Let your left hand be withered!' muttered the old man, and immediately the left hand dropped the sword and stayed withered in its place. Maddened by his helplessness, Alī made as if to kick the Jew in the belly with his right leg, but the other prevented him, saying: 'May your right leg be withered!' Thereupon Alī's right leg withered where it was and he stood balancing upon his left.

At this point Shahrazād saw the approach of morning and discreetly fell silent.

But when the four-hundred-and-sixty-second night had come

SHE SAID:

Alī tried to move his useless members, but all he effected was to fall over and roll about the floor until he was worn out. 'Do you renounce your attempt?' said the magician, but Alī answered: 'There is no help for it. I must have the robe and the other things.' 'Indeed there is no help for it,' replied the Jew. 'As you want the things, I must put you in good shape for carrying them.' So saying, he sprinkled Alī with water out of a cup, muttering and saying: 'Become an ass!' and Alī became an ass, with the face of an ass, vast pendulous ears and new-shod hoofs. He brayed like an ass, lifting his muzzle and his tail on high and sniffing the air. The Jew made further conjurations to give himself complete mastery and then obliged the ass to go downstairs on its hind legs and stand in the courtyard, where he himself traced a magic circle in the sand, which at once rose to be a solid enclosure round the animal, from which there was no hope of escape.

Next morning the Jew saddled, bridled and mounted Alī, whispering in his ear: 'We shall give my poor mule a rest.' As they left the enchanted palace, it disappeared into thin air.

Azariah rode to his shop and, after tying Alī where he was used to tether the mule, began to occupy himself with weighing his gold and silver. Alī, who kept all the faculties of man save speech, was obliged to crunch the dry beans of his feed in order not to die of hunger; but, as a consolation, he discharged his black humour in a series of sounding farts right in the face of the Jew's would-be customers. Soon there came to the Jew a young merchant who had been ruined. 'I have no money,' he said, 'and yet I must live and earn food for my wife. Here are the last gold bracelets which remained to her; I will exchange them for their value in money, if you will give me enough to buy an ass, so that I can turn water-carrier.' 'First tell me,' answered the Jew, 'if you are ready to ill-treat the ass and make his life a burden if he refuses to work for you?' 'As Allāh lives,' said the young man, 'if he will not work, I will thrust my stick into his most sensitive parts and force him to do as I wish.' Alī, the ass, heard all that was said and protested, as far as he was able, with a terrible fart; but the Jew said: 'If you promise that, I will let you have my own ass in exchange for the bracelets. Do not spare him or he will get lazy; load him heavily, for he is young and solid enough.' The man handed over the bracelets and led Alī away, while the poor beast said to itself: 'O Alī, I am sure this new master will load you with a heavy wooden saddle and make you carry waterskins until your back is broken; I think that you are lost.'

When the purchaser reached home, he bade his wife go down to the stable and feed the ass. The woman, who was young and pleasant to behold, carried beans to the stable and would have put them in Alī's nosebag. But the ass, after having looked at her out of the corner of his eye, sniffed the air furiously and butted her with his head, so that she fell across the trough with her clothes in the air. The beast then got over her, kissing her face with his great trembling lips, and displayed the considerable heritage which asses carry.

The woman uttered such piercing cries that all the neighbours ran into the stable and, seeing how matters stood, hastened to drive Alī from off the woman. When later her husband came and asked her what was the matter, she spat in his face, saying: 'O bastard, could you find no ass in all Baghdād except this woman-harrier? Either you will get rid of the beast or we shall talk about divorce.' 'But what has the ass done?' he asked. 'He tumbled me,' she said, 'and, if it had not been for the neighbours, would have terribly pierced me.' On this the young man gave the ass a good beating with his cudgel, and led him back to the Jew to whom he told the whole story. Azariah was obliged to return the bracelets, but, when the man had gone, he turned to the ass, saying: 'You would play the wanton with women, would you? Wait a bit! Since you are so fond of being an ass and cannot control your immoral caprices, I must find some other condition for you, in which you will be laughed at by great and small.' So saying he shut his shop, mounted the ass, and rode out of the city.

At this point Shahrazād saw the approach of morning and discreetly fell silent.

But when the four-hundred-and-sixty-third night had come

SHE SAID:

Again Azariah called his palace from the empty air. Then, after shutting the ass in its enclosure, he muttered certain incantations over it and sprinkled water upon the brown back until Alī returned to his own shape. Then said the Jew: 'Now will you take my advice and give up your foolishness or must I turn you into something worse?' 'As Allāh lives,' answered Alī, 'since your fortune is twined with mine, I must either kill you or take the robe from you and convert you to the faith of Islām.' He leapt towards the sorcerer, but the latter stretched out his hand and threw in his face drops of water from a cup graven with talismans. 'Become a bear!' he cried, and Alī became a bear, muzzled, fastened with a strong chain by an iron ring which pierced his nostrils, and already trained in dancing. 'You fool,' whispered the Jew in the bear's ear, 'you are like a nut which has to be cracked before it can be used.'

Alī spent the night fastened to a ring in the courtyard. But, when morning came, the Jew dragged him behind his mule to the shop and fastened him outside, while he went to attend to his gold. Poor Alī, the bear, heard and understood all that went on about him, but could not speak.

It was not long before a man, who was passing the shop, saw the bear and went in to Azariah, saying: 'My master, will you sell that bear? A doctor has prescribed bear's meat for my sick wife and bear's grease as a salve for her, but I cannot come by any.' 'Do you want to kill at once or will you be fattening the beast first to have more salve?' asked the Jew. 'He is fat enough for my purpose,' said the other. 'I will have him killed to-day.' 'As it is a lady who is ill,' cried the sorcerer joyfully, 'I will give you the bear for nothing.' The man haled Alī to his house and sent for a butcher, who soon appeared and, after rolling up his sleeves, began to sharpen two great knives one against the other. Love of dear life gave Alī a double portion of strength, so when the folk would have rolled him over and cut his throat, he threw them off and, leaping into the street, ran to the magician's palace as he had never run in all his life before.

'I will give you one more chance,' said Azariah when he saw the bear come back. He sprinkled Alī as before, until he returned to a man's shape, and then called his daughter Kamar. The girl found Alī so handsome that her heart went out to him in violent love. 'O beautiful young man,' she said, 'is it true that it is my robe you desire and not myself?' 'It is true,' he answered. 'I need your things for the most sensitive Zainab, daughter of that fine old woman Delilah.' This answer filled the girl with grief. 'You see,' cried the Jew, 'he will not repent.' So saying, he sprinkled Alī a third time with water from the talismanic cup, crying: 'Become a dog!' At once Alī was changed into a slinking hound of the street, and the magician spat in his face and kicked him out of the palace.

The dog, Alī, began to wander outside the walls, but soon, driven by hunger, he ventured into Baghdād. At once he was picked up by an immense outcry of all the dogs in the various wards through which he passed. Seeing that he was a stranger and yet ventured within those limits which they were guarding, they ran after him and chased him out of their domains with terrible biting. The poor intruder was bundled from one territory to another at the teeth of his fellows, until at last he fled into an open shop. The owner of this shop, who was a dealer in second-hand goods, took up a stick as soon as he saw the unhappy hound run in, with his tail between his legs and fleeing from a whole furious army of other dogs, and laid about him among the pursuers with such a will that they fled howling. Then the dog, Alī, lay down at the man's feet with tears in his eyes and gratefully began to lick his hand with many waggings of the tail. 'Better be a dog than an ape, or something worse,' he said to himself and, when evening came and the dealer shut his shop, kept close to the man and followed him to his house.

At this point Shahrazād saw the approach of morning and discreetly fell silent.

But when the four-hundred-and-sixty-fourth night had come

SHE SAID:

No sooner had Alī followed the dealer into the house than his daughter covered her face, crying: 'O father, what is this that you do, to bring a strange man into the presence of your daughter?' 'What strange man?' said the dealer. 'There is only a dog here.' 'But that dog,' she answered, 'is none other than Alī Quicksilver of Cairo, who has been magicked by Azariah, the Jew Sorcerer, because of the robe of Kamar.' 'Is that true?' asked the dealer, turning to the dog; when Alī nodded 'Yes' with his head, the girl went on: 'I am ready to bring him back to his human shape if he will consent to marry me.' 'As Allāh lives,' cried the dealer, 'bring him back now and he will surely marry you!' Then, turning to the dog, he said: 'Do you consent?' Alī wagged his tail and nodded his head again. At once the girl took a talismanic cup filled with water and was about to speak words of conjuration over it, when a loud cry was heard and a young slave belonging to the house ran into the room. 'What of your promise, my mistress,' she said. 'What of the pact between us? When I taught you sorcery, you undertook never to perform a magic operation without consulting me. I also want to marry young Alī Quicksilver, who is before us in the likeness of this dog, and I will never consent to the changing of him unless he belongs to the two of us in community and passes alternate nights with each.' The dealer's daughter consented to this arrangement and, when her astonished father asked how she had learned sorcery, answered: 'I learned from our new slave, who had herself acquired the knowledge when she was in the service of the Jew Azariah and could peep secretly into the grimoires and old books of that redoubtable man.'

Without more ado the two girls took a talismanic cup each and, after murmuring some Hebrew words over the water, sprinkled the dog Alī, saying: 'By the power and merit of Sulaimān, return as a man!' Alī Quicksilver leapt to his feet, younger and more beautiful than ever. But, even as he did so, a second loud cry was heard and the door flew open to admit a young woman of marvellous beauty, who carried on her outstretched arms two gold dishes, one above the other. The lower dish contained the gold robe, the gold crown, the gold belt and the gold slippers; the higher and smaller dish held the severed head of Azariah the Jew, bloody and with moving eyes.

This girl, who was none other than Kamar, set the two dishes before Alī Quicksilver, saying: 'O Alī, because I love you, I bring you those things of mine which you coveted and also the head of my father the Jew. I myself have adopted the faith of Islām. There is no God but Allāh! and Muhammad is the prophet of Allāh!'

'You are a woman,' answered Alī, 'and yet you bring me a fine wedding present. Therefore I am very ready to marry you at the same time as I marry these two, on condition that I shall be free to give the things to Zainab and take her to be my fourth wife, as the law allows.' Kamar and the other two women consented to this arrangement, and, when Quicksilver had promised the dealer that he would take no concubines to fret his wives, he was allowed to depart with Kamar's gifts and to set out for Delilah's house.

On his way he saw a strolling sweetmeat seller of unusually short stature, who carried a tray on his head filled with dry conserves, halwā and sugar-coated almonds. 'I will buy some of these sweets to take to Zainab,' said Alī to himself. Even as he framed this determination in his mind, the sweetmeat seller halted, as if he had guessed his thoughts, and said: 'Dear master, there is none in all Baghdād who can make carrot jam with nuts to equal mine. How much would you like? But first taste a little piece and tell me what you think of it.' Quicksilver took the morsel which was handed him, but no sooner had he swallowed it than he fell unconscious to the ground, for the jam was heavily drugged with banj and the sweetmeat seller was none other than little Mahmūd Miscarriage, who followed a lucrative trade along these lines. He had seen the rich presents which Alī was carrying and had used this trick in order to steal them. The moment Quicksilver was stretched on his back, Miscarriage collected the presents intended for Zainab and turned to flee. But he ran straight into the arms of the archers of Hasan-the-Pest, who had seen the theft and galloped up in the nick of time. Miscarriage was forced to confess his crime and to point out the body lying on the ground. At once Hasan, who had been scouring all the wards of Baghdād for Alī Quicksilver, had counter-banj fetched and administered it to his unconscious friend. Alī's first cry on coming to himself was for the gold garments. Hasan showed him that they were safe and congratulated him on his skill: 'As Allāh lives, you surpass us all!' He led Alī to Ahmad's house and had him tell his story. 'It is in my mind,' said Hasan, 'that the magician's palace belongs to you, since you are marrying Kamar. We will celebrate the fourfold bridal there. I shall carry these presents to Zainab at once and persuade her uncle Zuraik to consent to the match. I promise you that the old rascal will not refuse this time. As to Mahmūd Miscarriage, we can hardly punish him since you are marrying into the family.'

At this point Shahrazād saw the approach of morning and discreetly fell silent.

But when the four-hundred-and-sixty-fifth night had come

SHE SAID:

The Pest carried the gold robe, the gold crown, the gold belt and the gold slippers to the khān of pigeons, where he found Delilah and Zainab feeding the birds. After greetings, he begged them to fetch Zuraik and, when the fried fish seller had come, showed him the wedding presents which he had claimed as Zainab's dowry. 'You cannot refuse now,' he said. 'If you do, I, Hasan-the-Pest, will take the insult to myself.' But Zuraik and Delilah gladly accepted the presents and gave their consent to the marriage.

Next morning Alī Quicksilver took possession of the palace of Azariah the Jew, and that same evening, in the presence of the kādī and witnesses on the one side and Ahmad-the-Moth with his forty and Hasan-the-Pest with his forty on the other, contracts were written for the marriage of Quicksilver with Zainab, daughter of Delilah, with Kamar, daughter of Azariah, with the dealer's daughter, and the dealer's slave. A sumptuous feast celebrated the bridal, and all the women there declared that Zainab was the most beautiful and had the most provocative eyes beneath her marriage veil. She wore the gold robe, the gold crown, the gold belt and the gold slippers; the three other brides walked round her like stars about the moon.

On that night Alī Quicksilver penetrated his wife Zainab and, finding her to be a true unthreaded pearl, a right unridden filly, tasted all the delights of Paradise in her arms. On the next three nights he discovered that his other brides were perfect in beauty and virginity, so that he greatly enjoyed giving what he had to give and taking what he had to take, in mutual generosity.

The feasting lasted for thirty days and thirty nights, and no expense was spared, until the guests were weary with laughing, singing, eating and drinking. As soon as they departed, Hasan went to Quicksilver and, after renewed congratulations, said to him: 'O Alī, the time has now come for me to present you to our master the Khalīfah, that he may dower you with his favours.'

An audience was granted to the two and, as soon as Hārūn al-Rashīd saw young Alī Quicksilver, he felt his heart moved towards him because of his winning expression and great beauty. Pushed forward by the Pest, Alī first kissed the earth between the Khalīfah's hands and then, rising, whipped a piece of silk from a dish which Camelback handed him and exposed the severed head of Azariah the Jew.

'What head is that?' demanded the amazed Khalīfah. 'The head of your greatest enemy, O Commander of the Faithful,' answered Alī, 'the head of an evil sorcerer who could have destroyed Baghdād and all your palaces with a wave of his hand.'

He told Hārūn the whole story of his adventures from beginning to end, and the Khalīfah was so astonished that he instantly appointed him general supervisor of police, with the same rank, the same privileges, and the same emoluments as Ahmad-the-Moth and Hasan-the-Pest. 'Long live all gallant fellows of your kind, O Alī!' said al-Rashīd. 'Now ask me for something else.' 'I ask that the Khalīfah may live for ever,' answered Quicksilver, 'and also that I may send into Cairo, my native city, for my robber band, my forty old companions, that they may be my guards and make a train for me like those of my two colleagues.' The Khalīfah gave his permission and also ordered the ablest of the palace scribes to make a careful account of this story and to lock it in the archives of his reign, that it might serve as both instruction and amusement for the Mussulmān people and all those who in the future should believe in Allāh and in His prophet, Muhammad, the perfect man (upon whom be prayer and peace!).

They all lived the gayest and most delightful of lives, until they were visited by the Destroyer of joy, the Separator of friends.

Such, O auspicious King, is the true story, in all its details, of Delilah-the-Wily and her daughter Zainab-the-Cheat, with Ahmad-the-Moth, Hasan-the-Pest, Alī Quicksilver, and Zuraik the fried fish merchant. But Allāh (whose Name be glorified and exalted!) is wiser and sees further.

Then Shahrazād added: 'But you must not think, O auspicious King, that this tale is any truer than that of Jūdar the Fisherman and his Brothers.' And at once she told:

The Tale of Jūdar the Fisherman or the Enchanted Bag

IT is related, O auspicious King, that there was once a merchant called Umar who had three sons: Sālim the eldest, Salīm the second, and Jūdar who was the youngest. He had brought them all up to manhood, but ever preferred Jūdar, which caused the other brothers to hate and envy the lad. When Umar, who was a very old man, noticed this hate, he feared that Jūdar might be ill-treated after his death by the other two. Therefore he called together the folk of his family and certain learned men whose business, under the kādī, was with inheritance, and said to them: 'Let all my goods and the stock of my shop be brought before me!' This was done, and Umar continued: 'Good people, I beg you to divide these things into four equal parts, according to the law.' The goods were divided, and the old man gave one fourth to each of his three sons and kept the last for himself, saying: 'These possessions were all mine and I have divided them among my sons during my lifetime, so that after my death they will have nothing to claim from my estate or from each other. Thus discord will be avoided. When I am gone, the part which I have kept is to go to my wife that she may be free to nourish herself.'

Soon after this the old man died, and at once Sālim and Salīm claimed part of Jūdar's inheritance, saying: 'Our father's fortune has fallen into your hands.'

At this point Shahrazād saw the approach of morning and discreetly fell silent.

But when the four-hundred-and-sixty-sixth night had come

SHE SAID:

Jūdar was obliged to have recourse to the judges and to call those Mussulmāns who had witnessed the division. These gave testimony, and the judge forbade the two elder brothers to claim anything from

Jūdar. The expenses of the suit deprived all three of a part of their inheritance; but this did not prevent Sālim and Salīm from plotting against Jūdar a second time, so that he was forced to go to law again and lose yet more of his possessions. The other two suffered equally with him, but they went before a third judge and then a fourth and then a fifth, until the fortune of each had disappeared and none of the three had enough to buy an onion and a crust.

The two brothers, being unable to batten upon Jūdar in their ruin, ill-treated, deceived and robbed their mother. The poor woman came weeping to Jūdar and began to curse her elder sons, saying: 'They have stripped me of my all.' 'Dear mother,' answered Jūdar, 'do not curse them, for Allāh will find them a reward. I cannot sue them for a recovery of your goods as all my fortune has gone in suits already. We must resign ourselves in silence; you shall live with me and my bread shall be your bread for ever. Bless me, mother, and then Allāh will give me the means to care for you. Let the Great Judge see to my brothers, and do you console yourself with the poet's words:

> Of all avengers that there are
> Time's the most bloodthirsty by far.
> Also, a hill which overtops a hill
> Is dwarfed by mountains greater still,
> For such is Allāh's will.'

Thus Jūdar calmed his mother and persuaded her to live with him. To earn their living, he bought a fishing-net and went every day to cast it in the Nile at Bulāk, in the great pools or in other water. Sometimes he would earn ten copper pieces, sometimes twenty, sometimes as much as thirty; so that he and his mother ate and drank well.

The two brothers soon had nothing left, for neither knew a trade and the money which they had stolen from their mother had been quickly dissipated. They were obliged to show themselves as naked beggars before their mother, humbling themselves in the dust and complaining of their starvation. A mother's heart is ever pitiful; the women gave them crusts which were sometimes mouldy and fed them with the rests of yesterday's evening meal. 'Eat quickly,' she said, 'and go before your brother comes back, for if he saw you here he might harden his heart against me, and I be compromised.' As soon as they were fed they went their way. But one evening, as they sat eating of their mother's bounty, Jūdar unexpectedly returned. In shame and confusion his mother bowed her head to the ground, but Jūdar smiled at his brothers, saying: 'Be very welcome, O my brothers! What has happened to make you delight us at last with this eagerly expected visit?' He threw his arms about the necks of the two, and then continued: 'It was not good of you to let me languish in the sadness of your absence. I had no news of you at all.' 'As Allāh lives, dear brother,' they answered, 'we also have longed for you, but shame for what had passed prevented us from coming. It was all the work of the Devil (whom Allāh curse!) and now we have no other blessing but you and our mother.' Touched by these words, Jūdar made answer: 'I have no blessing but you, my brothers.' Then said his mother: 'My child, may Allāh whiten your face and increase your prosperity, for you are the most generous of us all!' 'Stay with me as welcome guests,' said Jūdar to his brothers. 'Allāh has been good to me and there is plenty in the house for all.' Thus he was reconciled with his brothers, who supped with him and stayed the night.

Next morning they ate together, and then Jūdar set forth with his net, confident in the generosity of Allāh, while the other two left the house until noon, when they returned to eat again with their mother. It was evening before Jūdar came home, loaded with meat and vegetables which he had earned by his fishing. The family lived together in this way for a month, Jūdar paying the expenses with his net and the other three eating and making merry.

At this point Shahrazād saw the approach of morning and discreetly fell silent.

But when the four-hundred-and-sixty-seventh night had come

SHE SAID:

One day Jūdar cast his net in the river and brought it back empty. The same thing happened again and yet again, so he changed his place and cast his net into new water. It came up as empty as before, therefore he changed his place again and then a third time; but he had not caught a single gudgeon by sundown. 'Are there no fish in the water,' he cried, 'or is there some other reason for this prodigy?' He took his net on his back in the gloaming and began to walk homewards sadly, torturing himself with the thought that his mother and brothers would have no food that night. His way lay past the baker's shop where he was accustomed to buy the evening bread, and he stopped with a sigh to watch the crowd of purchasers who surrounded the baker with their money. 'Welcome, Jūdar,' said the baker, 'do you want some bread?' Then, as the fisherman remained silent, he exclaimed: 'If you have no money, take what you want. I will give you time to pay.' 'Give me ten coppers' worth of bread,' answered Jūdar, 'and take my net as a pledge.' 'No, no,' said the baker, 'the net is your means of livelihood. If I took it I should be shutting the door of your sustenance. Here are the loaves and also ten coppers to buy other food. To-morrow you can bring me twenty coppers' worth of fish.' Jūdar thanked the man heartily and bought himself meat and vegetables, saying: 'Allāh will pay my debts for me to-morrow and drive my cares away.' That night his mother cooked the meal as usual and Jūdar ate and slept.

Next morning he went forth fasting and fished until noon, without catching anything. He had not the heart to try further, and so took up his net and made for home. The baker saw him and gave him more bread and ten coppers, saying: 'Take this and go your way. If luck has deserted you to-day, it will return to-morrow.' Jūdar would have excused himself, but the baker exclaimed: 'Do not say a word about it. If you had caught anything to-day you would have paid me. I am ready to give you the limit of credit; therefore come to-morrow without shame if you are not successful.'

On the next day Jūdar caught nothing and was obliged to accept the baker's offer. The same mischance followed him for seven further days and, at the end of that time, he said in the agony of his heart: 'To-morrow I will go and fish Lake Kārūn. Perhaps my Destiny awaits me there.'

Next morning Jūdar journeyed to Lake Kārūn, which is not far from Cairo, and was about to cast his net when he saw a Moor coming towards him on a mule. The man was dressed in a very beautiful robe, and was so muffled with his burnous and head-wrappings that only one of his eyes was to be seen. The mule was as richly-decked as its master, with silk and gold brocade, and on its rump bore a saddle-bag of coloured linen.

The Moor alighted from his mule, saying: 'Greeting, O Jūdar, son of Umar!' 'Greeting, O pilgrim!' answered Jūdar. Then said the Moor: 'I have need of you. If you will obey me, it will be to your great advantage; you shall be my friend and have charge of all my affairs.' 'Good master,' replied Jūdar, 'tell me what you have in your mind and I will obey you without reservation.' 'First recite the opening chapter of the Koran,' said the Moor, and Jūdar recited it. Then the stranger took certain silk cords from his bag, saying: 'O Jūdar, son of Umar, you must tie my arms behind me with these cords, as tightly as you can, then you must throw me into the lake and wait. If my hand comes up out of the water before my body, cast your net and bring me to the shore; but if my foot emerges first, you may know that I am dead. In that case take the mule with the bag and enquire in the market for one Shamaiah a Jew. He will give you a hundred dīnārs for the animal, and your sole remaining duty will be to keep the secret.'

At this point Shahrazād saw the approach of morning and discreetly fell silent.

But when the four-hundred-and-sixty-eighth night had come

SHE SAID:

At once Jūdar tied the Moor's arms, pulling tightly and more tightly at the man's request, and then lifted him up and threw him into the lake. After a certain time two feet came to the surface, and he understood that the man was dead. Without taking further thought for the body, Jūdar rode the mule to the market and found the Jew sitting at the entrance of his shop. 'There can be no doubt that the man has perished!' cried the merchant when he saw the mule. 'It was greed which killed him.' He paid a hundred dīnārs for the beast, and then dismissed Jūdar with a recommendation to keep the matter secret.

The fisherman hurried to the baker and gave him a dīnār, saying: 'Here is what I owe you, my master.' The baker made his account and assured Jūdar that the change would be good for bread on the two following days. Then Jūdar went to a butcher and a vegetable-seller, giving each a dīnār and asking them to give him credit for the change. When he reached home loaded with provisions, he found his brothers famished and their mother counselling patience. The three threw themselves upon the food like ghouls and ate all the bread, while they were waiting for the meat and vegetables to cook.

Before leaving the house next day, Jūdar gave the rest of the gold to his mother, bidding her see that none of the three lacked for anything while he was away. He returned to Lake Kārūn and was about to cast his net when he saw a second Moor, much like the first, approaching in far more expensive garments and upon a more sumptuously harnessed mule. The stranger dismounted, saying: 'Greeting, O Jūdar, son of Umar!' 'Greeting, O pilgrim!' answered the fisherman. Then said the Moor: 'Did you see a man like myself, mounted upon a mule, when you were here yesterday?' When Jūdar, fearing to be accused of the man's death, denied having seen anyone on the day before, the Moor answered with a smile: 'Poor Jūdar, I know everything that happened. The man whom you threw into the lake, and whose mule you sold to the Jew for a hundred dīnārs, was my brother.' 'Since you know all that,' retorted Jūdar, 'why do you ask me?' 'Because I have need of the same service as my brother,' said the man, and at once drew other silk cords from his costly bag, repeating the instructions of his dead brother: 'Fasten my arms tightly and throw me into the water. If my foot comes up first I shall be dead; then you may take the mule to the Jew and sell it for a hundred dīnārs.'

Jūdar tied the Moor's arms and threw him into the lake, where he sank to the bottom. In a short time two feet came up out of the water, and the fisherman said to himself: 'He is dead and damned. Allāh grant that a Moor be sent to me every day, that I may earn a hundred dīnārs!' When the Jew saw him returning, he cried: 'The second is dead! Such is the reward of overweening ambition.' He gave a hundred dīnārs in exchange for the mule, and Jūdar handed the whole sum to his mother when he reached home. 'My child,' cried the woman, 'whence comes all this gold?' Her son told her what had happened and she became very frightened. 'You should never return to Lake Kārūn,' she said. 'I fear these Moors for you.' 'It is with their consent that I throw them into the water,' he answered. 'It is foolish to bid me give up this trade, wherein I earn a hundred dīnārs a day as a professional drowner. As Allāh lives, I shall return to Kārūn every day until I have drowned the last Moor and there be no more such in all the world.'

On the third day Jūdar returned to Lake Kārūn and waited by its edge, until there came to him a third Moor, very like the other two but surpassing them in the splendour of his garments and the trappings of his mule. Another difference was that this man had a large glass jar on each side of his saddle-bag. 'Greeting, O Jūdar, son of Umar!' said the Moor, and Jūdar returned his salutation, thinking to himself: 'How is it that all of them know my name?'

At this point Shahrazād saw the approach of morning and discreetly fell silent.

But when the four-hundred-and-sixty-ninth night had come

SHE SAID:

'Have other Moors passed this way?' asked the stranger. 'Two,' answered Jūdar. 'Where did they go?' said the other, and the fisherman replied: 'I tied their arms and threw them into the lake, where they both drowned. I am ready to do the same for you if such an end is to your mind.' 'Poor fisherman,' exclaimed the Moor with a laugh, 'do you not know that the end of every life is fixed beforehand?' With this he got down from his mule and gave Jūdar silk cords from his saddle-bag, with which the fisherman bound his arms. 'I am in a hurry,' said Jūdar as he worked. 'You may have complete confidence in my skill as a drowner, for I have had some practice.' When he had thrown the third Moor into the water and seen him disappear, he waited for his feet to come to the surface; but, to his great surprise, two hands appeared instead, followed by the head of the Moor, who cried: 'Catch me in your net for I cannot swim!' Jūdar threw the net over him and, dragging him to land, saw that he held in each hand a coral-red fish. As soon as he got to his feet, the diver placed one of the fish into each of the glass jars and after securely closing the vessels, put them back in his bag. Then he took Jūdar in his arms and kissed him on the two cheeks with great effusion, crying: 'As Allāh lives, I would have died without you and never caught these fish!'

When Jūdar was a little recovered from his surprise, he said: 'O pilgrim, if you really think that I have had a hand in your salvation and the taking of the fishes, my price will be the true tale of your drowned brothers, the red fish and the Jew Shamaiah.' Then said the Moor: 'As you have guessed, the two Moors whom you drowned were my brothers; one was called Abd al-Salām and the other Abd al-Ahad. My name is Abd al-Samad, and the man whom you take to be a Jew is a fourth brother, a true Mussulmān of the Mālikī persuasion, whose real name is Abd al-Rahīm. Our father, Abd al-Wadūd, was a powerful magician, thoroughly versed in every mysterious science. He taught the four of us magic, sorcery, and the art of both discovering and opening the most deeply hidden treasures; and we applied ourselves so well to his teaching that we were able in the end to hold the Jinn, the Marids and the Afārīt at our command.

'When our father died, leaving us great possessions and incalculable riches, we divided in friendly fashion his gold, his various talismans, and his books; but over the possession of certain manuscripts we fell into a quarrel. The most important of these manuscripts was one entitled The Book of Eld, the worth of which may not be told; its weight in diamonds would not purchase a thousandth part of it. Our father had put the essential of all his knowledge into this work; it contains precise instruction of the place of every treasure hidden in the earth, with just rules for the solving of enigmas and the interpretation of signs.

'Discord had reached a high pitch between us when the venerable old man who had educated our father and taught him magic entered the house. This sage, whose name was al-Kāhīn al-Abtan, took The Book of Eld in his hand and said to us: "My children, you are the sons of my son and I cannot favour one before the rest. I therefore decree that the owner of this book shall be he who opens the treasure of al-Shamardal and brings me the celestial globe, the phial of kohl, the sword and the seal-ring which that hoard contains. These things have extraordinary powers. The ring is guarded by a Jinnī whose terrifying name is Thundering Thunder, and he who gets possession of it may front the powers of kings and sultāns without a qualm and dominate the length and breadth of all the world. The man who holds the sword may destroy armies with the bright flames which shoot forth from it. By means of the celestial globe a man may voyage to any part of the world without leaving his seat, and visit all the lands of East and West. He has only to touch with his finger the place which he wishes to reach and the globe will turn until that land, with its people and strange sights, appears as if it were in the same room. If the possessor of this globe has any fault to find with the people of a land or of a city, he has but to turn its equivalent on the surface of the globe to the rays of the sun and all the people there will be burnt up by a consuming flame. He who rubs his eyelids with kohl from the phial may see all treasures hidden in the earth. The Book of Eld shall belong solely to the one of you who opens this treasure; those who fail will have no redress. Do you accept these conditions?" "O teacher of our father, we accept them," cried the four of us, "but you must remember that we know nothing of the treasure of al-Shamardal."

At this point Shahrazād saw the approach of morning and discreetly fell silent.

But when the four-hundred-and-seventieth night had come

SHE SAID:

'Then said The Very Profound Kāhīn: "The treasure of al-Shamardal lies in the power of the two sons of King Red. Your father tried to gain possession of the treasure, but King Red's two sons, whom it is first necessary to enslave, escaped from him when they were hard pressed and threw themselves into Lake Kārūn, near Cairo, in the likeness of red fish. He came to me complaining of his failure, therefore I calculated the chances of the matter by astrology and discovered that the treasure of al-Shamardal could only be opened with the help and in the presence of a young man from Cairo, one Jūdar, son of Umar, a fisherman. This Jūdar may be met with by the banks of Lake Kārūn; only by him may that water be freed from enchantment; it is for him to fasten the arms of those who would go down into the lake and to cast them into it. The diver must contend against the two sons of King Red; if it be his fate to conquer and catch them, he will not drown and his hand will come first to the surface. In that case Jūdar must bring him to shore in his net. He who is fated to drown will come to the surface feet first and must be abandoned to his Destiny."

' "We will try even at the risk of our lives!" three of us answered, but our brother, Abd al-Rahīm, refused the adventure. We therefore decided to disguise him as a Jew merchant, and arranged that we should send the mule and the bag to him that he might buy them from the fisherman in case any of us perished in our attempt.

'You know what has happened since then. My two brothers perished in the lake, destroyed by King Red's sons. I nearly died also in my struggle with them; but, thanks to a conjuration which I made in my mind, I was able to undo my bonds, to free the water from enchantment, and imprison the two red fish in the glass jars. These sons of King Red are powerful Afārīt and their capture is the first step towards the opening of the treasure of al-Shamardal. It is, however, absolutely necessary, according to the horoscope cast by The Very Profound Kāhīn, that you should be present. Are you willing to come with me to a part of Maghrib, not far from Fez and Miknās, and help me to open the treasure? I will give you all that you ask and be your brother for ever in the sight of God. After the journey you may return joyfully to your own house.'

'O my lord pilgrim,' answered Jūdar, 'I have a mother and brothers to support. Who will feed them if I consent to go with you?' 'This is nothing but laziness,' retorted the Moor. 'But, if it is really care for your mother which prevents you, you may take her a thousand dīnārs from me and my promise that you will return at the end of four months.' At this talk of a thousand dīnārs, Jūdar cried: 'I will carry the money to my mother at once and then most willingly set out with you.' As soon as the Moor gave him the coins, he hurried to his house and put them in his mother's charge, saying: 'These thousand dīnārs are for the use of you and my brothers while I am away on a four months' voyage to Maghrib with an inhabitant of that place. Pray for me while I am gone, and your blessing shall help me.' 'O my child,' she answered, 'it is a long absence and I fear for you.' 'Dear mother,' he replied, 'there need be no fear for one who is under the protection of Allāh. Besides, the Moor is a very honest man.' He went on praising the stranger until his mother said: 'May Allāh incline the heart of this excellent Moor towards you! Go with him, my son, and may he prove a generous companion.'

'Have you consulted your mother?' asked the Moor when Jūdar returned to him. 'Indeed I have,' he answered, 'she has prayed for me and blessed me.' Without delay the Moor took Jūdar up behind him on the mule and they rode from noon until late in the day.

At this point Shahrazād saw the approach of morning and discreetly fell silent.

But when the four-hundred-and-seventy-first night had come

SHE SAID:

The movement through the air made Jūdar extremely hungry and, as he did not see any provision in the bag, he said to the Moor: 'My lord, I think that you have forgotten food for the journey.' 'Are you hungry?' asked the Moor and, when Jūdar answered that he was, stopped the mule and dismounted, saying: 'Give me the bag.' Then, with the bag in his hand, he asked: 'What does your soul desire, my brother?' 'Anything,' answered Jūdar. 'In Allāh's name, tell me what you would prefer to eat,' said the Moor. 'Bread and cheese,' answered Jūdar. 'Bread and cheese?' said the other with a

smile. 'That is scarce worthy of you. Ask for some excellent food.'
'Just now I would find anything excellent,' answered Jūdar. 'Do
you like roast chicken?' asked the Moor. 'As Allāh lives, I do,'
answered Jūdar. 'Do you like honeyed rice?' asked the Moor.
'Very much,' answered Jūdar. 'Do you like tomatoed birds' heads?
Do you like artichokes stuffed with parsley and colocasia? Roast
sheep's heads? Puffed barley with garnishment? Savoury vine
leaves? Pastries? And such and such and such?' In this way he
enumerated twenty-four dishes, while Jūdar thought to himself:
'Is the man mad? Or how is he going to give me these things when
he has neither cook nor kitchen? I must tell him that his meal is long
enough.' Then aloud he said: 'That is sufficient. Do you want to go
on making my mouth water with all these things, when you cannot
produce one of them?' But the Moor with a murmured 'Good
appetite, O Jūdar!' plunged his hand into the bag and took out of it a
gold dish on which were two roast chicken, piping hot; he dipped
again and there appeared another gold dish filled with skewered
mutton; and then came up, one after another, the rest of the twenty-
four courses which he had suggested.

'Eat, poor friend,' he said, but the astonished Jūdar cried: 'My
lord, surely before we started you must have put a little kitchen and
many cooks in the bag?' 'The bag is enchanted, that is all,' answered
the Moor with a smile. 'It is served by an Ifrīt who would, if we
wished it, instantly bring us a thousand Syrian dishes, a thousand
Egyptian, a thousand Indian, and a thousand Chinese.' The two ate
together until they were satisfied, and then the Moor, after throwing
away the remains and returning the gold dishes to the bag, drew
from the other side a gold ewer filled with fresh cool water. After
they had drunken their fill, made their ablutions, and recited the
noon prayer, the Moor returned the ewer to the bag, and the two
continued their journey on the back of the mule.

'O Jūdar,' said the Moor at length, 'do you know how far we have
gone from Cairo?' 'As Allāh lives, I do not,' replied the fisherman.
'In these two hours,' the other went on, 'we have covered a month's
journey; for this mule is none other than a Jinnīyah, and usually
achieves a year's travel in one day. On this occasion, however, she
has gone slowly, so as not to fatigue you.' They continued on their
way towards Maghrib, having all their needs supplied, morning and
evening, by the magic bag. However complicated and extraordinary
the food which Jūdar demanded, the bag was able to provide it,

cooked to a turn, upon a golden dish. At the end of five days they reached Maghrib and entered the city of Fez and Miknās.

As they went along the streets many folk recognised the Moorish lord, and he was either greeting or giving his hand to be kissed all the way, until they came to a certain house and dismounted before it. The door opened to their knocking, and on the threshold appeared a girl as bright as the moon, as beautiful and slender as a thirsting gazelle, who smiled a welcome at them. 'Rahmah, my child,' said the Moor paternally, 'open the great hall of the palace for us.' Rahmah went before them into the building, with such balancing of her hips that Jūdar's reason fled from its seat in his mind and he said to himself: 'Surely she is the daughter of some king!'

Before entering, the Moor took the bag from the mule's back, saying: 'O mule, return whence you came and the blessing of Allāh be upon you!' Immediately the earth opened, received the mule into its depths, and closed again. On this Jūdar cried: 'Praise be to Allāh who guarded us while we were on the creature's back!' But the Moor said: 'Why are you surprised, O Jūdar? Did I not tell you that she was a Jinnīyah? Enter now, and let us go to the great hall.'

At this point Shahrazād saw the approach of morning and discreetly fell silent.

But when the four-hundred-and-seventy-second night had come

SHE SAID:

Jūdar followed his host into the great hall, where his eyes were dazzled by the bright number of its ornaments, by the beauty of its silver lustres and hanging gold, and by the profusion of the gems with which it was studded. As soon as the two were seated, the Moor bade his daughter bring a certain packet and, when it was placed in his hand, drew from it a robe worth at least a thousand dīnārs, which he handed to Jūdar, saying: 'Dress yourself in this and be our very welcome guest.' Jūdar put on the robe and at once had the look of some King of Western Arabia.

Meanwhile the Moor had been taking a multitude of dishes from the magic bag, until he had arranged on the cloth forty various and different foods. 'Put forth your hand and eat, my master,' he called to Jūdar. 'For this once overlook the poverty of our service, as we do not yet know your tastes and preference in food. You have but to mention your favourite dishes and they shall be set before you instantly.' 'As Allāh lives, O pilgrim,' answered the fisherman, 'I like every food and hate none. Do not ask my tastes, but give me all the dishes which come into your head. Eating is my one accomplishment and sole delight. I flatter myself I eat rather well.' He did, in fact, eat well that evening and on the following days, without once seeing the smoke of a kitchen. The Moor had but to plunge his arm into the bag, while thinking of a dish, to bring it out served on a gold plate. It was the same with fruits and pastries. For twenty days Jūdar lived in the Moor's dwelling, changing his robe every morning and finding each more beautiful and costly than the last.

On the morning of the twenty-first day the Moor came to him, saying: 'Rise up, O Jūdar, for this is the appointed day when the treasure of Shamardal shall be opened.' The two went out together and, when they had come beyond the city walls, there appeared two mules, which they mounted, and two black slaves, who walked behind the mules. At noon they reached the banks of a certain river and dismounted. At a sign from the Moor, the two negroes led away the mules and then came back bearing a tent, carpets and cushions, with which they made a comfortable camp. When all was prepared, they set the two glass jars containing the coral-coloured fish before the Moor and then, after serving a banquet of twenty-four dishes from the bag, disappeared into thin air.

As soon as he had eaten, the Moor set the glass jars on a stool and began to murmur magic words over them, until the two fish cried from inside: 'We are here, O king of sorcery! Have mercy upon us!' He continued his conjuration and the fish their pleading, until the two jars burst in pieces and there appeared two beings of human form who abased themselves before the Moor, wailing: 'Grant us pardon and safety, O powerful one! What is our fate to be?' Then said the sorcerer: 'I will strangle you, I will burn you, unless you promise to open the treasure of al-Shamardal.' 'We will do so,' they answered, 'but first you must bring to this place one Jūdar, a fisherman of Cairo, for it is written in the book of Destiny that the treasure shall not be opened save in his presence, and that no other than Jūdar, son of Umar, shall enter into the place where the treasure is.' 'Behold, the man of whom you speak is here!' answered the Moor. 'He both hears and sees you.' The two apparitions looked long at Jūdar, and then said: 'The last difficulty is removed. We swear by the Name that you may count upon us.' At this the wizard allowed them to go about the business in their own way, and they disappeared beneath the surface of the river.

The Moor set two tablets of red carnelian upon a large hollow reed and, hanging a gold censer filled with charcoal above the tablets, breathed upon it until the charcoal became red. Then he sprinkled incense on the coal, saying: 'O Jūdar, the smoke rises and I shall soon recite the beginning of my magic; but, as I may not be interrupted without great risk of thwarting the Power, I will first instruct you in all which you have to do to reach our end.' 'I am ready, my master,' answered Jūdar.

At this point Shahrazād saw the approach of morning and discreetly fell silent.

But when the four-hundred-and-seventy-third night had come

SHE SAID:

Then said the Moor: 'When I begin to say my magic over the rising smoke, the water of the river will lessen little by little and, in the end, dry up completely, leaving the bed exposed. Then you will see, in the slope of the bank, a gold door, as high as a city gate, into which are fixed two rings of the same metal. Go up to that door, tap lightly with one of the rings, and wait for a moment; then knock more loudly and wait again; lastly, knock a third time very loudly and do not move. After the third knocking you will hear a voice cry from within: "Who knocks at the door of the treasure and yet does not know how to loose the enchantment?" When you answer: "I am Jūdar, son of Umar, the fisherman of Cairo!" the door will open and a man appear on the threshold with a sword in his hand. He will say: "If you are truly that man, stretch out your neck that I may cut off your head." You must stretch it out fearlessly; for then, even as he raises the sword above you, he will fall at your feet, a body without a soul. You will receive no hurt; but if you refuse, through fear, he will most certainly kill you.

'When you have broken the first magic, enter and you will find a second door on which you must knock once and very loud. Instantly, on the sill of it, will appear a rider menacing you with a tall lance. When he says: "What brings you to this place, where neither man nor Jinnī may set his feet?" you must answer by boldly baring your breast to the point of the lance. You will receive no hurt and the rider will fall at your feet, a body without a soul. But if you recoil he will kill you.

'You will come then to a third door, which will be opened by an archer aiming an arrow at you from his bow: thrust your breast forward as a mark, and he will fall at your feet, a body without a soul. But if you hesitate he will kill you.

'Go further and, from a fourth door, there will leap out upon you a terrible lion with wide jaws, and make as if to eat you. Put your hand into his mouth and he will fall dead at your feet, without having done you the least harm.

'The fifth door will be opened by a negro who will ask you your name. Answer: "I am Jūdar," and he will say: "If you are indeed that man, try to open the sixth door."

'At the sixth door you must cry: 'O Jesus, command Moses to open unto me." The door will swing wide and two enormous dragons leap upon you with open mouths, one on the right hand and one on the left. You must fearlessly stretch out a hand to each; before they can bite, they will roll powerless at your feet. But if you show fear, your death is certain.

'You will then knock at the seventh door, and it will be opened by your mother. She will say: "Be welcome, my son. Come near, that I may wish you peace." You must answer: "Stay where you are and undress!" "My child, I am your mother," she will say. "You owe me respect, because I suckled and educated you. How can you think of setting me naked?" You must cry out on her, saying: "If you do not take off your clothes I will kill you!" When you take down a sword, which you will find on the right hand wall, and bid her begin, she will try to move your pity. Be on your guard against her wheedling and, each time she takes off one of her garments, cry: "The rest, the rest!" and menace her with death until she is quite naked. As soon as she has no more clothes, she will vanish.

'Then, O Jūdar, you will have broken all the charms and loosened the enchantments without hurt to yourself. It will only remain to pluck the fruit of your labour.

'To that end you must enter by the seventh door into a hall piled with ingots of gold. Pay no attention to these, but make straight for a little curtain-hung pavilion in the middle of the hall. Raise the curtain and you will find the great magician al-Shamardal sleeping upon a gold throne. Near his head you will see a thing shining, round like the moon; that is the celestial globe. He will be girt with the sword, have the ring on his finger, and the phial of kohl hung by a gold chain about his neck. Take these four precious things without hesitation, and bring them out of the treasure chamber to me.

'Have great care not to forget or disobey any one of my instructions; for, if your wit or courage fail you, I greatly fear the result.'

The Moor repeated his directions to Jūdar once, twice, thrice and yet again, until the fisherman said:

At this point Shahrazād saw the approach of morning and discreetly fell silent.

But when the four-hundred-and-seventy-fourth night had come

SHE SAID:

'I have the thing pat; but what man alive could confront the magic of which you speak or support these terrible dangers?' 'Have no fear for that, O Jūdar,' answered the Moor. 'The guardians of the doors are but phantoms. You can be quite easy for them.' Then said Jūdar: 'I put my trust in Allāh!'

The Moor cast fresh incense upon the coals and started to pronounce his conjuration. Soon the water of the river began to diminish little by little, and the bed appeared, showing the great door upon the slope of it.

Without hesitation, Jūdar went down into the river bottom and, approaching the gold door, knocked three times in the manner prescribed. A voice from within cried: 'Who knocks at the door of the treasure and yet does not know how to loosen the enchantment?' When he answered that he was Jūdar, son of Umar, the door opened and a man appeared on the threshold with a naked sword, crying: 'Stretch out your neck!' Jūdar stretched out his neck and the man fell lifeless, even as he was in act to bring down the sword. The other doors opened exactly as the Moor had predicted, and each time Jūdar loosed the enchantment with great boldness. When his mother opened the seventh door and cried him welcome, he asked her who she was. 'I am your mother, my son,' she replied. 'I carried you within me for nine months and gave you suck and brought you up.' 'Take off your clothes!' cried Jūdar, and the woman exclaimed: 'You are my son! How can you tell me to strip naked?' 'Take off!' said he, snatching the sword from where it hung. 'If you do not undress, I will kill you.' She cast aside some of her garments and then, as he still cried: 'More, more!' gradually unclothed herself until nothing but her drawers remained. 'O my son,' she said in a shamed voice, 'it was indeed lost labour when I reared you! Is your heart of stone that you would make me show my middle nakedness? Do you not know that this is forbidden and a sacrilege?' 'You are right,' answered Jūdar. 'I allow you to keep on your drawers.' Hardly had he said the words when the old woman cried: 'Beat him, beat him, for he has drawn back!' Lusty blows fell on him like rain from the invisible guardians of the treasure, and he had received a thrashing which he would never forget in all his life before the unseen Afārīt had finished chasing him through the halls and had shut the last door behind him.

When the Moor saw him thrown outside the door, he hastened to drag him from the water, which was already pouring back into the river bed. He hauled him fainting to the bank and recited verses of the Koran over him until he came to himself. 'Alas, alas, what have you done?' he asked. 'I overcame each obstacle and broke the charms,' answered the fisherman. 'It was my mother's drawers which lost me all that I had gained and got me a thrashing such as has never been since the world began.' 'Did I not warn you that disobedience would be fatal?' said the Moor. 'When you allowed the woman to keep on her drawers, you did a wrong to me and a wrong to yourself. All is over for this year; we will have to wait for next year to renew our attempt. Until then you shall live with me.' At a word spoken in the air, the two negroes appeared and, after folding the tent and clearing the camp, brought back the mules, upon which Jūdar and the Moor returned to the city of Fez.

Jūdar stayed as the Moor's guest for a whole year, receiving a costly new robe every morning and feasting of the best by means of the enchanted bag. When the day for opening the treasure came round again, the Moor led Jūdar outside the city, where they were met by the two negroes with the mules. As soon as they reached the river, the tent was pitched and a meal prepared. Then the Moor arranged the hollow reed, the carnelian tablets, the censer and the incense, and said to Jūdar: 'I have a piece of advice to give you.' 'My lord,' cried the fisherman, 'it is not necessary. I will only forget your excellent instructions of last year when I forget my thrashing.'

At this point Shahrazād saw the approach of morning and discreetly fell silent.

But when the four-hundred-and-seventy-fifth night had come

SHE SAID:

'You are sure that you remember?' asked the Moor and, when Jūdar answered that he did, went on: 'Lift up your heart, Jūdar! Above all, do not imagine that the old woman is your mother; she is nothing but a phantom who has taken your mother's appearance to your harm. You came out alive the first time; but, if you make any mistake to-day, you will assuredly leave your body with the treasure.' 'If I make a mistake to-day,' Jūdar replied, 'I shall deserve to be burnt alive.'

As soon as the Moor threw incense on the charcoal and began his spells, the river dried up and Jūdar went down to the gold door. It opened in the same way as before and he succeeded in loosening each enchantment until he came to his mother, who wished him welcome. 'O hag,' he answered, 'since when have I been the son of such as you? Take off your clothes!' She undressed slowly, trying the while to soften his heart, but when only her drawers remained, Jūdar cried: 'Remove them, O hag!' and, as they dropped about her feet, she vanished.

Jūdar penetrated the central hall without difficulty and, disregarding the vast piles of gold, walked up to the little pavilion and lifted the curtain. Even as the Moor had said, mighty al-Shamardal slept there on a gold throne girt with the sword, wearing the ring, carrying the phial of kohl round his neck on a gold chain, and having above his head the moon-round and moon-bright globe.

Jūdar undid the sword, pulled off the ring, unfastened the phial, took down the globe and started to retire. At once a musical sound of unseen instruments broke forth to acclaim his victory and the voices of the invisible guards cried: 'Well done, well done, O Jūdar!' These sounds and voices only ceased when the fisherman found himself once more in the river bed.

As soon as he saw Jūdar come out with his burden, the Moor ceased from his fumigation and his spells, and, running towards him, clasped him to his breast. When he had received the four mysteries of the treasure, he called the negroes from the hollow air, who struck the tent and led up the mules.

When Jūdar and his host came to the palace and had eaten of a great banquet furnished by the bag, the empty dishes were returned, and Abd al-Samad said: 'O Jūdar, you left your native land because of

me and have brought my business to a successful end. I owe you
more than I can say. You have but to express a wish and Allāh will
grant it through my poor means. Have no false shame, for you have
deserved greatly.' 'My lord,' answered the fisherman, 'I ask from
Allāh and from you only the enchanted bag.' The Moor handed him
the bag, saying: 'You have earned it. Whatever you had asked, it
would have been as freely given. But this bag will only help you in
your eating and drinking. You have undergone dangers and fatigues
with me and, according to my promise that you should return well-
content to your own people, I ought to make you rich in more than
foodstuffs. Take, then, this second bag filled with gold and jewels,
so that you may become a great merchant in your own country,
satisfy your desires and those of your family, and never have a
second thought in using money. I will now tell you how to use the
first bag. All you have to do is to plunge in your hand and think
these words: "Slave of the bag, I order you, by virtue of the Magic
Names, to bring me such a dish!" Instantly you will find whatever
you have wished at the bottom of the bag, even were it a daily
thousand dishes of different form and hue.'

Abd al-Samad called one of the negroes and one of the mules
from the hollow air, and loaded the beast with a second bag, one
side bursting with coined and uncoined gold, the other filled with
jewels. On top of this he set the empty magic bag, saying to Jūdar:
'Mount the mule! This black man will walk before you and show you
the road until you reach the door of your own house in Cairo.
When you are home, take the two bags, but return the mule to the
negro who will bring it back to me. Never let a third person share
our secret. And now farewell in the name of Allāh!'

At this point Shahrazād saw the approach of morning and
discreetly fell silent.

But when the four-hundred-and-seventy-sixth night had come

SHE SAID:

'Allāh increase your prosperity, my lord!' said Jūdar, as he
mounted the mule and set off in the wake of the negro. The animal
faithfully followed its guide throughout the day and night and, as it
was this time going at its fullest speed, the walls of Cairo were in
sight when the second morning broke. Jūdar entered his native city
by the Victory Gate and, coming to his house, saw his mother

seated upon the threshold with outstretched hand, asking an alms in the name of Allāh.

Filled with a great anger at this sight, Jūdar threw himself from the mule and ran with open arms to his mother, who wept at the sight of him. When he had taken down the two bags and given the mule in charge of the negro, he led the old woman into the house and made her sit down upon a mat, saying: 'O mother, how goes it with my brothers?' 'It goes well,' she answered. 'Then why do you beg in the street?' he cried. 'I left you a hundred dīnārs for my first drowning, a hundred for my second, and a thousand when I went away.' 'My child,' she replied, 'your brothers plotted against me and took all that money, so that I was obliged to beg in the street or starve.' Then said Jūdar: 'Dear mother, your sufferings are over now that I have returned. See, here is a bag full of gold and jewels; also food shall not be lacking in our house.' Smiling through her tears, she exclaimed: 'My son, fortune was born with you. May Allāh grant you His favour and increase His benefits upon you! Go and buy us a little bread, for I slept last night without having eaten, and this morning I have fasted.' Jūdar laughed at the word bread, and answered: 'You have but to ask for those dishes which you desire and you shall have them at once, without any buying in the market or cooking in the kitchen.' 'But, my child,' said his mother, 'you have brought nothing with you but these two bags. Where is this food of which you speak?' 'I have it,' he answered. 'So tell me your fancy.' Then said she: 'It does not matter what, so it can cure the pains of hunger.' 'That is true,' he admitted, 'in necessity a man must be content with anything; but when there is abundance of all a choice of the delicate and delicious will not come amiss.' 'I would like a warm crust and a little cheese,' she said. 'That hardly suits with your degree, my mother,' he objected. 'Very well,' she said, 'you know better what is fitting. Tell me what we ought to have.' Then said Jūdar triumphantly: 'I would suggest lamb, roast chicken, and pimentoed rice; I would suggest sausages, stuffed vegetable marrow, stuffed mutton, stuffed ribs, a katāif with almonds, bees' honey mixed with sugar, pistachio fritters perfumed with amber, and almond cakes.' On hearing this seductive list, the poor woman thought her son was either making fun of her or had gone mad. 'What is wrong with you, Jūdar?' she cried. 'Are you dreaming or have you gone mad? What useful purpose do you serve by naming these astonishing and far-fetched dishes to your poor mother?' 'I have not mentioned one dish which you shall not eat of this very moment,' said he. 'Give me the empty bag.' She gave him the bag, feeling it by the way, and he drew from it a gold dish on which lay the sausages, moist, odorous, and swimming in their appetising sauce. Again and again he dipped, until all the dishes which he had suggested were ranged before his mother's astonished eyes. 'My child,' said the old woman, 'the bag is very small; moreover it is always empty. What is the explanation of this thing?' 'The bag is enchanted,' he answered. 'It was given me by the Moor. It is served by a Jinnī who provides any dish which is asked for in this fashion.' When he had told the old woman the formula, she asked whether she herself would be able to extract miraculous meals from the bag. 'Certainly,' he answered, and at once she thrust her hand deep down in the bag, saying: 'Slave of the bag, I command you by the virtue of the Magic Names to bring me a second helping of stuffed ribs.'

At this point Shahrazād saw the approach of morning and discreetly fell silent.

But when the four-hundred-and-seventy-seventh night had come

SHE SAID:

At once she felt a dish beneath her hand and drew it forth filled with a marvellously garnished rib, scented with cloves and fine spices. Then said she: 'I still want my hot crust and cheese; I am used to it and cannot get it out of my mind.' With that she repeated the invocation and obtained her bread and cheese. 'Remember,' said Jūdar, 'that, when the meal is over, the dishes must always be put back in the bag, for that is a part of its magic. Keep the thing shut away and only take it out when you have need to its services. Also, never tell the secret to anyone; though, of course, you are at liberty to give food to the neighbours and poor folk, and may feed my brothers as freely in my absence as when I am here.'

He had hardly made an end of these instructions when his two brothers entered the house and saw the superb feast spread about the cloth.

They had heard of Jūdar's return from a man, who said to them: 'Your brother has come back from his travels on a mule led by a negro; no one ever saw the like of his rich clothes.' 'Would to Allāh we had never despoiled our mother!' said Sālim. 'She will surely tell him of our act and we be for ever put out of his favour.' But Salīm answered: 'Our mother is very kind-hearted. Besides, even if she tells, our brother is more indulgent still. If we can think out any excuse for our conduct he will accept it.' Thus it was that they decided to venture back to the house.

When Jūdar saw them, he rose in their honour and wished them peace, saying: 'Sit down and eat with us.' So they sat down and ate abundantly, for they were thin with starvation. 'Dear brothers,' said Jūdar when they were satisfied, 'take what remains of these dishes and give to the poor of our district.' 'Would it not be better to keep the remains for supper?' they objected, but he laughed and answered: 'When supper comes, there will be as much and more.' Reassured by this, the two went out and distributed the broken meats to the poor, saying: 'Take and eat.' Then they brought the dishes back to Jūdar, who handed them to his mother and bade her return them to the bag.

When the hour came for the evening meal, Jūdar took the sack and drew from it forty different dishes, which his mother arranged on the cloth. Then he invited his brothers to come in and eat. Later he provided them with pastries to sweeten the repast and, when all was over, bade them take the broken fragments and give them to the poor.

After ten whole days in which they had been provided with such feasts as they had never dreamed, Sālim said to Salīm: 'Can you understand how our brother can serve us these fine meals every day, morning, noon, evening, and then pastries at night, such things as kings have on their tables? Even supposing that he has become very rich, the food must come from somewhere, and we never see him buying it or lighting a fire or staying in the kitchen.' 'I cannot understand it,' answered Salīm, 'but our mother will be able to explain the thing.' Thereupon they concocted a plan and went in to their mother, saying that they were hungry. 'You shall soon be satisfied,' said she and, going into the room where she had hidden the bag, returned with a hot meal. Then said they: 'These things are cooked to a turn and yet you have not entered the kitchen or blown the fire.' 'I took them out of the bag,' she answered. 'What bag is that?' they asked. 'An enchanted bag,' she said, and at once repeated the formula to them, begging them to keep it secret. 'We shall not say a word,' they answered, and tested the bag for themselves, each wishing for his favourite meat.

Next day Sālim said to Salīm: 'How long are we going to live as servants to our brother Jūdar, eating each meal as an alms thrown to a beggar? Can we not find some way of stealing the bag and keeping it for ourselves?' 'We need a plot,' answered Salīm. 'That is not far to seek,' continued the elder. 'All we have to do is to sell Jūdar to the chief captain of the sea of Suez.' 'How can we do that?' asked Salīm.

At this point Shahrazād saw the approach of morning and discreetly fell silent.

And when the four-hundred-and-seventy-eighth night had come

SHE SAID:

Then said Sālim: 'We will go to the captain, who is now in Cairo, and invite him to come to supper with us, bringing two of his sailors. You have only to back me up in the thing I have to say to Jūdar, and you shall see what I can compass before the night is out.'

The two sought the chief captain of Suez and greeted him, saying: 'We come upon a matter which will rejoice your heart.' 'Good,' said he, and they continued: 'We are two brothers, and there is a third, a good-for-nothing. When our father died, he left us equal shares; but our brother soon exhausted his in corrupt and licentious expense. When he was ruined, he brought us unjustly before a bribed and iniquitous judge, saying that we had cheated him out of our father's goods; and the judge fined us all our fortune. Our brother was not content with this however; he sued us a second and a third time, until we were reduced to utter want. Now he plots something else against us, we do not know what; therefore we have come to beg you to buy him from us and use him as a rower in one of your ships.'

'Can you think of some excuse for bringing him here?' asked the captain. 'If you can, I promise to have him speedily into one of my boats.' 'That will be difficult,' they answered. 'It will be better if you become our guest this evening and bring two of your men with you. When he is asleep, the five of us can fall upon and gag him; then you will be able to carry him from the house, under cover of dark, and smuggle him on board.' 'I agree to that,' said the captain. 'Will you let me have him for forty dīnārs?' 'That is very little,' they replied, 'but, as you are the purchaser, we consent. We will meet you at nightfall in such a street near to such a mosque. Do not forget to bring the two sailors with you.'

Théy returned to their brother Jūdar and, after they had chatted with him for some time on one matter and another, Sālim kissed his hand as if he had a favour to ask. 'What is it you wish, my brother?' asked Jūdar; and Sālim said: 'I have a friend who asked me many times to his house while you were away, and entertained me generously. To-day I visited him, and he asked me to stay to dinner. When I told him that I could not leave you alone, he suggested that I should bring you with me. Then said I: "I do not think he would accept it. It would be better if you and your brothers dined with us to-night." As the brothers were present I had to invite them, but I sincerely thought they would refuse; unhappily they made no difficulty and all three accepted, promising to meet me near the door of the mosque at the corner of our street. It is time that I was there, but I feel ashamed before you because of the liberty I have taken. I shall be obliged to you for ever if you will receive the men. But if, O generous brother, you do not wish to have these guests in the house, allow me to invite them to our neighbour's and wait upon them there myself.' 'But why ask them to a neighbour's house?' asked Jūdar. 'Is our own so narrow and inhospitable? Have we no food to give them? My dear brother, let them come and they shall dine without stint of meat and sweet or any other thing. Another time, if you wish to have guests while I am absent, you have only to ask our mother and she will provide more than is necessary for your entertainment. A blessing will follow from such guests, O brother.'

Sālim kissed Jūdar's hand and went to the door of the little mosque, where he found the three men waiting for him. As soon as he brought them into Jūdar's presence, the latter rose in their honour and, with words of kind welcome, made them sit down beside him. He was far from knowing of what cruel Destiny they were the instruments. At his request the old woman served a feast consisting of forty different coloured dishes, and the guests ate their fill, thinking all the time that the splendid things came from the generosity of Sālim and Salīm. A third of the way through the night, pastries and sweets were set on the floor, and eaten until midnight. Then, as Jūdar showed no signs of sleep, Sālim gave an agreed sign; the sailors threw themselves upon the youngest brother and, after thrusting a gag into his mouth, bound his hands and feet and carried him out of the house into the darkness. When they came to Suez, they threw the unfortunate young man on board one of the captain's vessels and, putting irons upon his feet, condemned him to toil at the rowers' bench among the other galley-slaves.

At this point Shahrazād saw the approach of morning and discreetly fell silent.

But when the four-hundred-and-seventy-ninth night had come

SHE SAID:

When the two brothers, Sālim and Salīm, woke in the morning, they went in to their mother and asked her whether Jūdar had yet risen. 'Go and wake him,' she said. 'Where is he sleeping?' they asked, and she told them he was sleeping in the guest-chamber. 'There is no one there,' they exclaimed. 'Perhaps he went off last night with the sailors; we know that he has a taste for travel and we even heard the stranger persuading him to go along with them to open certain hidden treasures of which they knew.' 'It is quite likely that he went with them without telling us,' said the old woman. 'We need not fear for him, for he was born lucky, and surely Allāh will send him back to us laden with riches.' But then, as any absence wrings a mother's heart, she began to weep. 'O wicked woman,' cried the brothers, 'you love Jūdar so much that if we were to go away or return you would neither weep nor rejoice. Are we not your sons as much as he?' 'You are indeed my sons,' she answered, 'and two more wicked and ungrateful woman never had. Since your father's death, neither of you has been good for anything; not on a single day have I obtained happiness or consideration from either. But Jūdar was always good to me; he had a heart to please me, to respect me, and to feed me. He is worthy of my tears, for his benefits are still upon me and upon you, O ungrateful ones.' At this the two vile fellows, after cursing and beating their mother, rummaged the house until they found the two bags. They took the gold and jewels from the second one, saying: 'These things are our father's.' But their mother cried: 'As Allāh lives, they belong to Jūdar. He brought them from the country of the Moor.' 'You lie,' they answered, 'for they are our inheritance, which we have a right to spend as we choose.' They divided the gold and gems into two equal parts, but fell into a quarrel about the enchanted bag. Then said their mother: 'My children, the other bag cannot be shared or divided without the charm being broken. Leave it with me, and every day I will take out of it for you such dishes as you desire, contenting myself with the broken pieces. If you consent to give me necessary clothes, it will be pure generosity on your part and not my due. But do not forget that you are my children and grant me this one favour: do not quarrel with or hurt each other, so that when your brother returns, you need not fear to meet him.' The two took no notice of her petition, but spent the night discussing and quarrelling over the magic bag in such loud voices that one of the King's officers, who was being entertained in the next house, heard all they said and understood the cause of the dissension in its details. Next morning he sought an audience of Shams al-Daulah, King of Egypt, and told him what he had overheard. The King at once had the two brothers brought into his presence and tortured them until they confessed their crimes. As soon as he understood the whole matter, the King took the two bags for himself, threw the brothers into a dungeon, and made Jūdar's mother a pension sufficient to supply her daily needs. So much for them.

Jūdar had already been a year slaving at the oar in a ship belonging to the captain of Suez, when a tempest rose about the boat and dashed it again and again against a rocky coast, until it was broken to pieces and all the men aboard drowned except Jūdar. He swam to shore and walked inland until he came to a camp of wandering Arabs, who entertained him and asked if he were a sailor.

While he was giving them details of the wreck, a merchant from Jiddah, who happened to be passing through the camp, took pity upon him and said: 'Would you like to enter my service, O Egyptian? In return I will furnish you with clothes and take you back with me to Jiddah.' Jūdar accepted this invitation with alacrity, and found himself generously treated when he came to the merchant's native city. Soon after their arrival, his employer went on pilgrimage to Mecca, taking Jūdar with him.

At this point Shahrazād saw the approach of morning and discreetly fell silent.

But when the four-hundred-and-eightieth night had come

SHE SAID:

When they came to Mecca, Jūdar hastened to join the procession round the sacred enclosure of the Kaabah, in order that he might make the seven ritual circles about it. As he walked among the people, he met his friend Abd al-Samad, the Moor, who greeted

him as a brother and asked his news. Jūdar told his story with
many tears, and at once the Moor led him to his own house and
clothed him in a robe of unparalleled richness, saying: 'Misfortune
has now passed you by, O Jūdar.' Then he cast the fisherman's
horoscope and found from it all which had overtaken the two wicked
brothers in the meanwhile. 'They have been cast into a dungeon by
the King of Egypt,' said he. 'But you are my welcome guest. Stay
with me until we have performed the rites of pilgrimage, and then
we shall see to your fortune.' 'Dear master,' answered Jūdar, 'let
me seek out the merchant who brought me here and ask for leave
and goodwill to come to you.' 'You owe him money?' asked the
Moor, and, when Jūdar shook his head, continued: 'Go and ask his
leave and goodwill then; for bread which is eaten has its obligations.'
Jūdar sought out the Jiddah merchant and told him that he had found
a friend who was dearer to him than a brother. 'Bring him here and
we will give a feast in his honour,' said the merchant, but Jūdar
replied: 'As Allāh lives, he has no need of feasts, being wealthy and
well-served.' The merchant then handed him twenty dīnārs, saying:
'Take these and free my conscience of responsibility.' 'I free it,'
answered Jūdar and took his leave. As he was returning to the
Moor's house, he met a poor man on the road and gave him the
twenty dīnārs; then he rejoined his friend and lived with him until
all the obligations of the pilgrimage had been fulfilled.

Before leaving Mecca, the Moor gave Jūdar that ring which had
formed part of the treasure of al-Shamardal. 'It will realise your every
wish,' he said. 'Its slave is the Jinnī Thundering Thunder. You have
but to rub the bezel and he will appear, to do your will and bring
you anything which you desire.' By way of illustration he rubbed
the bezel himself, and at once the Ifrīt appeared and bowed before
him, saying: 'Behold I am here, my lord! Command and you shall
be obeyed, ask and it shall be given to you. Would you rebuild a
ruined city, or ruin a living one? Would you kill? Would you snatch
the soul from a king, or only break his armies?' 'O Thundering
Thunder,' answered the Moor, 'behold your future master! Serve
him well.' Then he dismissed the Jinnī and turned to Jūdar, saying:
'Do not forget that this ring gives you power over all your enemies.
I would not that you should ignore the extent of its magic.' Said
Jūdar: 'If it be really so powerful, I very much wish to return to my
native land.' 'Rub the bezel then,' said the other. 'and the Jinnī will
take you there on his shoulders.'

Jūdar said farewell to Abd al-Samad, the Moor, and rubbed the ring. When the Ifrīt appeared, he said: 'I wish to be in Cairo to-day,' 'That is easy,' answered Thundering Thunder and at once, bending down, took the fisherman upon his back and flew into the air with him. The journey started at noon, and by midnight the Jinnī had set Jūdar down in his mother's house and disappeared.

His mother rose, weeping, and wished him peace. Then she told him how his brothers had been beaten, imprisoned, and robbed of the two bags. 'Do not concern yourself any more for that,' answered Jūdar. 'I will at once give you a taste of my power and bring my brothers back again.' As he spoke, he rubbed the ring and, when Thundering Thunder appeared, ordered him to free the two men from the King's dungeon and return with them.

Sālim and Salīm lay in agony on the damp floor of their prison, praying for death to deliver them. As they spoke bitterly of their sufferings, the earth opened beneath their feet and Thundering Thunder rose before them. Even as they fainted from fright, he took them under his arms and disappeared into the deeps of the earth. When they came to themselves, they found that they were lying on carpets between their mother and Jūdar, who were both caring for them. When Jūdar saw them open their eyes, he said: 'All greetings, O Sālim and Salīm! Have you forgotten me, do you know me?'

At this point Shahrazād saw the approach of morning and discreetly fell silent.

But when the four-hundred-and-eighty-first night had come

SHE SAID:

They bowed their heads and wept silently, but Jūdar said: 'Do not weep. Satan and greed compelled you to act as you did. And yet how could you have had the heart to sell me? But do not weep. It is some consolation for me to think that I resemble Joseph in that matter, for he also was sold by his brothers; they even behaved worse to him than you did to me, for they threw him into a dry cistern. Ask Allāh's pardon and He will forgive you even as I forgive you, since there is no limit to His mercy. Above all, have no fear or constraint in my presence.' He comforted them until their spirits were renewed; then, after telling them the story of his sufferings, he showed them the magic ring.

'Forgive us this once, dear brother,' they said, 'and, if we return to our old practices, you may punish us in any way that you consider fit.' 'Do not think any more of it,' he answered. 'Tell me instead what the King did to you.' They told him how they had been beaten and cast into prison; but, when they spoke of the confiscation of the two bags, he rubbed the bezel of the ring, saying: 'We must see into this.'

When Thundering Thunder appeared, the two brothers were terrified and thought that Jūdar had conjured him up to kill them. They threw themselves in front of their mother, crying: 'We put ourselves under your protection, dear mother. Sweet mother, intercede for us!' 'My children, do not be afraid,' she said.

Then said Jūdar to the Ifrīt: 'Bring me all jewels and precious things which are in the King's treasury and, at the same time, return me the two bags which were taken from my brothers.' The Jinnī disappeared and returned almost instantly with all the King's treasures and the two bags, which were quite unharmed. 'My lord, I left nothing in all the treasury,' he said. Jūdar put the bag of treasure and all the wealth of the King into his mother's charge; but kept the food bag by his side. 'Slave of the ring,' he said, 'I order you to build me a tall and splendid palace in the night, to paint it with liquid gold, to carpet and furnish it beyond the manner of kings. The work must be completed by to-morrow's dawn.' 'Your will be done!' answered Thunder and disappeared into the earth, leaving Jūdar to feast himself and his family from the enchanted bag.

The slave of the ring called together his companions of under earth and, choosing out the most skilful builders from among them, set these busily to work. Some shaped the stones, others set them up, others coloured them, others graved them with figures, others carpeted and furnished the halls when they were made; so that by dawn the palace stood splendid and complete. The slave of the ring came and stood before Jūdar, saying: 'My lord, will you come and see your palace, for it is finished.' Jūdar took his mother and brothers with him and they all examined the palace and found it to be without equal among the buildings of men, confounding the reason by the beauty of its architecture and happy plenishing. Looking up at the imposing front, Jūdar marvelled that all this had cost him nothing. 'Would you like to live there?' he asked his mother. 'I would indeed,' she answered and called down upon his head the blessings of Allāh. Jūdar rubbed the ring again and told the Ifrīt to bring him forty young and beautiful white slaves, forty well-built negresses, forty boys and forty eunuchs. At once the slave of the ring flew off, with forty of his companions, and fetched out of India, Sind and Persia, every handsome girl or boy they found there. When forty perfect of each sex had been chosen, they sought out eighty of the finest negroes and negresses, and carried all to Jūdar's palace. There Thundering Thunder made them walk one by one before Jūdar, who found them very much to his liking.

At this point Shahrazād saw the approach of morning and discreetly fell silent.

But when the four-hundred-and-eighty-second night had come

SHE SAID:

Then said Jūdar to the slave of the ring: 'Each must have a beautiful garment; also bring costly robes for my mother, my brothers, and myself.' Without delay the Jinnī clothed all the female slaves sumptuously, and then said to them: 'Now kiss the hand of your mistress, the mother of your master. Follow her with your eyes and obey her orders, O blacks and whites.' Next the Ifrīt dressed the boys and negroes, and sent them to kiss Jūdar's hand. Lastly he garmented Sālim and Salīm with peculiar care. Therefore, when all the palace was dressed, Jūdar seemed like a king and his brothers like wazīrs.

As his new home was of great size, Jūdar gave one of its wings to each of his brothers, with a full train of women and servants, and reserved the body of the palace for himself and his mother. Thus all three abode in their own places, like so many sultāns. So much for them.

When the King's chief-treasurer went in the morning to take from the treasury certain articles which his master needed, he opened the door and found nothing. The vast cupboard might well have recalled to any who saw it these words of the poet:

> Old hollow trees
> Look gay with murmuring multitudes of bees
> And golden droppings of the combs' increase;
> But when the honey's drained and dead
> And all the bees are fled,
> Remains this sorry sight instead:
> Old hollow trees.

The treasurer gave a loud cry and fell down in a swoon; when he came to himself, he ran to the King with upraised arms, crying: 'O Prince of Believers, the treasury has been emptied in the night!' 'Vile wretch,' cried the King, 'what have you done with my treasure?' 'As Allāh lives, I have done nothing with it,' answered the man. 'I know neither what has become of it nor how it could possibly have been removed. I checked it yesterday evening, but this morning the great cupboard is empty; yet the doors have not been forced or pierced, the locks are intact, and the chains unbroken. It was no ordinary robber who stole the treasure.' 'Have the two bags also gone?' asked the King. 'They have,' answered the treasurer.

The King felt reason waver in his head. He rose and, crying to the treasurer to follow him, ran to the cupboard, which he found untouched but perfectly empty. 'Who has dared to do this thing?' he cried and ran, flaming with anger, to assemble his dīwān. The amīrs and officers of the court hurried into the King's presence, asking each other the meaning of his dreadful rage. They were soon answered, for the King addressed them in these words: 'Know that my treasure has been emptied in the night and that I do not know what rash creature has dared thus to affront my anger. Ask the chief-treasurer if you would know more of the matter.' All crowded round the treasurer, who repeated his story, saying: 'Yesterday the treasure was full. To-day I found it empty, without a sign of breakage or perforation in the walls and doors.' As all stood with lowered heads before the burning glances of the King, there entered that same archer who had denounced Salīm and Salīm. 'O King of time,' said he, 'I have passed the night without sleep in watching the work of many excellent masons. At dawn I perceived a magnificent palace, such as is nowhere equalled in the world, which had grown to perfection under their hands in a single night. When I asked concerning the palace, I was told that it had been built by Jūdar, the son of Umar, who has just returned from a voyage, bringing numberless slaves, boys, gold, silver and jewels. I was also informed that he has delivered his brothers from captivity and now sits like a sultān in his palace.'

'Run to the dungeon!' cried the King and, when word was brought that Salīm and Salīm had disappeared, he shouted in his wrath: 'Now I know the truth! He who took Salīm and Salīm from prison also stole my treasure. The man is Jūdar, their brother. And he has taken away the two bags. O wazīr, send an amīr at once with fifty soldiers to seal up all their goods and bring the lot of them to me, that they may hang.'

At this point Shahrazād saw the approach of morning and discreetly fell silent.

But when the four-hundred-and-eighty-third night had come

SHE SAID:

Then, as his anger boiled yet more hotly within him, the King cried: 'Let all be done quickly, for I wish to see them die!' 'O King,' answered the wazīr, 'I pray you to be merciful and indulgent, even as Allāh is merciful and withholds His hand! The man who could build a palace in one night is not likely to be afraid of anyone in the world. I fear for the amīr you send to him. Therefore be patient until I find a better way and come upon the truth. When all is known, it will be easier for you to realise your desire concerning these people.' 'Advise me, then, O wazīr,' said the King, and the wazīr continued: 'Send an amīr, but only to invite Jūdar to come to the palace; when he is here, I shall know how to beguile him with friendship and questioning. After that we shall see. If his power is great, we will take him by craft: if it be small, by force; in either case you shall have him to treat as you list.' 'Let him be invited!' said the King.

The wazīr ordered an amīr, whose name was Uthmān, to seek out Jūdar and invite him to make one at that day's royal feast. 'And do not return without him,' added the King.

This Uthmān was foolish, proud and self-sufficient. When he came before Jūdar's palace, he saw a eunuch sitting at the threshold on a beautiful bamboo chair. He approached, but the man neither moved nor looked at him. Yet Uthmān and his fifty were distinctly visible. 'O slave, where is your master?' cried Uthmān. 'In the palace,' answered the slave, without turning his head or shifting his careless posture by so much as an inch. 'Calamitous and pitchy eunuch,' cried the amīr in a rage, 'are you not ashamed to loll there like a vicious boy while I am speaking to you?' 'Not another word from you!' answered the eunuch. 'Begone out of my sight!' In his indignation at these words, Uthmān lifted his mace of office and would have struck the eunuch, for he did not know that he had to deal with Thundering Thunder, the slave of the ring, whom

Jūdar had appointed to be palace doorkeeper. As soon as the Ifrīt saw this movement, he rose and, fixing the amīr with one eye while he kept the other shut, knocked him over with a single breath and beat him four times about the body with his own mace. Furious at this indignity shown to their master, the fifty soldiers drew their swords and threw themselves upon the eunuch. 'Would you draw your swords, you dogs? Wait a little!' he cried, and, with that, gathered up a handful of them and, plunging their own swords into their bellies, bathed them in each other's blood. Then he began to grind them to pieces, while the rest fled, with Uthmān leading them, and did not stop running until they reached the King. When they were out of sight, Thunder returned to and lolled upon the chair.

The King's rage knew no bounds when he heard the greeting which Uthmān had received. 'Let a hundred warriors be sent against this eunuch!' he cried. The hundred went, were soundly drubbed with the mace, and fled to tell the King. 'Let two hundred be sent!' said the King. The two hundred went up against the eunuch and a large part of them were broken in pieces by him. Then cried the King to his wazīr: 'Go yourself with five hundred and bring all these insolent fellows into my presence!' 'O King of time,' replied the wazīr, 'I would rather take no man with me and go myself unarmed.' 'Do as you think best,' said the King.

The wazīr threw aside his weapons and clothed himself in a long white robe; then he took a large rosary in his hand and walked slowly to the door of Jūdar's palace, telling his beads the while. He went up to the eunuch smiling and sat down opposite his chair with great politeness. 'Greeting, my lord,' he said. 'Greeting, O human,' answered the other. 'What do you wish?' As soon as the wazīr heard the word 'human,' he understood that the eunuch was a Jinnī and trembled in fear. 'Is my master, the lord Jūdar, within?' he asked humbly. 'He is in the palace,' answered the Ifrīt. Then said the wazīr: 'My lord, I beg you to go in and say to him: "Great Jūdar, King Shams al-Daulah invites you to visit him, for he is giving a feast in your honour. He sends you greeting and begs you to delight his home with your presence." ' 'Wait here and I will ask his pleasure,' answered Thunder.

At this point Shahrazād saw the approach of morning and discreetly fell silent.

But when the four-hundred-and-eighty-fourth night had come

SHE SAID:

The wazīr waited humbly, while the eunuch went in to Jūdar, saying: 'My lord, the King first sent a large amīr whom I beat, with fifty warriors whom I defeated. Next he sent a hundred warriors, whom I scattered; and then two hundred whom I destroyed; now he has sent his wazīr, disarmed and dressed in white, to invite you to eat the meat of his hospitality. What do you say?' 'Bring the wazīr to me,' answered Jūdar. Thunder brought the wazīr into the presence of his master, and the man saw Jūdar sitting upon a throne such as no king has had since time began, with a wonderful carpet spread out at his feet, and looking more proud and beautiful than any sultān. He was abashed and speechless because of the beauty of the palace; its ornament, its furniture and its carving made him feel like a beggar in the presence of his host. He kissed the earth between Jūdar's hands and called down blessings upon him. When Jūdar asked what he wanted, he said very politely: 'My lord, your friend, King Shams al-Daulah, sends greeting by me. He desires with all his heart to delight his eyes with a sight of your face, and for that reason is giving a feast in your honour. Will you deign to do him pleasure?' 'Since he is my friend,' answered Jūdar, 'carry my greeting to him and beg him instead to come and visit me.' Then he rubbed the ring and, when Thunder appeared, commanded him to fetch a beautiful robe. The Ifrīt did so, and Jūdar said to the wazīr: 'It is for you. Put it on. Then go and tell the King what you have seen and heard.' The wazīr dressed himself in the robe (no one in the world had ever worn the like) and, returning to the King, spread himself in the praise of the palace and its contents. 'Jūdar invites you,' he said. 'Come then, O warriors,' exclaimed the King, 'to horse and follow me! I will ride my battle charger to go and visit this Jūdar.'

Jūdar saw him coming with all his train of soldiers, and said to the slave of the ring: 'I desire you to bring me a troop of your companions in human guise, that they may make two ranks in the courtyard for the passage of the King. When he sees their number and quality, his heart will tremble and he will realise that my power is greater than his.' When the King entered the courtyard, he had to pass between a double line of two hundred Afārīt, terrible and tall, dressed in rich armour and having the appearance of picked guards.

Therefore his heart was troubled. He found Jūdar sitting more proudly upon his throne and with greater dignity than any king. He bowed before him and wished him well; but Jūdar neither rose in his honour nor returned his greeting nor invited him to sit down. Instead he left him standing so long, in order to increase his own importance, that the King lost countenance and did not know whether to go or stay. When at last Jūdar broke silence, it was to say: 'Do you think that you did well to oppress helpless folk and spoil them of their goods?' 'My lord,' answered the King, 'deign to excuse me; covetousness and ambition led me to act as I did towards your brothers; also it was my Destiny; also if there were no fault in the world there could be no pardon.' He went on for a long time, excusing himself and begging forgiveness; among other pleas he recited these lines of the poet:

> Forget the past, child of a noble line,
>   Forgive, O clement one;
>   For that is what I would have done
> Had but the fault been yours, the pardon mine.

He continued to humble himself in this way until Jūdar said: 'Allāh pardon you!' and permitted him to be seated. Then the fisherman dressed him in the robe of security and ordered his brothers to spread the cloth and serve numberless extraordinary meats. After the meal he gave rich garments to all who followed the King and showered benefits upon them. At last Shams al-Daulah took his leave; but it was to return every day and pass all his time with Jūdar. He held his dīwān in the other's palace and directed the affairs of the kingdom there. Their close friendship increased with the days and lasted for a long time.

But one day the King, finding himself alone with his wazīr, said to him: 'O wazīr, I fear that Jūdar may kill me and take my throne away.'

At this point Shahrazād saw the approach of morning and discreetly fell silent.

But when the four-hundred-and-eighty-fifth night had come

SHE SAID:

'O king of time,' answered the wazīr, 'I should have no fear for your throne; for Jūdar is richer and more powerful than any king and would have no use for a second and inferior throne. But, if you are serious in your apprehension that he may kill you, you have only to marry him to your daughter and divide your power with him, so that the two of you are on an equal footing.' 'O wazīr, can you bring this about for me?' asked the King. 'You have only to ask him to visit you,' said the wazīr. 'We will pass the evening in the great hall of your palace and you must arrange for your daughter to put on her best and pass like a beam of light across the doorway. Jūdar will see her and the apparition will so work upon his curiosity that he will fall violently in love with her and ask me who she is. I will lean to him mysteriously and, after whispering that she is your daughter, converse subtly with him, letting my words twist in and out of his, until I persuade him to ask for the girl, without having an idea that you know anything about the matter. When they are married, there will be certain peace between you and, on his death, you will inherit the greater part of his goods.' 'Excellently planned, O wazīr!' said the King, and at once prepared a feast and invited Jūdar to attend it. The young man willingly accepted, and the guests sat feasting joyfully in the great hall until the fall of day.

The King had sent word to his wife to dress the girl in her brightest and most costly ornaments, and instruct her to pass swiftly across the doorway of the hall. When the princess hurried, like a beam of light, past the door, shining in beauty and a cascade of gems, Jūdar uttered a cry and a sigh and called out: 'Ah, ah!' His limbs relaxed and his face turned yellow, for love, passion and hot desire had entered into him. Then said the wazīr: 'May sickness be far from you, my lord! Why do I see you so changed and suffering?' 'That girl, O wazīr,' answered Jūdar, 'whose daughter is she? She has taken my heart and my reason along with her.' Then said the wazīr: 'She is the daughter of your friend the King. If she really pleases you, I will speak to him and ask him if he will give her to you as a wife.' 'If you will do that,' cried Jūdar, 'you may ask of me all that your soul desires! The King shall receive whatever dowry he requires, and the two of us shall be friends and kinsmen for ever.' The wazīr approached the King, saying: 'O King Shams al-Daulah, your friend Jūdar desires to ally himself with your house. He has begged me to approach you in the matter of a marriage with your daughter, the lady Asiah. Accept my intercession, I pray. He will give you any dowry you ask.' 'The dowry has already been given,' answered the

King. 'My daughter is a slave to his service. If he accepts her as a wife he will be doing me great honour.'

Things only went so far that night. But, on the following morning, the King assembled his dīwān and called the sheikh al-Islām for that special occasion. In the presence of great and small, masters and servants, Jūdar proffered his request and the King granted it, saying: 'As for the dowry, I have already received it.'

At once the contract was written. Jūdar presented the King with a bag of gold and jewels. Drums and cymbals, flutes and fifes, played in the marriage. And, while the rest of the world were still feasting, Jūdar entered the marriage-chamber and took possession of his bride.

Jūdar and the King lived together in close unison for many months; and, when the King died, the armies called upon the fisherman to be their Sultān. At first he refused but, when they continued to importune, he accepted and ascended the throne. His first royal act was to build a mosque upon the tomb of Shams al-Daulah and to endow it richly. The tomb and mosque were in the quarter Bundukāniyah, but, since Jūdar's reign, the quarter and the mosque itself have been known as Jūdariyah.

King Jūdar appointed his brother Sālim to be wazīr upon his right side and Salīm to be wazīr on his left. The three lived together in peace for one year, but no longer.

At this point Shahrazād saw the approach of morning and discreetly fell silent.

But when the four-hundred-and-eighty-sixth night had come

SHE SAID:

At the end of that time Sālim said to Salīm: 'How long are we to stay as we are? Shall we serve Jūdar for the rest of our lives and never know the joy of absolute authority?' 'How can we kill him and take the ring and the bag?' answered Salīm. 'It is for you to find some strategy which will bring about his death, for you are cleverer than I am.' Then said Sālim: 'If I compass his death, do you agree that I shall become Sultān and make you my chief wazīr? I shall keep the ring and the bag, but you will have the use of them.' Salīm accepted, and thus the two agreed to murder Jūdar and enjoy the good things of this world in kingly fashion.

Sālim went to Jūdar, saying: 'Dear brother, will you give us the

pleasure of entertaining you this evening, for it is a long time since
you have crossed the threshold of our hospitality?' 'To which shall I
come for the feast?' asked Jūdar. 'First to me,' answered Sālim.
'Then, after you have tasted my food, you may eat with my brother
to-morrow.' 'There is no objection to that,' replied Jūdar and at
once accompanied Sālim to the wing in which he lived.

Little he knew what awaited him. Hardly had he swallowed the
first mouthful of the feast when he fell back in little pieces. So well
had the poison done its work that his flesh was scattered to one side
and his bones to the other.

At once Sālim tried to draw the magic ring from its finger and,
when it would not come, cut off the finger and gained possession of
the ring in that way. He rubbed its bezel and, when Thundering
Thunder appeared, saying: 'Behold I am here! Command and it
shall be done!' bade him take hold of his brother Salīm and put him
to death. 'Then take up what is left of Jūdar,' said he, 'and throw
the two bodies down before the chiefs of the army.' The Ifrīt,
whose lot was to obey the orders of any who rubbed the ring, put
Salīm to death and then, taking up the two bodies, carried them to
the feast-hall, where the chiefs of the armies were making merry,
and cast them down in the midst. The captains ceased from eating
and lifted their arms in the air, crying out to the Jinnī: 'Who has so
practised upon the persons of the King and his wazīr?' 'Their
brother Sālim,' answered Thundering Thunder, and, as he was
speaking, Sālim himself entered the hall. 'O chiefs of my armies, eat
and be of a quiet mind,' he said. 'I have become master of this ring,
taking it from my brother Jūdar. This Ifrīt is Thundering Thunder,
the slave of the ring. I ordered him to put Salīm to death that there
should be no rival to my throne. Besides, the fellow was a traitor
and I feared his plots. As Jūdar is dead, I am the only King. Will you
accept me as your Sultān, or would you rather I ordered the Ifrīt
to destroy you all, great and little, first and last?'

Because of their great fear the captains dared not protest, but
answered: 'We accept you as our King.'

Sālim ordered funerals for his brothers and, when all the people
had returned from burying them, he sat upon his throne and
received the homage of his new subjects. 'Now,' said he, 'I wish to
marry my brother's wife.' 'That may be done,' they said. 'But you
must wait until the four months and ten days of her widowhood
are passed.' But Sālim cried: 'I know nothing of such formalities!

By the life of my head, I will go in to her to-night!' Thus the kādīs were obliged to write out the marriage contract, and men went to warn the lady Asiah of what had happened.

At this point Shahrazād saw the approach of morning and discreetly fell silent.

But when the four-hundred-and-eighty-seventh night had come

SHE SAID:

'Let him come,' said the lady Asiah. So, when night had fallen, Sālim entered the chamber of his brother's wife and she received him with great demonstrations of joy. As a refreshment she offered him a cup of sherbert. When he had drunk it down, he fell in pieces, a body without a soul. Such was his death.

The lady Asiah took the magic ring and broke it in pieces, so that none might evilly use it in the future; also she cut the enchanted bag into two pieces, thus depriving it of virtue. Afterwards she sent to tell the sheikh al-Islām of what had passed and gave this message to the chiefs of the kingdom: 'Choose a new King!'

That, continued Shahrazād, is all I know of the tale of Jūdar and his brothers, of the magic ring and the enchanted bag. But I also know, O auspicious King, an astonishing tale which is called. . . .